S0-CRX-919

Preaching and Teaching
the
New Testament

Preaching and Teaching the New Testament

By

P. B. FITZWATER

Teacher at The Moody Bible Institute of Chicago for more than forty years

MOODY PRESS
CHICAGO

Printed in the United States of America

DEDICATION

This book is affectionately dedicated to the men of the Pastors Course and to the thousands of men and women who have sat in my classes during the forty-one years of my teaching ministry at the Moody Bible Institute.

The two significant words of the title of this book have been deliberately chosen as expressing the predominant characteristics of a graduate of the Moody Bible Institute. *Preaching* means the proclamation of good news of salvation to lost men through the shed blood of Jesus Christ on the cross of Calvary. *Teaching* means causing to know the meaning of the good news in the life and service of the believer.

It is the fervent wish and earnest prayer of the author that everyone into whose hands this book may come shall become a passionate soul-winner. Preaching and teaching is God's way of salvation for the sinner. "God so loved the world, that he gave his only begotten Son, that whosoever believeth in him should not perish, but have everlasting life" (John 3:16). The salvation of the world depends upon the preaching of the Gospel which is the power of God unto salvation. The only one who really can proclaim the good news and teach it is the one who has been saved by the Gospel. He must know by experience.

I sincerely hope that the study of this book may help you into the knowledge of the New Testament which will enable you to preach and teach it. If these things are accomplished I shall be abundantly repaid for the years of toil in its preparation.

CONTENTS

Preaching and Teaching
the
New Testament

INTRODUCTORY

THERE IS A GREAT DEARTH of real preaching and teaching today. This fact accounts for the moral and spiritual condition so widely prevalent. In order that there be faith and life, the Word of God must be preached and taught (Rom. 10:17). Through the centuries of church history, the index of spiritual power has been the vitality of the preaching. If there is to be a return to this power there must be a return to the real preaching of the Word of God. Young men are being sent out from the theological seminaries without having been taught how to preach the Bible.

Christ's parting commission to the disciples was: "Go ye into all the world, and preach the gospel to every creature" (Mark 16:15). Matthew says, "Go ye therefore, and teach all nations" (Matt. 28:19). Paul says: "The gospel of Christ . . . is the power of God unto salvation to everyone that believeth" (Rom. 1:16). The psalmist said: "God hath spoken once; twice have I heard this; that power belongeth unto God" (Ps. 62:11). Again Paul says: "Faith cometh by hearing, and hearing by the word of God" (Rom. 10:17). Preaching is a supernatural work—the preacher is called of God—His message is the power of God—the Holy Spirit makes the power operative in the believer's heart. Wherever the Gospel is preached some believe. God's purpose cannot fail. This ought to sober us and encourage us to prepare for preaching.

I. THE MEANING OF PREACHING.

Missionary work of all kinds centers in preaching. This has been true since the beginning of God's effort to redeem lost men. I heartily welcome every means which in this age is available and can be employed in bringing the Lord Jesus Christ to the attention of men, but when modern devices such as moving pictures, television, etc., displace the preaching of God's Word, it will be a sad day for the church.

The real meaning of preaching is gained from the different words used in the New Testament in conveying the Gospel message. The two most prominent of these words are *evangelizo,* meaning proclaiming the Gospel, the goods news of salvation; and *kerruso,* meaning to declare the Gospel message with authority. Preaching therefore means the proclamation of the good news of salvation to a lost world by the authority of the throne of God.

II. THE MEANING OF TEACHING (Matt. 28:19, 20).

The word here means becoming a disciple, a scholar; teaching is causing to know. After the pupil hears the good news of salvation, he needs to be taught the meaning of the good news of salvation in Christ in order to know how to appropriate it to himself and how to live a holy life and bear fruit for Christ. The disciple needs to be taught how to observe all that Christ has commanded (Matt. 28: 20). This means right living and fruitful service.

III. WHAT TO PREACH AND TEACH—THE BIBLE, THE WORD OF GOD (II Tim. 4:2).

Paul charged Timothy to preach the Word. In the early church we are told that the disciples went "everywhere preaching the word." We read further that they "preached Christ"—Christ as the Saviour from the guilt of sin, the power of sin, and Christ as the coming King. Observe that Timothy was not charged to preach *from* the Word, but to preach *the Word.*

In recent years two volumes have appeared which strikingly illustrate this, the one with the title, *Preaching from the Prophets,* and the other *Preaching from the Bible.* Perhaps these titles were inadvertently chosen, but they reveal an unfortunate condition. Instead of preaching *from* the Bible young men should be taught how to preach the Bible. To take a text from the Bible as a point of departure, as someone has said, is but a pretext. Dr. James M. Gray, the late president of Moody Bible Institute, said a generation ago to a group of ministers at a Winona Lake Bible Conference, "Brethren, you do not have to rack your brain to create sermons, but you must find them in the Bible." This is based upon the assumption that the Bible is a complete standard of faith and of conduct. There is no human need unprovided for in the Bible. The principles set forth therein are adequate to meet every conceivable human need.

In order to preach the Bible one must know the Bible. In order to know the Bible one must possess a knowledge of the factual content of every book of the Bible from Genesis to Revelation. Since the Bible is an organism, the preacher must know its very integral structure, and by structure is meant the formation, arrangement, and articulation of the several parts of the Bible. The absolute prerequisite to the understanding of the structure of the Bible is a grasp of the purpose of God in giving it to man. By purpose is meant that which one sets before himself to do; that is, an object to be attained. It likewise embraces the plan by which the end is to be achieved. The purpose of God implies that the self-existent, independent, and unchangeable God, moved entirely from within, created the universe according to His own plan. This plan was perfect in every detail, embracing all His works, great and small, from the beginning of time to the endless ages of eternity.

Dr. James Orr, in *Sidelights of Christian Doctrine,* says: "When we say with Scripture that God has a purpose, an eternal purpose; in Paul's language, 'the purpose of him who worketh all things after the counsel of his will' (Eph. 1:9-11), we mean simply that God has a plan, an eternal plan which He carried out in His creation and in His providence, and so is far from being a far-off metaphysical thing, but in truth a rock-fast foundation of all our Christian experience about God in His relation to the world. 'The counsel of the Lord standeth forever, the thoughts of his heart to all generations' (Ps. 33:11).

"That in this general sense God has a plan in all His actions, few, I think, will be disposed to doubt, if we attribute to God, as all Christians must, self-conscious personality and infinite knowledge and wisdom. This implies:

"1. That in all He does, God does not act blindly, but acts with intelligence and maturity.

"2. That in all that God does, He does not act arbitrarily, but on settled principles of wisdom and goodness.

"Intelligent action is action governed by the idea of an end, and wisdom in a good and holy being manifests itself in choosing the best ends and the best means to attain those ends. Thus far there will be general agreement. God's plan in the nature of the case must be eternal and does not alter. His purpose, formed in eternity, He executes in time."

The proper concept of the structure of the Bible must be historical, logical, and chronological. These characteristics must control all our thinking.

The place to begin Bible study is where God began to write. It must be assumed that the Bible is the record of the unfolding of His divine purpose. The Bible, composed of sixty-six books, must be viewed as the historical record of the outworking of the divine purpose. In viewing the Bible structure, we at once recognize its twofold division, the Old Testament and the New Testament. The Bible student must understand why the first division is called the Old Testament and the second division the New Testament.

I. THE OLD TESTAMENT

The broad structure of the Old Testament, held by the Jews and recognized by Jesus Christ, is, all things considered, most desirable. This concept appears in the record (Luke 24:44). The divisions of the Old Testament accordingly are the Law of Moses, the Prophets, and the Psalms. This triple division gives three clearly defined ideas: "The Law is the foundation of the whole revelation, the special discipline by which the chosen race was trained from a savage willfulness to the accomplishment of its divine work. The Prophets portray the struggles of the same people when they come into close connection with the kingdoms of the world, and were led to look for the inward antitypes of the outward precepts. The Hagiographa carried the divine lesson yet farther and shows its working in the various phases of individual life and relation to the great problems of thought and feeling which present themselves by a necessary law in the later stages of civilization" (Westcott).

A. *The Law of Moses, or the Pentateuch (five-columned book).*

It must be viewed as a historical book. It begins with the creation of the universe and ends with the death of Moses. The Pentateuch, or Law, is the foundation of the whole of revelation. It shows the origin of the universe, of sin, of judgment, promise of a Redeemer, nations, and especially the origin of the covenant nation, which was specifically to be the vehicle by which God's grace should reach the entire world.

The significance of the Pentateuch is indicated by the names given to the separate books composing it. Genesis suggests generation, production; Exodus means departure of Israel out of Egypt; Leviticus suggests ritual of worship as administered by the Levites; Numbers suggests the numbered people in their wanderings in the wilderness; and Deuteronomy, which literally means the second law, is the adaptation of the Law of Moses to the conditions of life of the chosen people in the Promised Land.

B. *The Prophets.*

The prophets vividly picture the struggles of the chosen nation as they come into close connection with the peoples and kingdoms of the world, thus severely testing them as to their loyalty to God and in their ability to stand alone for God before the world. Their lapses reveal their weakness and insecurity, while at the same time revealing the reality of their life with God.

When their testings were severest, and the tendency to apostasy of the chosen people was strongest, then God's prophets were most numerous and their evangelistic cries were most appealing and passionate. In such dark days the Gospel message was the clearest. The prophets were divided into two groups:

1. The Earlier Prophets.

In the Hebrew Bible Joshua stands at the head of a series of books called "The Earlier Prophets," which include Joshua, Judges, I and II Samuel, and I and II Kings.

a. Joshua. The land was conquered and apportioned among the tribes of Israel. Joshua wrote as God's prophet. A prophet in the Bible sense (see Exod. 7:1) means, one who speaks forth the message of God. There has been left no written message from Joshua.

b. Some thirteen judges witnessed for God and fulfilled the work of prophets. The people sinned; God permitted the enemy to enslave them; the people cried out in penitence to God for deliverance. The judges were God's appointed leaders in the deliverance of the people. This period covered some 300 years.

c. I and II Samuel. Samuel restored the theocratic rule and founded the kingdom of Israel (II Sam. 8:16).

d. I and II Kings. In these books the history of Israel is carried through the undivided kingdom, and also through the divided kingdom to the fall of Israel and the captivity of Judah.

2. The Later Prophets.

These later prophets are designated in Jewish literature as greater prophets and lesser prophets. These terms, *greater* and *lesser,* do not designate rank, but length. In our English Bible, they are designated as major prophets and minor prophets. In the structure of the Bible, we shall see these prophets in their true chronological position. A convenient way of viewing them is:

a. Precaptivity prophets. The prophets who prophesied before the Babylonian captivity.

b. Captivity prophets. The prophets who prephesied during the captivity.

c. Postcaptivity prophets. The prophets who prophesied after the Babylonian captivity.

3. The Psalms.

This last division included Psalms, Job, Proverbs, Ecclesiastes, and Song of Solomon. The Psalms, being the largest of the group, came to stand at their head, and came to be in connotation the title for the whole collection. This list of books, sometimes designated "wisdom literature," expressed the inner thoughts and experiences of the redeemed people.

II. NEW TESTAMENT

Structurally we find the New Testament made up of three parts, the same as the Old Testament.

Historical—the Gospels and Acts.

Didactic—the Epistles.

Prophetic—the Revelation.

The order of the Prophetic and Didactic is reversed in the New Testament because the Prophetic does not primarily have to do with the discipline of the people, but as presenting the consummation of the divine purpose—in the making full of all that God purposes.

The New Testament is the flower and fruit of the Old Testament. In the New Testament the Old Testament is revealed, while in the Old Testament the New Testament is concealed. Christ and His work is its supreme and great theme. In the Old Testament Christ's coming had been predicted, even indicating the tribe, the family, place, and date of His birth.

The Gospels portray the aforesaid redemptive work of Christ. The Acts reveal a new body—the Church—coming into existence, through whose agency the Gospel was to be made known to the whole world. The Epistles set forth the doctrinal and experimental teachings of Christianity. The Revelation is the setting forth of the consummation of the divine purpose in the restoration of all things through the power of the coming Mediator and Saviour.

The preaching of the Bible demands the analysis of every book of the Bible. In the analysis of a book of the Bible there must be grasped its central purpose and theme. It means the grasp of the Bible, including the central purpose and theme of every book with the mastery of its plan and structure. Furthermore, it requires the exegesis of the entire revelation of God as its redemptive purpose. This must be followed by a systematic examination of its teachings. The grasping of these truths will deter the novice from posing as a preacher and will be a challenge to everyone called of God to preach to fully qualify himself for his work.

III. THE ISSUE OF PREACHING THE BIBLE

A. *The Revelation of God As to the Wonders of His Being.*

Those who know God will put their trust in Him (Ps. 9:10). The only way back to righteous living is a knowledge of God. The only explanation of the collapse of the moral standards of this generation is the ruling out of God from the thought of men. Men do not love and serve God, because of their ignorance of Him.

B. *The Revelation of God As to the Wonders of His Grace.*

"God so loved the world, that he gave his only begotten Son, that whosoever believeth in him should not perish, but have everlasting life" (John 3:16).

C. *The Revelation of the Wonders of His Work.*

"The heavens declare the glory of God; and the firmament showeth his handiwork" (Ps. 19:1).

D. *The Salvation of Lost Men.*

E. *The Glory of the World To Be.*

F. *The Blessed News of Heaven.*

All these issues are dependent upon the preaching of the Word. God's appointed way of bringing into being all these is through preaching. What an honor and a responsibility! To be called to be a preacher is the highest honor that comes to men.

INTRODUCTION TO THE GOSPELS

GOSPEL means good news. According to correct Biblical speech, there is but one Gospel—the good news of salvation through the Lord Jesus Christ. From the earliest times of Christian history the term *Gospel* has been applied to each of the four narratives which together form the "four-sided Gospel," so called by Origen. In the oldest copies of the New Testament the titles are "According to Matthew," "According to Mark," "According to Luke," and "According to John," clearly implying that the one Gospel had been committed to writing by the evangelists in this fourfold account. There is clear evidence that those writings were received and read in the Christian assemblies for the worship of God as Scripture before the close of the second century A.D.

I. Why Four Gospels?

This is the problem which has engaged the thought of men through the centuries of Christian history. Why not three? Why not seven? Or since the Holy Spirit is the Author of all, why did He not gather together all the material presented by the four writers and set it forth in logical order as one complete treatise? Why leave us the bewildering task of harmonizing them?

Some attempted answers:

A. *They Are Supplementary or Corroborative.*

That they in some sense subserve this purpose is not denied; but it is not the main purpose, otherwise two, or at the most three, would have been sufficient; for in the mouth of two or three witnesses every word shall be established.

B. *A Biography or Life of Christ.*

Their brevity forbids this. Such would make that fullest and most marvelous of all lives to be compressed into the small compass of eighty to one hundred pages of our ordinary Bible. Besides, the accounts have to do with the last three and a half years of His life—only giving a single event between His birth and public ministry, passing over thirty years of His earthly sojourn in silence. Strictly speaking, there is no such a thing as "a life of Christ." That efforts along this line do some good is not to be denied, but it is a case where the good becomes the enemy of the best.

C. *Written for Four Classes of People.*

These classes are the Jews, Romans, Greeks, and the Christian church. The Gospels no doubt appealed to those classes, but to see this only or mainly is to miss their primary purpose and beauty.

II. THE TRUE VIEW.

In John 20:30, 31, John states his purpose in writing was to prove that the historic Person, Jesus Christ of Nazareth, was the promised Messiah, the Son of God, and that upon this fact faith might rest—that through it salvation might be received. Judging from the presentation of facts by Matthew, Mark, and Luke, John's words predicate the design of them all. The one central theme of them all is the stupendous work of redemption. The Messianic hope is the central theme around which every fact is gathered.

If this then be the true view, we are driven to the conclusion that there must be just four presentations of the work of Christ—could be no more, no less. The reasons for this must not be sought for in human reason or opinion but in the Word of God itself. Each writer, though using the same material in a large measure, had a special design in view and therefore selected and arranged it so as to set forth a definite phase of Christ's redemptive work. It is no more possible to merge into one account the narratives of Christ's redemptive work than for a photographer to show every side of a square building with one impression. Four impressions must be made to show the entire building.

A. *Old Testament Names.*

In the prophecies of the Old Testament is to be found an august portrait of the Saviour-Redeemer, a noteworthy feature of which is the variety of names ascribed to Him. These all can be grouped under four principal heads, corresponding to the number of the Gospels:

1. The Kingship of the Messiah.

It is set forth in the following passages—Psalm 2:6; Isaiah 32:1; Daniel 9:25; Zechariah 9:9; 14:9; Daniel 2:44. The prophets give great prominence to the Kingship of the coming Redeemer-Saviour. Matthew gives such emphasis to this heavenly personage—the nature and blessedness of His reign.

2. "Servant of Jehovah."

This title is given great prominence in the Prophets—Isaiah 42:1-7; 48:1-12; 50:4-9; 52:13-15; 53:1-12. This Servant will make known God's will and fulfill all its requirements. That which was lost in Adam shall be restored in Him. Mark presents Christ as the Servant fulfilling the divine will.

3. The Redeemer.

He is set forth as the Seed of the Woman—Genesis 3:15; Isaiah 7:14-16; Daniel 7:13. He is to be not only the Seed of the woman, but the offspring of David. He must be incorporated with the human race (Heb. 2:14). Only a blood relative could act in the redemption of another (Ruth 3:9; Lev. 25:47-50). This shows why the Saviour of men must become human. Luke presents Christ as the Son of man—the Kinsman-Redeemer.

4. The Lord of Glory.

The Prophets make Him none other—Isaiah 9:6; 40:3-8. The Word became flesh (John 1:14). Redemption is a divine act. Only the Son of God become human could redeem sinful man. John presents the eternal Word made flesh.

B. *The "Branch."*

The prophecies concerning the Redeemer are further centralized by the fourfold presentation in which the divine Redeemer is described as the "Branch."

1. The Branch as King (Jer. 23:5; 33:14-17).
2. The Branch as Servant (Zech. 3:8).
3. The Branch as Man (Zech. 6:12).
4. The Branch of the Lord (Isa. 4:2).

The fourfold account of the Gospels placed alongside these predictions fits exactly. Matthew exhibits Him as the promised King; Mark as the Servant of Jehovah; Luke as the Kinsman-Redeemer; John as the Son of God. Each writer was by nature and circumstances fitted for the peculiar task to which he was called. Matthew an officer under the Roman government could see Him as a King; Mark as servant of Paul and Barnabas would see Messiah as the Servant; Luke as the beloved physician would naturally see Him as the compassionate One, sympathizing with His people; and John who lay in the bosom of the Master would see Him in the bosom of the Father—the very Son of God, the Lord of glory.

THE GOSPEL ACCORDING TO MATTHEW

PART ONE—INTRODUCTORY MATTERS

In all ancient copies of the New Testament Scriptures, Matthew stands at the head. It sustains the same relationship to the New Testament that Genesis does to the Old Testament and is their connecting link. The Old Testament closes with predictions as to the coming King. Matthew has for its central theme the setting forth of that King with His kingdom. It is filled with references and quotations from the Old Testament; therefore, any exposition which ignores the predictions concerning the King and His kingdom stands self-condemned.

I. Authorship.

The author—Matthew, the taxcollector who was chosen by Christ as one of the apostles. From the earliest times authorship was ascribed to him and so far as known never questioned. In Mark and Luke he is called Levi (Mark 2:14; Luke 5:27). Throughout this Gospel he is called Matthew which means, "gift of Jehovah." Perhaps his original name was Levi, and after his call as an apostle, he took the name Matthew.

II. Theme.

Jesus Christ, the Son of David, the Son of Abraham is the theme (Matt. 1:1). In this book the two most important Old Testament covenants are brought together—the Davidic of kingship (II Sam. 7:8-16) and the Abrahamic of promise (Gen. 12:1-4; 15:18).

III. Analysis.

The Bible has a definite structure which must be grasped in order to understand its message. Every book of the Bible has its peculiar structure. The analysis of a book must be made in order to grasp its message. The theme of a book and its structural plan must be apprehended in order to have an intelligent exegesis of its words. The essential qualification for the preaching of Matthew is a knowledge of its structure and message. No one can preach that which he does not know.

PART TWO—DETAILED OUTLINE

I. THE KING'S BIRTH AND ITS ATTENDANT EVENTS (1:1—2:23).

A. *The King's Pedigree* (1:1-17).

The genealogy of a king is an all-important matter. This table shows His national and royal descent. Being the son of both David and Abraham, He is heir to the throne and to the promise. Only Matthew and Luke contain genealogies; they are not needed in Mark and John. The genealogy is given in three stages, representing the great epochs in the preparation of the people for their King —Abraham to David; David to the Captivity; Babylonian Captivity to Christ. Let us learn from this portion of Matthew—

1. That "All Scripture Is Profitable" Because Inspired of God (II Tim. 3:16).

Little attention is given to it. Usually passed over as of no value—only a list of hard names.

2. That God Always Keeps His Word.

God declared that deliverance would come through the woman's Seed (Gen. 3:15); that a Saviour would come through the family of David (Isa. 11:1); and that in Abraham's seed all the families of the earth should be blessed (Gen. 12:3).

3. That Those Who Reject Christ Shall Perish.

Sorrow and anguish shall come to the wicked as surely as salvation shall come to the righteous.

4. The Sinfulness and Corruptness of Human Nature.

Many godly parents have had wicked children. Grace is not inherited; virtue does run in families. Salvation is not through good advice and example, but through birth from above—regeneration by the Spirit of God.

5. That Christ Is a Compassionate and Mighty Saviour-Redeemer.

method, thus obviating the necessity of going to the cross. The kingdoms really were Christ's and Satan knew that they ultimately would become Christ's. The inducement was to get immediate possession without the suffering of the cross. This same temptation is before us today and is causing the church to bid for power by worldly means.

d. The defense—the Word of God (vv. 4, 7, 10). Christ met the Devil each time and repulsed him with, "It is written." Each time He quoted from Deuteronomy, the book which the modernists discredit as being reliable. Jesus had enough confidence in it to use it in the most crucial hour in the world's history.

e. The issue (v. 11). The enemy was completely routed. The strong man was bound so that the spoiling of his house was possible. May we all with full confidence in this same Word of God use it in meeting the temptations of the Devil. Jesus began His official work as Messiah at Jerusalem where He presented Himself to the Jewish nation.

3. The King His Own Herald (4:12-17).

a. The reason for this (v. 12). The news of the Baptist's imprisonment moved Jesus to forsake Judea and go into Galilee. The fate of John was accepted as foreshadowing His own. The rejection of the forerunner meant the rejection of the King whose advent he proclaimed. Because of this He withdrew from the metropolis and went to the remote regions where His work would attract less attention. This was an act of prudence on His part. When the people willfully reject the truth and do violence to the messenger, there should be a turning from them unless specially directed otherwise.

b. To whom the proclamation was made (vv. 13-16). It was to the people of Capernaum in fulfillment of Isaiah's prophecy (Isa. 9:1, 2). These people were not blessed with such privileges as those in and near Jerusalem. The darkest and most corrupt of the regions were getting the light first. This was a foreshadowing of the present age where the Gospel is being preached to the Gentiles.

c. His message (v. 17). "Repent for the kingdom of heaven is at hand." This is the same kingdom which John the Baptist and the Old Testament prophets proclaimed. It means the Messianic earth-rule of Jesus Christ. Their message differs from the message of

Christ's ministers today. We preach the Gospel of the grace of God —salvation through faith in the finished work of Christ. We should call upon people to repent and believe the Gospel of Christ's death for sin and resurrection for justification. The time is coming when heralds will again proclaim the coming of the King and His kingdom. It is for this we pray when we intelligently say, "Thy kingdom come."

4. The King Calling to Himself Assistants (4:18-22).

a. His command of authority (vv. 18, 19). He did not persuade them, but issued a mandate. To command is the King's prerogative, not to argue or entreat. Happy is the man who has learned this.

b. The station of the servants Christ called (vv. 18-24). They were men of lowly birth and occupation—fishermen. God chooses the foolish things of this world to confound the wise, and the weak things to confound the things which are mighty (I Cor. 1:26, 27). These men were busily engaged in service when the call was issued. The Lord always calls His servants from the ranks of the employed. There is no place for a lazy man in Christ's kingdom.

c. They were called to definite service (v. 19). He said, "I will make you *fishers of men.*" He had previously called them to be disciples (John 1:36-42). He now called them to service. This was not the Gospel call to sinners to believe on Christ for salvation, but the call to service of those who have already heeded His call to discipleship.

d. Their prompt obedience (vv. 20-22). They gave up their business and homes, not even inquiring as to where their salary was to come from. They put their trust in Him who called, believing that He was able to supply their needs. There is no time to delay when the King commands. There is no time for questions, for the King's business requires haste.

5. The King's Triumphant Progress (4:23-25).

He went the whole rounds of Galilee, teaching the Scriptures, preaching the Gospel of the kingdom and healing all manner of diseases. He did a threefold work:

a. Teaching the Scriptures in the synagogues (v. 23). The revelation of God needed to be explained. This is what He was doing in Nazareth (Luke 4:16-26). Such is the primary duty of every minister.

b. Preaching the Gospel of the kingdom (v. 23). The King was present and heralding His own mission. He was ready to establish His kingdom if they had been willing to receive Him. Despite His knowledge of their unwillingness to receive Him, He presented His claims as though the kingdom would then have been established.

c. Healing all manner of diseases (vv. 23-25). There was no form of disease which He could not cure, and so abundant was His success that "his fame went throughout all Syria: and they brought unto him all sick people that were taken with divers diseases and torments, and those which were possessed with devils, and those which were lunatic, and those that had palsy; and he healed them. And there followed him great multitudes of people from Galilee, and from Decapolis, and from Jerusalem, and from Judea, and from beyond Jordan."

C. *The King's Manifesto or the Royal Proclamation* (5:1—7:29). This section of Matthew is commonly called the "Sermon on the Mount." This proclamation of the Lord from the mountain was rather the announcement of the laws which should obtain in His kingdom. It should be further borne in mind that these laws do not set forth terms of salvation to sinners, but the principles of life which shall obtain when Christ shall reign on the earth.

1. The Characteristics of the Subjects of the Kingdom (5:1-12). These characteristics are set forth in the nine beatitudes.

a. Consciousness of utter spiritual poverty (v. 3). "Poor in spirit" does not mean to be without money (Isa. 66:2), but to come to the end of self in a state of absolute spiritual beggary, having no power to alter one's condition or to make oneself better.

b. Profound grief because of spiritual insolvency (v. 4). Mourning here is not because of external grief, but because of the keen consciousness of guilt before a holy God.

c. Humble submission to God's will (v. 5). This is the result of mourning over spiritual insolvency. Those who have taken to heart their sinful condition are meek in spirit.

d. An intense longing to conform to the laws of the kingdom (v. 6). The one who has received the righteousness of Christ as a free gift follows after the purity of character which expresses itself in deeds of righteousness. This is not doing deeds of righteousness to be saved, but the righteous living of the one who has been graciously put in Christ.

e. Merciful (v. 7). The subjects of the kingdom now take on the character of the King. Because of the mercifulness of Christ, His followers will be merciful.

f. Purity of heart (v. 8). Since the King is absolutely pure, the subjects who enjoy fellowship with Him must have heart purity. Those whose hearts are pure are able to see God now in everything.

g. Peacemakers (v. 9). The one who has received the peace of God through Jesus Christ will diffuse peace in others. The subjects of Christ's kingdom not only have peace, but follow after that which makes for peace.

h. Suffering for Christ's sake (v. 10). The world hated Christ the King, therefore those who reflect His spirit in their lives shall suffer persecution (II Tim. 3:12). Since the King went to the cross for these principles, His subjects can expect the same treatment (John 15:20).

i. Suffer reproach (v. 11). This means to be spoken against falsely. To have all manner of evil spoken against one for Christ's sake is an occasion for glorying. Great rewards in Heaven are promised to all such.

2. The Responsibilities of the Subjects of the Kingdom (5:13-16).

The world is in utter darkness because of its corruption. The subjects of the kingdom are to live such lives as to purify and enlighten. Their responsibilities are set forth under the figures of salt and light.

a. Ye are the salt of the earth (v. 13). The properties of salt are: penetrating, purifying, preserving. Since salt only preserves and purifies in the measure that it penetrates, the Christian must enter into the life of the world in order to preserve it from decay.

b. Ye are the light of the world (v. 14). Light illuminates and warms. This world is dark and cold. In this darkness the Devil has set many pitfalls and snares. The subjects of the kingdom should so live as to prevent the unwary from stumbling or falling.

3. The Laws of the Kingdom (5:17-48).

a. As to deeds of righteousness (vv. 17-20). The subjects of the kingdom will live in conformity to God's laws. Their obedience to laws will not be to win divine favor, but a demonstration of their kinship with Christ the King. Christ came to fulfill God's Law.

b. As to sanctity of life (vv. 21-26). The subject of the kingdom will seek to conserve his own life and that of the life of others. "Thou shalt not kill" means more than to refrain from taking life. Rash anger is heart murder (v. 22).

c. As to organized life (vv. 27-32). The family is the unit of society. There is no sin which so rots society as that against the relation of the sexes. The two awful sins against the family are: (1) adultery (vv. 27-30). Christ shows that adulterous thoughts which never ripen into open acts are a violation of the seventh commandment. There is heart adultery as well as heart murder. (2) Divorce (vv. 31, 32). Moses because of the hardness of the hearts of the people permitted a man in the case of adultery to put away his wife and give her a bill of divorcement.

d. As to oaths (vv. 33-37). Speech is the absolute test of character. The truth and that alone is to characterize the speech of the subject of the kingdom. Whatever is more than the simple form of affirmation or denial comes of the Devil.

e. As to behavior toward those who do not recognize the laws of the kingdom (vv. 38-48).

(1) Not revengeful (vv. 38, 39). Turning the other cheek after being smitten, means after one insult prepare for another without revenge. The best commentary on this is Christ's meek behavior when smitten in the presence of the high priest (John 18:22-33).

(2) Willingness to do more than required (v. 41). If compelled to go one mile, go two miles with the one compelling you. Rather than quarrel with the man compelling you to do that which you cannot help, show willingness to do more.

(3) Be charitable (v. 42). Our hearts should always be open, ready to give to all—worthy and unworthy. Even the borrower should not be turned away.

(4) Love your enemies (vv. 45-48). Loving them consists in:

(a) Blessing them that curse us.

(b) Doing good to them that hate us.

(c) Praying for those who despitefully use us.

Doing this displays the positive proof that we are God's children.

4. The Motive of Righteousness (6:1-34).

Having in the previous chapter set forth the standards of the kingdom, Christ now exhibits the underlying principles which actuate the subjects of the kingdom.

a. As to giving (vv. 1-4). Almsgiving was not to be done to be seen of men. To seek publicity in doing alms will be to miss the rewards of the heavenly Father. This is a most important and wholesome instruction for this advertising age.

b. As to praying (vv. 5-15).

(1) False prayer (vv. 5-7). This consists in praying to be *seen and heard of men* (v. 5). Many of the prayers in public are false, for more thought is given to what people think than to what God thinks, and also using vain repetitions. This does not forbid the asking more than once for the same thing. Christ and Paul asked three times for the same thing (Matt. 26:39-46; II Cor. 12:7, 8). The reason is that your Father knoweth what things you have need of before you ask Him.

(2) True prayer (v. 6). Since real praying is a transaction between the individual soul and God, there should be a real desire for fellowship with Him which moves one to meet God in the secret place. We should have our closet prayers where all the world is shut out and we are shut in with God.

(3) The model prayer (vv. 9-15). This involves:

(a) A right relationship—"Our Father" (v. 9).

(b) Right attitude—"Hallowed be thy name" (vv. 9, 10).

(c) Right spirit—"Give us this day our daily bread" (vv. 11-13).

c. As to fasting (vv. 16-18). The true reason for fasting is to be found in the opportunity it gives for a clear vision of God. Those who have thus seen God will make it manifest in a joyful countenance.

d. As to earthly riches (vv. 19-24). The Lord knew the

temptations which would befall His children on their earthly pilgrimage and the anxiety to which it would lead; therefore He set forth the proper attitude toward earthly riches.

(1) The nature of earthly riches (vv. 19-21).

(a) Uncertain (vv. 19, 20). Earthly treasures corrode or are taken away from us; therefore we should lay up for ourselves treasures in Heaven where they are absolutely safe from corruption and thieves.

(b) Seductive (v. 21). Christ called riches deceitful (Matt. 13:22). It is not wrong to possess earthly treasures, but when the treasures possess us they become a snare to us.

(2) The effect of earthly riches (vv. 22-24).

(a) They blunt the moral and spiritual perceptions (vv. 22, 23). Those who become enamored with the things of this world soon become irresponsive to spiritual things. It is impossible to serve God and mammon. When the heart is upon earthly treasures it is taken from God. The double eye is disastrous to spirituality.

(b) They render null and void all service (v. 24). As soon as one's heart is stolen by riches, he becomes unfit for spiritual service.

e. As to faith in the heavenly Father (vv. 25-34).

(1) Be not anxious about food and clothing (vv. 25-32). Because to do so shows:

(a) Distrust in God (v. 30). God is able to supply His children's need.

(b) It is useless (v. 31). Anxiety can bring nothing. While it brings nothing, it weakens our service.

(c) It is heathenish (v. 32). Those who have not learned to trust God may worry over temporal affairs, but those who trust God as their loving Father will be free from care.

(2) Be anxious to seek the kingdom of God and serve Him (vv. 33, 34). This means that worldly affairs should be subordinated to things of the Spirit. This does not preclude the proper foresight touching a reasonable support for oneself and family. The warning is not against proper forethought, but worry.

5. The Judgments of Righteousness (7:1-29).

a. Concerning censorious judgments (vv. 1-12).

(1) The sin and folly of (vv. 1-5). This prohibition does not forbid our making estimate of the lives of those about us, for "by their fruits ye shall know them." Neither does it prevent us from administering rebuke to those who deserve it. It is not wrong to condemn the errors and faults of those who are in ways of sin. It does not mean that sin should not be rebuked till we ourselves are perfect. It does rebuke that readiness to blame others and to magnify their weaknesses and error. We should spend much time in judging ourselves. The reason we are incapable of judging others is that the beam of our eyes prevents a clear vision of the mote of our brother.

(2) The duty of discrimination in dealing out holy things (v. 6). The Gospel should be preached to all, but it should be borne in mind that "dogs" and "swine" have no comprehension of holy things. We should turn from those who reject and treat with contempt the Gospel message.

(3) Qualification for discrimination in judging (vv. 7-12).

(a) A life of prayer (vv. 7-11). Only those are able to rightly divide the Word of truth who live a life of prayer. Those who "ask, seek and knock" will avoid mistakes in this respect.

(b) A disposition to treat others as one would be treated (v. 12). In all doubtful questions between us and man, we should deal with our fellows as we would have them deal with us; in fact, the whole law concerning human relations is compressed into this one rule. It is not merely to refrain from doing injury, but positively to do for others that which we would desire to have done unto ourselves under similar circumstances. Confucius set forth this principle negatively, but Christ positively. Between the negative and positive sides of this rule is found the difference between heathenism and Christianity. No man can live this rule unless he has been born from above and abides in Christ, and in the school of prayer till he becomes like Christ. The world has stolen this precept of Christ and is demanding of those who are under the power of the Devil to live it. Regeneration and submission to Christ constitute the essential preparation for keeping the golden rule.

b. Entrance into the kingdom urged (vv. 13, 14). There are

two ways only before each one—life and death, Heaven and Hell. The narrow gate is the way of life. While the gate is strait and the way is narrow, it is an open gate and the only way to life, and all are invited to enter. The gate which opens to every good thing in life is strait. The way of Jesus Christ is not the way of the crowd —the way of the crowd leads to destruction. Though the gate that leads to eternal life is strait and the way narrow in the beginning, it broadens out until the fullness of life is realized.

c. Warnings against false teachers (vv. 15-20).

(1) Their real existence (v. 15). Ever since God has had a people, false prophets and teachers have appeared among them. That they appear everywhere need not at all surprise us, for Christ foretold that such should be the case.

(2) Their nature (v. 15).

(a) They are hypocritical. The Devil does his most successful work by masquerading as an angel of light (II Cor. 11:14, 15). His ministers appear in this way and turn people from the narrow to the broad way. All through the centuries his success has come through his ability to deceive.

(b) They are destructive. This is suggested by their being ravening wolves. It is when the wolf is in sheep's clothing that it does its most destructive work. False teachers are doing their most deadly work while pretending to be loyal to the Bible and Jesus Christ.

(3) The unfailing test (vv. 16-18). "By their fruits ye shall know them." Every tree bears its own kind of fruit. Nature is inexorable in her laws as to this. One may search the universe in vain for an exception to this rule. It is equally true in the spiritual world. There is a vital connection between the faith of the heart and the fruit of the life. That which comes out of the life was first in the heart.

(4) Their ultimate end (v. 19). All false teachers shall be finally punished by being cast into the fire. Although God has infinite patience and bears long, He will see to it that this evil work does not go on forever.

d. The dangers of empty profession (vv. 21-23).

(1) Merely calling Christ Lord will not answer for doing His will (v. 21).

(2) One may do supernatural works and not be saved (vv. 22, 23). Not all supernatural works are divine. There is a supernatural work of evil. It is the responsibility of every believer to test the spirit (I John 4:1, 2). Every spirit that confesseth not that Jesus Christ is come in the flesh is not of God.

(3) They shall be separated from God (v. 23). One may have been a Sunday school teacher or a minister and have performed mighty works, and yet hear from Christ the awful declaration, "Depart from me; I never knew you."

e. The one and only safe way (vv. 24-29).

(1) Hear the sayings of Christ. To do this one must give attention to reading the Word of God.

(2) Do what Christ commands (vv. 24, 25). Hearing and doing the teaching of Christ is building upon the solid rock. Hearing and not doing Christ's sayings is to build upon the sand. Obedience must follow hearing Christ.

D. *The Dynamics of the Kingdom, or the King Demonstrates His Mighty Power* (8:1–9:34).

These mighty works or miracles are samples of what the King can do over the chief foes of mankind . . . sin, sickness, satanic power, death, sorrow and storms. They display the King's mighty power to establish and administer the affairs of the kingdom. It is fitting that they should be grouped here following the laws of the kingdom, for they show the King's power to produce within the subjects of the kingdom the graces of character set forth in these laws and to administer the affairs of the kingdom.

Because of the limited space and the purpose of this book the most outstanding of these miracles are selected.

1. A Leper Healed (8:1-4).

a. The dreadful disease (v. 2). It was leprosy; the most loathsome and hopeless disease known. In the Jewish ritual it was regarded as a symbol of sin and incurable by man. Just as leprosy was incurable by man, so only the divine Physician can cure sin.

b. The leper's faith (v. 2). His cry was most pitiable, but his faith was strong. He fully believed that Jesus was able, but was uncertain as to His willingness to heal him. Jesus is both willing and able to heal the sinner of his sins if he will cry to Him in faith.

c. Jesus' power (v. 3). Jesus put forth His hand and touched the leper, bidding the disease to depart, and instantly the man was cleansed. Jesus has the power and is willing to heal the moral leper today.

2. Jesus Healed the Centurion's Servant (8:5-13).

a. The disease (v. 6). It was paralysis. In paralysis a man is helpless and disqualified for service.

b. The centurion's humility (v. 8). He first sent the Jewish elders and then his friends (Luke 7:3, 6) because he felt his unworthiness. The case of his servant was so grave that he brushed aside his timidity and personally appealed to Jesus. Jesus is pleased
Him.
when men realize their helplessness and make personal appeal to

c. The centurion's faith (vv. 8, 9). In spite of his unworthiness he committed his case to the Lord. He believed that if Jesus would but speak the word, his servant would be healed.

d. The wonderful power of Jesus (v. 13). He did not even need to see the helpless man and touch him, but only needed to speak the word and it was done. He can heal miles away just as readily as when in the presence of the afflicted one.

3. Jesus Heals Peter's Mother-in-law (8:14, 15).

a. She was sick of a fever (v. 14). Jesus was invited into Peter's home to heal this woman (Luke 4:38).

b. He touched her hand and rebuked the fever, and it left her (v. 15).

c. The cure was immediate. She arose and ministered to Jesus and His disciples. When a woman arises from a sickbed and gets supper for thirteen men, you can be sure that the healing was genuine. Divine healing is immediate and full.

4. Jesus Stills the Waves (8:23-27).

a. Great tempest in the sea (v. 24). The ship was covered with the waves. The disciples were affrighted.

b. Their appeal to the Lord (v. 25). They knew that being saved from drowning was dependent upon the action of Jesus.

c. Jesus rebuked the winds and the sea. A great calm followed.

d. The disciples were filled with amazement. The wind and the sea obeyed the King.

5. Jesus Casts Out Demons (8:28-34).

After stilling the tempest, Jesus crossed to the other side of the sea into heathen territory.

a. Met by two men possessed by demons (v. 28). Their condition was desperate (see Mark 5:1-17; Luke 8:27). So fierce were they that no one could safely pass that way. They wore no clothes and no chains were strong enough to hold them. Many today are possessed with demons and their number is greatly increasing (I Tim. 4:1).

b. What they knew about Christ (v. 29). They knew that He was the Son of God and that He had come to destroy the Devil and his work. Among demons there is no doubt as to the deity of Jesus Christ and of the judgment to come. The reason men do not believe is because their eyes are blinded by the Devil (II Cor. 4:4).

c. The limitation of the Devil's power (v. 31). The devils knew that it was only a question of time until their torment should begin. Although the Devil is mighty in power he cannot even enter into a hog without God's permission.

d. Christ's power to deliver from the Devil (vv. 30-32). The demons quailed before Him, not daring to dispute His power but begged permission to enter the swine.

6. Jesus Heals a Woman with an Issue of Blood (9:20-22).

a. Her helpless condition (v. 20). She had been a great sufferer for twelve long years, not only for the disease but at the hands of the physicians (Mark 5:26).

b. Her faith (v. 21). She demonstrated her faith by pressing her way through the thronging multitude. Her faith was so strong that she believed contact with the Master's garment would secure the needed help.

c. Her confession (v. 21; cf. Luke 8:47). She thought furtively to get the blessing, but Jesus perceived that virtue had gone out from Him and had her make a public confession. Public confession of faith in Christ tends to strengthen one's faith.

d. Christ's words of encouragement (v. 22). He told her that it was her faith, not her touch that saved her.

7. Jesus Opening the Eyes of Two Blind Men (9:27-31).

a. Their persistence of faith (v. 28). These poor men had heard of the wonderful works of Jesus. This wrought in them a desire to be healed. They therefore followed Him along the way, crying out for help. The proof that faith is genuine is that it holds on.

b. The intelligence of faith (v. 27). They cried unto Him as the Son of David, showing that they recognized Him as the promised Messiah. The prophet had foretold such to be the works of the Messiah (Isa. 29:18; 35:5; 42:7). Faith is the highest form of knowledge. The exercise of faith is not a leap into the dark, but a leap into the arms of the Lord of life and light.

c. The challenge of faith (v. 28). In reply to His challenge they gave Him a definite answer. The Lord wants us to commit ourselves definitely to Him.

d. The triumph of faith (vv. 29, 30). Their faith brought them into touch with the Lord of life, who vindicated His power by opening their eyes.

E. *The Propagation of the Kingdom* (9:35–10:42).

Having noted the proclamation of the laws of the kingdom in chapters 5-7, and the demonstration of the power of the King to establish and administer the affairs of the kingdom by the mighty miracles recorded in chapters 8 and 9, we now come to the consideration of the measures adopted for its propagation.

1. A Plenteous Harvest Envisioned (9:35-38).

a. Christ's compassion (v. 36). As He went on His rounds preaching the Gospel of the kingdom, He saw the multitudes as sheep having no shepherd. This sight aroused His sympathy for them.

b. A plenteous harvest and the few laborers (v. 37). He saw the whole world as a field of grain ready to be harvested, but with few who were willing to labor in the harvest field.

c. Pray ye the Lord of the harvest that He will send forth laborers into His harvest (v. 38). Those whom He would send forth as laborers in His harvest He desires to be imbued with the Spirit of sympathy which would move them to pray for laborers to be thrust forth.

2. The Twelve Sent Forth (10:1-42).

The sending forth of the twelve shows the method adopted by Jesus Christ in the propagation of the kingdom. It should be definitely borne in mind that this chapter does not outline the policy of missionary endeavor in this present age. In order to show the dispensational aspects of this lesson the following divisions of the chapter are suggested:

a. Instructions bearing immediately upon the apostles' work to the death of Christ (vv. 1-15). In strictness of interpretation these teachings cannot be applied to any later periods.

(1) The ministers chosen (vv. 1-4). These twelve humble men were chosen and commissioned to carry forth work of propagation of the kingdom. These twelve stood in a peculiar relation to Israel.

(2) The sphere of their mission (vv. 5, 6). They were to go only to Jews. They had no message for Gentiles or even Samaritans. After Pentecost this sphere widened (Luke 24:46-49; Acts 1:8). No such restrictions obtain with reference to ministers today. The middle wall of partition was broken down by the death of Christ.

(3) Their message (v. 7). By "The kingdom of heaven is at hand" is meant that the kingdom of Israel was at hand; that Jesus Christ, the promised King was present and ready to set up His kingdom. After the Church is translated, the same message will be taken up for a brief time by the believing remnant. (See Acts 15:13-18; Rom. 11; Rev. 7.)

(4) The supernatural authentication of their mission (v. 8). They were clothed with power to work miracles. These wonderful works were really done by the twelve.

(5) Their maintenance (vv. 9, 10). They were to make no provision for their support, but to depend wholly upon the Lord who sent them. Since they had received the message and the power gratuitously, they were to give it out the same way.

(6) Responsibility of those to whom the message was delivered (vv. 11-15). If the people would not receive them and their message, they were to turn from them and pronounce judgment upon them.

b. Instructions concerning the testimony from Pentecost onward (vv. 16-23). After Pentecost, testimony for Christ would be fraught with great danger. Both Jews and Gentiles would assail the messengers with the most bitter persecutions. They were scourged in the synagogues before heathen magistrates. Instead of bringing peace to the homes, they brought divisions of the fiercest kind among families. In their defense they were to rely upon the Holy Spirit to aid them. These conditions were literally fulfilled in the period from Pentecost to the destruction of Jerusalem. Since the fall of Jerusalem no one has ever been scourged in a synagogue. Verse 23 seems to carry the work forward to the time of preaching the Gospel of the kingdom in the Tribulation time. The Lord's coming is then so speedy that their testimony will be cut short.

c. The teaching applicable in all ages (vv. 24-42). The disciple has the position of oneness with the Master. He is to courageously declare the whole counsel of God though violently opposed. Though the testimony result in the most bitter opposition, the witness should not be surprised or discouraged for so completely is the Lord identified with His disciples that He accepts treatment of them as treatment of Himself.

F. *How the Kingdom Was Received* (11:1-30).

In the teaching of this book the progress of thought in Matthew should be kept in mind. In chapters 5-7 the laws of the kingdom are set forth; in chapters 8 and 9 the mighty works demonstrate the King's ability to establish and administer the affairs of the kingdom; in chapter 10 the propagation of the kingdom through the sending forth of the twelve apostles; and in chapters 11 and 12 the reception of the kingdom is illustrated.

In showing the attitude of heart of the people toward Jesus Christ the King, four classes of hearers are described:

1. Perplexed Hearers like John the Baptist (11:2-11).

John believed that Jesus was the Christ (v. 2), but was somewhat perplexed as to the manner of the establishment of the kingdom (v. 3). In the Old Testament prediction there were two lines in the Messianic prophecies. The one set forth Christ as the Suffering One as in Isaiah 53; the other as the Invincible Conqueror as in Isaiah 63. Indeed in Isaiah 60:1, 2 we have the two advents in one view (Luke 4:17-20). The Baptist had in his preaching mainly emphasized the line of prophecy which made the Messiah the mighty conqueror

(Matt. 3:10-12). He declared that the "ax is laid at the root of the tree," and that there was to be a separation of the chaff from the wheat and a burning of the chaff; but now the King was occupied with the opening of the eyes of the blind, etc. John saw Christ as the One who would remove the sins of the people by the shedding of His blood (John 1:29), but failed to see the interval between the time of His suffering and the time of His triumph. Since the nature of the interval between the first and second comings of Christ (the age in which we live) was not known until Christ revealed it in the parables of chapter 13, we do not wonder at John's perplexity. John's faith was failing him; neither did he send this deputation to Jesus for the sake of his disciples. He was a true prophet and a faithful man, but was perplexed, because this situation had not as yet been revealed to him.

2. Violent Hearers (11:17-19).

They were willing to receive the kingdom according to their own way, but were unwilling to conform to its laws as proclaimed by Christ the King. They seized it with violent hands. Christ told them that before the coming of John the Baptist the prophets and the law were the courses of ascertaining the divine will and that if they would receive John, he would be the Elijah to lead them into the kingdom age. Elijah is to appear immediately before the coming of Christ in judgment (Mal. 4:5, 6), and direct the hearts of the people to the King. Their ears were closed to everything but their own carnality. They would not repent when called upon to do so by John, nor rejoice when called upon by Christ (vv. 17-19).

3. The Stouthearted Unbeliever (11:20-24).

In Chorazin, Bethsaida, and Capernaum Christ had done most of His mighty works, but the people deliberately set their hearts against Him and His message. It was not for lack of knowledge and opportunity that they were unsaved, but for the purposeful rejection of Christ. Tyre and Sidon were filled with immoral profligates and idolaters, but they will be more tolerably dealt with in the day of judgment than those who willfully reject Christ. To hear the Gospel is not enough, one must repent and be converted. God measures responsibilities by opportunities one may have.

4. Hearers Who Are Babes in Spirit (11:25-30).

There were some among the people who heard Jesus with child-like faith. They believed that Jesus was the Messiah and opened their hearts to receive Him. Christ invited those who have the child-like spirit to come to Him and receive rest—rest for their intellect, rest for their conscience, rest for their will and heart.

G. *The Antagonism to the Kingdom* (12:1-50).

In chapter 11 we saw the shameful indifference of the Jews to their King. In this chapter we see the positive and bitter opposition manifesting itself against Him. They are not only without a heart for Him, but do their best to destroy Him. The immediate occasion for their wicked determination was Christ's relation to the sabbath day. The sabbath was a peculiar sign between Jehovah and Israel (Exod. 31:13-17). It was therefore rightfully a special day for the Jews. Let no one confuse the resurrection day of the Christian with the sabbath. The one thing in common in respect to these days is that one day out of the seven is particularly set apart for the Lord.

With the increasing pressure in the propagation of the kingdom emerged the nature of the King's Person. He definitely declares:

1. The Son of Man Is the Lord of the Sabbath (12:1-8).

The hungry disciples were plucking ears of corn on the sabbath. With this the Pharisees found fault. They asserted that the disciples were breaking the law when in reality they were only doing that which was a violation of the traditions with which they had encrusted the law. To their cavils Christ replied and showed that God's purpose in instituting the sabbath was to serve man's highest interests and to contribute to his happiness. "The sabbath was made for man, and not man for the sabbath." In His reply He truly answered these carping Pharisees and pressed His transcendent claim as to the dignity of His Person, which moved them to plot His death. Note His claim:

a. He is greater than their greatest King David (vv. 3, 4). David when rejected was forced to do that which was unlawful for him to do.

b. He is greater than their sacrifices and priesthood (v. 5). If the priests because of their position and service could violate the sabbath laws and be blameless, much more could He who is greater than they in performing His work of sacrifice for their redemption be considered guiltless.

c. He is greater than the Temple (v. 6). The temple with its gorgeous rites and ceremonies was but typical of Himself. Much more then, did He have the right to do what He did.

d. He is greater than the sabbath (v. 8), for He is the very Lord of the sabbath.

2. Healing a Man with a Withered Hand on the Sabbath (12: 9-14).

In order that they might accuse Him, they asked: "Is it lawful to heal on the sabbath day?" Jesus' reply was both a question and a declaration. His question as to whether a man would not rescue an only sheep was practically saying that they were His sheep in a pit of sin and that He had come to lift them out. Following this question, He declared that it was lawful to do well on the sabbath day, implying that in keeping with His relation to them, He was endeavoring to lift them from the ditch. To accentuate His words He healed the man, demonstrating His power to rescue the unfortunate sheep. The man with the withered hand is a type of withered Israel, spiritually and nationally.

This was too much for them. They would not repent so the Pharisees held a council against Him as to how they might destroy Him. This widened His testimony. Multitudes followed Him and He healed them all. This was in fulfillment of Isaiah 42:1-8.

3. They Accuse Him of Being in League with the Devil (12: 22-37).

a. The occasion of this charge was the casting out of a demon (vv. 22-30). The case was a notable one. These people were amazed. Their conclusion was that the promised Messiah the Son of David was in their midst. When the Pharisees heard this, they declared: "This fellow does not cast out devils, but by Beelzebub the prince of the devils."

b. The effect of this miracle was twofold:

(1) Upon the multitudes. They were amazed and cried out, "Is not this the son of David?" Their question clearly implied that His mighty works commended Him as the Messiah.

(2) Upon the Pharisees. When they heard what the peo-

ple were saying their anger and satanic malice were aroused. They said He was casting out demons by the prince of demons. They did not deny the miracle, but sought to account for it without acknowledging Him as the Messiah, so they affirmed that He was in league with the Devil. Jesus claimed that He was the Messiah, the Son of God, and wrought miracles to prove His claim; but the Pharisees sought to slander Him, making Him an imposter. Such an accusation in the face of given light shows a moral perversity that renders salvation impossible.

In Christ's reply He exposes their folly and charges with awful guilt. He argued that every kingdom divided against itself must fall. This showed the absurdity of their charges. He was doing the works of God, not Satan, for before their very eyes He had driven the demon from the man. He was undoing the works of the Devil. Wherever He went men were blessed. He opened blind cyes, unstopped deaf ears, made the lame to walk, and raised the dead. He was thus binding the strong man, the Devil, and spoiling his house.

He met their accusations with unanswerable logic and demanded a verdict. He charged home upon them their awful guilt. They had attributed the work of the Holy Spirit to the Devil. This Christ calls blasphemy against the Holy Spirit for which there is no pardon.

c. The Pharisees demand a sign from Jesus (vv. 38-45). He called them an evil and adulterous generation and said that no sign would be given except the prophet Jonas. The death and resurrection of Christ was the only sign given. The condemnation passed upon them was not an arbitrary matter—they had shown themselves incapable of moral discernment—they did know good from evil.

H. *The Mysteries of the Kingdom Unfolded* (13:1-58).

By "mystery" in the Scriptures is meant truth undiscoverable by human reason made known by revelation. (See the Scofield Bible for a comprehensive list of mysteries in the Bible.) The seven parables of this chapter set forth in a most graphic manner the condition of affairs in the world in the interval between the crucifixion of Christ and His second coming. The kingdom of Heaven is not the Church. These parables display the admixture of moral and spiritual affairs in the world between Christ's ascension and His return to the earth.

The Bible student should be clear as to the purpose of teaching in parables. There is much misunderstanding concerning this matter. The parabolic method of teaching makes clear the truth to those who love it, but conceals it to those who have no heart for it. Jesus did not teach in parables until the rulers set their hearts against Him. When in the light of His miracles and wonderful works they turned against Him and attributed His works to the Devil, He denounced them in the most scathing terms and began in fulfillment of prophecy to teach in parables (Matt. 13:14, 15; cf. Isa. 6:9, 10). Jesus came, as did His forerunner, John the Baptist, proclaiming the kingdom as at hand. The people rejected and crucified Him. He arose from the grave and ascended into Heaven, assuring His disciples that He would come again and then set up His kingdom.

1. The Parable of the Sower (13:1-23).

a. The sower (v. 23). The sower is not named in this parable. In the parable of the wheat and tares the sower is the Son of man (v. 37). It is evident that the sower is the Lord Jesus Christ. Through the centuries He has been sowing the seeds of divine truth by means of the prophets, apostles, and ministers.

b. The kinds of soil (vv. 4-8, 19-33). The soil is the human heart (v. 19). The seed sown is the Word of God (v. 19). In this sowing the sower and the seed are the same, but the results are entirely different. The difference of results lies in the condition of the soil, which in turn is the state of the human heart. Notwithstanding the fidelity of the sower and the purity of the seed, the results of preaching God's Word depend upon the condition of the human heart. This parable reveals four kinds of soil or hearers.

(1) The wayside or hardhearted hearer (v. 4; cf. v. 19). The wayside means the track beaten down by the hoofs of animals and the feet of men. Because the soil was unbroken and uncultivated the seed could not get beneath the surface, therefore, was devoured by the fowls that came along. The great truth taught is that the heart unbroken or hard is not favorable for the Gospel. Such a heart it penetrates not, but lies loosely upon the surface. By such the Gospel is not recognized as God's means of restoring them to Himself. The fowls which devour the seed represent the wicked one. While the heart remains hard the Devil finds some way to snatch away the truth.

This explains the difficulty of the lodgment of God's Word in the hearts of men.

(2) The stony places—or superficial hearers (vv. 5, 6; cf. vv. 20, 21). This means not stones mixed with soil, but stones with a thin layer of soil over them. With such conditions the seed springs up quickly, but likewise scorches quickly as it has no depth of earth. The great lesson learned is that hearts superficially impressed receive God's Word with joy, but when trials and persecutions come because of God's Word, they wither away and die not being able to stand the test.

(3) The thorny ground or preoccupied hearers (v. 7; cf. v. 22). In this case the ground is good, but has thorns in it. It is mellow enough and has sufficient depth, but has not been cleaned of thorns. Such really hear the Word of God, but the cares of this world and the deceitfulness of riches and lusts of other things entering in choke the Word and it becomes unfruitful (Mark 4:19). Many are the "thorny-ground" hearers of this age. Good seed cannot mature because of—

(a) Worldliness. Men and women are completely absorbed in the things of business and are burdened with anxious cares.

(b) Deceitfulness of riches. Anxious care in business brings riches to many. The effect of riches blunts the spiritual perceptions of men, thereby rendering them unsusceptible and unresponsive to God's call to higher things in life.

(c) Lusts of other things entering in. This means the pleasures of life. All these things choke the Word of God. Many of the enjoyments of life may be innocent in themselves, but they attract so much attention and consume so much energy and time that one has no place for Bible reading, meditation, and prayer. This is a vivid picture of many Christian people today. If perchance they get to religious services they have not enough energy to take part or keep awake while God's Word is being preached.

(4) The good ground or fruitful hearers (v. 8; cf. v. 23). This ground differs from all the rest. It was soft, mellow, clean, deep, and moist, therefore it was capable of fruit; some one hundred, some sixty, and some thirtyfold, showing the different degrees of

fruitfulness. In the measure that the heart is kept free from worldliness, riches, and pleasures, the good seed matures.

2. The Parable of the Wheat and Tares (13:24-30).

Keep in mind that these parables set forth the admixture of moral and spiritual interests in the period between Christ's rejection and His triumphant kingdom. These things only apply to the Church as they permeate that Body by virtue of its being formed within this period. Observe that it is part of the mysteries of the kingdom.

a. The sowers.

(1) The Son of man (v. 24; cf. v. 37). He is the One who sows the good seed. In the former parables the seed sown was the Word of God. In this, the children of the kingdom are the seed. The Word of God sown results in the children of the kingdom which in turn are sown as seed. The field in which they are sown is the world.

(2) The Devil (v. 39). He is in a peculiar sense Christ's enemy. He intensely hates Him and with a relentless energy strives to defeat His purpose in saving men. This malicious person operates at night sowing tares among the wheat.

b. The growing crops (v. 26). While the contrast in the sowers is severe, there is a striking resemblance in the growing crops. Although they are not easily distinguished while growing, the effects produced when eaten are quite different. The wheat is wholesome, but the tares produce illness. The chief danger in the tares lies in their resemblance to the wheat. The chief peril of the Devil is in that he strives to imitate God, even to be transformed as an angel of light (II Cor. 11:14, 15). This is the danger in all the false religions of today.

c. The harvests (v. 30). There comes a time when the fruitage of the growing crop shall be gathered. The servants were disposed to root out the tares at once, but the time was not ripe. They must grow together until the harvest. There is a timed separation coming—the end of this age. The separation is not made with human hands, but by angels under the direction of the Son of man. For the tares there is a furnace of fire where there shall be wailing and gnashing of teeth. The righteous shall be gathered into the Lord's garner and shall shine forth as the sun in the kingdom of the Father.

3. The Parable of the Mustard Seed (13:31, 32).

a. Its unimportant beginning (v. 31). "The least of all the seeds, but grows to be the greatest among herbs." Christ the King was of humble parentage. His disciples were unlettered fishermen. The parentage and humble circumstances of the King greatly perplexed the people. That twelve unlettered fishermen should be selected as His royal advisers is still more amazing. The prophet said concerning Him, that He should be despised, rejected, and forsaken.

b. Its vigorous growth (v. 32). From the very small beginning the movement inaugurated by Jesus Christ has become the mightiest in the earth.

c. Its lodging capacity (v. 32). The birds which find lodgment in the trees do not represent the children of men which find safety and salvation in the church. The birds constitute no part of the tree; they are foreign to and independent of it. The branches increase the growth of the tree, but birds are injurious and burdensome to it. They are predatory—waiting to pluck the tender buds or to prey upon the ripened fruit. The effect of their lodging in the branches of the tree is evil, blighting and marring its beauty. In Christ's interpretation of the first parable He said that the fowls represent the wicked one (v. 19).

4. The Parable of the Leavened Meal (13:33).

When the scriptural significance of the meal, the woman, and the leaven is known, the interpretation is easy.

a. The meal. Meal is something wholesome and nutritious. It was used in one of the sweet-savor offerings which typified Christ (Lev. 2:1-3, A.S.V.); it was food for the priests (Lev. 6:15-17, A.S.V.); Abraham had Sarah knead a cake out of three measures of meal for the angelic messengers (Gen. 18:6); Solomon's royal table was provided with it (I Kings 4:22); Elijah was fed upon a cake made of meal (II Kings 4:41); Elisha used meal as an antidote for the poison of death in the pot (II Kings 4:38-41).

b. The woman. The woman is not the head of the home but its administrator. Her responsibility is to take the bread provided by the head of the home, prepare it and distribute it to the children and others of her household. Dealing with doctrine is forbidden to women (I Tim. 2:12). The meaning then of this parable is that the true doctrine, the meal, is given for the nourishment of the children of the kingdom (II Peter 2:2; I Tim. 4:6) and would be officially corrupted by false doctrine.

c. The leaven. In Scripture leaven is invariably a type of evil. Let the following examples suffice as proof:

(1) All through the Old Testament leaven is a continual and unvarying type of evil (Exod. 12:15; Lev. 2:11). It is inconceivable that Jesus should arbitrarily change without due notice an explanation of a word which the Spirit of God had so unchangingly used for 2,000 years from an evil to a good sense.

(2) Jesus Himself makes leaven to denote sin (Matt. 16: 6-12; Mark 8:15).

(3) Paul uses leaven in its usual Biblical sense (I Cor. 5: 6-8; Gal. 5:8, 9).

This is the only interpretation that will harmonize with Christ's interpretation of the first two parables. Further facts patent to all prove that the professed church today is feeding upon the leaven of sensuality, formality, and legalism, instead of the unleavened bread of sincerity and truth—the Word of God. Many are handling the Word of God deceitfully (II Cor. 4:2). Multitudes will not endure sound doctrine (II Tim. 4:3, 4).

5. The Parable of the Hid Treasure (13:44).

The common interpretation of this parable—that Christ is the hid treasure for which the sinner must give up everything in order to buy salvation—is incorrect for the following reasons:

a. Christ is not hidden in a field but has been lifted up and made a spectacle to the whole world.

b. No one has ever been obliged to buy the world in order to get Christ.

c. Salvation cannot be purchased, for it is God's free and gracious gift.

d. No warrant is ever held out to a man to conceal his religion after he has obtained it.

In order to find ground that is safe and that we may appreciate its beauty and symmetry, let us break up the parable into its component parts:

(1) The field (v. 38). Fortunately this landmark has been

set by Jesus Christ Himself. Any interpretation which ignores this fact stands self-condemned.

(2) The treasure. In Psalm 135:4 we are told that Israel, the chosen people, is His treasure. The same truth is set forth in different places and ways (Deut. 7:6-8; 14:2; 26:18; 32:8, 9). When Christ uttered this parable, the ten tribes were already concealed from human observation, and this concealment was partly a prophecy of that which was to follow. The kingdom of Heaven as to its true relation and bearing is now hidden. Christ was primarily sent to the Jews; it was for their sake, the hid treasure, that He bought the field.

(3) The purchaser was none other but the Lord Jesus Christ, God's only begotten Son (John 3:16). None else had sufficient resources to buy the world.

(4) The purchase price. This was the precious blood of Jesus Christ, God's beloved Son, which is worth infinitely more than silver and gold, even all the treasures of earth (I Peter 1:13-19; Isa. 53).

6. The Parable of the Merchant Man Seeking Pearls (13:45, 46). The view that this merchant man represents the sinner seeking salvation is contrary to the whole teaching of the Scriptures. This would make the sinner to be seeking for Christ, while Christ is as indifferent as a lifeless pearl. The whole burden of revelation is that man, since the fall of Adam in the garden of Eden, has been hidden away from God, and that the triune God, the Father, the Son, and the Holy Spirit are all actively engaged in seeking for lost men.

a. The merchant man. He is Christ who is specifically engaged in the search for pearls. In this search he discovers one pearl of great price.

b. The purchasing price. The merchant man sold all, impoverished himself, in order to buy the pearl. The Scriptures nowhere assert or intimate that the sinner, poor, blind, naked and worthless, miserable, all covered with filthy rags must either buy Christ or salvation. Christ did impoverish Himself (Phil. 2:6-8) to purchase the one pearl of great price by His own precious blood (I Peter 1:18, 19; Eph. 5:25). Salvation is without money and without price.

c. The pearl of great price. This is the Church. Christ the merchant will find other pearls of great value, but the peerless gem set above all others will be the Church which He has purchased with His own blood. This truth is in harmony with the general teaching of the Scriptures which set forth the different bodies of the redeemed. The redeemed family of God is made up of different orders, but the one order which is exalted to the highest place is the Church which He purchased with His own blood, and of which He became the vital Head through the resurrection from the dead (Col. 1:18). Therefore to be a member of the Body of Christ, the Church, is the highest dignity that shall ever come to humanity.

7. The Parable of the Dragnet (13:47-50).

This parable gives us a picture of the consummation of the kingdom. It stands in perfect harmony with all the rest of the parables of the chapter. Viewed in this harmonious relation we see the incorrectness of the common interpretation of these parables. If leaven means the triumph of the Gospel and the conversion of the world by the activity of the Church, we have a strange ending of affairs—the dragnet filled with good and bad fishes; the triumphant (?) church full of men whom the angels cast into a place of eternal burning. Note the parts of the parable:

a. The sea. This word, when used in a figurative sense, denotes peoples or multitudes (Dan. 7:3; Rev. 17:15). This means then that out of this world shall be gathered a multitude of people good and bad.

b. The dragnet. The word *net* should be dragnet. The dragnet cast into the sea then means the preaching of the Gospel in this present age.

c. The dragnet drawn to the shore when full. This means that when God's purpose is made full regarding the preaching of the Gospel in this age, account will be taken of the results.

d. Assortment made by the angels. In the day of this accounting the angels will be the agents which shall separate the saved from the unsaved.

e. The destiny of the bad fish. The angels which are sent forth shall sever the wicked from among the just, and shall cast the wicked into the furnace of fire where there shall be wailing and gnashing of teeth.

I. *The Ministry and Teaching of the King in the Place of Rejection* (13:53–23:39).

1. Without Honor in His Own Country (13:53-58).

Jesus shared the common fate of men unacknowledged in His own country. Even His own brothers did not believe on Him till after His resurrection (John 7:3-8; cf. Acts 1:14). Familiarity has a paralyzing effect. At times it breeds contempt. Because of unbelief only a limited work could be done there.

2. John's Death a Precedent of Christ's Death (14:1-13).

News of the murder of John the Baptist is accepted as His own rejection and a precedent of His own death. Herod's conscience troubled him. He wanted to undo his wicked act, but it seemed that his adulterous passion held him fast. Multitudes today are in like condition. The news of the murder of John brought grief to the Master's heart and He withdrew to a desert place to commune with the Father. The people followed Him. Where Jesus is, the multitudes gather. Though the rulers had broken with Jesus, He did not abandon His work. He continued to preach and to heal. No case was found which He could not heal. He is the same sympathizing Saviour and mighty Lord.

3. Feeding the Hungry Multitudes (14:15-21).

The purpose of this miracle was to reveal Himself as the Bread of life sent down from Heaven (John 6:1-14).

a. Jesus' conference with the disciples (vv. 15-18).

(1) The disciples' request (v. 15). They asked that the multitude be sent away. They knew that they were in a desert place, therefore prudence would dictate that they should go to the villages to buy food. The disciples knew little of His power.

(2) Jesus' command (v. 16). "Give ye them to eat." Such a command would have been utter foolishness had He not possessed the power to create the supply, but as always with the command goes the power to do.

(3) The disciples' perplexity (v. 17). They said, "We have here but five loaves, and two fishes." They considered their meager resources and left Christ out. Christ knew that they had but

five loaves and two small fishes, still He commanded them to do the impossible. He wanted them to know that the things which are impossible with men are possible with God. To be face to face with the humanly impossible is a threefold benefit: to make us feel our dependence upon Christ; to drive us to Him for help in our need; to lead us to give glory to Him for the results. Though our gifts be small and our powers limited, yet in the hands of Christ we may accomplish much. Though our ability to teach, to preach, or give money be meager we should remember that our Lord with His ability is equal to any demands made.

b. Jesus' method in feeding the multitude (vv. 18-21).

(1) The Lord's part. He created the provisions. He is able to bring into existence that which will meet the needs of the hungry multitude. He blessed and gave thanks. He is able to meet all temporal and spiritual needs. His power is unlimited.

(2) The people's part. They were to sit down and eat. They were not responsible for the creation of the supply, but had a part in its distribution. Obedience to His command was necessary. Even after the food had been blessed and distributed the people would have perished with hunger had they not eaten. So today unless the people receive that which the Lord has provided, they will eternally starve.

4. Jesus Walking on the Sea (14:22-36).

The storm-tossed disciples on the sea at night are an example of the struggling followers of the Lord in the darkness of this present age, as they are tossed about by the tempest of the Evil One.

a. The disciples on the storm-tossed sea (vv. 22-24).

(1) They are sent across the sea by Christ (v. 22). Jesus constrained His disciples to get into the ship. Doubtless His reason for this was to keep them from entanglements in the movement of the people to make Him king, for in John 6:14, 15 it is shown that the people were excited by the feeding of the five thousand and they were about to make him king by force. Though they were somewhat unwilling to go, it was a mercy for Him to constrain them.

(2) Christ dismisses the multitude (v. 22). "He sent the multitudes away." This act may be considered as typical of His rejection of the nation whose rulers had already rejected Him.

(3) Christ praying alone in the mountain (v. 23). Temptation to earthly honor and power had come to Him; therefore, He went to the Father in prayer for relief and strength. The need for prayer is greatest at such times. We are not informed as to the object of His prayer. It is no doubt proper to surmise that He prayed for Himself and for His disciples. According to Mark 6:48, He saw the disciples toiling on the storm-tossed sea. We should learn from this that the disciple is never out of the sight of his Lord, even when he must struggle against the storms of life. The disciple is saved to the uttermost because His Lord ever liveth to make intercession for him.

b. Jesus went to the disciples (vv. 25-27).

(1) It was in the fourth watch of the night (v. 25). He did not come to them at once, but waited till almost dawn. However, it was the darkest part of the night. Their physical danger was great, but no doubt their mental perplexity was greater. They knew that the Lord had sent them, but why should they be in such straits if He sent them? The stormy sea is no evidence that the disciple is not in the Lord's appointed way. The disciple's concern should be to obey the command of the Lord, being assured that while doing His will, He will protect them.

(2) The disciples alarmed at the appearance of the Lord (v. 26). At the sight of Him they cried out for fear. They said, "It is a spirit." It was the coming of their best Friend to deliver them from danger. He frequently comes to us in such ways that we are affrighted.

(3) Jesus' words of comfort and good cheer (v. 27). In the midst of their distress they heard the Master's words, "Be of good cheer; it is I; be not afraid." This changed their fear to joy.

c. Peter walking on the water (vv. 28, 29).

(1) Peter's request (v. 28). As soon as Peter recognized the Lord's voice he cried, "Bid me come to thee on the water."

(2) Jesus' response (v. 29). At the Lord's, "Come," Peter left the boat and walked on the water. While he kept his eyes on the Lord he walked on the waves. His faith linked him with divine power and was thus upheld. Vital faith in Jesus Christ will enable the disciple to outride the storms of life.

d. Peter sinking (v. 30). He took his eyes off the Lord and

placed them upon the raging sea. This separated him from divine power. We should learn to fix our eyes upon the Lord instead of upon circumstances. Failure will surely follow if we give consideration to our circumstances and our own ability to master them.

e. Christ rescuing Peter (v. 31). When Peter began to sink he did the sensible thing. He cried out, "Lord, save me." Immediately Jesus stretched forth His hand and caught Peter. His salvation from death at the bottom of the sea was the result of the Lord taking hold of him. Jesus Christ in the incarnation was the divine hand reaching forth to rescue a sinking world. The significance of the expression, "caught him," is made clear in Hebrews 2:16. It is there declared that Jesus took not upon Himself the nature of angels, but the seed of Abraham. The same Greek word occurs in verse 31 of this chapter. We should understand from this that the eternal Son of God did not come in the form of man in order to show man the way to God, but to identify Himself with man through incorporation with man. He did not come as an example, but as a Saviour.

5. The King Demands Holiness of Life (15:1-20).

Life in the kingdom is more than conformity to commandments. Israel, God's covenant people, were called for a specific purpose and given definite marks of separation unto God. They mistook the things which were designed to make them separate for the demands of a holy life. This is a common error today among Christians. God's children must show by their lives their relation to their heavenly Father. The scribes and Pharisees came to Christ with the question as to why the disciples ate their meals with unwashed hands.

Christ severely rebuked them, calling them hypocrites for pretending to honor Him while in their hearts there was hostility. He accuses them of making the commandment of God of none effect through their traditions, showing that Isaiah had prophesied of them (Isa. 29:13). Christ called the multitude together and asked them to hear and understand that defilement comes out of the heart of man and not that which enters the body from without. Evil thoughts, murders, fornication, lying, etc., come out of the heart and thus defile a man.

6. The Rejected King Ministers to a Gentile (15:21-28).

In verses 1-20 is presented the apostasy of Israel and her rejection of Christ. In this ministry to the Syrophoenician woman we see a type—salvation reaching out to the Gentiles.

a. The mother's awful distress (vv. 21, 22). Her daughter was grievously vexed with a devil. The daughter was the one who was afflicted, but it was the mother who carried the burden. Perhaps the mother's sufferings were more intense than those of the child. If children would realize how completely their mother's sufferings are one with their own, they would be more careful to lighten their burdens. Would that mothers were as much interested in their daughter's spiritual interests as they are in their temporal. No doubt this Gentile woman had heard of the fame of Jesus and His power to heal, and many times had longed for Him to come that way that her daughter might be healed. Now that Jesus was in her neighborhood she came straightway to Him. Let us bring our children to Jesus. Perhaps they may be demon-possessed. He is able to heal them spiritually.

b. The mother's fervent appeal for help (vv. 22-25). She humbly fell at Jesus' feet and pleaded for mercy. She besought Him to cast the devil out. Hers is a model prayer.

(1) It was sincere and earnest. From the depth of her heart she cried to the Lord for help. Only such prayers avail.

(2) It was brief and definite. In a few well-chosen words she besought the Lord in behalf of her daughter. The Lord wants us to ask definitely for what we want.

(3) It was personal and humble. The Lord is pleased when we beseech Him in behalf of our children and friends. We should mention by name the objects of our prayers. She came humbly—she fell at His feet (Mark 7:25).

(4) It was believing and persistent (vv. 25-27). Though she was outside of the covenant people, she believed that the Lord would answer her cry of need. She persistently begged help of the Lord. She would not accept His apparent refusal. The Lord is pleased with the soul who will not let Him go until the blessing is granted (Luke 11:5-10; 18:1-8).

c. The woman's faith rewarded (vv. 26-28).

(1) Christ's apparent refusal (v. 23). "He answered her not a word." This seems passing strange that to this woman's distress He was irresponsive. Scarcely ever did anyone have to ask the second time. Frequently He did not wait to be asked. The reason for this silence was that a real difficulty lay in the way. He was sent to the lost sheep of the house of Israel. She was a stranger to the covenant people. Furthermore she appealed to Him on the wrong basis. She addressed Him as the Son of David, which only a child of the kingdom had a right to do. Only an Israelite had a right to seek His blessing as the "Son of David." His refusal was from His love. She must come in the right way.

(2) The woman's quick response (vv. 25-27). As soon as she perceived the difficulty, she worshiped Him as Lord and cried for help. While only an Israelite could approach Him as the "Son of David," all could come to Him and own Him as Lord. She willingly took her place as a Gentile "dog," recognizing that "salvation is of the Jews." Many times we would get what we ask if we would be willing to take our rightful place before Him. The word *dog* is a diminutive term, showing the pet or household dog which had a right to the crumbs which fell from the table.

(3) The glorious issue of her faith (v. 28). She got more than she asked. Her daughter was healed at once and the instructions she received were worth much to her, and she goes down in history with the Lord's commendation for her faith. True faith is invincible. It will not take "no" for an answer.

7. The King Healing a Great Multitude (15:29-31).

Although the rulers have broken with Jesus, He does not abandon His work, but continues to preach and work for the good of those who would hear. The multitudes pressed in upon Him and broke up His quiet time with the Father, but the great heart of the King was moved with compassion as He beheld the multitudes of suffering ones—sick, lame, blind, and palsied. The people brought their desperate and hopeless cases to Him, but there was nothing too hard for Him. He is just as compassionate and powerful to heal and save those who are ruined by sin.

8. The King Feeding Four Thousand (15:32-39). According to the connection in John 6:33-48, the real purpose of this miracle was to show Himself as the Bread of eternal life.

a. Jesus' conference with the disciples (vv. 32-34).

(1) He called the disciples to Him to tell them that in view of the multitudes having tarried now three days with Him, He is determined that they shall not go away fasting lest they faint by the way. A crowd of men and women always incited His sympathy. If we have His spirit, the condition of lost men will move us to pity.

(2) The disciples' perplexity (vv. 33, 34). They said: "Whence should we have so much bread in the wilderness?" They were looking on their meager resources and leaving out Christ. He knew that they had but seven small loaves and two fishes, but He commands them to do the impossible. He wished them to learn that the things which are impossible with men are possible with God. To be face to face with the humanly impossible has a threefold benefit—to make us feel our dependence upon Christ; to drive us to Him for help: and to lead us to give Him the glory for the results. Though our gifts be small and our powers limited, yet in the hands of Christ we may accomplish much.

b. The method of Christ in feeding the multitudes (vv. 35-39).

(1) The Master's part. He created the provisions. He was able to create the food which was required to meet the needs of the hungry multitudes. He is now able to meet all our needs—temporal and spiritual. His power is unlimited. Observe that the Lord has methods in His work.

(2) The disciples' part. This was to take that which He had blessed and distribute it. We are laborers with God. God has made us His partners in the salvation of the world.

(3) The people's part. This was not to create nor distribute, but to sit down and eat. They were responsible for obedience. Even after the bread had been blessed by the Lord and distributed by the disciples they would have fainted with hunger had they not eaten. So it is today, unless the people receive that which the Lord has provided they will eternally starve.

9. The King in Conflict with the Pharisees and Sadducees (16:1-12).

These two sects among the Jews were usually enemies, but here they make common cause against Christ. This is common today. Men of opposite opinions and purpose form unholy alliances against the Gospel of Christ. Here these opposing sects join in opposing Christ. They demanded a sign from Him. They pretended that they needed a demonstration by a sign from Heaven of His Messiahship. He rebukes them for their blindness (vv. 3, 4). He calls them a wicked and adulterous generation. Their opposition was not because of a lack of evidence, but to moral perversity. He then exposes their hypocrisy by interpreting the symbol of leaven. He revealed that their teaching was characterized by deception and intrigue. He refused to give a sign. He knew their murderous purpose and that His death and resurrection would be the only sign. This sign is the abiding sign. He issued a solemn warning against the Pharisees and Sadducees.

10. The King Taking Account of His Ministry (16:13-20).

The disciples had been with the Lord for several years. They had heard His wonderful words and witnessed His mighty works. Various opinions were extant about Him. Since Jesus was soon to go to the cross it was necessary for the disciples to have a definite and true conception of Him. Jesus knew the importance of the disciples having the right understanding as to His Person and mission. In order to help them into the right perception He provoked this confession from Peter as the spokesman of the disciples.

a. The place (v. 13). It was at Caesarea Philippi, the northern limit of Jewish territory. It was practically in Gentile territory. It was significant that the announcement concerning the Church should take place in this region.

b. The time in Christ's ministry. It marked a turning point. His ministry was largely restricted to His disciples after this. The cross was only a few months away. The King had already been rejected. They had charged Him with being in league with the Devil and sought to kill Him. It was highly important that the disciples have clear views as to Christ's Person in order to stand the test of the trial and crucifixion of Jesus.

c. Peter's confession (vv. 13-16).

(1) The occasion (vv. 13, 15). Two questions asked by Jesus Christ provoked this confession.

(a) As to the opinion of the people concerning Him (vv. 13, 14). They recognized Him as a teacher and prophet of more than human authority and power. Today, as then, there is a diversity of opinion concerning Jesus. Some think that He is only a man; others that He is a great teacher but nothing more. Had He been content with this, He would not have been molested in Jerusalem, for the Jews willingly acknowledged Him as being more than a human teacher. It was His persistent claim to be the God-man, the very Son of God, that sent Him to the cross.

(b) As to the personal opinion of the disciples (v. 15). It was not enough for them to be able to tell what opinion the people held concerning Jesus. It was necessary that they have clear personal knowledge. There must be definite, correct, and personal knowledge of and belief in Him. This is highly important. It is worth infinitely more than to know the opinion of others, for upon it hinge character and destiny.

(2) The content (v. 16). It consisted of two parts:

(a) "Thou art the Christ." This means that Jesus of Nazareth was the Messiah, the fulfiller of the Jewish hopes and expectations. The coming of the Messiah was to mark the dawn of the new day.

(b) "The Son of the living God." This acknowledged Him to be divine. It was the recognition of His glorious Person in keeping with the Jewish hope (Isa. 9:6, 7).

d. Christ's confession of Peter (v. 17). Peter had made a noble confession. Now Christ confesses him. Those who confess Christ shall be confessed by Him (Matt. 10:32, 33). Christ pronounced a blessing upon Peter, not in the nature of a reward, but the declaration of the spiritual condition of Peter because of the clear apprehension which he had gained of his Lord. This knowledge was revealed to him by the Father, but since Jesus is the revealer of the Father, Peter's knowledge was the result of Christ's work.

e. Christ's charge to the disciples (v. 20). He asked them

not to tell any man that He was the Messiah. The time was not ripe for such testimony. It would have increased His difficulties.

11. The New Body, the Church, Announced (16:18, 19).

Following the confession of Peter, Jesus declared His intention of bringing into existence a new Body. To the members thereof He would give eternal life and into whose hands He would entrust the keys of the kingdom. Peter was to have a distinguished place in this Body. The keys entrusted to him were used at Pentecost and again in the case of Cornelius. Association in this new Body cannot be broken by death, for the gates of Hades shall not prevail against it. The origin, unity, and destiny of that Body are fully set forth in Ephesians.

12. The King Predicts His Death (16:21, 23).

This prediction was no doubt startling to the disciples. They did not yet realize that redemption was to be accomplished through the passion of the cross. So unwelcome was this announcement that Peter cried, "This shall not be unto thee." Later Peter saw through the darkness to the sunlight on the hilltops beyond. A new hope filled his breast (I Peter 1:3, 4). Victory through death is yet the stumbling block of many. Many are stumbling over the doctrine of salvation through the sufferings of the Christ. All such are influenced by the Devil. The Devil hates the doctrine of salvation by blood.

13. The Cost of Discipleship (16:24-27).

To follow Christ means suffering. To follow Him is to turn one's back upon the world. Life can only be saved by losing it. If we are going to be Christians, we must share Christ's suffering. We cannot go to Heaven on flowery beds of ease.

a. There must be denial of self (v. 24). There is a wide difference between self-denial and denial of self. All people practice self-denial, but only real disciples of Christ deny self.

b. "Take up his cross" (v. 24). This cross is the shame and suffering which lie in the path of loyalty to Christ. To do our whole duty will bring suffering (II Tim. 3:12).

c. Follow Christ (vv. 24-27). This means to have the mind of Christ, to be like Christ. All such shall be rewarded when Christ comes in glory.

14. The King's Transfiguration—a Foregleam of the Coming Kingdom (16:28—17:21).

a. The meaning of the transfiguration (II Peter 1:16-18). These verses are an inspired interpretation by one who was present and knew all that transpired. The hope of the disciples was crushed. When Christ announced His death, which was to take place on the cross, they were unable to see how victory could issue from death. Jesus took with Him Peter, James, and John, and they went into the mountain by themselves. According to Luke, they went there to pray (Luke 9:28). While doubtless He longed for fellowship and sympathy as the shadows of the cross were falling upon Him, His chief desire was to get the disciples apart and into a state of receptivity so that He might show them the methods of the kingdom.

Before going into the mountain He declared that there were some standing in His presence who would not taste of death till they had seen the kingdom of God come with power (v. 28). That their drooping spirits might be revived and full confidence restored He was transfigured before them. If the faith of the disciples was to be kept through the dark hour of the cross, which was looming large before them, the light of the eternal must beam forth.

The two men from the upper world were sent to converse with Jesus about His approaching death at Jerusalem—the very thing about which the disciples refused to talk. Then, too, God's own voice was heard in words of approval of Christ's course, directing them to hear the Master. With a foregleam of the coming kingdom and the approving words of God Himself, the disciples could not doubt the ability of Jesus to carry into execution His kingdom plans.

b. Jesus Christ glorified on the mountain (17:2, 3). He took the disciples "by themselves" and was "transfigured before them." This shows that the purpose of the transfiguration terminated upon the disciples and not on Christ. Christ's rebuke of Peter for his unwillingness to hear concerning His death apparently for a time estranged the disciples from Him. To heal this breach an unusual transaction was required. His shining raiment was typical of that glory which shall be manifest when Christ comes back to the earth.

His appearance on the mountain typifies His visible appearance on the Mount of Olives (Zech. 14:4, 9).

c. Peter, James, and John represent Israel in the flesh in connection with the kingdom (v. 2). Christ is peculiarly the King of Israel. According to Ezekiel 37:21-27, the Israelites are to be the central people in the kingdom. This people shall be gathered from among the nations and united as one in that kingdom, in their own country.

d. Moses and Elijah appeared in glory with Jesus (vv. 4-13). These men in the glorified state are typical of the state of the saints in glory. Moses, who was once denied an entrance into Palestine, appears now in glory representing the redeemed of the Lord who shall pass through death into the kingdom. Multitudes of the Lord's own who have fallen asleep shall be awakened at Christ's coming and pass into the kingdom. Elijah represents the redeemed who shall pass into the kingdom through translation. Some shall be living upon the earth when the Lord shall come and they, without dying, shall be changed and thus pass into the kingdom (I Cor. 15:50-53; I Thess. 4:14-18).

(1) Peter's proposal (vv. 5, 6). So definitely was the method of the kingdom unfolded before Peter that he proposed to erect tabernacles for Christ, Moses, and Elijah. It is true that the unveiling of the majestic Person of Christ and the panoramic display of the kingdom somewhat disconcerted Peter; yet he grasped its central meaning and proposed to celebrate the advent of the kingdom which had been prefigured in a tangible way.

(2) The divine voice out of the cloud (vv. 7, 8). God declared Jesus to be His beloved Son in whom He was well pleased. If one would know what is pleasing to God, let him study Jesus Christ, who perfectly did His Father's will.

(3) Jesus' charge (vv. 9-13). He charged them that they should tell no man concerning the things which they had seen until He had risen from the dead.

e. A demonstration of the purpose of the establishment of the kingdom (vv. 14-21). When they descended from the Mount of Transfiguration they witnessed a great multitude in a state of perplexity. The immediate cause of this state was the grievous condition of a young man possessed with a demon (v. 18). The father of the young man had appealed to the disciples to cast out the demon, but they were unable to do so. When they brought him unto Jesus, the foul spirit was rebuked and came forth. This young man's state is representative of the nations who are oppressed by the Devil. Just as this young man was grievously oppressed, causing him to cast himself into the fire and into the waters, so the nations today in their great perplexity are doing the things which will result in their own destruction. The Devil will be peculiarly active in the oppression of men and nations in the last days. Just as he was peculiarly active when Christ was here, so the Scriptures set forth his unusual activities just preceding Christ's second coming. This may account for the turmoil among the nations today.

15. Second Announcement of His Death (17:22, 23).

16. The Miracle of the Tribute Money (17:24-27).

Offenses in the world are many. Failure to conform to certain customs among us may seriously offend. Where no principle of righteousness is involved, we should jealously seek to avoid giving offense. This miracle shows Christ's concern about this matter.

17. The Exalted Position of the Subjects of the Kingdom (18: 1-14).

a. The kingdom belongs to the childlike (v. 3). Conversion is essential to membership in the kingdom. Birth from above must precede entrance into the kingdom.

b. The humblest are the greatest (v. 4). The sure mark of conversion is humility. Pride and selfishness always characterize the unregenerate.

c. The danger of putting stumbling blocks in the way of believers (vv. 6-11).

d. The heavenly Father's care over them (vv. 12-14). The shepherd seeks the lost sheep. The Son of man came to save the lost. The Father is not willing that any of the little ones be lost.

18. The King Teaching Forgiveness (18:15-35).

This is a most needed instruction. We are surrounded by wicked men. Ill-treatment we shall most surely receive, for all who will live godly in Christ Jesus shall suffer persecution (II Tim. 3:12). Here we have divine instruction in such cases.

a. How to gain an erring brother (vv. 15-20). A sinning brother is lost. To bring him to a knowledge of his sin and restore him to fellowship with believers is to gain him. One soul is of greater value than the whole world. The method to be used is:

(1) Personal (v. 15). Go tell him his fault alone. Personal effort is most valuable in winning an erring brother. It is usually an effective method. The aim is not to charge him with sin, but to bring him to see his sin.

(2) The help of a comrade (v. 16). "Take with thee one or two more." The presence of one or two more helps in making known his fault.

(3) Tell it to the church (v. 27). Sometimes the church can accomplish what the individual and the comrades fail to do.

(4) The binding authority of the church's decision (vv. 18-20). When the church follows the Lord's instructions, gathers in the name of Jesus Christ, and is activated by the Holy Spirit, its decision is final. The church sets moral standards.

b. How often should one be forgiven? (vv. 21, 22).

(1) Peter's question (v. 21). His question was perhaps occasioned by ill-treatment he was receiving at the hands of his fellow disciples. Christ's confession of Peter brought him into the limelight. The question of the disciples, "Who is greatest in the kingdom?" shows that there was some jealousy of Peter among the disciples. The disciples perhaps taunted him with jeers. The limits of his patience brought him to Jesus with the above question. From the Lord's teaching as to efforts to bring about reconciliation in case of offense between brother and brother, he knew that the spirit of forgiveness would be required. The rabbis taught that one, two, and three offenses should be forgiven, but the fourth should be punished. Peter disposed to be gracious inquired, "Until seven times?" showed his willingness to forgive his brother, not three times, but twice three times and a little more.

(2) Jesus' answer (v. 22) was an astonishing revelation to Peter. Jesus said: "I say not unto thee, Until seven times: but, Until seventy times seven," showing that our willingness to forgive should be practically without limit.

c. The parable of the two creditors (vv. 23-35) illustrates the Christian principle of forgiveness.

(1) The gracious creditor (vv. 23-27). The king here represents God. The servant who is greatly in debt represents the sinner—any sinner, every sinner. You and me. We were hopelessly in debt to God. Ten thousand talents are equal to some twelve millions of dollars. To meet this obligation would be utterly impossible. This man's plea for time, promising to pay all, resembles man's vain imagination that he can pay his debt to God; that by his future good works he can atone for his past grievous sins. The law says, "pay all," but Christ forgives all. By the justice of God's law we were hopelessly condemned; by the grace of God we are freely pardoned.

(2) The cruel creditor (vv. 28-35). The man who was forgiven so much found a man who owed him a small sum, about seventeen dollars. He shut his ears to the man's entreaty to be patient with him, flew at his throat, and cruelly put him into jail. The great mercy shown him did not touch his heart so he refused to be merciful. Everyone who is unforgiving shows that the forgiveness of God in Christ has not been experienced. Being set free from so great a debt as our sins against God, we should not take up some slight consideration against our brother, but should make God's act of unlimited forgiveness toward us a standard of unlimited forgiveness toward others. We should keep always before us our need of forgiveness from God, and never forget that there is a day of judgment coming when we shall be treated as we have treated others.

19. Some Discourses of the King (19:1-30).

a. Sacredness of marriage (vv. 1-12). The question touching divorce, which the Pharisees temptingly put to Christ, brought forth teaching which shows how subjects of the kingdom should regard the holy relationship of marriage. They should with holy jealousy guard against degradation by divorce. In verses 4-6, the Master shows that the ideal law of life for the subjects of the kingdom is marriage, not celibacy. Yet he recognizes that some will live a life of celibacy.

A life of celibacy is not to be condemned when the circumstances of birth, and the actions of wicked men make marriage impossible, or when one voluntarily chooses a life of celibacy in order to give the life unreservedly to the Lord's service, as Paul did. Divorce is absolutely wrong, save for one cause. It is contrary to God's original plan. It was never sanctioned but suffered by Moses because of sin. God's original and primal intention was that the man have a helper in the person of the woman, thus laying the foundation for family life. This is fundamental to all society—the fountainhead of all life. Corrupting influences here are fatal.

b. Relationship of children to the kingdom (vv. 13-15). It is pre-eminently fitting that following the divine law of marriage, the basis of home and family life, the Master should set forth the divine estimate of children and His interest in them.

The disciples regarded it beneath the dignity of the Master to spend time with the children. There are many professing disciples today, even mothers, who think it beneath their dignity to take time with their children, choosing public life instead. They should ponder well the Master's words and acts, for all child life belongs to His kingdom. This should not only cause us to give proper consideration to work among children, but should be eagerly appropriated by us in regard to our own children. We should regard them as the property of the King, and that it is our high and holy privilege to train them for Him. We should also be assured that if we thus bring them to Him, he will put His hands upon them in blessing, and fold them to His bosom, shielding them from the ravening wolves of society.

c. The relationship of earthly riches to the kingdom (vv. 16-26). This young ruler lacked but one thing, and yet was lost. Perhaps the records of lost men furnish us with no character more beautiful and lovable than this man. The Saviour's own heart is enraptured by him. He was moral, religious, honest, earnest, and courageous. With all these excellent traits he fails. He is self-deceived. He no doubt thought that he had kept the law. The Lord, knowing his heart, put His finger right on the weak spot.

When it came to parting with his possessions in order to help his neighbors, he parted company with the Lord and went away sorrowful. This revealed the fact that he was a covetous man, a violator of the tenth commandment. Besides this, he had a defective theology. He thought that eternal life could be obtained by good works. Although claiming to have kept the law, there was an aching void within his soul which he thought to fill by doing some good thing which he believed the Lord could show him. The Lord pointed out the defect in his life, but when it was seen, his great wealth proved too much for him to give up. When the time came in his life to choose between eternal life and wealth, he chose the wealth and parted company with Christ, perhaps forever.

The heart of this lesson is that a rich man can hardly enter into the kingdom of God. The difficulty does not lie in the fact that a man possesses riches, for a man may possess great riches and still be an heir of the kingdom. Wealth is a mighty power. Money in itself is not other than good. It will provide bread for the widow and orphan, amelioration for the suffering, and will enable men to preach the Gospel in all lands. Many of the most useful men in ancient and modern times have been men of wealth, but they, like Abraham, chose to live in tents, looking to a city which had foundations. The difficulty lies in trusting in riches. The step, however, from possessing to trusting in them, is a very short one. The tendency of growing wealth is to destroy the nobler life of the soul. Then riches possess the man.

d. Rewards for following Christ (vv. 27-30). Those who turn their backs upon their kindred and possessions for the sake of Christ shall receive an hundredfold in this life and eternal life in the world to come. Those who forsake all to follow Christ shall reign with Him in glory.

20. Parable of Laborers in the Vineyard (20:1-16).

This parable is variously interpreted by writers and teachers. That the penny or denarius represents eternal life or salvation we reject, for that would make salvation to come through works instead of grace. Everywhere the Scriptures declare that eternal life is a gift of God, not something merited by obedience and works. Some, while recognizing that the teaching of the parable has to do with rewards in the kingdom, assert that there will be no different degrees of reward in the kingdom. This is also wrong for it is flatly in opposition to scriptural teaching.

The only way to get a right understanding is to examine it in the light of its context. The key is to be found in the circumstance of the rich young ruler coming to Christ and the question of Peter which grew out of Christ's instruction to him (19:27). Christ's teaching to the disciples as to the extreme difficulty, and yet the possibility of a rich man's entering the kingdom, moved Peter to inquire, "Lo, we have left all, and have followed thee; what then shall we have?" This question showed somewhat of a mercenary spirit—a disposition to follow Christ for what honor and profit there was in it. The Lord wants followers whose love is so great for Him that they never think of wages. Such service is that of a hireling. The true mother, as she toils day and night for her family, never thinks about the pay—her service is a service of love. So should we serve our blessed Master.

The central teaching of the parable is that the true disciple heeds the call of the King, and enters His service because he loves Him, not for the gain it brings. However, it should be distinctly remembered that the Lord gave to Peter a straightforward answer, declaring that for those who had left all and followed Him, there was a full reward and the inheritance of eternal life (19:28, 29). That there will be eternal life with the addition of reward, Jesus gives the positive assurance, but He is displeased with the mercenary spirit which follows Him for the "loaves and the fishes." This parable is a rebuke to that spirit. Observe:

a. The call for laborers (20:1-7). The householder made five distinct calls during the day for help: first, early in the morning—at day dawn; the second at the third hour; the third at the sixth hour; the fourth at the ninth hour; the fifth about the eleventh hour. All the laborers seem to obey the call at once. This teaches us that no one can enter the Lord's service until called by God Himself. We should remember that the call is a call to service. God does not want idlers in His vineyard. When He calls, we should instantly obey. God is not going to drag us into His vineyard. Our entrance upon the work must be of our own free will.

b. The reward of the laborers (vv. 8-10). This took place in the evening. We should not expect rewards till after the day is at an end. The same reward was given to all, beginning with the last who went to work at the eleventh hour. This should not be so construed that those who enter the service of Christ early in life, serving Him faithfully to the end, will not receive a more abundant reward than those who enter later in life and serve Him a short while. It should be noted that the first called made a bargain (v. 2) as to their wages, and that all the rest simply willingly entered into service, trusting the householder's own gracious will and sense of justice.

c. The complaint of the laborers (vv. 11, 12). This shows an evil eye—that service was not rendered out of a heart of love, but of desire for gain. All service for Christ should be regarded as a privilege. We should not think that the one who enters His service at a later hour is rewarded above us. We should regard the privilege of serving the Lord so many years as one highly to be prized. The true Christian does not complain that he has served so long—but grieves that he has done so little. We should work for love's sake, not for reward. God will take care of the reward.

d. The householder's vindication (vv. 13-16).

(1) He paid the laborers all that he had promised (v. 13). The agreement had been exactly carried out.

(2) He declared that he had a right to do as he pleased with his own (v. 15). God is sovereign.

(3) He gave to those who trusted his grace the same as those who toiled long.

21. The King's Third Announcement of His Death (20:17-19). Twice before, Jesus had told of His death. The first time followed Peter's confession (16:21, 22). To this Peter violently reacted, even rebuked the Lord. That which motivated Peter's reaction we do not fully know, but love for Him was strong calling forth this protest. Perhaps an element of self-interest was involved—the prospect of an honorable position in the kingdom. Whatever the motive Christ severely rebuked Peter, saying: "Get thee behind me, Satan: for thou art an offense unto me," meaning that Peter's protest was made through the Devil who had entered into him and taken charge of his personality. Peter confessed that Jesus was the Messiah, the Son of the living God. When Christ announced that His rejection and crucifixion was at hand, the Devil was aroused and entered Peter's life and moved him to protest. The death of Christ meant the destruction of the Devil (Heb. 2:14). The Devil hates the cross because it means his death-blow. The one who preaches the cross of Christ and all it stands for will have opposition. The second an-

nouncement of the death of Christ caused the disciples great sorrow (Matt. 17:23).

a. Time and circumstances (v. 17). The King was on His last journey to Jerusalem the beloved city. He took the disciples aside from the traveling pilgrims to make known unto them what was before them. As they journeyed He went ahead of the disciples. The courage thus shown by the Lord amazed the disciples who were following in fear (Mark 10:32). "Christ the conscious and certain sufferer is courageous. His followers who had nothing to fear were afraid."

b. His betrayal and death foretold (vv. 18, 19). He went forward fully conscious of the awful tragedy of the cross. He now for the third time since the transfiguration tells the disciples of His suffering and death, but they are so filled with their ambitious schemes that they do not understand Him. The treachery of Judas Iscariot; the fierce persecution of the chief priests and scribes; the unjust judgment; the delivery to Pilate; the mocking and scourging; the crown of thorns; the cross; the hanging between two malefactors; the nails; the spear—all were spread before His mind like a picture. Though He knew all this He pressed on not of necessity but deliberately. The joyous outlook upon the victory which would be accomplished by the shedding of His blood led Him forward. He went courageously for He knew the time had come for the accomplishment of His Father's will. We should from this be eager to do God's will regardless of what sufferings it may bring.

c. The resurrection foretold (v. 19). Truly this would have been a dark picture had not the resurrection been made known. The resurrection life beyond is always seen as the issue of the cross. The blessedness of the life beyond this "vale of tears" should urge us on. In this we have Christ as the grand example. "Looking unto Jesus the author and finisher of our faith; who for the joy that was set before him endured the cross, despising the shame, and is set down at the right hand of the throne of God" (Heb. 12:2).

22. The Ambitious Request of James and John (20:20-23).

a. The request (vv. 20, 21). This request was made by their mother for a place of prominence in the kingdom. This is not the last mother whom children have used to carry out that which they are ashamed to do themselves. It is right for mothers to be ambitious for their children, but they know that earth's pinnacles are exceedingly dangerous. It is very desirable to get places for our children near to Jesus, but we should keep out of our minds the vanity of the world. Unfortunately many parents think about the pinnacle of the world for their children and forget about nearness to Christ.

b. Jesus' answer (vv. 22, 23). He spoke directly to the men, not to their mother, declaring that they knew not what they were asking. He showed them that the way to this position of glory was through suffering. The cup of which they were to drink was of great suffering and agony. The positions which they craved were attainable but in a very different way from what they apprehended. The way to places of glory in the kingdom of Christ is through the path of lowly and self-forgetful service and even great suffering. How often we blindly ask for that which we should not, and because of this the Lord many times has to rebuke and reprove us!

23. How To Be Truly Exalted (20:24-28).

a. The angry disciples (v. 24). When the ten heard of the request of James and John they were filled with indignation against them. Their displeasure did not arise from the fact that they were free from the same selfish spirit, but that these two had thrust themselves to the front; it was an admixture of indignation and jealousy.

b. Greatness among the heathen (v. 25). The rule of the world has always been by the strong arm. Their standards have always been not moral excellence, but wealth, station, and power. Even today the reason one nation rules the other is that ruling nations possess sharper swords and heavier clubs than the other. The atom bomb is now the determent to aggressive war.

c. Greatness among Christ's disciples (vv. 26, 27). Here the standard is in sharp contrast to that of the world. The way to places of prominence in Christ's kingdom is the way of self-abasement. To give is greater than to receive. The way up is down. To be serving someone is infinitely better than to be served. It is not wrong to be ambitious to be great, but the basis of true greatness is that which human selfishness seeks to avoid. There will be degrees of rank in Christ's kingdom, but this rank will be character and not position or authority. The Spirit of Christ substitutes "the greatness of love for the love of greatness." The greatness is not won at the expense of others. It is perfectly right to be great if that greatness has been attained by the enrichment of others.

d. Christ the supreme example of greatness (v. 28). All who would be great should study and imitate Christ. Let them forget self and serve others, even to give their lives to do so. This will eliminate all scrambling for place and power. The one grand test by which to know whether Christ's Spirit controls one is whether he is serving or seeking to be served.

24. The King Healing Two Blind Men (20:29-34).

With the weight of the cross upon Him, Christ was never too much occupied to keep from performing gracious acts. Two blind beggars are healed.

a. Their request (vv. 29, 30). They cried to Him for mercy. Their method of addressing Him shows that they recognized His Messiahship. They called Him "The Son of David." They had faith in Him as such. They could not see, so as soon as they heard that He was passing by they cried to Him for help. It was a simple matter, but it was enough. Jesus not only can hear our cries, but He can tell even when a soul yearns after Him, and will respond to that act.

b. The rebuke by the multitudes (v. 31). This only moved them to cry out with more earnestness. They believed that Jesus could and would help them. The fact that God has brought salvation within our reach should convince us that it is His time for us to cry for help, and we should not let the opposition of men keep us from Christ.

c. The blessing granted (vv. 32-34). Their earnest cry caused Jesus to stand still. He knew their desire, but wanted them to commit themselves definitely. God wants us to come to Him with our definite needs. Jesus had compassion on them and opened their eyes. As they looked upon the world they saw many interesting things, but they were above all interested in Christ for they followed Him. They turned their backs upon Jericho and followed Jesus.

25. The King's Final Presentation to the Jewish Nation (21:1–23:39).

This picture is a dark one. The usual designation, "triumphal entry," should be discarded, for it is only such in appearance. Back of the cry, "Hosanna," the awful cry, "Crucify," was taking form, and doubtless this awful word, "crucify," was uttered by some of the same persons who cried, "Hosanna." Though they were utterly blind to the fact, God was about to carry out His plan of "Hosanna," which means "save now," through the crucifixion of the Son of God.

a. The entrance of the King into Jerusalem (vv. 1-11).

(1) The preparation (vv. 1-6).

(a) Sending of disciples (vv. 1-3). He told them just where to find the colt, and told them how to answer the inquiry of the one who owned it. This shows how perfectly our Lord knows our ways. Whether by day or by night, His matchless gaze beholds all we do and think. God uses unlikely and apparently insignificant things in the accomplishment of His purposes. To go and find the ass was a small thing for the disciples. The providing of the animal was not man's plan, but was the working of all things according to Christ's foreknowledge.

(b) The fulfillment of prophecy (vv. 4, 5). Some five hundred years before, Zechariah had made this prediction (Zech. 9:9). This coming of Christ was in exact fulfillment of the prediction. This is highly instructive to those who would understand unfulfilled prophecy. If the predictions of His first coming were thus literally fulfilled, there is no alternative but to believe that those of His second coming likewise will be fulfilled literally. They stand or fall together. The first is established beyond a doubt. The second we should just as heartily believe. The prediction of Zechariah 14: 3-11 will be just as literally fulfilled as that of Zechariah 9:9.

(c) The obedience of the disciples (v. 6). The request may have seemed strange and unreasonable but they fully obeyed. True disciples will render full and glad obedience no matter how strange the command may seem. Let us thus prove that we are disciples indeed.

(2) The formal entrance of the King (vv. 7-11).

(a) The disciples put their garments upon the ass and set the Lord upon them (v. 7). This act showed that they recognized Him as their King (II Kings 9:13).

(b) The multitude. Some spread their garments in the

way; others who had no garments to spare cut down branches and did the same with them, which was just as acceptable to Him. To give what we have and do what we can is all that He asks of us. They likewise sing, "Hosanna," but how soon the cry is changed! The human heart is inconstant.

(c) The city shaken (vv. 10, 11). This was a stirring time, but one even more stirring is coming. That will be when the Lord comes in power and glory.

b. The King rejected (vv. 12-17). The immediate occasion of this rejection was the cleansing of the temple. A like cleansing had been made some two years before (John 2:13-17), but the worldlings had gone back to their old trade. The matter of exchange was not wrong in itself. To sell oxen and sheep and doves was legitimate as well as to exchange money in doing it, but doing it for gain was wrong. As soon as the spirit of avarice enters, the house of prayer is converted into a den of thieves. This is fearfully prevalent today. On every hand is manifest a tendency to secularize the Gospel.

The envy and jealousy of the chief priests is due to the fact that Jesus is praised. Many today manifest this same envy and jealousy. They cannot stand for another to receive praise when they do not.

c. The nation rejected by the King (21:18—22:14). Having in this official presentation shown their unwillingness to receive Christ, He turns from them and by parables makes known their awful condition.

(1) Cursing of the fig tree (vv. 18-22). It was on the morrow after His official presentation as He was returning to Jerusalem that Jesus observed the unfruitful fig tree. Because of hunger He sought for figs, and finding none He caused to fall upon it a withering curse. This fig tree full of leaves but barren of fruit is a type of Israel. With its leaves it gave a show of life, but being destitute of fruit it had no right to encumber the ground. Israel at this time had all the externals, but lacked the real spiritual life which bears fruit. The nation thus stood like a mountain in the way of the Gospel. He encouraged the disciples by showing them that if they had faith even this great mountain should not stand in their way. This should serve as a warning to all who are resting in their forms and

works, lest the withering curse of Christ's judgment strike them. The branch that beareth not fruit is taken away.

(2) The two sons (vv. 28-32). Both sons were told by the father to work in the vineyard. The one, like the profligate publican, refused outright to obey, but afterward repented and went. The other pretended willingness to obey, but in reality did not. The first one represents the publicans and harlots; the second, the proud and self-righteous Pharisees, priests, and elders. The Lord declared that the publicans and harlots would go into the kingdom before them. It is often true that the self-righteous, proud legalist, who may even be a member of the church, is harder to reach with the Gospel than the profligate sinner.

(3) The householder (vv. 33-46).

(a) The householder. This was God Himself.

(b) The vineyard. This means Israel (see Isa. 5:1-7; Jer. 2:21; Ps. 80-89). The Lord went to particular pains to gather out this nation and make it separate, bestowing peculiar favors upon it. This vineyard so well kept and provided for did not bear fruit.

(c) The husbandmen. These were the spiritual guides, the rulers, and teachers of Israel, the members of the Sanhedrin.

(d) The servants were sent for the fruit of the vineyard. These were the various prophets whom God sent to the nation. The maltreatment and rejection of the prophets is fully set forth in the Scriptures. They were beaten and killed.

(e) The Son, He is the Lord Jesus Christ, God's only and beloved Son. He came into their midst. They knew Him to be the Son, but they did not receive His message nor bow to His authority. They cast Him out of the vineyard and slew Him. They knew this was intended for them. Jesus knew that in a few days He would be crucified. He now asked them for their own verdict upon such ingratitude. He took the place of a judge and pronounced judgment upon them on the basis of their own verdict. They not only rejected the kingdom, but the King who was the Son.

(4) The marriage feast (22:1-14). In the previous parable the responsibilities of the subjects of the kingdom were before us for consideration in the light of the obligation to render to the house-

holder the fruits of his vineyard. In this one the ethic is changed, and the privileges and blessings of the kingdom are placed on exhibition. This parable lifts the conception of the kingdom and places it on a high plane. It is much more than paying rent to a king; it is feasting at the King's table on fat things which He has prepared with great expense to Himself.

Let every teacher strive to show that Christ's kingdom is infinitely more than a system of laws and regulations to be obeyed. It is a system to provide rich benefits and blessings even as infinite love provides for dear children. It will be a great day for the church and the world when man can be made to see that the kingdom of God is not an organization which demands conformity to laws, but one which makes its richest and most abundant provision for humanity's deepest needs. The figure of marriage is most suggestive; it represents the highest ideal of love and friendship.

(a) The King's feast despised (vv. 1-7). The previous parable exhibits the attitude of the Jewish people toward the King up to the crucifixion of Christ. This one carries us beyond the cross, even through the present age of the Gentiles. The marriage feast which the king made for his son and to which he invited guests represents the gracious offer of God to give joy and blessing to certain of His creatures. This feast has been made in honor of his Son and is an exceedingly rich one. His oxen and fatlings are ready. His repeated invitations show God's earnestness in seeking to bless men. God does more than simply invite men once; He presses His invitation again and again most earnestly. How many times from our childhood has He not pressed His invitation upon us! The attitude of those invited toward the invitation and the King is passing strange and exceedingly sinful. To treat the king's invitation with such contempt after he had made such costly preparation deserves the severest punishment. They not only neglected it but made light of it and hurried on to their worldly business, showing that they regarded it as of more importance than the salvation of their souls. Some went forth and even did violence to the messengers of the king, killing them.

While this is a picture of the attitude of the Jews from Christ's crucifixion to the destruction of Jerusalem, it has its counterpart in the day in which we live. Some today are indifferent to God's invitation; some are making light of God's way of salvation, and others are even hostile to the messengers of Christ. Their attitude and behavior incited the anger of the king, and he executed vengeance upon them, burning their city. This was historically fulfilled in the destruction of Jerusalem by the Romans in A.D. 70, and is typical of what He will do to those who are neglecting or rejecting His invitation at the close of this dispensation.

(b) The king's invitation accepted (vv. 8-10). When those who were first invited refused, the king sent his servants to others; for his table must be provided with guests. The King of kings has prepared this feast at infinite cost, and though He urgently invites He will not compel anyone to accept. Those that were shut out were shut out because they refused to accept, not because the king was unwilling. Christ sent His servants among the Gentiles, which is shown by their going into the highways and hedges.

(c) The king inspecting the guests (vv. 11-14). As he made this inspection the king found one among the guests who had not on a wedding garment—had not conformed to the regulations of the feast. The custom in the East was for the king to furnish the guests with a suitable garment. There could thus be no excuse for not wearing one. Therefore, this act of the man showed that he only accepted the invitation for selfish ends not desiring to conform to the regulations of the king. The wedding garment which the king provided in this case pictures the righteousness of Christ, which alone will entitle one to a place at the King's marriage feast. This righteousness is obtained by faith in the atoning blood of Jesus Christ. Christianity is more than uniting with the church or even being baptized; it is conforming to God's plan.

d. The open breach between the Jews and the king (22:15—23:36).

(1) The effort of Pharisees to entrap Jesus (vv. 15-40). Seeing that Jesus was gaining the favor of the people they thought to discredit Him by causing Him to become tangled in His words. This they thought to accomplish by means of three entangling questions.

(a) Concerning tribute money (vv. 15-22). The Herodians sought to test His loyalty to the Roman government; therefore, they came to him with the subtle question, "Is it lawful to give tribute unto Caesar, or not?" At this time the Jews were galling under the yoke of the Roman government. For Christ to have answered either yes or no would have involved difficulties. "Yes" would have conveyed the impression of endorsement of the Roman government. "No" would have brought Him into conflict with the government. Christ's reply to this question is the final word on the Christian's relationship to civil government. The obligation of the citizen is to render obedience to civil authority. However, this is not all, but the correct principle of life. Those enjoying the benefits of civil government should support that government, and those enjoying the blessings of God should render full allegiance to Him. This can only be done in worship and praise.

(b) Concerning the resurrection (vv. 23-33). The Sadducees did not believe in the resurrection. To entrap Him they placed before Him a hypothetical case of a woman who had had seven husbands with the question as to whose wife she would be in the resurrection. Christ's wisdom was shown in pointing out to them that the source of their difficulty was in their ignorance of the Scriptures and of the power of God. The Scriptures make it clear that marriage is for this life; that in the resurrection human beings will be as angels of God in Heaven. Among the angels there is no marriage relation. The angels constituted a company, whereas humanity is a race. God's purpose as to the race was expressed in the creation of Adam and Eve and their endowment with the power of propagation.

(c) Concerning the great commandment of the law (vv. 34-40). For the third time in one day the Lord is tried by hard questions. Though the questioners were occupied by wrong motives, we may be glad for the valuable truths set forth in His answers.

i) The first commandment (vv. 34-38). "Thou shalt love the Lord thy God with all thy heart." This means that supreme and undivided love to God is the first and great commandment. It shows that man's supreme obligation is to God. Real righteousness is doing the right with God. The greatest immorality is failure to respond to the demands of God.

ii) The second commandment (vv. 39, 40). This is like the first, in that it centers in love. It is not equal to the first, because the object is finite, whereas in the first the object is infinite. Even then, one is not under obligation to love his neighbor supremely. The measure of love to my neighbor is my self-love. We should love God better than ourselves because He is worthy of all our affections and demands them all. However, love to our neighbor is involved in love to God, since our neighbor bears the likeness and image of God. The one who loves God will love the one who bears His image (I John 4:20).

(2) Jesus questions the Pharisees (vv. 41-46). Christ's answers to the questions which had been asked to entangle and discredit Him not only frustrated His enemies, but set forth principles for the guidance of His followers for all time. Now Jesus puts forth a counter question involving the supreme problem in right thinking, right living, and eternal destiny. It has to do with the Person of Christ. Is He God or man? Or is He the God-man? How could David intelligently speak of the Messiah as both His son and His Lord? There is but one answer. He is both human and divine. The incarnation is the only solution to the central problem of the Christian faith. Jesus by word and deed presented Himself as the Messiah. His enemies could not answer Him. The historic virgin birth is the crux of the Christian message.

(3) Jesus warning against the Pharisees (23:1-12). Having put to silence His opponents in argument, Christ now issues sober warnings against them. The very core of His rebuke is embodied in the repeated and reproachful term "hypocrites." His most bitter denunciations were directed against those whose outward lives were respectable and whose religious professions were the loudest. These Pharisees were ostentatious; what they did was "to be seen of men." They were inconsistent; they "say and do not." They required of others what they did not do themselves. They loved the pre-eminence. They sought the chief seats in public places.

(4) The King pronouncing judgment upon the scribes and Pharisees (vv. 13-36). In these verses are found the charges denounced against the Jewish teacher. He publicly dealt with chief errors of the scribes and Pharisees. Eight times He used the solemn

expression, "Woe unto you." Seven times He calls them "hypocrites." Twice He speaks of them as "blind guides," and twice as "fools and blind." Once as "serpents and generation of vipers."

In these burning words of denunciation there is no trace of malice or suggestion of loss of self-control. There is such a thing as "the wrath of the Lamb." In these judgments there is some suggestion of pity and sorrow. Someone has said that the word *woe* which Jesus pronounced may possibly be interpreted as meaning, "Alas, for you." His words of pity and His weeping over Jerusalem favor this view. Note the "woes."

(a) The first woe is directed against the opposition of the scribes and Pharisees to the progress of the Gospel. They "shut up the kingdom of heaven." They would not go in themselves nor suffer others to go in (v. 13).

(b) The second woe is directed against the covetousness and self-aggrandizing spirit of the scribes and Pharisees. They devoured "widows" houses, and for a pretense made long prayers (v. 14).

(c) The third woe was directed against the zeal of the Pharisees for making partisans. They compassed land and sea to make one proselyte. This they did to get men to join their party and adopt their opinions (v. 15).

(d) The fourth woe is directed against the doctrines of the scribes and Pharisees about oaths. They taught that some oaths were binding while others were not (vv. 16-22).

(e) The fifth woe was directed against the scribes and Pharisees for exalting minor things while disregarding the things of great importance, such as tithing garden herbs while indifferent to obligation of justice, charity, and honesty.

(f) The sixth woe was directed against the scribes and Pharisees for being careful about the externals of religion while disregarding the purity of the heart (vv. 25, 26).

(g) The seventh woe is directed against the scribes and Pharisees for their outward appearance of being clean while being full of hypocrisy and iniquity (vv. 27, 28). He likened them to "whited sepulchers," but inwardly filled with dead men's bones.

(h) The eighth woe is directed against the appearance of

veneration for the saints while plotting to kill the Lord of glory (vv. 29-32). He closes this picture by calling them "serpents" and a "generation of vipers."

(5) The King laments over Jerusalem (vv. 37-39). His farewell to those who rejected Him was that the guilt of all the murderers from Abel to that time was resting upon them. He reminds them that in spite of their awful sin and guilt He was coming back in glory and that they would look upon Him whom they pierced. The hope of Israel and the world centers in the coming of the Lord.

III. THE PROPHETIC PICTURE OF THE INTERVAL BETWEEN CHRIST'S ASCENSION AND HIS SECOND COMING (24:1—25:46).

Our knowledge of this interval is limited to the matters revealed by Jesus in the Olivet discourse. We should jealously guard against adding to or taking from that which was revealed by Him.

A. *The Present Age* (24:1-14).

Two great facts confront us here—the destruction of Jerusalem and the second coming of Christ. The one is near, having taken place within forty years after Christ's crucifixion, and the other still future. This is the period covered by the parables of chapter 13, and will be characterized by false Christs, wars and rumors of war, kingdom arrayed against kingdom, earthquakes, famines and pestilences, murder, unfaithfulness to contract; false prophets shall arise and deceive many. Who but the Son of God could have pictured with such clearness two thousand years ago conditions which would prevail over the world today?

B. *The Appearance of the Antichrist* (24:15-26).

The prophet Daniel foresaw the appearance of this wicked one (Dan. 9:27). Under his leadership will come the Great Tribulation with violent persecution of God's people unknown in the world before or after. This awful situation will be aggravated by the appearance of false prophets who shall deceive many. Under such conditions the only hope of survival of the elect is through divine intervention.

C. *The Return of the King in Glory* (24:27-51).

The deliverance from the power of the Antichrist and the hand of the persecutors will be through the coming of the Son of man in glory and power. He will send His angels to gather His elect. The only hope of the world is the second coming of Christ. The kingdom does not come by the church witnessing for Christ, but through the "stone . . . cut out of the mountain without hands" smiting the feet of the image and grinding it to powder and then filling the whole earth (Dan. 2.44, 45). The kingdom is not built by man but established by the mighty King. Note the following features concerning the coming of the Lord:

1. New Life for Israel (24:32, 33).

The fig tree is a picture of Israel (Matt. 21:19, 20; Luke 21:29-33). The tree that was withered will live again. The teaching here is that just immediately preceding the second coming of Christ there will be new life and fruit to the Jewish nation. When this is seen, the coming of the Lord draweth nigh. With the increased activity among the Jews and their rapid return to their own land, we are warned of the nearness of the end. "When ye shall see all these things, know that it is near, even at the doors."

2. The Jews Will Remain a Separate People Until the Lord Returns (24:34, 35).

The word *generation* here means race, family, stock, etc., therefore it means that the Jewish race will remain intact to the end of the age. The outstanding miracle of the ages is the continued identity of Israel. Without a government, land, or king they have not lost their identity like other nations. This fact is a perpetual pledge, a guarantee of the return of our Lord. Besides, the eternal words of Christ are back of it. "Heaven and earth shall pass away," but Christ's words never. With such a guarantee we can afford to hope in Him even though scoffers are found on every side.

3. The Time of the Coming of the Lord Unknown (24:36).

It is not only foolish but extremely sinful to speculate as to the time of the coming of the Lord. Beware of men who attempt to figure out the time of the Lord's return. Such effort dishonors God's Word, reproaches prophecy, and shipwrecks the faith of many of God's children.

4. The State of the World When Christ Returns (24:37-39).

This is not a converted world. It will be as it was in the days of Noah. The mass of men and women will be occupied, absorbed in worldly pursuits, utterly disregarding the call of God's righteous servants to repentance. There were two representative classes in that day—a small number with an affection for God ready to obey Him, and the great mass in unbelief and rebellion. "Noah lived at the close of an age, was saved with his house through a great judgment, and then became the beginning of a new age." As the age of Noah closed with a deluge, so this age will close with a judgment. The judgment came suddenly and unexpectedly; so will it be when Christ returns. Let no one be deluded with the false notion that the world will be converted then, for the word of Christ flatly contradicts this.

5. There Will Be an Awful Separation When Christ Returns (24:40-42).

This is an age of mixture; in the home, in the field, in business, and in the church, the children of God and the children of the Devil are found side by side. Two will be in the field, one will be taken and the other left. Wives will be separated from husbands; children will be separated from parents; brothers will be separated from sisters, forevermore. For those who are taken there will be happiness forever; for those who are left, sorrow and anguish forever. In view of this all should watch.

6. Christ's Coming Will Be Unexpected (24:43, 44).

As the thief comes unannounced and unexpected, so will the Lord come. The way to be ready for the thief is to be constantly awake—on the watch. We should be constantly ready that we be not taken without preparation.

7. The Right Attitude in View of Christ's Coming (24:45-51).

We should be faithfully doing the duties which the Lord has given us to do. For such, there is blessed news and promotion. The Lord will make him ruler over all His goods. But to say that the Lord delayed His coming, and then cruelly treat His fellow servants and eat and drink with the drunken, will result in being brought unexpectedly into judgment to receive the just doom; where there will be weeping and gnashing of teeth.

D. *The Parable of the Ten Virgins* (25:1-13).

This parable has reference to the behavior of believers in view of the coming of the Lord. Its teaching has continuous application in this present age. (See I Thess. 3:13; Titus 2:11-13.)

1. The Equipment of the Virgins (25:1-5).

a. The foolish virgins took lamps, but no oil with them (v. 3). Lamps signify Christian profession (5:16) and oil the Holy Spirit (Zech. 14). Having lamps but no oil shows that they were professors of religion without possessing its reality. The Christian life is sustained by the Holy Spirit. As soon as a man is regenerated, the Holy Spirit takes up His abode within him. The Spirit's indwelling therefore is an advance work upon regeneration. The proof that one is a child of God is that he has the Holy Spirit dwelling within him (Rom. 8:9). The foolish virgins were professors, but not possessors.

b. The wise virgins possessed both lamps and oil (v. 4). They backed their profession with a real life of righteousness. Both the wise and the foolish virgins slumbered and slept. Their eyes had grown heavy and they fell under the spell of sleep (v. 5). This shows that as the present age lengthens, the real and the professing church will cease looking for the coming of the Lord. It is unspeakably sad that so many, even of God's chosen—the wise virgins—should give up the expectancy of the return of the Lord.

2. The Coming of the Bridegroom (25:6-12).

a. The midnight cry (v. 6). In the midst of the night when all the virgins were asleep the cry was heard, "Behold, the bridegroom cometh." Who knows but what the time of this cry is close upon us?

b. Activity of the virgins (v. 7). They all arose and trimmed their lamps. When the Lord comes there will be great activity on the part of both believers and those who only make a profession. It will be a day when the reality of one's faith will be tested.

c. The foolish virgins' request of the wise to share their oil (vv. 8, 9). The revelation of Christ will make manifest the genuineness of our faith and expose the folly of mere profession. When the Lord comes it will be too late to mend one's ways.

d. The wise enter in to the marriage (v. 10). While the foolish were seeking to amend their ways, trying to buy oil, the bridegroom came and those who were ready were admitted to the marriage.

e. The pitiful petition of the foolish virgins (v. 11). They begged the Lord to open the door that they might enter into the marriage feast.

f. The awful judgment (v. 12). The Lord declared, "I know you not."

3. The Solemn Obligation (25:13).

"Watch therefore, for ye know neither the day nor the hour wherein the Son of man cometh." Two solemn facts should engage the attention of everyone.

a. Entering with Christ into the marriage depends upon faithfulness to the end.

If oil and light be wanting when Christ comes, no admittance will be granted to the heavenly banquet.

b. Borrowed religion will not avail at that day. Despite the value of godly companions and associates, they can render no service in the day of Jesus Christ. Personal contact with the Lord Jesus through faith in His blood is the absolute essential.

E. *The Parable of the Talents* (25:14-30).

This parable, like that of the ten virgins, has a vital relationship to the second coming of Christ. In both instances the unpreparedness for His coming on the part of the people is shown. In that of the ten virgins their unreadiness consisted in their lack of the inward life—absence of the Holy Spirit. In the parable of the talents their failure was to properly use the gifts which God had entrusted to them. The first was failure *to watch;* the second was failure *to work.* To each of His servants God entrusted certain gifts and will hold each responsible for their use. By talents is meant whatever gifts of grace, such as physical strength, reason, energy, knowledge, influence, time, money, the gifts of speech and song.

1. The Distribution of the Talents (25:14, 15).

a. It was a sovereign act. The lord called his own servants and distributed to them his own money. The Lord did not consult us as to our gifts. The One who created us and absolutely owns us has assigned us our place and given us several powers, intending that we put them to the best possible use. This is the first principle if we would fulfill God's highest purpose.

b. It was an intelligent act, "according to his several ability."

The God who created us knew our ability to use gifts, therefore made the distribution upon that basis. The reason why some have greater gifts than others is that they possess the ability to use them. A recognition of God's sovereignty and intelligence regarding the distribution of His gifts will make us content in our sphere of labor.

c. It was a purposeful act. The talents were given for trading. They were not given to be used for one's own gain and profit, but as stock in trade for the enrichment and glory of the Master.

2. The Employment of the Talents (25:16-18).

a. All servants are stewards. All the servants recognized that the talents were not their own, that they were therefore responsible to the Lord for the use made of them. This is the first principle of right Christian service. We should remember that we are all stewards of the manifold blessings and grace of God. We are not responsible for the creation of gifts, but for the employment of such gifts as have been given to us.

b. Two servants used their talents. The five-talent man put his to use and gained five more, and the two-talent man put his two talents to use and gained two more. This shows that God's gifts can be increased. The exercise of any gift increases it. The faithful use of what we have in the place where we are will prepare us for greater usefulness and honor. It is not primarily a question as to what we receive, but as to what use we have made of what we have received.

c. The one hid his talent. The fact that one possesses but one talent should not discourage him, but rather make him strive harder. God does not reward according to what we possess, but according to our faithfulness. The crime of the one-talent man was not that he had but one talent, but what he did with the talent which the Lord gave him. "To do no harm is the praise of a stone, not of a man." To hide a talent may be more difficult than to use it.

3. The Accounting for the Talents (25:19-30).

a. Its certainty (v. 19). There is a day coming when all must give an account of their stewardship. Answer must be given as to the use made of God's gifts. Escape is absolutely impossible.

b. The time (v. 19). It will be at the coming of the Lord. Those who have done well will then receive praise. The unfaithful shall be censured.

c. Judgments announced (vv. 21-30).

(1) Reward of the faithful (vv. 21-23).

(a) Praise, "Well done." All like to be praised. From childhood through life, commendation is pleasing. How blessed it will be to hear from the lips of the Lord Himself, "Well done."

(b) Promotion. The great consideration for all is not how many talents we possess, but as to how faithful we are in their use.

(2) Punishment of the faithless (vv. 24-30). Just as the natural eyes lose their power if we live in darkness, so it is spiritually. The one who ceases to grow in knowledge and grace loses the capacity to grow.

(a) Reproach, "Thou wicked and slothful servant." To be called lazy is a reproach disliked even by a lazy man.

(b) Stripped, "Take therefore, the talent from him." Even the talent which had been given to him was now wrenched from him.

(c) Cast out, "Cast into outer darkness." This servant was condemned on his own ground. The very fact that he knew the character of his lord should have been an incentive for him to have exerted himself. His condition was his own fault. In the day of accounts no excuse will avail.

F. *The Judgment of the Nations* (25:31-46).

According to the legitimate textual and contextual signification it is the judgment of the living nations which still lies in the future (v. 32). The idea of a general judgment which is of such frequent occurrence in religious literature and teaching is a fundamental error. It is not once found in the Bible, nor the idea which it is intended to convey. Dr. Pentecost most truthfully says: "It is a mischievous habit that has led the Christian world to speak of the judgment as being one great event taking place at the end of the world when all human beings, saints and sinners, Jews and Gentiles, the living and the dead, shall stand up before the Great White Throne and there be judged. Nothing can be more wide of the Scriptures." The Bible speaks of several judgments, different in respect to the subjects to be judged, the place of judgment, the time of judgment, and the result of the judgment. The judgment which we are considering here, therefore, is not that one set forth in Revelation 20:11-14. It precedes that one by at least 1,000 years. A careful analysis of this portion will show how entirely distinct this judgment is from the final judgment.

1. The Judge (25:31).

It is the Son of man, the One who came and died to redeem the human race. He is now seen clothed with majesty and power sitting upon His throne acting as Judge. Those who accept Jesus Christ now as their Saviour shall not come into judgment (John 5:24).

2. The Time (25:31).

This judgment will take place when the Lord comes in His glory accompanied by a retinue of glorious angels. This will take place after He has gathered the elect remnant of Israel. There will be no resurrection in connection with this judgment.

3. The Place (25:31).

The prophecies of Joel 3 and Zechariah 14:1-5 show that it is to be in or near Jerusalem. The angel said to Mary: "Thou . . . shalt call his name Jesus. He shall be great, and shall be called the Son of the Highest: and the Lord God shall give unto him the throne of his father David: and he shall reign over the house of Jacob forever; and of his kingdom there shall be no end" (Luke 1:31-33). As David was a literal king and reigned in a literal place, there shall be a literal Judge occupying a literal place of judgment.

4. The People Judged and Basis of Judgment (25:32-45).

These will be the living nations upon earth after the Church has been translated (I Thess. 4:16, 17). These are the nations to whom the Gospel of the kingdom shall be preached just prior to the coming of the end. "And this gospel of the kingdom shall be preached in all the world for a witness unto all nations; and then shall the end come" (Matt. 24:14). This Gospel is distinct from the grace of God, which is now being preached. The preachers of this Gospel will be the Jews (see Rev. 7; Rom. 11). These are the brethren of the Lord in the flesh—they that move among the nations of the world with the startling message of the news of the Lord's approaching kingdom. Some of the nations will gladly receive the message and most kindly receive the kingdom messengers, giving them clothing, food, shelter, etc. Others will persecute them, thrusting them into prison, etc. Here the former will visit the messengers of the King and provide for their wants. At this time the Judge will separate the nations, placing the sheep on the right and the goats on the left hand. The sheep are those who have given proper treatment to Christ's brethren. The goats are those who rejected and maltreated His brethren. If these three classes—the sheep, the goats, and the brethren—be kept separate, all confusion will be avoided.

5. The Issue of the Judgment (25:46; cf. vv. 34, 41).

a. The sheep entering upon the inheritance of a prepared kingdom.

b. The goats going into everlasting fire prepared for the Devil and his angels. This judgment shall determine their destiny.

IV. THE PASSION OF THE KING (26:1–27:66).

A. *The King in the Shadow of the Cross* (26:1-46).

1. Plotting for the Death of Jesus (26:1-5).

Christ with divine insight predicted not only the fact of His death, but its time and manner. He was not taken by surprise, since for this pre-eminent purpose He came into the world (Heb. 2:14). He deliberately walked up to death. He knew that the Passover would find its fulfillment in His death, for He was the antitypical lamb thereof. The Jewish authorities in secret conclave were plotting to silence His voice by putting Him to death. It was the divine purpose that He die. In their wickedness they were plotting to do that which God had ordained. In spite of themselves, they were moving in the line of God's decree.

2. Mary of Bethany Anoints Jesus (26:6-13).

a. The meaning of the act (vv. 6, 7). This anointing occurred when Jesus was at meat in Simon's house. Mary had the keenest apprehension of all the disciples. By sitting at His feet in loving fellowship, she obtained a grasp of truth which none of the other disciples had. She saw that His body was to be broken and that His precious life was to go out. She entered into fellowship with His sufferings and the joys of His resurrection. This she showed in the symbolic act of bringing her most precious possession and lavishing it upon Him. Knowing that no living person could minister to Him in that dread hour, she did this service in loving anticipation.

She regarded no sacrifice too great, no gift too costly for her Lord. Genuine love is not calculating.

b. The indigation of the disciples (vv. 8, 9). The action of the disciples is in strange contrast with Mary's love. Judas Iscariot is the leader, but the whole apostolic company are won over by him. The real thing that hurt Judas was the losing of the money for which the ointment might have been sold; not that he cared for the poor.

c. Mary defended by Christ (vv. 10-13). Jesus could not allow His most appreciative disciple to be under this censure, so He came to her rescue. In spite of their criticism, He had nothing but the highest praise. What need we care for the condemnation of men if we can have His praise! As a result of Christ's defense, Judas is so stingingly rebuked that he hastens away to betray his Lord. The supreme expression of Mary's love arouses the very opposite attitude in the soul of Judas. Mary's act of worship and adoration brought out the traitor's heart.

3. Jesus Betrayed (26:14-30).

a. The bargain of betrayal (vv. 14-16). Satan has so completely the mastery over Judas that he sold his Lord for the price of a slave (Exod. 21:32). Judas was not suddenly overtaken by this sin. His action was of deliberate purpose.

b. The betrayal announced (vv. 20-25). It was while they were eating the Passover that Jesus made this announcement. Who knows but that the reason for this announcement at this time was to give Judas a last opportunity to repent. The sorrowful question in verse 22 indicates that the disciples did not seem to suspect one another, but directed personal attention to themselves. The darkness of this crime is shown in that "he that dippeth his hand with me in the dish, the same shall betray me." In the face of all that Christ said, Judas went forward and tried to cover up his purpose by asking, "Master, is it I?"

4. The Disciples Warned (26:31-35).

This took place as they walked from the upper room to the Garden of Gethsemane. He plainly told them: "All ye shall be offended because of me this night," quoting Zechariah 13:7 as proof. While He did tell them of the darkness which was gathering, yet He gave them a glimpse of the coming light. He said: "After I am risen again, I will go before you into Galilee." Peter vehemently protested that though all should forsake Him, he would not. How little Peter knew of his weakness! His self-confidence was his snare.

5. Jesus Praying (26:36-46).

a. The place—the Garden of Gethsemane (v. 36). Gethsemane means oil press. It was a place some three-quarters of a mile east of Jerusalem where oil was crushed out of the olives.

b. His companions (v. 37). Peter, James, and John. The same who had been with Him on the Mount of Transfiguration are permitted to go with Him into the deep shadow of the garden. They slept while He prayed.

c. Jesus sorrowing even unto death (vv. 37, 38). The cause of His suffering was not primarily physical, but spiritual. The physical is not to be minimized, but the burden of sin, the world's sin, was pressing heavily upon Him. He was being made sin for us (II Cor. 5:21).

d. The prayer itself (v. 39). "O my Father, if it be possible, let this cup pass from me." What was this cup? It was not prayer to be delivered from the cross. The idea that He desired to escape from the cross and thus stop short of His redemptive work is not to be entertained. Redemption through the sacrifice of Himself was the supreme purpose of His coming into the world. The holiness and perfection of His nature moved Him to shrink from the mountain of sin which was resting upon Him. Though the cup was bitter, He bowed in submission to the Father's will. After this prayer He returned to find His disciples asleep. They had boasted of their fidelity, but now could not watch with Him one hour. He withdrew the second and third time and prayed practically the same words. Each time upon His return He found the disciples asleep. The last time he bade them, "Sleep on." He no longer needed their sympathy. The battle had been fought and gloriously won without them.

B. *The King on the Cross* (27:1-66).

To miss the significance of the crucifixion of Christ will be to render valueless all the preceding accounts. It is not a matter of learning the lessons taught by a great teacher or imitating the examples of a great and good man, but of apprehending the atonement made by the world's Redeemer. Let everyone see by a personal experience that Christ died for him and then strive to get others to see that Christ's death took place instead of their own death. We escape judgment because judgment fell upon Him. He was made to be sin for us that we might be made the righteousness of God in Him (II Cor. 5:21).

1. The Place of Crucifixion (27:33, 34).

They led Him away to Golgotha, a hill north of Jerusalem, resembling a skull. He was crucified without the gate (Heb. 13:12). At first He was compelled to bear His own cross, but when physical weakness made it impossible for Him to continue, they compelled Simon, the Cyrenean, to bear it for Him (v. 32). No such procession was ever seen before or since. Can it be that the Man of Sorrows suffered thus for me! In order that He might not succumb to death before He was nailed to the cross, the soldiers offered Him a stimulant of vinegar mixed with gall. If they had known Him as the Lord of life, they would have been saved that trouble. No one could take His life from Him. At the appointed time, His work being done, He dismissed His spirit. He refused the stimulant offered and consciously drank the cup of sin to its bitter dregs.

2. Gambling for the Clothing of the Lord (27:35, 36).

It was the custom for the soldiers who had charge of the crucifixion to receive the garments of the one crucified. We have here a fulfillment of Psalm 22:18: "They parted my garments among them, and upon my vesture did they cast lots." What sacrilege for them to gamble for His seamless robe under the very cross where He was dying! Their heartless cruelty is seen in that they sat down and waited while the Lord was dying. If they had but eyes to see they could have beheld a robe of righteousness being provided in His death to cover their own sinful nakedness.

3. The Accusation (27:37).

It was customary to place over the victim on the cross his name and crime. This superscription was placed over Jesus by Pilate to vex the Jews. He was their King in absolute truth. They had long looked for Him and now when He had come, this is the kind of treatment they gave Him. Though they rejected Him and placed a crown of thorns upon His head, the throne of His father David is His by right of the unfailing covenant of God to David (II Sam. 7:8-16).

He shall come again with a crown of glory and before Him shall Jews and Gentiles bow.

4. Two Malefactors Crucified with Him (27:38).

We are not told who they were. Perhaps they belonged to the band of Barabbas. This was another fulfillment of Scripture: "He was numbered with the transgressors" (Isa. 53:12). In these three crosses we have set forth a spiritual history of the whole world. These malefactors by their attitude toward Jesus were separated from Him. One of them afterward changed His attitude.

5. The Dying Saviour Reviled (27:39-44).

He was reviled by the passersby, the chief priests, the scribes, elders, and the malefactors who were crucified with Him. In their mockery they unwittingly spoke great truths.

a. "He saved others; himself he cannot save" (v. 42). This jest was meant to show the absurdity of Jesus' claims, but it demonstrated them and showed the reason for His suffering. He could not save Himself and others, so He chose to give Himself to save others. This is the very heart of the Gospel. He gave Himself for us. His only way of saving us was by taking our sins, sorrows, and stripes upon Himself. This law finds expression all about us. The lamp burns out by giving light. We help others by giving ourselves.

b. "If he be the king of Israel, let him now come down from the cross" (v. 42). His refusal to abandon the cross established His rightful claims. The Devil offered Him the kingdom of the world if He would escape the cross (4:8-10). Through His death He came into His place of kingship over all who bow to Him. The very fact that He did not abandon the cross proves that He was what He claimed to be, for it was unto the cross that He came.

c. "He trusted in God; let him deliver him now" (v. 43). His refusal to abandon the cross proved God's full delight and satisfaction in His Son. His obedience unto death was the sacrifice which met God's full approval. Their very reasoning established Christ's claims instead of breaking them down.

6. The Death of Christ (27:45-50).

Who is sufficient to comment upon this tragedy? Let us contemplate it in adoration and wonder. So shocking was this crime that nature threw around the Son of God a shroud that the godless company could not gaze upon Him. Darkness was upon the land at noonday. Upon the termination of the darkness, He cried with a loud voice: "My God, my God, why hast thou forsaken me?" This darkness was the outer sign of that which hung over the Lord. He became sin for the world, and the world's sin hid God's face from Him. God forsook Him, turned from Him who had taken the sinner's place. God was dealing with sin on the innocent Substitute. No one can understand that but God, but we can believe, and do enjoy the experience. When the price of sin was paid He cried out with a loud voice, showing that He still had vitality, that His death was not from exhaustion, but by His sovereign will. He yielded up the ghost and sent away His spirit. He died like no other man in all the world's history. He did not even die of a broken heart.

7. Intervening Events (27:51-66).

In order to fully appreciate the meaning of the resurrection of Christ, we should glance at the events intervening between His crucifixion and resurrection.

a. We note the rent veil (v. 51). This veil was rent from top to bottom, indicating an unusual event. The veil excluded men from the Holy of Holies. The rending of it showed that Jewish ritual was at an end and that all who accept the atonement affected by the shedding of Christ's blood had the right of approach to God.

b. The tombs were opened (vv. 52, 53). The death of the King shook the earth and rent the rocks. The open tombs were the glorious declaration that Christ's death had broken the power of death. The bodies of the saints did not come forth till after Christ's resurrection. By the death of Christ deliverance was accomplished. Through death judgment was passed upon the Devil who had the power of death (Heb. 2:14), and deliverance from the grave was effected. Christ was the first fruits of the resurrection, therefore these saints could not arise until after He came forth.

c. Gentiles confess Christ. So marvelous were these events that the Gentiles confessed Christ as the Son of God. Not only did the Gentiles confess Him as the Son of God, but Joseph of Arimathaea now boldly avowed his discipleship and came openly to Pilate to ask for the dead body of his Lord, that he might lay it tenderly away in his own sepulcher. In the guarding of the body of the Lord we see the utter folly of His enemies (vv. 62-66). They did their best to make all secure. Their very efforts furnish us with the strongest evidence of His glorious resurrection.

V. THE RISEN KING AND THE GREAT COMMISSION (28:1-20).

A. *The Empty Sepulcher* (28:1-7).

1. The Earthquake (28:1-4).

This occurred when the glorious angel descended from Heaven to roll the stone away from the tomb. This work of the angel was not to allow Jesus to escape, but to show that the tomb was empty. Christ needed not even the help of the glorious angel, for He came forth from the grave by His own power as the seal of His atoning work on the cross (Rom. 1:4). The open tomb and the angel sitting upon the stone with calm dignity is a graphic picture of Christ's triumph over the Devil, and the terror of the keepers is a sample of what all of Christ's enemies shall one day experience when He comes in glory to reign as King.

2. The Angel's Message to the Women (28:5-7).

a. Fear not (v. 5). While the enemies had occasion to fear, these women who loved the Lord received good news from the empty tomb. The Lord will not leave in suspense and dread those who follow Him and love Him. The empty tomb puts an end forever to all doubts and fears. It is the evidence that the question of sin has been dealt with and that God is satisfied and eternal victory is secured. Let everyone endeavor to show the greatness of the fact that the tomb was empty, for it shows that we have a living Christ. The resurrection of Christ should be the major theme of those who give out the Christian message.

b. "Come, see" (v. 6). The angel told the women that the Lord had risen and invited them to see the place where He lay. The reason He invited them to come was that He desired them to make sure about the facts. The Lord made special effort to convince the disciples of the reality of His resurrection. He remained with them for forty days, giving them many "infallible proofs."

c. "Go quickly" (v. 7). Having seen for themselves, their responsibility was to go and tell the message. While it is important to be convinced of facts, one should not stay too long because there is work to do. Experience is necessary before testimony. They were to go quickly to the disciples with the message, assured that the Lord would go before and meet them.

B. *The Risen Lord Meets the Women* (28:8-10).

The women quickly obeyed the command of the angel and were running to bring word to the disciples. Jesus met them on the way. Those who have an experimental knowledge of Christ should go speedily to tell others of it. The Lord Himself will meet on the way all who go quickly with this message. When they saw Jesus that He was really the Lord, they worshiped Him. They knew that He was the Son of God, therefore entitled to be worshiped.

C. *Paying Money to Circulate a Lie* (28:11-15).

That Jesus arose from the dead could not even be denied by the Sanhedrin. They saw only one way out of the difficulty; that was to bribe the keepers to tell a lie. They had paid money for His betrayal; now they paid more money to circulate a lie about His resurrection. This shows the wonderful power that money has over the lives and consciences of men. It not only induces people to lie, but it even muzzles the mouths of some teachers and preachers.

D. *The King's Great Commission* (28:16-20).

1. The Royal Authority (28:18).

By virtue of His divine authority, He issued this command to the disciples. In order to prepare them for the reception of this command, He declared unto them that all power in Heaven and earth had been given unto Him. Only as the disciples realized the authority of the Lord will they go out to proclaim His message.

2. The Commission Itself (28:19, 20).

a. "Go teach all nations." This is the first and primary business of the disciple. This command has been issued to all disciples by the risen and mighty Lord.

b. Baptize them in the name of the triune God. Those who have become disciples of the Lord should receive the rite which signifies that relationship to Him.

c. Teach them to observe all Christ's commandments (v. 20). Those who have become Christ's disciples should be taught obedience to all His commandments.

3. The Available Power (28:20).

Those who obey Christ in carrying out this commission shall enjoy His abiding presence. The guarantee of the success of the enterprise is Christ's abiding presence.

THE GOSPEL ACCORDING TO MARK

PART ONE–INTRODUCTORY MATTERS

Of the four writings called the Gospels, the one bearing the name Mark is least frequently read and prized. This neglect and indifference may be accounted for by two reasons: (a) It was supposed to have been written first, and served both Matthew and Luke in their writings, who copied from it or made additions here and there. (b) It was regarded as a sort of abridgment of Matthew; therefore, in its study to note variations was thought sufficient.

Neither of these opinions trouble those who believe that Mark is a real part of the "scriptures given by the inspiration of God" (II Tim. 3:16). In keeping with the presentation in the Old Testament prophets of the Messiah as the Servant of Jehovah (see Isa. 42:1-4; 52:13; Zech. 3:8), Mark, who was a servant of Paul and Barnabas (Acts 12:25), selects and arranges his material so as to exhibit Jesus Christ as the blessed Servant of the Lord who went about doing good, giving himself up in unselfish service. All matters not bearing on this theme are omitted.

The neglect of the study of Mark accounts for the unwillingness of many, who call themselves Christians, to serve. May the example of the Son of God, abridging His hours for sleep and rest, quicken us all to greater zeal in the service of the living God. When once the central purpose of the Gospel According to Mark is grasped, it is found that this book has a beauty of its own. The "girded one" is as attractive and lovely as the "arrayed one." If the study of Mark does not send us forth with a greater zeal for Christ's service, it will be because we have not seen God's Servant energetically doing God's will.

I. Authorship.

The title, The Gospel According to Mark, expresses the belief of the primitive church. Mark is twice called "John whose surname is Mark." Mark was not an apostle but closely associated with two apostles. He was assistant to Paul and Barnabas and later became a fellow laborer with Peter (I Peter 5:13).

In preaching a series of sermons on Mark's Gospel, the first one should be biographical, setting forth the circumstances of his mother and home life. The preparation for this sermon would demand the examination of all the passages in the New Testament on his life and service.

A. *Mark's Home Life* (Acts 12:12).

He had the wholesome influence of a Christian home, for his mother was a godly woman. Even when it was perilous to be known as a follower of Jesus, she was not afraid to have a prayer meeting in her home. There is no heritage to be compared with that of a godly home. Nothing has such a far-reaching influence upon the life of a young man as the memory of a praying mother. Children coming from such homes usually make good in life.

B. *Mark with Jesus in Gethsemane* (Mark 14:51, 52).

At the sight of the Roman guard, the disciples "all forsook him and fled." This timid lad still followed the Lord till laid hold of by the young men. He then fled, leaving behind him his linen garment. This Gethsemane experience doubtless had a decided effect upon his life.

C. *Mark a Servant of Paul and Barnabas* (Acts 12:25–13:5).

Mark was with the company when Peter told of his wonderful release from prison. This doubtless made a great impression upon him and was the beginning of his desire to accompany the missionaries of the cross. He was not a missionary on the same footing as Paul and Barnabas, but an attendant upon them to look after their needs.

D. *Mark Deserting Paul and Barnabas* (Acts 13:13).

We are not told the cause of this desertion. Three conjectures are offered, one or all of which had a bearing upon his actions.

1. Homesickness.

His home was one of easy circumstances, if not wealthy. As they were carrying the Gospel into the rough, mountainous country, occupied by rough, half-civilized people, the mettle of this young servant was tried. We ought not to condemn him too readily, for we know how trying it is to leave home when struggling against the rough world. While sympathizing with him, we must remember that duty is stronger than the tender ties of life. The time comes when the soldier must spurn the ties which bind him to father, mother, wife, or children in response to the call of duty. The missionary must turn his back upon home, native land, and friends in devotion to his Lord.

2. Disbelief in Foreign Missions.

There was a common prejudice among the Jews against taking the Gospel to the Gentiles. When he saw that these missionaries were going to the "regions beyond," his prejudice may have caused him to turn back. Some today, not Jews, are prejudiced against foreign missions.

3. Cowardice.

The dangers before them were not imaginary but real. The missionary today often faces awful dangers, unhealthy climates, wild beasts, deadly serpents and insects, savages and cannibals. All are more or less fearful although they may try to conceal the fact. However, fear is no excuse for cowardice, for we are linked to the Almighty by faith; there is nothing in Heaven or earth that can harm us. Courage is required of those who would do the Lord's work. "Quit you like men" is the ringing challenge to all.

E. *Mark with Peter in Babylon* (I Peter 5:13).

Some years after Mark's desertion, when Paul and Barnabas were arranging for a second evangelistic tour, they had a sharp dispute over the question of taking Mark with them. Paul would not consent to Mark's accompanying them, so "they departed asunder one from the other." Mark went with his uncle. By this time he must have been cured of his cowardice, for we see him associated with Peter in Babylon. He had found himself, and therefore was not afraid of the enemies in that city.

F. *Mark Honored by Paul* (II Tim. 4:11).

Paul is now an old man in prison. Mark is a middle-aged man associated with Timothy at Ephesus. Mark had proved himself, for

Paul gives the pleasing testimony that "he is profitable unto me for the ministry." Mark is an example of one who made good in spite of his early backsliding. Those who are genuine will redeem themselves from all failures. Failures can be made steppingstones to higher and nobler things.

II. THEME.

Jesus Christ Jehovah's Servant—the Branch (Zech. 3:8). He is the mighty worker rather than the unique teacher. The key thought is: "For even the Son of man came not to be ministered unto, but to minister, and to give his life a ransom for many" (10:45).

Dr. Charles R. Erdman in his *Gospel of Mark* says: "This service is one of strenuous activity. Task follows task, with almost breathless rapidity. Every scene is one of life, movement, vigor. This impression is produced by the frequent use of verbs in the present tense; it is deepened by the surprising repetition of the conjunction *and* which begins two verses out of every three in the Gospel and occurs in practically every verse of some of the chapters. The characteristic word, however, is *straightway* which represents a term translated also as 'forthwith' and 'immediately.' It is found in its Greek form forty-two times in this brief Gospel, more frequently in fact, than in all the other books of the New Testament. His incessant deeds of gracious service were always accompanied by acts of mighty power, as someone has said: 'Mark is the Gospel of miracles instead of parables.' "

III. ANALYSIS.

There does not appear a structural plan. Mark seems to record the events chronologically as they took place. It is proper to note that Mark deals almost exclusively with the Lord's Galilean ministry. He does not allude to any ministry in Judea till the Redeemer goes to Jerusalem to finish His supreme ministry in His sacrificial death.

Since there does not seem to be a structural plan for the Gospel of Mark, I have adopted the following plan for its analysis:

I. The Servant Manifested (1:1-11).
II. The Fidelity of the Servant Demonstrated (1:12, 13).
III. The Servant at Work (1:14—13:37).

IV. The Servant Giving His Life a Ransom for Many (14:1–15:47).

V. The Servant Exalted (16:1-20).

PART TWO—DETAILED OUTLINE

I. THE SERVANT MANIFESTED (1:1-11).

A. *Who Is This Servant of Jehovah?* (1:1).

It is none other than God's beloved Son. As we have seen, the theme of Mark's Gospel is that Jesus Christ is the Servant of Jehovah, according to the prophet Zechariah. The first emphasis is placed upon His deity. No virgin birth appears here. No genealogy is given, because the Servant needs no genealogy. No record of the visit of the Wise Men. All these omissions are in keeping with Mark's purpose in writing. The great truth before us is that the Servant is the Son of God. Sonship and real service go together, for only a real Son can serve. If our service is faulty, it is because *we are not* sons, or *do not realize* our sonship. The coming of this servant as announced by John the Baptist was foretold by the Old Testament prophets (Mal. 3:1; Isa. 40:3).

B. *The Forerunner of the Servant* (1:2-8).

1. Who He Was (1:2, 3).

He was John the Baptist who was prophesied of more than five hundred years before (Isa. 40:3). His mission was to prepare the way for Jesus Christ's coming. He represented himself as but a voice of one crying in the wilderness. He was, therefore, God's voice sounding forth the divine will and purpose. He was content to be but a voice.

2. John's Message (1:3-8).

a. "Prepare ye the way of the Lord" (v. 3). It was the custom for servants to go before distinguished personages and prepare the road over which they were to travel. In this preparation there was the removal of stones, the leveling of the surface of the ground, etc. John's message meant, therefore, that the people should remove from their hearts everything which hindered the incoming of the Lord. He called upon them to humble themselves, to bring down the high places of pride, straighten out the crooked places, and con-tess their sins.

b. The baptism of repentance (v. 4). In preparation for the coming of Christ, the people were to repent of their sins. Those who repented of their sins were to be baptized. Baptism was to be administered to those who repented, as an expression of penitence which led to forgiveness of sin.

c. The coming of the Messiah (vv. 7, 8). The coming One was to be much greater than himself; so great that John was unworthy to loosen the latches of His shoes. The superior dignity of Christ was not only in His Person, but in the work He was to perform. John merely baptized with water, but Jesus would baptize with the Holy Ghost.

3. John's Success (1:5).

People from all over Judea and Jerusalem went out and were baptized. John's dress and demeanor were in keeping with his stern mission. He was clothed with camel's hair and had a girdle of skins. Locusts and wild honey constituted his food. His food and dress indicated that he had withdrawn from the world as a protest against its follies and sins.

C. *The Servant Dedicated to His Work* (1:9-11).

This dedication was symbolized in His baptism. Jesus was not baptized because He had sinned and therefore needed repentance, but because He was now about to accomplish a work which would constitute the basis of all righteousness. He was now dedicating Himself to the task of bringing in righteousness through His sacrificial death. Christian baptism has meaning only in the fact that it is symbolical of the believer's identification with Jesus Christ in His death and resurrection. Observe in connection with His baptism:

1. The Opened Heavens (1:10).

This indicated His connection with Heaven.

2. The Descent of the Holy Spirit upon Him (1:10).

This was the fulfillment of John's prediction concerning Him and gave the divine seal to His work.

3. The Voice of Approval from Heaven (1:11).

This made clear to John that Jesus was the Messiah. It was this voice of heavenly approval that gave meaning to Mark's opening sentence: "The beginning of the gospel of Jesus Christ, the Son of God." The word *Gospel* means "good news." *Jesus* means "Saviour." *Christ* means "anointed." The Gospel is good news, therefore, because it is the good tidings that God had anointed Jesus Christ to be the Saviour of the world. This Gospel has as its grand center the Person Jesus Christ. He is both human and divine. In His connection with the human race He is the seed of David (Rom. 1:3). In His connection with the realm above He is the very Son of God (Rom. 1:4). This enables us to determine as to what the Gospel really is. Any doctrine that does not center in the Person of Christ as a divine-human being is not the Gospel. May we again call to mind the central theme of Mark and the key verse: "For even the Son of man came not to be ministered unto, but to minister, and to give his life a ransom for many."

II. THE FIDELITY OF THE SERVANT DEMONSTRATED (1:12, 13).

This demonstration took place immediately after the heavenly recognition.

A. *The Place—the Wilderness* (1:12).

Adam was tested in the beautiful Garden of Eden with Eve as his needed partner. Jesus Christ was tested in the wilderness surrounded by wild beasts. The Spirit which came upon Him at His baptism directed Him into the wilderness.

B. *The Purpose.*

It was to demonstrate the reality of the incarnation and His loyalty to God.

C. *The Result* (1:13).

The victory was a glorious triumph over the Devil. Because of this victory believers can be assured that the Son of God is able to "save unto the uttermost" those who come to God by Him.

III. THE SERVANT AT WORK (1:14—13:37).

Jesus came not to be ministered unto but to minister.

A. *He Began by Preaching the Gospel of the Kingdom of God* (1:14, 15).

He said: "The time is fulfilled. . . . The kingdom of God is at hand." "Repent ye and believe the gospel." The redemptive work of Jesus Christ is threefold—prophetic, priestly, and kingly. The prophetic was begun by Christ when He was here on earth; the priestly was effected by giving Himself a ransom for many, and will be completed by His coming in power and glory. He began His ministry by preaching this truth. If ministers would preach the New Testament, the people would know about the second coming of Christ to establish the kingdom of God.

A quotation from a sermon by John Calvin on the "Final Advent of Our Lord Jesus Christ" will emphasize this truth. "Our Lord Jesus Christ must appear from Heaven. It is one of the principal articles of our faith. His coming must not be useless. Then we should look for it, waiting for our redemption and salvation. We need not doubt it. For that would violate all that our Lord Jesus did and suffered. For why did He descend into this world? Why was He clothed in human flesh? Why was He exposed to death? Why was He raised from the dead and lifted into Heaven? It was to gather us unto His kingdom when He shall appear. Thus this coming of the Lord is to seal and ratify everything He did and endured for our salvation. Now that should fully suffice to brace us up to resist all the temptation of the world."

B. *The Call for the First Disciples* (1:16-20).

Jesus, having proclaimed the good news that the "kingdom of God is at hand" and knowing that His own career would be short, called helpers to assist Him in preaching this Gospel in all the world. As He walked along by the Sea of Galilee He saw Peter and Andrew casting their net into the sea. He said: "Come ye after me, and I will make you to become fishers of men." They at once left their nets and followed Him. As He went a little farther, He saw James and John who also were fishermen and called them. They left their father and his servants and followed Jesus.

The work to which Jesus called these disciples is still unfinished. The Lord is calling His disciples today to finish the task by proclaiming the good news of salvation to "every creature." Concerning this call note:

1. It Is Definite and Personal.

The Lord is not here in the flesh, but He is calling by the Holy Spirit who works in the believer.

2. It Is to a Definite Work.

It is to become fishers of men. H. Clay Trumbull said a generation ago, that "fishers of men" means "taking men alive."

3. It Is a Call Requiring Sacrifice and Separation.

James and John gave up their business and home and followed Jesus.

4. It Is a Call with Rich Reward.

They gave up being fishermen and enjoying the comforts of home and became immortal on the pages of history. But best of all is the experience of abiding fellowship with the Lord Himself. In issuing the commission to preach the Gospel to every creature, He said, "Lo, I am with you alway."

C. *The Divine Servant Teaching with Authority* (1:21, 22).

The purpose of Mark in this section is to show Christ the Servant bearing the divine message, and clothed with power to perform a saving work. Coupled with the superhuman strength is the *unwearied* sympathy giving itself out in helpful and saving service.

1. Place—Synagogue in Capernaum.

To this place, Christ with the four disciples went "straightway" upon His entrance into the village. He availed Himself of the regular channel of instruction. Many abuses were endured in connection with the synagogue, but He chose to associate the new with the old order.

2. Time—Sabbath Day.

His faithfulness in observing the sabbath brought Him to worship, giving Him an opportunity to expound the Scriptures. He came not to destroy but to fulfill the law, even of the sabbath. Disregard of established order is no sign of one's being sent of God, but the reverse.

3. The Impression—Astonishment (1:22).

Two things about His teaching profoundly impressed His hearers.

a. The substance of His message.

b. The authority of its deliverance. The scribes, the professional teachers of the law merely quoted the authorities, but Jesus, with firsthand knowledge, set forth the truth with the enthusiasm of freshness and personal conviction. This distinction was quickly detected by those who heard Him.

D. *The Servant Curing a Demoniac at Capernaum* (1:23-28).

1. The Outcry of the Demon-possessed Man (1:23).

Perhaps he interrupted Jesus while He was teaching. When the power of God is manifested, there is bound to be an outcry of the evil spirits.

2. The Demon's Confession (1:24).

"Thou art, the Holy One of God." The one whose chief business was to waste and destroy human life, who was in such miserable state as to desire to have nothing to do with Christ, was forced to confess Him as the Holy One. So powerful is Christ that the demons are forced to confess His holiness.

3. Christ's Attitude Toward Him (1:25).

He asked and accepted no testimony from him, but sternly rebuked and cast out the foul spirit. He not only is Himself pure, but is able to deliver others from impurity. Christ wants confession only from pure lips.

4. The Obedience of the Demon (1:26).

The spirit was reluctant to leave, and malicious to the end, for he tore the man whom he had to leave. He had to acknowledge his defeat, and with a howling rage went out.

5. The Impression Made upon the People (1:27, 28).

They were startled by two things:

a. The new doctrine which He brought.

b. The authority over demons. This news spread rapidly over the district around Galilee.

E. *The Servant Healing Peter's Mother-in-law* (1:29-31).

This act shows His tenderness. The scene takes place in the home of one of the disciples. He went home with Simon and Andrew. They told Him of the condition of Peter's mother-in-law. He came at once and lifted her up, and the fever left her. She immediately ministered to Him. The hand of the omnipotent Servant was ready to tenderly heal His own. This was a case of real divine healing.

F. *The Servant Ministering at Sunset* (1:32-34).

Though the day was strenuous in its labors, He came unwearied, "even when the sun did set," to meet the needs of the multitudes who had gathered from all parts of the city. He healed many diseases, cast out many demons, but would not allow the demons to speak. They knew Him, but the poor blind people did not.

G. *The Servant on a Preaching Tour in Galilee* (1:35-39).

It will greatly help us in the understanding of the Lord's action and teachings to fix in mind the strenuousness of the life He was living. He had scarcely time to eat and sleep.

1. Retirement to a Solitary Place (1:35).

He arose "a great while before day . . . and departed into a solitary place, and there prayed." What a lesson for us in our time! If the mighty Son of God needed to go alone with the Father before going on a preaching tour, much more do we need this preparation. There must be a time and a place for this preparation. The *early morning and alone with God* is the answer. Let every minister acquaint himself with the New Testament record of the prayer life of Christ in relation to His teaching and preaching ministry, and then imitate Him.

2. He Preached in the Synagogue Throughout all Galilee (1:39).

To the news of the disciples that "all men seek for thee," He replied: "let us go into the next towns, that I may preach there also: for therefore came I forth." His mission was urgent and the time was short. The good news of the Gospel must be preached to those who had not yet heard. His preaching was in mighty power, for the demons were cast out. Let it be known that Christ's mission was preeminently preaching, miracles were but the credentials of His being sent of God. The Gospel is the "power of God unto salvation." To be a preacher of the Gospel is the highest honor ever conferred on any man.

H. *Jesus Cleanses a Leper* (1:40-45).

1. The Terrible Disease.

It was hopelessly incurable by man. It was a most loathsome disease. The uncleanness of the afflicted one was such he was obliged to live apart from others. He was required to give warning of his approach by crying, "Unclean!" "Unclean!" His disease was corrupting physically and ceremonially. Leprosy is a fitting emblem of sin.

2. The Leper's Approach to Jesus (1:40).

As he knelt down to Jesus he makes a most startling request. "If thou wilt, thou canst make me clean." This request embraces a confession of his faith. He was asking Jesus to do what no physician on earth could do. He was certain that Jesus had the power to heal him, but was not sure of His willingness.

3. Jesus' Compassion (1:41).

The man's awful condition called forth the Master's compassion. The helpless, ruined condition of the sinner always elicits Christ's sympathy.

4. Jesus' Action (1:41).

He . . . put forth his hand, and touched him, and saith unto him, I will; be thou clean."

5. The Blessed Result (1:42).

"Immediately the leprosy departed from him." No sinner who has come to Jesus in real faith, has ever had to wait long for salvation, despite the awfulness of his sinful condition. Jesus saves fully and immediately.

I. *The Servant Forgiving Sins* (2:1-12).

1. Jesus Preaching (2:1, 2).

a. The surging crowd (vv. 1, 2). The crowd was gathered about the home where Jesus was stopping. The house may have been the home of Peter, where He had healed his wife's mother of a fever. As soon as it was noised about that Jesus was in the house, the multitudes gathered.

b. What Jesus preached unto them (v. 2). He preached unto them the Word. He always preached the Word before He wrought miracles, for to make known the will of God is His supreme mission. The people came partly out of curiosity and partly to be healed. He gave them that which they needed, regardless of the motive which actuated their coming.

2. Jesus Forgives Sin (2:3-5).

The man was suffering from the dread disease of palsy, but this disease was only typical of a more deadly one with which he was afflicted—sin. This mighty miracle wrought by Jesus in confirmation of His message was vitally connected with faith.

a. Faith in coming to Jesus (v. 3). The palsied man and the four friends who carried him were actuated by faith.

b. Faith in overcoming difficulties (v. 4). Though prevented by the crowd from coming into the presence of Jesus, they ascended the outer stairway and let the man down through the roof into the presence of Jesus. They disregarded conventionalities, knowing that the all-important thing was to go to the Lord with their need.

c. Faith is rewarded (v. 5). No word was uttered either by the paralytic or his bearers. None was needed, their act was enough. The paralytic got more than he expected. He desired healing of the body. He got that plus forgiveness of sins—the healing of the soul.

3. Jesus Answering the Scribes (2:6-9).

a. Their objections.

(1) "Why doth this man thus speak?"

(2) "Who can forgive sins?" They were right in their reasonings that only God can forgive sins, but they were wrong in esteeming Him less than God.

b. Jesus' answer. In this He shows divine knowledge. He knew their inner thoughts and reasonings and gave them a test of His deity. "Thy sins be forgiven thee or . . . Arise, and take up thy bed, and walk." He was willing that His power in the invisible realm should be tested by His power in the visible.

4. Jesus Healing the Paralytic (2:10-12).

a. He did it by speaking the Word. Christ's words are enough. This poor man was helpless and of himself unable to move, but when Christ commands, He gives the strength to obey.

b. Obedience of the man (v. 12). The cure was immediate. The poor helpless man walked away with his bed upon his shoulder. At the words of Christ disease and death flee away.

c. The people were amazed and glorified God, saying, "We never saw it on this fashion."

J. *The Servant-Saviour Calling Levi (Matthew)* (2:13-17).

1. It was a Personal Call.

It was definitely given to a person, for a definite purpose, to follow Jesus, i.e., to become a disciple.

2. It Was Seemingly an Abrupt Call (2:14).

It was given as Jesus passed by. However, Jesus doubtless had given particular attention to the taxgatherers, and Levi was most likely well acquainted with the work of Jesus. Perhaps he had heard Him preach many times. His business required alertness of perception. Jesus knew his capabilities. His choice was an intelligent one, for He is omniscient.

3. It Was a Call to Great Worldly Sacrifice.

It meant the loss of wealth. He could not be a part-time disciple. It meant giving up all for Christ.

4. His Response Was Immediate (2:14).

He arose and followed Jesus.

5. The Result of His Action.

It was immediate salvation, and immortal fame. He became a blessing to his people and a crown of glory. Wherever the Bible is known, he is known as the author of the Gospel According to Matthew.

6. The Feast in Levi's House (2:15-17).

Presumably this feast was prepared as a token of allegiance of the new disciple to his Lord. He invited a large company of his friends to come to a feast where Christ was the Guest of honor. The natural desire of the new disciple is to bring his friends into the presence of his Lord and Saviour that they too may come to know Him.

The willingness of Jesus to come to such a feast was not in any way to encourage sinners to continue in their sinful practices, or sanction the joining in business and social practices which are contrary to the mind of Christ. It clearly manifests Christ's willingness to come to sinners. He came to give His life a ransom for sinners. The reason Christ mingled with sinners was that He was the Great Physician, and that as such He came to save sinners. The fact that they were sick proved their need of the Physician. Only the sick need the doctor.

K. *The Servant-Saviour Answering a Question Concerning Fasting* (2:18-22).

The question asked was: "Why do the disciples of John and of the Pharisees fast, but thy disciples fast not?" Christ answered: "Can the children of the bridechamber fast, while the bridegroom is with them? As long as they have the bridegroom with them, they cannot fast. But the days will come when the bridegroom shall be taken away from them, and then shall they fast." Christ was the Bridegroom whom they would soon take away from the disciples and crucify, and then the disciples would fast.

By means of the two parables of the new cloth sewn on the old garment and the new wine in old bottles, He shows the folly of mixing the new dispensation with the old.

Fasting means abstention from food. Normal life demands wholesome food at proper periods. Dr. Davis in his *Dictionary of the Bible* says: "There are no injunctions laid upon Christians to fast, and the revisers on the ground of textual criticism have removed the word from Matthew 17:21; Mark 9:29; Acts 10:30; I Corinthians 7:5."

Christ's forty days of fasting were not, in the author's opinion, a preparation for His struggle with the Devil in the wilderness. Luke says: "Jesus being full of the Holy Ghost returned from Jordan, and was led by the Spirit into the wilderness, being forty days tempted of the devil. And in those days he did eat nothing: and when they were ended, he afterward hungered" (Luke 4:1, 2). He did not fast to get strength to meet the Devil, but was so desperately struggling in the conflict with the Devil that He did not have time or inclination to eat.

L. *The Servant Is Lord of the Sabbath* (2:23–3:6).

The mingling of Jesus with publicans and sinners and His disregard of the law of the Pharisees regarding fasting aroused opposition. But when He exposed their erroneous teaching regarding the sabbath, their hatred became intense.

1. The Disciples Plucking Ears of Corn (2:23-28).

a. The charge made against the disciples (vv. 23, 24). Perhaps they were on their way to the synagogue to worship when they plucked the ears of corn. For this act the Pharisees accused them of lawlessness.

b. Jesus defends them against the charge (vv. 25-28).

(1) He cites a precedent (vv. 25, 26). The very law which they charged the disciples of breaking recorded the fact that David, the great king of Israel, had gone into the house of God and eaten the bread which should be eaten only by the priests. The higher law of human need warranted David's breaking the law in this case, and

his action had met the approval of the people of his time and the succeeding generations.

(2) He shows the nature of the sabbath law (v. 27). It was made for man, and when man's good is subserved by breaking it, it is permissible to do so. The laws of honesty, truth, purity, and love differ from the law of the sabbath, and there is no circumstance under which they may be broken with impunity. The sabbath should not be man's cruel master, but his helpful servant.

Jesus is Lord of the sabbath (v. 28). It was He who instituted it when Creation was finished; therefore He had a right to use it as it pleased Him for man's good.

2. Jesus Healing the Withered Hand (3:1-6).

a. Place—the synagogue (v. 1). Jesus' example shows what He did on the sabbath. He went to the place of worship. Entering into the worship of God is more important than a selfish observance of forms and ceremonies. The presence of a man with a withered hand gave Jesus an opportunity to administer a rebuke to the Pharisees.

b. The Pharisees watching (v. 2). They knew that Jesus would be interested in this helpless man. They surmised that some work would have to be performed to heal him. The motive which actuated their watching was evil.

c. The man made an example (v. 3). Jesus wanted the case to be open to all, so He commanded the man to stand forth where all could see him.

d. The questions asked (v. 4). "Is it lawful to do good on the sabbath days, or to do evil? to save life, or to kill?" He made the issue clear. He plainly showed them that to fail to do good, to show works of mercy, to save life is to be guilty of wrongdoing, even of murder. The obligation to show mercy and to save life is universal.

e. The man healed (v. 5). Christ healed him by speaking the word, so they could not accuse Him. Their hardness of heart grieved and angered Him.

f. The result (vv. 4, 6). The Pharisees were silenced. There was no ground upon which to accuse Him; but since their hearts were bent upon His destruction they sought how they might put Him to death.

M. *The Servant Ministering by the Sea* (3:7-12).

1. Why He Withdrew (3:6).

It was because of the murderous plotting of the Pharisees against His life. So violent was their hatred against Him that they conspired with the Herodians, whom they regarded as traitors to their nation and country, to put Him to death. Their opposition was aroused when Jesus claimed to have power on earth to forgive sins (2:10). It grew in intensity when He mingled with publicans and sinners (2:16), and was fanned into violent flame when He set at naught their false interpretations of the sabbath law (2:23-28).

2. To Whom He Ministered (3:7, 8).

A great multitude represented a wide stretch of territory. They came from Jerusalem and Idumea on the south, from beyond Jordan on the east, and from Tyre and Sidon on the northwest. Jesus was the magnetic attraction, the Hero of the hour. The interest of the whole country centered in Him.

3. The Result (3:9-12).

a. So great was the pressure that His very life was in danger of being crushed out by the thronging multitudes. Some came out of curiosity, "when they had heard what great things he did" (v. 8). Others came for the physical benefit, to be healed of their diseases. To escape this crush, He ordered the disciples to prepare a small boat for Him.

b. The unclean spirits prostrated themselves before Him, confessing Him as the Son of God (vv. 11, 12). This testimony He refused to receive because:

(1) The time was not ripe.

(2) They were not the beings to make Him known. He would be proclaimed only by those who loved and honored Him.

N. *The Servant Choosing the Twelve Apostles* (3:13-19).

He makes provision for the carrying forward of the work after He was gone. Before choosing the twelve He spent a whole night in prayer (Luke 6:12). What He immediately did shows this to be the burden of His prayer. From among His disciples He chose twelve whom He ordained for a twofold purpose:

1. "That They Might Be with Him" (3:14).

Fellowship with the Lord is not only the highest privilege of the disciples, but it is the indispensable qualification for witnessing. Personal association with Jesus Christ, which is often made a secondary matter, is a preparation for Christian service of the highest importance. It is needful to be with Him to catch His spirit and to be impressed with His personality.

2. "That He Might Send Them Forth to Preach" (3:14).

To proclaim the good news of salvation was the supreme mission of the disciples. Their credentials for this commission was the induement with power "to heal sicknesses, and to cast out devils" (v. 15). Concerning those who were to be the messengers of Christ, note:

a. Twelve were ordained (v. 14). This was the beginning of the process by which the Triune God was to make manifest His grace to the whole world: hence He selects and qualifies the number of men corresponding to that purpose; for the number twelve is the product of heavenly three and earthly four, thus indicating the purpose of the Triune God to reveal Himself unto the four quarters of the earth.

b. Their characteristics:

(1) From the middle ranks of society—walks of life. They were neither rich nor paupers. God usually chooses men and women for places of largest service from among those who can understand the feelings, language, and needs of the common people.

(2) Men of average ability. Christ did not go to the schools for His apostles, yet it is clear that He chose men of mental grasp and efficiency. Here and there God uses men and women of conspicuous learning and ability, yet it still remains true that "not many wise men after the flesh, not many mighty, and not many noble, are called" (I Cor. 1:26).

(3) Men of diverse temperamental gifts. The grouping of the apostles shows: (*a*) men of impulse and leadership; (*b*) men of a reflective and questioning type; and (*c*) men of practical business ability. Such are needed in every enterprise for God.

O. *The Servant Misunderstood and Opposed* (3:20-35).

1. The Occasion (3:19, 20).

A series of important events in the ministry of Jesus had immediately followed in rapid succession. The twelve had been chosen and He with His disciples had just returned from a trip of preaching and healing in Galilee. Such great interest was aroused that though Jesus was weary and hungry He did not have time to eat. Doing the works which the Father sent Him to do was more important than eating.

2. What His Friends Purposed to Do (3:21).

They went out to lay hold on Him. They saw Him giving Himself with absolute abandon to His work, so they attempted to forcibly rescue Him by taking Him from His work.

3. What They Said (3:21).

"He is beside himself." His passionate devotion to saving the lost seemed to them a kind of insanity. Many today who turn from gainful occupations to spend and be spent in winning lost souls to Christ are called crazy.

4. Jesus Opposed by the Scribes (3:22-30).

a. Their charge (v. 22). They charged Him with casting out demons by Beelzebub. According to Matthew 12:22-24, the Pharisees joined the scribes in this charge. The occasion which provoked this charge was the healing of a man who has been possessed with a demon. Not being able to explain his unwearying service for needy men by attributing his zeal to a religious frenzy, they accused Him of being in league with the Devil. The miracles wrought were so real that they could not deny them. Being unwilling to confess Him as the Messiah, they sought to slander Him by calling Him an impostor.

b. Christ's reply (vv. 23-27). He exposed their folly by a question and by parables.

(1) "How can Satan cast out Satan?" If after Satan gets control of a man he should voluntarily relinquish that hold, he would thus become his own enemy. In view of the nature of the Devil, this is unthinkable. If Satan should rise up against himself, then he and his works would end (v. 26). There is no such thing as a double personality. Despite Stevenson's presentation, there is no Dr. Jekyll and Mr. Hyde. Such psychological manifestations as suggested are delusions of a disordered brain.

(2) "If a kingdom be divided against itself, that kingdom cannot stand" (v. 24). Civil war is national suicide.

(3) "If a house be divided against itself, that house cannot stand" (v. 25). House here means family. The family that wars against itself will surely perish.

(4) "No man can enter into a strong man's house, and spoil his goods, except he will first bind the strong man" (v. 27). Satan here is the strong man, the house is the world, the goods of the house are the human beings whose welfare and happiness Satan is seeking to destroy. On the cross of Calvary Christ bound the strong man and He with His servants is endeavoring to keep Satan from destroying the souls of men which are the Lord's goods.

c. Christ's charge (vv. 28-30). Since He was doing the works of God and not of Satan (for before their very eyes He had driven the demon from the man), He was undoing the works of the Devil. He went about doing good. Wherever He went, men were blessed. The eyes of the blind were opened, deaf ears were unstopped, the lame were made to walk, and the dead were raised. Having with unanswerable logic met their accusations, He charged them with the most awful guilt, that of blasphemy against the Holy Ghost. Blasphemy against the Holy Ghost is attributing the works of the Spirit to the Devil. For this great sin there is no pardon. Those who commit it are exposed to the danger of eternal damnation.

5. Jesus Misunderstood by His Family (3:31-35).

His brothers and mother came with the object of taking Him home because they thought He had lost His reason. Of course His brothers did not believe on Him as the Messiah, but their filial interest moved them to try to get Him home. No doubt this was most painful to Jesus. Their motive may have been right, but they were used of the Devil to hinder Him. Growing out of this came that wonderful declaration, that relation to Christ is more vital than that of human kinship. The highest relationship in the world is oneness with God through Christ.

P. *The Servant Teaching by Parables* (4:1-34).

1. Parable of the Sower (4:1-20).

a. The place—the seaside (v. 1). A great multitude gathered to Him at the seaside, so that He was obliged to enter a boat to escape the pressure of the crowd. From this boat as a pulpit He taught many things in parables.

b. The reason He taught in parables (vv. 9-12). This method of teaching was not employed until the rulers had set their hearts against Him. When in the light of His wonderful works they turned against Him and attributed His works to the Devil (3:22), He denounced them in most scathing terms and began teaching in parables, in fulfillment of Isaiah 6:10. The parabolic method of teaching makes clear the truth to those who love it, and conceals it from those who dislike it.

c. The parable of the four kinds of ground (vv. 3-8; 13:20). The seed and the sower are the same in all these instances, but the results are entirely different. The difference lies in the condition of the soil. The central purpose of this parable is to show that the results of preaching the Word depend upon the condition of the heart.

(1) The wayside (vv. 4, 15). The wayside means the track beaten down by the hoofs of animals and the feet of men. Because the soil was unbroken and uncultivated, the seed could not get beneath the surface, therefore was devoured by the fowls that came along (v. 4). The great truth taught is that the heart unbroken and hard is not fit soil for the Gospel. Such a heart it penetrates not, but lies loosely upon the surface. It is not recognized as God's means for restoring them unto Himself. While in this condition the Evil One finds some way to snatch away the truth. The fowls which devour the seed represent the agents of Satan (v. 15).

(2) The stony ground (vv. 5, 6, 16, 17). This means not stones mixed with soil, but rocks with a thin layer of soil upon them. With such conditions the seed springs up quickly, and likewise scorches quickly since it has not much depth. The great lesson is that hearts superficially impressed receive the Word with joy, but when affliction or persecution arises for the Word's sake, immediately they are offended. They wither away and die.

(3) The thorny ground (vv. 7, 18, 19). In this case the ground is good, but has thorns in it. It is mellow enough and has sufficient depth, but has not been cleared of the thorns. Such really hear the Word, but the cares of this world and the deceitfulness of

riches and the lusts of other things entering in choke the Word, and it becomes unfruitful (v. 19). The thorny-ground hearers of this age are those—

(a) Who are so immersed in worldliness, business, and anxious care that the good seed cannot mature.

(b) Who are rich. Anxious care in business brings riches, and the effect of riches is the blunting of the spiritual perceptions of men and women, thereby rendering them unsusceptible to the call of God to higher things in life.

(c) Who are running after the pleasures of life. All these things choke the Word. Many of the enjoyments of the world may be innocent in themselves, but they attract so much attention and consume so much energy and time that one has no time for Bible reading, meditation, and prayer.

(4) The good ground (vv. 8, 20). This ground differs from all the rest. It is soft and mellow, deep and moist; therefore it is capable of bringing forth fruit, some a hundred, some sixty, and some thirtyfold, indicating different degrees of fruitfulness even of good ground. In the measure that the heart is kept free from worldliness, riches, and pleasures, the good seed matures.

2. Parable of the Candle (4:21-25).

In the parable of the sower (vv. 1-20) the Word which is sown is not only to bear fruit, but to shine forth in testimony. Dr. James M. Gray says: "The 'bushel' stands for the cares and material things of life, and the 'bed' for ease and comfort." The meaning then would be that the Word of God should so permeate our being, that in our business and social life we may have a testimony for Christ. This obligation is enforced by a solemn command and warning. "Take heed what ye hear" (v. 24) means that we should not only be attentive to what is taught, but wholehearted in its reception. We should receive the whole of what the Lord has to say to us. All such shall have their understanding enlarged and knowledge increased (v. 24). Indifference and unbelief will result in limitation, and even degeneration (v. 25).

3. The Parable of the Growing Grain (4:26-29).

This parable is peculiar to Mark. In the light of the purpose of Mark, it is clear why it should appear here. It is the parable for the servant. In the previous parables (vv. 24, 25; cf. vv. 1-21), the responsibility of the hearer is set forth. The teaching in this parable is for the servant who proclaims the message.

a. The attitude of mind of the Gospel preacher (vv. 26, 27). He should with the utmost fidelity "cast seed into the ground," preach the Word, and leave the results to God. The spiritual processes of God's Word in the soul of man are shrouded in the deepest mystery. The seed should "spring and grow up, he knoweth not how" (v. 27). When the sowing has been faithfully done, the sower should not be burdened with anxiety. He can "sleep, and rise night and day," confident that the Almighty will take care of the processes and results. It may require hard and even painful efforts to prepare the soil and sow the seed, but when that is done he should rest, for the processes and results are beyond his wisdom and power.

b. The processes of the spiritual life are gradual (v. 28). "First the blade, then the ear, after that the full corn in the ear." We should not expect maturity of Christian character at once, any more than the farmer should expect his crops to mature at once. He has a time of sowing, a time of growing, and a time of harvest.

c. The consummation of the spiritual processes (v. 29). Though the sowing of the seed be done under difficulties and the processes of development long drawn out, the harvest will surely come. When the grain is ripe, the farmer thrusts in the sickle.

4. The Parable of the Mustard Seed (4:30-34).

In this parable the plant with its great branches (called a tree in Matt. 13:32), which springs out of the small seed, exhibits a mystery of the kingdom (Matt. 13:11). It shows the condition of things in the world in the interval between Christ's going away and His coming again. It was not designed to make known church conditions, but the admixture of things in what is known as Christendom. In this parable three things claim our attention:

a. The unimportant beginning (v. 31). It begins as the least of all seeds, and grows to be the greatest among herbs. The parentage and humble circumstances of Jesus greatly perplexed the people. That twelve unlettered fisherman should be selected as His royal advisers was still more amazing. The prophet had said of Him that he would be "despised," "rejected," "forsaken," "cut off," "having nothing."

b. The vigorous growth (v. 32). From the very small beginnings of the movement inaugurated by Christ, His influence has gone forth so that there is no power or influence today in the earth so great as that which calls itself Christian.

c. The lodging capacity (v. 32). The birds which find lodgment in the branches do not represent, as is commonly interpreted, the children of men who find safety and salvation in the church, because church truth is not now under consideration. It is a mystery of the kingdom which was proclaimed as at hand by John the Baptist, Jesus, and the disciples; passed into abeyance when Jesus was crucified, and shall come into realization when Jesus comes back to earth again. The believer in Christ becomes a vital part of His Body, and is necessary even to its strength and fruitfulness. The branches increase the growth of the tree, but the birds are injurious and burdensome to it. They are predatory—waiting to pluck off the tender buds, or to prey upon the ripened fruit. The effect of such lodging is evil and blighting to the tree.

In Christ's interpretation of the parable of the sower, He said that the fowls which devoured the seed represent Satan (v. 15). He who would make the lodgers here anything else makes Christ's interpretation a farce. The same Greek word is used in both cases, and the circumstances are the same. Besides Christ's interpretation, if we have eyes to discern, we shall see these fowls of the air polluting the tree which the Lord is causing to grow up. The idolatrous and licentious bird of Mormonism, the anti-Christian birds of Christian Science, Russellism, Spiritualism, etc., are notable examples.

Q. *The Divine Servant Doing Mighty Works* (4:35—5:20).

Jesus was a great Teacher, as was shown in the foregoing parables. But Mark's aim is pre-eminently to exhibit Him as the divine Servant doing mighty deeds; hence following the parables are presented deeds which show Him to be the Master of the forces of nature, demons, diseases, and death.

1. Jesus Calms the Sea (4:35-41).

a. Crossing the sea (vv. 35, 36). Weary with the teaching of the day, He proposed that they take ship to the other side of the sea, doubtless to escape the crush of the multitude.

b. Overtaken by a storm (v. 37). Even though Jesus was in the boat with the disciples, they were overtaken by a storm. It is not God's will that we should escape the storms, but those who have Christ cannot go down.

c. Jesus asleep in the storm-tossed boat (v. 38). In the midst of the turbulent elements, He was resting in sleep. The day had been a very strenuous one, and He was weary. He who had made the sea could well lie down and sleep, though the storm violently raged.

d. The terrified disciples (v. 38). In their minds nothing but disaster and death awaited them. There was absolutely no danger, for no boat can go down, regardless of the violence of the storm, which has Christ on board. The disciples were not only terrified, but they also chided Him for sleeping while they were in such danger.

e. The Servant rebukes (vv. 39, 40).

(1) The wind (v. 39). This showed that the elements of nature were subject to Him.

(2) The disciples for their lack of faith. They were looking at their circumstances instead of at their Lord.

f. The effect upon the disciples (v. 41). They were filled with great fear. A little while ago they were afraid in the face of the storm; now they are afraid in the presence of the Lord.

2. Jesus Heals the Gadarene Demoniac (5:1-20).

After stilling the tempest, Jesus crossed to the other side of the sea into heathen territory.

a. Met by a demon-possessed man (vv. 1-6). This man was in a desperate condition. He was so fierce that no one could safely pass that way; he wore no clothes (Luke 8:27). No chains were strong enough to hold him, and no one was able to tame him. In the nighttime his hideous cries could be heard while he vented his rage by cutting himself with stones. Many today are demon possessed. Much of the insanity of the age is traceable to this cause. As the coming of the Lord draws nigh these things will increase (I Tim. 4:1). However, no demon can enter a man without his consent.

b. What the demons knew about Christ (vv. 7-9). They knew

that He was the Son of God, and that He had come to destroy the Devil and his works. Among the demons there is no doubt as to the deity of Christ and the judgment to come, though we have many theologians and preachers who say they do not believe it. The Devil blinds their eyes so that they cannot understand (II Cor. 4:4). He knows that this is a good way to hinder the Lord's work.

c. Christ's power to deliver from the Devil (vv. 10-13). He cast out the demons from the man (v. 8). The demons quailed before Christ, not daring to dispute His power, so they begged to be permitted to enter the swine. As soon as the Lord issued the permission they hastened away to hurl the swine to destruction.

d. The effect upon the people of the city (vv. 14-17). The keepers of the swine fled to the city and reported what had occurred. This miracle brought out the people, but when they realized the loss of their hogs, they besought Him to leave their coasts. They cared more for their hogs than for Christ and the cure of this man. These Gadarenes have many successors today.

e. The man who was healed sent home to testify (vv. 18-20). No doubt it would have been safe and pleasant to abide with Jesus but his friends needed his testimony. The best witness for Christ is one who has been saved by Him. The best place to begin that testimony is at home where one is well known.

R. *The Mighty Servant Restoring Life and Health* (5:21-43).

In the last section Christ's power over the forces of nature and demons was exhibited; in this His power over disease and death is a fitting climax. The stories of the raising of the damsel and the healing of the woman are so interwoven as almost to constitute one narrative; but since the persons are diverse and places separate, and the one an interruption of the other, they should be treated separately.

1. Jairus' Daughter Raised from the Dead (5:21-24; 35-43).

a. Jairus' urgent mission (vv. 21-23). His only daughter (Luke 8:42), perhaps his only child, lay dying. In this time of utter helplessness he came to Jesus, for he had faith in His ability to raise her up. In the providence of God sorrow, sickness, and death are often used to bring needy men and women into contact with Jesus. He showed the proper attitude toward Jesus; "he fell at his feet" (v. 22).

b. Jesus goes with Jairus (v. 24). Jairus believed that if Jesus would lay His hand upon his daughter she would live. Such faith always gets a response from Jesus.

c. News of the daughter's death (v. 35). This was a startling message. The messengers who brought the news suggested that Jesus should be excused from going farther as it was now too late.

d. Jairus' faith strengthened (v. 36). Jesus said, "Be not afraid, only believe." Only the mighty Servant of God could speak thus.

e. The mourners rebuked (vv. 37-39). He now dismissed the crowd, and allowed only three of His disciples and the parents of the damsel to enter this chamber of death with Him. A tumultuous wailing showed the despair of the friends. Such unbelief met His rebuke.

f. Jairus' faith rewarded (vv. 41-43). Christ took the damsel by the hand and issued the command for her to arise. She straightway arose and walked and partook of food. He charged them to keep silent concerning this miracle, as premature notoriety might interfere with His work.

2. The Woman with an Issue of Blood Healed (5:25-34).

a. Her helpless condition (vv. 25, 26; cf. Luke 8:43). She had been a great sufferer for twelve long years, not only from the disease itself, but from the physicians as well.

b. Her faith (vv. 27, 28). It was earnest. For a poor emaciated woman, after twelve years of suffering, to press her way through a thronging multitude shows that she possessed a determined purpose. The test of the actuality and quality of one's faith is the activity which characterizes the life. Her faith was so strong that she believed contact with the Master's garments would secure the needed help. Though strong, her faith was very imperfect. She only knew Him as a wonder worker, but through this experience she learned to know Him as a compassionate Saviour.

c. Her healing (vv. 29-32). As soon as she touched the hem of His garment, she experienced in her body His healing power.

d. Her confession (v. 33; cf. Luke 8:47). She thought furtively to get the blessing of healing, but Jesus perceived that virtue had gone out from Him and had her make a public confession. This was for her good, for faith in Christ unconfessed will naturally weaken.

e. Jesus' words of encouragement (v. 34). With the communication of His healing virtue, He spoke most gracious and comforting words to this poor woman. He tells her that it was her faith, not her touch, that saved her.

S. *The Servant Doing Mighty Works at Nazareth Without Honor* (6:1-6).

As God's obedient Servant, Jesus energetically gave Himself to His work. Having just completed a series of marvelous miracles, He came back to His own country, accompanied by His disciples, to continue His work.

1. Teaching in the Synagogue (6:2).

This He did on the sabbath. He could let no opportunity to do good pass. As the people gathered together on the sabbath, He taught them.

2. The Result of His Teaching (6:2, 3).

a. The people were astonished. In their astonishment they asked questions.

(1) "From whence hath this man these things?"

(2) "What wisdom . . . is given unto him?"

(3) "Is not this the carpenter?"

(4) "Are not his sisters here with us?" That His wisdom and power were superhuman, they could not doubt. They were unable to account for them. The only answer to their questions is Christ's absolute deity. Had they apprehended Him as the Son of God the matter would have been clear to them.

b. The people offended (v. 3). Not being able to answer their own questions and to believe their own eyes and ears, they rejected Him. This rejection was not because they knew Him too well, but because they knew Him not at all. The more one knows about Jesus, the more he will honor and respect Him. If people were to judge Jesus on the basis of His own claims and upon what He did, they could not help but believe on Him.

3. Jesus Misunderstood by His Fellow Townsmen (6:3-6).

The citizens of Nazareth were unable to question the reality of Christ's work and the power of His words, but because He was one of them they were offended at Him. This is a marvelous example of the blighting effects of prejudice. Because of this attitude of soul on the part of the people His wonder-working was very limited among them. At their unbelief He greatly marveled.

4. Christ Marveled at the Unbelief of the People (6:6).

But He continued His teaching in the villages.

T. *The Divine Servant Sending Forth the Twelve to Preach* (6: 7-13).

Though Jesus' fame had spread abroad and multitudes thronged Him, the people of His own town Nazareth rejected Him (vv. 1-6). He answered their taunts and jeers by declaring that a prophet is not without honor but in his own country, and among his own kin, and in his own house. Because of their unbelief, He could do no mighty works there so He went round about the villages teaching, knowing that though the leaders turned a deaf ear to His message, some would hear and believe.

Two pressing considerations moved Him to send them forth—the increasing multitudes who were eager to hear the message, and the fact that His own career would soon end. Others must be ready to carry on the work which He had begun.

1. They Were Sent Forth in Pairs (6:7).

Three reasons may be assigned for sending them two by two:

a. A wider scope of country could be covered than if they would go in company.

b. A companionship would be provided for the workers which would be mutually cheering and comforting.

c. Their testimony would be confirmed, for in the mouth of two or three witnesses every word shall be established. Wise missionary administration will take account of this. There should not be too great concentration, neither should there be too great isolation.

2. The Supernatural Authentication of Their Mission (6:7).

He gave them power over unclean spirits. They were endowed with power to work miracles, to show that they were commissioned by Heaven for their work.

3. Their Maintenance (6:8, 9).

They were to make no provision for their support, but to depend wholly upon the Lord who sent them. They had received the message and power gratuitously, so they were to give it out in the same way (Matt. 10:9). Christ's messengers should not be burdened with needless equipment, but go forth in faith depending upon the Lord to move upon those to whom they minister to provide them entertainment and support, not as a matter of poverty, but that which is legitimate, for the laborer is worthy of his hire.

4. Contentment with Hospitality (6:10).

According to Matthew, inquiry was to be made upon entering a city as to a reputable place to stay. When such place is determined upon, the missionary should be content.

5. Responsibility of Those to Whom the Message Was Delivered (6:11).

Judgment was to be pronounced upon those who rejected their message. Their doom would be more hopeless than that of Sodom and Gomorrah.

6. Their Message and Work (6:12, 13).

They went out and preached that men should repent. Matthew adds, "The kingdom of heaven is at hand" (Matt. 10:7), which means that the kingdom promised to Israel was at hand, that Christ was present and ready to set up His kingdom. In confirmation of their message they cast out many demons and anointed with oil many that were sick, and healed them.

7. Effect of Their Ministry (6:14-29).

The fame of Christ spread far and wide through the teaching and miracles wrought by the twelve. Various explanations were offered of this marvelous work. Their preaching had the Messiahship of Jesus as its central content. Some said that He was one of the prophets, others that He was Elias; but Herod said that He was John the Baptist whom he had beheaded. Herod's guilty conscience troubled him, but he was too weak to obey its voice. John had rebuked Herod for his unlawful marriage with his brother's wife. Herod recognized the righteousness of John's indictment, but was so bound with the shackles of sin that he was unable to free himself from them. He did not desire to kill John, nor was he willing to give up his illegal relationship, so he compromised by imprisoning John. In the midst of his temporizing, Satan wins the victory over him. On the occasion of the disgraceful dance on Herod's birthday, he was caught by the conspiracy of Herodias and beheaded John. His sleeping conscience which had been violated was aroused by the strenuous preaching and mighty works of the twelve.

8. The Twelve Making Report of Their Work to Jesus (6:30, 31).

After their strenuous campaign, at the invitation of Jesus they retired with Him and told Him what they had taught and what they had wrought. Such retirement with the Lord has a twofold benefit; it would fix their minds upon the Lord instead of upon themselves as to their successes, and prevent despondency for their failures.

U. *The Servant Ministering to the Multitudes* (6:32-44).

1. The Servant Teaching the Ignorant Multitude (6:32-34).

a. Departing for the desert place (v. 32). The Master invited the twelve to retire from the crowd for a rest. Periods of withdrawal from the crowd in fellowship with the Lord are necessary after evangelistic campaigns.

b. Thronged by the people (v. 33). Seeing the Lord and His disciples depart, the people from all the cities anticipated their landing.

c. The Lord moved with compassion (v. 34). Instead of becoming irritated by the intrusion of the crowd, His heart was moved with pity. His personal interests were forgotten as the needs of the shepherdless sheep pressed upon His notice. He is now the same compassionate Saviour touched with the feelings of our infirmities (Heb. 4:15). Under these circumstances He taught them many things.

2. The Servant Feeding the Hungry Multitude (6:35-44).

a. Conference with the disciples (vv. 35-38).

(1) Disciples request that the multitude be sent to the surrounding villages to buy bread (v. 36). According to Matthew, Christ made the proposition that the multitude be fed.

(2) Jesus commands them to feed the multitude (v. 36).

(3) The disciples' perplexity (v. 37). They began to calculate as to the amount of provision required. They asked the Lord as to whether they should go and buy two hundred pennyworth of bread. The perplexity of the disciples was due to the fact that they were

depending upon their own resources instead of on Christ. To be face to face with the humanly impossible has a threefold benefit:

(a) To make us feel our dependence upon Christ.

(b) To drive us to Him for help in our need.

(c) To lead us to give the glory to Him for results. Though the disciples' ability to teach, preach, or give be meager, when coupled with the Lord's ability it is equal to any demands which may be made.

b. Jesus' method in feeding the multitudes (vv. 39-44).

(1) The Master's part. This was to issue the instructions as to the method of procedure, and to create the provisions. Though they had but five loaves and two fishes, He so increased them that the needs of the hungry multitude were met.

(2) The disciples' part. They were to have the people to sit down in companies to facilitate distribution. They then took that which the Master had blessed and distributed it to the people. The disciples were not responsible for the creating of the provisions, but only to get them to the people.

(3) The people's part. Their part was not to create nor distribute, but obediently to sit down and eat. Even after the bread had been blessed by the Lord and distributed by the disciples, they would have famished with hunger had they not eaten. Unless the people receive that which the Lord has provided for their salvation they shall eternally starve. The Lord has done His part; the disciples are under solemn obligation to do their part; and the final responsibility rests upon the people.

V. *The Servant Walking on the Sea, and Healing at Gennesaret* (6:45-56).

1. The Servant Walking on the Sea (6:45-52).

a. The disciples on the stormy sea (vv. 45-47).

(1) They were sent there by Christ (v. 45).

(2) The multitude dismissed by Christ (v. 46).

(3) Christ praying on the mountain (v. 46).

(4) The ship in the midst of the sea and Christ alone on the land (v. 47).

b. Jesus cometh to the disciples (v. 48).

(1) This was at the fourth watch of the night (v. 48).

(2) The disciples were alarmed (v. 49).

(3) Jesus' words of comfort (v. 50).

(4) Jesus went to them into the ship and the wind ceased (v. 51).

(5) The disciples were amazed and wondered for they had forgotten the miracles of the loaves (v. 52).

(For fuller details see Matt. 14:22-32.)

2. The Servant Healing at Gennesaret (6:53-56).

a. The multitudes at once recognized the Lord as He reached Gennesaret with His disciples (v. 54). Mark gives a vivid picture of the arrival of Jesus. The people opened their hearts to Him.

b. They not only knew Him, but immediately began to carry on their beds those who were sick when they knew where He was. They even laid their sick in the streets that they might touch but the border of His garment, and as many as touched Him were made whole.

W. *The Divine Servant Rebukes the Pharisees* (7:1-23).

1. The Emptiness of Formal Worship (7:1-7).

The tendency of the human heart is to depart from the life, and rest in the form which was calculated to express the life. The traditions and customs adopted by men for the temporary help of the spiritual life frequently are crystallized into laws and made to supersede the laws and institutions of God.

a. The charge against Christ (v. 2). This was that Christ's disciples ate bread with unwashed hands. Their finding fault was not on the basis of physical uncleanness, but their disregard of the custom to thoroughly wash the hands before eating.

b. Examples of empty forms (vv. 2-4).

(1) Washing of the hands before eating (v. 3). They not only washed their hands often but diligently and intensely.

(2) Washing of cups, tables, pots, and brazen vessels. The ceremonial washing applied to the vessels as well as to the hands.

c. Explanation demanded by the Pharisees (v. 5). They asked Christ to explain why His disciples ignored the tradition of the elders with reference to this ceremonial cleansing.

d. Christ's answer (vv. 6, 7). He declared that worship which centered in forms was as empty and meaningless as was lip service while the heart was away from God. This He calls hypocrisy, even such as foretold by Isaiah the prophet. Men of his day made much of external observance and of religious rites while their hearts remained unchanged. Many today are practicing the same hypocrisy. They are going through the forms of religion while their hearts are destitute of spiritual interest and understanding.

2. Making the Word of God of None Effect (7:8-13).

a. How it may be done (v. 8). It was done through tradition by so punctiliously observing the precepts of man, such as washing of the hands, pots, etc., while ignoring the commandments of God. This is being done by those who make much of the externalities of religion while at the same time are indifferent to the moral requirements. They even participate in the sacred ordinances of the church of God while the stains of sin are on their souls. Christians ought to ask themselves often as to whether they observe the body of Christ.

b. An instance cited (vv. 9-13). The Law of God as given by Moses said: "Honor thy father and thy mother; and, Whoso curseth father or mother, let him die the death: but ye say, If a man shall say to his father or mother, It is Corban, that is to say, a gift, by whatsoever thou mightest be profited by me; he shall go free. And ye suffer him no more to do ought for his father or his mother." The Law of God demands of children that they care and provide for parents in their need. According to an accepted tradition among the Jews, if a man should consecrate his goods or possessions to the Lord's service by pronouncing over them the word *Corban,* which means "the gift," his goods would be thus dedicated to God.

While the property was not thus available for help to his parents, it seems that the man was free to use it for his personal gratification. It was possible, therefore, for a man to be enjoying wealth while his parents were destitute. Those who are allowing their parents to go to the poorhouse while living in ease are making the command of God of no effect. They are living in the externalities of religion, thus making void the Law of God. This instance convicted the Pharisees of sin. It is most perilous to be content with the forms of religion while the heart is selfish and wicked.

3. The Real Source of Defilement and Impurity (7:14-23).

This passage discloses a truth of tremendous importance. Clearness of perception of this truth is essential to right living. Christ called the multitudes to hear this explanation. So striking was the reflection upon them that the issue could not be escaped.

a. Sin is moral and spiritual. Uncleanness before God is not of the body save as the body is directed by the soul. A man is not defiled by that which enters his mouth, but by that which springs out of his soul. Temptation of the severest kind is not sin.

b. That which springs out of the heart—the deliberate choice of the will is the source of defilement (v. 20).

c. A list of evils springing out of the heart (vv. 21, 22). The awful list is as follows: evil thoughts, adulteries, fornications, murders, thefts, covetousness, wickedness, deceit, lasciviousness, an evil eye, blasphemy, pride, foolishness, which all come from within. This catalogue includes every possible form of evil. Every one of them originate in the heart, and when they become acts of the will and life they defile the man. Moral acts are matters of the heart. It is only when temptations and solicitations lead to indulgence by the deliberate act of the will that they corrupt a man. This should bring home to our consciences with terrific force the necessity of looking to the source of our acts. We should not neglect the inner shrine of life while zealously carrying on life's activities.

X. *The Servant Making Men Free* (7:24-37).

1. Jesus in the Borders of Tyre and Sidon (7:24).

His own nation had rejected Him; even His own townsmen at Nazareth had done so. The multitudes thronged Him, but they mainly perceived Him as a mighty healer of the body. He retired to this region where He might instruct His disciples in the deeper things of His mission, since He must soon go to the cross.

2. Jesus Healing the Daughter of the Syrophenician Woman (7:25-30).

In sharp contrast with the apostasy of Israel and their rejection of the Saviour, we see in the Syrophenician woman a foregleam of the offer of salvation to the Gentiles.

a. The mother's awful distress (v. 25). Her daughter was grievously vexed with a devil. The daughter was the one afflicted, but the mother carried the burden. Doubtless this Gentile woman had heard of the fame of Jesus, His power to heal, and many times longed for Him to come that way that her daughter might be healed. Now that He was in her neighborhood, she came straightway to Him.

b. Her fervent appeal for help (vv. 25, 26). She humbly fell at His feet, and besought Him to cast out the devil. She had faith to believe that the Lord could heal her daughter.

c. Her faith rewarded (vv. 27-30).

(1) The Saviour's apparent refusal (v. 27). Jesus, according to Matthew, answered her not a word. The reason for His silence was that she appealed to Him on the wrong basis, addressing Him as the Son of David (Matt. 15:22). Only a child of the kingdom had a right to address Him thus. Only an Israelite had the right to seek His blessing as the Son of David. He was sent to the lost sheep of the house of Israel. She was a stranger to the covenant people. His silence was not from indifference, but He desired her to come in the right way. Jesus said: "Let the children first be filled: for it is not meet to take the children's bread, and to cast it unto the dogs." The Jews regarded the Gentiles as dogs.

(2) The woman's quick response (v. 28). As soon as she perceived the real difficulty, she addressed Him as Lord and cried for help (Matt. 15:25-27). While only an Israelite could approach Him as the Son of David, all could come to Him and own Him as Lord. She willingly took her place as a Gentile "dog," willing to receive but the crumbs from the children's table. The word for dog seems to be a diminutive term, showing the pet or household dog, which had a right to the crumbs which fell from the table.

(3) The glorious issue of her faith (vv. 29, 30). Jesus said: "Go thy way; the devil is gone out of thy daughter." And when she came to her house she found it so.

3. Jesus Healing a Deaf Mute (7:31-37).

a. The place (v. 31). This is the region where He had healed the Gadarene demoniac, and where the people had requested His withdrawal from their country (5:20) because of the loss of their swine. The man whom Jesus healed must have made good as a witness for Him, for as soon as Jesus came into their country, "they bring unto him one that was deaf, and had an impediment in his speech" (v. 32).

b. The method (vv. 33, 34).

(1) "Took him aside from the multitude" (v. 33). He did this to avoid publicity, also that the man might without distraction attend to what He was doing and fix his mind upon Jesus.

(2) "Put his fingers into his ears, and he spit, and touched his tongue" (v. 32). This was a sign language, designed to objectify to the man what Jesus was going to do for him; namely, to open his deaf ears, and loosen his helpless tongue.

(3) He looked "up to heaven" (v. 34) to show to the man that his help was from God.

(4) A command issued (v. 34). The cure was immediate and complete, quite different from most of the so-called cases of healing today (v. 35).

c. The effect (vv. 36, 37). Though He charged them to "tell no man" so much the more a great deal they published it, saying: "He hath done all things well: he maketh both the deaf to hear, and the dumb to speak."

Y. *The Compassionate Servant Feeding the 4000* (8:1-9).

The healing of the deaf mute made such an impression that multitudes thronged the Lord and lingered for three days without food. Therefore there was a human need to be met. The Lord did not work miracles for the mere display of power, but to reveal His mercy. There is reason to believe that this mighty miracle is separate from the feeding of the 5000. It may be that other than the time recorded He showed His compassion in feeding the hungry people.

1. Jesus' Compassion (8:2).

He is really human and can be touched with the feeling of our infirmities. He knew that if they did not get food they would faint by the way.

2. The Disciples' Question (8:4).

"Whence can a man satisfy these men?"

3. Jesus' Inquiry As to Their Supply of Food (8:5).

This He did to cause the disciples to see their need of looking to the Lord for help.

4. What Jesus Did To Supply the Need (8:6, 7).

He took the seven loaves and few fishes, gave thanks and blessed them and gave to the disciples to set before the people. The result was that 4,000 did eat and were filled, and had left over seven basketfuls.

Z. *The Servant Warning Against the Leaven of the Pharisees and Herod* (8:10-21).

The Pharisees came seeking a sign from Heaven, perhaps demanding some portent from the skies pretending that if they had sufficient evidence of His Person and mission they would follow Him. He responded to their demand with a deep sigh, knowing their hypocrisy, and declared that no sign would be given to their generation. The leaven of the Pharisees was their false doctrine and the leaven of Herod was worldliness and irreligion in pretending to be Jews while living as the heathen.

AA. *Healing of the Blind Man at Bethsaida* (8:22-26).

1. The Blind Man Brought to Jesus (8:22).

His friends brought him for the touch of the Master. They believed that the divine touch would issue in healing.

2. Led Out of Town by Jesus (8:23).

From the fact that Jesus instructed the blind man not to go into the town nor to tell anyone in the town of his healing, we gather that the situation was now so critical that publicity would increase His difficulty.

3. The Blind Man Healed by Jesus (8:23-25).

The method used in this healing seems quite strange. He "spit on his eyes, and put his hands upon him, and asked him if he saw ought." The Lord is not restricted to any particular method of healing. He even healed at a distance. We can be assured that He always uses the best method.

Let us view this miracle as an acted parable illustrating the salvation of sinners.

a. All members of the human race are blind and helpless because of sin.

b. Only by the sovereign act of the Holy Spirit are their eyes opened.

c. Our solemn obligation is to introduce them to the blessed Saviour and Lord.

BB. *The Servant Demanding Confession of Faith* (8:27-38).

The time has now come for Jesus to take account of His ministry.

Having been rejected by the rulers, He goes into retirement with His disciples. His primary object in His teaching during this time is to prepare the disciples for the tragedy of the cross, which He knew was so near. His teaching gathers around the great cardinal doctrines of the Christian faith. He instructs them regarding His Person, atoning death, resurrection, and glorious coming again. He knew that in the measure that they intelligently apprehended these things they would be able to pass through the ordeal before them. The same is true today. Those who clearly apprehend the divine Person, the vicarious atonement, the glorious resurrection, and the second coming of Christ are undisturbed by the world tragedies of the present hour.

1. Peter's Confession of Christ (8:27-30).

Two questions of Christ provoked this confession:

a. "Whom do men say that I am?" (vv. 27, 28). This question referred to the opinions of the people regarding Jesus. Some believed Him to be John the Baptist, some Elijah, and some one of the prophets. They all recognized Him to be a teacher or prophet with more than human authority and power. Jesus was not content with this acknowledgment. Had He been satisfied with this, He would not have been molested in Jerusalem, for the Jews willingly acknowledged Him as much more than a human teacher.

b. "Whom say ye that I am?" (vv. 29, 30). Jesus persistently claimed to be the God-man, the very Son of God. He wanted the personal opinion of the disciples concerning Himself.

2. Jesus Teaching Concerning the Cross (8:31-33).

Christ charged the disciples not to make public His Messiahship, as that would precipitate the crisis. The disciples needed much instruction yet to prepare them for the crucial hour of the cross.

a. What He taught (v. 31).

(1) "The Son of man must suffer many things." He suffered physical weariness and hunger, ridicule and contempt, and even misunderstanding and lack of appreciation on the part of His friends and disciples.

(2) "Be rejected of the elders, and of the chief priests, and scribes." These were the nation's official representatives, the very ones who should have known and received Christ and recommended

His reception on the part of the nation. Truly, "he came unto his own, and his own received him not" (John 1:11).

(3) "Be killed." This announcement was startling to the disciples. They had not yet come to realize that redemption was to be accomplished through the passion and the cross. Jesus now states with definiteness and certainty that He must die on the cross. This necessity was due primarily to the fact that it was the divine purpose to make the death of Christ the heart and core of the atonement, and also to human hatred and opposition.

(4) "Rise again." Though this was utterly incomprehensible to the disciples, He shows them that this would be the glorious issue of His death.

b. How the disciples received His teaching (v. 32). So unwelcome was His teaching about the cross that Peter, the spokesman of the disciples, rebuked Him. Peter later saw through this darkness the light of glory on the hilltops beyond (I Peter 1:3, 4).

c. Jesus rebukes Peter (v. 33). He told Peter plainly that his attitude was due to his being under the influence of the Devil.

3. The Cost of Discipleship (8:34).

The law of the Christian life is suffering. To follow Christ means to turn one's back upon the world. To repudiate the world means to incur the hatred of the world. To be Christians, therefore, means to share Christ's sufferings.

a. There must be denial of self (v. 34). There is a wide difference between self-denial and denial of self. All people practice self-denial, but only Christians deny self. The way to Heaven is the way of sacrifice and denial of self.

b. The cross must be taken up (v. 34). This means the sufferings and shame which lie in the path of loyalty to God. To live the godly life means suffering (II Tim. 3:12).

c. Christ must be followed (v. 34). This means to have the mind of Christ (Phil. 2:5) and to perform the service of Christ.

4. The Issue of Discipleship (8:35-38).

The blessed issue of following Christ is a life of freedom here and now, and eternal life hereafter. Such sacrifice enriches the life that now is, and prepares for the enjoyment of the life which is to come. To barter the future life for present enjoyment is most foolish for the choices of life are fraught with eternal issues. Those who refuse to follow in Christ's footsteps shall be separated from Him at His glorious appearing (v. 38; cf. II Thess. 1:7-10).

CC. *The Transfiguration of the Divine Servant—a Foregleam of the Kingdom of God* (9:1-29).

The hopes of the disciples were crushed when Christ announced His death on the cross. They were unable to see how victory could issue from death. Jesus took Peter, James, and John and went into the mountain apart by themselves. According to Luke, they went there to pray (Luke 9:28). While, doubtless, He longed for fellowship and sympathy as the shadows of the cross were falling upon Him, His chief desire was to get the disciples apart and into a state of receptivity so that He might show them the method of the kingdom. Before going to the mountain He declared that there were some standing in His presence who would not taste of death till they had seen the kingdom of God come with power (v. 1). That their drooping spirits might be revived and their confidence restored, He was transfigured before them.

If the faith of the disciples was to be kept through the dark hour of the cross, which was looming large before them, the light of the eternal must beam forth. Two men from the upper world are sent to converse with Him about His approaching death in Jerusalem—the very thing about which the disciples refused to talk. Then too God's own voice was heard in words of approval of Christ's course, directing them to hear the Master. With a foregleam of the coming kingdom, and the approving words of God Himself, the disciples cannot doubt the ability of Jesus to carry into execution His kingdom plans. That this is true is not only shown by the context and circumstances, but by the inspired interpretation of one who was there with Him and knew all that transpired (see II Peter 1:16-19, A.S.V.). There is absolutely no need to seek further for an explanation of the purpose of the transfiguration.

1. Jesus Christ Glorified on the Mountain (9:2, 3).

He took the disciples "by themselves" and was "transfigured before them." This shows the purpose terminated upon the disciples and not on Himself. Christ's rebuke of Peter for his unwillingness to hear concerning His death apparently for a time estranged the disciples from Him. To heal this breach, an unusual transaction was required. His "shining raiment" was typical of that glory which shall be manifest when He comes back to the earth.

2. Peter, James, and John Represent Israel in the Flesh in Connection with the Kingdom (9:2).

Christ is peculiarly the King of Israel. According to Ezekiel 37:21-27, Israelites are to be the central people in the kingdom. This people shall be gathered from among the nations, and united as one in that kingdom in their own country.

3. Moses and Elias Appeared in Glory with Jesus (9:4-13).

These men in the glorified state are typical of the state of the saints in glory. Moses, who was once denied an entrance into Palestine, appears now in glory, representing the redeemed of the Lord who shall pass through death into the kingdom. At Christ's coming the thousands of the Lord's own who have fallen asleep shall be awakened and pass into the kingdom. Elijah represents the redeemed who shall pass into the kingdom through translation. Many shall be living upon the earth when the Lord shall come and they, without dying, shall be changed and pass into the kingdom (I Cor. 15:50-53; I Thess. 4:14-18).

a. Peter's foolish proposal (vv. 5, 6). Moses and Elias, who had been a long time in glory, would be ill at ease in a tabernacle on the mountainside. It would have been to Peter's credit to have been silent, since he knew not what to say.

b. The divine voice out of the cloud (vv. 7, 8). He is declared to be the beloved Son in whom God is well pleased. When one desires to know what pleases God, look at His perfect Son Jesus Christ.

c. Jesus' charge (vv. 9-13). He instructed them that they should tell no man concerning the things which they had seen until He had risen from the dead.

4. The Mighty Power of the Divine Servant (9:14-29).

When they descended from the mountain, they saw a great multitude in a state of perplexity. The immediate cause of their perplexity was the grievous state of a young man who was possessed with a demon (v. 18). The father of the young man had appealed to the disciples to cast out the demon, but they were unable. When they brought him unto Jesus, the foul spirit was rebuked (v. 25) and came forth. This young man's state is representative of the nations who are oppressed by the Devil. The people were grievously oppressed. There are times when the Devil is especially active in the oppression of men. During Christ's sojourn on earth he seems to have been very active, and we have reason to believe from the Scriptures that just preceding His second coming he will be even more active, for he knows that his time is short.

DD. *The Divine Servant Rebukes Selfishness* (9:30-50).

1. The Stupidity of Selfishness (9:30-32).

Jesus with the disciples is on His way to Capernaum for the last time. He is soon to leave for Jerusalem where He is to die on the cruel cross for the world's sins. He still seeks the way of retirement in order to be alone with His disciples, His object being to lead them into the meaning of the cross. The teaching which was interrupted at Caesarea by Peter's rebuke is now resumed, and with definiteness He declares the future event as already present.

a. "The Son of man is delivered into the hands of men."

b. "They shall kill him."

c. "He shall rise the third day."

While pressing upon them continually the fact and necessity of the cross, He never failed to show them the bright side, His triumphant victory over death in the resurrection. The hearts of the disciples were so steeped in selfishness that they failed to understand His teachings. If the disciples had more definitely attended to His teaching concerning the cross, they would have been better prepared for the hour of temptation which was soon to overtake them.

2. The Wrangling of Selfishness (9:33-37).

a. The searching question (v. 33). The omniscient Christ knew the secrets of their hearts. The fact that the disciples were wrangling about official position, while the Lord was facing humiliation and death for them and for the whole world, shows how completely the Lord was alone in His sorrow.

b. The silent disciples (v. 34). They were ashamed in His presence, because the selfishness of their hearts was revealed.

c. The stinging rebuke (vv. 35-37). "If any man desire to be first, the same shall be last of all." The greatest among men are those who are willing to take the lowest place and serve others. This truth He enforced in a concrete way by placing a child in their midst. The child was an illustration of dependence and ignorance. By example and word He shows that true greatness is expressed by willingness to aid the weak, to instruct the ignorant, and serve those in need. All such render service not merely to those in need, but unto Christ and God. True greatness, therefore, consists not in self-seeking but rendering cheerful service to the needy in the name of Christ.

3. The Intolerance of Selfishness (9:38-41).

a. John's guilty conscience (v. 38). In the light of the teaching of Jesus, John was a little disturbed over having forbidden a worker for Christ who did not follow after Him. Doubtless this intolerance was in part due to jealousy for Christ, but also a selfish ambition. Many times Christians mistake bigotry for zeal for Christ.

b. Whom to tolerate (vv. 39-41).

(1) Those who are casting out demons (v. 39). We should really satisfy ourselves that supernatural works are being done. Are demons being cast out? However this is not final, as there is a supernatural work not of God.

(2) Those who are doing this work in Christ's name (v. 41). Any worker going forth in the name of Christ and for the glory of Christ should be bidden Godspeed. If he be doing a good work, even though not in your way, or if not a member of your church or school, "forbid him not."

4. The Awful Issue of Selfishness (9:42-50).

Selfishness results in ruin to others (v. 42), and also to the individual (vv. 43, 45, 47). In either case, the issue is eternal torment in Hell. Selfishness is opposed to God and that which is opposed to God must be eternally separated from Him. Self-renunciation should be so complete that we should be willing to abandon the most necessary and lawful things in life—hands, feet, and eyes—when they become an occasion for stumbling either to ourselves or to others.

EE. *The Servant Sets New Standards of Living* (10:1-31).

1. Regarding Marriage (10:1-12).

The question touching divorce, which the Pharisees temptingly put to Christ, brought forth teaching which exhibits marriage in its true light.

a. Should not be degraded by divorce (vv. 1-6). Divorce was not instituted by God. The marriage relationship was intended to be indissoluble. Moses suffered divorce, limited and regulated it. Its existence and its practice are indicative of the coarseness and perverseness of man. Sin is its real cause.

b. Marriage is God's primal law (vv. 6-9). The ideal law of life for the subjects of the kingdom is marriage. This is proved by the fundamental fact of sex. The union of the male and female natures is physical, mental, and spiritual. In marriage the male and female natures are mutually complemented. God's intention is that man should not be without the woman, nor the woman without the man (I Cor. 11:11).

c. Remarriage of the divorcer is adultery (vv. 10-12). The marriage relationship can be broken only by death and sin. In view of the fact that marriage is for life, men and women should not enter this relationship without very serious consideration. Divorce for other than marital infidelity does not give the right to remarry.

2. Regarding Children (10:13-16).

The union of the male and female natures, according to God's purpose, lays the foundation for family life. The issue of such union is children. In connection with the divine law of marriage, it is fitting that Jesus should set forth His estimate of children and interest in them. Those who think it beneath their dignity to give attention to children should ponder well the words of Jesus. This will give the disciples proper consideration of work among children, and also of the nurture and discipline of their own children. Christian men and women will regard children as the property of the Lord, and will esteem it a high and holy privilege to train them for Him. Due attention to Christ's teaching regarding children would transform the home life of society.

3. Regarding Riches (10:17-31).

a. The young ruler's question (v. 17). This question reveals a void in his heart. He was a young man with a lovable character. He was moral, honest, earnest, and courageous. He thought that eternal life could be obtained by good works. Though he claimed to have kept the law, he was conscious of something to fill up that which was lacking; therefore he came to Jesus to make inquiry as to that lack.

b. Jesus' reply (vv. 18, 19). He knew the young man's heart, and put His finger on the weak spot. When it came to parting with his possessions in order to help his neighbor he parted with the Lord, going away sorrowful. This revealed the fact that he was a covetous man, a violator of the tenth commandment.

c. Lacking one thing and yet lost (vv. 21, 22). When the Lord pointed out that the defect in his life was the love of his money, he was unwilling to pay the price. When the time came to choose between eternal life and riches, he chose wealth and parted company with Christ, perhaps forever.

d. The peril of riches (vv. 23-31). The difficulty does not lie in the fact that a man possesses riches, for a man may possess great riches and still be an heir of the kingdom. Wealth is a mighty power. In itself it is good. It will provide bread for the widow and orphan, amelioration for the suffering, and send the Gospel of Christ to the ends of the earth. The difficulty lies in trusting in riches. The step from possessing riches to trusting in them is a very short one. The tendency of growing wealthy is to destroy the nobler life of the soul. As long as a man possesses riches he is safe, but as soon as riches possess the man he is in deadly peril.

FF. *The Divine Servant Facing the Cross* (10:32-52).

1. Jesus Foretells His Passion and Resurrection (10:32-34). This is the third time He makes this prediction. The circumstances are most tragic.

a. Jesus going to Jerusalem (v. 32). He was going with the full consciousness of the awful tragedy of the cross before Him—the treachery of Judas—the fiery persecutions of the priests and scribes—the unjust judgment—the delivery to Pontius Pilate—the mocking—the scourging—the crown of thorns—the cross between malefactors—the nails—the spear—all were spread before Him. He moves on to this goal, not by external necessity, but a fixed purpose. The Servant had not come only "to minister, but to give his life a ransom for many." That which He had voluntarily set out to do was moving on to its glorious issue. The joyous outlook upon the victory which would be accomplished through the shedding of His blood led Him forward (Heb. 12:2). The notion that the death of Christ was incidental to His career is most fallacious. The purpose of the incarnation was the vicarious death (Heb. 2:14). His example of heroism is unique.

b. The disciples following after (v. 32). They were in dread bewilderment. His utterances and demeanor filled their minds with perplexity and their hearts with awe. In this state of confusion, Jesus called them to Him and patiently instructed them.

c. "What things should happen unto him" (vv. 33, 34).

(1) "Delivered unto the chief priests, and unto the scribes."

(2) "They shall condemn him to death, and shall deliver him to the Gentiles."

(3) "They shall mock . . . scourge . . . spit upon . . . and kill him."

(4) "The third day he shall rise again."

2. The Ambitious Request of James and John (10:35-45).

a. The request (vv. 35-37). It was for a place of prominence in the kingdom. According to Matthew, their mother was the intercessor.

b. Jesus' reply (vv. 38-45).

(1) To James and John (vv. 38-40). He speaks directly to the men, declaring that they know not what they ask. He showed them the way to this position of glory was through suffering. The cup which they were to drink was all that was embraced in the agony of the cross. He concedes that the positions which they craved were obtainable, but in a very different way from what they apprehended. The way to places in glory in the kingdom of Christ is through the path of lowly, self-forgetful service.

(2) To the ten (vv. 41-45). The ten were displeased with James and John, but doubtless they were not free from the same selfish ambitions. Christ showed them that to give is greater than to receive; that to serve is greater than to be served. The standard of His kingdom is to forget self and serve others, even to giving one's life. Christ is the supreme example to be imitated by all who would follow Him.

3. Jesus Cures Bartimaeus of Blindness (10:46-52).

Though the weight of the cross was upon Him, He had time for gracious deeds. Blind Bartimaeus receives his sight.

a. Bartimaeus' request (vv. 46, 47). He cried to Jesus for mercy. The fact that he addressed Him as the Son of David shows that he recognized His Messiahship; his faith enabled him to take hold of Jesus. As soon as he heard that Jesus was passing by he cried to Him for help.

b. Rebuked by the multitude (v. 48). This rebuke provoked a more earnest cry from Bartimaeus. He believed that Jesus could and would help him, and knew that it was now or never with him.

c. The blessing granted (vv. 49-52). Though Jesus knew his desire, He wished him to definitely commit himself. When his eyes were opened he doubtless saw many interesting things in the world, but the supreme object of interest was Christ, for he followed Him. Note the progress in the experience of Bartimaeus:

(1) A blind beggar (v. 46).
(2) His cry for mercy (v. 47).
(3) Persistence in his cry (v. 48).
(4) Responded to the call of Jesus (vv. 49, 50).
(5) Made specific request (v. 51).
(6) Received his sight immediately (v. 52).

How quickly one can pass from sore need to jubilant discipleship!

GG. *The Divine Servant Exercising His Royal Authority* (11: 1-33).

1. Jesus Officially Presented to the Jewish Nation as King (11: 1-11).

This should not be designated the triumphal entry for it was so only in outward appearances. The shouts were empty and meaningless. It was the promised King publicly offering Himself to the nation.

a. The preparation (vv. 1-6).

(1) Two disciples sent for the ass (vv. 1-3). He told them just where to go to find it, and how to answer the owner's inquiry. The providing of the animal was the working out of the divine plan according to Christ's foreknowledge.

(2) Obedience of the disciples (vv. 4-6). Without asking

why, they go at His bidding. The command may have seemed strange and unreasonable, but they rendered explicit obedience.

b. The entry into Jerusalem (vv. 7-10).

(1) The disciples put their garments upon the ass and set the Lord upon it (v. 7). This act showed recognition of Him as their King (II Kings 9:13).

(2) The multitude (vv. 8, 9). Some spread their garments in the way; others who had no garments to spare cut down branches and strewed them in the way, which was just as acceptable to Him. This entry was in fulfillment of a prophecy uttered some 500 years before (Zech. 9:9). They uttered the very cry which the prophet predicted. This is a clue to enable one to understand the prophecies which are unfulfilled as yet. If the prediction of His first coming was thus literally fulfilled, we must believe that those of His second coming will likewise be literally fulfilled. The prediction of Zechariah 14:3-11 will be just as literally fulfilled as that of Zechariah 9:9.

(3) The Lord's action (v. 10). Upon entering the temple He looked around upon all things, but as it was eventide He withdrew to Bethany with the twelve.

2. Jesus Exercising His Royal Authority (11:12-19).

a. The barren fig tree (vv. 12-14, 20, 21). The fig tree is typical of the Jewish nation. The fruit normally appears on the fig tree ahead of the leaves. The presence of the leaves is the assurance of fruit. This was an acted parable of the Lord's judgment on Israel for pretending to be the chosen people without the fruits thereof. It indicated the spiritual state of the Jews.

b. The temple cleansed (vv. 15-19). For the various sacrifices in the Temple many oxen, sheep, and doves were needed. Many persons came from distant parts of the land; therefore it was impracticable to bring their sacrifices with them, so they brought money and bought the animals needed. This privilege the law had granted to them (Deut. 14:24-26) for the exchange was necessary. When evil men used it as an opportunity for gain, it became an offense before God. It defiled His house. He made Himself a scourge of cords and drove out the money-changers, overthrowing their tables and pouring out their money. By this act He declared Himself to be the Lord of the temple and one with God. That which God intended to be a "house of prayer for all nations" was made a "den of thieves." This action symbolized the call of the nation to repentance. The scribes and chief priests grasped the meaning for they were aroused to murderous hate, and sought to destroy Him. This act is further typical of a day when Christ shall come in wrath and execute judgment upon all who profane His house and service.

3. Jesus' Authority Challenged (11:27-33).

They challenged Him to show by what authority He accepted the honors of the Messiah, and who gave Him the authority to cast out the money-changers. This placed Jesus in a dilemma. He responded by a question which placed *them* in a counter dilemma. Since John was His forerunner, the divinity of His commission rested upon that of John. They were powerless to discredit John, because the people accepted John as such. If they had accepted John's message, they would have been prepared to accept His. They cowardly confessed that they did not know. These rulers had no affection for Jesus, so they rejected Him and sought to destroy Him.

HH. *The Divine Servant Silences His Adversaries* (12:1-44).

1. The Parable of the Husbandmen (12:1-12).

Having put the scribes, chief priests, and elders to confusion by a skillful counter question when they demanded His authority, Jesus by means of a story lays before them His claim to divine authority, and charges them with betrayal of trust and plotting to murder the very Son of God. His teaching in this parable cut them to the quick, and they sought to lay hands upon Him, but desisted for fear of the people. This parable is simple, yet very comprehensive.

a. The vineyard (v. 1) represented Israel (see Ps. 80; Isa. 5).

b. The husbandmen (v. 1) represented the rulers who were charged with responsibility of the spiritual interests of the people.

c. The messengers (vv. 2-5) represented the prophets whom God sent to Israel, even including John the Baptist.

d. The son (vv. 6-8) represented Jesus Himself.

e. The judgment of the Lord of the vineyard (v. 9). This represented the time when the Jews shall be brought to account for their treatment of the servants of God and of Jesus Himself.

2. The Tribute Money (12:13-17).

They already would have gladly taken Him by violence and killed Him, but they feared the people. In order to destroy Him they seek to discredit Him among the people. To this end they send the representatives of both factions, "certain of the Pharisees and of the Herodians, to catch him in his words" (v. 13).

a. Their question (v. 14). "Is it lawful to give tribute to Caesar, or not?" The Pharisees contended that since God was the real King of Israel, it was not obligatory, yea, it was even sinful to give tribute (taxes) to a heathen king. The Herodians were supporters of Herod; with flattery on their lips they put this subtle question. For Him to answer "Yes" would have discredited Him with the people, and to have said "No" would have made Him liable to arrest by the Roman authorities as an enemy of the government.

b. Jesus' reply (vv. 15-17). He asks for a coin to be brought and inquires as to whose image and superscription it bore, declaring that those who accept the coin of Caesar should pay taxes to Caesar. In this reply the Lord escapes their trap and enunciates a principle which applies to all time and conditions as to the Christian's responsibility to civil government. Those who accept the protection and blessing of civil government should support that government. There is no conflict between being a citizen and a Christian. Being a loyal citizen is not enough; there is a duty to God. To render to Caesar that which belongs to Caesar is all right, but there is even a higher obligation—render "to God the things that are God's." Just as the one who acknowledges the benefits of civil government should support it, so being the recipients of God's favors, all should render unto Him that which is His due.

3. The Resurrection of the Dead (12:18-27).

The Pharisees and Herodians being silenced, the Sadducees came with a question which involved not only the immortality but the resurrection of the body. The Sadducees were the rationalists of their day. They denied the reality of the resurrection, and believed not in angel or spirit (Acts 23:8).

a. The case proposed (vv. 19-23). The Law of Moses made it not only legal but morally binding for a man to take his brother's wife whose husband died before they had children (Deut. 22:5). They propose the case of a woman married successively to seven brothers. They ask whose wife she shall be in the resurrection. This was doubtless a hypothetical case.

b. Jesus' reply (vv. 24-26). By a quotation from the Mosaic Law (Exod. 3:6) He proves the resurrection of the dead, and their continued existence beyond the dead as human beings. The immortal spirit clothed with a deathless body is His thought. He shows that marriage is only for this present life and does not belong to the resurrection life. Since there will be no death after the resurrection, there will be no necessity for births. In this respect humankind will be as the angels in the resurrection life. He points out to them that their great error was due to two things.

(1) Ignorance of the Scriptures (v. 24). In the very Scriptures which they professed to believe was positive proof of the resurrection (Exod. 3:6).

(2) Ignorance of the power of God (v. 24). God is able to provide a life where there is no death, no births, or marriages. In Heaven life will be on a plane infinitely higher than the most blessed relationships of this life. Our chief concern is to find out what is written, and then believe that God is able to accomplish that which He has promised.

4. The Great Commandment of the Law (12:28-34).

Christ's answer shows marvelous insight. He sums up man's whole duty in one word—love: love to God and love to man. The first and great commandment is supreme and undivided love to God. The second is like unto it in that love is its center, but love is for our neighbor in the measure that we love ourselves. Love for God is to be supreme; He is worthy of all our affections. Love is the actuating power behind all our service. Having put His questioners to silence, Jesus now puts to them a question which involves the central doctrine of the Christian faith—the Person of Christ (vv. 35-40). Is He human or divine, or both? Whose Son is He? is the supreme test of a man's orthodoxy.

5. The Widow's Mite (12:41-44).

This is a picture in striking contrast to that of the Pharisees and Sadducees. This poor woman was doing that which in the sight of the world was insignificant, but in the sight of the Lord was of great moment. The words of the Lord reveal to us that in God's sight a gift is measured by the heart motive and not by its amount. The widow's mite was all she had. Our gifts are not mites unless they are our entire possessions.

II. *The Divine Servant's Prophetic Outline of Events Between His Crucifixion and His Coming Again* (13:1-37).

In order to avoid confusion in this study, let it be clearly borne in mind that two matters are presented—the destruction of Jerusalem by the Roman armies, and the glorious return of the Lord. The two are sometimes so closely interwoven as to make the threads difficult to disentangle, but if we see the coloring in the graphic picture of the destruction of Jerusalem as adumbrating the revelation of the Son of God in glory, we shall have no serious trouble.

1. The Occasion of the Prophecy (13:1-4).

As Jesus was passing through the Temple for the last time on His way to the Mount of Olives where He gave this discourse, the disciples reminded Him of the splendor of the building, to which He replied that not one stone should be left upon another. When seated upon the mount, the disciples came privately with a threefold question (Matt. 24), requesting further information:

a. "When shall these things be?"

b. "What shall be the sign" of Thy coming?

c. And the end of the age?

That which follows is given in answer to these questions.

2. The Characteristics of the Age during the Absence of Christ (vv. 13:5-23).

a. Appearance of deceivers (vv. 5, 6). From time to time, many false Christs have pressed their claims as being the Christ, since Jesus went back to Heaven. As the age draws to a close, these claims doubtless will increase.

b. Wars and strife among the nations (vv. 7, 8). The history of the centuries since Christ is written in blood, and the river increases in volume as the age goes on toward its consummation. Jesus warns against making any particular war the sign of His coming. Many good people have seriously blundered in this respect because they did not heed this warning.

c. Earthquakes and famines (v. 8). Though these calamities grow increasingly severe as the days lengthen, the intelligent, believing disciple is not surprised or alarmed, for these are the precursors of a new order, the birth pangs of a new age, the establishment of the kingdom of Christ upon this earth. Let the child of God in this present darkness look up, for his redemption draws nigh (Luke 21:28).

d. Universal evangelism (v. 19). The Gospel of the kingdom (Matt. 24:14) shall be preached in all the world for a witness. This is not the Gospel of the grace of God which we now preach, but the new evangelism which shall be proclaimed by elect Israelites immediately preceding the coming of Christ to establish His kingdom (see Rev. 7:4-19; Rom. 11:15).

e. Universal hatred of the believing Israelites (vv. 10-13). They shall be severely persecuted. Civil government shall be against them, and even their relatives and near kin shall hate, hunt, and kill them. Their one duty notwithstanding shall be to preach the Gospel, depending upon the Holy Spirit for wisdom and power. For this specific duty they are sealed with the seal of God in their foreheads (Rev. 7:3). This will be the real Pentecost, of which the outpouring of the Spirit at the beginning of the Church was a type (Joel 2:28-32; Acts 2:16). Eternal salvation is promised as an encouragement to fidelity (v. 13). It is the great tribulation (vv. 14-23). This is the consummation of the age immediately preceding the glorious appearing of Christ. Out of the missionary propaganda of converted Israel shall eventuate the unparalleled horrors so glowingly pictured here. Daniel's "abomination of desolation" is the Antichrist, the "man of sin" (Dan. 9:26, 27; 11:36; II Thess. 2:3, 4) will direct this reign of horror. In men's desire for deliverance from this reign of terror they will be led astray easily by false Christs who shall peculiarly appear at this time. Happily, divine interposition shall cut short these days.

3. The Lord's Glorious Return (13:24-27).

This is the superlative event, the one to which all prophecies have pointed, and all ages are moving with unfailing precision. It will usher in the golden age of which the wise and great of all ages have dreamed, and for which they have longed. The coming of the Lord will put an end to earth's sorrows; wars and strife will not end until the kingdoms of this world become the kingdoms of our Lord and

His Christ (Rev. 11:15). This event will be accompanied by great physical disturbances, and Jesus will gather His elect from the ends of the earth.

4. Applications of the Prophecy (13:28-37).

a. As these events multiply in the earth we know that the coming of the Lord draws nigh (vv. 28, 29), as the putting forth of the leaves of the fig tree prove the approach of summer.

b. The Jewish race shall retain its integrity until the end (v. 30). The perpetuity of Israel is the miracle of the ages.

c. Certainty of fulfillment (v. 31). The unfailing guarantee are the words of Christ.

d. The time of Christ's coming unknown (v. 32). In view of this it is utter folly to set the time. The Devil keeps people from the truth of Christ's coming as long as possible. When he can no longer succeed in this, he then tries to get them to set the time.

e. The proper behavior in view of Christ's imminent coming is watchfulness and prayer (vv. 33-37).

IV. THE SERVANT GIVING HIS LIFE A RANSOM FOR MANY (14:1–15:47).

A. *Judas' Bargain with the Chief Priests* (14:10, 11).

This black crime was committed immediately following the beautiful act of devotion by Mary (vv. 3-9). The motive actuating Judas was avarice. This awful depth of infamy was not reached at one bound. Because he did not master this besetting sin at the beginning he was conquered by it.

B. *The Last Passover* (14:12-25).

1. The Preparation (14:12-16).

In reply to the disciples' inquiry as to where they should prepare the Passover for Him, Jesus told them to go into the city where they would meet a man bearing a pitcher of water, whom they should follow. In the house to which they were thus led would be found a guest chamber—a large upper room—where they could make ready the Passover. He not only knew that the disciples would meet this man, but He knew that Judas had bargained with the priests for His betrayal. For this reason He kept secret the location of the upper room, thus preventing interruption by those into whose hands Judas had betrayed the Lord.

2. The Betrayal Announced (14:17-21).

The betrayal was to be by one of the disciples who was eating with Jesus. This betrayal had been predicted, though such prediction did not interfere with the free act of Judas in the betrayal. It was because of this act of treachery being freely committed by Judas that Jesus pronounced upon him the awful doom: "Good were it for that man if he had never been born."

3. The Sacrament of the Bread and Cup (14:22-25).

These were symbols of His broken body and shed blood by which He made atonement for man's sins, thus ratifying the new covenant. This is not only a memorial service, but has a forward look to the perfected kingdom of God which shall be ushered in with the coming of the Son of God (I Cor. 11:26).

C. *The Disciples' Cowardice Foretold* (14:26-31).

In spite of their cowardly turning from the Saviour, He assures them that after His resurrection He would go before them into Galilee. Peter protested against such an act of disloyalty by the disciples, and assured the Lord that though all the rest should forsake Him yet he would not. The Lord showed him what little he knew of his own best resolve, telling him that on that very night he would deny Him thrice. All the disciples said the same thing.

D. *The Agony of Gethsemane* (14:32-42).

The clear vision of the coming anguish of the cross, accentuated by the utter failure of the disciples to understand or believe, brought upon Him an indescribable anguish of soul, so He took Peter, James, and John and went apart to pray. The cup of agony was not mere death, but the sacrificial death for sin under the weight of the world's guilt.

1. The First Prayer (14:35, 36).

Notwithstanding the darkness of the hour, He prayed in faith accompanied with a willingness to obey. When He came and found the three sleeping instead of praying, He commanded them to watch and pray that they enter not into temptation.

2. The Second Prayer (14:39-48).

He went apart and uttered the same words, and upon His return again found the disciples asleep.

3. The Third Prayer (14:41, 42).

When He came the third time and found the disciples asleep, He announced that the Son of man was betrayed, and that the betrayer was at hand.

E. *The Betrayal and Arrest of Jesus* (14:43-52).

1. The Sign to the Mob (14:43-47).

With the basest of hypocrisy Judas pointed out Jesus, to the mob by a kiss, the sign of love.

2. Jesus Forsaken by All (14:48-52).

At the sight of the Master's betrayal and arrest, one of His disciples attempted to defend Him by resorting to the sword; but seeing that Jesus made no attempt at resistance they all fled. Their courage failed them in the hour of trial. How little man knows his weakness until the crucial hour!

F. *Jesus Before the Sanhedrin* (14:53-65).

1. Contradictory Testimony of False Witnesses (14:53-59).

The high priest's questions (vv. 60-65):

a. "What is it which these witness against thee?" To this Jesus was silent, showing that no evidence had yet been given worthy of answer.

b. "Art thou the Christ?" To this He definitely replied, "I am," and quotes a scripture passage which they recognize as referring to the Messiah. This claim they answer with buffeting and the most shameful treatment.

G. *Peter Denies the Lord* (14:66-72).

Though Peter loves Jesus, yet in the hour of supreme trial he fails. Grievous as his sin is, it is not like that of Judas. His failure was due to

1. Boasting Self-confidence (14:29-31).
2. Lack of Watchfulness (14:37).
3. Neglect of Prayer (14:38).
4. Service in the Energy of the Flesh (14:47).
5. Following Jesus Afar Off (14:54).
6. Seeking Comfort Among the Lord's Enemies (14:67; cf. Luke 22:55).

7. Open Denial (14:68-72).

Peter's backsliding really began when he shrank from the cross.

H. *The Son of God Giving His Life a Ransom for Many* (15:1-47).

The grand climax is reached here. If the significance of the crucifixion is not apprehended all else is meaningless. It is not a matter of learning lessons taught by a great teacher, or imitating the example of a great and good man, but of apprehending the vicarious atonement made by the world's Redeemer. Christ saves, not by His ethics, but by His shed blood. His death was purposeful and absolutely voluntary.

1. Jesus Arraigned Before Pilate (15:1-15).

In the early morning, after the mock trial before the high priest they bound Jesus and delivered Him to Pilate. They acted freely in this according to the evil desires of their own hearts, yet He was delivered up by the determinate counsel and foreknowledge of God. The Jews would gladly have killed Him, but they had not the authority to do so. They delivered Him to the Gentile governor, thus involving the Jews and the Gentiles in the crowning act of the world's sin. Pilate questioned Him without delay, for they accused Him of pretending to be a king—a rebel. "Thou sayest," was His only reply. To the slanderous accusations of the chief priests and elders He made no reply, to the utter astonishment of Pilate. Pilate sought to release Him, because he was convinced of His innocence. After several unsuccessful efforts to escape the responsibility, the expedient of letting the people choose between Barabbas and Jesus was resorted to. He no doubt thought that they would choose Jesus rather than the notorious Barabbas.

2. Jesus Crowned with Thorns (15:16-20).

Knowing that Jesus had been condemned for claiming to be Israel's king, they in mockery crown Him with a wreath of thorns and salute Him, "King of the Jews." Not only this, but they smote Him on the head and spat upon Him, and went through a form of mock worship. The crown of thorns typifies the curse which He bore for man's sin (Gen. 3:17, 18).

3. Jesus Crucified (15:21-41).

a. Led away to the place of crucifixion (vv. 21-23). At first they compelled Him to bear His own cross, but when physical weakness made this impossible, they compelled Simon the Cyrenian to bear it for Him. It is beautiful to note that the son of this Cyrenian who bore the cross of Jesus came to believe on Him (Rom. 16:13). Because of the scourging and cruel indignities heaped upon Him, they actually were obliged to bear Him to Golgotha. His face was marked by the thorns and cruel blows, so that there was "no form nor comeliness" (Isa. 53:2). All this He endured for us. He drank this bitter cup to its very dregs, and refused to drink the "wine mingled with myrrh," which would have deadened His pain. He went all the way in His sufferings.

b. Gambling for the clothing of the Lord (vv. 24, 25). Having nailed Him to the cross, they gambled for the seamless robe under the very cross where He was dying, and in their heartless cruelty they sat down to watch Him die (Matt. 27:36).

c. The superscription (v. 26). It was customary to place over the victim on the cross the name and crime of the offender. Though Pilate did this in mockery to vex the Jews, the title was absolutely true. He was indeed their King. They had long looked for Him, and now when He came they crucified Him.

d. Between two thieves (vv. 27, 28). This added to His shame. His identification with two robbers was the fulfillment of the Scripture, "numbered with the transgressors."

e. The dying Saviour reviled (vv. 29-32). This reviling was engaged in by the passersby, the chief priests, and the thieves who were crucified with Him. In the nameless agony and shame they taunted Him by bidding Him come down from the cross, and derisively saying, "He saved others; himself he cannot save." They unconsciously uttered a great truth. He could not save Himself and others, so He chose to die to save others. Hallelujah, what a Saviour!

f. Darkness upon the land (v. 33). This was at noonday. So shocking was this crime that nature threw around the Son of God a shroud to hide Him from the gaze of a godless company.

g. The cry from the cross (vv. 34-37). What awful anguish when God laid the world's sins upon His beloved Son! When the price was fully paid, Jesus dismissed His spirit. No one took His life; He gave it up. His death was unlike that of any other.

h. The rent veil (v. 38). This symbolized the giving up of His life (Heb. 10:20).

i. The centurion's confession (v. 39).

j. The lingering group of women (vv. 40, 41). They who had lovingly ministered to Him in life were waiting to see where they could bury His precious body.

4. Christ's Burial (15:42-47).

Loving hands now take the precious body and lay it in Joseph's new tomb. This man who did not consent to the foul treatment of the Lord now risks his reputation, and by his action makes a bold confession of the Lord. The sinless Son of God is placed in a new tomb.

V. THE DIVINE SERVANT EXALTED (16:1-20).

A. *The Ministry of Love* (16:1-4).

1. By Whom? (16:1).

Mary Magdalene, the mother of James, and Salome.

2. When? (16:2).

Early in the morning, the first day of the week.

3. Their Perplexity (16:3, 4).

They questioned as to who should roll away the large stone from the mouth of the tomb. To their surprise they found the stone removed.

B. *The Angel in the Tomb* (16:5-8).

Jesus knew that these women would come to the sepulcher with unbelieving hearts, so He had an angel waiting there to announce to them the fact of His resurrection. The angel's message:

1. "Be Not Affrighted" (16:6).

2. "Ye Seek Jesus of Nazareth, Which Was Crucified" (16:6).

This threefold designation with marvelous clearness shows

a. His humanity—Jesus.

b. Lowly residence—Nazareth.

c. Ignominious death—crucified.

3. "He Is Risen; He Is Not Here: Behold the Place Where They Laid Him" (16:6).

These words throw light upon His birth, humility, and shameful death. He who was born in lowly circumstances and suffered the shameful death of the cross is now the conqueror of death. His resurrection gives meaning to His death. "If Christ be not risen, your faith is vain; ye are yet in your sins" (I Cor. 15:17).

4. "Go Your Way, Tell His Disciples and Peter" (16:7).

As soon as it was known that Christ had risen from the dead, they were to tell it to the disciples. The disciples all needed this blessed news, but Peter especially since he had so openly denied Him. Wonderful grace!

5. "He Goeth Before You into Galilee: There Shall Ye See Him" (16:7).

Christ had told the disciples that He would arise from the dead and meet them in Galilee, but their unbelief kept them from this blessed truth.

C. *The Appearances of the Risen Christ* (16:9-14).

These appearances had as their object the restoration of the disciples from their awful failure and discouragement, and the convincing of them, without the peradventure of a doubt, of Christ's resurrection. Since His resurrection was to be the central theme of apostolic preaching, it was necessary that they have certainty of knowledge as to this matter (Acts 1:3). Without the resurrection of Christ His death would be meaningless. Out of the ten or more appearances Mark selects three:

1. To Mary Magdalene (16:9-11).

Mary's heart responded to the Saviour's gracious deliverance from demons. Her sufferings were no doubt terrible. She is the first to the tomb. Her devotion is amply rewarded by being the first to meet the risen Lord, though faith is weak. She went at once and told the sorrowing disciples, but they refused to believe.

2. To Two Disciples on the Way to Emmaus (16:12, 13).

Luke gives full particulars concerning this appearance. Jesus had walked, talked, and eaten with them, convincing them that the Lord was risen indeed (Luke 24:13-35). The testimony of such is trustworthy.

3. To the Eleven Disciples (16:14).

Christ appeared to them while sitting at meat and reproved them for their unbelief, "because they believed not them which had seen him after he was risen." The fact that they stubbornly resisted the testimony that Christ had risen, and afterward were willing to risk their lives in the proclamation of this truth, is strengthening to our faith.

D. *The Commission of the Risen Lord* (16:15-18).

After the disciples were convinced of the truth of His resurrection, Christ sent them forth to "preach the gospel to every creature." What a glorious and supreme task is this! "He that believeth and is baptized shall be saved; but he that believeth not shall be damned" (v. 16).

E. *The Activity of the Enthroned Christ* (16:19, 20).

After giving the disciples their commission He ascends on high, and from the unseen sphere He directs their activities. Wherever they went He confirmed their word. He does the same for His faithful disciples today.

THE GOSPEL ACCORDING TO LUKE

PART ONE—INTRODUCTORY MATTERS

SOMEONE HAS CALLED Luke the most beautiful book in the world. Those who know it best and have experienced its message are in full agreement with this declaration, because it portrays Jesus the perfect Man, giving Himself up to the redemption of the human race. He is beautiful in Himself and beautiful in what He does. He is the unique and ideal Man.

I. DESIGN.

Luke's purpose was not only to show the perfection of the Son of man, but to show Him as the world's Redeemer (Luke 19:10; cf. 1:68). A redeemer's function was twofold—to redeem the inheritance (Lev. 25:25); and to redeem the person (Lev. 25:47-50). The essential qualification of a redeemer was to be a blood relative (Lev. 25:25). No other could act in that capacity. See this illustrated in the Book of Ruth. Boaz could redeem the forfeited inheritance because he was near of kin to Naomi's husband.

A. *Purpose.*

Some of the characteristics of Luke are an indication of his peculiar purpose in writing:

1. A Friend Writes to a Friend (1:3, 4).
2. Birth of John the Baptist (1:5-25, 57-80).

This aged couple longed for a child.

3. Outburst of Praise at Expected Motherhood (1:42-56).
4. Real Human Birth and Development (2:6, 7, 40).
5. Much Emphasis upon the Praying of the Lord Showing Human Dependence:

    a. At baptism (3:21).
    b. Choosing the twelve (6:12, 13).

c. "Whom say the people that I am?" (9:18).

d. The transfiguration (9:29).

e. Request of disciples (11:1).

6. It Exhibits Human Interests.

It is the story of real life—suffused with human emotion, filled with gladness and sorrow, songs and tears, praise and prayer.

a. It is the Gospel of childhood. Glory surrounds infancy. It is only in Luke we find a picture of the childhood of Jesus.

b. It is the Gospel of womanhood. Note the immortal group of women associated with the Lord. See Elisabeth and Mary, aged Anna, widow of Nain, Bethany sisters, the repentant sinner, etc.

c. It is the Gospel of the home. See the glimpses of family life at Nazareth; scenes in the house of Simon; hospitality of Martha; importunate friend at midnight; prodigal son, etc.

d. It is the Gospel of the poor and lowly sounding forth in the song of Mary—the parable of the rich fool—rich man and Lazarus.

e. It is the Gospel of praise and prayer opening with the Magnificat of Mary through the songs of angels and Zacharias, and closes with the benediction of the Lord.

B. *Jesus Is Pictured as an Ideal Man.*

1. His Courage.

He "passed through the midst of them, went his way." Censuring Herod He said, "Go tell that fox, etc."

2. Tender in Sympathy.

3. A Man of Faith.

"Must be about my Father's business"; "I commend my Spirit."

II. AUTHORSHIP.

Luke is called by Paul the "beloved physician" (Col. 4:14). The same man who wrote Luke also wrote the Book of Acts. In Luke he records what Jesus "began to do," and in Acts he records what Jesus continued to do after Pentecost (Acts 1:1).

A. *Luke, the Historian* (1:1-4; cf. Acts 1:1).

Luke was a writer of great distinction. His style is clear and picturesque. The pieces of writing left us are the Gospel of Luke and the Acts. According to Acts 1:1, 3, the Gospel was written to set down in order the things which Jesus began to do and to teach, and to show what the risen and ascended Lord was continuing to do and to teach. While here on earth He only began to do and to show certain things, but from His place of glorious exaltation He is continuing His mighty works by the Holy Spirit through the disciples. Concerning the contents of the Gospel, he asserts first, that the source of his information was recorded statements of eyewitnesses. He assures us that these statements have been verified by him. Second, that he had made a systematic statement of these facts in order to strengthen the faith of his friend Theophilus.

B. *Luke, the Beloved Physician* (Col. 4:14).

He evidently was a skilled physician as his description of the diseases which Jesus cured show. His description of the symptoms of the diseases shows his capability. It was left to the physician to portray with vivid exactness the Virgin Birth by means of which the eternal Son became incarnate. He was not only skillful but tenderly sympathetic. This sympathy is shown in his portrayal of the Great Physician in His compassion for the poor, helpless, and suffering people. What untold good a skillful and sympathetic Christian physician can do! No one gets so closely in touch with human life as a physician.

C. *Luke, the Companion of Paul* (Acts 16:9-15).

1. Paul's Need for a Physician.

There is clear evidence that Paul had some physical ailment which made the service of a skillful physician most desirable. When the call came to go to Europe with the Gospel, Luke joined Paul and became one of his most helpful companions. This is one example of what a faithful Christian physician can do for a fellow man.

2. Luke's Fidelity.

"Only Luke is with me." He was no mere faraway friend. He stood by Paul in storm and calm. Paul was now in jail awaiting execution. What a great comfort it must have been to know that this faithful physician was with him! He was with him at Philippi, Miletus, Jerusalem, Caesarea, before Felix and Festus, on the voyage to Rome, with him in the Roman jail, through the Roman trial, and perhaps a spectator of his execution. It cost Luke a great deal to do this, but he no doubt considered it a labor of love, even feeling the call of God as really as Paul. Nothing is known of Luke after

Paul's death. Tradition has some interesting things to say, but no word of certainty.

III. THEME (Zech. 6:12).

The key phrase is "Son of man"; key verse, 19:10. By the Gospel is meant the Good News of salvation for the lost race. In Luke we do not have the Magi asking: "Where is he that is born King of the Jews," as in Matthew, or the record of the beginning of His ministry as in Mark. But we hear the angels saying to the shepherds: "Fear not: for, behold, I bring you good tidings of great joy, which shall be to all people" (2:10). At His circumcision, Simeon said that He was to give light to the Gentiles (2:32). At the very beginning He is thus placed in the broadest relation to the human race.

PART TWO—DETAILED OUTLINE

I. INTRODUCTION (1:1-4).

A. *The Motive of the Writer* (1:1).

It was to furnish a treatise conveying certainty touching the "things" of the Christian faith. He assures us that he has investigated the incidents of the life and ministry of Jesus Christ so that he could give established facts.

B. *The Order* (1:1).

His treatise sets forth the order—the sequence in time of the incidents and the proportion properly characterizing a historical treatise.

C. *The Source* (1:2).

He assures us that the source of his information is the information given him by eyewitnesses.

D. *The Recipient* (1:3).

It was addressed to Theophilus, a Gentile of some rank. He called him "most excellent," indicating a personage of superior merit among his fellows. This is further accentuated by the meaning of his name, "Theophilus—loved by God."

II. THE REDEEMER'S INCORPORATION WITH THE HUMAN RACE (1:5—3:38).

Through the Incarnation, Jesus came to be akin to us (Heb. 2:14).

In setting forth the human relations of the Redeemer we have presented to us:

A. *The Forerunner, John the Baptist* (1:5-25, 57-80).

1. His Parents (1:5-7).

a. When they lived (v. 5). "In the days of Herod the king." They lived in a day when ungodliness was rife. The priesthood was very corrupt and the ruling classes were wicked. Zacharias and his wife lived in a time when it was not easy to be godly.

b. Their character (v. 6). They were righteous before God. To be righteous before God is a high tribute. Many appear to be righteous before men who are not righteous before God. Their lives were so mated that they walked blameless in the commandments of the Lord. How beautiful it is when husband and wife are united in the Lord and walk together in fellowship with God! The highest in wedded life can only be attained when both are united in Jesus Christ. Their practical living was manifested in obedience to God's commands.

c. They were childless (v. 7). Though this godly couple were well-mated and they possessed the joy of the Lord in their souls, there was a real lack in that home. No home is quite ideal into which no child has come to gladden the hearts of the husband and wife.

2. His Birth Promised (1:8-17).

a. By whom (v. 11; cf. v. 19). The angel Gabriel appeared and made known the good news to Zacharias. This exalted being, the special messenger of God, was sent to make this disclosure.

b. When (vv. 8-14). While officiating as priest this good news came to him. Zacharias must have been definitely praying about this very matter (v. 13). As he burned incense, which typified prayer, the multitude without were praying.

c. Characteristics of the child (vv. 15-17).

(1) Shall be great in the sight of the Lord (v. 15). Though the people did not greatly esteem him, he was highly esteemed by the Lord. This is infinitely better than if he had been greatly esteemed in the eyes of men or in his own eyes.

(2) Shall drink neither wine nor strong drink (v. 15).

The child shall become a Nazarite, separating himself from sensuous things and dedicating himself to the service of the Lord.

(3) Shall be filled with the Holy Ghost (v. 15). The energy of the divine Spirit would enable him to lead the people to repentance (v. 16).

(4) Shall go in the spirit and power of Elijah (v. 17). In this power he was to prepare the people for the coming of the Saviour and the salvation which He was to bring.

3. Zacharias Asks for a Sign (1:18-23).

Although the aged priest was earnestly praying for the salvation of Israel the gracious promise of the angel, which was the beginning of that salvation, staggered his faith. He was unable to believe that what he fondly hoped and prayed for would be realized. The angel gave to Zacharias a sign. He was smitten with dumbness which was to continue until the fulfillment of the promise. Because he refused to praise God in faith for this gracious promise, God caused his tongue to be silent until the promise was fulfilled and his lips could open in thanksgiving and praise. Though he was thus rebuked, his faith was strengthened by the manifestation of the supernatural. God wants us to believe His promises no matter how contrary to reason they may seem.

4. The Promise Fulfilled (1:57-63).

When the time came for the birth of John, Elisabeth brought forth a son, and the neighbors rejoiced with her. On the eighth day they circumcised the child and gave him a name according to the instruction of the angel (v. 13). The name John was contrary to the family custom. By means of writing, Zacharias made known the name for the child which was given by divine instruction. At this time God opened the mouth of Zacharias and he offered praise.

5. Zacharias' Prophecy (1:64-80).

The following quotation from Dr. Charles R. Erdman's exposition of Luke will be helpful:

"This hymn is named the Benedictus from the first word in the Latin version. It is an ecstatic expression of gratitude to God for His boundless goodness. The poem possibly may be divided into five stanzas of four lines each; but there is a definite pause after the third of these stanzas when the thought turns from the work of Christ to the specific mission of John.

"The first strophe (vv. 68, 69) speaks of the redemption of Israel as already accomplished in the gift of the Christ who is about to be born and who is described as 'a horn of salvation,' that is, a manifestation of saving power. He is to appear as a son and heir of David the king.

"The second stanza, or strophe (vv. 70-72), indicates that the salvation from all enemies is a fulfillment of the promises made through the prophets and cherished by the ancient fathers and embodied in the holy covenant made with Israel of old.

"The third stanza (vv. 73-75) describes the nature of this salvation which was assured by the oath to Abraham; it is to be such a deliverance from political oppression as to make possible for Israel a true, priestly service of God, as a nation holy and righteous before him.

"In the fourth stanza (vv. 76, 77) the singer turns to address his own son whose birth has given occasion to the song. He declares that John is to be recognized as a prophet of God whose divine mission will be to announce and to define the promised salvation as in its essence not a political but a spiritual redemption consisting in the remission of sin. John was not to be a revolutionist but a reformer. He was to call a nation to repentance that those who obeyed his message might be ready to receive the salvation of Christ.

"This mission of John is linked with that of Christ as the description of the latter reaches its climax in the closing strophe (vv. 78, 79). The source of all the blessings Christ will bring is found in 'the tender mercy of our God'; the essence is a visitation of the 'dayspring from on high' when the Sun of righteousness arises upon the helpless, terrified wanderers of the night who are seated 'in darkness and the shadow of death'; the result will be, 'to guide our feet into the way of peace.'"

B. *Mary the Mother of Jesus* (1:26-38, 46-56; 2:1-20, 41-52; John 19:25-27).

1. Mary at Nazareth (1:26-38, 46-56).

Mary was a Jewish maid of the town of Nazareth. Our first information is that she was engaged to be married to Joseph, a carpenter of the same village. It seems that the custom among the Jews was for betrothal to take place a year before marriage. During this interval the woman remained with her parents.

a. Gabriel was sent from God to Mary (vv. 26-38). It was during this interval of betrothal before Joseph and Mary were married that God sent the angel Gabriel to announce unto Mary that she was to be the mother of Jesus. Isaiah more than 700 years before prophesied declaring that a virgin should give birth to a Son whose name shall be called Immanuel—God with us (Isa. 7:14).

Though at first perplexed, she accepted the annunciation with remarkable courage and devotion. To be told that she was to be a mother was nothing startling, for this was the normal desire of every married Jewish woman. But under the circumstances she accepted motherhood at a tremendous cost. She was conscious of her virgin purity. She knew that to become a mother under such circumstances would expose her to unutterable suspicion and shame. This was the view that certain Jews took of the matter, for they cast this insinuation into the face of Jesus that He was born of fornication (John 8:41).

Her faith was such that she responded with noble courage. She said: "Behold the handmaid of the Lord; be it unto me according to thy word" (1:38). She accepted motherhood under these circumstances as God's command. It was made clear to her that the begetting was by the Holy Ghost and that the Most High would embody Himself with humanity divinely begotten, that the resultant thing born would be holy and called the "Son of God."

b. Her wonderful song (vv. 46-56). In her embarrassment she set out on a visit to a kinswoman named Elisabeth. Having sought the sympathy and encouragement of this friend, her triumphant faith carried her beyond the misunderstanding, the scorn, and the shame which awaited her, and caused her soul to burst out in the most wonderful song of praise. This is called the Magnificat, because of the first word in the Latin version, "My soul doth magnify the Lord." As pointed out by another, three features of her character stand out in this song:

(1) Her purity of heart. Only a pure heart rejoices when God comes near.

(2) Her humility. She forgot herself and gave her heart to God's praise.

(3) Her unselfishness. She did not primarily think of the undying honor which through the ages would be attached to her, but the blessedness which would come upon future generations through her.

2. Mary at Bethlehem (2:1-20).

What Gabriel announced to Mary was now being fulfilled. Caesar's decree concerning taxation brought Joseph and Mary to Bethlehem at the opportune time for the fulfillment of Micah 5:2. Because of the crowded condition of the inn, the birth of the world's Saviour took place in a cave-stable. This was a most wonderful night—the angel's song to the shepherds in the field; the shepherd's visit to the manger-cradle to verify the truthfulness of the announcement, and their proclamation of the event to all within their reach. Mary did not understand all these things, but as a wise mother she kept and pondered them in her heart.

3. Mary in Jerusalem and Galilee (2:41-52).

Jesus was twelve years old and was now a child of the Law, for at that age the child took his responsibility as a worshiper. Here we see Mary characteristically a mother with human limitations.

a. Failure in vigilant care (v. 43). They had left the city and gone a whole day's journey without knowing where the Child was.

b. Failure to understand fully Jesus' action and words (v. 50). No particular censure should attach to this, as it is beyond our ability even now to understand all these things.

c. Failure to properly sympathize with Jesus' deepest longings and emotions. "How is it that ye sought me? Wist ye not that I must be about my Father's business?"

d. Failure to perceive her limit of guardianship. The time comes when duty to God takes precedence over duty to parents. The wise mother recognizes her limits. Later Jesus declared that "he that doeth the Father's will, the same is my mother." All these limitations should be viewed with the background of her deep devotion to God. She was pure in heart, faithful in attendance upon the Temple worship. Her whole life was lived in a spiritual atmosphere. She was just the kind of woman to whom God would trust the upbringing of His Son. Jesus went back with them to Nazareth and was subject unto them.

4. Mary at the Cross (John 19:25-27).

This was a great trial. For any mother to see her son die is a trial, but what must it have been for this mother in the face of all the sacred memories that clung to her soul! It is beautiful to note the tender care which Jesus in His dying hour manifested for His mother. He committed her to the care of John. Since she had other sons we wonder why she was committed to John. It may have been that John was better prepared to give her the needed care. And since it was not until after the crucifixion that his brothers believed on Him, He might have judged that she would fare better in the hands of the beloved disciple than in the hands of her unconverted children. John accepted the responsibility of a son and took her to his home.

C. *The Birth of Jesus* (2:1-20).

1. The Birth of the Saviour (1:1-7).

a. The time of the birth (vv. 1, 2). It was when the Jews were coming under control of the Roman power—a most propitious time. In the providence of God, the birth of Christ occurred at a time when all the systems of religion and morality were tottering upon their foundations. It was at a time, indeed, when a new force was needed to be brought into the world. Furthermore, it occurred at a time which was the most suitable for the introduction of the Gospel. The whole world being under one rule made it possible for ministers to move from city to city and from country to country without molestation. We should learn from this that the Almighty is ruling in all things and that He is never ahead nor behind in His administrations.

b. The place of the birth (vv. 3, 4). It took place at Bethlehem as the prophet had foretold some 700 years before (Micah 5:2). A little while previous to this it seemed very unlikely that the words of Micah would come true. Mary, the mother of Jesus, was in Galilee, miles away from Bethlehem. God moved the emperor to enforce the decree of taxation just at the time to cause Mary to be at Bethlehem at the proper time. Little did the emperor realize that he was an instrument in the hands of God! We should not be greatly exercised over what man does, knowing that he can do nothing but what God allows.

c. The circumstances of His birth (v. 7). The surroundings were of the most humble sort. The almighty Creator condescended to take upon Himself humanity—to be born in a manger, becoming the poorest of the poor, that none might be hindered from coming to Him.

2. The Birth of the Saviour Announced (2:8-14).

a. To whom (v. 8). His birth was announced to the shepherds who were keeping watch over their flocks by night. This shows that poverty is no barrier to the reception of the blessed Gospel. God does not reveal Himself mainly to the princes and great men of the earth, but oftentimes these things are concealed from such, and disclosed to the poor. "Hath not God chosen the poor of this world, rich in faith and heirs of the kingdom, which he hath promised to them that love him?" (James 2:5). Their being busy with the duties of this life did not prevent them from being favored with this glorious message from God. Moses, Gideon, Amos, and Elisha were called by the Lord from the busy activities of life. The Lord never calls the idle. The Gospel is peculiarly fitted for the laboring man.

b. By whom (v. 9). The first Gospel sermon was preached by the angel of the Lord. This exalted being had part in the announcement of the plan of salvation. Angels earnestly sympathize with poor, fallen, sin-cursed men.

c. The nature of the message (vv. 10-14). It was good tidings of great joy. Surely this was a gladsome message. It was good tidings because the darkness of heathendom which had for so long covered the earth was beginning to vanish. The casting out of Satan, the prince of this world, was about to take place. Liberty was soon to be proclaimed to those who were in bondage. The way of salvation was now about to be opened to all. No longer was the knowledge of God to be confined to the Jews, but offered to the whole world. So glorious was this good news that a multitude of the heavenly hosts appeared, joining in the song of praise.

3. The Prompt Investigation by the Shepherds (2:15, 16).

They did not stop to argue or question, though no doubt these things seemed passing strange to them, but they hastily went to

Bethlehem where they found everything just as represented. They had the privilege of first gazing upon the world's Saviour, the Lord of glory. They returned with gratitude in their hearts, praising God for all these wonderful things which He had revealed to them.

4. The Shepherds Witnessing (2:17-20).

They could not remain silent. All who have truly heard the good tidings of salvation through Jesus Christ must tell it to others. These shepherds went back to their work praising God.

D. *The Boyhood of Jesus* (2:40-52).

1. Jesus Growing (2:40).

While Jesus Christ was God, yet His deity did not interfere with His development as a human being. The processes of His physical, mental, and spiritual growth were the same as those of any normal human being.

a. "Grew and waxed strong." It was necessary for His body to develop. His brain, nerves, and muscles must not only attain to their proper size but must come to act together, become correlated.

b. "Filled with wisdom." His training was largely in the hands of His mother. She was a Bible woman as evinced by her song of praise when it was announced to her that God's favor was to come upon her. She was, therefore, a suitable teacher. She, no doubt, taught Him to memorize Bible verses and taught Him the great stories of the Old Testament from the Creation through the patriarchs and prophets. It would seem that it was the custom among the Jews that at the age of six years a boy was sent to the synagogue school, where the Old Testament was the textbook with comments by the rabbis.

c. "And the grace of God was upon him." By the grace of God doubtless is meant God's loving favor and tender care. Because of this grace upon Him we may be sure that as a boy He was a model for His associates in and around Nazareth.

2. Jesus Tarrying Behind at Jerusalem (2:41-43).

At the age of twelve years the Jewish child took his place as a worshiper in the Temple. He was then considered "a child of the law." Being conscious of His mission, when His mother and Joseph were returning from attendance at the Passover, Jesus tarried behind in the Temple and inquired into the meaning of the ordinances of

God's house. He had an alert, eager mind which inquired after truth, especially the truth concerning His Father's house; His heart yearned for His Father.

3. Jesus Found in the Temple (2:44-47).

When His mother and Joseph had gone some distance on their return journey, they perceived that Jesus was not with them and sought Him among their kinfolk and acquaintances. Not finding Him there, they returned to Jerusalem where they found Him in the Temple.

a. He was sitting (v. 46). This shows that He was no passing visitor or sightseer. He was perfectly at home in His Father's house.

b. He was hearing the teachers of God's Word (v. 46). This shows that He was eager to learn God's will.

c. He asked questions (v. 46). His growing mind was inquisitive. It more than received what was taught, it inquired after truth.

d. He answered questions (v. 47). His answers showed great wisdom which astonished those who heard Him, yet we should not surmise that He was consciously displaying His wisdom. It was not an exhibition of His divine wisdom, but the expression of the workings of a perfect human mind suffused by the Holy Spirit.

4. Mary's Complaint (2:48-50).

She remonstrated with Him for His behavior. To this He replied in a dignified, yet tender manner. He made no apology, showing that He was more than the son of Mary, God was His Father. Though Mary did not understand these things, as a wise mother she kept them in her heart.

5. Jesus' Obedience (2:51).

Though He was fully conscious of His divine being and mission, He lived a life of filial obedience, thus teaching us that obedience to parents is pleasing to God and a duty which will be discharged faithfully by those who have the Spirit of Christ.

6. Jesus' Development (2:52).

a. Mental. He increased in wisdom. Although the divine nature was united with the human, the human was left free to develop as a normal human mind.

b. Physical. He increased in stature. This shows that His body developed according to the laws of a normal human being.

c. Spiritual. He increased in favor with God and man. As His mind increased, and His apprehension of God became fuller, the divine Being could more fully express Himself through Him and, as the perfect life was lived, men could recognize in Him superior qualities, and therefore their hearts would open to Him.

E. *The Ministry of John the Baptist* (3:1-22).

1. The Degeneracy of the Times (3:1, 2).

The Jews had sunk to a very low level of civil, moral, and religious life. Luke carefully enumerates the civil and religious rules in order to show the profligacy of the times, and therefore the need of a messenger to call the people back to God and virtue. Pontius Pilate, a little later, attained notoriety by unjustly, and in a cowardly manner, condemning Jesus to death. Herod, the son of Herod the Great, was a murderer. Annas and Caiaphas were corrupt ecclesiastical rulers. The political, moral, and religious affairs of the world strongly call for a John the Baptist to call it to repentance.

2. The Nature of John's Ministry (3:3-6).

In the wilderness he underwent a discipline which fitted him for his task. While there he heard the call of God and came forth with a message from Him. Out of the wilderness he flashed forth, preaching the baptism of repentance for the remission of sins (v. 3). The baptism was the sign of repentance. This ministry is declared to be a fulfillment of Isaiah's prophecy. The message was described as one calling upon the nation to prepare for the coming of the Messiah. The only hope for the world is God's salvation through Jesus Christ. Let men accept Christ and all war and contention will end. Men will then love each other instead of hating one another. They will then co-operate in helpful service instead of seeking to destroy.

3. The Content of John's Message (3:7-18).

a. Denunciation of sin (vv. 7, 8). He called them "a generation of vipers." This shows that he charged them with deceitfulness and wickedness. Men in all ages have been awakened by such indictments of sin. Knowing the subtle hypocrisy of these Jews, he demanded evidence of their sincerity; the genuineness of their repentance was to be demonstrated by their works.

b. Announcement of judgment (v. 9). He declared that the ax was laid at the root of the tree, and that the tree not bringing forth fruit was to be hewn down and cast into the fire. Face to face with judgment, men become sober. John made it very plain that for their sins they should be called into judgment. Paul's preaching of a judgment to come made Felix tremble (Acts 24:25). This kind of preaching is needed today. While John preached sin and judgment, he accompanied it with assurance of pardon on condition of repentance.

c. Instructions to the inquirers (vv. 10-14).

(1) The people (vv. 10, 11). Each man was to turn from his besetting sin and show love and kindness to his fellow man. Clothing and food were to be given those who had need. They were to turn from a life of selfishness and greed, and do unto others as they would be done by.

(2) Publicans (vv. 12, 13). These taxgatherers who were guilty of greed and oppression were not asked to give up their occupation, but to exact only that which was appointed by law.

(3) The soldiers (v. 14). These were probably the policemen of that day, at least men on military duty.

(4) Testimony to Jesus (vv. 15-18). The people were musing in their hearts as to whether John was indeed the Messiah. When John perceived this, he with deep humility declared that his mission was so lowly in comparison with Christ's that he would be unworthy to perform the menial act of a slave in loosing the latchet of His shoes. John baptized with water, but Christ, he declared, would baptize with the Holy Ghost and with fire. Water was a material element and at best was only symbolic, but Jesus would exert upon their souls the divine cleansing and quickening power. He showed that Christ would come with mighty power to punish the wicked and impenitent, even separating them as chaff from the wheat, gathering the wheat into the granary and burning up the chaff.

4. John's Imprisonment (3:19, 20).

For his reproof of Herod's lewdness and other sins John went to the dungeon. God's faithful prophets are usually despised by the world, even cast into prison, burned, and beheaded.

5. Jesus' Baptism (3:21, 22).

a. Jesus praying while being baptized.

b. The opened heavens.

c. Descent of the Holy Spirit in the shape of a dove.

d. Open declaration from Heaven: "Thou art my beloved Son in whom I am well pleased."

F. *The Genealogy of Jesus' Mother* (3:23-38).

The genealogy links Jesus with Adam the head of the human race, showing that Jesus Christ is the Redeemer of the world of human beings.

III. THE TEMPTATION OF JESUS—A DEMONSTRATION OF THE REALITY OF THE INCARNATION (4:1-13).

Having shown this organic connection of the Redeemer to the human race through the action of the Son of God in the historic Virgin Birth, the Holy Spirit drives Him into the wilderness to be tempted by the Devil. He experienced terrific tests through a period of forty days, proving beyond any doubt that the union of the divine and human natures was real and unbreakable. The Devil does not like the doctrine of the Virgin Birth.

A. *The Place* (4:1).

The wilderness of Judea. The first man, Adam, was tempted in a garden with the most pleasant surroundings. The second Man, Jesus Christ, was tempted in a barren wilderness, surrounded by wild beasts (Mark 1:13). Adam shamefully failed; Christ gloriously triumphed. The temptation continued for forty days.

B. *The Purpose* (4:1).

He was led into the wilderness by the Spirit. Christ's temptation was Messianic. We are not tempted as He was, but the same methods are employed on us. During the eighteen years of retirement Satan no doubt tempted Christ as he tempts us. As a carpenter He was no doubt tempted by Satan to do imperfect work and use unsound material. The Holy Spirit, not the Devil, led Jesus into temptation. Satan no doubt would have gladly escaped this hour, but the time had come for the Redeemer to enter upon His mediatorial work. Therefore He went from the place of anointing and heavenly recognition as the Son of God to meet and despoil the archenemy (Heb. 2:14). Satan is a real personal being filled with cunning and malice.

1. It Proved His Ability to Despoil Enemy.

It was not a preparation for His work, but rather part of the work

He had come to do. In baptism we have the symbolic act of dedication of Himself to the work of redemption through the cross—the making full a righteousness. In the temptation, the strong man is spoiling the enemy.

2. It Proved His Steadfastness.

It was not to see if Christ would stand fast, or would fail under the most crucial test. Christ could not fail.

3. It Proved His Stability.

It was to show Christ as an object upon which we may rest our faith with unshaken confidence. He came as the second Man, the Head of a new race, its very source and life. It was a demonstration of the inseparableness of the divine and human natures in the incarnation. In the act of the incarnation was found a union which the Devil could not break.

C. *The Method* (4:2-12).

Christ as the world's Redeemer sustained a threefold relationship —Son of man, Son of God, and Messiah; therefore Satan made each one a ground of attack.

1. As Son of Man (4:2-4).

Satan made his first assault upon Him as a man by appealing to the instinct of hunger. Satan urged Him to use His divine power and convert a stone into bread. Hunger is natural and sinless. Real human life experiences hunger. The appetite of hunger was right and normal. The temptation was in satisfying a right hunger in a wrong way. To have yielded in this case, though His hunger was desperate, would have been to renounce the human limitations which He had taken for our sakes. To use divine power to satisfy human needs would have been to fail as Saviour and Redeemer. To do right in a wrong way is to sin. In the Incarnation He became identified with humanity, so He chose to abide in fellowship with man.

2. As Messiah (4:5-8).

Here the temptation was to grasp His rightful dominions by false means. The Devil offered to surrender unto Him the world if He would adopt his methods—would worship Him. The force of this temptation was in the fact that the kingdoms of the world are Christ's by God's covenant with Him. Satan is only a usurper. God's method by which Jesus was to possess the world was the cross. The temptation Satan is pressing upon the Church today is to get possession of the world by other means than the cross. We fall into the hands of the tempter today when we resort to worldly means of doing the Lord's work. To depart from unswerving loyalty to God and His Word is to fall into Satan's temptation. To bid for power by using worldly means is to follow after Satan. To worship the Devil would be to set up his kingdom.

3. As Son of God (4:9-12).

Here Satan tries to induce Christ to presume upon God's care. He quotes a Messianic psalm to induce Him to so act. To do the spectacular thing in order to get notice is to fall into Satan's temptation. For Jesus to have placed Himself in danger in order to get God's special help in delivering Him would have been to sin. To test God as to whether He will keep His promise is the greatest distrust—it is to sin and fall. To put oneself in moral and spiritual peril in order to test God's faithfulness is to sin. Satan is never quite so dangerous as when he quotes Scripture. Beware of Satan when he comes with a Bible under his arm.

D. *Christ's Defense* (4:4, 8, 12).

It was the Word of God. He met and repulsed the enemy with, "It is written." Our defense is God's Word. May every Christian know how to use it!

E. *The Issue* (4:13).

Satan is vanquished. If we will but trust God and use His Word we too can overcome.

IV. THE MINISTRY OF THE SON OF MAN (4:14—9:50).

A. *Jesus Preaching in the Synagogue at Nazareth* (4:14-30).

1. His Custom Was To Go to the House of God (4:16).

He now had come back to the town of His boyhood days and entered the place of worship as was His custom while growing up as a lad. The time to acquire the habit of churchgoing is while young.

2. Jesus Reading from the Scriptures (4:17-19).

He opened the Book to Isaiah 61, and read the Scripture passage which set forth His entire mission. In this passage we find the divine character of that mission and His special enduement for it.

a. Character of His mission (vv. 18, 19).

(1) Preach the Gospel to the poor. The glory of the Gospel is that it comes to the help of those most in need. The Gospel puts a premium upon what man is, not upon what he possesses. Character is before property. It puts dignity upon labor. Indeed, it puts a ladder at the feet of a man and enables him to climb as high as his ability will permit him.

(2) Heal the brokenhearted! How welcome should the Gospel message be to such! The Gospel of Christ really heals.

(3) Preach deliverance to the captives. Those who are in captivity to sin and Satan Christ can and will deliver (John 8:34-36).

(4) Recovering of sight to the blind. Christ not only can open the physical eyes, but the eyes of the spirit as well. Only those in Christ have an understanding of the real situation in life.

(5) Set at liberty them that are bruised. Satan has been most mercilessly bruising men, but the mighty One has come who can set them free. How blessed the Gospel!

(6) Preach the acceptable year of the Lord. This was the Year of Jubilee which looked forward to the glorious millennial age (Lev. 25:8-13, 50-54).

b. His enduement (v. 18). The Holy Spirit came upon Christ for the express purpose of fitting Him for His divine mission. Because of this enduement He cannot fail in His glorious work. It should be noted that Christ stopped His quotation from the prophet at a comma. This shows how exactly the Scriptures are inspired. That which follows, "The day of vengeance of our God," refers to the awful judgment which shall follow the Year of Jubilee because the Gospel of God's grace has been rejected.

c. His testimony (vv. 20, 21). Having completed the reading, He declared that the Scripture had fulfillment then and there in Himself. This was a critical hour for the people. May there not be rejection like that which followed His testimony at Nazareth!

This seems to be the first sermon preached by Christ. It is given a place here by Luke because it contains the program of the saving ministry of the Kinsman-Redeemer. Note program as wrought out by:

(1) Christ's first coming (vv. 18, 19).

(2) Christ's second coming (Isa. 61:1, 2).

This first recorded sermon is a fine illustration of what preaching the Bible is.

(a) The text (vv. 18, 19).
(b) The exposition of the text (vv. 20-27).
(c) The result (vv. 28-30).
(i) Wondered at His gracious words.
(ii) Hostility to the preacher.

B. *Jesus Working Miracles at Capernaum—the Great Physician* (4:31—5:26).

1. Jesus Heals a Demoniac (4:31-37).

While engaged in teaching in the synagogue He was interrupted by a man who had an unclean spirit. Jesus rebuked the demon and compelled him to come out of the man. This was no doubt a wicked, supernatural, personal being who entered into and controlled the poor man. This healing shows Jesus not only to be gracious, but powerful to set free the whole brood of diabolical passions such as lust, envy, anger, and jealousy which rule men.

2. Jesus Heals a Woman of a Fever, and Many Others (4:38-44).

Peter's mother-in-law was prostrate with a great fever. They of Peter's household besought Jesus for her. Jesus rebuked the fever and it left her, so that she immediately rose and ministered unto them. No earthly physician has ever been known to heal in that way. Divine healing is immediate and complete. We should distinguish between divine healing and faith healing. Faith healing is the result of the action of the mind upon the body and is measured by the degree of the faith. Divine healing is the action of the power of God upon the diseased one and is always complete and immediate, because it is measured by the power of the Healer—God. His fame spread abroad and many sick of divers diseases were brought unto Him and He healed them all, even casting out demons and forbidding them to testify of Him.

3. The Miraculous Draught of Fishes (5:1-11).

Let us learn—

a. To be ready for every good work. The people were crowding upon Him. Jesus did not wait for a place to be prepared for teaching, but used a boat standing idle.

b. To render unquestioning obedience to the Lord's command. Though Peter had toiled all night without any success, at Christ's command he let down the net and enclosed many fishes.

c. To be conscious of our sinfulness because of a sense of God's presence.

d. To be capable of catching men. "Fear not, from henceforth thou shalt catch men."

4. Jesus Heals a Leper (5:12-16).

Leprosy was a most loathsome and terrible disease. Because of its foulness one afflicted therewith was an outcast. The disease is thought incurable by man, therefore the leper was regarded as hopeless and dead. In response to the leper's earnest request Jesus touched him and bade the leprosy to depart, and immediately he was healed and cleansed. Leprosy is a type of sin. Though sin is loathsome, hideous, and separating, Jesus has power to save those who come to Him by faith. He has power to heal and cleanse and restore.

5. Jesus Heals a Paralytic (5:17-26).

a. Watched by the Pharisees and doctors (v. 17). Jesus' fame spread abroad and this only incited jealousy on the part of these men. They did not want to get too close to Him, but close enough to know what was going on. These human teachers were watching the divine Teacher.

b. The paralytic brought to Jesus (vv. 18, 19). This is a fine lesson in Christian service. They could not heal the man, but being moved by sympathy they co-operated in bringing him to Jesus who could heal and restore. Their efforts in bringing the man shows their willingness to go to pains and trouble to bring him to Jesus.

c. The man's sins forgiven (v. 20). Jesus looked back of the palsy to its cause—sin. The effect of his sin was before Jesus, but he proceeded to deal with the cause of it. All disease and death are the result of sin. The Lord deals first with that which was at the root of the trouble. Jesus saw the faith of those not only who brought him, but of the man himself. No doubt He saw the man's sorrow for his sins.

d. The purpose of miracles (vv. 21, 22). The Pharisees accused Christ of blasphemy when He declared the man's sins forgiven. Jesus showed them that back of the beneficent deed to the man was the demonstration of His deity. The main purpose in the working of the miracles is the authentication of the divine mission of the one performing them. The healing of the man was done by divine power. The working of the miracle was to demonstrate His authority to atone for sin and to grant forgiveness. While the divine power and authority are thus shown, the wisdom and love of God are shown that in all cases the supernatural work is for the good of the individual.

e. Relative value of physical ills and moral and spiritual maladies (v. 23). Physical ills are less serious than the sins which cause them. In dealing with them we should follow the example of Christ, and first deal with the cause.

f. The cure and its effects (vv. 24-26).

C. *The Call of Levi or Matthew* (5:27-39).

1. Who Matthew Was.

Of Matthew little is known, even his birthplace is concealed. Our first sight of him is while sitting at the toll booth collecting taxes. He was no doubt a Jew, but from the fact that he was engaged in collecting taxes for the Roman government, we judge that he did not belong to the religious or educated class. The taxgatherer was hated by the loyal Jews because he was engaged in collecting taxes for the alien government whose yoke was galling, and also because of the extortion usually practiced by them. From the meager accounts we find that he was—

a. A man of decision. We do not know as to whether he had ever seen or heard of Jesus before this time, but we note that he at once arose and followed Jesus. No doubt, many things concerned him. It was no little task to break off from his business because it would seem that he had a lucrative business.

b. He was a humble man. In Matthew 10:3, the order in which he gives his own name and the fact that he designates himself a "publican" would show that he did not overestimate himself.

c. He possessed force of character. This is shown in the fact that he gave a feast and invited his friends to see and hear his Lord.

He had two names—Levi, which means "attached" or "joined"; and Matthew which means "gift of Jehovah." Most likely Matthew is the name taken after his conversion.

2. Matthew's Call or Conversion (Matt. 9:9).

a. As Jesus passed by, He "saw a man." He saw the possibilities which were in Matthew. The divine grace was revealed in this call. The Lord saw through the hated profession of a taxgatherer, the shining possibilities of his manhood and apostleship. He saw in him the fit man to perceive and portray the Messiahship of the Redeemer. Jesus sees what is in man regardless of his name or profession. May He see in us the possibilities of useful service.

b. Matthew's response (v. 9). He acted with decision and promptness; he left his business behind him. When Jesus said, "Follow me," Matthew perceived that One greater than man had spoken to him. May we yield ourselves unto Him and render such simple obedience that our actions may be but the echoes of the divine voice in commanding. Two things in Matthew's compliance prove the genuineness of his conversion:

(1) "He left all" (5:28). Real conversion always results in the forsaking of all that is contrary to Jesus, such as illegitimate business, wicked associates, and worldly pleasures, etc.

(2) "Followed Jesus." Following Jesus means the commitment of one's life to Him for full salvation, abandonment of the will to Him to do whatsoever He wills, and a willingness to suffer, and even die, if need be, for Him.

3. Matthew Makes a Great Feast (5:29-39).

This feast was made in honor of his newly found Saviour. His conversion was so real that he wanted his friends to become acquainted with his Saviour. He was not ashamed to confess his Lord before his friends. He showed real tact in making a supper. Men will come to a feast much more readily than they will to a sermon. We should use every lawful means to bring men under the sound of the Gospel. A great company of sinners came. These doubtless had been Matthew's companions in sin. He now desires them to become his brothers in Christ.

The scribes and Pharisees were astonished that Jesus would appear in company with such a motley crowd of disreputable persons. They were too cowardly to speak to Jesus but they came to the disciples. Jesus championed their cause and baffled His adversaries. His reasoning was unanswerable. A physician's place is among the sick. Only those who are diseased should come to the doctor's house. Since spiritual matters are of more importance than physical, Jesus was more than justified in being in the center of those who were morally sick that He might heal them of their maladies. He now declared that His purpose in coming among men was to save the bad, not to be served by the good. He came to call sinners to repentance.

D. *The Sabbath Controversy* (6:1-11).

This controversy arose over Christ's permitting the disciples to pluck ears of corn on the sabbath to satisfy their hunger, and Christ's healing a man's withered hand on the sabbath. Christ answered by showing them that the Son of man was Lord of the sabbath. The sabbath was made for man's good and not as a burden—it is a time for rest and worship. Human sympathy shows in doing deeds of mercy on the sabbath to relieve hunger and suffering. The necessities of man and beast must be attended to on the sabbath.

1. The Son of Man Is Lord of the Sabbath (6:1-8).

The hungry disciples were plucking corn on the sabbath. With this the Pharisees found fault. They asserted that the disciples were breaking the Law, when in reality they were only doing that which was a violation of the traditions with which they had encrusted the Law. To these cavils Christ replied showing that God's purpose in instituting the sabbath was to conserve man's highest interests and contribute to his happiness. In this reply He shrewdly answered these carping Pharisees and pressed His transcendent claim as to the dignity of His Person, which moved them to plot His death.

a. He is greater than their greatest king—David. David when rejected was forced to do that which was unlawful for him to do.

b. He is greater than their sacrifice and priesthood. If the priests because of their position and services could violate the Sabbath laws and be blameless, much more should He who is greater than they in performing His work of sacrifice and redemption for them be considered guiltless.

c. He is greater than the Temple. The Temple with the gorgeous rites and ceremonies was but typical of Himself. Much more then did He have the right to do what He did.

d. He is greater than the Sabbath, for He is Lord of the Sabbath.

2. Healing the Withered Hand (6:9-14).

In order that they might accuse Him they asked, "Is it lawful to heal on the sabbath days?" The Saviour's reply to this was both a question and a declaration. His question as to whether a man would not rescue an only sheep was practically saying that they were His sheep in the pit of sin, and that He had come to lift them out. Following this He declared that it was lawful to do well on the Sabbath days, implying that, in keeping with His relation to them, He was endeavoring to lift them from the ditch. To accentuate His words He healed the man, demonstrating His power to rescue the unfortunate sheep. The man with the withered hand is a type of withered Israel, spiritually and nationally. Following this the Pharisees held a council to devise means to destroy Him.

E. *The Son of Man Choosing the Twelve Apostles* (6:12-19).

Jesus, knowing that the rising tide of opposition and violent hatred of the scribes and Pharisees meant death at the first opportunity, saw the need for organizing His work, therefore, He chose the twelve and ordained them to evangelize the world. He esteemed the need so great that He spent the preceding night in prayer. He found His refuge and help in God. He had a twofold purpose in choosing them.

1. That They Might Be "with Him" (Mark 3:14).

He was so really human that He needed their companionship in the lonely, dark hour of His passion, and they needed His help in preparing them for the difficulties which they faced.

2. That They Should Preach the Gospel to All Nations.

Only as they had firsthand knowledge of what they were to preach and endure would they be able to execute their "great commission."

F. *The Son of Man Proclaiming the Laws of the Kingdom of God* (6:20-49).

1. Characteristics of the Subjects of the Kingdom (6:20-26).

Only those who are subjects of the kingdom know what blessedness is. The spiritual experience of the subjects of the kingdom are marked by the following steps:

a. Poverty of spirit (v. 20). This means consciousness of one's lost condition and worthlessness. It is spiritual bankruptcy. It means to come to the end of oneself and to show sorrow for sins.

b. Hunger for righteousness (v. 21). The one who has come to know his poverty desires the true righteousness of Christ.

c. Weeping because of his lack (v. 21). This is the godly sorrow which worketh repentance (II Cor. 7:10).

d. Treatment which the subjects of the kingdom may expect (vv. 22, 23). When the subjects of the kingdom become like the King they incite the hatred, contempt, and persecution of the world. Those who pass through this for Christ's sake should rejoice, for there is great reward laid up in Heaven for them. Those who are rich, self-centered, and seeking the applause of the world have woes pronounced upon them (vv. 25, 26).

2. The Governing Principles of the Kingdom (6:27-46).

a. Love your enemies (v. 27). To love friends is easy, but to love enemies is only possible to those who have been made partakers of the divine nature.

b. Do good to those who hate you (v. 27). Love acts according to its own nature. Enmity only stimulates love to act in harmony with its own laws.

c. Bless them that curse you (v. 28). Injury by words is hard to let go unchallenged.

d. Pray for them which despitefully use you (v. 28). Christ's own example is the best commentary on this precept (23:34; cf. Acts 7:60).

e. Patiently endure wrong and injury (v. 29). The Christian is not to bristle in defense of his rights, but rather to suffer injury and even loss. This should not be pressed so far that evildoers can go on unchecked. It expresses the law which should govern individual action.

f. Give to everyone that asketh (v. 30). We should give to everyone that asketh, but not necessarily the thing asked for.

g. Do as you wish to be done by (v. 31). This is called the Golden Rule. If men were to live by this rule the labor problem would be solved. An end would be put to war. International relations would be peacefully adjusted and all profiteering in business would end. This is the grand and unfailing test of all that calls itself Christian. The practicing of this precept proves that we are children of God (v. 35).

h. Be merciful (v. 36). The mercy of the heavenly Father is the grand example.

i. Censorious judgment condemned (v. 37). We should not seek out the evil in others for our satisfaction. This should not be interpreted to prohibit the estimation of another's character by his deeds.

j. Danger of following false teachers (v. 39). The one who does not know God and the way to Heaven will lead others to ruin. Happily we have the Scriptures, and the Holy Spirit is ready to make their meaning known, so there is no excuse.

k. Those who reprove others should strive to live blameless lives (vv. 31-46). It is easy to see others' faults, but hard to see our own. We should remove evildoing from our lives before bringing others to account. This should not be so interpreted as to prevent from reproving another until his own life is faultless.

l. The sin of profession without fruits (v. 46). The one who professes a life and fellowship with God should practice the principles which reveal the nature of God.

3. The Judgment to Be Applied to the Subjects of the Kingdom (7:47-49).

a. The one who hears and does the sayings of Christ the King shall be as secure as the house built upon the solid rock. The storms of the judgment cannot destroy him, for the Rock of Ages is immovable.

b. The one who hears and does not Christ's sayings shall be overwhelmed in the judgment and go down to utter ruin and destruction.

G. *Jesus Heals the Centurion's Servant* (7:1-10).

1. The Disease of Palsy (Matt. 8:6).

In palsy the victim is helpless and disqualified for service.

2. The Centurion's Humility (7:3-5).

First he sent the Jewish elders and then his friends because he felt his unworthiness. The case of his servant was so grave that his master brushed aside his timidity and personally appealed to Jesus. Jesus is pleased when men realize their helplessness and make their personal appeals to Him.

3. The Centurion's Faith (7:7, 8).

In spite of his unworthiness he committed his case to the Lord Jesus. He believed that if Jesus would but speak the word, his servant would be healed.

4. The Wonderful Power of the Son of Man (7:10).

He did not even need to go to see the centurion's slave and touch him, but only needed to speak the word and it was done. He could heal miles away just as readily as when in the presence of the victim.

H. *The Son of Man Raising the Widow's Son* (7:11-17).

1. The Sorrowful Scene (7:12).

A dead man was being carried out—the only son of a mother who was a widow. Duplicates of this scene are multiplied by the millions in every generation all over the world. The cause of all this is sin which has entered into the human race. Every funeral procession, every cemetery, every funeral parlor is a reminder of the awful fact of sin.

2. The Compassionate Son of Man (7:13, 14).

The sight of this mother's sorrow aroused His pity. He had compassion on her. Jesus knows all about our sorrows and cares. He said, "Weep not," and touched the bier and said, "Young man, I say unto thee, Arise."

3. The Almighty Power of Jesus Christ (7:15).

"He that was dead sat up and began to speak." He will display this power in the coming day in calling forth from the grave the dead in Christ (John 5:28, 29). He is able now to quicken into life souls which are dead in trespasses and sins (John 5:21). This is the only hope of the world.

I. *Jesus' Testimony Concerning John the Baptist* (7:18-35).

Because John did not see the interval between the "sufferings of Christ" and the "glory that should follow," he was perplexed; therefore, he sent a deputation to Jesus for light. The prophets did not see, or at least did not make clear, the interval between the crucifixion of Christ and His second coming. The two events were so presented as to appear to be in close succession. John in his preaching had stressed the mighty judgments which should take place at the appearance of the Messiah. The turn things were taking—he himself being imprisoned with the gloomy prospect of death—was in great contrast with the coming of the Messiah in fiery judgment—"the ax is laid at the root of the tree" and "the chaff to be burned up with unquenchable fire" (Matt. 3:10, 12).

The Messiah had to be the Lamb of God which taketh away the sin of the world (John 1:29). The trend of events puzzled him. It was not lack of faith, but confusion of mind that prompted his inquiry. Christ's testimony defends him against such an accusation. He declared that John was inferior to no prophet that had appeared. Christ vindicated him against a vacillating mind because of the storms of persecution. He was not like a reed shaken by the wind (v. 24) or the hardships of prison life (v. 25). John had lived a life of self-denial, therefore he did not leave his faith in Christ because of the dungeon. Jesus declared that no greater prophet had arisen. That which perplexed John was the delay in judgment—the day of God's patience while gathering out the Church. This was a truth not disclosed to the prophets—that which Paul made known because a special revelation had been granted.

J. *The Son of Man the Friend of Sinners* (7:36-50).

1. A Penitent Woman's Act of Love (7:37, 38).

a. The place (v. 37). It was in the home of Simon the Pharisee while Jesus was sitting at meat. When she knew of Christ's visit in this home she came to lavish upon Him her affection.

b. The act (v. 38). She washed Jesus' feet with her tears and wiped them with her hair. Through some means she had heard of Jesus' pardoning grace, and God had opened her heart to receive Him as her Saviour. Out of a heart of gratitude she kissed His feet and anointed them with precious ointment.

c. Who she was (v. 37). Her name is not mentioned. There is no good ground for assuming that she was Mary Magdalene. She was a notoriously bad character. Though known to the public as a bad woman, something had happened which transformed her. She was a saved sinner because she believed on Jesus Christ. The moment one believes on Christ he is saved regardless of what his former life has been.

2. The Pharisee's Displeasure (7:39).

Simon felt scandalized by such a happening at his table. He was a respectable man. For Jesus to tolerate such familiarity on the part of a woman of such evil repute greatly perplexed him. Though he believed Jesus enough to invite Him to dine with him, he questions within himself as to whether after all he was not mistaken. He reasons if Jesus were a prophet, He would have known the character of this woman and would have either withdrawn His feet or thrust her back with them, or if He knew her character His tolerance of such familiarity proved that He was not a good man. Simon's righteousness was of that sort which gathers up its skirts and gives the sinner a backward push into his filth. If he had known who Jesus was and what a change had been wrought in the woman's heart, he would not have been so severe.

3. Jesus Teaches the Pharisee (7:40-48).

He taught him by means of the parable of a creditor and two debtors. Observe that Jesus made it very clear that He not only knew the woman, but knew Simon also.

a. The common debt (v. 41). The woman was a sinner, so was Simon, though he was not the same kind of a sinner that she was. There were two debtors, though the one owed ten times as much as the other. This is still representative of all sinners. The Bible declares all to be sinners, yet recognizes degrees of guilt. Full credit ought to be given to the man who is honest, virtuous, generous, and kind. Yet such a life will not secure entrance into Heaven. On the other hand, the Saviour's words are a severe rebuke to the respectable Pharisees who are sitting in judgment against the sinners of a coarser type.

b. The common insolvency (v. 42). "And when they had nothing to pay." Jesus freely granted the difference in the degree of the woman's sins and those of the Pharisee, but drove home to him the fact that they were both debtors and had nothing with which to pay (Rom. 3:23). As sinners we may quit our sinning and hate our deeds, but that does not make satisfaction for the sins of the past. What we have done is irrevocable—it has passed from our reach. Every transgression shall receive a just recompense of reward (Heb. 2:2). We must come to our Creditor, God Almighty, and acknowledge our insolvency and accept the kindness of Jesus Christ who bore our sins in His own body on the tree (I Peter 2:24). We are all paupers, and instead of judging each other as to relative guilt, we should come to God and sue for pardon.

c. The relation of forgiveness and love (vv. 44-48). Simon's reluctant answer to Jesus' question shows that he got the point of Jesus' teaching. In order to make His teaching concrete He turned to the woman, calling Simon's attention to what she had done in contrast to what he had done. Simon had neglected to extend to Jesus the common courtesies of a respected guest, but this forgiven woman had lavished upon Him her affection and gifts. The measure of one's love is determined by the measure of the apprehension of sins forgiven. The one most forgiven will love most. Frequently the worst sinners make the best saints. The wasted life of the sinner often spurs him on to the utmost endeavor; but let no one think lightly of sin. Through the grace of God forgiveness of sins is possible, yet sins leave their scars.

K. *The Son of Man the Great Missionary* (8:1-39).

1. The Great Missionary's Field (8:1-3).

He went throughout every city and village. The true missionary goes to everyone, for all need the Gospel.

a. His message (v. 1). He preached the glad tidings of the kingdom of God. The Gospel message is truly good tidings, for the great King is offering to rebellious sinners salvation through Jesus Christ.

b. His helpers (v. 1). The twelve apostles were with Him. The missionary should utilize the help of others. Those who have heard the good tidings of the Gospel gladly join in preaching it to others.

c. Supported by saved women (vv. 2, 3). Out of grateful hearts certain women who had experienced the saving power of the Gospel ministered unto Jesus of their substance. This throws light on how Christ and the apostles were supported. Saved men and women delight to supply the temporal needs of God's missionaries.

2. The Great Missionary Teaching (8:4-21).

Jesus was not only a Gospel Preacher, but a great Teacher. When the people from every city gathered unto Him, He taught them.

a. The parable of the sower (vv. 4-18).

(1) The Sower—Jesus (Matt. 13:37).

(2) The Seed—the Word of God (v. 11).

(3) The kinds of ground (vv. 5-8). This shows the condition of the human heart as the Word of God is preached.

(a) Wayside (v. 5). This foot-trodden path pictures the hardhearted upon which no impression can be made. The preached Word finds no entrance, and Satan snatches it away as birds pick up the grain from the hard-beaten path. In such cases faith cannot spring up and result in salvation (v. 12).

(b) Stony ground (v. 6). This is not stones mixed with earth, but a thin layer of earth on a ledge of rock. The seed falling upon such earth springs up quickly, but the plant soon dies when exposed to the sun. This pictures the hearer who receives with joy the message of the Gospel, but when persecution and trials come because of following Christ, they give up and desert the cause (v. 15).

(c) Thorny ground (v. 7). This ground is good but it has thorns growing in it. The seeds spring up but the plant has no room to develop. This pictures the Christians who bear no Christian fruit because of being preoccupied with cares, riches, and pleasures of this life (v. 14).

(d) Good ground (v. 8). The seed here sprang up and bore fruit to the full measure. This pictures the honest heart which receives the Gospel message and allows it to produce in its life a full harvest of grain (v. 15).

This parable graphically represents the different classes of hearers wherever the Gospel is preached. The application of this parable is found in verses 16-18. The Word of God is compared with a lamp or lighted candle. A Christian who has received the Seed in an honest heart is as a lamp. A lamp is of use only as it sends out light. One who hears God's Word and does not witness for Christ is as a lamp covered up. Moreover, to fail to witness for Christ will result in having his light taken away. May this be a warning to everyone!

b. Kinship with Jesus Christ (vv. 19-21). Jesus teaches here that there is a relationship to Him which is closer than the tie of blood. Only those who receive the message of God's Word and render glad obedience to it can claim relationship with Christ.

3. The Great Missionary Doing Wonders (8:22-39).

a. Calming the storm (vv. 22-25).

(1) Jesus asleep (v. 23). While the disciples were sailing the ship, the Master fell asleep.

(2) The frightened disciples (vv. 23, 24). The storm was an unusual one. These sturdy men were used to the storms, which were common to that sea, but as their ships filled with water, they awakened Jesus with their cry of peril.

(3) Jesus rebuked the wind and water (v. 24). At His word there was a great calm.

(4) Jesus rebuked the disciples (v. 25). After rebuking the raging elements, He turned to the disciples. He did not rebuke them for waking Him, but for their lack of faith.

b. Casting out demons (vv. 26-39). Demon-possession was in that day, and is today, an awful reality.

(1) Jesus met by the demoniac (vv. 26-29). This poor man's suffering and nakedness were awful. Sin imposes upon its victims anguish and shame. He was helpless under the demon's power. His cry of anguish shows his consciousness of torment. There is no doubt in the minds of demons as to the reality of a place of torment. The Devil blinds men's minds to it.

(2) Jesus' question (v. 30). The purpose of this question doubtless was to bring the real man to consciousness to enable him to distinguish between the demon and himself. The answer shows that the man thought his case hopeless. He said that many demons were entered into him. If he had known just who was speaking to him he would have known that deliverance from even so many was possible. The Devil delights in getting men to believe their case is hopeless.

(3) The demons' request (vv. 31, 32). They asked permission to enter into a herd of swine. It seems that the demons have a dislike for disembodiment. In the presence of Jesus the demons quaver and beg permission to act. The Devil cannot act without divine permission.

(4) The request granted (vv. 32, 33). Just why this was done we do not know. Since Jesus did it we must believe that it was wise.

(5) The effect upon the people (vv. 34-37).

(a) The keepers of the swine made it known in the city and country.

(b) The people made investigation. They saw the man clothed and in his right mind, and heard the testimony of those who had seen what was done.

(c) Besought Jesus to depart from them. How sad in the face of the mighty works of Jesus that men will not open their hearts unto Him!

(6) Request of the man whom He healed (vv. 38, 39). He desired to be with Jesus. This was natural and right, but his responsibility was to go home and show them what great things God had done for him. He went his way and published throughout the city what great things Jesus had done unto him.

L. *The Daughter of Jairus Raised and a Woman with an Issue of Blood Healed* (8:40-56; cf. Mark 5:21-43).

Jesus had just returned from the country of the Gadarenes where He had healed the man with an unclean spirit. In the preceding portion Christ's power over the forces of nature and demons was exhibited; in this, His power over disease and death is shown, which is a fitting climax. The accounts of the raising of the damsel and the healing of the woman are so interwoven as almost to constitute one narrative. But since the persons are diverse and places separate, and the one an interruption of the other, they should be treated separately.

1. Daughter of Jairus Raised (8:41, 42, 49-56).

a. Jairus' urgent mission (Mark 5:22, 23). His only daughter (8:42), perhaps his only child, lay dying. In this time of utter helplessness he came to Jesus, for he had faith in His ability to raise her up. In the providence of God sorrow, sickness, and death are often used to bring needy men and women into contact with Jesus. He showed the proper attitude toward Jesus—"he fell at his feet" (v. 22). Frequently men and women will not go to Jesus for themselves, but will pray to Him for loved ones.

b. Jesus goes with Jairus (v. 24). Jairus believed that if Jesus would lay His hand upon his daughter, she would live. Such faith always gets a response from Jesus. No blessing can come to the one who is destitute of faith.

c. News of his daughter's death (v. 35). This is a most startling message. No doubt Jairus' patience was greatly tested because Christ tarried to speak to and heal the woman who had been so grievously afflicted. The messenger who brought the news of her death suggested that Jesus should be excused from going farther as it was now too late.

d. Jairus' faith strengthened (v. 36). As soon as Jesus heard the words spoken concerning the death of this girl, He said to the father, "Be not afraid, only believe." Only the Son of God could thus speak. This is His message still to every distressed soul!

e. The mourners rebuked (vv. 37-39). He now dismissed the crowd and allowed only three of His disciples and the parents of the damsel to enter this chamber of death with Him. A tumultuous wailing showed the despair of the friends. In connection with this death wail the Lord was ridiculed when He declared that the girl could be awakened from her sleep of death.

f. Jairus' faith rewarded (vv. 41-43). He took the damsel by the hand and issued the command for her to arise. The expression, *Talitha cumi,* in the Aramaic seems to be freely expressed, "Wake up, little girl." She straightway arose and walked and partook of food. Her walking was the proof of the reality of the miracle. There seemed to be none of the weakness which usually followed a severe sickness. Jesus charged them to keep silent concerning this miracle as premature notoriety might interfere with His work.

2. The Woman with an Issue of Blood Healed (8:43-48).

a. Her helpless condition (v. 43). She had been a great sufferer for twelve long years. In addition to the physical suffering her malady involved ceremonial uncleanness, which perhaps was as hard to bear as the physical suffering.

b. Her faith (Mark 5:27, 28). She possessed a real and earnest faith. She may have come a considerable distance, having heard of the fame of Jesus. For a poor, emaciated woman, after twelve years of suffering, to press her way through a thronging multitude shows that she possessed a determined purpose. The test of the actuality and quality of one's faith is the activity which characterizes the life. Her faith was so strong that she believed contact with the Master's garments would secure the needed help. Though her faith was strong, it was imperfect. She only knew Him as a wonder-worker, but through this experience she came to know Him as a compassionate Saviour.

c. Her healing (vv. 29-32). As soon as she touched the hem of His garment, she experienced in her body His healing power. Jesus Himself was conscious of the outgoing of virtue from Himself, therefore inquired, "Who touched me?" to which the disciples replied with amazement: "Thou seest the multitude thronging thee and sayest thou, Who touched me?"

d. Her confession (v. 33; cf. 8:47). She thought secretly to get the blessing of healing, but Jesus perceived that virtue had gone out from Him and had her make a public confession. It was for her good, for faith in Christ unconfessed will naturally weaken.

e. Jesus' words of encouragement (v. 34). With the communication of His healing virtue, He spoke most gracious and comforting words to this poor woman. He told her that it was her faith, not her touch, that had saved her. Faith does not need to face dangers and to exhaust itself in active endeavor in order to gain Christ's blessing. All that is required is a trust in prayer. She attained the blessing immediately. Not only did she gain the blessing, but had the distinction of being the only woman on record as ever having been addressed as "daughter," which shows His spirit of tenderness to those who come to Him with their needs.

M. *The Closing Period of Christ's Galilean Ministry* (9:1-50).

1. The Sending Forth of the Twelve Apostles (9:1-9; cf. Mark 6:7-31).

Though Jesus' fame had spread abroad and multitudes thronged Him, the people of His own town Nazareth rejected Him (vv. 1-6). Their taunts and jeers He answered by declaring that a prophet is not without honor but in his own country, and among his own kin, and in his own house. Because of their unbelief, He could do no mighty works there so He went round about the villages teaching, knowing that though the leaders turned a deaf ear to His message, some would hear and believe.

a. The twelve sent forth (Mark 6:7-13). Two pressing considerations moved Him to send them forth—the increasing multitudes who were eager to hear the message, and the fact that His own career would soon end. Others must be ready to carry on the work which He had begun.

(1) They were sent forth in pairs (v. 7). Three reasons may be assigned for sending them two by two:

(a) A wider scope of country could be covered than if they would go in company.

(b) A companionship would be provided for the workers which would be mutually cheering and comforting.

(c) Their testimony would be confirmed, for in the mouth of two or three witnesses every word shall be established.

(2) The supernatural authentication of their mission (v. 7). He gave them power over unclean spirits. They were endowed with power to work miracles, to show that they were commissioned by Heaven for their work.

(3) Their maintenance (vv. 8, 9). They were to make no provision for their support, but to depend wholly upon the Lord who sent them. They had received the message and power gratuitously, so they were to give it out in the same way (Matt. 10:9). Christ's messengers should not be burdened with needless equipment, but go forth in faith depending upon the Lord to move upon those to whom they minister to provide them entertainment and support; this, not as a matter of poverty, but that which is legitimate, for the laborer is worthy of his hire.

(4) Contentment with hospitality (v. 10). According to Matthew inquiry was to be made upon entering a city as to a reputable place to stay. When such a place is determined upon, the missionary should be content.

(5) Responsibility of those to whom the message was delivered (v. 11). Judgment was to be pronounced upon those who rejected their message. Their doom would be more hopeless than that of Sodom and Gomorrah.

(6) Their message and work (vv. 12, 13). They went out and preached that men should repent. Matthew adds, "The kingdom of heaven is at hand" (Matt. 10:7), which means that the kingdom promised to Israel was at hand, that Christ was present and ready to set up His kingdom. In confirmation of their message they

cast out many demons and anointed with oil many that were sick, and healed them.

b. Effect of their ministry (vv. 14-29). The fame of Christ spread far and wide through the teaching and miracles wrought by the twelve. Various explanations were offered of this marvelous work. Their preaching had, as its central content, the messiahship of Jesus. Some said that He was one of the prophets, others that He was Elias; but King Herod said that He was John the Baptist whom he had beheaded. Herod's guilty conscience troubled him, but he was too weak to obey its voice. John had rebuked Herod for his unlawful marriage with his borther's wife. Herod recognized the righteousness of John's indictment, but was so bound with the shackles of sin that he was unable to free himself from them. He did not desire to kill John, nor was he willing to give up his illegal relationship, so he compromised by imprisoning John. In the midst of his temporizing, Satan wins the victory over him. On the occasion of the disgraceful dance on Herod's birthday, he was caught by the conspiracy of Herodias, and beheaded John. His sleeping conscience which had been violated was aroused by the strenuous preaching and mighty works of the twelve.

c. The twelve report their work to Jesus (vv. 30, 31). After their strenuous campaign, at the invitation of Jesus they retired with Him and told Him what they had taught and what they had wrought. Such retirement with the Lord has a twofold benefit—it would fix their minds upon the Lord instead of upon themselves as to their successes, and prevent despondency for their failure.

2. The Son of Man Feeding the Five Thousand (9:10-17). According to the connection in John 6:1-14, the real purpose of this miracle was to show Himself as the Bread of eternal life sent down from Heaven.

a. Jesus' conference with the disciples (vv. 12, 13).

(1) The disciples' request (v. 12). They asked that the multitude be sent away. They knew that they were in a desert place, therefore prudence would indicate that they would go to the villages to buy victuals. How little they knew of His power!

(2) Jesus' command, "Give ye them to eat" (v. 13). Such

a command would have been utter foolishness had He not possessed the power to create the supply; but always with the command of Jesus goes the power to do.

(3) The disciples' perplexity (v. 13). They said: "We have but five loaves and two small fishes." They were counting on their meager resources, leaving Christ out. Christ knew they had but five loaves and two fishes, still He commanded them to do the impossible. He wishes them to learn that the things which are impossible with men are possible with God. To be face to face with the humanly impossible is a threefold benefit:

(a) To make us feel our dependence upon Christ.

(b) To drive us to Him for His help in our need.

(c) To lead us to give the glory to Him for results. Though our gifts be small and our powers weak, yet in the hands of Christ we may accomplish much. Though our ability to teach, preach, or give be meager we should remember that our Lord with His ability is equal to any demands which may be made.

b. Jesus' method in feeding the multitude (vv. 14-17).

(1) The Lord's part. He created the provisions. He is able to create that which will meet the needs of the hungry multitude. He is able to meet the needs of all, temporally and spiritually. His power is unlimited.

(2) The people's part. They were to sit down and eat. They were not responsible for the creation of the supply or its distribution, but they were responsible for obedience. Even after the bread had been blessed by the Lord and distributed by the disciples, they would have fainted with hunger had they not eaten. So it is today, unless the people receive that which is provided by the Lord, they will eternally starve. The Lord has done His part; we should be doing our part, and then the final responsibility will be resting upon the people.

(3) The disciples' part. This was to take that which the Master had blessed and distribute it. We are laborers together with God. God has made us partners in the salvation of the world.

3. The Son of Man Predicting His Death and Resurrection (9:18-27).

He took account of His ministry before going to Jerusalem to be offered up. The cross loomed large upon His horizon as He set His face toward Jerusalem for the last time. His supreme concern was that His disciples be prepared for the ordeal which awaited them at His crucifixion. It seems that the first clear prediction of His death took place immediately after Peter's confession of Jesus as the Christ of God.

a. The occasion was while alone praying. The disciples were with Him (v. 18). The praying was being done by Christ alone while the disciples were with Him. The purpose of the praying was primarily for the disciples—that they might understand the meaning of the cross and be able to preach the Gospel effectively after the Lord was gone. The crucified and resurrected Christ is alone the Gospel.

b. The questions asked (vv. 18-20).

(1) "Whom say the people that I am?" The disciples answered: "John the Baptist; but some say Elias; and others say one of the prophets is risen again." The import of their answer was that a reformer, a great preacher, a messenger of God has appeared again. Such opinion did not satisfy Christ. Millions today say such things about Christ, who deny His essential deity and Saviourhood.

(2) "Whom say ye that I am?" (v. 20). Christ demanded a personal answer. Peter as spokesman for the disciples said, "The Christ of God."

This great affirmation of Peter Christ accepted, but commanded that they tell no man that thing, for it would not be understood. "Christ of God" meant the fulfillment of the Messianic hope and embraced three things: the Prophet who would bring forth God's full and final revelation, the Priest who would exercise a complete mediation, and the King who would reign and rule as the absolute monarch.

As Dr. Morgan says: "Here was a man, blunt in speech of that nation saying to Jesus, 'Thou are the Prophet, the Priest, the King promised, looked for, waited for, now come from God. Thou art the Revealer, thou are the Redeemer; thou art the Ruler.' "

c. The revelation of Christ's coming death, suffering, and triumphant resurrection, and the affirmation of the necessity of the personal experience of the value of the cross in order to prove the grace of salvation to the lost. This is the message for the preacher in our day and generation. "The gospel of Christ is the power of God unto salvation to everyone that believeth" (Rom. 1:17).

4. The Son of Man Transfigured (9:28-43).

It includes the unveiling of the incarnation and exhibition of His redemptive program.

While it is true that in this section the disciples are witnesses of Christ's glory, the full truth is that the manifestation of Christ in glory was to give to the discouraged disciples a foregleam of the Messianic kingdom. The hopes of the disciples were crushed when Christ announced His death on the cross. They were unable to see how victory could issue from death.

Jesus took with Him Peter, James, and John and went into the mountain to pray. His chief aim in retirement was to get the disciples apart and into a state of receptivity so that He might show them the method of the kingdom. Before going to the mountain He declared that there were some standing in His presence who would not taste of death till they should see the Son of man coming in His kingdom (9:27; Matt. 16:28). That their drooping spirits might be revived and their confidence restored, He is transfigured before them. Two men from the upper world are sent to converse with Him about His approaching death in Jerusalem (v. 31) the very thing about which the disciples refused to talk. Then, too, God's own voice was heard in words of approval of Christ's course, directing them to hear the Master. Surely they cannot doubt His ability now to carry into execution His kingdom plans.

The purpose then of the transfiguration is to give the disciples a foregleam of the coming kingdom, to enable them to see the kingdom in embryo. That this is true is not only shown by the context and circumstances but by the inspired interpretation of one who was with Him and knew all that transpired. Peter said: "For we did not follow cunningly devised fables when we made known unto you the power and coming of our Lord Jesus Christ, but we were eyewitnesses of his majesty, for he received of God the Father honor and glory when there came such a voice to him from the excellent glory; This is my beloved Son in whom I am well pleased: and this voice we ourselves heard come out of heaven, when we were with him in the holy mount. And we have the word of prophecy made more sure; whereunto ye do well that ye take heed, as unto a lamp shining in a dark place, until the day dawn, and the daystar arise in your hearts" (II Peter 1:16-19, A.S.V.). To those who believe in the inspiration of the Bible these words are final. Let us therefore note the outstanding features of the kingdom as displayed in the transfiguration.

a. Jesus Christ the glorified King on Mount Zion (v. 29). The glorified King on this mount was intended to symbolize the Messianic kingdom when Christ returns to the Mount of Olives in Jerusalem (Zech. 14:4-17). This is still in the future, and will be literally fulfilled.

b. The glorified saints with Christ (vv. 30, 31).

(1) Moses, who was once denied an entrance into Palestine, appears now in glory, representing the redeemed of the Lord who shall pass through death into the kingdom. Many thousands of the redeemed have fallen asleep and at the coming of the Lord shall be awakened to pass into the kingdom.

(2) Elijah, now glorified, represents the redeemed who shall pass into the kingdom through translation. Many shall be living upon the earth when the Lord shall come, and shall without dying be changed, and thus pass into the kingdom (I Cor. 15:50-53; I Thess. 4:14-18).

(3) They talk of the very thing which the disciples refused to believe, namely, the death of Christ.

c. Israel, in the flesh, in connection with the kingdom, represented by Peter, James, and John (v. 28). Israel shall be called from their hiding places among all nations of the earth and shall be gathered to Jesus Christ the King, as the central people in the kingdom (Ezek. 37:21-27).

d. Peter proposes to build three tabernacles (v. 33). The Feast of Tabernacles looked forward to the glorious reign of Christ. Peter caught a glimpse of the significance of the transfiguration. His proposition showed that he thought of the Feast of Tabernacles and therefore of the Millennium.

e. The divine voice (v. 35). At this time God Himself uttered His words, assuring them that this One in glory was His Son Jesus Christ.

f. The multitude at the foot of the mountain (vv. 37-43).

This is representative of the nations to be brought into the kingdom which shall be established over Israel. (See Isa. 11:10-12.) The people here were grievously oppressed by the Devil. There are times when the Devil is especially active in his oppression of men. About the time of Christ's first coming he did his best to harass men. Just before Christ's coming again he will be especially active, for he knows that his time is short.

5. Pride, Selfish Ambition, and Bigotry Rebuked (9:46-50).

V. THE KINSMAN-REDEEMER SETTING HIS FACE TO GO TO JERUSALEM (9:51–19:27).

Jesus was increasingly conscious that the time of His being offered up was drawing near. He repeatedly reminded His disciples of the near approach of His death and resurrection. He wanted them to be fully aware of that which awaited them. As for Himself, with unfaltering courage He pressed on. The climax of His mission about to be realized. For our knowledge of incidents of this journey to Jerusalem we are dependent upon Luke's record.

A. *The Inhospitality of the Samaritans* (9:51-56).

1. Messengers Sent To Arrange Entertainment (9:51, 52).

2. The Samaritans' Refusal (9:53).

Their excuse was somewhat flimsy—they accused the Lord of having shown no interest in them. His primary purpose was to go on to Jerusalem.

3. The Reaction of James and John (9:54).

They interpreted the actions of the Samaritans as an insult to their Lord. They proposed to have fire sent down from Heaven and burn them up, as Elijah had done.

4. Jesus Rebuked James and John (9:55, 56).

He said: "Ye know not what manner of spirit ye are of." He reminded them that such an act would be a contravention of His mission. "The Son of man" came to save men, not to destroy them. Their love for the Lord moved them to brook no insult to Him. John was true to the truth of the name *Boanerges* given him by the Lord. Jesus made it clear that there was no place in the life of the disciple of Christ for anger, intolerance, or revenge.

B. *Tests of True Discipleship* (9:57-62).

In the company of those who followed the Lord there were three classes:

1. The Thoughtless (9:57, 58).

They were those who were swept along with the emotions of the crowd—those who had not considered that to follow Jesus might involve much sacrifice and great pain. It was for this reason that Jesus turned to him with implied rebuke, saying: "Foxes have holes, and birds of the air have nests; but the Son of man hath not where to lay his head." This disciple was guilty of rashness—he had not counted the cost of discipleship.

2. The Procrastinator (9:59, 60).

The second man when bidden by Jesus to follow Him offered an excuse. He said: "Lord, suffer me first to go and bury my father." The Lord who knew the man's heart said to him: "Let the dead bury their dead; but go thou and preach the kingdom of God." By "burying my father" the man doubtless meant that after his father's death he would be willing to follow Jesus. Prompt obedience was necessary as Jesus was passing that way for the last time—the proclamation of the Gospel of life was an urgent necessity.

3. The Irresolute (9:61, 62).

The third man said: "Lord, I will follow thee, but let me first go bid them farewell, which are at home at my house." He expressed a willingness to go, but asked for a delay long enough to say good-by to his family and friends. His request indicated that he had not fully made up his mind as to his obligation. The Lord's reply (v. 62) was a stinging rebuke showing that his indecision was due to a lack of discernment.

C. *Jesus Sending Out Missionaries* (10:1-24).

1. The Seventy Sent Forth (10:1, 2).

a. Appointed by the Lord (v. 1). Only those should go forth who are appointed by the Lord.

b. Sent forth two by two (v. 1). The purpose of this was that they might mutually help, counsel, and support each other. These seventy were to be pioneer missionaries.

c. Reason for their appointment (v. 2). The harvest was great but the laborers were few. Missionaries should have an intense realization of the enormous task set before them. The task before the Christian Church after more than 1900 years is still great. Not only the workers who go forth, but the Church itself should have this vision.

d. Pray the Lord to send forth laborers (v. 2). The realization of the prodigious task before us will cause us to pray to the Lord to send forth more laborers. The Church will never have the necessary number of missionaries until she realizes her obligation before God and earnestly prays Him to send forth laborers.

2. Instructions Given (10:3-16).

a. He reveals the dangers confronting them (v. 3). They were thrust forth by the Lord to proclaim His name, though by so doing they would expose themselves to deadly peril, even as lambs surrounded by hungry wolves. It matters not what the dangers are if the Lord sends forth.

b. Free from all encumbrance (v. 4). The mission was urgent, so all that would in any way hinder the speedy execution of the task were to be left behind.

c. Distraction of social intercourse to be omitted (v. 4). Eastern salutations were long-drawn affairs. To go into such formalities would greatly delay Christ's messengers. This does not mean that Christ's ministers should not be courteous.

d. Behavior in the homes where received (vv. 5-9).

(1) Offer the peace of the Gospel (vv. 5, 6). This is to be done regardless whether it will be received or not. There is a reflex blessedness in preaching the Gospel. Even when the message is rejected the effort is not wasted, but comes back to the one who has made the effort. All efforts to bless others bless themselves.

(2) Do not shift quarters (vv. 7, 8). Missionaries should remain in the home where they have been received, content with what is given them. They should not demand better food and more comfortable quarters than what is commonly provided. However, that which is given should be gratefully given, for the laborer is worthy of his hire.

(3) Healed the sick (v. 9). These disciples were given power to heal the sick. The ministers of Christ should seek to give relief to those in distress and use every opportunity to proclaim the Gospel message.

e. The awful fate of those who reject Christ's message (vv. 10-16). Their case is more hopeless than that of Sodom. The thought of those who would reject Him through rejection of His messengers reminds Jesus of those cities which had already rejected Him. The measure of one's judgment is determined by the measure of his privileges. Those who reject Christ's messengers reject Christ and reject the heavenly Father who sent Him. Where they were not received, they were to turn away shaking the very dust from their feet, showing that they would take away not one thing belonging to the city.

3. The Return of the Seventy (10:17-24).

a. Their report (v. 17). They were highly elated. They seemed to be agreeably surprised. They not only found that they could heal the sick, but cast out demons also. They seemed to be filled with self-satisfaction. It is easy, even in Christian service, to be spoiled by our successes.

b. Jesus' answer (vv. 18-24).

(1) He told them that it was no surprise to Him (vv. 18, 19). With prophetic eye He saw their success as indicating that time when the prince of this world would be overthrown (John 12:31). By virtue of His mighty triumph over Satan He assures them that they need have no fear of what would befall them. Nothing could harm them. Nothing could prosper which opposed them. Indeed, nothing can harm the servant who goes about his Master's business.

(2) Real cause for rejoicing (v. 20). He promptly rebuked them, telling them that their chief joy should be because of their heavenly relation, not because of these miraculous gifts. That above all which should provoke gratitude is the fact that God has chosen us in Christ and saved us, inscribing our names in Heaven.

(3) Jesus' exultation (vv. 21, 22). The consciousness that soon the victory would be won because God had committed all things unto Him, and that only as men received Him could they know the Father, caused Him to rejoice in what was being accomplished.

(4) Jesus congratulates the disciples (vv. 23, 24). He assured them that they were sharing privileges which had been denied

to many of the prophets and kings. To share in the opportunity of making known Jesus Christ is greater than being king.

D. *The Good Samaritan* (10:25-37).

1. How to Inherit Eternal Life (10:25-28).

a. The lawyer's question (v. 25). *Lawyer* here means one versed in religious law, the Scriptures—not lawyer in our modern sense of that term. It would more nearly correspond to a theological professor. The lawyer's object was to trap Jesus—to induce Him to take such a stand as would weaken His influence as a Teacher. He expected Jesus to set forth some new ceremonies which would conflict with or disparage the Law.

b. Jesus' question (v. 26). Though Jesus knew the motive of the lawyer he did not evade his question. He sent him to the law, the field which was familiar to him. He thus was robbed of his own weapon.

c. The lawyer's reply (v. 27). He made an intelligent answer declaring that the entire content of the law was embraced in love to God and man. This expresses the whole of human duty.

d. Jesus' reply (v. 28). This straightforward answer went to the heart of the lawyer. Perfect love to God and man is truly the way of life. No man has yet had or can have such love. His sinful condition precludes its possibility. Man's failure to measure up to this requirement is his condemnation. The lawyer keenly felt this thrust. He was defeated on his own grounds and convicted of guilt.

2. "Who Is My Neighbor?" (10:29-37).

a. The lawyer's question (v. 29). This question reveals the insincerity of the lawyer. Christ's answer had reached his conscience, and now he seeks to escape the difficulty by asking a captious question. Lawyer-like he sought to get off by raising a question as to the meaning of words.

b. Jesus' answer (vv. 30-37). This more than answered the lawyer's question. In the parable of the Good Samaritan He makes clear who is a neighbor, and also what it means to be a neighbor, or what loving a neighbor means. Christ's answer had a double meaning. He not only made clear who is my neighbor, but made it clear that the lawyer was not playing the neighbor. He thus was convicted of not having been a neighbor.

(1) "Who is my neighbor?" This destitute, wounded man left on the highway by the robbers is the man who needs a neighbor. My neighbor, therefore, is the one who needs my help, whether he lives next door or on the other side of the world. Those who have the Spirit of Christ can see their neighbors on every hand.

(2) What being a neighbor means. Our supreme concern should not be, "Who is my neighbor?" but, "Whose neighbor am I?" To be a neighbor is:

(a) To be on the lookout for those in need of our help (v. 33).

(b) To have compassion on the needy (v. 33). Christ's compassion was aroused as He came into contact with those who were suffering and in need. All those who have His nature will be likewise moved.

(c) To give to those in need (v. 34). Many are willing to give money to help the poor and needy, but are unwilling to personally minister to them. Many times the personal touch is more important than the material aid. We should give ourselves as well as our money.

(d) To bind up wounds (v. 34).

(e) To set the helpless ones on our beasts while we walk (v. 34). This is proof that love is genuine. Christians will deny themselves in order to have something to give to those who have need. This kind of sympathy is greatly needed today.

(f) To bring to the inn and take care of the unfortunate (v. 34). Genuine love does not leave its service incomplete. Much Christian service is spasmodic—helps and then leaves a man to take care of himself.

(g) To give money (v. 35). It costs a good deal to be a neighbor. Love is the most expensive thing in the world. It cost God His only Son. It cost Christ His life. May we go and do likewise!

E. *Jesus with Martha and Mary* (10:38-42).

There is no place where true character is so clearly revealed as at home. The world is much richer because of this scene in the Bethany home.

1. His Reception (10:38).

Martha was the head of the home, therefore she received Him. We are not told as to why it was her house; perhaps it was because she was the oldest of the family. Jesus must have greatly appreciated the fact that there was one home into which He was welcome. It would be a fine thing if all homes were open to receive Jesus.

2. Mary Sits at Jesus' Feet (10:39).

She, of fine spiritual discernment, knew that sitting at the Lord's feet and hearing His word was that which would please Him most. He was more concerned with opportunity to reveal Himself to human hearts than with the eating of well-prepared meals. Mary's way of entertaining Jesus was more acceptable to Him than that of Martha. She was getting that for which her heart yearned, and at the same time pleasing the Lord.

3. Martha Is Cumbered About Much Serving (10:40).

Both sisters loved the Lord. It would be impossible to say which loved the more; but Martha was bent on providing a fine meal for Him. She was trying to do so many things that she was on the verge of distraction. This had so upset her that she found fault with Jesus for permitting Mary to leave the kitchen to listen to His teaching. Not only did she criticize her sister and Jesus, but she assumed the authority to command Him to send Mary back to the kitchen to help.

4. Jesus' Answer (10:41, 52).

a. Rebukes Martha (v. 41). He did this tenderly, for He knew that she loved Him sincerely. Many today who truly love Jesus are distracted with the many things in serving.

b. Defends Mary (v. 42). He declared that but one thing was needful and that Mary had chosen that good part which could not be taken away from her. The one thing needful is a heart for the Lord, which brings to Jesus its possessor to hear His teaching. Those who have chosen this good part can never be robbed of it. Because of this choice and what she gained through the Lord's teaching, in the day when death entered the home she was calm, and in the hour when all the rest of the disciples were slow to discern, she rendered loving service to the Lord in anointing Him in anticipation of His burial.

F. *Jesus' Teaching Concerning Prayer* (11:1-13).

Prayer ought to be a matter of great concern to every believer, for the Lord is nigh unto all them that truly call upon Him; He will hear their cry and will save them (Ps. 145:18). The range of prayer is from the depths of the soul to the very thoughts of God. There was something about the praying of Jesus that so impressed the disciples that they requested Him to teach them to pray (v. 1). We nowhere read of their asking Him to teach them how to preach. Praying is more important than preaching. No one is fit to teach or preach who does not know how to pray. May each one enroll at once in the school of prayer with Christ as Teacher. In response to the disciples' request He outlines the following principles of prayer:

1. The Right Relationship of the One Praying (11:2).

a. Filial—"Father." In order to pray to God, the suppliant must be a child of God. God is a Father; His gifts and blessings are for His children. This relationship can only be entered into through regeneration. Not all men have a right to say "Our Father" when addressing God. Only those who are children of God by faith in Jesus Christ can so address Him.

b. Fraternal—"Our Father." God has more than one child. His children are bound up together in nature and interests. Even in our secret prayer we should address Him as "Our Father," which is a recognition of the interests of others alongside ours.

2. The Right Attitude in Prayer (11:2).

a. Reverent adoration. As children we have certain privileges, and yet holy reverence becomes us. We should hallow His name; we should adore Him as the eternal God.

b. Loyalty. When praying to God we should come with the spirit of loyalty which cries out, "Thy kingdom come." We should not only receive Him as the Lord of our lives, but should dedicate our lives to bringing in the rule of God in the earth.

c. Submission—"Thy will be done." We should have no will of our own regarding the rule of God. We should let Him direct us in all things.

3. The Right Spirit (11:3-8).

a. Dependent faith—"Give us our daily bread" (v. 3). We should realize that not only what we have, but life itself is ours to enjoy because of Him, and that He is able to do for us exceeding abundantly above all that we ask or think.

b. Penitence and love—"Forgive us our debts" (v. 4). We should come to Him realizing that we have sinned and cry unto Him for forgiveness. Our hearts should be so filled with love for others that we will forgive those who sin against us as God is willing to forgive us.

c. Holiness and caution—"Lead us not into temptation" (v. 4). Because we are God's children, and realizing the depravity of our natures and the consequent tendency to practice that which displeases Him, we should shrink from that which if indulged in would dishonor Him, and earnestly cry unto Him to lead us not into the place where we would likely fall.

d. Intercessory (vv. 5, 6). The man who asked for bread did not ask for himself, but for a friend. Prayer which pleases God is unselfish in its requests. It takes in the needs of all those in need, rather than those of the one praying.

e. Perseverance (vv. 7, 8). Though his friend refused at first and offered excuse, because he would not take no for an answer, he arose from his bed and gave him as many as he needed. Prayer which pleases God and gets results is importunate, perseveres until the object is achieved.

4. Encouragement to Pray (11:9-12).

a. God's promise (vv. 9, 10). True prayer cannot fail of an answer, because God definitely promises that everyone that asketh receiveth, he that seeketh findeth, and to him that knocketh it shall be opened.

b. The example of an earthly father (vv. 11-13). No father will give a stone to his son who asks for bread, or a serpent instead of a fish, or a scorpion instead of an egg. God is infinitely more willing to answer the prayers of His children than earthly parents are to give good gifts to their children.

5. The True Goal of All Prayers (11:13).

God's best gift is Himself in the Person of His Holy Spirit. All those who practice the principles which Jesus taught in this model prayer shall be blessed with the gift of the Holy Spirit.

G. *Jesus Enduring the Contradiction of Sinners Against Himself* (11:14-54).

1. Charged with Being in League with the Devil (11:14-23).

Being unwilling to receive Him as the Son of God, and yet unable to account for His mighty works, they declared that He was casting out demons through Beelzebub, the chief of the demons. He exposed the fallacy of their reasoning by showing that such would array Satan against himself, and he would thus destroy his own kingdom.

2. Refusal to Believe His Miracles (11:29-32).

They asked for a sign, to which He replied that they would have a sign from Heaven in His death and resurrection. He reminded them, however, that their request showed unbelief surpassing that of the heathen queen of the South, and the wicked people of Nineveh.

3. Wickedness Denounced (11:37-54).

He pronounced six woes upon those who were opposing Him and seeking His destruction—three upon the Pharisees and three upon the lawyers. Religion with these had degenerated into matters of form and ritual. This should be taken to heart by all, for it is ever the tendency among us. Sometimes there are to be found unrealities in our lives of which we may not be conscious.

a. The Pharisees (vv. 37-41). These He denounced for:

(1) Punctiliously observing some minute rites while at the same time breaking the Ten Commandments. They carefully tithed the small herbs of the garden while practicing injustice to their fellow men and withholding love from God. He pointed out to them the folly of attending to these external acts while the heart was filled with wickedness. It was as absurd as merely washing the outside of an unclean cup. A more important preparation for eating would be to make some gift to the poor, rather than the washing of the hands. However, He does not disregard the desirability of washing before eating. "These ought ye to have done, and not to leave the other undone."

(2) Desire for public recognition (v. 43). This is a common sin today. Vanity and pride may be asserting themselves while we are unconscious of their presence. Love for titles of respect and position of prominence is a very common sin.

(3) Feigning humility (v. 44). He compares their hypocrisy to graves which are on a level with the ground and may be stepped upon unconsciously by someone and thus defiled. We can avoid those who made their vanity known by arrogant boasting, but

some are filled with this same wickedness who do not thus make it known.

b. The lawyers (vv. 45-54). Jesus' strictures on the hypocritical Pharisees aroused the lawyers, one of whom indignantly declared, "You are insulting us also." In replying to this, Christ pronounced three woes upon them:

(1) For placing burdensome requirements upon the people to which they themselves would not submit (v. 46). Religion should not be made irksome. To do so is displeasing to God.

(2) For the murder of God's prophets (vv. 47-51). He shows that their attitude toward Him was the same that was shown to the prophets by their fathers. Their diabolical murdering was done in the name of religion. Religious fanaticism has done much wickedness, even killing God's holy prophets and messengers. Jesus declares that their guilt was the same as that of their fathers and that their generation would be held responsible for all that the fathers had done.

(3) For keeping back the knowledge of God by false interpretation of the Scriptures (vv. 52-54). There is no wickedness perhaps so great as that of supposed teachers of God's Word who keep its precious truths from the people by perverting its meaning. These woes apply to many professed teachers today. What awful judgment must befall those who are thus withholding the knowledge of God from the people! This exposure of their hypocrisy set them in a rage, causing them to hate Him more violently.

H. *Warning Against the Leaven of the Pharisees* (12:1-7).

This leaven was hypocrisy. They testified with their lips, but their hearts were away from God. Their manner of life revealed the falsity of their testimony. Violence is to be expected in the world. Those whose words and manner of life are true to Christ shall suffer persecution.

I. *Importance of Confessing Christ* (12:8-12).

1. Not Easy (12:8, 9).

To confess Christ is not easy; it has never been easy. To do so means exposure to ridicule, contempt, and persecution. Regardless of its issue, the true disciple will confess his Lord.

a. Christ will confess before the angels of God those who confess Him before men (v. 8). The true disciple will not be ashamed to let all men know that he knows, loves, and serves Christ.

b. Christ will deny before the angels of God those who deny Him before men (v. 9). To deny Christ before men may get one a little of human applause, but will surely bring one to loss of Heaven and the sufferings of Hell forever.

2. A Pernicious Testimony Is Unpardonable (12:10).

This testimony is the expression of a heart utterly perverse, attributing the mighty works of the Holy Spirit as wrought by Christ to the Devil (Matt. 12:32; Mark 3:29). The unpardonable sin will only be committed by one whose heart is incurably bad, one whose moral nature is so vile that he fails to discern between God and the Devil—a reprobate.

3. Divine Aid Given in Testimony (12:11, 12).

In the most trying hour the Holy Spirit will teach the disciple what to say, and how to say it.

J. *Warning Against Covetousness* (12:13-21).

1. The Occasion (12:13-15).

One of the company requested Jesus to be judge in a disputed estate. Two brothers were in trouble over an inheritance. We are not told who was to blame, perhaps the trouble was the result of covetousness on the part of both. Christ refused to enter the sphere of the civil law and warned against the spirit of avarice. Christ's mission was pre-eminently spiritual. His action is a warning against the church or against the minister departing from the spiritual to perform a civil and commercial service. His teachings embrace principles which will adjust all such matters. The minister who devotes his attention to inculcating these principles into the hearts of the people will accomplish infinitely more than to invade the realm of the civil and commercial. The Church and State should be separate.

2. Enforcement of the Warning (12:16-21).

The parable of the rich man shows clearly that to be concerned with earthly riches while neglecting God is the height of folly. The Lord's warning is of great importance today; for many are seeking gold and forgetting God.

a. His increase in goods (v. 16). His riches were rightly obtained, for the ground brought forth plentifully. This shows that a man may be rich because of the Lord's blessing upon him. It is not sinful to be rich. The money of some rich men is unquestionably without taint.

b. His perplexity (v. 17). His land was producing more than his barns would hold. His perplexity was to know what to do. He did not want it to go to waste. No frugal man wants to see the legitimate fruits of his toil perish. If he had possessed right views of life and a sense of stewardship before God, he would have seen that his barns, at least, had enough for his personal needs, and that he could have distributed his surplus to the needy and for benevolent purposes. He could have found pleasure in this service and escaped the task of building larger barns. Many honest and honorable rich men have been caught in the trap of avarice.

c. The fatal choice (vv. 18, 19). He chose to enlarge his barns and give up his life to ease and luxury. It ought to be a delightful task for men whom God has made rich to devote their time and energy to the distribution of their possessions to benevolent purposes. How sad to see capable men the victims of their circumstances! Man owns nothing; he owes everything to God.

d. The awful indictment (vv. 20, 21). God calls him a fool. This is no arbitrary judgment. Riches furnish neither contentment in life nor guarantee continuance of life. It is not only foolish, but madness to forget God while engaged in heaping up riches. Soon the man must die, and his riches may get into the hands of unworthy men or even curse the lives of the children who inherit them.

K. *The Certain Cure for Anxiety* (12:22-34).

Having shown the folly of the rich man who gained gold and lost God, He now urged the disciples to trust God and dismiss all anxious care. He assures them that they need not be anxious even for the necessities of life.

1. The Arguments (12:22, 23).

This is summed up in one brief sentence: "The life is more than food, and the body is more than raiment." The God who gave the life and made the body should be trusted to provide food and clothing.

2. The Illustrations (12:24-28).

a. God's care for the fowls (vv. 24-26). The ravens do not

sow or reap—they have not storehouse or barn, yet they live, for God feeds them. If God does not forget the fowls, certainly He would do more for His children, created in His likeness and image, and redeemed by the precious blood of Christ.

b. God's care for the flowers of the field (vv. 27, 28). If God is so careful of those flowers which appear but for a day, how much more will He clothe His children!

3. The Exhortations (12:29-34).

a. The getting of good clothes should not be the chief concern. To give these things anxious concern is to imitate the heathen, who lack the knowledge of God's care over His children.

b. Seek the kingdom of God (v. 31). Those who make God's kingdom first shall have all their needs supplied (Phil. 4:19).

c. Be not afraid (v. 32). God's good pleasure is upon His own, and all good things He will give.

d. Practice self-denial in order to be able to give gifts to those in need (vv. 33, 34). The doing of such deeds will tend to lift the thoughts upward to God—to trust Him.

L. *Be Ready for the Coming of the Lord* (12:35-40).

Having warned the disciples against the acquisition of worldly goods while forgetting God, and having shown them the needlessness of anxiety for food and clothes, He shows them the blessedness of being in a state of readiness when the Lord shall come. Conviction as to the certainty of the Lord's coming is the sure cure for worldliness and anxious care. This attitude of heart He made clear by two parables—that of the returning of the Lord and that of the thief. The Lord will be so pleased with those who are waiting for Him that He will take delight in sitting at the banquet with them, and will even serve them. The parable of the thief shows that the time of the Lord's coming is not known. The only way to act is to be ready at all times.

M. *The Parable of the Steward and Servants* (12:41-48).

The parable of the Steward and Servants was spoken in answer to Peter's question as to whom the previous parable applied—whether to the disciples or to all men. The coming of the Lord is the touchstone of human destiny. To the believer it will mean full salvation and an eternity of blessedness in Heaven and to the unbeliever it will mean condemnation and eternal woe. All men have been created in the likeness and image of God, all are morally responsible to God. "For God so loved the world, that he gave his only begotten Son, that whosoever believeth in him should not perish, but have everlasting life" (John 3:16). All men are stewards. All rational beings have a sense of obligation. Preaching the Bible is God's way of salvation for all men. The Gospel of Christ is the power of God unto salvation to everyone that believeth. Observe the two kinds of servants.

1. The Faithful and Wise Servant (12:42-44).

He knows his Lord and his duties and wisely administers the affairs of the Lord's household. He serves with the consciousness of the imminent coming of his Lord. He is rewarded by being given rulership over all that the Lord hath.

2. The Unfaithful and Unwise Servant (12:45-48).

He says in his heart, "My lord delayeth his coming," and begins "to beat the menservants and maidens, and to eat and drink, and to be drunken." The hope of the Lord's coming is the supreme, grand incentive to right living and efficient service. The neglect and rejection of the doctrine of the second coming of Christ has resulted in worldliness in living and unfaithfulness in service. The only remedy for this deplorable condition is the return to the faithful preaching of the truths of the Bible.

Sure punishment awaits the unfaithful servant. His lord "will come in a day when he looketh not for him . . . and cut him in sunder, and will appoint him his portion with the unbelievers." More than that he shall be beaten with many stripes.

N. *Christ a Divider of Men* (12:49-59).

Christ's answer to His own question put to the disciples—"Suppose ye that I am come to give peace on earth?"—seems to be a contradiction to the song of the angels to the shepherds when they sang: "Glory to God in the highest, and on earth peace, good will toward men." The angels expressed God's attitude and desire for men. Christ's answer is a declaration of the fact that His coming would issue in strife and bloodshed among men. According to Matthew's record, Christ said: "I came not to send peace, but a sword" (Matt. 10:34).

For an understanding as to why strife and war are so widely prevalent we must go back to the fall of man. God's penalty on man's rebellion was undying enmity between Satan and the woman, and their respective seeds (Gen. 3:15). The Devil sees to it that division and strife in the home and between nations characterize every generation. The unregenerated heart violently reacts toward Christ and His Church. "The natural man receiveth not the things of the Spirit of God" (I Cor. 2:14). Birth from above is necessary. When Christ said: "Suppose ye that I am come to give peace on earth? I tell you, Nay; but rather division," He referred to His Incarnation. His Incarnation was for the purpose of dying on the cross. "Forasmuch then as the children are partakers of flesh and blood, he also himself likewise took part of the same; that through death he might destroy him that had the power of death, that is, the devil" (Heb. 2:14). The cross was clearly in view when these words were uttered. "Now is the judgment of this world: now shall the prince of this world be cast out" (John 12:31). The cross of Christ divides men. Peace cannot come by compromise. There is no substitute for victory. Life out of death is the law of the universe both physical and spiritual. "Except a corn of wheat fall into the ground and die, it abideth alone" (John 12:24).

The time is coming when individuals and nations shall be at peace. When the kingdom of Christ shall be established there will be peace and good will on earth.

O. *A Call to Repentance* (13:1-9).

Repentance is necessary on the part of all, since all are sinners. "The wages of sin is death" (Rom. 6:23). While God is unalterably opposed to sin, He is infinitely gracious. His holy nature compels Him to cause judgment to fall upon those who will not turn from their sins to serve Him. Repentance is not merely a matter of privilege, but of absolute necessity. It is not a question as to how great a sinner one is as to whether he needs to repent, since God cannot look upon evil: "Thou art of purer eyes than to behold evil, and canst not look on iniquity" (Hab. 1:13). God commands men to repent (Acts 17:30).

P. *Jesus Releases a Woman from an Infirmity* (13:10-17).

What Jesus did on the sabbath frequently brought Him into serious conflict with the Pharisees. Through the petty rules and regulations they had made this holy day, which God designed as a day of rest and the doing of deeds of mercy, a day of burden and hardship. Jesus did not disregard the sabbath, but broke through their traditions and showed that the sabbath was made for man, and not man for the sabbath. Religious rites and ceremonies should not be hardened into fetters to bind the worshiper.

1. Jesus Teaching on the Sabbath Day (13:10).

It was the Lord's custom to go to the place of worship on the sabbath day. His disciples will imitate Him in this. At the place of worship there is opportunity to be nearest to God to worship Him, and to our fellow man to sympathize and to show mercy and kindness.

2. Jesus Healing on the Sabbath (13:11-13).

Jesus was first a Teacher and afterward a Healer. It is the business of the ministry of the church today to make known God's will by preaching and teaching.

a. A woman in need (v. 11). This poor woman's back was bowed down with eighteen years of great suffering. Though thus afflicted she found her way to the place of worship. Men and women are in great need today. Their bodies may not be bowed down with physical suffering, but there are many bowed down with the burden of sin and sorrow.

b. Called to Jesus (v. 12). He is always quick to discern those who are burdened. He spake the word of healing to her. How welcome must have been His words. He is calling today to the many who are weighted down with guilty consciences to come to Him.

c. Laid His hands upon her (v. 13). At His touch she was made straight and glorified God. It was not enough to teach. He showed His sympathy by coming into touch with the suffering woman. Christ's followers are to imitate Him in teaching and also in coming into direct touch with the needy, sinful, and burdened world.

3. The Indignation of the Ruler of the Synagogue (13:14).

This man feigned indignation. Under a pious pretense of loyalty to God he showed that ritual is of more importance than mercy and love. It was not primarily concern for ritual, but hatred for Jesus that moved him to indignation. He was too cowardly to attack the Lord directly, so he turned to the people and struck at Him over their backs. He pretended great concern for the healing of the people, but advised that they come in the six days and not thus have the sabbath profaned by such sacrilegious act as the healing of this poor woman. This man is a type of the many hypocrites among us today. The liquor interests today are hypocritically talking of the sacred rights of personal liberty. They go on trampling down the sacred rights of men and women until their own interests are involved. Their claim is as hollow as that of doing away with the Ten Commandments because they interfere with the personal liberty of the murderer and thief. We should all examine ourselves as to whether there may not be a hypocritical Pharisee lurking in our own bosom, when even in the ministry a rival appears with gifts exceeding ours. Sometimes the charge of heresy may be an utterance of the old Pharisee. The party accused may be more orthodox than the accuser.

4. The Lord's Reply to the Ruler (13:15, 16).

Jesus removes the mask of hypocrisy from the ruler as He points out his own custom as a condemnation of his pious pretense. He argues from the lesser to the greater. If it was right to take animals, which had only been tied for a few hours, to water on the sabbath day, certainly it was right to bring relief to this woman who had been bowed down for eighteen years. Human beings are of more value than animals. This woman was a daughter of Abraham and not a sinner of lowdown character. The principle which Jesus set forth restored the sabbath to its true purpose.

5. Shamed Adversaries and Rejoicing People (13:17).

The tide was now turned. Their exposure was so great that their consciences smote them. The arguments against morals and the church are of the same type today. The opponents of the so-called blue laws are hiding behind the same hypocrisy. The exposure of this hypocrisy will bring joy and rejoicing to multitudes today.

Q. *Jesus Teaching on the Way to Jerusalem* (13:18-35).

1. Parable of the Mustard Seed (13:18, 19).

a. Its unimportant beginning (v. 19). "The least of all the seeds, but grows to be the greatest among herbs." Christ the King was of humble parentage. Some of His disciples were unlettered fishermen. The parentage and humble circumstances of the King greatly perplexed the people. That twelve unlettered men should be selected as His royal advisers is still more amazing. The prophet said concerning Him, that He should be despised, rejected, and forsaken.

b. Its vigorous growth (v. 19). From the very small beginning the movement inaugurated by Jesus Christ has become the mightiest in the earth.

c. Its lodging capacity (v. 19). The birds which find lodgment in the trees do not represent the children of men which find safety and salvation in the Church. The birds constitute no part of the tree; they are foreign to and independent of it. The branches increase the growth of the tree, but birds are injurious and burdensome to it. They are predatory—waiting to pluck the tender buds or to prey upon the ripened fruit. The effect of their lodging in the branches of the tree is evil, blighting and marring its beauty. In Christ's interpretation of the first parable of Matthew 13, He said that the fowls represent the wicked one.

2. The Parable of the Leavened Meal (13:20, 21).

When the scriptural significance of the meal, the woman, and the leaven is known, the interpretation is easy.

a. The meal. Meal is something wholesome and nutritious. It was used in one of the sweet-savor offerings which typified Christ (Lev. 2:1-3, A.S.V.); it was food for the priests (Lev. 6:15-17, A.S.V.); Abraham had Sarah to knead a cake out of three measures of meal for the angelic messengers (Gen. 18:6); Solomon's royal table was provided with it (I Kings 4:22); Elijah was fed upon a cake made of meal (II Kings 4:41); Elisha used meal as an antidote for the poison of death in the pot (II Kings 4:38-41).

b. The woman. The woman is not the head of the home but its administrator. Her responsibility is to take the bread provided by the head of the home, prepare and distribute it to the children. In Scripture we find false doctrine being taught by a woman (Rev. 2:20); dealing with doctrine is forbidden to women (I Tim. 2:12). In I Timothy 4:1-3; II Timothy 2:17, 18; 4:3, 4; II Peter 2:1-3 we find that the apostasy will be brought in through false teaching within the ranks of God's people. The meaning then of this parable is that the true doctrine, the meal, given for the nourishment of the children of the kingdom would officially be corrupted by false doctrine (II Peter 2:2; I Tim. 4:6). The children's food would be corrupted by the mother.

c. The leaven. In Scripture leaven is invariably a type of evil. Let the following examples suffice as proof:

(1) All through the Old Testament leaven is a continual and unvarying type of evil (Exod. 12:15; Lev. 2:11). It is inconceivable that Jesus should arbitrarily change without due notice and explanation a word which the Spirit of God had so unchangingly used for two thousand years from an evil to a good sense.

(2) Jesus Himself makes leaven to denote sin (Matt. 16:6-12; Mark 8:15).

(3) Paul uses leaven in its usual Biblical sense (I Cor. 5:6-8; Gal. 5:8, 9).

This is the only interpretation that will harmonize with Christ's interpretation of the first two parables of Matthew 13. Further facts patent to all prove that the professed church today is feeding upon the leaven of sensuality, formality, and legalism, instead of the unleavened bread of sincerity and truth—the Word of God. Many are handling the Word of God deceitfully (II Cor. 4:2). Multitudes will not endure sound doctrine (II Tim. 4:3, 4).

3. The Narrow Gate (13:22-30).

a. A question asked (v. 23). We are not told the name or the motive of the questioner. Most likely it came from a self-righteous Jew who thought that only a Jew could be saved. At any rate the Lord gave a serious answer.

b. The Lord's answer (vv. 24-30).

(1) Salvation is a matter of personal responsibility. Early in His ministry Christ said: "Strait is the gate, and narrow is the way, which leadeth unto life, and few there be that find it" (Matt. 7:14). Instead of idle speculation as to whether many or few be saved, the Lord urgently exhorted the people to "strive to enter the strait gate."

(2) The reason for personal and immediate action (vv. 24, 25). The invitation is limited. When the master shuts the door,

knocking for entrance will be futile. It will be too late when the Lord declares, " I know you not."

(3) A most solemn and awful day is awaiting the world; the Master of the house shall arise and shut the door; some shall sit down in the kingdom of God; others shall be shut out forevermore. There will be weeping and gnashing of teeth when it is too late.

4. A Message to Herod (13:31-33).

Certain Pharisees informed Jesus that King Herod purposed to kill Him and advised Him to flee for His life. Jesus sent a message of courageous defiance. He said: "Go ye, and tell that fox, Behold, I cast out devils, and do cures today and tomorrow, and the third day I shall be perfected." Christ called the king, "that fox," because He saw Herod's cunning trick which was to induce Jesus to flee to Jerusalem where He would fall into the hands of the Jews. His message was a solemn one, for it reminded Herod that in a little while He would go to the cross, the third day would arise from the grave, and His redemption purposes would be perfected. "For it cannot be that a prophet perish out of Jerusalem."

5. Jesus Laments over Jerusalem (13:34, 35).

He loved the city and people of Jerusalem. He knew that His rejection would hasten the doom of the city. He would gladly have given them salvation and protection, but they would not accept Him. Ruin was inevitable. "Behold, your house is left unto you desolate: and verily I say unto you, Ye shall not see me, until the time come when ye shall say, Blessed is he that cometh in the name of the Lord."

R. *Jesus a Sabbath Guest* (14:1-14).

1. Dining with a Pharisee (14:1).

Jesus was not an ascetic. He entered freely into the common social customs of the day. We see Him at a wedding, a dinner party, in the home of sickness, and at a funeral. He was truly a Man among men. He was unlike John the Baptist in this respect. The Christian's influence is best when mingling with his fellows in all right relations and positions in life, even though selfish and evil-minded men are found among them. This does not mean that he should be a partaker of their deeds. Jesus in thus moving in all circles of human society showed the divine sympathy. This prominent social function was on a sabbath day. While Jesus was *in* society, He was not *of* it. So should the Chrisitan be. Jesus was in a company outwardly courteous but inwardly hostile. Doubtless the motive of the invitation was to find an occasion against Him. This is implied in the statement, "they watched him."

2. Healing a Dropsical Man (14:2-6).

a. Why this man was present (v. 2). There is no way of absolutely determining it, but likely it was part of a plot of the Pharisees to trap Jesus by getting Him to violate the sabbath rules.

b. Jesus' question (v. 3). Jesus' question was an answer to the thoughts of the lawyers and Pharisees who were watching Him, for they had not spoken. Before healing this man He submitted the case to their judgment. They were free on the sabbath day to hold a feast where their selfish pride and vanity could be displayed, but they were horrified that a fellow man should be healed on the sabbath. They were silent because their consciences made them ashamed of their heartlessness.

c. Healing the man (v. 4). While they were in a state of embarrassment, Jesus healed the man and let him go.

d. Jesus rebuked them (vv. 5, 6). He laid bare their hypocrisy by showing them that their willingness to show mercy to a beast on the sabbath should induce them to regard as not sinful the relieving of a human being of distress on the sabbath. They were again silent, for they perceived their inconsistency and inhumanity. Surely man is more than a beast.

3. Jesus Rebukes Selfish Ambition (14:7-11).

a. The occasion (v. 7). He observed that the guests while taking their places at the table chose the best seats for themselves. This is still true of men and women. In the trains, hotels, streetcars, busses, etc. they scramble for the best places. In the homes even members of the same family will try to get the best food, etc.

b. Instruction given (vv. 8-11). When bidden to a feast take the lowest place, lest you suffer humiliation of being asked to take a lower seat. This is more than a lesson on courtesy or table manners; it is a severe rebuke of that selfishness which fills the human heart, causing it to seek to be ministered unto instead of ministering to others. Unselfishness will express itself in humbly taking the lowest place, esteeming others better than ourselves. Jesus declares that the fundamental principle of the philosophy governing the moral world is: "Whosoever exalteth himself shall be abased; and he that humbleth himself shall be exalted." Those who live humbly and modestly, unconcerned about their own selfish interests, shall receive the very best for themselves. The one who has experienced the redeeming love of Christ will gladly take the place assigned him. faithfully doing his work without effort to be noticed, and courteously recognizing the rights of others.

4. The True Motive in Deeds of Charity (14:12-14).

Jesus takes advantage of this social occasion to teach a great principle. The Jews, like many of the rich today, made social dinners occasions for display. They invited only those whose wealth would enable them to invite in return, even with the prospect of greater display. Jesus took note of the selfishness thus displayed and set forth to them the right principle, namely, that they should extend their hospitality to the poor and afflicted. All charitable deeds should be done with unselfish motives. Our aim should be to confer benefits not expecting a recompense. Jesus assured them that recompense would be made at the resurrection of the just. This does not mean that friends and neighbors of certain rank should never exchange pleasant hospitalities. Wealth should be used to confer blessings upon the poor and needy instead of ministering to the pride and vanity of the possessor.

S. *Jesus Teaching in Parables* (14:15–15:32).

1. A Great Supper (14:15-24).

a. Partaking of food periodically is necessary and pleasurable. Activities of life consume vitality. Replacement is necessary to continued existence and service. The consciousness of need and the pleasure of eating furnish a double incentive for eating. With normal people the call to supper is eagerly looked for and greatly enjoyed. The "certain man" who made the supper is the living God who has sent Jesus Christ, the "Bread of Life" to hungry and needy humans. The supper is a great one because of the greatness of the One who prepared and the greatness of the need of the human race.

b. The invitation given—"Come for all things are now ready" (v. 17). The purpose of God was on the eve of fulfillment. The fullness of redemption through the sacrifice of Jesus Christ on the cross was at hand. Salvation so full and free to all who will accept Christ.

c. The flimsy excuses offered (vv. 18-20). Not one valid reason for nonacceptance was offered. Pleasure and profit were placed before need and honor. Every excuse offered was a pretext for ignoring the invitation.

d. The anger of the Lord (vv. 21-24). The action of the invited guests was an insult to the Lord, who declared that none of the men bidden "should taste of my supper." What a picture of the sinning human race for nearly 2,000 years!

2. A Test of Discipleship (14:25-33).

The Lord did not wish to discourage men from following Him, but wanted them to fully count the cost of their action. He wants His disciples to know that following Him meant great sacrifice and suffering, willingness to part with all they possessed, even to giving up their lives. Hating their kindred did not mean to cease loving them, but to give Christ the pre-eminence in their lives.

The Lord further illustrated the necessity of counting the cost by the folly and shame which follow the effort to build a tower, without being able to finish it even after the foundation has been laid; and the peril of a king going to war without being sure that he has at his command a mightier army to overcome his enemy.

3. The Lost Sheep and Lost Coin (15:1-10). Jesus answered the murmuring of the Pharisees and the scribes that Jesus receiveth sinners and eateth with them. "The Son of man came to seek and to save that which was lost" (19:10). The sheep was lost so it needed a shepherd to find it. The coin was lost so it needed a finder. Christ associated with the lost in order to save the lost.

McClaren says: "The sheep was lost because it had only animal instinct; it only followed its taste for grass and wandered away from the shepherd. The coin was lost because it was without life; it had weight so it fell." The Lord's reason for association with sinners was because they were lost and needed a Saviour.

4. The Prodigal Son (15:11-32).

The center of interest in this parable is not the prodigal or his brother, but the "certain man who had two sons." In this parable, in a most picturesque and dramatic manner, the history of man is portrayed, from his fall to his reconciliation with God. The whole orbit of revelation is swept as it pertains to a sinning race and a pardoning God. He who fails to see the heart of our Father God will miss the purpose of the parable.

a. The son's insubordination (v. 12). There is every indication that this was a happy home. But the Devil entered it and stirred up discontent in the heart of the younger son. He became tired of the restraints of home. His desire for freedom moved him to willfully choose to leave home, throwing off the constraints of his father's rule. Sin is the desire to be free from the restraints of rightful authority and for selfish indulgence. It starts out with wrong thoughts about God. At the request of the son, the father "divided unto them his living." Man is a free being. He has been given this freedom by his Creator. God has committed to man his own destiny. Man can go away from God if he wills.

b. The son's departure (v. 13). Having made the fatal decision he went posthaste to the enjoyment of his cherished vision, so he got his goods in portable shape. Having thrown off the restraints of his father's rule he eagerly withdrew from his father's presence. This is always the way sin works. Adam and Eve hid themselves after they had sinned. The son could not now stand the presence of his father, so he hastened away. He "gathered all together." When the sinner casts off allegiance to God he takes all that he has with him. He not only wastes his money, but his character is sacrificed.

c. The son's degeneration (vv. 13, 14). He had a good time while his money lasted, but the end came quickly. The indications are that his course was soon run. From plenty in his father's house to destitution in the far country was a short journey. The sinner soon is made to realize the famine when the very powers which ministered to his pleasure are burned out.

d. The son's degradation (vv. 15, 16). He had no friends now to help him when his money was all gone, so he was driven to hire out to a citizen to feed swine. It was quite a change from a son in his father's house to feeding hogs in the far country. So it is; those who will not serve God are made slaves to the Devil to do his bidding (Rom. 6:16). How vividly this portrays the history of many men and women about us! And yet it is a picture of the inevitable consequences of sin. In his shame and disgrace he could not even get the necessary food. The coarse food of the hogs was denied him.

e. The son's restoration (vv. 17-24).

(1) He came to himself (v. 17). When he reflected a bit he was made conscious that though he had wronged his father and ruined himself, yet he was a son of his father. In the days of his sinning he was beside himself. The sinner continues in his sin because he is insane. The world calls the sinner who leaves off his evil ways crazy, but in reality he just becomes sane. If we could only get sinners to think seriously of their condition it would be easier to get them to turn from their sins.

(2) His resolution (v. 18). His reflection ripened into resolution. The picture of his home, where even the hired servants had a superabundance, moved him to make a decision to leave the far country and to go home.

(3) His confession (vv. 18, 19). He acknowledged that his sin was against Heaven and his father, that he had forfeited his right to be called a son, and begged to be given a place as a hired servant. The sinner not only should make a resolution, he should confess his sin. "For with the heart man believeth unto righteousness; and with the mouth confession is made unto salvation" (Rom. 10:10).

(4) His action (v. 20). Action was needed. Resolution will not avail unless accompanied with action. When the confession is genuine, action will follow. Someone has said that the road to Hell is paved with good resolutions.

(5) His reception by his father (vv. 20-24). The father had not forgotten his son. During these years he longed for his return. He must have looked for him, for he saw him when he was a great way off. So anxious was he for him that he ran to meet him and fell upon his neck and kissed him. So glad was the father that he even did not hear his confession through, but ordered the tokens of honor to be placed upon him, receiving him back into a son's position. Then the feast was made, expressive of the joy of his heart. God is love. Jesus came to reveal God. This parable makes bare God's heart. Every teacher should strive to present this lesson so as to show God's forgiving mercy, His willingness to receive back His wayward child.

f. The behavior of the elder son (vv. 25-32). The father accepts unchallenged the elder son's statement as to his fidelity and the prodigality of his brother, but insists that the return of the prodigal is an occasion for rejoicing. When the prodigal returned he was not watching with the father, he was in the field; "when he learned that his brother had been welcomed to the home he was filled with anger. He refused to enter the house and when his father came out to entreat him, he accused him of partiality and unkindness. His words described admirably the self-righteous Pharisees, 'Neither transgressed I at any time thy commandment'; they also show how little he appreciated his true privileges, 'Thou never gavest me a kid.' The reply of his father intimates the possibilities which he never enjoyed: 'Son, thou art ever with me, and all that I have is thine.' " The elder son is a graphic portrayal of the Pharisee who was without love for the salvation of the repentant publicans and sinners.

Dr. Erdman says: "The elder brother knew nothing of the experience of a true son."

T. *The Unrighteous Steward* (16:1-13).

1. His Accusation (16:1).

He was accused of having wasted his lord's goods.

2. Called to Account (16:2).

The master called the man to account and apparently discharged him without giving an opportunity to defend himself. The case was so notorious that the steward knew his case was hopeless.

3. His Perfidious Act (16:3-7).

After some cogitation he declared, "I cannot dig; to beg I am ashamed." This was followed by the resolution to defraud his lord and involve his lord's debtors in his perfidy (vv. 5-7).

4. The Reaction of the Lord of the Steward (16:8).

He commended the steward for his sagacity, not the act of fraud by which he was robbed, but his worldly shrewdness. Remember that commendation is not that of the Lord Jesus Christ, but of the lord of the steward. Christ could not commend rascality, even the shrewd rascality of the world.

5. The Application of the Parable (16:9-13).

This story doubtless was intended to illustrate the stewardship of temporal possessions. It has no reference to salvation, for salvation is a matter of grace through faith (Eph. 2:8).

a. The proper use of money applies to the rich and the poor. Christ says: "He that is faithful in that which is least is faithful also in much: and he that is unjust in the least is unjust also in much" (v. 10).

b. The actuating motive of meritorious service is love for the one served (v. 13). The secret of the failure of the unjust steward was disloyalty to his lord. He was really seeking to serve himself rather than his master who employed him. The one who really loves his Lord will be faithful in the use of that which has been entrusted to him. He was merely a slave.

The danger to the Christian is divided allegiance. "No servant can serve two masters: for either he will hate the one, and love the other; or else he will hold to the one, and despise the other. Ye cannot serve God and mammon."

U. *The Rich Man and Lazarus* (16:19-31).

In this scripture portion we are afforded a look into two worlds where we see disclosed extremes of character and conditions. In this world we see a rich man reveling in luxury, and a poor man in sore affliction begging at the rich man's gate. In the other world we see the same men with reversed positions—the poor beggar is enjoying the richest blessings of Heaven, while the former rich man is suffering the torments of Hell. No more graphic picture could be drawn showing the contrast of two lives. These lives were intended to be representative. The rich man descends from the highest pinnacle of worldly enjoyment to the depths of endless misery. The poor beggar ascends from utter wretchedness and misery to the loftiest heights of blessing. The application of this story is as vital today as when Jesus uttered it.

1. Contrasted Lives (16:19-21).

a. The rich man (v. 19). He lived in a mansion secluded from the common people. He was clothed in costly raiment; his outer garments were of purple and his inner garments of fine linen. This dress was most expensive. He fed upon the richest food that could be provided. No expense was spared to furnish that which would gratify his appetite. Observe that this man is not said to have illicitly gained his riches; neither is any good deed recorded. His sin was to selfishly indulge his appetites without consideration for others.

b. The beggar (vv. 20, 21). He was laid at the rich man's gate with the hope of getting at least the crumbs from his table. No consideration was given him by the rich man. The dogs of the street were kinder to him than the rich man. Though destitute and helpless the poor man's name is most suggestive. Lazarus means "God is a help," indicating that a godly life shone through his poverty. We learn from these contrasted lives that worldly condition is no sure test of a man's state in the sight of God. Rich men are not all wicked or selfish, and not all poor men are godly.

2. Contrasted Deaths and Burials (16:22).

a. The beggar. He was found dead and his body hurried off to a pauper's grave. No notice was taken of it by the world. The only loss to the world was that he was no longer to be seen at the gate of the rich man.

b. The rich man. He also died. His gold could not bribe the messenger of death. Doubtless a costly funeral was held, attended by those who moved in his class of society. No doubt great eulogies were pronounced by the officiating priest. Death is the common end to which all classes must come. It is here that the lines of all lives meet.

3. Contrasted Destinies (16:23).

a. The beggar. He was at once carried by the angels into Abraham's bosom. The souls of believers are especially cared for at the hour of death. They go immediately to be with the Lord. Those who live right at the hour of death are set free from this mortal body and are ushered into the presence of Christ. Destinies are determined in this life.

b. The rich man. Though he had an elaborate burial he lifted up his eyes in Hell, being in torment. When the veil of futurity is lifted we see that the positions of these men are reversed. The poor man is in the company of just men made perfect, because of his godly life while on earth, and the rich man is stripped of his purple and fine linen and cast into Hell with all wicked men, because while on earth he only lived for selfish ends. There is a time coming when the inequalities of this life shall be righted.

4. The Reality and Fixedness of Life Beyond the Grave (16:24-31).

a. The cry for mercy (v. 24). Dives, which is the Latin name for "rich man," was now willing to claim relationship to Abraham. He is keenly conscious, and the appetites which controlled him while on earth were still with him. Instead of a means of gratification they were now an instrument of torture. Part of the torment of Hell will be the cravings of appetite and lust, with no means of their gratification.

b. Abraham's reply (v. 25). This reply cast the matter back upon the man's memory. He said, "Son, remember." The lashings of a guilty conscience will be most real in Hell. The only thing to do will be to remember the cause which led to the awful destiny. And there it will be remembered that the doom is just.

c. Their fixedness (v. 26). Human destinies are fixed by the choices made during life. When one passes out of this life he enters into a state and condition unchangeable.

d. God's Word the all-sufficient light (vv. 27-31). Dives now requested that Lazarus go on an errand of mercy to his brethren. He regarded the testimony of a spirit of more value than the Word of God. Abraham declared that God's Word is sufficient, that those who reject Moses and the prophets would not repent though visited by one who had risen from the dead. The greatest miracles will not affect the hearts of men who reject the Bible. Men will learn the value of a soul when it is too late.

V. *Warnings to the Disciples* (17:1-10).

1. As to Offenses (17:1, 2).

a. They are inevitable—variableness of human temperaments, the universality of sin, the power, cunning, and malice of the evil one render offenses as certain.

b. "Woe unto him, through whom they come" (v. 1)! Death at the bottom of the sea would be better than to cause a believer to stumble. This should be a solemn warning to those who might cause an offense.

2. As to Forgiveness of the Offender (17:3, 4).

The offender should be rebuked. If he repent, he should be forgiven. Should this offense occur repeatedly—even seven times a day —forgiveness should follow sincere repentance.

3. As to the Destitution of Their Faith (17:5, 6).

The disciples recognizing their lack of such faith asked the Lord for an increase of faith. To this the Lord replied: "If ye had faith as a grain of mustard seed, ye might say unto this sycamine tree, Be thou plucked up by the root, and be thou planted in the sea; and it should obey you."

4. By a Parable of Service (17:7-10).

This parable should be a rebuke to all human expectation of reward for doing one's duty. This generation greatly needs to be shown the meaning of duty. There is a certain *oughtness* in the very constitution of personal beings which regulates conduct. Parents train their children to expect pay for doing what is their duty. "Jesus taught that no human works however perfect have any claim upon God—they are the fulfillment of duty." *Unprofitable* does not mean worthless, but that one has not gone beyond obligation or duty. Godly living and unselfish service to one's fellow men are required of all human beings because they bear the "likeness and image" of God. Reward, praise, and promotion dare not be substituted for duty and obligation.

W. *Healing of the Ten Lepers* (17:11-19).

Jesus is now on His way to Jerusalem where He shall be offered up for the sins of the people. It is fitting that He should pass through the country of the Samaritans, for He was the Saviour of all men. On this occasion He came into touch with a group of ten lepers, and His healing of them exhibits the condition of human nature and the workings of His divine grace.

1. Their Awful Affliction (17:12).

They were lepers. Leprosy is a contagious disease. It may be unnoticed in the blood of the person for years. It is of such a foul nature that the one thus afflicted was cast out from society. This segregation was in accordance with the Mosaic Law (Lev. 13:46). It was a kind of quarantine measure. Leprosy has always been regarded as a type of sin, even at times visited upon people for some sin. Examples, the leprosy of Naaman (II Kings 5); Gehazi (II Kings 5); Miriam (Num. 12); Uzziah (II Kings 15:5), etc. Sin has come into the world and flows from generation to generation through the racial stream, so that all are sinners (Rom. 5:12). Though sin may be hidden, it eventually breaks out and destroys the body. This is but a prophecy of the consequences of sin. Evidences of this are seen on every hand. There is no need of Bible proof of its reality.

2. Their Cry for Mercy (17:13).

They were in great need. No human help was available. They had somehow heard how Jesus had healed some lepers. Where there is real healing it is bound to be noised about. This roused faith in them. "Faith cometh by hearing, and hearing by the word of God" (Rom. 10:17). As He came their way, the lepers called for mercy. It is the privilege of all sinners to call upon Jesus Christ for mercy. He has healed many, and no failure has been recorded.

3. Bidden To Go to the Priests (17:14).

Before the lepers were healed, they were to show themselves to the priests, according to the Mosaic Law (Lev. 14:1-32). As they went in faith they were healed. While God goes before in the work of salvation, yet He demands faith of the sinner. This faith is the cause of His action. Activity on the sinner's part is necessary so that God's grace can flow into him. Faith expresses itself in action. By this means the divine power and human need are united. The only faith needed is for the sinner to realize the healing power of Christ, and as this is acted upon, there is the consequent increase which results in complete salvation. Cleansing is realized through obedience.

4. The Gratitude of the One (17:15, 16).

Perceiving that he was healed of his leprosy, the one turned back and with a loud voice glorified God. He even fell down on his face and gave thanks. The one least expected to show gratitude for this great mercy was the one who sincerely expressed it.

5. The Ingratitude of the Nine (17:17-19).

Presumably they were Jews. The very ones who should have been most grateful did not show any appreciation. They were content to get much from Christ without giving Him anything. He expects those who experience His salvation to give Him their love and gratitude. It greatly grieves the Lord when saved sinners go off with the blessing of salvation as though they had stolen it. Many take all they can get from Christ and give nothing in return. All the blessings of civilization are ours through Christ, yet how few thank Him for them. The proportion of those who are ungrateful for the blessings which Christ brought is perhaps nine to one. The fact that gratitude was expressed by a Samaritan shows how often we are shamed by the devotion of those less favored than ourselves.

X. *The Coming of the Kingdom* (17:20-37).

The coming of the kingdom is a matter of great importance, and yet strange to say is greatly misunderstood even among earnest believers. The kingdom will be the personal reign of Jesus Christ on this earth. The personal return of the Lord will precede His reign as King. It is manifestly improper to be looking for signs of His coming. He will appear in great splendor and mighty power to set up His kingdom. The believer looks for a Person to appear, not for signs of His appearing. The kingdom of Heaven is the kingdom which the God of Heaven shall set up (Dan. 2:44, 45). This kingdom can never be destroyed.

The occasion of Christ's teaching was the demand of the Pharisees as to when the kingdom of God cometh. Note His reply:

1. To the Pharisees (17:20, 21).

"The kingdom of God cometh not with observation: neither shall they say, Lo here! or, lo there! for, behold, the kingdom of God is within you." He doubtless meant that it would not come in such a manner as they were expecting, or as a visible development. In the Person of the King it was already "in the midst" of them and they did not recognize Him. "Within you" could not apply to these godless Pharisees, but the word should be translated "in the midst of you."

2. To the Disciples (17:22-37).

a. The King who will come to reign must suffer and die—those who rejected Him will not be expecting Him. His return will be sudden and His glorious splendor shall flash across the heavens like lightning.

b. Conditions of the world when He comes (vv. 26-30). The race will be careless, living under the power of carnal lusts, absorbed in the usual occupations of life as were the people before the Flood and the inhabitants of Sodom in the day of its doom.

c. The attitude of those expecting to share the glories of the kingdom will be that of earnestly looking for His coming (vv. 31-33). Such do not come down from the "top of the house" to secure their goods; return from the field; not even look back as Lot's wife. They are ready to go forward with their Lord. It will be a time of separation of those who have been closely related.

Y. *The Ungodly and Unrighteous Judge* (18:1-8).

The purpose of this parable is to encourage Christians to pray to God at all times and under all circumstances in life.

1. Men Ought Always To Pray (18:1).

Prayer is absolutely necessary to the spiritual life. It is to the spiritual life what breathing is to the physical life. Men ought to pray under every variety of circumstances—in times of sorrow and burdens for strength to endure; in times of joy and success for grace to behave aright. Prayer ought to be persisted in even when the answer is not immediately seen. "All men pray at times; to the Christian alone belongs faith-filled and persistent prayer." God hears and answers prayer even when we do not understand the mysteries of delay.

2. The Urgent Prayer of a Widow (18:2-8).

The picture here is of a helpless widow who was being cheated out of her property rights, coming to a godless judge for redress. Her only means of getting help was to prove the justice of her claim by her persistence. Even this did not gain access to his heart, for he feared not God nor regarded man. He complied with her request to get rid of her. The point here is not that God is like this unjust judge that He can be teased into compliance, but rather the teaching is by contrast. If such action can be secured on the part of a godless judge by persistence, how much surer will the help of God be given to His elect who cry unto Him day and night! The helpless widow pictures the Church in this age suffering the deprivation of her rights. It is not the Church praying for vengeance upon her enemies, but suing for the possession of her rights by virtue of her covenant relation in Christ. The inheritance of the Church will be actualized at the coming of Christ. This is why the truth concerning the coming of Christ is so vital to Christianity, and why such disastrous consequences follow the loss of the "blessed hope." Every prayer offered by the Church will surely be answered. The apparent delay in the vindication of the Church may dishearten some and cause others to mock (II Peter 3:4). Jesus' question should be a solemn warning against allowing apparent delay of the coming of the Lord to crowd out our praying. Though many may give up we should be assured that genuine faith will abide, and that the divine promise concerning the coming of Christ shall be fulfilled.

Z. *The Parable of the Pharisee and the Publican* (18:9-14).

This parable was spoken unto certain who trusted in themselves and despised others.

1. The Prayer of the Proud Pharisee (18:9-12).

a. He took a striking attitude (v. 11). The Jewish custom was to stand while praying, but the word *stood* implies the assumption of an ostentatious position. He was self-righteous and trusted in himself.

b. He prayed with himself (vv. 11, 12). He used the name of God, but it was really a soliloquy. He pretended to be thanking God when really he was rehearsing his own goodness—complimenting himself. His whole thought centered on himself, he congratulated himself for his morality (v. 11). He thanked God that he was not as other men are, such as extortioners, unjust, adulterers, or even as the publican who was standing afar off. One who has been kept from these gross sins ought to be grateful to God but should not set himself above his fellow men because of it. He congratulated himself for his religious merits (v. 12). He fasted twice a week and gave tithes of all he possessed. He thus informed God that he did more than what was required, implying that God was under obligation to him.

2. The Prayer of the Humble Publican (18:13).

In striking contrast with this supposed saint stood the publican whose shame kept him from even looking up to Heaven, beating upon his breast as a sign of anguish of soul, crying out to God to be merciful to him, a sinner. He took his place as a sinner and called upon God for mercy.

3. Christ's Testimony (18:14).

He declared that the publican went away justified rather than the

Pharisee. The one great and urgent need on the part of men is a confession of sin and a willingness to cry unto God for mercy.

AA. *Jesus Receives Little Children* (18:15-17).

1. Bringing Babes to Christ (18:15).

The Greek word translated "little children" means infants. Parents were bringing their babes in arms to Jesus for His blessing. This scene is unsurpassed in literature and art in its beauty, purpose, and charm. It appeals to children and adults.

2. Rebuked by the Disciples (18:15).

The disciples regarded the mission of the Lord as too important and urgent to be diverted and delayed by attention to children. In the home in teaching and in preaching let it be recognized that the supreme obligation of society is to bring the children into a saving and sanctifying relation to Jesus Christ. Failure in this supreme obligation is the explanation of the youth problem today. The solution is not in the club or the police, or the fidelity of the warden of the jail. "Train up a child in the way he should go: and when he is old, he will not depart from it" (Prov. 22:6). "Christian nurture of children is the supreme problem of the times" (Dr. Erdman).

3. Disciples Taught by Jesus (18:16, 17).

"Suffer little children to come unto me, and forbid them not: for of such is the kingdom of God." There was something about children that appealed to Christ. Christ has a special appeal to children. The problem of waywardness of children lies with parents. Christian parents bringing up their children in the nurture and admonition of the Lord is the nation's only hope.

BB. *The Rich Ruler* (18:18-30).

1. His Question (18:18).

"What shall I do to inherit eternal life?" This young man was in earnest. He came running and knelt before Jesus. This question reveals a void in his heart. He was a young man with a lovable character. "Jesus beholding him loved him" (Mark 10:21). He was moral, honest, earnest, and courageous, but had a defective theology. He thought that eternal life could be obtained by good works. Though he claimed to have kept the law, he was conscious of lacking something. He was willing to do something to fill up that which was lacking, therefore he came to Jesus to make inquiry as to that lack.

2. Jesus' Reply (18:19, 20).

He knew the young man's heart and put His finger on the weak spot in his life. Jesus reiterated the commandments, but when it came to parting with his possessions in order to help his neighbor, the ruler parted with the Lord, going away sorrowful. This revealed the fact that he was a covetous man, a violator of the tenth commandment.

3. Lacking One Thing and Yet Lost (18:21, 22).

When the Lord pointed out to him that the defect in his life was the love of money, he was unwilling to pay the price. When the time came in his life to choose between eternal life and riches, he chose wealth and parted company with Christ, perhaps forever.

4. The Peril of Riches (18:23-27).

Jesus said: "How hardly shall they that have riches enter into the kingdom of God!" When He discerned the astonishment of the disciples, He answered again and said: "How hard is it for them that trust in riches to enter the kingdom of God! It is easier for a camel to go through the eye of a needle, than for a rich man to enter into the kingdom of God" (Mark 10:24, 25). The difficulty does not lie in the fact that a man possesses riches, for one may possess riches and still be an heir of the kingdom. Wealth is a mighty power. In itself it is good. It will provide bread for the widow and orphans, amelioration for the suffering, and send the Gospel of Christ to the ends of the earth. The peril of riches lies in trusting in them. However, the state from possession of riches to trusting in them is a very short one. The tendency of growing wealth is to destroy the noble life of the soul. As long as a man possesses riches he is safe, but as soon as riches possess the man he is in deadly peril.

5. Christ's Encouraging Word to Peter (18:28-30).

"And he said unto them, Verily I say unto you, There is no man that hath left house, or parents, or brethren, or wife, or children, for the kingdom of God's sake, who shall not receive manifold more in this present time, and in the world to come life everlasting."

CC. *Jesus Again Foretells His Death and Resurrection* (18:31-34).

This is the third time He makes this prediction. The circumstances are most tragic.

1. Jesus Going to Jerusalem (18:31).

He was going with the full consciousness of the awful tragedy of the cross before Him—the treachery of Judas—the fiery persecutions of the priests and scribes—the unjust judgment—the delivery to Pontius Pilate—the mocking—the scourging—the crown of thorns—the cross between malefactors—the nails—the spear—all were spread before Him. He moves on to this goal, not by external necessity but a fixed purpose. The Servant had not come only "to minister, but to give his life a ransom for many." That which He had voluntarily set out to do was moving on to its glorious issue. The joyous outlook upon the victory which would be accomplished through the shedding of His blood led Him forward (Heb. 12:2). The notion that the death of Christ was incidental to His career is most fallacious. The purpose of the Incarnation was the vicarious death (Heb. 2:14). His example of heroism is unique.

2. The Disciples Following After (18:32).

They were in dread bewilderment. His utterances and demeanor filled their minds with perplexity and their hearts with awe. In this state of confusion, Jesus called them to Him and patiently instructed them (cf. Mark 10:32).

3. What Needs Should Happen unto Him? (18:32, 33).

a. Delivered unto chief priests and scribes.

b. They shall condemn Him to death, and deliver Him to the Gentiles.

c. They shall mock, scourge, spit upon, and kill Him.

d. The third day He shall rise again.

These things were not understood by the disciples.

DD. *Jesus Cures Bartimaeus of Blindness* (18:35-43. See Mark 10:46).

Though the weight of the cross was upon Him, He had time for gracious deeds. Blind Bartimaeus receives his sight.

1. Bartimaeus' Request (18:36-38).

He cried to Jesus for mercy. The fact that he addressed Him as the Son of David shows that he recognized His Messiahship. Though he was blind, his faith enabled him to take hold of Jesus. As soon as he heard that Jesus was passing by, he cried to Him for help.

2. Rebuked by the Multitude (18:39).

This rebuke provoked a more earnest cry from Bartimaeus. He believed that Jesus could and would help him, and knew that it was now or never.

3. The Blessing Granted (18:40-43).

Though Jesus knew his desire, He wished him to definitely commit himself. When his eyes were opened, he doubtless saw many interesting things in the world, but the supreme object of interest was Christ, for he followed Him. Note the progress in the experience of Bartimaeus:

a. A blind beggar (v. 35).
b. His cry for mercy (v. 38).
c. Persistence in his cry (v. 39).
d. Responded to call of Jesus (v. 40).
e. Made specific request (v. 41).
f. Received his sight immediately (v. 43).

How quickly one can pass from sore need to jubilant discipleship!

EE. *The Conversion of Zacchaeus* (19:1-10).

1. Jesus Passing Through Jericho (19:1).

Jericho is noted as the stronghold of the Canaanites, which was miraculously delivered into the hands of Israel in response to their faith (Josh. 6); and also for the faith of Rahab which saved her from destruction with the city (Heb. 11:30, 31). It was thus noted as a city where faith and unbelief played against each other. It was fitting that Jesus should pass through Jericho. Faith and unbelief again were manifested. Two notorious sinners, Rahab and Zacchaeus, were saved at Jericho.

2. Zacchaeus Seeking Jesus (19:2-4).

a. His object (v. 3). He sought to see who Jesus was. Though perhaps prompted by curiosity he eagerly sought Jesus. He doubtless had heard of Jesus' kind treatment of publicans, so was prompted to see what kind of a man he was.

b. His difficulties (vv. 2, 3).

(1) His infamous business (v. 2). He was a taxcollector for the Roman government. The very fact that a Jew held such an

office under the hated Romans would make him extremely unpopular. Then since he was rich, it was evident that he had practiced extortion in collecting taxes. By virtue of his traitorous act in accepting such an office from the Romans and his extortion in collecting taxes he was ostracized from society. Therefore, when Jesus came along, he had a hard time, as the people thrust him aside. Many men and women have a hard time in coming to Christ because of their unpopular business relations.

(2) His shortness of stature (v. 3). He was too small to crowd his way through to Jesus, and being hated by the people, they had thrust him aside, no doubt with taunts and jeers.

(3) His persistence (v. 4). He ran before the multitude and climbed into a tree. What he lacked in stature he was determined should be made up by the height of the tree. Zacchaeus was of that choleric temperament which knows no defeat. Obstacles placed before him were brushed aside, and those he could not brush aside he climbed over because he had set his heart upon the goal. Desire must be translated into action if one be saved. Though Zacchaeus' legs were too short to enable him to see Jesus they were long enough to run past the crowd and enable him to climb the tree. It was somewhat undignified for this rich man to climb a tree, but he was so desirous of seeing Jesus that he cast his pride to the winds. Many a man is kept from Jesus because of his pride. Those who sincerely desire to see Jesus will succeed.

3. Jesus Finding Zacchaeus (19:5, 6).

While Zacchaeus was trying to see Jesus, Jesus was looking for him. This is always the case. When desire is stirred up in a heart to see Jesus, Jesus is seeking that one. When Jesus saw him, He commanded him to come down from the tree and declared His intention of going home with him. Zacchaeus got more than he expected. Jesus called him by name. He did not utter a word which would humiliate Zacchaeus. Jesus knew his heart's desire and dealt accordingly with him. All souls who earnestly seek Jesus shall be found of Him. How wonderful His grace, that regardless of one's past life Jesus will receive him as a friend and enter into fellowship with him! Zacchaeus quickly responded. He came down and with joy received Jesus. He acted wisely in that he did not hesitate. A moment's indecision and waiting would have kept Zacchaeus from Jesus—from Jesus and salvation. Many lose their souls through indecision.

4. Zacchaeus' Conversion (19:7-10).

His conversion was sudden and thorough. He was converted before he had reached the ground. It does not take Jesus long to save a soul.

a. What the crowd said (v. 7). They said just what they say today when sinners come to Christ. They call to mind the man's former sins. They also reproached Christ, saying that He had gone to be a guest with this notorious extortioner, the taxcollector. That for which they reproached Jesus was His glory. His supreme mission was to save sinners (v. 10). Jesus came not to condemn us, but to save us; not to shame and destroy us; but to save from sin and reconcile us to God our Father.

b. What Zacchaeus said (v. 8). His conversion was thorough. It took hold upon his heart. His new life was begun with resolution and restitution. He dedicated the half of his goods to the poor. The man who a little while ago was a grafter was now a generous giver. His conversion got hold of his pocketbook. His determination to make restitution wherein he had wrongly exacted taxes shows the genuineness of his conversion. While God forgets the past of a sinner when he comes to Christ, the sinner who is converted will seek to make right all wrongs—unkind words or unrighteous deeds. Sorrow for sin is not enough when restitution is possible.

c. What Jesus said (vv. 9, 10). "Today is salvation come to thy house." The publican was now a child of God, a son of Abraham. Salvation is a present reality when one receives Christ.

FF. *Parable of the Pounds* (19:11-27).

The purpose of this parable was to correct the misapprehension of the disciples as to the immediate establishment of the kingdom. They were on the way to Jerusalem and they thought that immediately upon their arrival there Jesus would begin the exercise of His kingdom rule. It is to be noted that Jesus did not correct them for believing in the reality of the kingdom, but for believing that it would appear immediately. Christ taught the disciples the reality of His coming and the setting up of a real kingdom, but indicated that there would be a long delay after His ascension before He would return. This parable was to make clear and to show the personal responsibility of His servants during His absence.

1. The Absent Lord (19:12).

He pictures His going back to God as a nobleman going to receive a kingdom. This was a common occurrence among them. They knew how some of the Herodian family had thus done—had gone to Rome and secured their appointment to rule over Palestine. Jesus ascended on high to receive from God, the Father, a kingdom. He will return when the fullness of the Gentiles come in. Let no one mistake the certainty of His return, though the time be unknown and the event delayed. Though the interim of His absence be lengthened, He will surely come again.

2. The Distribution of the Pounds (19:13).

These pounds represent Christ's gifts to His servants. When Christ ascended He gave gifts to men (Eph. 4:7, 8, 11, 12). To each servant was given the same amount showing that to all a certain gift has been given and therefore all will be held responsible for its use. The distribution was made by the sovereign. The servants did not choose as to whether they would have a gift or the amount of the gift. It was also a purposeful distribution. They were to put their gifts to use during his absence. What the nobleman demanded was faithfulness. The pounds were to be used for the master, not for the selfish enjoyment of the servant. Our business is to use all our gifts for Jesus Christ.

3. The Rebellious Citizens (19:14).

They hated him and sent messengers after him, notifying him of their refusal to be subject to him. This pictures the unbelief of the Jews after Christ's ascension and their repudiation of His rule. It also pictures the unbelieving world in its hatred and rejection of Christ. How wicked is this world! How violently it hates Jesus!

4. The Accounting (19:15-27).

a. Its certainty. Christ will surely bring everyone to account for the use made of His gifts. It is appointed unto men once to die, and after that the judgment. Men may go on in proud unbelief and rebellion, but God never forgets. He has appointed a day in which He will judge the world (Acts 17:31).

b. Time (v. 15). It will take place when Jesus comes back to the earth. At that time He will summon His servants and reckon with them. This will take place when He has received His kingdom. He will receive His kingdom when He asks the Father (Ps. 2:8). That He delays His asking is His long-suffering mercy, extending grace to as many as will receive Him as Saviour and Lord.

c. Rewards given for faithfulness (vv. 16-19).

(1) The first report (vv. 16, 17). The pound had gained ten pounds. He did not say, "I have made ten pounds," but, "Thy pound hath gained ten pounds." He recognized the lord's ownership. To this the lord replied by commendation. He praised and promoted him. He was made ruler over ten cities.

(2) The second report (v. 18). In this case the pound had gained five pounds. He did not get the lord's commendation, for he had not done so well, but he was appointed to a place of rulership over five cities. The reward in each case was proportioned to faithfulness during the lord's absence. The principle of reward was shown to be that faithfulness in very small things prepares for larger responsibilities. This principle finds application all through life and will doubtless obtain throughout eternity.

d. Judgment upon the unfaithful (vv. 20-27).

(1) His report (vv. 20, 21). This report was entirely bad. He had not put the pound to use, but laid it away throwing the blame upon the lord. He asserted that the character of the lord was such as to produce fear. Men are failing today in their service because they have wrong conceptions of Christ.

(2) Condemnation (vv. 22, 23). The wicked servant is judged out of his own mouth. His excuse increased his guilt. He is called wicked. He doubtless regarded himself as unfortunate. To fail to use our opportunities to serve Christ is the basest wickedness. In the judgment the sinner's excuse will be his undoing.

(3) Stripped of the pound (vv. 24-26). To fail to use one's gifts means to lose them. One of the losses of the next world will be the deprivation of what we have now.

(4) Warning (v. 27). Those who reject Christ, refusing to submit to His authority, will share the same deprivation as those who are unfaithful in His service.

VI. THE SON OF MAN MINISTERING AND TEACHING IN JERUSALEM—(19:28–21:38).

A. *The Official Presentation of the Son of Man as the Messiah* (19:28-48).

The common title given this section is somewhat misleading. Strictly speaking, this was far from a triumphal entry. It was rather the official presentation of the King to the Jewish nation. Back of the cry, "Hosanna," the awful word *crucify* was taking form. Likely this awful word *crucify* was uttered by some of the same persons who cried, "Hosanna." Though they were utterly blind to the fact, God was about to carry out His plan of Hosanna, which means "save now," through the crucifixion of the Son of God.

1. The Preparation (19:29-34).

a. Sending the disciples for the ass (vv. 29-31). He told them just where to go to find it and told them how to answer the inquiry of the one who owned it. This shows how perfectly the Lord knows all our ways. He knows our whereabouts by day and by night. He even knows our thoughts. He uses unlikely means and insignificant things in the accomplishment of His purpose.

b. The fulfillment of prophecy (Matt. 21:4, 5). Some 500 years before Zechariah had predicted this event, Christ's entry into Jerusalem was an exact fulfillment of this prediction. This is highly instructive to those who would understand unfulfilled prophecies. Since the prediction of His first coming was literally fulfilled, we can be assured that those of His second coming will be likewise fulfilled. The first is established beyond a doubt. The second we should as heartily believe. The prediction of Zechariah 14:3-11 will be just as literally fulfilled as that of Zechariah 9:9.

c. Obedience of the disciples (vv. 32-34). Though the request may have seemed strange, and even unreasonable, they fully obeyed. The true disciple will render glad obedience to the Lord no matter how strange His commands may seem. Obedience to that only which seems reasonable is not obedience at all. May we prove that we are real disciples.

2. The Entry of the King (19:35-38).

a. The disciples set Jesus upon the ass (v. 35). This act of putting their garments upon the ass and setting Jesus upon it showed that they recognized Him as their King (II Kings 9:13).

b. Acclaimed as King by the disciples (vv. 36-38). Some spread their garments in the way. Others perhaps having no garments to spare cut down branches of trees and strewed them in His way, which was no doubt just as acceptable to Him. They praised God for all the mighty works which they had seen and cried out: "Blessed be the King that cometh in the name of the Lord."

3. The Critical Pharisees (19:39, 40).

Although swept along by the demonstration of the multitude they deemed it prudent to ask the Lord to rebuke the disciples as such behavior might be interpreted by the Roman government as an insurrection. To their demand Jesus replied that such homage was not only fitting but necessary. He declared that if the multitude were silent, the very stones would cry out in adoration of Him.

4. Jesus Weeps over Jerusalem (19:41-44).
(See comment on Luke 13:34, 35.)

5. Second Purification of the Temple (19:45-48).
(See comment on John 2:13-17.)

6. The King Rejected (19:47, 48).

Christ knew what awaited Him in Jerusalem. Though surrounded by loyal hearts, He knew that the rulers of the nation had no heart for Him. His coming trial and death loomed before Him so that He wept over Jerusalem. He knew what awful days awaited it, and that loyal hearts would gladly welcome Him if they only knew. He showed that their inability to see Him as their King and Saviour would result in bringing upon them the awful horrors of the destruction of their city. He entered the city and rebuked the rulers for allowing the house of God to become degraded by carrying on traffic for gain. The cleansing of the Temple only increased their hatred and opposition to Him.

This action only intensified the determination to destroy Jesus.

B. *Jesus' Authority Questioned* (20:1-8).

1. The Demand Made of Jesus (20:1, 2).

After the official presentation of the Messiah-King to the Jewish people, His popularity among the people greatly increased. In the Temple He taught the people and preached the Gospel. The leaders among the Jews had already determined to put Him to death, but they thought it wise to first discredit Him before the people by questioning His authority, so they sent a deputation from the Sanhedrin to find out His authority for receiving Messianic honors and driving traders from the Temple. Their questions were shrewdly framed. If Jesus had answered that authority had been delegated to Him, they would have accused Him of disloyalty to the Jewish state. If He had claimed inherent divine authority, they would have condemned Him for blasphemy.

2. Jesus Silenced His Enemies by a Counterquestion Which Put Them in a Dilemma (20:3, 4).

"The baptism of John, was it from heaven, or of men?" They could not say "from heaven" for they had rejected and beheaded John. They did not dare to say "from men," for they feared the people who regarded John as a prophet.

3. Their Cowardly Professed Ignorance (20:5-7).

They were hypocritical liars. They pretended to desire His credentials but really wanted to trap and discredit Him. It turned out to be a boomerang. Modern enemies of Christ are clamoring for proof of the integrity of the Bible and the deity of Christ, when in reality they are unregenerate sinners. What is needed is not more proof, but willingness to believe.

C. *Parable of the Husbandmen* (20:9-18).

Having put the scribes, chief priests, and elders to confusion by a skillful counterquestion when they demanded His authority, Jesus by means of a little story lays before them His claim to divine authority, and charges them with betrayal of trust and plotting to murder the very Son of God. His teaching of this parable cut them to the quick, and they sought to lay hands on Him, but desisted for fear of the people. The parable is simple yet very comprehensive.

1. The Planter (20:9).

A certain man who planted the Vineyard represents God Himself.

2. The Vineyard (20:9).

This means Israel, the chosen nation. (See Isa. 5:1-7; Jer. 2:21; Ps. 80:8.) The Lord went to particular pains to make this nation separate. He bestowed peculiar favors upon it.

3. The Husbandmen (20:9-14).

These were the rulers and teachers of Israel, even members of the Sanhedrin. They were the spiritual guides of the people.

4. The Servants (20:10-12).

These were the various prophets whom God sent to the nation. The maltreatment and rejection of the prophets is fully set forth in the Scriptures. They were beaten and killed.

5. The Well-beloved Son Sent (20:13-15).

The Son here is the Lord Jesus Christ, God's only and beloved Son. He came into their midst. They knew Him to be the Son, but they would not receive His message or bow to His authority, so they cast Him out of the vineyard and slew Him. They knew that this parable was intended for them. Jesus knew that within a few days He would be crucified.

6. The Punishment of the Householders (20:16-18).

Jesus now asked them for their own verdict upon such villainous ingratitude. He took the place of a judge and pronounced judgment upon them on the basis of their own verdict. They not only rejected the kingdom, but the Son who was the King. Therefore, the kingdom was taken from them and given to a nation bringing forth fruits thereof.

D. *The Question of Paying Tribute* (20:19-26).

The popularity of Jesus after the triumphal entry greatly troubled the rulers of Israel. He met their wicked challenge as to His authority in such a skillful way as to place them under condemnation for their unbelief. This condition was accentuated by the parable of the householder (vv. 9-18), which made it clear that the wicked husbandmen represented them in the murderous plot against Him, and that their schemes would result in their utter undoing.

1. Spies Sent To Trap Jesus (20:20).

These men were too cowardly to do this themselves, so they employed underlings to do their mean work while they hid. This diabolical method is employed today in political and religious life. Many times questions are raised under the guise of sincerity, when the real purpose is to do mischief.

2. Wicked Flattery (20:21).

They complimented His truthful teaching, His impartiality and courage. They certified to His faithfulness even to the extent that He would face Caesar himself. This compliment was true, though insincerely given. Back of this flattery was the base purpose to destroy Jesus. Many today praise to the face in order to stab in the back.

3. The Cunning Question (20:22-26).

"Is it lawful for us to give tribute unto Caesar, or no?" At this time the Jews were galling under the yoke of the Roman government. To have answered this question either by Yes or No would have involved difficulties. To have answered Yes would have conveyed the impression of endorsing all that the Roman government did. To have answered No would have at once brought Him into conflict with the government. It is not always an easy matter for a Christian to determine his right relation to civil government. Christ's reply to this question properly understood and applied is the final word on the subject. Until the civil authorities demand that which is a violation of God's Law we are bound to render unto them obedience. Render unto Caesar the things that are due him within the realm of the rights of government. But while Christ's answer sets forth their duties to civil authorities, He used the occasion to impress upon them their duties to God. Render unto God the things that are God's. Man bears the image of God. Therefore he should honor and serve Him. Since he enjoys God's protection and care, it is his duty to own allegiance to Him, yield his life to Him in service, worship, and praise. Everyone who enjoys the benefits of civil government is obliged to pay the taxes which are necessary for the support of that government, and everyone who receives God's favor is placed under a like obligation to Him.

E. *Jesus Answers the Sadducees Concerning the Resurrection* (20:27-38).

The Pharisees and Herodians being silenced, the Sadducees came with a question which involved not only immortality but the resurrection of the body. The Sadducees were the rationalists of their days. They denied the reality of the resurrection, and believed not in angel or spirit (Acts 23:8).

1. The Case Proposed (20:19-23).

The Law of Moses made it not only legal, but morally binding in the case of a man dying without children, for his brother to take his wife (Deut. 22:5). They proposed the case of a woman married successively to seven brothers. They ask whose wife she shall be in the resurrection. This was doubtless a hypothetical case.

2. Jesus' Reply (20:24-26).

By a quotation from the Mosaic Law (Exod. 3:6), Jesus proves the resurrection of the dead, and their continued existence beyond death as human beings. The immortal spirit clothed with a deathless body is His thought. He shows that marriage is only for the present life. Since there will be no death after the resurrection, there will be no necessity for births. In this respect human kind will be as the angels in the resurrection life. He points out to them that their great error was due to two things:

a. Ignorance of the Scriptures (v. 24). In the very Scriptures which they professed to believe was positive proof of the resurrection (Exod. 3:6).

b. Ignorance of the power of God (v. 24). God is able to provide a life where there is no death, no births, or marriages. In Heaven life will be on a plane infinitely higher than the most blessed relationships of this life. Our chief concern is to find out what is written, and then believe that God is able to accomplish that which He has promised.

F. *Jesus Questions the Scribes* (20:39-47).

Having triumphed over His enemies in debate, He so answered their crafty questions, which were designed to discredit Him as a Teacher and furnish some ground for His arrest, that they were put to silence—"Durst not ask him any question at all." Jesus took advantage of the situation by asking a question which would bring into focus His supreme claim as being the divine Son of God. "How say they that Christ is David's son? And David himself saith in the book of Psalms, The Lord said unto my Lord, Sit thou on my right hand, till I make thine enemies thy footstool. David therefore calleth him Lord, how is he then his son?" His motive was to ask the question in such a way and at such a time that its answer would bring before the people and its rulers His claim of being divine. At that time as well as today, the supreme question is, "What think ye of Christ? Whose son is he?" The Person of Christ is the center of all ecclesiastical and philosophical problems. The universe is Christ-centric. Christian thought and life center in the Incarnation.

1. Warning Against the Scribes (20:45-47).

The lives of these unworthy religious leaders were characterized by:

a. Vanity. They were ambitious for display, high position, and love of flattery.

b. Cruel avarice. They devoured widows' houses.

c. Hypocrisy. They for pretense made long prayers.

G. *Jesus' Estimate of Giving* (21:1-4).

1. Jesus Watches the People Giving (21:1).

He was greatly interested in observing the way the people cast their gifts into the treasury. Perhaps there is no more vital index to one's character than the way he behaves before the Lord's treasury. Jesus sits over against every treasury and knows every dollar cast into it. He knows how the dollars come and how they go. No trickery can deceive Him. He not only knows this in the church, but He knows it in the business world.

2. The Rich Gave of Their Abundance (21:1, 4).

They no doubt gave much, but in proportion to what they had left their gifts were small. The size of the gift is not primarily to be measured by how much it is, but how much the giver has left.

3. A Widow Gave Two Mites (21:2, 4).

In value a mite was less than a cent. Though the two coins were of small value themselves, they represented her all—not merely her surplus, but her living. Let no one deceive himself by pretending to give the widow's mite, for to give the widow's mite means to give everything.

4. Jesus' Verdict (21:3, 4).

He declared that she had given more than they all. Jesus looks into the heart and estimates our gifts not by their size but by the motives prompting them.

H. *The Olivet Prophetic Discourse* (21:5-38).

Jesus knowing that His public ministry was nearing its end, that the Shepherd would soon be smitten and the sheep scattered, sought to prepare the disciples for the tragic ordeal through which they soon should be called to pass. This is a part of the well-known Olivet discourse. It gives a prophetic view of the course of time from its utterance just before the crucifixion to the second advent of Christ. Two great events are before us in this prophetic utterance—the destruction of Jerusalem and the second coming of Christ. The one was near, having taken place within forty years from the crucifixion of Christ; the other is still future.

The occasion of this prophecy was the threefold question asked by the disciples as they gazed upon the splendor of the Temple which Jesus had declared would be utterly destroyed, "not be left one stone upon another, that shall not be thrown down" (vv. 6, 7).

Christ's answer to their question sketched the following:

1. The Character of the Present Age (21:8-19).

In this age many shall come saying, "I am Christ," and shall deceive many. There shall be wars and rumors of wars. Nation shall be pitted against nation and kingdom against kingdom, with earthquakes in divers places accompanied with famine and pestilence. Witnesses of Christ shall be persecuted and arraigned before rulers and kings. Brother shall betray brother to death and the father the son. Children will arise against their parents and cause them to be put to death. The preachers of the Gospel shall be hated for Christ's sake and some of them put to death.

2. The Destruction of Jerusalem (21:20-24).

Christ had repeatedly told of the doom of Jerusalem and wept over it, but now He declared that the sign of the impending doom would be the siege of the city. "When ye shall see Jerusalem compassed with armies, then know that the desolation thereof is nigh." He advised those in Judea to flee to the mountains; those in the midst of the city to depart; and those in the country not to enter. This took place in the year A.D. 70. He declared that they would fall by the sword and be led into captivity among all nations, and that "Jerusalem shall be trodden down of the Gentiles, until the times of the Gentiles be fulfilled."

3. The Glorious Coming of the Son of Man (21:25-28).

This is the hope toward which all the ages are moving. His glorious appearing will be preceded by certain startling and even terrifying signs (v. 25). For unbelievers this event will be a time of distress, but for the true Church it will be a time of exultant joy—the fulfillment of blessed expectation.

4. Encouragement to Steadfastness and Vigilance (21:29-38).

Having referred to certain signs by which believers may know the coming of the Lord is near, He now uses a parable of the foliage of the trees in the springtime as a certain harbinger of summer. Even so, "ye, when ye see these things come to pass, know ye that the kingdom of God is nigh at hand" (v. 31). The kingdom of God is the kingdom which shall be established when the Lord comes in glory. In view of this blessed hope the heart of the Christian is to be set upon the Lord instead of on the things of the world. They are warned to be vigilant—watching and praying so that they may escape the judgments which shall befall the guilty world.

VII. THE SON OF MAN REJECTED, CRUCIFIED, RESURRECTED AND ASCENDED (22:1—24:53).

A. *The Treachery of Judas* (22:1-6; cf. vv. 21-23).

1. Satan Entered into Him (22:3).
2. Covenanted with Chief Priests and Scribes (22:4, 5).
3. Time of Its Manifestation (22:21).

It was while they were eating the last Passover that Jesus made the announcement of the betrayal. Perhaps the reason this feast was disturbed by such an announcement was that Judas might be given an opportunity at the last moment to repent.

4. The Betrayal Was by the Determinate Counsel of God (22:22; cf. Acts 2:23).

Nothing takes place by chance. Even the evil, sinful acts of men come within the permissive providences of God, but this does not lessen the guilt, for Jesus said: "Woe unto that man by whom he is betrayed!" Such a sinful act as committed by Judas, in the face of his great opportunity, is to put one into a place which is worse than nonexistence.

5. A Sorrowful Question (22:23).

The disciples did not seem to suspect one another but made the question a personal one. We should always examine ourselves rather than others.

B. *The Last Passover Supper* (22:7-38).

The last meal that Jesus ate with His disciples was the Passover. The Passover was a memorial of a national deliverance and pointed to the supreme deliverance which would be effected on the cross of Calvary. In connection with this the feast of the new covenant was instituted. This too has a double import. It looks backward to the great deliverance through His atoning death on the cross and forward to the greater deliverance which He shall accomplish at His second coming.

1. The Passover Prepared (22:7-13).

a. The disciples' inquiry (vv. 7-9) They inquired of Jesus as to where they should prepare for the Passover. They no doubt were anxious to be of service to Him. The disciple should not be ready only to do his Lord's bidding, but should inquire what He would have him do.

b. The Master's strange directions (vv. 10-12). They were to go into the city where they would meet a man bearing a pitcher of water. It was usual for the women to carry the water. This unusual occurrence would make it easier for them to find the man of whom they were to ask, "Where is the guest chamber, where I shall eat the passover with my disciples?" He assured them that they would then be shown a large upper room furnished.

c. The obedience of the disciples (v. 13). The disciples did as Jesus had instructed them. They did not stop to question the sanity of the command but like true disciples they obeyed. Jesus, because He is omniscient, knew just how the matter would turn out.

2. The Passover Eaten (22:14-18).

a. By whom (v. 14)? Those who sat down to this last Passover feast were the Master and the twelve apostles.

b. His words unto them (vv. 15-18).

(1) "I have desired to eat this passover with you before I suffer." How anxious He was to show them the meaning of the passion through which He was to go; also He craved their human sympathy as He passed through this trying ordeal!

(2) "I will not any more eat thereof, until it be fulfilled in the kingdom of God." His death was the antitypical fulfillment of the Passover meal. He declared that this would be the last time

they could share this ordinance this side of the completion of His mediatorial work. He looked forward to that time when the process of redemption would have been completed and a perfect union between the disciples and the Lord would be consummated.

(3) "Take this [cup], and divide it among yourselves." The disciples were now partaking of that symbol of His blood. He assured them that He would not drink again of the fruit of the vine until the kingdom of God should come. Drinking anew in the kingdom does not mean that in Heaven this service will be renewed, but that this was symbolic of the heavenly reality.

3. The Feast of the New Covenant Instituted (22:19, 20).

This took place at the close of the paschal supper.

a. The bread, a symbol of Christ's body (v. 19). As bread nourishes and strengthens our bodies, so Christ is food to our spiritual lives. Unless we feed upon Him we shall perish. Christ giving the physical bread to the disciples signified the giving of Himself to them. In order to get benefit from physical bread it is necessary to receive it. In order to get benefit from Christ one must receive Him.

b. The cup, a symbol of Christ's blood (v. 20). This was symbolic of the atonement which was made by the shedding of His blood on the cross. He said: "This cup is the new testament in my blood, which is shed for you," indicating that each one must personally accept the atonement made by the shedding of His blood. This was not only a seal but a memorial of the new covenant.

4. Sundry Incidents of the Passover Feast (22:21-38).

Strange and unpredictable reaction of human beings to the cross of Christ.

a. Jesus announces the betrayal (v. 21).

b. Strife for pre-eminence (vv. 24-27). This would seem the time of all times when the Christlike spirit would prevail. The Christian should follow the example of his Lord. Christ came not to be ministered unto, but to minister and give His life a ransom for many.

c. The apostles' place in the kingdom (vv. 28-30). Christ assures them that those who continue with Him in His trials would be appointed unto a place in the kingdom which would entitle them to eat and drink at His table in His kingdom and sit on thrones judging the twelve tribes of Israel.

d. Jesus predicts Peter's denial (vv. 31-34).

(1) He told Peter of Satan's desire to sift him.

(2) He assures Peter of His prayer for him that his faith would not fail.

(3) Peter's pledge of loyalty even to prison and death.

e. Warning of coming conflicts (vv. 35-38). Church history through the centuries records the struggle of Christ's followers to maintain themselves and carry the Gospel to the world.

C. *Jesus in Gethsemane* (22:39-46).

The place called Gethsemane was an enclosure containing olive and fig trees beyond Kidron about three-quarters of a mile from Jerusalem. The name means, "olive press." The name is significant of the occasion. Edersheim says, "It is an emblem of trial, distress and agony." Perhaps the garden was owned by one of Jesus' friends. It afforded Him a suitable place to retire with His disciples in this trying hour.

1. His Agony (22:44).

The "cup" (v. 42) expresses intense suffering. The reality of the cross was now clearly seen by Him. However, it was not primarily the prospect of physical suffering that was crushing Him, it was the suffering as the Sin-bearer—the sensations of His pure soul coming into contact with the awful sin and guilt of the world. Only pure and refined natures can understand this. In addition to this there was the judgment stroke from the holy God as it fell upon His Son instead of the sinner. God caused the iniquities of the world to strike upon Jesus Christ (II Cor. 5:21; cf. Isa. 53:6). Christ's prayer was not "agonizing" prayer but "being in an agony he prayed *more earnestly."*

2. His Praying (vv. 41, 42).

Though Jesus prized human sympathy in the hour of supreme need, His only recourse was prayer. The sympathy of our friends is helpful, but in life's great crises we can only find the needed help as we go to God in prayer. "Is any among you afflicted, let him pray" (James 5:12).

D. *Jesus Betrayed and Arrested* (22:47-54).

1. The Betrayer (22:47).

The betrayal was by Judas, one of the twelve. He had enjoyed the most intimate relations with the Lord—eating with Him, listening to His teaching, witnessing His marvelous miracles, and enjoying His confidence. This intensifies the sadness of his actions. Now he is guiding the mob to arrest the blessed Saviour.

2. The Sign of Betrayal (22:47).

It was the kiss, the token of the tenderest affection and friendship. He now degrades it by making it the token of disloyalty and treason. Jesus' tender words to this infamous disciple shows the infinite tenderness of His heart. If Judas had been at all human, this pathetic appeal would have smitten him to his very heart. How many professing disciples have proved their disloyalty to the Master and even betrayed Him! All who bear the name of Christian and especially ministers and teachers who deny the virgin birth of Christ, His deity, and vicarious atonement are following in the footsteps of Judas. May each one inquire, "Lord, is it I?"

3. Jesus Arrested (22:54).

The multitude with swords and clubs, led by Judas, invaded the sacred precincts of the garden, arrested Jesus, and brought Him before the high priest.

Note the calm behavior of Jesus in contrast with that of His followers. His followers thought that the time had come to defend the Master by the sword (v. 38). He rebuked His enemies for coming with swords and staves as against a thief, when He had been with them daily of His own choice.

E. *Peter's Denial* (22:54-62).

Peter really loved the Lord and he never lost faith in Him, but in this hour of supreme trial which Jesus had predicted (v. 32), he lost his courage.

From the height of fellowship with God, which Peter enjoyed when he confessed that Jesus was the Messiah, the Son of the living God (Matt. 16), to the depth of emphasizing a lie by foul oaths is a long way, but the steps were quickly taken, for the time was short. In order to grasp the real secret of Peter's fall, we must sweep into view Mark 14:29-71. Peter's downfall began when he refused to hear, and ended when he with a foul oath declared, "I know not the man." When the disciples would no longer hear Christ's message about the cross, they not only ceased to grow in knowledge, but they began to deteriorate in moral discernment and were, therefore, exposed to the possibility of the shameful denial of their Lord. In order that we may be saved from such a fall, let us note carefully the steps in Peter's backsliding:

1. Overweaning Self-confidence (Mark 14:29-31).

His unwillingness to face the cross alienated him from Jesus, and when apprised of the fact that the disciples would all forsake Jesus, Peter declared that Jesus was certainly mistaken, saying: "Although all shall be offended, yet will not I." Our condition is most perilous when we are surest of our safety. "Let him that thinketh he standeth, take heed lest he fall."

2. Sleeping at the Post of Duty (Mark 14:37).

In one short hour the very one who was so confident of his self-sufficiency had fallen asleep instead of watching. The only way to escape from backsliding is to watch. The one who is filled with self-sufficiency will not be careful to watch. The one who overrates himself underrates the power of the Devil. Underrating the strength of the Devil results in unwatchfulness.

3. Lack of Prayer (Mark 14:38).

The legitimate inference from the Lord's words, "Watch ye and pray," is that He had commanded them to pray as well as to watch. The reason there is so little prayer is due to a lack of the sense of need of God's help. Conscious weakness is a power of incentive to prayer.

F. *Jesus Before the Sanhedrin* (22:63-71).

1. Buffeted by His Captors (22:63, 64).

He was not only mocked and reviled but beaten. They blindfolded Him and blasphemously demanded that He prove Himself a prophet by telling who smote Him. Such treatment can only come from those who have rejected the Saviour. "And many other things blasphemously spake they against him" (v. 65).

2. Contradicting Testimony of False Witnesses (Mark 14:53-59).

The chief priests and all the council sought for witnesses against

Jesus to put Him to death but found none because there was no unity of testimony. They accused Him of having declared that within three days He would build again the Temple if it were destroyed.

3. The High Priest's Questions (22:67-71).

a. "Art thou the Christ?" (v. 67). To this He definitely replied: "If I tell you, ye will not believe." "Hereafter shall the Son of man sit at the right hand of the power of God" (v. 69).

b. "Art thou then the Son of God?" (v. 70). He answered them, "Ye say that I am." To this they answered: "What need we any further witness? For we ourselves have heard of his own mouth." The highest court regards His own words as incriminating Himself. They were not honest men seeking after the truth of His Messiahship, but to find some evidence for His condemnation.

G. *Jesus Arraigned Before Pilate* (23:1-25).

In the early morning after the mock trial before the high priest they bound Jesus and delivered Him to Pilate. They acted freely in this according to the evil desires of their own hearts. Yet He was delivered up by the "determinate counsel and foreknowledge of God" (Acts 2:23). The Jews would gladly have killed Him, but they had been deprived of the authority of capital punishment by their Roman conquerors. They sought confirmation of their purpose to crucify Jesus. This mock trial turned out to be an exhibition of a disgraceful contest between these murderous Jewish rulers and the vacillating Roman governor who was compelled to act contrary to his conscience and desire in submitting his will to the desires of his hated subjects. Pilate's reply to the accusation of the multitudes, that he "found no fault in him," only increased vehemence. Pilate sought to escape the responsibility of making a decision, but this only increased his difficulty.

1. Sent Jesus to Herod (23:6-12).

Learning that Jesus was from Galilee, Pilate was glad to get Herod's opinion concerning the accusation made by the Jews. Herod and Pilate were personal enemies but became friends that day. Herod had heard much about Jesus' works and gladly welcomed the opportunity to see Him. To Herod's many questions Jesus was silent. Jesus was always responsive to the cry of the penitent sinner, but silent only to the question of the profligate murder of John the

Baptist. He responded by silent contempt. Herod reacted to Jesus' silence by an act of petty revenge. Herod with his men of war set Him at naught and mocked Him and arrayed Him in a gorgeous robe and sent Him back to Pilate (v. 11).

2. Offered a Compromise (23:13-26).

Pilate called together the chief priests and rulers of the people, informed them that he had examined Jesus before them, declaring that he found no fault in Him. He informed them that Herod had joined him in deciding that Jesus had done nothing worthy of death. He offered to chastise or scourge Jesus and to release Him. To scourge an innocent person would be a crime of the first magnitude, but it would not be murder and less heinous than murder. Seeing that Pilate hesitated, the enemies pressed their claim with greater vigor. To this he yielded. After several unsuccessful efforts to escape responsibility, he resorted to the expedient of letting the people choose between Jesus and Barabbas. He no doubt thought that Jesus would be chosen rather than the notorious Barabbas.

H. *The Crucifixion of Christ* (23:26-49).

We now face the record of the greatest tragedy of all time. No record in the annals of all history approaches it. It is indeed the climax of all history. Though unique in its blackness, from it flows streams of life and liberty for all the world. It is highly important that every preacher and teacher have the personal experience of Christ's death for himself, and then get the people to see that Christ's death was instead of their own death. We escaped judgment because judgment fell upon Christ. He was made to be sin for us that we might be the righteousness of God in Him (II Cor. 5:21). No one lacking this experience can really teach this truth.

Christ's death was the judgment of this world (John 12:31), and the guarantee that the prince of this world shall be cast out. It was for this purpose that the Son of God became incarnate (Heb. 2:14). This explains why the vicarious atonement of Christ and the virgin birth of Christ are rejected by modern liberals.

1. On the Way to Calvary (23:28-32).

a. Simon the Cyrenian compelled to bear the cross after Jesus (v. 26). What a spectacle! The sinless One in bonds journeying to the place of death, with the cross upon which He was to die borne by Simon.

b. A weeping multitude with certain godly women following Jesus to the place of death (v. 27).

c. Jesus' words to them (vv. 28-30). "Daughters of Jerusalem, weep not for me, but weep for yourselves, and for your children." He did not rebuke them for their expression of sympathy, but to tell them that their coming suffering would exceed His. He had in mind their suffering in the destruction of Jerusalem. He predicted that the horrors would be so great that men would call upon the mountains to fall upon them and the hills to cover them.

2. The Place of Crucifixion (23:33).

a. They led Him away to Calvary, a hill north of Jerusalem resembling a skull. *Calvary* is the Latin word, and *Golgotha* is the Hebrew word. This is a most significant name for the place where man's redemption was accomplished. The skull is an apt picture of man's condition as the result of sin—life and intelligence are gone, leaving only the dark empty cavern which once contained them. Jesus was not crucified in the city, for He was to suffer without the gate (Heb. 13:12).

b. Foretold in Jewish prophecy. "The mode of Christ's death had been foretold under a variety of types and figures. The brazen serpent signified that He was to be lifted up. The lamb upon the altar showed that His blood must be shed. His hands and feet must be pierced. He must be wounded and tormented; His ears were to be filled with revilings; upon His vesture lots were to be cast and vinegar was to be given Him to drink. These and divers requirements as to the Messiah's death had been foretold in Jewish prophecy, and now the Gentile world came forward with a mode of death that marvelously combined them all. This was the cross."

3. His Companions on the Cross (23:33).

Two malefactors were crucified with Him. Their names are not given. This is fulfillment of the Scriptures. "He was numbered with the transgressors" (Isa. 53:12). He was sinless, but became sin for us.

4. His Forgiving Love (23:34).

He cried, "Father, forgive them." He doubtless had in mind not only the soldiers who acted for the government, but the Jews who in their blindness were ignorant of the enormity of their crime. He had no hatred in His heart. His compassionate soul yearned for their salvation.

5. The World Revealed (23:34-43).

Jesus Christ on the cross is the supreme touchstone of human life, and discloses the world's heart. Take a cross section of the world at any time since Christ was crucified, and representatives of the various classes therein were found around Jesus on the cross. The cross is the judgment of this world (John 12:31).

a. The covetous (v. 34). They gambled for His seamless robe right under the cross where He was dying. This represents those whose primary interest in Christ is a means to get gain. If they had had eyes to see they could have beheld a robe of righteousness being provided in His death to cover their sinful nakedness.

b. The indifferent (v. 35). "The people stood beholding." They gazed upon Him with indifference. The great mass of the world gazes upon the crucified Christ with stolid indifference.

c. The scoffers (vv. 35-39).

(1) The rulers reviled Him for His claim to be the Saviour but not a crucified Saviour. Many today are religious but have only contempt for a salvation which centers in an atonement made by blood. They uttered a great truth when they said, "He saved others," but He could not save Himself and others, because God's plan was to save others by giving Himself.

(2) The soldiers reviled Him for claiming to be a King. The title, "King of the Jews," had been placed over Him in bitter irony, but it was true, for by right of the Davidic covenant He shall be one day King over Israel (II Sam. 7:8-16). Through His death He came into the place of Lordship over all who will acknowledge Him. The fact that the superscription was in Greek, Hebrew, and Latin shows that He was to be King over all the world.

(3) The impenitent malefactor (v. 39). This brutal man joined in reviling the Saviour, even though he was under condemnation.

d. The penitent malefactor (vv. 40-43). The conscious sinner who discerned the heart of the Saviour prayed for mercy. The salvation of this penitent man is a remarkable picture of the saving power of Christ. The man confessed his sin as against God and cried to Jesus for salvation. He saw that the dying Man was the forgiving God.

The fact that he acknowledged his sin as against God showed that he was penitent. His request for Christ to remember him when He came into His kingdom shows that he recognized that the One who was dying on the cross was making atonement for sin, and that He would come to reign as King. His salvation was immediate. Christ said: "Today shalt thou be with me in paradise."

6. The Death of Christ (23:44-46).

So shocking was the crime that nature herself threw around the Son of God a shroud to hide Him from the godless crowd. Darkness was upon the land at noonday. When the price of sin was paid, He "cried with a loud voice," showing that He still had vitality, that His death was not through exhaustion but by His sovereign will. He died like no other in all history.

I. *The Burial of Christ* (23:50-56).

While Christ died an ignominious death, He was given an honorable burial. Before leaving the scene of His death note the reaction of the three groups of witnesses: the *centurion,* the official who had crucified Jesus as a criminal, glorified God and testified that He was a "righteous man"; *"all the people* that came together to that sight, beholding the things which were done, smote their breasts, and returned" (v. 48) in agony of remorse, a prophecy of Israel's repentance as they "look on him whom they pierced"; the *group of perplexed and saddened disciples* who "stood afar off, beholding these things" (v. 49). To this last group the light dawned on the resurrection morning.

Joseph of Arimathaea, a counselor, a good man and just, who had not consented to the counsel and deed, went to Pilate and begged the body of Jesus, prepared it for burial, and laid it in a new sepulcher "wherein never man was laid." He risked the possible scorn of the rulers, begged the Lord's body, and reverently laid it away.

J. *The Resurrection of the Son of Man* (24:1-12).

The supreme test of Christianity is the resurrection of Jesus

Christ from the dead. It matters little what Jesus said and did while alive if His body remained in the grave. If He did not come forth in triumph from the tomb, then all His claims are false. On the other hand, since He did arise, all His claims are true. Happily, there is no better authenticated fact in all history than that of the resurrection of the body of Jesus Christ.

1. The Empty Sepulcher (24:1-3).

a. The coming of the women (v. 1). As an expression of affectionate regard for the Master, they came with spices for His body. This was a beautiful expression of sentiment, but showed their lack of faith. If they had believed His words, they would have known that His body could not be found in the sepulcher.

b. What they found (vv. 2, 3). When they came to the sepulcher they found the stone had been removed. How the stone was to be removed greatly perplexed them on their way. Upon their arrival they discovered that their difficulty had already been removed. Many of our difficulties vanish as we approach them. They found the stone rolled away, but found not the body of Jesus. For them to have found His body in the sepulcher would have been the world's greatest tragedy. The empty tomb spoke most eloquently of the deity and power of the Son of God (Rom. 1:4).

2. The Message of the Men in Shining Garments (24:4-8).

a. "Why seek ye the living among the dead?" (v. 5). This question has been reverberating through the centuries since uttered by the angels.

b. "He is not here, but is risen" (v. 6). Jesus had made all these matters quite plain. He had told them that the Lord must be betrayed and crucified and that on the third day He would rise again. If they had given heed to His words, they would have been relieved of their perplexities. This is equally true today. If we believe God's Word, we will be saved great embarrassment and perplexity.

3. The Women Witnessing to the Eleven (24:9-11).

Their thrilling testimony concerning the empty tomb and the words of the angels appeared to the apostles as idle tales, and they refused to believe.

4. Peter Investigating (24:12).

While the testimony of the women seemed as idle tales, Peter was not of the temperament to dismiss the matter from his mind, therefore he ran unto the sepulcher. Upon close investigation he found the linen clothes lying in such a way as to prove the reality of the resurrection.

K. *The Postresurrection Ministry of the Son of Man* (24:13-48).

1. The Walk of the Two Discouraged Disciples (24:13-15).

Emmaus was seven and a half miles northwest of Jerusalem. Just why they were walking this way we do not know. Perhaps their home was there, or they were merely walking to seek relief from their stunning sorrow. If they had believed what Jesus told them about His death and resurrection, they would have escaped this great disappointment. Unbelief causes many heartaches and disappointments. One of these disciples was Cleopas, but the other is unknown. The topic of conversation was the tragedy of the cross and the resurrection rumors. So little had His teaching about His resurrection impressed the disciples that the reports which the women brought were as idle tales to them. If they had believed what He said about coming forth from the grave, they would have been expecting to hear just such reports as were being circulated.

2. The Unrecognized Companion (24:16-24).

a. Who He was—Jesus (v. 15). While they reasoned together on the wonderful events of the last few days on this journey, Jesus joined them. Even when He questioned them concerning their sadness they did not recognize Him. Many times we are so taken up with our sorrows and disappointments that we do not recognize Jesus, though walking by our side.

b. His question (v. 17). Perceiving their sadness and perplexities, He sought to help by calling forth a statement of their grief.

c. Their answer (v. 18). His question so surprised them that they jumped at the conclusion that He was a stranger in Jerusalem, for the condemnation and crucifixion of the great Prophet of Nazareth were so recent and notorious that no one who had lived in Jerusalem could be ignorant of them. One valuable feature of the unbelief of the disciples was that it revealed they were not credulous enthusiasts, but hard to convince. Out of this incredulity of the disciples developed the unshaken faith in Christ's resurrection.

3. The Scriptures Opened (24:25-31).

a. His rebuke (vv. 25-30). He did not rebuke them for not believing the strange stories that they had heard, but for ignorance and lack of confidence in the Old Testament Scriptures. They had only accepted such parts of the Old Testament as suited their notion. Men and women who do not believe all that the Scriptures say about the work of the blessed Saviour are entirely blameworthy. The very center and heart of the Old Testament Scriptures set forth the death and resurrection of Christ. It is ignorance of the Scriptures and unbelief of the wonders and complete redemption wrought by Christ that rob us of many joys and power and efficiency as workers for Christ. Christ will be the Teacher of all who will open their hearts to Him.

b. Jesus recognized (vv. 31-35). While they were sitting at meat with the disciples, their eyes were opened as they saw Him bless the bread and distribute it to them. We, too, can see the Lord on such common occasions as eating a meal if we have open eyes. Indeed we ought to see Him when eating, selling, buying, and in our recreations, for He has promised His presence. They were so filled with joy over this revelation of the Saviour that they hastened back to Jerusalem to tell the other disciples of His resurrection. Those who have had the Scriptures opened to them, touching the death and resurrection of Christ, cannot help but hasten to make it known to others.

4. Jesus Standing in the Midst of the Eleven (24:36-47).

a. He said, "Peace be unto you" (vv. 36, 37). But they were terrified and affrighted. Sinful man in the presence of God is ill at ease.

b. He showed them His hands and His feet (vv. 38-40). In order to convince them of His personal identity He gave them tangible evidence that He was not a mere spirit.

c. He ate before them (vv. 41-45).

d. He commissioned them to evangelize the world (vv. 46-49). They were to testify concerning His shed blood and resurrection, and on this ground they were to preach repentance and remission of sins to all nations.

L. *Jesus Christ Ascends into Heaven* (24:49-53).

Having given the disciples the parting message to evangelize the world, He ascended into Heaven. Just as we treasure the words of our departed loved ones we should ponder this farewell message of our Lord.

1. The Proof of Christ's Ascension (24:50-53).

"And he led them out as far as to Bethany, and he lifted up his hands, and blessed them. And it came to pass, while he blessed them, he was parted from them, and carried up into heaven. And they worshiped him, and returned to Jerusalem with great joy: and were continually in the temple, praising and blessing God. Amen."

"And he said unto them, It is not for you to know the times or the seasons, which the Father hath put in his own power. But ye shall receive power, after that the Holy Ghost is come upon you: and ye shall be witnesses unto me both in Jerusalem, and in all Judea, and in Samaria, and unto the uttermost part of the earth. And when he had spoken these things, while they beheld, he was taken up; and a cloud received him out of their sight. And while they looked steadfastly toward heaven as he went up, behold, two men stood by them in white apparel; which also said, Ye men of Galilee, why stand ye gazing up into heaven? This same Jesus, which is taken up from you into heaven, shall so come in like manner as ye have seen him go into heaven" (Acts 1:7-11).

Christ visibly departed from the disciples and ascended into Heaven. The One who ascended was the One whom the disciples had known intimately for several years. He tarried with them for forty days after His resurrection to furnish them infallible proofs of its reality. He then ascended into Heaven.

2. The Purpose of Christ's Ascension.

a. To be our Forerunner. Jesus entered Heaven that the believer might follow Him there. As He now occupies a joint place with the Father on His throne, the victorious believer shall one day enjoy joint occupancy with Jesus on His throne. "Which hope we have as an anchor of the soul, both sure and steadfast, and which entereth into that within the veil; whither the forerunner is for us entered, even Jesus, made an high priest forever after the order of Melchisedec" (Heb. 6:19, 20). We can rest assured that He will not leave one of His own behind. "Behold, I stand at the door, and knock: if any man hear my voice, and open the door, I will come in to him, and will sup with him, and he with me. To him that overcometh will I grant to sit with me in my throne, even as I also overcame, and am set down with my Father in his throne" (Rev. 3: 20, 21).

b. To prepare a place for His disciples. Before He went away, He declared that in His Father's house are many mansions, or abiding places, and that He was going there to prepare a place for them. "In my Father's house are many mansions: if it were not so, I would have told you. I go to prepare a place for you" (John 14:2).

c. To appear before God for the believer. Although the believer enjoys the assurance of eternal life, he has many urgent needs while living here. The believer's triumph depends upon the efficiency of Christ's ministry. Because of His intercession He is able to save His own to the uttermost. "For Christ is not entered into the holy places made with hands, which are the figures of the true; but into heaven itself, now to appear in the presence of God for us" (Heb. 9:24).

THE GOSPEL ACCORDING TO JOHN

PART ONE—INTRODUCTORY MATTERS

I. Author—John the Apostle.

In preaching from the Gospel According to John it is highly important that the preacher possess a knowledge of the chief characteristics of John's personality. A study should be made of these as revealed in New Testament Scriptures. The following traits are suggested as examples:

A. *He Was Reserved.*

John was decidedly reticent as to himself. This quality is most desirable on the part of a minister of the Gospel.

B. *He Possessed Keen Mental Penetrative Insight.*

This is a rare gift. He did not reach conclusions by processes of reasoning, but by insight. He was indeed the seer. He could see the truth in its entirety.

C. *He Was the Apostle of Love.*

He said: "Let us love one another, for love is of God." His very nature was steeped in God's redeeming love. This love was not a soft, yielding sentiment, but an overmastering passion which seizes its object with all its might and repelled whatever tends to disgrace its loved one. It is this trait that accounts for the vehemence of utterance in his writing: "Who is a liar but he that denieth that Jesus is the Christ" (I John 2:22). His love was not only for God, but for the children of God—his brethren. In fact, love for the brethren was the evidence that he loved God his Father (I John 4:20).

D. *He Possessed Fiery Vehemence.*

John was not the effeminate weak man usually thought of, but was characterized by fiery zeal. He was thoroughly masculine with strong affection. Note his ambition for pre-eminence in the kingdom and his stern judgment upon the inhospitable Samaritans for their refusal to furnish lodging for the Lord and His disciples (Luke 9:54). John was truly a "Boanerges"—so named by the Lord who knew men's inner selves.

II. PURPOSE.

The author's purpose in writing is plainly declared in 20:30 and 31.

A. *It Is Twofold:*

1. "That Ye Might Believe That Jesus Is the Christ, the Son of God."

2. "And That, Believing, Ye Might Have Life Through His Name."

It is to present the Messiahship and deity of Jesus to the end that belief might be produced and eternal life received.

B. *The Key Words—Believe and Testify.*

Believe or some form of it occurs more than ninety times in the book; *witness* or its equivalent occurs more than forty times. Having this purpose before him the author proceeds, lawyer-like, to lay down his propositions and then to introduce his witnesses one by one to establish them.

III. ANALYSIS.

The analytical outline embraces three divisions: between the Prologue (1:1-18) and the Epilogue (20:1—21:25) is found the main part of the book, which is composed of three parts:

A. *Manifestation of the Son of God to the World* (1:19—12:50).

B. *Revelation of the Son of God to His Disciples* (13:1—17:26).

C. *Revelation of the Son of God as the Fulfiller of Prediction and Prophecy* (18:1—19:42).

PART TWO—DETAILED OUTLINE

I. THE PROLOGUE (1:1-18).

A. *Jesus Christ the Word of God* (1:1-4).

He is the Word of God because He is the expression of God to man; He is the One who utters to men the Father's will (v. 18; cf. Heb. 1:1, 2). Note the wonderful implications in these verses:

1. The Personality of the Word (1:1).

"With God"—He is a Person separate and distinct from the Father.

2. The Eternity of the Word (1:1).

"In the beginning"—He was with God in the beginning—before Creation (Col. 1:17).

3. The Deity of the Word (1:1).

"The Word was God"—He is a Being one in essence with God.

4. The Word as the Creator (1:3).

"All things were made by him."

5. The Word as the Source of All Life (1:4).

6. The Word as the Light of Men (1:4).

He is the source of men's power to reason and the human conscience. In this light we perceive the truth as to:

a. Our origin.
b. Our destiny.
c. Our nature.
d. Our present salvation.
e. Our eternal blessedness.

B. *The World's Attitude Toward the Word of God* (1:5-13).

1. Men Are Insensible to the Presence of the True Light (1:5-10).

Man's ignorance is so dense that he does not recognize the presence of the Light of glory; the very Lord who created the world and is in the world governing its destiny was unrecognized by the world. In this state God in His grace sent John the Baptist as a witness that all men might believe.

2. The Desperate Wickedness of Men's Hearts (1:11).

Jesus Christ was rejected by His own chosen nation; they would not receive the One whom God had anointed to be their King.

3. Some Received Christ and Thus Became Sons of God (1:12, 13).

Though rejected by the nation, some individuals of the nation received Him.

C. *The Word of God Made Flesh* (1:14-18).

In these verses we are taught that Jesus the eternal Son of God became a Man born of a woman, passed through childhood and youth into manhood, was tested, suffered, and died in order that He might become identified with the human race and lift it to God, and thus restore the broken fellowship.

II. MANIFESTATION OF THE SON OF GOD TO THE WORLD (1:19–12:50).

The writer having set forth his thesis, namely, the Messiahship and deity of Jesus Christ (1:1-18), proceeds at once to introduce evidence to prove it.

A. *John's Testimony to the Jewish Deputation* (1:19-28).

The purpose of these Jews in sending this committee was not a good one—they were not seeking light. Their aim was ecclesiastical regularity. They were inquiring into his right to make disciples by baptism. As his fame was spreading abroad, they thought that this irregularity needed investigation. In his testimony before them he defines:

1. His Own Position (1:19-26).

a. Negatively (vv. 20, 21). "I am not the Christ," "I am not Elias." The apparent contradiction between the words of Christ (Matt. 11:14) and these words of John is removed by the words of Luke (Luke 1:17). Malachi had announced that before the day of the Lord, Elijah the prophet should come (Mal. 4:5). These Jews wished to know whether this was the fulfillment of that prophecy. John did come in the spirit and power of Elijah, which must be the thought of Christ in Matthew 11:14, "I am not that prophet." The "prophet" here referred to, no doubt, was the one announced in Deuteronomy 18:15-18, about which they seemed not to have clear knowledge.

b. Positively (vv. 22-28). "I am the voice of one crying in the wilderness" (v. 23; cf. Isa. 40:3). This answer shows John's humility. He did not wish to direct the attention of the people to himself. He declares his unworthiness to even unloose the latchet of Christ's shoes. With reference to their question as to his authority to baptize, he seems to say, "I do not baptize by my own authority but by commission from One far higher than myself. I only baptize with water, and I do not do it to make disciples for myself but for my Master. I form no party, I ask no man to follow me. I tell all whom I baptize to believe on that mighty One, who is coming after me. I am only the servant of One far greater than myself, who is even now standing among you if you had eyes to see Him."

2. The Position of Christ (1:23).

He is the Lord. He announced that in fulfillment of the prophetic prediction he was the forerunner of the Lord.

B. *John's Testimony Before His Disciples* (1:29-34).

1. Jesus Is the Lamb of God (1:29).

The lamb was familiar to the Jewish mind. It was used to denote His substitutionary sacrifice for sin. Christ was the true Lamb to which every sacrificial offering pointed. He was the Lamb which Isaiah showed should be brought to the slaughter (Isa. 53:7) upon whom the Lord laid man's iniquity. The Passover lamb was the type of Christ (Exod. 12). He was God's Lamb because He was the One whom God had set apart from the foundation of the world to make an antonement for men's sins (I Peter 1:18-20). John invited those who stood by to behold the Lamb. This is the business of every Christian worker. Christ's mission was not merely to be a great teacher but to save men. His mission is as broad as the world. The reason men are lost now is because they are unwilling to accept Him as their Sin-bearer (John 3:18, 19; Heb. 10:28, 29). The atonement made by Christ is sufficient to blot out the sins of this world. Christ was not only the Sin-bearer who has taken away past sins but continues to daily remove the sins of those who will confess Him.

2. The Spirit Descended from Above and Abode upon Him (1:32).

Isaiah foretold that the Spirit was to be upon the Messiah (Isa. 11:2). When John thus saw the Spirit descending from Heaven upon Christ, he knew that He was the Son of God, the Messiah. John waited until he knew for a certainty; then proclaimed the news. It becomes us as His witnesses to be sure of the truth and then to speak it boldly. We must first have an experimental knowledge of the saving power of Christ before we can recommend Him to others.

3. Christ Is the Baptizer with the Holy Ghost (1:33).

He not only received the Spirit but is the sovereign Bestower of Him. He will give unto us that Spirit if we ask Him (Luke 11:13).

4. He Is the Son of God (1:34).

This testimony sent them away to be Christ's disciples. This is every true minister's testimony. He sends people away from himself to Jesus Christ.

C. *The Testimony of Christ's Deity by His First Disciples* (1:35-51).

This section shows us the value of continuous testimony for Christ. Just the day before, John delivered the same message, no doubt to the same disciples. His theme was the Lamb of God, the Sin-bearer of the world. His audience was small and his message the same, but John knew it was the message for the occasion. If one has the right message and knows the time to deliver it, he need not hunt for something new.

1. The Disciples Following Jesus (1:35-37).

As a result of the testimony of John the Baptist, his disciples left him and followed Jesus. Their look upon the Lord in compliance with John's request induced them to follow Jesus. When they looked they believed. The proof that they believed in Him was their following Him. John did not become envious of Christ's success, but rather rejoiced in it (3:26, 29). As Sunday school teachers let us deliver such a message and so conduct ourselves that those who hear us may look away from us to Christ and follow after Him. John speaks—the disciples hear and follow. The whole plan of salvation is wrapped up in this.

2. The Disciples Abiding with Jesus (1:38, 39).

The reply of the disciples to the inquiry of Jesus as to why they were following Him, shows their desire to go apart privately where they can disclose their hearts to Him. Knowing their sincerity, He invites them to His place of abode. There for the remainder of that day they held sweet intercourse with the Master. This privilege is open to everyone who will follow Jesus.

3. The Disciples Bring Others to Jesus (1:40-46).

These disciples go at once to tell others of the priceless treasure they have found. This is always characteristic of the true disciple. Andrew goes and brings his brother. The best place to begin our testimony for Christ is among our kinsfolk (Luke 8:39). This was a great day's work for Andrew, for Peter became one of the pillars in the church of God. As soon as Christ found Philip, Nathanael was found by Philip and witnessed to him concerning the Messiahship of Jesus. He tells him that this is He of whom Moses and the prophets spake. Christ is the sum and substance of the Old Testament. Nathanael was somewhat skeptical but he was honest. Philip had wisdom not to argue with him but at once brought him to Jesus. The one who is honest when brought into the presence of Jesus will soon have all doubts removed (7:17). The best way is not to rebuke the skeptic for his lack of faith, but invite him to put Christ to the test. Christianity courts inquiry. The reason men do not believe in Jesus Christ is because Satan hath blinded their eyes so as to prevent their seeing His glory (II Cor. 4:4).

4. The Disciple Seeing and Hearing Jesus Testifies as to His Divinity (1:47-51).

As soon as Nathanael saw and heard Jesus, all his doubts rolled away. This proves at once that He is the omniscient One. Perhaps Nathanael under the fig tree was praying for heavenly light and guidance. Jesus saw him while there. He who is willing to be led and to do shall surely come to the light (7:17). He who acts upon the light, shall see greater things (1:50, 51). The angels of God ascending and descending upon the Son of Man with the open heavens shows Jesus Christ as the means of communication between earth and Heaven (Heb. 10:19, 20; Eph. 2:18; cf. Gen. 28:12).

The Lord's experience with the first disciples exhibited the following stages of Christian experience:

a. Hearing about Jesus (v. 36).
b. Looking upon Jesus (v. 36).
c. Following Jesus (v. 37).
d. Abiding with Jesus (v. 39).
e. Witnessing for Jesus (vv. 41, 45).
f. Bringing others to Jesus (vv. 41, 45). This all argues for the divinity of Christ.

D. *Deity of Christ Demonstrated by a Miracle at Cana* (2:1-11).

This miracle at the marriage in Cana was designed to prove the deity of Christ. The glory of His majestic presence was perceived and accepted by the disciples, for they believed on Him.

1. The Marriage Feast (2:1, 2).

Marriage was ordained by God, and the first wedding was sanctioned by His presence (Gen. 2:22-24); indeed, He must have performed the first marriage ceremony. It is not only honorable in all (Heb. 13:4), but when based on true affection it is the highest and best of human relationships next to union with the Lord. It was ordained for the propagation of the race and for its happiness and well-being. It promotes the physical, moral, and spiritual well-being of both husband and wife and makes possible an atmosphere for the nurture of children. Marriage is not only an honorable relationship, but a wedding is a most beautiful occasion for many human beings. The one unfailing touchstone indicating man's human and moral qualities is his attitude toward marriage.

a. Attendance by Jesus' mother and His disciples (vv. 1, 2). The friends at this marriage feast were related to Jesus by blood and grace. To be united to Jesus Christ by the bonds of grace does not interfere with normal human relations but sanctifies them. Being the Son of man He can enter into human relations.

b. Attendance by Jesus (v. 2). God attended the first marriage on earth (Gen. 2:22), and Jesus, who was about His Father's business (Luke 2:49) set a mark of honor upon every spring of human life by gracing this marriage feast with His presence. The Redeemer of man as He entered upon His exalted career thus lifted the holy ordinance of marriage to its proper dignity and beauty. Man by polygamy, adultery, divorce, and fornication has basely degraded it.

2. The Anxiety of Jesus' Mother (2:3-5).

a. The wine failed (v. 3). Although this was a trying social exigency it seems to have been quite natural. The arrival of Jesus and His disciples put a drain upon the resources of the host, for these guests were bidden after they had reached Cana.

b. Mary presents the need to Jesus (v. 3). The clear implication is that she requested Him to embrace this opportunity to present His Messianic claims by working a miracle to supply the lack of wine. We may learn two lessons from Mary:

(1) In our great needs when our resources are exhausted, we, like Mary, should come to Jesus for help. Let us cast our cares upon Him, for He careth for us (I Peter 5:7).

(2) Let us not prescribe to Jesus the manner in which His

help is to be given. While it was right for Mary to come to Him in her need, it was not her province to dictate how help should be given.

c. Jesus' assertion of authority (v. 3). He respectfully reminded His mother that He had passed from her authority—that His Father's will was supreme. He frequently must rebuke those whom He loves.

d. Mary's confidence (v. 5). Although with calm dignity He asserted His authority, there must have been some sign by which He gave her to understand that He would not fail her in this embarrassing emergency. Frequently the Lord must rebuke us, and yet He always accompanies the rebuke with such mercy and kindness that we are encouraged to trust Him for the supply of our needs. She directed the servants to be ready to carry out whatever instructions He should issue. We should always be on the alert to hear and be ready to carry out any instructions Jesus may give.

Just a little thought that came to me as I wrote the reasons for Mary asking Jesus to meet the need of the host when the wine was gone. Somehow I wondered since Jesus was and is God, and He lived at home with the family, there must have been times when they were in need and don't you suppose Jesus supplied that need in His own home—otherwise why would Mary say that they should do as He said? She probably knew that He could and would supply the need for wine at the wedding feast and she was used to having Him do these things. Is that too far-fetched?

3. The Water Made Wine, a Display of Jesus' Creative Power. (2: 6-9).

A miracle is the display of the supernatural. It is not against the laws of nature but the execution of issues beyond nature. This creative act so mirrored the glory of Jesus that His disciples believed on Him.

a. The measure of this miracle (v. 6). The six vessels had perhaps a capacity of 120 gallons. Jesus is unstinted in His gifts. He gives a superabundance. Twelve baskets were left over from feeding the 5,000. God is bounteous in all His gifts.

b. Its freedom from display (vv. 7, 8). The mighty works of the Lord are not for display, not for the gaze of men. While not for display, it was so real that the disciples and guests knew that it was wrought by divine power.

c. Its design (v. 11). Its primary aim was to show the divine glory. Though Jesus would not use His divine power to relieve His own hunger, He responded to the plea to supply the wants of others. He came not to detract from human happiness, but to add to it.

d. Its reality (v. 9). This was not a sham, a make-believe. To prove its reality it was brought to the governor of the feast, presumably the bridegroom.

4. The Surprised Table Master (2:10, 11).

The excellency of the wine was praised by the ruler of the feast. Christ gives, not only quantity, but quality. This miracle proves that Jesus was in reality the glorious Lord, for His disciples believed on Him when they saw His glory shine forth.

E. *The Cleansing of the Temple, a Demonstration of His Messiahship and Deity* (2:13-22).

1. Jesus Attending the Passover (2:13).

He went up to Jerusalem very often to attend the various feasts. Beginning at the age of twelve He kept this custom to the end of His ministry. He was under the law and therefore He obeyed it (Deut. 16:16), but primarily He went up because it was His Father's house. It is important that all people from their youth up should make attendance upon the house of God a habit of their lives. They should be taught that it is not only their duty but high privilege to observe the ordinances of God's house.

2. The Temple Defiled (2:14).

For the various sacrifices in the Temple many oxen, sheep, and doves were needed. Many persons came from distant parts of the land; therefore, it was impracticable to bring their sacrifices with them, so they brought money and bought the animals needed. This privilege the Lord granted to them (Deut. 14:24-26). This exchange was necessary, but when evil men used it as an opportunity for gain, it became an offense before God. If Christ were to come to many of our so-called houses of God today, He would find them polluted in just as aggravating a way. His purging the Temple courts shows the need of purity and order in all matters connected with divine worship.

3. Jesus Cleansing the Temple (2:15-17).

a. Driving out the merchants and animals (v. 15). Being the Lord of the Temple, the very Messiah who should come to His Temple, He had the right to cleanse it, to drive out those who polluted it. It is not said that He used the scourge of cords but, at any rate, it was the symbol of authority. This act is typical of the day when Jesus will come in wrath and execute judgment upon all who profane His house and service.

b. His command (v. 16). "Make not my Father's house an house of merchandise." Merchandise is legitimate in its place. Any use of the Lord's house other than to worship and honor Him is to make it a place of merchandise, to pollute it. There is great danger of a worldly spirit intruding into the domain of religion. Men who unite with the church for temporal interests, men who come to the house of worship with worldly matters uppermost in their thoughts, ministers who serve as professionals, men who bring their ill-gotten gains to help further the work of the Lord—in fact, all who do not behave properly in the Lord's house are defiling it and therefore all such must meet His judgment.

c. His zeal (v. 17). He was so completely dominated by the passion to do the will of God that He unreservedly gave Himself to His work. This was according to the prophecy: "The zeal of thine house hath eaten me up." We should take His act as an example to us in the divine service and manifest commendable zeal. This reform did not prove permanent. A few years later He cleansed it again. This shows how quickly the human heart is under the control of sin. The only permanent reformation is that which is wrought in regeneration. The new birth is necessary.

4. The Jews Demanding a Sign (2:18-22).

They demanded of Jesus that He show His authority for such behavior. He told them that the only sign that would be given was His death and resurrection. Destroying the Temple and raising it up in three days refers to His crucifixion and resurrection. The resurrection is an unalterable proof of His divine Sonship (Rom. 1:4). Jesus came forth from the grave by His own power. The Jews did not want a sign. They were only finding excuses for their wickedness. Men today who are demanding proof of Christ's divinity do not really wish the proof but are only trying to find excuses for their sins. Jesus had the ability to justify His ways before God and man. After the resurrection the disciples remembered the words of Jesus on this occasion. This shows that no sowing of the truth shall eventually fail. The fruit shall be gathered though it may be many days hence. This ought to be a great comfort for Sunday school teachers and Christian workers.

F. *Christ's Deity Proved by His Knowledge and Teaching* (2:24–3:21).

The subject of the conversation with Nicodemus was the new birth. This topic has peculiar significance in the light of Nicodemus' station in life. He was a learned rabbi, a doctor of the law and presumably a man of good character. His coming by night indicates his timidity. Like Joseph of Arimathaea he was afraid to openly espouse the cause of the new Teacher of Galilee lest he be put out of the synagogue. Though timid, as an honest man he must investigate and get firsthand information.

1. The Necessity of the New Birth (3:1-7).

It is not a matter of choice as to whether one is to be born again, but of necessity if he is ever to see and enter the kingdom of God. Regeneration is the first demand the Gospel of Christ makes upon men. The reasons for this are:

a. The kingdom of God is a spiritual kingdom (vv. 3, 5). Therefore, there must be a spiritual birth in order to see and enter it. As we enter the physical kingdom by a natural birth, so we enter the kingdom of God by a supernatural birth.

b. The natural birth (v. 6). The nature which we get through the natural birth is radically and essentially bad. Christ declares that that which is born of the flesh is flesh. In Galatians 5:19-21 Paul gives a catalogue of the works of the flesh. The flesh cannot be improved (Jer. 13:23). Culture and educate, do all you please, and it still remains flesh. Furthermore, in order to enter into the kingdom of Heaven there must be a nature fitted for Heaven. To be in Heaven with a carnal nature would be undesirable. There is nothing that can be substituted for the new birth. Men are trying to substitute morality and education for the new birth. Nicodemus possessed these; yet Christ declared that he needed something more.

Regeneration is an act, not a process. It is an act of God through the Holy Spirit which quickens a man from spiritual death and plants within him God's own nature (II Peter 1:4). It is no more possible to have a physical being without a physical birth than it is to have a spiritual nature without being born of the Spirit.

2. The Mystery of the New Birth (3:8-13).

Its process is mysterious, but its results are definite. You may not be able to discern from whence the wind cometh or whither it goeth, but you know that it blows by its effects. The fruit of our lives demonstrates our nature, whether it is heavenly or carnal. We need not be told that we have a physical birth, for our bodies with their various faculties in exercise prove it. Even so the presence within us of a nature which has no affinity for the things of the world, a strong affection for God, and a disposition to yield prompt obedience to His commands proves that we have been born from above. Just as a tree is known by its fruits, so tastes, desire, and ambition prove it. Galatians 5:22, 23 is an infallible test. The truthfulness of this declaration is vouched for by the fact that Jesus Christ came down from Heaven to make it known. Even the great teacher Nicodemus could not understand it without a revelation.

3. The Ground upon Which the New Birth Rests (3:14-18).

Christ's atoning death on the cross makes regeneration possible. He took the place of sinners. His infinite merit was placed to their account. He suffered in the sinner's stead. Just as the Israelites had only to look on the brazen serpent in the wilderness, so the sinner must look to Christ uplifted on the cross. (See Num. 21:4-9; John 12:32; II Cor. 5:21; I Peter 2:24.) Our salvation cost on the part of God the giving up of His only begotten Son, and on the part of Christ the sufferings and shame of the cross.

4. For Whom Salvation Was Provided (3:16, 17).

"Whosoever believeth on him."

These verses give in a condensed form the whole plan of salvation.

a. The source—God so loved.
b. The ground—the death of Christ.
c. The recipients—whosoever.
d. How appropriated—believeth on Him.
e. Results—should not perish, have everlasting life.

5. Men's Attitude Toward Christ (3:18-21).

a. Some believe and are saved. Those who believe are now free from condemnation (5:24). They are not only saved now, but forever (10:28, 29; Rom. 8:33, 34).

b. Some will not believe and are resting, therefore, under the condemnation of God. The awful sin which causes men to be eternally lost is unbelief in Christ. The cause of their unbelief in Him is their love of sin. Refusal to come to Christ proves that men's deeds are evil and that they love darkness rather than light.

G. *The Last Testimony of John the Baptist* (3:22-36).

1. The Occasion (3:22-26).

John and Jesus baptizing in the same locality caused a controversy as to which was subordinate. Some supposed that Jesus was subordinate because He had received His commission from John.

2. The Content (3:27-36).

a. Relationship between John and Jesus (vv. 27-30).

(1) Christ's popularity due to the special favor of God (v. 27), therefore no room for jealousy.

(2) John was sent before Christ (v. 28).

(3) John was the friend of the Bridegroom (v. 29).

(4) John must decrease while Christ must increase (v. 30).

There is no need of a friend where the bridegroom received the bride, therefore, his mission being accomplished, he must retire.

b. Relation of Jesus to the world (vv. 31-36).

(1) He is above it (v. 31). He existed in Heaven before His Incarnation.

(2) He has a supernatural message (v. 32). What He saw and heard in His preincarnate state with God, He utters.

(3) He was sent into the world by God (v. 32).

(4) He is loved by God and all things are given into His hands (v. 35).

(5) Eternal life or death dependent upon men's attitudes toward Him (v. 36).

H. *The Testimony of Christ to the Samaritans* (4:1-42).

1. Jesus Must Needs Go Through Samaria (4:4-6).

The growing popularity of Jesus aroused the envious opposition of the Pharisees, which obliged Him to leave Judea and go into Samaria. There was another way to reach Galilee—one used by many Jews to avoid contact with the despised Samaritans—on the eastern side of the Jordan. He must "needs go through Samaria" in order to find this poor sinful woman and the needy citizens of Sychar. The great necessity which was upon Him was to seek and to save that which was lost (Luke 19:10). The wearied Jesus waiting at Jacob's well to speak to this poor lost woman gives us a concrete picture of the divine-human Saviour in His work of seeking lost humanity.

2. Jesus' Testimony to the Woman (4:7-26).

a. A favor asked (vv. 7-9). Jesus tactfully made a request which appealed to the woman's sympathy. Not only did the thirst of the weary traveler appeal to her, but the fact that He being a Jew asked a favor of her, showed His sympathy for her. In introducing the conversation, He referred to that which was uppermost in her mind, namely, water. This was the teacher's point of contact. He soon passed from earthly water to the water of everlasting life which was in Himself. His aim was to bridge the chasm which separated them. Every Christian worker should imitate Him. Every human mind has a handle. Our success as Christian workers depends upon our ability to grasp and use it.

b. Jesus' tender dealing with this woman (vv. 10-15). He first appealed to her curiosity by declaring: "If thou knewest the gift of God" (v. 10). He knew the deep unrest of the soul of this sinful woman as she went on her way. He knew that if she really knew Him she would believe on Him and be saved from her sins; therefore, the first thing was to get her attention. When we can get one to give attention to the claims of Christ, there is good chance of winning him. He followed this appeal to her curiosity by a promise which directed her attention to her deepest needs. There is a consciousness of deep need in every soul. Just what the need is, is not always known. The world with its honors, gains, and pleasures never really satisfies us. In her efforts to satisfy her nature, this poor woman respected neither the law of God nor the rights of men. The deepest need of a soul only Jesus can satisfy. There is real and lasting satisfaction in Him and His gifts. The woman's reply: "Sir, give me this water that I thirst not," is the inarticulate cry of every heart.

c. The woman convicted of her sins (vv. 16-19). Jesus succeeded in arousing her interest, but she did not really understand Him. Before she could understand what the water of life is, she must be convicted of her sins. He skillfully gave the command which brought her face to face with the facts of her life which she was unwilling to confess. She did not argue with Him, but became a humble inquirer. The soul must be convicted of sin before it can be converted.

d. The problem of worship submitted to Christ (vv. 20-24). This she did as soon as she perceived Him to be a prophet. This indicates that He was succeeding in bringing her mind to spiritual things. Jesus, knowing the inner life of this woman, told her of the glad time even then present when true worshipers could hold intercourse with God anywhere. He showed her that the place of worship is unimportant, that the all-important thing is to have the true conception of God as brought through the Jews. He exposed the folly of a religion of form only and showed that acceptable worship depends upon the condition of the heart. Since worship is spiritual, only those who have been regenerated can worship God in spirit. Except a man be born from above he cannot see the kingdom of God (3:3).

3. The Woman of Samaria Witnessing for Christ (4:27-39).

When the disciples perceived that Jesus talked with the woman, they marveled, yet they hesitated to ask Him for an explanation. The woman left her water-pot and went into the city and said: "Come, see a man which told me all things that ever I did. Is not this the Christ?" As soon as she was converted she became an enthusiastic missionary. This is as it ought to be and always will be. The soul that acknowledges Jesus cannot be still (1:41-45). The result of her testimony was that many believed on Jesus.

4. Jesus Testifying to the Citizens of Sychar (4:40, 41).

The woman's testimony brought the request from the Samaritans that Jesus tarry with them. He abode with them two days. Though they heard the woman's testimony, their belief was due to Christ's own word (v. 41).

5. The Samaritans Witnessing for Christ (4:42).

They declared: "We know that this is indeed the Christ, the

Saviour of the world." They confessed to the woman that their belief was not due to her testimony, but to having heard Him themselves, that they were sure that He was the Messiah.

I. *The Healing of the Nobleman's Son a Testimony to the Deity of Christ* (4:46-54).

The glorious revival among the Samaritans being over, Jesus with yearning heart for His countrymen goes back into Galilee (vv. 43-45). When He began His work there, it was not appreciated as it should have been. His own testimony is that a prophet hath no honor in his own country. Having made a reputation elsewhere He now came back to them. His fellow countrymen had witnessed His wonderful works at the capital city, Jerusalem. Now they will listen to Him.

1. The Nobleman's Earnest Plea (4:46, 47).

This father's heart is in deep anguish because of the critical illness of his son, but he had the good sense to go to Jesus in his distress. Parents should eagerly bring their children to the Great Physician. This affliction was used to bring him to Jesus. Many do not think of Jesus until overwhelmed with grief and distress. It is need that always brings men to Jesus. Even when human physicians fail, the case is not hopeless, for there is no case too hard for Christ, and there is no disease too difficult, or sorrow too great, but what relief can be found in Him. This is true of our physical ills, but it is pre-eminently true of our souls. We see here that a rich and influential man in distress, showing that the rich and exalted are no more exempt from afflictions and anxiety than are the poor. Cares and troubles come to all alike. The young are liable to disease and death as are the old. This nobleman learned of Jesus through the testimony of another (v. 47). Had not someone told him about Jesus he may not have called upon Him. Before lost men can call upon the Lord someone must tell them about Him (Rom. 10:14, 15). May the urgent need of the world to hear of the power of Jesus to save compel us to preach the Gospel unto them.

2. The Testing of the Nobleman's Faith (4:48, 49).

In his experience we find an illustration of the development of belief. He had faith but not an intelligent faith. Before help could be given, his attitude of mind must be changed. Jesus declared: "Except ye see signs and wonders, ye will not believe," showing that the nobleman's faith was such as was based upon signs and wonders. The man needed something more than the healing of his son. He must needs know Christ as Saviour as well as Healer. He did not allow himself to be put off, but insistently demanded, "Sir, come down ere my child die." This shows that he was now willing to make any experiment to save his boy. His very impotency forced him to lay hold upon the Lord. Jesus desired this man to possess a faith which was based upon His naked word, not mere signs and wonders. The Samaritans with whom Christ had just had good success took Him at His Word, did not look for signs. The way of Jesus is to first reveal Himself as a Saviour and then as a Healer.

3. The Nobleman's Faith Victorious (4:50-54).

Through his testing he passed with good advantage. He is now ready to receive the Lord's own words, "Go thy way; thy son liveth." These words created true faith and the man stepped out upon them. Because he believed the words that Jesus spoke to him, he went his way. Faith increases in brightness the longer it is exercised. The foundation upon which he reposed his faith was the words of Jesus. On his return, his faith met with confirmation. His servant met him and told him that his son was alive. Upon inquiry he found that the recovery of his son was from the very hour in which Jesus spoke the words. This was such an unmistakable evidence of the deity of Jesus that not only the nobleman, but his household was won for Christ. This affords us an example of the beauty of household religion. May we all learn that the words of Jesus are reliable! That which He promises is just as sure as though it had already come to pass. The salvation of the one who believes in Jesus is just as sure as though he had been in Heaven and seen his name in the book of life. Anxiety for the son brought salvation to the whole house.

J. *The Healing of the Impotent Man at Bethesda, a Testimony to Christ's Deity* (5:1-27).

1. The Dire Need Confronting the Lord (5:1-5).

Perhaps no more miserable spectacle ever confronted the Lord. Before Him were a multitude of sick, blind, halt, and withered folk, waiting to be healed. With great anxiety they watched every move of the waters. At such time intense was the struggle to get into the waters, and great was the disappointment of those who were prevented from doing so. The most impotent were left to wait as the others would beat them to the pool. This group of suffering folk is but a picture of the many thousands of the like in every age, and their physical infirmities betoken their moral and spiritual wretchedness. All the misery in the world, be it physical or moral, has been brought in through sin. The Lord singles out one case from among the rest, which seems to be the most aggravated. This one was an invalid for thirty-eight years. Who can estimate the meaning of so many years of suffering?

Are there not cases of equal malignity about us today? The awful misery, pain, despair, and death about us on every hand ought to cause us more and more to hate sin, for they are all traceable to sin. He who knows the awful effects of sin, will not be so careless about it. Many are not only careless about it, but delight in it. There is no surer mark of man's depravity than his delight in sin. "Fools make a mock at sin" (Prov. 14:9). While we acknowledge that sin has entered the world and wrought such dreadful ruin, we can prevent its dominion in our own lives, for the Great Physician is ready to heal all who will call on Him. There is no case too hard for Him; He is able to save unto the uttermost.

2. The Impotent Man Made Whole By Christ (5:6-9).

This man's misery caused the compassion of Christ to go out to him. His very helplessness was an appeal. Our very needs give us a claim upon the Lord. Christ's method with this man was:

a. To kindle hope within him by the question, "Wilt thou be made whole?" (v. 6). Many times this man had come with the expectation of having his body healed, only to have his hopes shattered.

b. To inspire confidence.

c. To expect obedience. When his hopes were merged into confidence, then he is ready to express his confidence by rendering willing obedience to the Lord's commands.

d. To bestow blessing. This willing obedience was crowned with unspeakable blessings. This is the method always. Hope, confidence, obedience, and blessing indicate the steps in the Lord's dealing with helpless sinners.

3. The Antagonism of the Jews to Christ (5:10-13).

Their attitude toward this man reveals their real condition of heart. They do not seem to notice the blessed experience which has come to him. They only see him carrying his bed on the sabbath. This shows how gross was their perversion of the gracious institution of God. The man could only tell them that the One who had healed him had bidden him so to do. When Jesus found this man again in the Temple and revealed Himself to him, the man went immediately to tell the Jews that it was Jesus who had healed him. Their opposition now turns against Christ. The reply of Jesus shows that the sin of man had broken God's rest, and thus ended the sabbath. Christ's work of healing and removing sin was the beginning of the restoration of the sabbath. This only incited more intense hatred. They now attempt to kill Him because He made God His Father.

4. The Great Lesson that Recovery from Sickness Should Teach Us (5:14).

Every affliction that comes to us is God's voice to us. We should learn that nothing in this world happens by chance—that the hand of God is in all our experiences. This man's sickness was the result of sin. May God's intervention in our behalf in raising us up from beds of sickness be a call to a higher and more useful life. To go back in sin again will bring worse results.

5. The Discourse of Jesus in Explanation of the Healing of the Impotent Man at Bethesda (5:17-47).

a. Asserts His equality, oneness, and intimacy with God (vv. 17-30).

(1) He gives life (v. 21).
(2) All judgment committed to Him (v. 22).
(3) Honor done to Him is honor done to the Father (v.23).
(4) The Father and Son act in conjunction (v. 19).
(5) The Father tells the Son everything (v. 20).
(6) Salvation can come only through hearing Christ's words (v. 24).
(7) Christ's work in resurrection:
   (a) Gives life to the dead (v. 25).

(b) All shall come forth at His call (vv. 28, 29).

b. Christ proves His deity by four witnesses (vv. 30-47).

(1) John the Baptist (v. 33).

(2) Mighty works (v. 36).

(3) The Father (v. 37; cf. Matt. 3:17).

(4) The Scriptures (vv. 39-47).

K. *The Testimony of the Miracle of the Loaves to the Deity of Christ* (6:1-14).

In the previous chapter Jesus showed Himself to be the source of life. He here proves Himself to be the Sustainer of life.

1. Jesus' Compassion for the Multitude (6:1-5; cf. Matt. 14:14).

The sight of the crowd always incited the Lord's sympathy. He knew that they were as shepherdless sheep (Mark 6:34). They were going forth with no one to care for them. Besides, they were ignorant, so much so that they had no appreciation of Him. Added to this was their awful physical hunger. This condition roused the Saviour's pity. This is true of the multitude today. The crowd surges about us daily as shepherdless sheep. There is no one to care for them. Then, too, they are ignorant. Sin has so thoroughly blinded them that they are not conscious of their lost condition. Down deep in their heart is a hunger for truth and God. The millions of earth are hungering for Christ, though ignorant of their real needs. The human heart can never find rest apart from Christ.

2. The Lord's Conference with the Disciples Touching the People's Need (6:5-9).

This was not done for His benefit, for He knew what He would do (v. 6). He is equal to any occasion. His object in this conference may be summed up as follows:

a. To teach them their sense of obligation to the multitudes. Men are slow to recognize their obligation to the great shepherdless multitudes. We need to be taught the wonderful truth that God has made man His partner in the salvation of the world. We are workers together with God (II Cor. 6:1). It is a most solemn obligation to co-operate with Him in saving the millions who are groping in darkness. God will hold us responsible for the execution of the charge to be our brother's keeper.

b. To teach them their true helplessness in the face of such great needs. The loaves and fishes were as nothing in the presence of 5,000 men, besides women and children. Well might Andrew exclaim, "What are these among so many?" We may plant and water, but the increase entirely comes from God. It is a good thing to realize our true needs, that we may be driven to Christ, who is able to supply them all.

c. To teach them that their sufficiency is from the Lord. The mission worker needs to know that Christ is the only source of supply. Without Him we can do nothing (15:1-8). We can no more carry on the work ourselves than the branch can bear fruit without the vine. The branch supplies the life and strength for the production of fruit. Philip's arithmetic is of no use in the face of such need. The Lord Jesus has all power. We should not count any case too hard for Him. He can soften even the hardest heart. May we put our trust in Him!

3. The Lord's Method of Accomplishing His Work (6:10-13). We observe here the orderliness of Christ's work. He does everything decently and in order. He pauses to give thanks for their scanty supply, teaching us that we should always bring our abilities and gifts to God that He might bless them to His use.

a. The Lord's part was to bless and break the bread; yea, even to create the needed supply. This part the disciples could not perform. The Lord must begin the work. The same kind of bread was provided for all, rich and poor, young and old, women and children.

b. The disciples' part was to distribute that which He had blessed and consecrated. This is true of the missionary today. His part is to take from the hands of the Lord that which He has blessed and consecrated, and distribute it among the starving multitudes. We are not responsible for the supply; but we are responsible for its distribution to all those who are hungering and perishing for the bread of life.

c. The people's part was to sit down and eat. They had no part in the provision, neither its distribution; but only to take from the hands of the disciples and eat. This is exactly our situation. The people are responsible for the taking and eating of the bread of life. Obedience is their part. This is an illustration of the part obedience plays in our salvation. When all had eaten to the full, much was left, illustrating the superabundance of Christ's salvation. The Gospel is ample for the salvation of the world.

4. The Effect (6:14).

The people recognized Him at once as the Prophet who should come. They believed Him for His works' sake.

L. *Christ's Deity Demonstrated by the Miracle of Walking on the Sea* (6:15-21).

1. Attempt to Make Christ King by Force (6:15).

The impression made upon the masses by the feeding of the 5,000 was so tremendous that they were about to elevate Him to the Kingship by a mass movement. Christ's elevation to the Kingship will be a divine act (Ps. 2:6). This is the lesson that the Church must learn. The eternal decree of redemption will be actuated by the coming of Christ clothed with divine authority to reign over the universe (Ps. 2:7). The kingdom will not come as a result of the efforts of the Church, but by the Stone hewn out of the mountain without hands smiting the image and grinding it to powder. Gentile rule must be supplanted by the Redeemer-King (Dan. 2:44).

2. Christ's Strategy (6:16).

He dismissed the multitude and instructed the disciples to get into the boat and meet Him on the other side of the lake. He Himself withdrew to a lonely place for prayer. This would give the disciples time to receive a right perception of Christ's deity and power.

3. Jesus Walking on the Sea (6:17-19).

A tempestuous storm had arisen giving an opportunity for the disciples to see Him as the Almighty Ruler of the forces of nature. Dr. Erdman says: "It reveals, not a political leader with power restricted, earthly sphere, but a divine Creator who has supreme power in the universe." This was not a case where the law of gravitation was suspended but a revelation of Himself as superior to natural forces in His being independent of space.

4. The Frightened Disciples (6:19, 20).

They were calmed by His words of cheer, "It is I; be not afraid."

5. The Disciples Willingly Received Him into the Ship (6:21).

Immediately the ship was safely at the destination. So it will even be to the believing disciple who obeys and trusts the Lord Jesus.

M. *The Discourse on the Bread of Life, a Testimony of Christ's Deity* (6:22-71).

1. Searching for Jesus (6:22-27).

a. The searchers (vv. 22-24). This search was not made by the disciples, but by the people who honored Him only as a miracle-worker. Doubtless they were ones who sought by force to make Him king (v. 15). They concluded that such a Man could deliver them from the Roman yoke and supply all their needs.

b. Their motive in seeking Jesus (vv. 26, 27). They sought Jesus, not to honor Him, but for what they thought He could do for them. They failed to see the real purpose of the miracle of the loaves and fishes. Instead of seeing the Saviour through the miracle, they see only the bread. Outwardly, these people seemed to be honest seekers, but He who knoweth the very motives of the heart declared that they were coming with wrong motives. He detected their hypocrisy. "Man looketh on the outward appearance, but the Lord looketh on the heart" (I Sam. 16:7). The hypocrisy of those today who are seeking Jesus through false motives shall one day be exposed. It will be impossible to deceive Christ. Though their motives shall have not been right, their case is not hopeless. The right way is pointed out to them (v. 27). They are forbidden to labor for the imperishable. This does not mean that it is wrong to engage in legitimate business or labor, for Jesus Himself toiled at the carpenter's bench at Nazareth. Labor is honorable in all. Even before the fall of man he had employment in Paradise. His words are a continuous rebuke to that excessive devotion after earthly things to the exclusion or neglect of the soul's interests. The thing He would have us to do is to take great pains to find that food for the soul which is so abundantly provided in Himself. He who is diligent in the pursuit of his soul's interests shall have the Son of man—the meat which endureth unto everlasting life. Would that men were as anxious for this as they are for the things of this life. We should aim to center our interests and energies upon that which we can take with us beyond the grave.

2. Working the Works of God (6:28-31).

When the Lord had commanded them to labor and strive after the bread of everlasting life which was in Himself, they at once wanted to know what works they must perform. This is ever the cry of the natural heart. Many today think that the only way to Heaven is by doing works. Many admit that faith is essential, but it must be supplemented by works. This is the error with which Paul deals in the Epistle to the Galatians. We find in the world three kinds of errorists.

a. The pure legalist who maintains that justification is through works alone.

b. The antinomian who disavows works entirely.

c. The Galatianist who insists upon an admixture of law and grace—that justification begins with faith and is completed in works. To all this Christ says: "This is the work of God, that ye believe on him whom he hath sent" (v. 29). If we would but get a scriptural definition of terms there would be an end to this quibbling. Faith involves the action of the affections and will as truly as that of the intellect. Bible faith and heart belief are identical. The heart in Scripture stands for the whole man. When a man has saving faith, he has an intelligent apprehension of the truth of Christ's Person; his affections go out toward Him and his soul yields itself to Him. Thus believing on Christ is the work of God. The content of the word *faith* is the entire man laying hold of God through Christ and then working for Him. Works, genuine works, is faith in action. Bible faith is not a dead entity but a vital, living thing inciting to action. We are justified by faith which works. This is the teaching of James 2:16-26. Faith in Jesus is the first work, and provides the force necessary for all deeds, which will please the Lord.

3. The Bread of Life (6:32-35).

a. Jesus Christ is the Bread of life (v. 35). Bread is a necessary food. No other article of food can take its place. Christ is the necessary food for the soul. Many substitutes have been offered but only He can permanently satisfy. He provides satisfaction in sunshine and shadow, in joy and sorrow, in prosperity and adversity, in life and in death. Christ is the food of the soul by God's appointment. He is indefinitely more to the soul than bread is to the body, for He both gives and sustains life. Apart from Christ men have not true life in them. Men must have this Bread from Heaven or die in their sins. Bread is a universal food; so Christ is for all men in all ages.

b. How to obtain this Bread of life (v. 35). It is by coming to Christ and believing on Him. By this is meant "that movement of the soul which takes place when a man, feeling his sins and finding out that he cannot save himself, hears of Christ, applies to Christ, trusts in Christ, lays hold on Christ, and leans all his weight on Christ for salvation." It is not a question of personal merit or of doing good works, or the ability to purchase, but come and take. We must eat of physical bread before we derive benefit from it, so we must appropriate Christ in order to obtain salvation.

c. The blessed issue of taking this bread (v. 35).

(1) "Shall never hunger." The one who takes Christ never feels an emptiness or a deficiency. Christ absolutely satisfies.

(2) "Shall never thirst." We drink of natural water and thirst again, but when we drink at the fountain of living water there is no more thirsting.

4. The Will of God (6:36-40).

a. That none of those given to Christ should be lost (v. 39). All that the Father gave to Christ shall come to Him, and those who come to Him shall not be cast out, but shall be raised again at the last day.

b. That everyone who seeth the Son and believeth on Him shall have everlasting life (v. 40).

5. Outline of Discourse.

For a comprehensive and detailed outline of Christ's discourse on the Bread of life, note the following:

a. Its content (vv. 22-59).

(1) The introduction—historical (vv. 22-25).

(2) Reproof for unworthy motive in seeking Jesus (v. 26).

(3) Exhortation to labor for the meat that abideth unto eternal life (v. 27).

(4) Christ declares that He is that abiding Bread (vv. 28-40).

(a) He is the true Bread (v. 32).

(b) The Bread of God (v. 33).

(c) The Bread out of Heaven (v. 32).

(d) The Bread of life (v. 35).

(5) God's will is that everyone who believes in Christ

should have eternal life (vv. 36-40). Believing on Christ is the evidence that God is working in you.

(6) Christ replies to certain objections (vv. 41-59).

(a) Affirms the need for divine aid in coming to Christ (vv. 41-46).

(b) Reiterates His claim to be the Bread of life (vv. 47-57).

(c) Explains the way of this Bread is to be received (vv. 52-55).

(d) Declares the issue of partaking of this Bread—"Live forever" (vv. 56-59).

b. Its issue (vv. 60-71).

(1) Many of His disciples turned back (vv. 60-66).

(2) Peter's confession (vv. 67-69).

N. *The Testimony of Christ at the Feast of Tabernacles to His* Deity (7:1—8:59).

1. The Occasion (7:1-13).

a. His unbelieving brethren urged Him to go to Jerusalem that His disciples might see His works and show Himself to the world (vv. 1-9).

b. Difference of opinion as to Christ prevailed among the Jews (vv. 10-13).

2. The Content of John (7:14—8:58).

He boldly entered the Temple and taught to the astonishment of the Jews.

a. "My doctrine is not mine, but his that sent me. If any man will do his will, he shall know of the doctrine, whether it be of God or whether I speak of myself" (vv. 16, 17).

b. His mission was for the glory of the One who sent Him (v. 18).

c. He was sent by God (vv. 28, 29). Christ charged them with deliberate purpose to destroy Him even when they knew who He was and from whence He came. He also said that in a little time He would go to Him who had sent Him.

d. He declared that He was the Bestower of the Holy Spirit (vv. 37-39). Here is the great prophecy concerning the power of the Holy Spirit in the pentecostal age which would follow the death of Christ.

e. "I am the light of the world" (8:12).

f. "I am from above" (v. 23).

g. Oneness with the Father (vv. 28, 29).

h. Reality of discipleship and spiritual freedom (vv. 31-37). Salvation is more than the removal of sin's penalty. It is a setting free from its power and bringing the sinner as the child into the family of God. To be free in Christ is to be a disciple, a learner (v. 31). It is not mere profession, but persistently following of Christ which proves our discipleship. Freedom is through the knowledge of the truth (v. 32). So long as people are ignorant of Christ they remain in bondage of sin. Sin is a hard taskmaster, and has, as its end, death (Rom. 6:23). Through Christ's blood we are justified and pardoned, and can look forward with boldness to the coming judgment. The one in Christ shall not come into judgment (5:24), but he has passed out of death into life. This freedom issues in an enduring relation of sonship (v. 35), which saves from death.

i. "Before Abraham was, I am" (v. 58).

3. The Issue Of (8:59).

They took up stones to cast at Him.

O. *The Healing of a Man Born Blind, a Powerful Testimony to the Deity of Christ* (9:1-41).

This miracle was so unusual that it was declared since the world began that it was not heard that any man opened the eyes of one that was born blind.

1. Working the Works of God While It Is Day (9:1-5).

a. The disciples' problem (vv. 1, 2). In their minds all affliction, negative and positive, was God's retribution for sin. Therefore, they argued that this man's blindness proved his sin. They recognized, too, that the effect of sin is sometimes hereditary. No doubt they inferred this from the second commandment (Exod. 20:5). The implication is that they held the view that men have pre-existence, and that suffering in this life may be the result of sins committed in that pre-existent state. Many about us today are disposed to associate sickness, disease, and all sorts of calamities with judgment for sin.

b. The Lord's answer (vv. 3-5). The Lord affirmed that in this case there was neither sin on the man's part, nor on the part of his parents, but it was an occasion for the display of the works of God, and He had come to execute this task while it was day, because the night would come when no man could work. In this saying, Jesus conveyed the message that there are limited hours for the task which we are sent to do; and that if we neglect our opportunity for service it will be lost forever as the night will soon come when no work will be possible. Since Christ is the light of the world, the task which challenged His attention was the opening of this man's eyes. The purpose of Jesus in working miracles was not a mere exhibition of miraculous power, but "to illustrate in the physical sphere His power in the spiritual sphere." With this as our viewpoint, we observe that this man's absolute helplessness in bettering his physical condition is illustrative of man's utter helplessness in the salvation of his own soul. The natural man is blind and dead (II Cor. 4:4; Eph. 2:1). God by His spirit must quicken the soul dead in trespass and sin before it can see to take hold on Christ, the remedy for sin.

2. The Man's Eyes Opened (9:6, 7).

a. The means. Jesus spat on the ground and made clay of the spittle and anointed his eyes. Observe that the means used in this miracle were little less than foolish in themselves. How ill-adapted a plaster of mud would be when applied to the eye, the most delicate and sensitive of all the organs of the body! What is more to be avoided than applying sand to the eye? The object must have been to teach this man the utter inadequacy of the means to the accomplishment of the end that he might be caused to look from the means to the One who used them, that he might be convinced that the power was of God. Then, too, the washing in the pool would teach him the absolute necessity of immediate, implicit obedience in order to enjoy God's blessings.

b. His obedience (v. 7). He immediately obeyed. He did not stop to question the reasonableness of the command. Obedience only to that which seems reasonable is not obedience at all. He did not inquire as to what would be the result. God's Word is the standard, not human reason.

3. The Man's Testimony (9:8-36).

In his testimony we have a fine example of the development of faith. The opening of this man's eyes aroused inquiry among his neighbors. When a man's spiritual eyes are opened there will be a stir among his friends. While they were debating and investigating the matter, he gave his testimony.

a. He testified to his personal identity (v. 9). This was very easy. His self-consciousness enabled him to know that he was the same man who was born blind.

b. He testified as to how it was done (vv. 11-15). So definite was his experience that he was able to tell just how it was done. When he repeated it, there was no conflict.

c. He testified that the One who opened his eyes was a Prophet (v. 17).

d. He testified that this Healer no doubt was sent of God (vv. 30-33). He declared that He was the greatest worker of miracles who had appeared since the world began.

e. He worshiped Him as the Son of God (v. 38).

4. The Results of His Confession.

a. As to the people, they were divided in sentiment (v. 16). Some believed He was from God because of His works, others that He was a sinner because He did His work on the Sabbath day.

b. As to the man, they cast him out (v. 34). Faithful testimony will often result in ostracism from even religious people, but whatever the cost we must be faithful.

c. As to Jesus, He found the man (v. 35). Being cast out by men, he found himself in the arms of Jesus. It is quite often true that separation from human fellowship results in more vital fellowship with Jesus. Had he not been cast out by men, perhaps he never would have experienced the deeper fellowship of Jesus. He was led on to a deeper faith. He saw Him first as a miracle worker, then as a prophet, and finally as the Son of God; and when he perceived Him to be the Son of God, he worshiped Him. Those who manifest their fidelity will experience His love.

5. Summary of Chapter (9:1-41).

This whole chapter may be reviewed from three angles:

a. As an acted parable of the life that issues in faith in Christ (an illustration of the spiritual sphere in terms of the physical).

b. A testimony to the deity of our Lord. This testimony is fourfold:

(1) The miracle itself, an unheard of work, that a man born blind should receive his sight.

(2) The unwilling admission of the enemies themselves who made a public and official investigation.

(3) The testimony of the man himself.

(4) The testimony of his parents.

c. An illuminating example of faith's development.

P. *The Testimony of Christ Being the Shepherd of God's Flock* (10:1-42).

The occasion for the parable of the good shepherd was the excommunication of the blind man who had been healed by Christ. When Jesus saw the Pharisees, who posed as shepherds of God's flock, casting out of the fold this poor, helpless sheep (9:34, 35), He boldly declared that He was the Good Shepherd. Behind this we can see His compassion for the poor man and indignation at the Pharisees. The relationship of the Messiah to His own is set forth in the Old Testament under the figure of the Shepherd and His sheep (Ps. 23; Ezek. 34).

1. The Good Shepherd (10:1-18).

a. He is the true Shepherd (vv. 1-6). He came by the divinely appointed way. The power exercised by the Pharisees in casting out this man was not obtained by lawful means. It was stolen by them and exercised in the bold spirit of robbers. John the Baptist and others of the prophets had performed the function of the porter and opened the door to the Shepherd (v. 23). Despite the deceit, audacity, theft, and robbery of these Pharisees, those who were Christ's sheep were declared to be forming a new flock and following Him as the true Shepherd (v. 4). The reason the man suffered excommunication for Jesus' sake was that he recognized Him as the true Shepherd and the Pharisees as strangers. We can afford excommunication at the hands of men when we can have the leadership of Christ.

b. He is the Door of the sheep (vv. 7-10). The way to fellowship with God is through Christ. He is the only door (Acts 4:12). There is absolutely no way to get into the fold of the redeemed but by Him. All who attempt it are thieves and robbers (v. 8). Those who become members of the flock through Him enjoy marvelous gifts (vv. 9, 10).

(1) Salvation—"Shall be saved" (vv. 27, 28). Not only saved now but saved eternally.

(2) Liberty—"Shall go in and out" (v. 9). Only those who accept salvation in Christ know what freedom is. "If the Son therefore shall make you free, ye shall be free indeed" (8:36).

(3) Contentment—"Shall go in and out and find pasture" (v. 9). The one who really enters the fold by Christ the door receives that which is all-satisfying to the soul. The world's attractions lose their hold upon him. He has no want which is not satisfied, (Ps. 23). Not only is every way supplied, but every fear removed.

c. He is the Good Shepherd (vv. 11-18). He is so devoted to His sheep that He willingly lays down His life for them. The hireling abandons his sheep in time of danger. The Good Shepherd has perfect knowledge of His sheep and they know Him (vv. 14, 15). The mutual relationship which exists between Christ and the Father. Knowing His sheep so well, He looks after their welfare. He enjoys such personal intimacy with His sheep that He knows them by name and goes before them to lead the way and defend them from every danger. This He will do even unto death. On Calvary this was historically fulfilled. The hireling, represented by the Pharisees, takes up the work and continues it for his own sake, for the profit that is in it. It was Christ's love for such sheep as this poor blind man that caused Him to give up His life in order to find for them the abundant life (v. 10). This sympathy is world-wide—"other sheep I have which are not of this fold." This suggests that the Gentiles have a place in His fold. All who believe in Christ form one flock. In order to save His sheep He voluntarily laid down His life (vv. 17, 18). Such devotion enjoys the love of the Father (v. 17). In view of that time when Christ shall gather His widely separated flock into one fold, let us now be brought under that spirit of unity which will please Him.

2. The Sheep (10:19-30).

a. Unbelievers are not His sheep (vv. 19-26). Christ's assertion that He was the Good Shepherd caused a division among the people. Some accused Him of being mad, others that He had a Devil. To their request that He would tell them plainly if He were the Christ, He referred them to the testimony of His works, declaring that the secret of their inability to recognize Him was their unbelief.

b. They recognize His voice (v. 4). There are many voices in the world, the voice of the hireling, the voice of the thief and the voice of the stranger, but none of these will the sheep hear. The voice of the true Shepherd is recognized by His sheep even amid the babel of voices in the world today. They not only know it as His, their souls are in accord with it. It is sweet music to their ears.

c. His sheep follow Him (vv. 3, 27). This is the proof that they are His. The one who does not hear, heed, or obey the Lord's voice is clearly not His sheep. His sheep have unquestioned faith in His ability to lead them. Regardless of the darkness, dangers, and difficulties of the way they turn from the voice of others and follow Him. The true sheep will flee from strangers (v. 5). This is a solemn warning to many professing Christians who are following strangers.

d. His sheep are eternally secure (vv. 27, 28). The sheep are entirely dependent upon the Shepherd. It is the Shepherd's business to look after and care for the sheep. This He does, for He knows them by name and is acquainted with their weaknesses and trials.

3. The Almighty Shepherd (10:22-42).

a. Works in the Father's name (v. 25). He declares that His works bear witness that He is the divine Son of God.

b. He gives eternal life to His sheep (v. 28). Only God can give eternal life.

c. He jointly with the Father makes the sheep eternally secure (vv. 28, 29).

d. Oneness with the Father (v. 30).

e. Sanctified by the Father and sent into the world (vv. 36-38).

Q. *Jesus Raises Lazarus from the Dead, a Witness of His Deity* (11:1-57).

1. Mary and Martha Send for Jesus (11:1-6).

The family of which Lazarus was a member held a peculiar place in the affections of Jesus. When the doors of other homes were closed against Him, the door of this one flung wide open to receive Him. When misunderstood by others, and weary with His arduous labors, He could come into this home, enjoy intelligent fellowship, and find rest. In these days of social and spiritual sunshine this family had come to know Jesus as more than a mere man. So when the shadow of death was cast over this home, they instinctively turned to their best Friend for sympathy and help. We should all learn to know Jesus while we are well and happy so that we can turn to Him in our times of distress; for those who receive Him into their homes when all is well can be sure of His sympathy and help when sickness and death visit them.

When sickness seized the brother in this home, his sisters dispatched a messenger after Jesus. His behavior in tarrying several days after receiving the message no doubt greatly perplexed Martha and Mary. This action is strangely prefaced by the statement that "Jesus loved Martha and her sister and Lazarus." They sent for Him because He loved Lazarus and yet He tarries because of His love for them. This apparent mystery is explained by noting the use of two different words in referring to His love. The one is human, and the other divine love. Human love would have hastened to that home, but divine love, which has as its basis perfect knowledge, tarried. All the apparent delays of the Lord are occasioned by His love.

2. Jesus Goes to the Bethany Home (11:7-17).

At length the time came for Him to turn His face toward this sorrowing household. He told the disciples that His purpose in going was to awaken Lazarus out of his sleep to the intent that they might believe (vv. 11, 15). His mission to this home was twofold: to restore to these sisters their brother, and to strengthen the faith of the disciples. The word *sleep* reveals Jesus' estimate of death —it is only a sleep. This is a most comforting word to those in deep sorrow. Jesus is fearless in the discharge of duty—even though they had threatened His life. He labored with the conviction that God's purposes were changeless and that no enemy nor accident could shorten by a single hour His life. This is true of every follower of

Christ. This belief will give courage in time of peril and darkness and hardship.

3. Jesus Teaching Martha (11:18-27).

As He was nearing the village, Martha meets Him with a complaint because of His delay. He ignores her complaint and teaches her concerning the resurrection and life.

a. "Thy brother shall rise again" (v. 23). Most blessed words, these, to fall upon the ears of a sorrowing one for a dead brother, wife, husband, child, or parent.

b. "I am the resurrection and the life" (vv. 25, 26). He is the source of life and all who are joined to Him by a living faith experience such a vital fellowship as to be unaffected by any bodily change. The believer cannot die. That which we call death is to Him but an incident in the course of an endless life. May we have our faith centered in the Person of our Lord that we can meet these experiences.

4. Jesus Weeping with Mary (11:28-37).

Mary fell at Jesus' feet uttering the same words used by Martha, but no doubt with a different tone of voice and attitude. She had been sitting at His feet in the days of sunshine, therefore, she knew where to go in time of sorrow. He responded to her words with His tears—"Jesus wept." He is revealed here as a sympathizing Saviour who can be touched with the feeling of our infirmities (Heb. 4:15). Being a real man He suffered with these bereaved sisters, and though He knew the joy that was so soon to come in the restoration of life to Lazarus, He wept, thus mingling His tears of sympathy with those He loved and who loved Him.

It was a great privilege to hear His instruction to Martha, but much more comforting to receive an expression of His personal, tender sympathy. May we, in the time of our bereavement, fall at the feet of our sympathizing Lord!

5. Jesus Raising Lazarus (11:38-44).

This miracle of the mighty power of Jesus, and His tears of sympathy and love linked with omnipotence make eloquent His ministry.

This gives us an illustration of the awakening into spiritual life of those dead in trespasses and sins:

a. Lazarus was dead, even putrefaction had set in (v. 39).

This is a type of the sinner dead in trespasses and sins, morally corrupt (Eph. 2:1).

b. The stone must be rolled away (v. 39). This is our business as Christian workers to remove every obstacle, between dead sinners and the life-giving Saviour.

c. Martha in unbelief protested against the stone being removed and insisted that Lazarus had already undergone putrefaction (v. 39). Unbelief in God's people is saying the same about sinners as being without hope of salvation, Christ is able to save the sinner regardless of the degree of his sins.

d. Christ's intimacy and fellowship with the Father (v. 42). In His prayer He declared that it was not for His sake that He prayed but for those who stood by.

e. Christ's manner of dealing with Lazarus (v. 43). It was by a call. He is calling men and women today by His Spirit, Word, and providence. His call is an individual one, even by name. Have you heard it? If not, respond now.

f. The response of Lazarus (v. 44). This shows that the call of Jesus is with authority and power. With the call goes the power to hear and obey; even though one be dead in trespasses and sins, and therefore helpless. There is nothing too hard for the Lord.

g. The command to the people (v. 44). They were to remove the graveclothes and set him free. They could not make Lazarus alive, but they could remove the graveclothes which bound the man whom Christ made alive. It is our business to teach God's Word to those who have been made alive by Christ for the truth shall make them free (8:32). This miracle is a mighty demonstration that Jesus Christ is the Son of God. May we come to know that Jesus Christ is the Son of God and enter upon the triumphant life in the power of Him who overcame death, Hell, and the grave.

6. The Effect of This Miracle (11:45-57).

a. Some believed (v. 45).

b. His enemies sought to put Him to death (vv. 46-53).

c. His withdrawal (v. 54).

R. *Jesus Anointed at Bethany, A Testimony to Christ's Death* (12:1-11).

So powerful was the testimony of the raising of Lazarus that the rulers feared lest all men should turn unto Him, and the Jewish nation be lost. This so aroused their hatred that they plotted His death. The unwilling prophecy of Caiaphas (11:49-52), only accentuated their desire to get rid of Jesus. For prudential reasons Jesus withdrew to a place of safety until the time arrived for the offering of the Passover lamb (11:54).

1. Jesus Revisits Bethany (12:1).

Christ's ministry is now nearing its close. The cross looms large upon the horizon—its shadows are falling upon His pathway. Feeling keenly, no doubt, the pangs of the cross, He seeks the fellowship of the loved ones in the Bethany home. This longing for fellowship in the hour of trial reveals His humanity.

2. Jesus Entertained at Bethany (12:2-8).

Since the resurrection of Lazarus, Jesus was a much talked-of Man. This wonderful work had been the topic of many a conversation.

a. They made Him a supper (v. 2). The members of this beloved family took the lead in the matter. This they did in honor of Him—in grateful appreciation of His help and sympathy in their days of trial and anguish. Jesus' reception of this hospitality shows that He is ever willing to mingle with the people in a social way, even to eat with publicans and sinners. At this supper Martha is back at her old business, that of serving; but seemingly with an unruffled disposition. Because the Master rebuked her in a former time for excessive anxiety in serving, she does not go to another extreme and refuse to serve. There is a right way to serve. Happy is the one who learns the lesson from the Master's rebukes, and ever afterward puts the right spirit into service.

Lazarus sits with the guests at the table and partakes of the feast, which is an unmistakable evidence of the genuineness of his resurrection. He had lain in the grave four days, even till putrefaction had set in; but now he is seen by all sitting at the feast. He has a real body, for he eats and drinks material food. No one can say that the people were deluded. The proof of the resurrection of Jesus is just as valid, for He was seen by many witnesses, eating material food after the resurrection (Luke 23:42).

b. Mary anoints the feet of Jesus (v. 3). This was a token of her great love and devotion. She is back at her accustomed place at the feet of Jesus. In order to appreciate her service now, we must glance backward in her history and see her life as a composite picture. While all is well–days of sunshine in that home–she sits at the Master's feet listening to His teaching. The cruel hand of death had done its work and cast its shadow across that home, and in her dire distress she casts herself at the feet of Jesus for sympathy, and she gets it. If we would be ready for the day of trial and sorrow we should sit at Jesus' feet when all is well.

Finally, the cross casts its shadow across the life of the Master. Mary, with the keen intuition of true love, reads His sorrow, and brings her costliest gift as an evidence of her love which withholds nothing from Him. She anticipates His death and burial, and knowing that she could not minister to Him then, she does this against His burial. This act of hers represents a service which costs. It is the self-sacrificing service which love delights in giving. The great trouble with the Christian church is the desire to take things easy, to save oneself. The Christian worker, the businessman, or the student will lose out whenever he begins to spare himself. The Lord received this act of love at its full value. It is much better that we show our love for our friends while they live, than after they can no longer appreciate it. So profuse was this outpouring that the whole house was filled with its fragrance. Wherever there is the unsparing service of love today, there goes up from it a sweet-smelling savor.

c. The foul criticism of Judas (vv. 4-6). The uncalculating zeal of Mary was too much for Judas. Under the hypocritical pretense of caring for the poor he offers caustic criticism upon her act. It was not his love for the poor, but the avaricious craving to get hold of the money for himself that prompted him to do it.

d. Jesus' defense of Mary (vv. 7, 8). Christ fully appreciates the act of love bestowed upon Him. He declares that it is no more a waste than the ointment placed upon the bodies of the dead for embalming. It was but doing that very act beforehand for Him.

3. Attitude Toward Jesus (12:9-11).

a. The Jews were attracted through curiosity. His miracles attracted some, but the curiosity to see Lazarus brought many. This even resulted in good, for "many of the Jews went away and believed on Jesus."

b. The wicked purpose of the chief priests (v. 10). This is a proof of great hardness of heart. They could not deny the wonderful work, the miracle was outstanding. The only way was to shut the mouths of both Lazarus and Christ by killing them.

S. *The Public Entry into Jerusalem, A Testimony of His Messiahship* (12:12-26).

The divine consciousness told Jesus that it was now time to come forth from the Bethany seclusion. This public presentation of Jesus as the Messiah was prearranged by Himself. This testimony of the multitude to His Messiahship was the most picturesque of all that was presented. Once before when the enthusiastic multitude attempted to force Him to be King He refused, but now the presentation is at His command.

1. The Presentation of the King to the Jewish Nation (12:12-19).

a. Homage of the multitude (vv. 12, 13). The people proclaim Him as the predicted Messiah in symbol and song. They wave palm branches and sing from the Psalm which was recognized by the Jews as a prophecy of the coming Messiah (Ps. 118:25, 26). "Hosannah: Blessed is the King of Israel that cometh in the name of the Lord."

b. Jesus' response to the faith of the people (vv. 14, 15). Jesus knowing what the people would do prearranged the ass's colt so that He could meet their faith with the fulfillment of a Messianic scripture. "Fear not, daughter of Zion; behold thy King cometh, sitting on an ass's colt" (Zech. 9:9).

c. The stupidity of the disciples (v. 16). Doubtless the multitude little understood the meaning of what they did or heard. Even the disciples, did not understand at first. After the resurrection and glorification of the Lord they remembered. Men may be in the midst of great blessings and marvelous transactions—even actors in great movements—and not know their meaning, or who it is that is ordering things. Fortunately, we have a Saviour who will not take advantage of our ignorance, guides us so that we may not stumble, and afterward makes things clear. Many will be the happy surprises of the memory when we no longer see as through a glass darkly but face to face!

d. The source of the people's faith (vv. 17, 18). The "sign" of the raising of Lazarus was not forgotten. The people who were with Him when He called Lazarus out of his grave gave their testimony which created within the multitude the faith to go out to welcome Him as the King.

e. The attitude of the Pharisees (v. 19). That which created faith within the hearts of the multitude exasperated the Pharisees and goaded them to the accomplishment of Christ's death. The Gospel is either a savor of life or of death. The sunshine which melts the wax hardens the clay, so with the grace of God in its effect upon men's hearts.

2. The Request of the Greeks (12:20-26).

They ask for an interview with Jesus. What heart desire prompted this request we know not, neither are we sure that it was granted. They must have been Gentiles who had come to worship in the Temple. They made their request through the disciples as they, doubtless, did not enjoy the intimacies in the Temple accorded to the Jews. Whether they obtained what they sought, Christ's reply gave them what they supremely needed to know.

a. The hour had come for the glorification of Jesus (v. 23). The title "Son of Man" used at the approach of the Gentile, links Him with the whole human race and was prophetic of that time when men of every nation should be gathered unto Him.

b. The gateway by which these blessings only could come (v. 24). It was to be through the cross of Jesus that all men could come into Messiah's blessings. They did not primarily need to see His miracles, etc., but they did need to see the cross. His death was absolutely necessary to fruitfulness; just as the seed must decay, perish as a grain, in order for the production of a multitude like itself. Life through death is the universal law.

c. Success is to be achieved through self-sacrifice (vv. 25, 26). This is to be the law of the disciple. Let us follow in His steps!

3. The Meaning of the Cross (12:27-31).

a. To Jesus it meant anguish of soul (v. 27). The sin of the world was laid upon Him, causing Him to shrink from it. The reaction of His pure nature from being made sin was more painful than the physical suffering.

b. To the world of sinners it meant judgment (v. 31).

c. To the Devil it meant to be cast out (v. 31).

4. The Dynamic Which Draws All Men unto Christ (12:32).

"Lifted up" refers to His crucifixion on the cross of Calvary, not to preaching.

III. THE REVELATION OF THE SON OF GOD TO HIS DISCIPLES (13:1–17:26).

These events and instructions all transpired in a single evening in the upper room and on the way to the garden of Gethsemane. These had value only in the light of the cross which now loomed higher upon the horizon. May God enable us to view them now in this light.

A. *The Preparation* (13:1-38).

1. Reveals Himself as the Disciples' Lord (13:1-17).

He shows the need of cleansing in order to have fellowship with Himself.

This chapter begins the second section of the body of the Book of John—the inner revelation of Christ to His disciples. Because the nation rejected Christ, He devotes the few remaining hours to comforting and instructing His own disciples. Likely the immediate occasion for this incident was the strife among the disciples as to who was to be the greatest. It was at such a time that the Lord of glory stooped to wash the disciples' feet.

a. Christ's amazing love for His own (vv. 1-3). Christ was fully conscious of what was upon Him; He knew that the cross with all its anguish was just before Him; He knew that His disciples would shamefully forsake Him in a very few hours; He knew that one of His disciples would be an instrument in the hands of the Devil in His betrayal; He knew that all things were in His hands, being fully conscious of His deity. Notwithstanding all this, He displayed patient and untiring love; He did not withdraw His love from them because of their weakness and the shameful failure which would soon be made manifest; He loved them to the uttermost. His thoughts might well have been of the eternal light and glory upon which He would soon enter, but it seemed mainly to be upon His own disciples. Christ's love never fails.

b. Christ washing His disciples' feet (vv. 4-11).

(1) Steps in this service:

(a) He rises from supper (v. 4).

(b) Laid aside His garments (v. 4).

(c) Took a towel and girded Himself (v. 4).

(d) Poured water into a basin (v. 5).

(e) Washed His disciples' feet (v. 5).

(f) Wiped their feet with the towel wherewith He was girded (v. 5).

These steps symbolize the entire work of redemption. His rising from supper represents His rising from His place of enjoyment in the heavenly glory; His laying aside His garments, His putting aside His vesture of majesty (Phil. 2:7, 8); His girding Himself, His taking the form of a servant (Phil. 2:7); the water in the basin, His cleansing blood; His washing of their feet, His sanctification of men's lives through His Word (15:3; Eph. 5:26); His taking His garments again, His resumption of glory upon Himself.

(2) Peter's impetuous ignorance (vv. 9, 10). He went from one extreme to the other; it was his failure to understand the significance of this service that caused him to behave so unseemly. Peter needed to learn that to be a disciple means to be surrendered to the Lord and to give up having his own way. Only as we give ourselves wholly to Him and obey Him in whatever He bids can we have fellowship with Him. It is not ours to reason why, or to make reply—it is ours only to obey.

(3) The significance of this service to the disciples.

(a) A spiritual cleansing (v. 8). Fellowship with Jesus is only possible as we are continually cleansed from our sins. The constant cleansing by His blood is needed. This is the cleansing of sanctification, not of regeneration (v. 10), "He that is washed needeth not save to wash his feet, but is clean every whit." He that is washed in the blood of Christ, symbolized by baptism, does not need to repeat the act; he only needs the cleansing of sanctification, symbolized by the washing of the feet.

(b) A badge of brotherly affection. This act showed His

abandonment to the service of His own. One can only prove his love by his service. This is a lesson that we need to learn today. We need to love each other more and manifest it so that the world may see it.

(c) The proof of humility (v. 14). There is much pride and vanity and arrogance in the church. If the Son of God was not ashamed to stoop to such lowly service, the disciple should be willing to follow Him.

(d) Equalization. This service, practiced in the spirit of the Master, will be the sure destruction of caste among brethren; it is the great leveler of humanity.

c. An example for us (vv. 12-17). The disciples of the Lord are under obligation to do to each other as He did unto them. This obligation is based upon His Lordship (v. 14). All who call Him "Lord" should render unto Him obedience. Besides the delight in rendering unto the Lord obedience, He promises happiness to those who practice these things.

2. The Traitor Revealed (13:18-30).

His deity revealed in His ability to point out the false disciple.

3. Declares the Arrival of the Hour for the Son's Glorification (13:31-35).

He reveals the sign by which His disciples could be known.

4. Peter Forewarned (13:36-38).

B. *The Instruction* (14:1—16:33).

1. Christ Is the Way to God (14:1-6).

The last words of Jesus were words of comfort. These words have comforted untold thousands of God's children. Profound truths are set forth in these words in such simple language that even children can comprehend. The hopes of the disciples were utterly shattered when Jesus told them about the cross. He had told them that He was going away and that they could not follow Him. Their hearts flooded with grief. He consoled them by:

a. Pointing to the reunion in the Father's house (vv. 1-3).

(1) He asked them to trust in Him even as God (v. 1). Faith in the God-man Christ Jesus will steady the heart no matter how intense the grief, nor how great the sorrow. We all have our

burdens and sorrows, so let us learn to cast them upon Him, for He careth for us.

(2) He informed them that He was going to the Father's house in Heaven to prepare a home for them (v. 2). He assured them that there was abundant room for all. Heaven is an eternal dwelling place. It is not an imaginary place, but a real place prepared for a prepared people. Only those can enter who have made the necessary preparation here.

(3) He assured them that He would come again and escort them to Heaven (v. 3). Jesus will not wait for His own to come to Him, but will come and call forth from the grave those who have died and will transform living believers and take them all to be with Himself in the heavenly home forevermore. He will not be satisfied until His own are with Him. This has been a comfort to many of God's people in all ages, in all climes, and in all circumstances.

b. Revealing the way to the Father's house (vv. 4-6). Jesus informed the disciples that they knew the place and the way to which He was going. To this Thomas interposed a doubt, in answer to which Christ asserts:

(1) He is the way to God (v. 6). He is more than a mere guide or teacher; He is the way itself. He is the door of the sheepfold, yea, the very entrance to the tree of life.

(2) He is the truth (v. 6). He is not merely the teacher, but the truth incarnate. In His Incarnation the spiritual and material worlds were united. Therefore every line of truth, whether spiritual or material converges in Him. No one can ever have the real truth about anything who does not have Christ. In Him we have the truth about man, as to what he is, what he ought to be, and what he shall be in eternity. In Him especially we have the truth about God. To pretend to know God, while at the same time rejecting Jesus Christ, is utter folly. Only as Christ reveals God can man know Him (1:18).

(3) He is the life (v. 6). Christ is not merely the giver of life, but He is the essence of life. Only those who receive Christ have life in the true sense. Since He is God incarnate, to know Him is to know God. This is a truth which cannot be arrived at by intellectual

processes. It is a mystery which can only be penetrated by faith. We do not see in order to believe, but believe in order to see.

2. Christ Is the Mediator Between the Father and the Believer (14:7-15).

Being in the Father and the Father in Him, He makes known the Father and secures from the Father anything that the disciples ask in His name. He assured them that His work was to continue (vv. 12-15). Jesus' going away was not to end the work which He had begun. This no doubt means that through the ministry of the Spirit-filled disciples the work which He had begun would assume larger proportions. There would be a much greater number of conversions than under His ministry. After the Day of Pentecost the Gospel took a much wider range. During His ministry the message was confined to the Jews, while under the ministry of the disciples it was only limited by the world itself. The disciples' ministry was ushered in by the conversion of 3,000 in one day. The means by which they were to get this power to do such wonders was prayer. God will surely answer prayer, not only because He loves His children, but through answered prayer His own name is glorified.

3. He Is the Sovereign Bestower of the Holy Spirit (14:16-31).

a. He promised another Comforter (vv. 16, 17). The word *comforter* means literally "one called to the side of another to give help, protection, and deliverance." This comforter was the Holy Spirit. Jesus was the Comforter while here in the body. The Holy Spirit was to be another Comforter. The condition upon which they might enjoy Him was loving obedience. The help and presence of the Spirit were to continue forever.

b. He assured them of His return to them (vv. 18-24). Although Christ went away, He did not leave His disciples as orphans. He is spiritually present with them always. The Father and the Son make their abode with the disciples who love and obey Jesus Christ.

c. He assured them that the Holy Spirit would aid them in remembering and understanding His words (vv. 25, 26). This the Holy Spirit does by illuminating the minds of the disciples.

d. He gave the legacy of His peace (vv. 27-31). By His peace is meant the serenity of soul which one enjoys who is reconciled to God, who knows that his sins are forgiven.

4. The Vital Union of the Disciples and the Lord (15:1-17).

Under the beautiful allegory of the vine and the branches Jesus set forth the spiritual oneness of Himself and His disciples. In the most solemn hour, just before going to the cross, He bore witness that the source of the believer's life was in Him and that apart from Him they were powerless to do anything. No mere man, even a prophet or an apostle, ever made such a claim. He shows them that though He was going away, they would be in vital touch with their unseen Lord, and that through them His life was to be manifested and His purposes accomplished.

a. The relationship of Jesus and the Father to the disciples (vv. 1-3).

(1) Jesus as the source of the disciple's life (v. 1). He is the true vine. Through the Incarnation Jesus identified Himself with humanity, and by virtue of His atoning death and resurrection it is possible for the believer to be a partaker of His life so that between the disciple and his Lord there is a community of life. As the vine pours its life into the branch, so Christ pours His life into the believer. Our life is a derived life. Whatever is worth while in the believer is derived from Christ. The stream of heavenly life flows from Him. Our salvation is eternal life because it is the life of the eternal Son in us.

(2) The Father has in His hands the discipline of the disciple (v. 1). The "Father is the husbandman." Just as the culture of the vine is in the hands of a husbandman so the discipline of the believer's life is in the hands of the Father. While this is a serious fact, yet we should rejoice in it, for His hands are skillful and His knowledge is infinite. He knows exactly how deep to cut with His pruning knife. He can be absolutely trusted to cut no deeper than necessary, for He is our affectionate Father. In this disciplinary process He:

(a) Removes the unfruitful branch (v. 2). He does not take the trouble to prune the fruitless branch. The nominal church member, the mere professor He removes. This may be an explanation of the unseemly death of some professing Christians.

(b) Purges the fruitful branch that it may produce more fruit (v. 2). He restrains our natural tendencies and desires in order that the virtues of the Lord, the fruit of the Spirit, may shine forth. To be without His discipline, His chastisement, is a bad sign (Heb. 12:8).

(3) The instrument by which the pruning is accomplished is Jesus' words (v. 3). The disciples already were cleansed by Christ's words, for Judas the traitor has been cast out. If the believer's life is to be fruitful in character and service, the pruning knife, Christ's words, must be intelligently and regularly applied. Failure to apply this knife is the secret of unfruitfulness on the part of many.

b. The conditions of fruit bearing (vv. 4-7). The supreme and grand object in pruning, the culture of the vine, is fruit. The energy of the vine is to be used in growing fruit, not producing wood fiber. God's whole design in producing the vine and making men branches was to obtain fruit, much fruit, more fruit.

(1) Abiding in Christ (vv. 4-6). As the branches draw sap and life from the vine, so the believers must abide in Christ from whom they derive their purity, strength, and wisdom. Indeed, it is a mutual abiding, the disciple in Christ and Christ in the disciple. It is Christ's life expressing itself through the believer. The one thus indwelt by Christ will bear much fruit. So great is the displeasure of the Lord with lifeless, unfruitful branches that they are to be "cast forth," "withered," even "burned" (v. 6). This ought to seriously concern us as to the necessity of abiding in Christ. The vine is dependent upon the branches for the bearing of fruit, so Christ can only be made known through us. Christ's way to fill the world's hunger and need and to supply that need is through His disciples.

(2) Christ's words abide in us (v. 7). So mighty is the power of the one who abides in Christ and His words abide in him that Heaven can withhold no gift from him. In fact, the one who is united to Christ by faith and prayerfully meditates upon His words will be so led by the Spirit to pray as to have success without limit (Col. 3:16).

(1) The glorification of the Father (v. 8). Through much fruit bearing the Father will be glorified (Matt. 5:16). The unfruitful life fails in this respect.

(2) Credentials of discipleship (v. 8). The only way to prove that one is a child of God is to manifest the characteristics of God in our acts and service.

(3) Abiding in Christ's love and keeping His commandments (vv. 9, 10). The way to abide in Christ's love is to keep His commandments. The one who neglects the words of Christ is destitute of His love. It is folly to talk of being in the love of Christ while disobeying His teachings. The supreme example for our imitation is Christ's obedience to the Father.

(4) Fullness of joy (v. 11). The way to have fullness of joy is to have Christ's joy in us.

(5) Intimate friendship (vv. 12-17).

5. Christ Is the Support of the Believer in Conflict with the World (15:18–16:33).

a. The attitude of the world toward the believer is that of hatred (vv. 18-25). The believer has been chosen out of the world to be a witness against it. The world hates the real Christian because the world hates Jesus Christ. The hatred of the world expresses itself in persecution. "All who will live godly in Christ Jesus shall suffer persecution" (II Tim. 3:12). Being organically united to Christ, the Christian enjoys real intimacy with Him. He is a friend of Christ, "therefore all things that I have heard of my Father I have made known unto you" (v. 15).

b. The Holy Spirit and the believer (15:26–16:15).

(1) The Holy Spirit, Christ's representative (vv. 26, 27). In 14:16 Christ says that in view of His absence in preparing a home in Heaven for His disciples He would send another Comforter, Someone to act as His substitute. That substitute is the Holy Spirit. He calls out from the nations those who are to be members of His Church and presides over the Church. He does not act for Himself but for Christ. The more we know, therefore, of the Spirit the more we shall know of Christ. If we would please Christ, we must receive and honor His substitute. The Holy Spirit's testimony is to be supplemented by that of the disciples. Their testimony was of particular value for they had been with Him, and therefore had a personal experimental knowledge of Him. The more intimate they were with

Him, and the more accurate their knowledge of Him, the more valuable their testimony became; for the more they knew the more beauty they saw in Him. They never saw in Him any imperfection for He never made a blunder in speech or deed.

(2) The Holy Spirit the believer's Comforter in time of trial (16:1-7). The word *comforter* according to its etymology signifies "one who is called to another's side to aid him, as an advocate in a court of justice." The Holy Spirit therefore is Christ's representative who stands by the side of His own disciples, strengthens, encourages, defends from the enemy and pleads their cause before God the Father. The bitter persecutions which awaited the disciples as soon as the Lord had gone away had been told them by Jesus. He told them that they should be cast out of the synagogue (v. 2). This was an awful experience. It meant the exclusion of a disciple from all religious and social intercourse. People would avoid him as they would a leper. Curses were pronounced upon him. Stones were cast upon his coffin when he was dead, and all mourning for him was forbidden. He tells them that they would not even stop at that but would kill them, believing that it would be a service well pleasing to God. This service to God carries the meaning of a religious sacrifice. This wonderful prophecy has been and still is being fulfilled.

As Christ forewarned His disciples, so Paul in a later time showed what would be. "All that will live godly in Christ Jesus shall suffer persecution" (II Tim. 3:12). But the same Holy Spirit who gave strength and grace then will keep us from falling. These words so grieved the disciples that they had scarcely inquired as to where the Lord was going (vv. 5, 6). Nevertheless He tells them that His going is expedient else the Spirit, the Comforter will not come. With the Holy Spirit in and upon them giving wisdom and courage, they could better endure all these sufferings. That same Spirit is for us now. With the Lord Jesus as our High Priest in the presence of the Father, and the Holy Spirit in and upon us, it is much better than if we had Christ's bodily presence.

c. The Holy Spirit the Judge of the world (vv. 8-11). This was encouraging to the disciples. Through the coming of the Comforter and His working in and through them victory was to be achieved.

(1) He will convict the world of sin (v. 8). The peculiar sin of the world is not believing on Christ. The essence of all sin is unbelief in Christ, an unwillingness to surrender to the divine will (v. 9; cf. 3:18, 19). Christ, the Son of God, came to bring to the world salvation, therefore no sin so great can be conceived as the unbelief in and rejection of Him. The way the Spirit convicts the world is through the testimony of those who are filled with Him; that is, He operates upon the world through the lives and testimony of those who have been saved. Let us realize that if ever the men and women in the world are to believe on Jesus it will be through us. Our concern should be to place ourselves completely under His control.

(2) He will convict the world of righteousness (v. 8). This was to be through the resurrection and ascension of Christ (v. 10). His coming forth from the grave and ascension into Heaven was an indisputable proof that He was no impostor. It proved that He was what He claimed to be. Thus they would see that He was a righteous One whose merit is imputed to all those who believe on Him.

(3) He will convict the world of judgment (v. 8). He tells of judgment to come. The guarantee that there is a judgment to come is that Satan is already judged (v. 11; cf. 12:31).

d. The Holy Spirit the Guide into all truth (vv. 12-16). The disciples were not ready to receive all that Christ had to teach them (v. 12). Their own prejudices had entered in and made it impossible for Him to teach them concerning His death. They had ceased to grow because they refused to believe and act upon what the Lord desired to teach them. That which He said they would afterward understand was to be made real by the Holy Spirit. This Spirit came on Pentecost. The coming of the Spirit is the guarantee that the Gospel record is true; and also that the teaching of the apostles is from God, even the revelation which shows us things to come. The Spirit will lead His disciples into a deeper and fuller knowledge of the truth. No man in the power of his intellect can know the truths of the Bible. The Spirit is the interpreter of the truth revealed in

His Word. His supreme mission is to make Christ known. He does not witness to Himself, but remaining unseen, points men to Christ. Let us receive that Spirit as our teacher for He is eminently successful; and when once Christ is made known unto us by Him, we shall see Him as the fairest of ten thousand and the One altogether lovely.

e. Christ testifies to the unity of Himself, and the Father foretells His death, resurrection, and second coming—the sorrows and trials through which the disciples must pass—assuring them of His oneness with the Father in order that they may have peace. "Be of good cheer, I have overcome the world" (vv. 16-33).

C. *Christ's Intercessory Prayer* (17:1-26).

Christ had repeatedly announced His death to the disciples. Though unwilling to believe this at first when they awoke to its reality, their hopes were crushed. They said, "We trusted that it had been he which should have redeemed Israel" (Luke 24:21). They were sorely troubled. He gave them reasons for not sorrowing (14:1-31). Fully conscious of what lay before them—persecutions, struggles, temptations, their ignorance, inability to meet their trials and face their perils—He commended them to God. This is really the Lord's Prayer. Three definite objects are mentioned in it.

1. His Prayer for Himself (17:1-5).

Fully conscious that the hour of His crucifixion was at hand, He prayed to the Father saying: "Glorify thy Son, that thy Son also may glorify thee." His coming into the world had as its supreme mission the glorification of the Father. In order that the Father might be glorified it was necessary that the Son should be glorified.

a. To Him had been given the power to give eternal life to God's chosen ones (vv. 2, 3). Eternal life is knowledge of and a right relation to the true God and Jesus Christ. Thus we see that eternal life is a relationship and not an entity.

b. He declared that He had finished the work committed unto Him (v. 4). The definite work which He came to do was to give eternal life to the chosen of God. Having now finished that work, He prayed that He might be received back into that specific relationship to the Father which He had eternally enjoyed.

2. His Prayer for His Immediate Disciples (17:6-19).

a. Their preservation (vv. 9-16). He did not pray that they would be taken out of the world, but that they might be kept from the Evil One. He did not ask that they escape temptation, suffering, and sorrow, but kept, preserved while passing through them. It is not the divine will that we go to Heaven at once when we believe because:

(1) Christ needs our ministry. Those who have been made partakers of the divine life are His representatives in the world. He is depending upon them to carry on His work.

(2) We need His graces strengthened and developed in us. Heaven is a prepared place and only those who have been prepared for it can be admitted into it. Further, only such would be at home in it if admitted. The tribulations of life are not pleasant but necessary. Just as certain flowers need to be crushed in order that they might give off their fragrance, so the disciples need trials of life to cause the graces of the Lord Jesus Christ to shine forth.

(3) The world needs us. Christ declares that the disciples are the light of the world, the salt of the earth (Matt. 5:16). Only as the light of the Lord shines forth through the disciples can the people in the world find their way. The Christian then should be willing to suffer in order that he might represent his Lord and guide the lost world to the Lamb of God which taketh away its sin.

b. Their sanctification (vv. 17-19).

(1) Sanctify means: First, to set apart. That means then that the disciples were to be set apart to do the specific work of representing Christ. Second, to cleanse. Those who are set apart as His representatives need special cleansing grace to make them vessels fit for the Master's use.

(2) The instrument used (v. 17). They were to be sanctified through God's truth. God's truth is His Word. Therefore, the instrument used in the sanctification of believers is the Word of God.

(3) The purpose (v. 18). They were sanctified in order that they might be qualified for His service in the world. Sanctification is not for personal satisfaction and honor but to be witnesses of the saving grace of the Lord Jesus Christ.

(4) Jesus' own sanctification was for that purpose (v. 19). He is the grand Example. The one who has the hope of meeting the Lord will separate himself from all uncleanness in order that he might be separated unto His service.

3. His Prayer for His Future Disciples (17:20-26).

a. Their unification (vv. 20-23). His great concern was that all believers should be united.

(1) The great pattern of this spiritual union is the union that exists between the Father and the Son (v. 21). The believer is a member of the Body of Christ, since he is brought into fellowship with eternal life. The believers are to be in vital union as the Father and the Son are one.

(2) The incentive making possible this union (v. 22). The vision of the glory of God in Christ (II Cor. 3:18) is the grand incentive which incites the believers to unity.

(3) The purpose (v. 23). The supreme objective in the unification of the believers is to convince the world that God sent Jesus Christ to save it. The lack of union between believers is a mighty stumbling block to the world.

b. Their glorification (vv. 24-26). The disciple of Christ enjoys fellowship with the Father and the Son and fellowship with his fellow believer, but he also looks forward to the time when he shall be glorified.

(1) "I will that they be with me where I am" (v. 24). There is a present glory enjoyed by believers.

(a) They are now children of God, although it does not yet appear what they shall be.

(b) They now possess eternal life and therefore shall never perish. While there is the present glory, Jesus wants His disciples to be with Him in Heaven. He said: "Except a grain of wheat fall into the ground and die, it abideth alone." We can reverently say that unless the believer is taken to Heaven Christ will be lonely.

(2) "Behold my glory" (v. 24). The believer shall share the ineffable glory of Christ (I John 3:13). That which makes possible that glory is the fact that through the Incarnation there has been effected an organic union between Him and His disciples.

IV. Revelation of the Son of God as the Fulfiller of Prediction and Prophecy (18:1–20:31).

The most solemn and important hour in the world's history had now come. Christ dies that His own might go free.

A. *Jesus Betrayed and Denied, A Proof of His Messiahship and Deity* (18:1-18).

We now enter upon the study of the last main division of the Book of John. Jesus now passes from the fellowship of His disciples to the preparation of the great sacrifice which He is about to make for the sins of the world. It is a short step from His great intercessory prayer to the cross.

1. Jesus Betrayed (18:1-3).

a. Place of betrayal (v. 1). Gethsemane, a place of prayer to which He with His disciples often resorted. It meant much to Him in His loneliness and trials to be alone in communion with the heavenly Father.

b. His companions in trial (v. 1). Peter, James, and John (Mark 14:33). He took with Him the three who apparently were closest to Him, but even they slept while He endured His greatest agony, even sweating, as it were, great drops of blood.

c. The traitor (vv. 2, 3). The blackest of the world's crimes was committed by a trusted disciple. This infamous deed began in the greed for money (12:6). Judas had been with Jesus for three years, enjoying the most intimate fellowship. His holy teachings had fallen upon his ears again and again. He witnessed the many mighty works which the Lord wrought. He no doubt preached in Christ's name. He had been with Him in seasons of retirement, so much so that the place where Christ was apprehended was familiar to him. Now because he has no heart for the Lord, he uses this knowledge to bring Christ's deadliest enemies upon Him. What infamous perfidy this! This awful condition of heart was not reached at one bound. Judas allowed the love of money to get between himself and the Lord (I Tim. 6:10). This had a paralyzing effect upon his conscience. It is always true that blessings misused become curses. The love of money, or of the world, may lead one into a careless life. Let him that thinketh he standeth take heed lest he fall (I Cor.

10:12). Let this act of Judas be a warning to us all lest we too should cherish some besetting sin.

2. Jesus' Voluntary Surrender of Himself (18:4-8).

He went forth with the full consciousness of meeting His enemies. There was no moment of His life when He was freer than when the mob came to arrest Him. The outcome of that night was clearly before Him. He did not wait for them to seek Him out, but went calmly to them and inquired as to whom they sought. And when they told Him that they sought Jesus of Nazareth, He told them that He was that One. His surrender was entirely the act of His free will; there was no necessity laid upon Him. Accompanying His utterance, "I am he," was His invisible divine power, for those sturdy Roman soldiers fell backward to the ground. This may be taken as typical of the confusion and disaster which shall overtake His enemies when He comes in glory. His giving Himself up illustrates His work of redemption.

3. Jesus' Tender Consideration of His Disciples (18:8, 9).

The awful agony of the cross was before Him. He knew full well what He must suffer, but He did not forget His own. He knew the weakness of His disciples, so He yields Himself up and makes a way of escape for them. He secured the deliverance of His own by surrendering Himself to shame and death. "If, therefore, ye seek me, let these go their way" (v. 8). This is ever His way: the Good Shepherd lays down His life for His sheep. He is doing the same now. No one who trusts Jesus can be lost. Let us more and more yield ourselves to Him.

4. Peter's Denial (18:15-18, 25-27).

The Lord had warned the disciples of their danger. He even gives them the hint that they are to go away. He told Peter that he could not follow Him now (13:16), but Peter with overweening confidence was determined to show the Lord that he would stand by Him. Peter little knew himself. He not only proved to be a coward, but even indulged in oaths, as he denied the Lord. This should be a solemn warning to us all. We should heed it that we may not make the same shipwreck of our lives.

Note the steps in Peter's fall:

a. Self-confidence: "Although all shall be offended, yet will not I" (Mark 14:29). Jesus had just told them that all of them should be offended, but Peter was determined to show the Lord that He was mistaken in him. May we beware of self-confidence.

b. Failure to watch: "Simon, sleepest thou? Couldest not thou watch one hour?" (Mark 14:37). Self-confidence is always followed by unwatchfulness.

c. Failure to pray (Mark 14:38). It is the one who realizes his weakness who always seeks communion with God in prayer.

d. Zeal without knowledge (vv. 10, 11; cf. Mark 14:47). Peter thought now to make up for his lack of watchfulness in prayer by outward acts. Many today are equally foolish.

e. Following Christ afar off (Mark 14:54). Christ's rebuke to Peter for his ignorant zeal cut him to the quick. He is not ready to forsake Him, but is following him afar off, no doubt wondering what will be the outcome.

f. Warming himself at the enemy's fire (vv. 18, 25; cf. Mark 14:54).

g. Open denial (vv. 25-27; cf. Mark 14:66-72). After having so far allied himself with Christ's enemies as to warm himself at their fire, the next step was open denial. May we seriously ask ourselves, Are we betraying Christ today? We may betray Him by failing to speak for Him, by neglecting the study of His Word, by denying His deity and authority, by craving selfish ease or desiring the things of the world. The penalty which we must pay for such denial will be His denial of us.

5. Jesus' Preliminary Trial Before the High Priest (18:12-14, 19-24).

a. He was bound and sent to Caiaphas (vv. 12-14). Note the wise counsel of Caiaphas.

b. Questioned as to His disciples and doctrine (v. 19).

6. Jesus' Trial Before Pilate (18:28–19:16).

Though condemned by the Sanhedrin, convoked by Caiaphas, the sentence could not be executed without the consent of Rome. The power of death had been taken from the Jews.

Note the scenes in this trial:

a. The judge and accusers—outside the palace (vv. 28-32).

b. The judge and the prisoner—inside the palace (vv. 33-38).

c. The judge and the accusers—outside the palace (vv. 39-40). The judge declared the prisoner innocent. The accusers chose Barabbas.

d. The judge and prisoner—inside the palace (19:1-3). The prisoner scourged and mocked.

e. The judge and accusers—outside the palace (19:4-7). The prisoner twice declared innocent—accused of calling Himself the Son of God.

f. The judge and the prisoner—inside the palace (vv. 8-11). The prisoner declares the source of the judge's authority and the measure of his guilt.

g. The judge and the accusers—outside the palace (vv. 12-16). Pilate's last effort breaks down and Christ is delivered into the hands of His enemies.

7. The Crucifixion of Christ (19:17-37).

a. The place (v. 17). It was on a hill called in Latin Calvary, in Hebrew Golgotha, which in shape resembled a skull. This hill is a few hundred yards outside Jerusalem.

b. His companions—two malefactors (v. 18; cf. Luke 23:32). This shows how completely Jesus was identified with sinners.

c. The inscription over Him (vv. 19, 20). It was customary to place an inscription over the cross stating the crime for which the victim suffered. Although Pilate did this in bitter irony and contempt he uttered a great truth, affirming more than he intended. This truth is in harmony with John's purpose to show that Jesus is the Messiah.

d. Gambling for the garments of Jesus (vv. 23, 24). This was a fulfillment of Scripture. "They parted my garments among them and upon my vesture did they cast lots." This is an exhibition of how men's heart may be so callous as to plan and act for present gain under the shadow of the cross of Christ.

e. Utterances from the cross (vv. 25-30).

(1) "Behold thy son. . . . Behold thy mother" (vv. 25, 26). In this crucial hour He forgot His own bitter anguish and interested Himself in those He loved. It is a touching example of human sympathy and especially of filial love at its best. Though He was leaving the earth and its struggles, He made provision for the dear ones

left behind. It is very true that true love forgets its own sorrows and concerns itself in the interests of others.

(2) "It is finished" (v. 30). While no one can fathom the depth of meaning in these words, they no doubt indicate (a) that the calumnies and indignities heaped upon Him were at an end. His trial was grossly illegal. False witnesses were employed to incriminate Him. (b) His awful sufferings were at an end. The penalty of the unnameable and indescribable sins of the world was resting upon Him, wringing from Him the pathetic cry, "My God, my God, why hast thou forsaken me?" (c) The fulfillment of every type and prophecy. (d) His life of perfect obedience. (e) The great work of redemption. Finished means more than ended; it means accomplished. All that He started out to do was now completed. (f) The judgment of the world and the casting out of Satan (see 12:31).

f. His death (v. 30). His death was voluntary. No one took his life from Him. He had the power to lay it down and the power to take it again (10:18). With full consciousness that all things which He had come to do had now been accomplished, He dismissed His spirit.

g. Not a bone to be broken (vv. 31-37).

h. Christ's burial (vv. 38-42).

(1) Joseph of Arimathaea for fear of the Jews secretly besought permission of Pilate to take away Christ's body.

(2) Nicodemus who came to Jesus by night found Joseph and they prepared Jesus' body for burial according to Jewish custom and laid it away in a new sepulcher where never was man laid.

V. The Epilogue (20:1—21:25).

A. *The Resurrection of Christ* (20:1—21:14).

1. The Empty Tomb (20:1-10).

John does not enter into a description of the resurrection, or attempt its proof other than that the tomb was empty and that Jesus had repeatedly manifested Himself after the tomb was found empty. In these verses John describes the process of his own conviction touching Christ's resurrection.

a. The testimony of Mary Magdalene (vv. 1, 2). This woman,

out of whom Jesus had cast seven demons (Mark 16:9; Luke 8:2), announced the fact of the empty tomb to Peter and John.

Prompted by love for Him for His kindness to her, she went early to the tomb, even when it was yet dark. "She was last at the cross and first at the grave. She stayed longest there and was soonest here." Her love for the Master was genuine, though her knowledge was defective. She had realized great good at His hands; therefore she could not rest until she had done her utmost for Him. That morning was a dark one for this woman and the rest of the disciples, but the darkness did not long remain, for the Lord revealed Himself. All who love Jesus and seek Him shall not remain in darkness (7: 17).

b. Personal investigation by Peter and John (vv. 3:10). The news of the empty tomb which Mary brought with breathless haste so moved John and Peter that they both ran to investigate. Upon arrival at the tomb, John gazed into it, but Peter entered it. The removal of the stone from the sepulcher and the arrangement of the graveclothes convinced them that an enemy could not have done this. Every sign of the action of thieves was absent.

2. The Manifestations of the Risen Lord (20:11–21:14).

a. To Mary Magdalene (vv. 11-18).

(1) Mary weeping at the empty tomb (v. 11). Peter and John went home, but Mary could not; she stood weeping. Home was nothing to her while her Lord was missing. She should have been rejoicing that the grave was empty, for the empty tomb was an eloquent proof of His Messiahship and deity. Had His body been there, she would have had real cause for weeping.

(2) Mary questioned by the angels (vv. 12, 13). She viewed through her tears angels at the tomb who inquired as to the cause of her sorrow.

(3) Jesus reveals Himself to Mary (vv. 14-16). She saw first the angels, and then her eyes lighted upon the Lord. She did not recognize Him in His resurrection body, but His voice was familiar to her. As soon as her name was called, she recognized Him, and worshiped at His feet.

(4) Jesus forbids her to touch Him (v. 17). This shows that she was now coming into a new relationship with Him. Besides,

there was no time for such familiarity while the disciples were in darkness. "Go tell my brethren," was the urgent message she was to take.

(5) Mary's testimony (v. 18).

b. To the disciples (20:19–21:14).

(1) When Thomas was absent (vv. 19-23). Thomas was absent at the first appearance of Jesus—just why we may never know. His absence deprived him of a vision of the Lord. Absence from the assembly of believers always occasions loss. The other disciples went to Thomas with the glad news of the Lord's resurrection, but he would not believe. His stubborn disbelief was such that he doggedly declared that unless he saw the prints of the nails and put his finger in the print of the nails and thrust his hand into His side, he would not believe. It is right to demand evidence, but to prescribe terms is rank unbelief.

He came to them with the message of peace (v. 19), showed His hands and side (v. 20), commissioned them (v. 21), and bestowed upon them the Holy Spirit (v. 22).

(2) When Thomas was present (vv. 24-29).

(a) The Lord's kindness to those who have difficulties (vv. 26, 27). Thomas deserved rebuke, but the Lord kindly supplied the evidence which he demanded.

(b) The Lord revealed Himself to Thomas (vv. 27, 28). When He thus revealed Himself, Thomas was transformed from a doubter into a confessor. He cried out, "My Lord and my God."

(c) The superior blessing of belief without sight (v. 29). Jesus patiently furnished Thomas with tangible evidence of His resurrection, but assured him that belief on Him without the tangible evidence was to be in a frame of mind to receive the blessings of the Lord. Victory over Thomas' skepticism was realized by the sight and touch of the Lord. Greater blessings are promised for those who believe, not having seen (v. 29).

(3) To seven disciples at Sea of Tiberias (21:1-14).

(a) The occasion (vv. 1-3). At Peter's suggestion the disciples go fishing. They do not go back to their old calling without hope in Christ. They should not be accused of forsaking their Lord—they were poor men, therefore obliged to work. Furthermore, honest toil should not be considered incompatible with witnessing for Christ. Sensible men and women will be busy at so-called secular occupations until called from them by the Lord. Indeed, when the Lord wants men to work for Him, He goes to those who are busy. The disciples toiled all night and got nothing. No doubt they were greatly discouraged and very tired.

(b) The risen Lord the Supplier of the disciples' needs (vv. 4-14). At dawn He appeared on the shore and inquired as to their success. The Lord appears at the point of their extremity. When the disciples confessed their failure, He directed them and success followed. This success was preceded by their obedience. If they had not cast their net on the other side, no fish would have been caught. No success can come to one while in the path of disobedience. The Lord Jesus now on the shore of Heaven is just as anxious to help us if we but follow His directions. Coming to the shore tired and hungry, they receive the invitation from the Lord to dine with Him. In the service of Christ it is not all work, but work then enjoyment. They needed some teaching, but their physical needs must first be supplied. This whole scene put into symbolic language is the Saviour preparing for the blessed feast above while His disciples are toiling on the sea of time. After awhile we shall go ashore and He will feed us with the Bread of Heaven.

B. *The Charge of the Risen Lord to Peter* (21:15-17).

Christ put to Peter the thrice repeated question, "Lovest thou me?" before He gave him a commission. This shows that supreme love to Christ is the one essential qualification for serving Him. "Lovest thou me more than these?" means no doubt, "Do you love Me more than you do these disciples and all things besides?" He asked this question three times to show that supreme love for Christ is an indispensable qualification for serving Him. Love is the spring from which all activity flows. He asked also to show that there are three classes in the church which demand care and attention. Three classes in the church need special care and food adapted to their several estates.

1. "Feed my Lambs" (21:15).

This first charge relates to those who are beginning the Christian life, the babes in Christ. The word "feed" means more than instruction. It means in addition to instruction, surroundings, influences, examples, etc. As a Christian minister, Peter was to be an example —provide the proper surroundings and do the proper teaching for the young Christians and those beginning the Christian life. Supreme love only can qualify for this.

2. "Tend my Sheep" (21:16).

This charge shows a different class. It means to shepherd the sheep. The duty here enjoined is to deal with the mature class. He must feed them, give them the proper instruction, guide them, lead them and correct them. The essential qualification for this is love.

3. "Feed my Sheep" (21:17).

This third charge means the caring of aged Christians. The word "feed" is much the same as in the first case. It means that for the aged Christians the instructions ought to be such as will be suited to their needs. This needs emphasis today because much attention is given to the young people, but in many instances the old people are neglected.

C. *Command of Risen Lord—"Follow Me"* (21:18-23).

Christ here gives a prophecy concerning Peter's death. It was to be by crucifixion (v. 18). Peter once shrank from the cross, but now the Lord holds it up before him. It is not the Lord's death on the cross, but Peter's own. He teaches here that the Christian's faith is for the glory of God. Whatever may be before, even the cruel cross, the disciples are directed to follow Him. The Lord is to be our Leader, whatever may be our experience in following Him.

THE ACTS OF THE APOSTLES

PART ONE—INTRODUCTORY MATTERS

THE HISTORY OF ACTS covers but a brief period, perhaps thirty years. No similar period in world history has witnessed such social and religious changes.

When Christ left the earth, He had not founded a Church, neither instructed His disciples to do so. This book shows the series of acts by which Christ created the Church.

Failure to understand the origin and nature of the Church has resulted in gross confusion among Christian leaders and has rendered abortive much of their endeavors.

I. The Setting of the Book.

Acts has a unique place in the New Testament. It bears a vital relationship to the Gospels and to the Epistles. It is indeed the bond binding them together.

A. *Relationship to the Gospels.*

Acts is a continuation of the Gospel According to Luke. It has the same author and is similar in style and aim. In Luke Jesus Christ is presented as the Kinsman-Redeemer and Saviour of men. This theme is continued in Acts. Christ resurrected and glorified gives the Holy Spirit who anoints His servants and sends them forth with His Gospel, first to the Jew and then to the Gentile. Hence Luke opens this book with a significant reference to his Gospel. He joined his narrative with the Gospel where he closed it (1:1; cf. Luke 24: 51).

B. *Relationship to the Epistles.*

Acts serves as a bridge, carrying us from the Gospels to the Epistles. In this book alone we find a history of Paul who wrote thirteen of the twenty-four Epistles of the New Testament. No trace of this great character is found in the Gospels. Here is found the history of the transformation of this savage persecutor who became the devoted servant of Christ. Furthermore, when we wish knowledge concerning the founding of the different churches to whom the Epistles were addressed, we must go to the Book of Acts as the only source of information. Our loss would indeed be great without this book.

II. THE DESIGN OF THE BOOK OF ACTS.

The title *Acts of the Apostles* is not sufficiently broad and comprehensive. Only a few of the apostles figure in the great movements of the book. Many do not appear at all, while, the names of two deacons, Stephen and Philip, appear prominently. Some regard it as a history of the spread of the Gospel from India to the uttermost parts of the earth. Others, that it is a history of the establishment of the Church through Peter and Paul. Still others, that it is a history of the advent and mission of the Holy Spirit into the world, or the personal action of Jesus Christ in the establishment of His Church. Dr. A. T. Pierson calls it "The Acts of the Holy Spirit"; Plumtree calls it "The Gospel of the Holy Spirit." All these views contain some truth, but in order to obtain a satisfactory view we must combine these views into one comprehensive view. The apostles figure in the work, the Church is established, the history of the spread of the Gospel is given, the work of the Holy Spirit is emphasized.

A. *Advent of the Holy Spirit.*

1. The Frequent Repetition.

The word *Spirit* is used eleven times and *Holy Spirit* forty-one times.

2. Promise of His Coming Is Given (1:5, 8).

Disciples were to be baptized with the Spirit, receive power, and become witnesses in all the earth.

3. The Spirit Was To Be Poured Out by Christ at Pentecost (2:33).

4. Disciples Were Filled with Him (4:31).

5. Lied to by Ananias and Sapphira (5:3).

6. Gives Witness to Those Who Obey Him (5:32).

7. Deacons Chosen and Filled with Him (6:5).

8. Received by the Samaritans (8:15-18).
9. Sends Philip to the Ethiopian (8:26).
10. Saul Filled with Him (9:17).
11. Cornelius and Friends Baptized with Him (10:44, 45).
12. Separates Barnabas and Saul for Special Work (13:2-4).
13. Guides to a Decision at the Jerusalem Council (15:28).
14. Guides Missionaries to Europe (16:6-10).

In these pages we see the Spirit active as general superintendent of the Church in qualifying His servants, selecting missionary fields, etc.

B. *The Work of Christ Stands Out in a Striking Way:*

1. In the Election of One To Succeed Judas (1:21-26).

They appealed to Christ to choose. Did Christ respond? (See 2:24; 6:2; I Cor. 15:5.)

2. Sent Forth the Holy Spirit at Pentecost (2:33).
3. In Connection with Martyrdom of Stephen (7:55, 56).

Now from the statement made in Acts 1:1, which is the link connecting Acts with Luke's Gospel, we are enabled to convert or merge these views into one true view. Luke's Gospel gives the account of what Jesus "*began* both to do and teach." The Book of Acts gives what Christ *continues* to do and teach. The correct theme of Acts is "The Acts of the risen and ascended Christ in the establishment of His Church and the carrying forward of His work in the world by the Holy Spirit through the apostles." The Holy Spirit acts conjointly with Jesus Christ. He is the only *vicar* of Christ on the earth.

III. THE BROAD OUTLINE OF ACTS.

A grasp of the structure of a book is essential to an understanding of its message. After the comprehension of the design of a book the rational mind inquires after its literary structure. Every book of the Bible has its own particular design and structure. The application of this truth will revolutionize Bible study and greatly increase the effectiveness of preaching.

The key verse of the book is Acts 1:8. The book falls into three concentric circles like the sections forming the growth of a tree. The divisions are based upon the epochs in the spread of the Gospel, or church history as set forth by Christ. They are:

A. *The Church Witnessing for the Lord Jesus Christ at Jerusalem* (1:1–7:60).

B. *The Church Witnessing for Christ in Judea and Samaria* (8:1–12:25).

C. *The Church Witnessing for Christ to the Uttermost Parts of the Earth* (13:1–28:31).

PART TWO—DETAILED OUTLINE

I. THE CHURCH WITNESSING FOR CHRIST IN JERUSALEM (1:1–7:60).

A. *The Lord Ascending on High* (1:1-26).

Chapter 1 of Acts gives us a view of the order of things before the Church was formed. Out of the ministry and sacrifice of the Lord Jesus Christ there was a group of 120 disciples ready for the new order of things.

1. The Postresurrection Ministry of the Lord (1:1-8).

The forty days of communion of the Lord with His disciples before His ascension had a fourfold object:

a. To convince the disciples of the absolute certainty of His resurrection. This was most fundamental (v. 3). His resurrection must be put beyond the shadow of a doubt, for the whole fabric of Christianity would stand or fall upon its truth or falsity. The resurrection of Christ was the burden of apostolic Christianity. He who was *dead* was now *alive forevermore.*

b. To instruct the disciples in things pertaining to the kingdom of God (v. 3; cf. vv. 6, 7). The disciples were not wrong in expecting the kingdom, but were wrong as to its *time.* Much confusion exists today after nearly 2,000 years both as to what the kingdom is and as to the time of its establishment.

c. To bring the disciples to understand how a new *body* was to be formed to become a channel of grace, how they were to be Christ's witnesses to the ends of the earth, and that they would receive the Father's promise which would qualify them for their work (vv. 4, 5; cf. Luke 24:48, 49).

d. To cause them to comprehend the scope of their missionary activity and to inspire them with the proper zeal for it (v. 8).

2. The Grand Incentive for Missionary Endeavor (1:9-11).

The Lord ascended "while they beheld," in order to show them the source of their power and to furnish them with a supreme, grand incentive for their work. The ascension of the Lord showed them that henceforth He would operate from above. Their work was to be on earth, but their Head and source of power were in Heaven. The words of the two men in white apparel have a double significance:

a. To inform them that He will return. "This same Jesus"; "in like manner" indicate that His coming will be personal and visible.

b. To show them that the source of their power is in Heaven. The teaching of the blessed hope of the Lord's coming has largely disappeared and therefore the grand incentive is largely lost.

3. The Disciples Wait for the Holy Spirit (1:12-14).

This was not a frustrated, sorrowing assembly, but they were intelligently expectant. Christ had declared that they were to be witnesses of His death and resurrection through which there should come repentance and remission of sins. The enduement of the Spirit was the power needed for preaching the Gospel (1:8). They waited with "one accord" with "the women" and "Mary the mother of Jesus" and "his brethren" (1:14). They definitely prayed for the fulfillment of the Father's promise (Luke 24:49).

4. A Successor to Judas Chosen (1:15-26).

Two were nominated. Matthias was chosen by lot, scripturally chosen. Before Pentecost the will of the Lord was ascertained by the casting of the lot. Since Pentecost we hear nothing of the lot.

B. *Day of Pentecost* (2:1-40).

1. Significance of the Day.

It gets its meaning from the Greek word *pentecoste* meaning "fifty." It was one of the great feasts of the Jews held fifty days after the wave sheaf was offered (Lev. 23:15, 16), which was a part of the Passover feast when a sheaf was presented as a vicarious offering "accepted for you." Here no leaven appeared, for it typified the cutting off of Jesus—His presentation without sin for the sins of the people. In contradistinction at Pentecost two loaves were presented with leaven (Lev. 23:17). This typified the disciples who had sin in them. Their offerings were not vicarious. A sin offering was made at this feast (Lev. 23:19) to make it acceptable. The two loaves represented Jews and Gentiles.

2. The Gift of the Holy Spirit (2:4).

It was the evidence that the offering was accepted. By this manifestation we know that Christ's sacrifice was accepted. When is the gift of the Holy Spirit received? Must time elapse between regeneration and the baptism of the Spirit? This was the sovereign act of God by His Spirit fusing the disciples into the one Body called the Church. This is what Paul calls the baptism of the Spirit (I Cor. 12:13).

3. The Marks of Pentecost (2:2-4).

a. External.

(1) Sound of a rushing mighty wind, though no wind.

(2) Tongues of flame. Fire means purifying energy; and tongues, the practical purpose.

b. Internal.

This is evidenced in the transformation wrought in the disciples. They came before the people with courage and self-possession. They boldly declared that the Jews had murdered their King. This transformation is seen particularly in Peter's memorable sermon. His wisdom and skill are no less marvelous than the gifts of tongues because the sermon was the work of a Galilean fisherman without culture and literary training.

His analysis is perfect. He begins with a brief defense and a scriptural explanation of the phenomenon of tongues (vv. 14-21). This is followed by a threefold argument to prove the Messiahship of Jesus (vv. 22-36). The conclusion is an appeal to repent and be baptized in the name of Jesus. In marshaling his arguments there is great skill. The Messiahship of Jesus is not announced till the close of his address because it was distasteful to his hearers. The announcement at the start would have received scornful rejection at once, but at the close it came with irresistible proofs.

c. Outline of Peter's sermon which displays his homiletical skill.

(1) The introduction or apology (vv. 14-21).

(a) "Not drunk with wine."

(b) "Filled with the Spirit."

This he declared to be that which the prophet Joel predicted (2:28-32) that before the Messianic judgment there would be an outpouring of the Holy Spirit and the salvation of all who call upon the name of the Lord. The behavior of the disciples under the influence of the Holy Spirit is a sign that the prophecy was being fulfilled. Yet all who call upon the name of the Lord would be saved from the impending judgment. The argument which follows shows that Jesus was the Lord upon whom they were to call.

(2) The argument (vv. 22-36). To prove that Jesus was the Lord upon whom they were to call if they were to be saved Peter used a threefold argument.

(a) Jesus approved of God by His works (v. 22). His wonderful works were witnessed by His hearers.

(b) Jesus approved of God through death and resurrection (vv. 25-31). The Messiah was to die and arise again according to the Old Testament Scriptures (Ps. 16:8-10). Therefore Jesus is the Messiah, the Lord upon whom they were to call. The disciples were witnesses of Christ's resurrection (v. 32).

(c) Jesus ascended on high, to the right hand of God (v. 32). The Messiah was to ascend, therefore Jesus is the Messiah (vv. 34, 35). The ascension of Jesus Christ was certified by the coming of the Spirit at Pentecost.

The conclusion is that Jesus is Lord and Messiah and therefore Jews are guilty of an unparalleled crime in crucifying Jesus. The manner of life is the proof of the reality of the baptism of the Holy Spirit. Those fused into the Body of Christ will demonstrate by their mode of life rather than by speaking with tongues and working of miracles.

(3) The appeal (vv. 38-40). He called upon the Jews who had crucified Jesus—

(a) To repent (v. 38).
(b) To be baptized.
(c) To receive the Holy Spirit.
(d) To be saved.

C. *The New Community* (2:41-47).

This beautiful fellowship of believers was a sample of the work of the Holy Spirit which was poured out at Pentecost.

1. They Continued in the Apostles' Doctrine (2:42).

They were learning about Jesus Christ, being taught by the apostles instead of the scribes. They turned away from their blind guides and followed new ones.

2. They Continued in Fellowship in the Spirit Around Jesus Christ as Their Vital Head (2:42).

The Church is one Body illustrated by breaking of bread—the one loaf, one Body.

3. They Continued in Prayers (2:42).

Real praying is in the Holy Spirit. The proof of the reality of Christian experience and the efficacy of Christian endeavor is made known by the indwelling of the Spirit and His outworking through our activities.

4. They Recognized the Oneness of the Body in the Lord (2:44, 45).

This they did through the indwelling of the Holy Spirit. They sold their possessions, sharing the proceeds with their needy fellow members. This was the evidence of the power of the Holy Spirit. To abandon one's title to earthly possessions is not natural. This action was not the outburst of miguided enthusiasm. It has been the pattern of Christian behavior through the centuries. Pentecostal experience is thus normally expressed. Only those born from above, truly regenerated, will behave that way. To make this a standard of life for a mixed society would be a blunder of the first magnitude.

5. They Continued in Praise (2:47).

The grace of God brought them in favor with the people, and the Lord added to the Church such as were being saved. Christians witness to the Lord by their manner of life—"epistles known and read of all men."

D. *Christ the Unfailing Guide of the Church* (3:1—4:37).

Most likely several months elapsed since Pentecost. The new community was being taught by the apostles. Mighty works were the credentials of these teachers (2:43). The one in this lesson was of very great importance.

Christ the Head of the Church was its guide, though this guidance was not fully understood. It was nevertheless most real. Under His leadership observe what Christ does:

1. Going to the House of Worship (3:1).

a. Peter and John, friends and mutual complements, went together. This was a fitting arrangement made by the Lord.

b. They went to worship. They knew that Judaism was corrupt, but they went to worship. They were not separatists. John Wesley, Martin Luther, and many others through the centuries contiued with the established order though that order was very corrupt.

2. Healing the Lame Man (3:2-11).

a. The place (v. 2). Why at the entrance of the place of worship? Doubtless because at the place of worship man comes closest to God and man. Common human instincts discern this. Beggars are seldom found at the doors of infidel lecture halls.

b. The man (v. 2). He was infirm from his birth. He brought his ailment into the world with him. He was now past forty years old (4:22). He had been known by the people for many years.

c. The meaning of the miracle. It should be considered as a parable illustrating the work or mission of the church.

(1) The beggar was helpless; he had been carried there. Men and women out of Christ are dead in sin, spiritually helpless. They need to have the life of Christ applied to them. They must be brought to Christ.

(2) Putting out the right hand shows the manner of the church's help. Ministers and Christians may not have silver and gold, but they have something infinitely better to give. Besides, money is not what people mainly need—they need Christ. The poor human race needs Christ the Saviour, not charity!

d. The man's response (v. 8). He thoroughly advertised the miracle. He stood, he walked, he leaned, and shouted praise to God. The one who has experienced the life of Christ will most surely make it manifest. Reality of conversion will be proved by the activity and the testimony of the saved. Some people profess to be saved but stay where they were before. What would you think of this lame man if he had remained in the position of a helpless beggar?

3. Peter Witnessing Before the Multitude (3:12-26).

The healing of the lame man was such a wonderful miracle that the crowd in amazement ran together unto Solomon's porch. Peter took advantage of this opportunity to witness to them of Christ.

a. The power of the miracle was ascribed to Christ (vv. 12-16). Peter disclaims any honor and glory. It is a marvelous thing that Christ should choose us as channels of good to others, but if we are His true servants we will refuse compliments to ourselves and magnify Christ. Such behavior is a mark of a true servant of Christ. Peter then uses a series of antitheses to characterize the guilt of the Jew in rejecting Christ (vv. 13-15). He declares that Christ's power was shown in the soundness of the healed man (v. 16).

b. The appeal (vv. 17-19). He calls them to repent. Though their guilt was awful—they had murdered their Messiah—they could yet receive salvation and blessings from the crucified One. Peter does not excuse their sins but accounts for them as the result of gross ignorance.

c. The promises (vv. 19-26).

(1) Sins blotted out (v. 19).

(2) Refreshing times from the presence of the Lord (vv. 19-26). When Jesus returns, there will be restitution of all things.

4. Peter and John in Prison (4:1-37).

a. The arrest (vv. 1-4).

(1) By whom (v. 1). His antagonists were of two classes, priests and Sadducees. The priests were intolerant because these new teachers were encroaching upon their ministerial functions. Their jealousy was real. The Sadducees opposed them from doctrinal considerations. Sadducees were the liberalists of their day, but they were likewise intolerant.

(2) Chains could hold the apostles, but Christ continued to work (v. 4). The Pentecostal believers now numbered 5,000. Opposition helps God's cause. The storms of opposition only fan the flames.

b. The arraignment (vv. 5-7). They were brought before an august assembly. Note the question asked in verse 7. The inquiry admitted the reality of this miracle. They wanted to know its significance.

c. The answer (vv. 8-12). Peter is not now quailing before a Jewish maid, but with confidence, being filled with the Holy Spirit, answers:

(1) Courteously, yet with quiet irony (v. 9). He reminds

them that they are charging him of a recognized superhuman deed of benevolence, not of a crime. He thus put them to a great disadvantage at the start.

(2) He declares that this miracle had been done in the name of Jesus Christ (v. 10) whom they had crucified.

(3) He shows them that their action was a fulfillment of the Scriptures (v. 11).

(4) He then declared that there is no salvation in any other name (v. 12). No way to reach Heaven except through that name.

d. The impression made (vv. 13, 14).

(1) They were convinced that Peter and John had been with Jesus.

(2) They were unable to speak against the miracle (v. 14), or to gainsay Peter's accusation. They were the persons on trial.

e. Preaching in Christ's name forbidden (vv. 15-22).

(1) Confessed the reality of the miracle (v. 16).

(2) Threatened them (v. 17).

(3) Defied by the apostles (vv. 19, 20). Under the leadership of Christ they expressed their determination to disobey—we thus see the old order passing. They were determined to obey God instead of man.

(4) Apostles dismissed from the assembly (vv. 21, 22).

f. The church at prayer (vv. 23-31).

(1) Laid the matter before the Lord.

(2) Asked the Lord to sustain them (vv. 29, 30).

(3) Filled again with the Holy Spirit (v. 31). Thus they came out with increased determination.

g. The ideal Christian household or church (4:31-35).

(1) A praying church (v. 31).

(2) A Spirit-filled church (v. 31).

(3) Boldness in testifying (v. 31).

(4) A united church (v. 32).

(5) A charitable church; "all things common" (v. 32).

(6) Ministers had a powerful testimony (v. 33).

(7) Great power, great grace were upon all (v. 33).

E. *The Lord's Supreme Concern for His Church* (5:1–7:60).

We should remind ourselves that the Church is composed of the people called out of the world, regenerated and fused into one Body of which Christ is the Head, by the baptism of the Holy Spirit uniting them to Jesus Christ as Head and to each other as members of that Body. Nothing can touch the Church without affecting Christ the Head.

1. The Vindication of the New Community Now Called the Church (5:1-16).

The situation now before us is in strange contrast with that at the close of chapter 4. The break with Judaism has come. They had resolved to be led by the Spirit, hence the title, "All the church" (v. 11). Recognition must be given to the Church. It must be shown to be a holy Body. The sanctity which belonged to the tabernacle and Temple is transferred to this new Body, which is God's dwelling place (Eph. 2:19-22). The Church itself, as well as the people about it, did not recognize this sacredness till God's judgment shone forth among them.

a. The occasion (vv. 1-9; cf. 4:36, 37). It was the dishonest dealing—tempting the Holy Spirit. Barnabas sold his property and brought the proceeds and laid it at the feet of the apostles. Ananias and Sapphira imitated him.

b. The judgments (vv. 5, 10). Swift and terrible was the penalty meted out upon those who would deal treacherously with the Holy Spirit of God. This judgment utters a solemn warning to all who make an outward profession which is not in keeping with inward reality, e.g., unregenerate persons sitting at the Lord's Table. Participating in the communion presupposes a regenerated heart (I Cor. 11:27-30). Preaching sermons not one's own, etc. Men are slow to learn this lesson. This is illustrated by Nadab and Abihu, Uzziah and Achan. Ananias and Sapphira wanted the honor of those who gave all without paying the price.

c. The result (vv. 11-16).

(1) Great fear came upon the church and all who heard these things (v. 11). They recognized that God was dwelling in the church.

(2) Multitudes of men and women were added to the Lord

(v. 14). This caused the fame of Peter to be spread far and wide so that the people were anxious to come under his shadow. Did Peter know it?

(3) The hypocrites did not dare join (v. 13). May we learn from this that nothing unhallowed or no unsanctified person has a place in the Christian church. The offerings in the church should be a serious matter.

2. The Apostles Given Divine Credentials as Teachers (5:17-42).

Just as the new Body needed a demonstration of its sanctity, so the new teachers needed credentials. They not only needed this for themselves, but needed it for the sake of the people. They had declared: "We cannot but speak the things which we have seen and heard" (4:20). They needed Heaven's approval for they were being bitterly opposed by teachers who supposedly were properly appointed. Observe:

a. The occasion (vv. 17, 18). The apostles were arrested and imprisoned at the behest of the priests and Sadducees.

b. They were delivered by the angel of the Lord (vv. 19, 20), who commanded them to go and speak in the Temple to the people "all the words of this life." Note the significance of the Sadducees in connection with the angel.

c. The apostles emboldened by the words of the angel entered the Temple and taught the people (vv. 21-25).

d. The apostles reproved by the officers (vv. 26-28). They feared the people would storm them, therefore, they brought the prisoners out and rebuked them for disobeying their orders.

e. The reply of the apostles (vv. 29-32). They declared that they were acting under the compulsion of the will of God. The will of God supersedes the will of man. They announced the great fact of the mission of Jesus Christ and boldly declared that their divine commission was to witness to these things in co-operation with the Holy Spirit.

f. They were saved by the speech of Gamaliel (vv. 33-39). He counseled inaction.

g. The dismissal (vv. 40-42). They beat the apostles, commanded them not to speak in the name of Jesus, and let them go.

The apostles rejoiced that they were counted worthy to suffer shame for His name, and continued daily in the Temple and in every house to teach and preach Jesus Christ.

3. The Church Overcoming Internal Difficulties (6:1-7).

This is the first organization in the church. Hitherto the difficulties were external. Now a grave difficulty arises from within. Partiality, it was charged, was shown in the distribution of alms. They were confronted by a twofold danger: disruption, and the turning of the apostles away from their real work to a secondary one. They faced a most serious situation. Will the church be able to meet it? Yes! How? They appointed seven men to look after the lesser affairs of the church while the apostles did that which Christ had commissioned them to do.

Observe the wisdom shown by the apostles. They did not attempt to heal the difficulty by the exercise of authority, but they put the matter into the hands of the church. The church selected the men with the approval of the apostles.

Note the qualifications of the deacons:

a. Integrity—"of honest report" (v. 3). Integrity goes far in inspiring confidence.

b. Sagacity (v. 3). Great wisdom is required even in handling the benevolences of the church.

c. Spirituality (v. 3). It is evident that these deacons energetically discharged their obligations. Nothing of this kind is recorded afterward. Social and financial considerations did not enter. The result was a great increase in membership (v. 7). This is always true when the church is in good working condition.

4. The Martyrdom of Stephen (6:8–7:60).

Observe that the appointment of the deacons was the entering wedge to the wider dissemination of the Gospel. It brought the Hellenists to the front. The very apparent neglect of these widows was the occasion in the providence of God for this change. Note:

a. Stephen's work of distributing alms to the widows gave him an opportunity of witnessing concerning Christ (v. 8).

b. His witnessing provoked the encounter with certain of the synagogue (vv. 9, 10).

c. Stephen's arrest and charge of blasphemy (vv. 11-15). These were false witnesses. Perhaps they were bribed to testify against him.

d. Stephen's defense (7:1-53). He denies that he dishonors the Temple. He shows respect to it but is not in bondage to it. Four things stand out in this defense:

(1) God's dealings with the people showed progress and development. This is proved by:

(a) God's dealings with Abraham. He did not get into the land at once (v. 4). It was only by promise even after finally reaching it (v. 5).

(b) Progression is seen in Abraham's seed. They go into Egypt and only increase rapidly when the time of the promise draws nigh (v. 17). Even after Moses, their deliverer, was born they rejected him and had to wait forty years while he was in Arabia. So with the Temple. The idea of the Temple was given in the tabernacle and was finally built by Solomon (vv. 44-50).

(2) The Temple is not the *only* holy place. God appeared to Abraham in a heathen land (v. 2). Joseph spent his whole career in Egypt. Moses was born there. The lesson is that God is not confined to the Temple. Wherever God is, there His sanctuary is to be found (vv. 48-50; cf. Isa. 66:1).

(3) Israel rejected their deliverer, suffered as a consequence, and afterward accepted him (vv. 27-36). It was the same with Joseph, and later with Christ. This opens hope for the Gentiles.

(4) He is not disloyal to Moses and the Law, but constantly refers to it and makes Moses the writer of it, even the prophet of Jesus Christ (v. 37). He now presses home upon them the guilt of rejecting and crucifying Christ. This was too much for them. They gnashed upon him, being cut to the quick, or heart (v. 54).

e. His death (vv. 55-60). They stoned him as he knelt down and committed his spirit to the Lord. He cried with a loud voice, saying, "Lord, lay not this sin to their charge." This must be expected by everyone who truly witnesses for Christ. The Holy Spirit will give wisdom and courage for such ordeals. Such loyalty and devotion to Christ will issue in:

(1) A vision of the Lord (v. 55).

(2) A forgiving spirit (v. 60).

(3) The peace of Christ (v. 60). "Fell asleep."

(4) The crown of Christ (II Tim. 4:8; Rev. 2:10). Stephen wears a crown.

II. THE CHURCH WITNESSING FOR CHRIST IN JUDEA AND SAMARIA (8:1–12:25).

A. *The Broadening of the Church* (8:1—9:21).

The Church now begins her witness throughout Judea and Samaria. It should never be forgotten that the entering wedge for wider testimony was the appointment of deacons. The people at Jerusalem were not all against Stephen. Devout Jews, not Christians, gave him a respectable burial.

As soon as Stephen was dead, the bloody persecutors rushed back to the city and fell upon the Church. The believers took flight and "went everywhere preaching the word" (v. 4). Preaching was not now confined to the Twelve. This persecution was a great blessing. The enlarged field required more workers. The wrath of man accomplished the purpose of God. Though they were scattered they did not cease their work.

1. The Samaritans Receiving the Gospel from Philip (8:4-25).

Note how God in His providence prepared these "halfway" people, the Samaritans, to bridge the chasm between the Jews and Gentiles. They were neither Jews nor Gentiles.

a. Philip's ministry (vv. 5-8).

(1) He preached (v. 5).

(2) Wrought miracles (vv. 6, 7).

(3) Effect upon the city (v. 8).

b. Simon the sorcerer (vv. 9-13, 18-24).

(1) Who he was and his influence (vv. 10, 11).

(2) Professed conversion (v. 13).

(3) Offers to buy the Holy Spirit's gift (vv. 18, 19). All who want the Spirit's gifts for selfish ends are guilty of the same sin. Let us learn from this:

(a) What the Gospel must endure and overcome.

(b) Philip could preach the Gospel and baptize the people, but the Holy Spirit could only be bestowed by the apostles.

c. The new work was not independent of the mother church

at Jerusalem. The apostolic office must be recognized and honored (vv. 14-17).

d. The presence of the apostles shows the work to be genuine. It seemed the proper recognition (v. 25).

2. The Conversion of the Eunuch (8:26-40).

Observe the work of the church is still spreading, not only as to its geographical location but as to nationality.

a. Philip was directed by the Holy Spirit to the eunuch (vv. 26-29).

b. The eunuch needed the help of the preacher (v. 31; cf. Rom. 10:14).

c. The baptism (vv. 36, 38). Philip preached Christ to the eunuch and baptized him. This is the evangelist's duty.

d. Caught away as soon as his work was done. Philip is a good example of evangelism.

(1) Philip only man called "evangelist" (21:8), not ordained. World will be evangelized when laymen take hold.

(2) The message: "Preached Christ"—

(a) As the Saviour from sin; vicarious atonement (vv. 32, 33; cf. Isa. 53).

(b) As the Lord of the life symbolized in baptism (v. 38).

(c) As a king and kingdom (v. 12). This looks to a time when all the world shall be under the sway of one King in the Person of Jesus Christ.

(3) The method:

(a) Public preaching. This will be the first duty of the evangelist.

(b) Personal soul-winning (v. 35). Individual work in winning individuals. Preaching must be supplemented by personal work.

(c) Right home life (21:9). Philip had four daughters who prophesied. This is the needed method today. The last requirement is the most important.

(4) The power—the Holy Spirit. Filled with the Holy Spirit was the basis of his choice (6:3-5; cf. vv. 24, 25, 29). The Holy

Spirit is the only power in which the work of the evangelist can be done.

3. The Conversion of Saul (9:1-30).

He is the new apostle, the prepared instrument for world-wide evangelization.

a. Starts to Damascus with letters of authority (vv. 1, 2). He is zealous in his work of stamping out this new religion.

b. Stricken down while on the way (vv. 3-9). The proud persecutor is humble enough now. Why did not the Lord appear to him in Jerusalem? The answer is He appeared in the circumstance most favorable for his understanding of his call.

c. Baptized by Ananias (vv. 10-19). Note how the Lord can use humble men. Even in conferring the Holy Spirit He can designate one who is not an apostle. This was to show that Saul's ministry was not dependent upon the apostles. This is in striking contrast with the case of the Samaritans.

d. Saul's preaching (vv. 20-22). His theme differs from that of Peter. Saul stresses the deity of Christ while Peter, His Messiahship. The reason for this must be in the mission of his ministry.

e. The Jews took counsel to kill him (vv. 23-30). After his sojourn in Arabia (Gal. 1:17, 18) Saul was not welcomed at Jerusalem. There was no place for him in Judaism. His life was in danger except among the Gentiles where he was called to labor.

f. Saul's conversion was a parable of the Israelitish nation. Observe:

(1) His conversion was through the direct appearing of Jesus Christ to him. So it will be with Israel.

(2) Saul goes immediately with the Gospel to the Gentiles. Even so it will be with the conversion of Israel.

B. *The Preparation of the Church for the Admission of the Gentiles* (9:32–12:25).

1. Peter's Missionary Journey (9:32-43).

On this journey Peter had reached the limit of the Jew's country. When the Gospel had reached this limit, the Holy Spirit records the working of two mighty miracles. The reason for this is to show that the Gospel has lost none of its original power. It does not weaken by dissemination. Why? Because it is the power of God (Rom. 1:16, 17).

a. Aeneas cured of palsy (vv. 32-35). This was a case of semi-death raised to life.

b. Dorcas raised up. It was the case of the departed soul re-tenanting the dead body (vv. 36-44).

Nothing like these had taken place before in the history of the Church. The greater wonders (works) appear when the Church enters upon its widest ministry.

2. The Conversion of Cornelius (10:1—11:18).

Intense hatred lingered in the breast of the Jews for the Gentiles. This barrier must be broken down. This can *best* be accomplished by the Gentiles taking the *first* step.

a. The man (vv. 1, 2).

(1) He was a devout man.

(2) He was charitable.

(3) He was respected by his own family. He feared God with all his house. He was a good man but not a *saved* man. Why should God choose a man of such a character? Only a man of good character and position or standard could have filled the bill.

b. The preacher. Peter was a man of narrow vision. He said, "Not so, Lord." However, he was willing to do the Lord's will when he saw it.

c. The meeting (vv. 3-33). It was of divine arrangement. When the Lord desires the coming together of two persons, He sees to it that they meet. No barriers are too great to prevent it. Two visions are given:

(1) Vision of Cornelius (vv. 3-8). The angel of God announced that his prayers and alms had come up as a memorial before God, and instructed him to send to Joppa for Peter. Why did Peter lodge with Simon the tanner? It must have been to encourage Cornelius, by showing him that Peter was somewhat liberal in his associations.

(2) Vision of Peter (vv. 9-16).

(a) It was while praying on the housetop.

(b) A sheet let down from Heaven with all manner of beasts.

(c) Directed to slay and eat. It was while dinner was delayed that this vision occurred. This was one time when a late dinner was a good thing. It was an important factor in the world's salvation.

(3) Messengers from Cornelius (vv. 17-22). The Holy Spirit spoke at the time when inquiry was made for Peter, clearing up doubts in his mind.

(4) Peter took with him six brethren and met Cornelius. Peter shows great wisdom in this. When Peter and Cornelius meet each made an explanation.

d. Peter's sermon (vv. 34-43).

(1) The introduction (vv. 34, 35). He does not mean to say (vv. 33-37) that Cornelius is *saved* and has no need for faith in Christ, but that he is *savable.*

(2) History of the work of Christ (vv. 36-41).

(a) In His life (vv. 36-39a).

(b) In His death (v. 39b).

(c) In His resurrection (vv. 40, 41).

(3) The office of Christ (vv. 42, 43).

(a) To judge the quick and the dead.

(b) To give remission of sins.

e. The Holy Spirit poured out (vv. 44-48). This was a new Pentecost as the Gospel makes a wider embrace. Note this as an ideal Gospel service:

(1) The preacher sent by God (vv. 28, 29). He was prepared by God to speak the divine message.

(2) The people were present in a right frame of mind (v. 33).

(a) Before God, not merely the minister.

(b) To *hear* all things, not to be entertained.

(3) The proper message (v. 33). They desired a certain message.

(a) Not the preacher's opinions but what God had commanded.

(b) All that God had commanded, not a part withheld. They desired to hear even though the message may not be a pleasant one, or it might be against their prejudices, or against their secular interests.

f. Contention with Peter at Jerusalem (11:1-18). Peter rehearsed the story of the conversion of Cornelius. This story was corroborated by the six brethren who had accompanied him. Peter's account given to the Jerusalem church only settled the *possibility* of Gentile salvation, not the *method of receiving* them. The method of their reception was settled at the Jerusalem council (15).

3. A New Religious Center Established (11:19-30).

Jerusalem because of prejudices could not be the center of worldwide evangelization. It never sent out missionaries, but thrust them out by persecution. Antioch was fitted for such a center, geographically, commercially, and ethically.

The disciples were first called Christians at Antioch. They were not thus called in derision but because of the teaching which had been done by Paul and Barnabas. To Paul had been given a special revelation concerning the Church. This designation was also in keeping with the place and circumstances.

4. The Church in Conflict with the State (12:1-25).

The Church had triumphed over persecution, broken the fetters of legalism, but now the sword of the State is unsheathed against her. Will the Lord deliver her? Herod was the agent in this persecution. He was in sympathy with corrupt Judaism. Because it pleased the Jews, he laid hands upon the Church. James, one of the twelve apostles, was killed and Peter was in prison awaiting execution. Note:

a. How securely Peter was imprisoned. They had heard how Peter had broken jail before.

b. The minute details about his delivery.

c. The hesitancy of the church to believe that he had escaped.

d. The death of Herod.

III. THE CHURCH WITNESSING FOR CHRIST TO THE UTTERMOST PART OF THE EARTH (13:1—28:31).

A. *The Evangelization of the World Begun* (13:1—14:28).

After a number of years, the Church is prepared to begin the execution of its commission to preach the Gospel (Mark 16:15, 16).

Jewish caste is now broken; a new center of operation is formed at Antioch; the apostle who is to lead in this enterprise is ready to begin his work.

Barnabas and Saul return from their benevolent work at Jerusalem, accompanied by John Mark who was to be a servant to them.

1. The Preparation (13:1-3).

a. Prophets and teachers ministering to the Lord (v. 2). Doubtless this ministry included Bible study.

b. Seeking the will of the Lord through fasting and prayer (v. 2).

c. Ministers or missionaries set apart (v. 3). It was while the Church ministered to the Lord and fasted that the Holy Spirit ordered the ministers set apart. Observe the order of the names "Barnabas and Saul." The work which brought Saul to the front was not yet begun. *Rank* is determined by *men's work.*

2. The Points Touched on This Journey (13:4—14:20).

a. The island of Cyprus (vv. 4-12).

(1) Salamis (v. 5). Here they preached to the Jews in the synagogue.

(2) Paphos (vv. 6-13). Here they encountered the sorcerer.

(a) This "child of the devil" attempts to bar the mission to the Gentiles, the heathen. This finds illustration in the appearances of the Devil to Adam and to Christ.

(b) Sergius Paulus desired to know the Gospel. Elymas tries to keep him in ignorance. This the Devil always seeks to do. He is busy at this work all the while the minister preaches. (See II Cor. 4:4.)

(c) Saul's name changed to Paul (v. 9). Saul was his Hebrew name and Paul was his Gentile name. He now is known by the name which fits his mission. Paul now takes the lead.

b. Perga (v. 13). No record of preaching here. John Mark returns, perhaps because of difficulties lying before them.

c. Antioch in Pisidia (vv. 14-52). Here they entered the synagogue on the sabbath day. They were invited to preach. Paul "used the liberty" and showed that God by a series of changes increasing in helpfulness has always provided for the good of His people—this series culminating in the gift of His Son.

(1) God chose and exalted the people (v. 17).

(2) Delivered them from Egyptian bondage (v. 17).

(3) Gave them a country (vv. 18, 19).

(4) Provided judges (v. 20).

(5) Gave them a king at their request (v. 21).

(6) After removing this king He raised up David, a man after His own heart (v. 22).

(7) From David's seed Jesus sprang (v. 23).

(8) Jesus proved to be the great gift (vv. 24-27).

(9) Appeal and warning (vv. 38-41.

(10) Effect upon the people (vv. 42-52).

(a) Some Jews believed.

(b) Gentiles anxious.

(c) Expelled from the coast, they shook off the dust from their feet.

d. Iconium (14:1-5). Jews and Greeks believe, but Jews incite rebellion.

e. Lystra (vv. 6-20). Missionaries were worshiped as gods when they saw the wonderful miracles.

3. Revisiting the Churches (14:21-28).

They had a threefold object in this ministry:

a. To establish the new converts in the faith (v. 22).

b. To prepare them to endure hardship and opposition (v. 22).

c. To complete the church organization (v. 23). This was necessary for the perpetuation of the work.

Note the application of this first missionary to the modern missionary enterprise:

(1) The home base. A church engaged in prayerful Bible study. They did not wait till all were converted at home.

(2) An organized enterprise. The church at Antioch sent them out, implying that the home church supported them in the work, paid their expenses.

(3) The kind of men sent out:

(a) Spirit-filled men.

(b) Called men, but not perfect men; John Mark deserted them.

(4) The message. The crucified and risen Christ; justification by faith in Christ's shed blood; the missionary's message never changes.

(5) The method employed. They relied exclusively upon the Gospel; medical and industrial interests not used. These things, as well as education, are secondary. They are the fruits which follow—by-products of the Gospel.

B. *The Gospel Triumphant Among the Heathen* (15:1—18:28).

1. The Condition of Gentile Salvation (15:1-35).

a. The difficulty (v. 1). A serious controversy arose in the church at Antioch, one which threatened the disruption of the church into a Jewish and a Gentile church. The vital question was not as to whether Gentiles should be received into the church—that had been settled before (11:18)—but the *condition* upon which they could be received.

The Pharisaic party claimed that they should keep the Mosaic Law; i.e., be circumcised after the manner of Moses (vv. 1, 5), or they could not be saved.

Paul and Barnabas, the newly returned missionaries could not silence these Judean opponents as the Scriptures were on their side (Gen. 17:13, 14). This was an ordinance forever, for both Jew and Gentile.

b. The discussion (15:2-18). Not being able to come to a decision or agreement, Paul and Barnabas go up to Jerusalem about it. In this council Peter speaks first, giving his experience with Cornelius (vv. 7-13). Paul and Barnabas follow (v. 12); James comes last, showing by the Scriptures a way out of the difficulty (vv. 13-18). Peter, Barnabas, and Paul placed God's speaking through His wonderful works over against the spoken words, and James shows a harmony between them.

c. In his citation from Amos, we have a most luminous outline of God's purpose in the present age and that which is to follow.

(1) Taking out of the Gentiles a people for His name (v. 14). This is the distinctive work which is now going on in the world. The Church is the "called out assembly"—the *ecclesia*. This

is not the Gentile blessing which shall ultimately come through the Jews, foretold by the prophets, but a new thing. This was elective. God taking out of them a people and forming an elect body, composed of Jews and Gentiles, a Church. This was unknown to the Old Testament prophets. A special revelation was given to Paul to disclose it (Eph. 3:1-12).

The history of Church activity through the centuries shows how true were the utterances of James. Some have believed everywhere—all have believed nowhere. This *new thing*—the Church—Peter declares is not in contradiction to the prophets.

(2) The re-establishment of the Davidic rule over Israel (v. 16). After the Church has been completed, the Lord will return and rehabilitate the Jewish nation and raise up the fallen house of David (Amos 9:11-15; Isa. 11:1, 10-12; Jer. 23:5-8; Luke 1:31-33; II Sam. 7:8-17). This will bring the rest of the Jews to acknowledge their King.

(3) The conversion of the world through the instrumentality of converted Israel (v. 17; cf. Micah 4:2; Zech. 8:21-23; Rom. 11:24-27; Matt. 17:1-21).

d. The decision (15:19-31).

(1) Liberty—Magna Charta of Christian liberty (vv. 19, 28).

(2) Purity (vv. 20, 29).

(3) Charity (v. 23).

e. The result (vv. 30, 31)—a united church.

2. The Companions in Travel (15:36—16:5).

a. Silas (v. 40). Because of dissension between Paul and Barnabas, they separate, Barnabas taking Mark, and Paul, Silas. The latter go with the blessings of the church. We do not know who was to blame, but we know that God's work goes on though His workers disagree. In fact, God does His work through fallible men (James 5:17). Their differences did not seem to spread among the church members.

b. Timothy (16:1-5). He was a half-Jew. His father was a Greek and his mother a Jewess. He was of good reputation and being part Hebrew and part Gentile (of mixed parentage) was in sympathy well fitted for the work. Paul circumcised him, not as a *ground of salvation,* but for *expediency.*

3. The Call to Europe (16:6-10).

The churches seem to have been hastily revisited. When the work was done, the Spirit beckoned to Europe. The very Spirit who hindered in Asia helped them to Europe.

4. Cities Visited in Europe on This Journey (16:11–18:28).

a. Philippi (vv. 11-40). Note Philippi was a Roman colony (v. 12), a *miniature Rome.* Why should the Gospel begin in such a city? Typical of its ultimate triumph.

(1) Lydia was the first convert in Europe (vv. 14, 15). Note what women have done for the church. Note that Lydia's is a typical conversion. Steps:

(a) Attendance at the place of prayer (v. 13).

(b) Listened to the preaching of the Word of God (vv. 12, 14).

(c) Her heart was opened by the Lord (v. 14).

(d) She was baptized (v. 15).

(e) Her household believed also (v. 15). This was as it should be.

(f) Practices hospitality (v. 15).

(2) Demon cast out of a female slave (vv. 16-18). Satan opposes the Gospel again; would not have testimony from such a source (cf. Christ's action in such a case).

(3) Paul and Silas delivered from jail (vv. 19-40). Note jailer converted; Paul refused to go privately. He insisted on his rights as a Roman citizen. Had he left without a public example, the church would have been at a great disadvantage.

b. Thessalonica (17:1-9). In his preaching here he expounds the Scriptures on three lines:

(1) They show that Messiah must be a sufferer.

(2) Messiah must arise from the dead.

(3) The historic Jesus did suffer and rise, therefore, He is the predicted Messiah.

c. Beroea (vv. 10-15). More noble hearers. Why? *More noble* means better bred.

d. Athens (vv. 16-34). Paul met the culture of this place.

Theism must precede Christianity or teaching about Christ. His sermon at Athens:

(1) Nature of God:
(a) Creator.
(b) Preserver.
(c) Ruler.
(2) Guilty ignorance of man.
(3) Repentance necessary.
(4) Results.

e. Corinth (18:1-17). Associated with Priscilla and Aquila because of same nationality and craft. Note importance of craft among the Jews.

Note God's encouragement to Paul in Corinth:

(1) "I am with thee."
(2) "No harm to come."
(3) "I have much people."

f. Return to Antioch (vv. 18-22). Priscilla and Aquila left behind at Ephesus as a nucleus of work.

C. *Paul's Third Missionary Journey, or Purpose of the Church to Evangelize the World with Rome as Center* (18:23—21:16; cf. Rom. 15:23).

1. Witnessing at Ephesus (18:23—19:41).

2. Apollos (vv. 23-28). Portrait of a great preacher with a vital lack.

a. Note characteristics:

(1) Eloquent—"learned" (Williams' trans.); both essential to a preacher.

(2) "Mighty in the scriptures."

(3) "Fervent in the spirit"—felt his message—zealous.

(4) Diligent—taught accurately.

(5) Limited in his knowledge of Jesus. He knew only the Messiahship of Jesus. He knew not the value of the cross, the victory of the resurrection, nor the Spirit's indwelling and graces.

(6) Bold (v. 26).

(7) Teachable (v. 26). Willing to be taught by a humble woman. She taught him concerning the *cross* and the Holy Spirit. Many an eloquent preacher can be taught by some humble Christian

woman. An evidence of his greatness is his willingness to be taught.

b. John's disciples become Christians (19:1-7). Apparently these twelve men were the fruits of Apollos' ministry. If so, they lack just what their teacher lacked. A teacher can never impart that which he knows not, and cannot lead his people into a place of blessing which he does not occupy himself. Notwithstanding his learning, sincerity, and eloquence, he only succeeded in gathering a group of half-instructed disciples. Just as Pentecost was impossible before the crucifixion, so the one who lacks the vision of the cross lacks the graces of the Spirit.

As soon as they were taught the meaning of the cross, they were baptized, thus symbolizing their identification with Christ in death, burial, and resurrection. Then the Holy Spirit came upon them. Same results will follow today.

c. The power of God's Word (vv. 8-20; note vv. 10, 20). First in the synagogue and then in the Greek school, Paul preached the Word of the Lord Jesus, so that all Asia heard the Gospel. The very opposition in the synagogue was overruled to the success of the Gospel as the Greek school afforded a convenient meeting place.

Another factor which contributed to the success of the Gospel was the miraculous power at the hands of Paul. Such wonderful power provoked imitation, only to have the imitators discomfited by the demons. The result was that:

(1) Fear came upon all (v. 17).

(2) The name of the Lord Jesus was magnified (v. 17).

(3) Many confessed their deeds (v. 18).

(4) Books on magic burned (v. 19). The only way to get rid of vicious books is to preach the Word of God in the energy of the Holy Spirit.

d. Plan to see Rome (vv. 21, 22). Great was his success but no present victory can satisfy the heart of the minister who has the vision of Christ with reference to the world. He desires to see the Gospel reach the central city of earthly power.

e. Uproar of the silversmiths at Ephesus (vv. 23-41). This was provoked by the fact that the spread of the truth undermined the prevailing trade of the city (vv. 26, 27). This shows the method by which Christianity acts. It touches the inner springs of life, and expresses itself in the outer conduct. When the heart becomes the shrine of God, then all false shrines cease to interest. If we want men to give up evil callings, wrong habits, false worship, we must get them to take God within. Demetrius was not much concerned as long as Christianity did not touch his business, and it is the same today. When vested interests are touched, look out! Christ in the heart will change habits, religion, and business.

2. Paul's Final Journey to Jerusalem (20:1—21:17).

a. Macedonia and Greece (vv. 1-5). Action characterizes all in this section.

b. At Troas (vv. 6-12). Preaching till midnight when Eutychus went to sleep and fell out of the window from the third loft and was killed. Happy would we be if all who go to sleep would have Paul to deal with them!

c. At Miletus (vv. 13-38). Farewell address to Ephesian elders is very touching. Note:

(1) Retrospect (vv. 18-21).

(a) Humility (v. 19).

(b) Tenderness (v. 19).

(c) Faithful (v. 20).

(2) Prospect (vv. 22-27). Perils confronted him but he courageously pushed on, conscious that he had discharged his obligation.

(3) Exhortation (vv. 28-31).

(a) Take heed to selves and to flock.

(b) Feed the church of God.

(c) Wolves shall enter.

(d) Perverse men shall arise from among themselves.

(e) Watch, remembering Paul's example.

(4) Farewell (vv. 32-35).

d. At Tyre (21:1-5). Warned not to go to Jerusalem, Paul sought out the disciples while waiting.

e. From Tyre to Jerusalem (vv. 6-17). Note stop with Philip at Caesarea (vv. 8, 9); received gladly at Jerusalem. Agabus made known Paul's sufferings; Paul was entreated not to go. He was obliged to trample under foot natural affection for higher love of the Lord Jesus. However, he was not callous or insensible to human affection, e.g., "What do ye weeping and breaking my heart?"

D. *The Gospel at Rome—the Capital of the World Empire* (21:18—28:31).

Paul's work with reference to the *establishment* of the church seemed to have reached its consummation at Ephesus, as indicated by his letter to the church at Ephesus, and his committal of the work to others, declaring that they should see his face no more.

1. Paul a Refugee in the Roman Castle (21:18—23:35).

a. The Gospel offered for the last time to the Jews at Jerusalem (vv. 18-40). Paul taught that Gentiles need not keep the Law, and that Jews should not keep it as a ground of justification, but could keep it for prudential reasons (see I Cor. 9:20, 21).

(1) In order to remove prejudice, Paul acceded to the request of the elders as to taking a vow (vv. 17-26). Was it right? It succeeded with the church but not with "Jews from Asia."

(2) Paul in the hands of an angry mob (vv. 27-32).

(3) Paul rescued by Roman captain (vv. 32-40).

b. Paul's defense before the people (22:1-30). He affirms that:

(1) Present beliefs are not due to an original difference between himself and his hearers (vv. 3-5).

(2) God's interposition was the explanation (vv. 6-16). Change was wrought by God; change was at the hands of a reputable Jew—Ananias.

(3) God sent him as a messenger to the Gentiles (vv. 17-21).

(4) Paul claiming the right of citizenship (vv. 22-30). His argument, though dignified and courteous, failed; the fury of the crowd broke out at the mention of Gentiles.

Perhaps the church at Jerusalem from the first followed a course of policy. This did not pay, it never does; eventually brings trouble.

c. Paul's defense before the council (23:1-35). He was once a member of this council and now is on trial before it. The very council that had rejected and condemned Jesus had another chance to accept Him.

(1) Rebukes the presiding officer (vv. 1-5). Though earnestly seeking a hearing from the council, he fails.

(2) Appeal to Pharisees (vv. 6-10). Effort to get a hearing. Was it legitimate?

(3) Succored by the Lord (v. 11). He was assured that his purpose was to come to fruition. What cheer! The Lord never fails us when the heart's purpose is right, even though we may fail in our trials.

(4) Jews' vow of murder (vv. 12-22). Thwarted by Paul's nephew; all cunning and wrath are foolish when God moves. Though the heathen rage, God's own are safe in His will. Though Paul believed what the Lord had said to him, yet he used his common sense to bring it to pass. True faith exercises precaution.

(5) Paul escorted by Roman soldiers to Caesarea (vv. 23-35).

2. Paul's Defense Before Felix (24:1-27).

a. Circumstances (v. 1).

b. Charge (vv. 2-9). The accusers brought a lawyer along. Note hypocritical fawning of these Jews—flattery (vv. 2-4).

(1) Evil character (v. 5).
(2) Sedition—insurrectionist (v. 5).
(3) Heresy (v. 5).
(4) Sacrilege (v. 6).

c. Defense (vv. 10-21).

(1) Reply as to sedition (vv. 11-13).
(a) Time too short (v. 11).
(b) Conduct (v. 12).
(c) No proof (v. 13).

(2) Reply as to heresy (vv. 14-16).
(a) Believes the Jewish Scriptures (v. 14).
(b) Same hope (v. 15).
(c) Lives in view of this hope (v. 16).

(3) Reply as to sacrilege (vv. 17-21).
(a) His alms (v. 17).
(b) Was found purified (v. 18).
(c) No competent witness (v. 19).
(d) Present witnesses challenged (vv. 20, 21).

d. Result (vv. 22-27).

(1) Acquitted (vv. 22, 23). Indirect acquittal in that he

is committed to indulgent imprisonment and thus protected.

(2) Felix convicted of guilt (vv. 24-27). Paul was no *trimmer;* no time to accommodate message to selfish ends; he reasoned of righteousness, self-control, and of judgment to come.

Note application of righteousness to a man who was seeking a bribe; self-control (temperance) to a man and woman whose lust had swept them away into the damning sin of adultery; and of judgment to come as the outcome of such sins. Note further:

(a) Personal appeal.

(b) Profound impression.

(c) Pitiful excuse.

3. Paul's Appeal to Caesar (25:1—26:32).

a. Refused to be tried by the Jews (vv. 1-12). Festus succeeded Felix. The Jews plotted to kill Paul on the way but were overruled by the Lord, who had said that Paul would see Rome. Purposes of men cannot succeed against God's plan.

b. Defense before Agrippa (25:13—26:32). Agrippa, the king, visited Festus, who used the occasion to present Paul's matter before him for advice. It is of interest to note the puzzled Roman before the profligate Jewish monarch. Note the pomp as the king and his company assemble. Paul has another opportunity to present Christ.

(1) The argument (vv. 1-23).

(a) Introduction—conciliatory (vv. 2, 3).

(b) Absurdity of the charge (vv. 4-8). Charged with holding a belief in Messiah which all Jews accepted.

(c) Paul's career and doctrine (vv. 9-23).

(i) Early career (vv. 9-11).

(ii) His vision (vv. 12-15).

(iii) His commission from Christ (vv. 16-20).

(iv) Teaching in harmony with Old Testament Scriptures (vv. 21-23).

(2) The appeal (vv. 24-30). Note Agrippa's answer. Was it scorn, indifference, indecision?

4. Paul's Journey to Rome (27:1—28:14).

a. Contrary winds rendered slow progress (vv. 1-8).

b. Ship in the grip of the storm (vv. 9-26).

c. Shipwreck (vv. 27-44).

(1) Difficulties beset the way. Yet *the way* is *God's program.*

(2) Though the severest tests were applied the Lord was very near to comfort, care for, and direct.

(3) Though the ship went to pieces, God's servant must see Rome. God appears at just such times. Though stormy seas must be sailed by us and hope sometimes fails, yet He never fails us.

d. Rescued company on island of Melita (28:1-10).
  (1) Gathering sticks for a fire.
  (2) Bitten by a viper.
  (3) Believed to be a murderer or a god.
  (4) Publius' father cured of a fever (vv. 7-10).
  (5) Voyage completed (vv. 11-14).

5. Gospel Preached in Rome (28:15-31).
  a. Rejected by Jews in Rome.
  b. Sent hence among the Gentiles.

EPISTLE TO THE ROMANS

PART ONE—INTRODUCTORY MATTERS

THE BOOK OF ROMANS does not appear in our Bible in its chronological place, as I and II Thessalonians, I and II Corinthians, and Galatians were written before it. As to content of doctrine, however, it appears in its logical place at the beginning of the didactic or teaching portion of the New Testament; that is, the Epistles.

I. CONTENT OF ROMANS.

A grasp of the content of Romans is absolutely necessary in order to understand God's scheme of redemption. It deals with the very heart of Christianity. In its relation to Christian doctrine it is the most important book of the Bible. In it we find the following vital and profound principles of Gospel truth:

- Man's ruined condition by nature.
- Man's helplessness and hopelessness in the midst of his highest attainment in culture and religion.
- The wonderful redemption accomplished through Jesus Christ.
- The application of this redemption by the Holy Spirit.
- The bestowal of this redemption is based upon God's sovereign grace.
- The security of the believer who has appropriated this redemption.
- The life filled with love to God and man—the fruit of salvation, even in spite of a corrupt nature.

II. ORIGIN OF ROMAN CHURCH.

The origin of the church at Rome is unknown. The claim that it was founded by Peter is evidently false. It has no historic basis.

There is no historic record of any apostle having visited Rome before Paul.

Two conjectures may be offered as to its origin:

"Strangers of Rome" who heard the Gospel at Pentecost went back and preached the Word to their countrymen.

The door opened to the Gentiles on Peter's visit to the household of Cornelius. Perhaps some representative of this household carried the Gospel to Rome.

This epistle was sent by Phebe (Rom. 16:1).

III. THE FRAMEWORK OF THIS EPISTLE IS SEEN IN THE FOLLOWING BROAD OUTLINE.

A. *The Introduction* (1:1-17).
B. *The Doctrinal Teachings* (1:18—11:36).
C. *The Practical Exhortation* (12:1—15:13).
D. *The Conclusion* (15:14—16:27).

PART TWO—DETAILED OUTLINE

I. THE INTRODUCTION (1:1-17).

There is sufficient material in this introduction for a sermon.

A. *The Address or Salutation* (1:1-7).

1. The Author—Paul (1:1).

a. His relationship to Jesus Christ (v. 1). It was that of a bondslave. Every true minister of Jesus Christ sustains the same relation.

b. His office (v. 1). He was an apostle—that is, one sent. He was specifically called to that office. His office was limited. He was separated unto the Gospel of God. Everything else was excluded, even things which may be good in themselves. This is true of every minister of the Gospel today.

2. His Message (1:2-6).

a. It was received from God (v. 1).

b. It was not a novelty (v. 2). It was revealed long before by God's prophets.

c. It was in harmony with the Scriptures (v. 2). The prophetic message was recorded in the Bible of that day. This is a peculiarity of the message of those sent from God. People are not left to guess as to the message of the true minister.

d. The content of his message (vv. 3-5). It was "concerning Jesus Christ," God's Son. His message centered in the Person of Jesus Christ. Though one Person, He belonged to two realms:

(1) In his connection with the human race, He (Christ) came through the royal line. He was of the seed of David (v. 3).

(2) In His connection with the realm above, He was the very Son of God (v. 4). Both of these connections were absolutely necessary. Without the Incarnation salvation is utterly impossible.

3. To Whom Addressed (1:7).

Paul declared that the Romans were included in the Gospel-intent; observe:

a. The titles applied:

(1) Called of Jesus Christ.

(2) Beloved of God.

(3) Called to be saints.

b. The greeting. Grace and peace. Grace always precedes peace and is its very source.

B. *Personal Interests* (1:8-13).

1. "I Thank My God (1:8).

a. "For you all" (v. 8).

b. For their widely known faith; their testimony was a matter for real thanksgiving on the part of the apostles (v. 8).

2. "I Make Mention of You Always in My Prayers" (1:9, 10).

His unceasing prayer was for a prosperous journey to come to them.

3. "I Long To See You" (1:11-13).

He longed to see them that he might help them and be helped by them. There is always a reactionary beneficent effect upon the true minister's life. It is always true that the Christian witness receives something from those to whom he imparts the Gospel message.

C. *The Obligation* (1:14-16).

1. "I Am Debtor" (1:14).

Paul was under obligation to men of every tongue—"Greeks and Barbarians"; and to men of every degree of culture—"wise" and "unwise." The deposit of the Gospel which he had received from God made it obligatory for him to preach it to the Romans.

2. "I Am Ready" (1:15).

In view of this obligation Paul was ready to preach the Gospel to those at Rome.

3. "I Am Not Ashamed" (1:16a).

Paul had full confidence in the Gospel for that field because he knew it to be the power of God unto salvation. Men everywhere honor power.

D. *The Theme* (1:16b, 17).

The Gospel of Christ is the power of God unto salvation and the revelation of God's righteousness to the Jew and to the Greek on the condition of faith. Note the wealth of meaning in this brief sentence:

1. What the Gospel Does.

It saves—brings salvation.

2. To the extent of—"Everyone."

3. How Appropriated—"Everyone That Believeth."

Observe it is from faith to faith. It is obtained by faith and leads to a life of faith.

II. THE DOCTRINAL TEACHINGS (1:18–11:36).

A. *The Universal Sin and Guilt of the Human Race, or the Supreme Need of the Gospel* (1:18–3:20).

The sin question must be properly answered before there can be right thinking about Jesus Christ and salvation. All heresy is the result of ignorance as to the meaning of sin. No one who knows the truth concerning sin ever objects to the atonement through the shedding of Christ's blood. Rejection of the vicarious atonement is due to ignorance of the nature of sin.

In enunciating the principle upon which the universal sin and guilt of the race is determined the following query should be raised —Why did God give a righteousness? The answer is that man was destitute of a righteousness of his own. Because of this destitution the wrath of God is upon him (v. 18). Correlative with the revelation of God's righteousness is the revelation of His wrath. This fact discovers for us the reason for man's dislike for the Gospel. It is because the Gospel reveals sin and the consequent wrath of God, along with the good news of salvation, that men are indifferent to its preaching and oftentimes hostile to the Gospel preacher.

Sin is of two kinds—ungodliness and unrighteousness. Ungodliness is the root, and unrighteousness is the fruit. While being ungodly, men cannot do right with each other. It is highly important that men have the right view of sin. All heresies spring out of wrong view of sin. The corrective for heretical views is the Bible view of sin.

1. The Guilt of the Race (Gentiles) (1:18-36).

Human guilt has been expressed in all ages by all men. Men have conceived Heaven as frowning upon them for their deeds.

a. The race had adequate opportunity (vv. 19, 20). God was their Teacher. This teaching was through conscience and divine works. Two phrases (v. 19) disclose this—"in them" and "unto them." By *in them* is meant the conscience, and *unto them* is meant the creation. We see therefore that sin was not for lack of knowledge but in spite of it. Sin is not infirmity but positive willfulness. Sin entered the human race through the deliberate act of Adam in rebellion against God. It was this act of rebellion which introduced schism in the human being. Observe carefully that the schism in the human nature is not because of the bringing together or a lower and a higher element in man. Sin is spiritual not material. Sin is not inherent in matter. It is because of this fact that the race is without excuse.

b. The race rejected the light (vv. 21, 22). Because of this deliberate rejection, God sent them darkness. Note the triple declaration. "God also gave them up to uncleanness" (v. 24). "God gave them up to vile affections" (v. 26), and "God gave them over to a reprobate mind" (v. 28). Deliberate refusal of the light issues in darkness and confusion. There is absolutely no neutral position possible on the part of moral beings.

c. In this darkness the human race fell into:

(1) Idolatry (vv. 23-25). Man was originally a monotheist, a worshiper of one God. His first step downward was idolatry which is a caricature of God. In this worship the imperishable and incorruptible God was likened to the corruptible:

(a) Likened to a man.
(b) Likened to birds.
(c) Likened to four-footed beasts.
(d) Likened to creeping things (snakes).

Paul's statement here is corroborated by history. Man's progress has been downward instead of upward. Paul's teaching here puts the lie to evolution. The very opposite is true. In this evolution careful distinction should be made between primitive man and the savage. The savage is degenerate man. There is much more reason to regard the ape as a degenerate man than to regard man as an evoluted ape.

(2) Sensuality (vv. 26, 27). Man originally was chaste. When cast off by God, his passions were unchained. The secret of all virtue is retaining God in our thoughts. The reason for the present moral degeneration is leaving God out of man's thinking. The knowledge of God is preserved through the Bible. What a sad reflection upon America that even the reading of the Bible should be forbidden in our schools! Observe the striking phrase, "Even their women" (v. 26).

(3) Every kind of immorality (vv. 27-32). Who can say which of these sins are not practiced among men and women today? Note the charge of an intelligent heathen, who had read the first chapter of Romans, against the missionary. He declared that the missionary had written this account as a description of what he had observed as to the common practices of the heathen. May we learn from this section of Romans:

(a) God gives sufficient light to me through the testimony of His works.

(b) Man's course has not been upward, but downward. Man at first had the light but refused it.

(c) God punishes sin with sin. Man's awful crimes provoked God's judgment. All man's efforts to cure the ills of the race apart from the dynamic of the Gospel of Christ are utterly futile.

(d) We should not be ashamed of the Gospel because it is the power of God for the salvation of men for his awful sins. Through Christ's redemption lost men may be snatched from perdition.

2. The Guilt of the Self-righteous—or Better Classes—both Jews and Gentiles (2:1-16).

Observe that in chapter 1 the Gentile is not named—there was no need of it. This was illustrated in the case of a heathen accusing the missionary for writing the first chapter of Romans as cited before. It is probable that the self-righteous were mainly Jews. It was most difficult to prove the Jews guilty since they rested in the formal obedience to the Law.

Principles—their test was made:

a. The judgment of God according to the truth (vv. 2-5).

(1) The principle stated (v. 2). It is not on the ground of appearance, station, or life, or birth, but upon what one actually is.

(2) The principle applied (vv. 3-5). Instead of hiding behind others they should repent.

b. The judgment of God according to deeds (vv. 6-10). The application of this principle is that evil doing issues in suffering, while doing good issues in rewards.

c. The judgment of God is impartial (vv. 11-15). The specific application is in verses 12-15. If a Gentile kept the Law, his being a Gentile would not be against him. Being a Jew and disobedient to the Law would not avail anything. God has no favorites.

d. God's judgment will reach the secrets of men by Jesus Christ (v. 16). God's judgment of men is on the basis of their attitude toward the Gospel of Jesus Christ.

3. The Guilt of the Jews (2:17–3:18).

Though the Jew had the Law and boasted therein he was continually breaking it. This merited the greater condemnation.

4. The Conclusion (3:19, 20). All the world is under the righteous judgment of God (v. 19). Since the Law only reveals sin (v. 20), it is manifest that if there is to be any righteousness, it must be apart from law-keeping or inherent goodness. It must be a righteousness which meets all of God's requirements. In this light "there is none righteous, no not one." The sin question must be met. There is no quarrel about Christ's atonement by those who understand the *meaning of sin.*

B. *The Divine Remedy for Man's Sin* (3:21–4:25).

The righteousness of God provided in Christ is revealed in the Gospel.

1. Righteousness in Christ (3:21-31).

That which man had not, nor ever could have, is graciously provided in Jesus Christ. The righteousness of God means what God is in Himself and what He has provided. Both requirements met in Jesus Christ. Observe:

a. The source of this righteousness (v. 21). It came from God, it could not come from man. It was revealed at a time when there was no righteousness in existence so far as man was concerned.

b. Its relation to Law (v. 21). It was apart from Law, for Law reveals sin.

c. It was attested by Scripture (v. 21). Every type and ceremony pointed to this righteousness.

d. How to appropriate (v. 22). It must be obtained, as it cannot be attained. There is no virtue even in faith, for faith is but the hand that reaches out for salvation.

e. The scope—all who believe (v. 22).

f. The need—all have sinned (v. 23).

g. The ground—redemption in Christ (v. 24). It comes to us freely. While free to us, it cost God a great deal—the life of His Son.

h. The method (v. 25). It was propitiation through Christ's blood. Note the meaning of *propitiate.* It means that justice and love met together.

i. It excludes boasting (v. 27). Since it is not of works, but by faith, all boasting is excluded.

j. It is equally suited to all (vv. 29, 30). Jew and Gentile meet on the same basis. The atonement of Christ is not only adequate, but full and complete. This righteousness satisfies the justice of God and secures the justification of the sinner. In the appropriation of Christ's righteousness, the believer is saved on the basis of justice. God found a way to be just while at the same time he justifies the sinner. The sinner is reconciled to God and given all the privileges of a child of God.

2. Righteousness Was Set Forth in the Old Testament Scriptures (4:1-25).

It finds illustration in God's dealing with Abraham (4:1-5, 9-25). To this David adds his testimony (4:6-8).

C. *The Results of Receiving God's Righteousness, or Salvation Experienced* (5:1–8:39).

1. Justification (5:1-11).

By justification is meant that by the judicial act of God on the ground of the sinner's acceptance of the righteousness which has been provided in Jesus Christ, man is declared righteous. Justification is a legal term; it is more than forgiveness, it is restoration. It means to have a righteous standing. The believer is positionally as righteous as though he had never sinned. Justification is an act which can never be repeated. What God does, He does forever.

Observe the fruits of justification:

a. Peace with God (v. 1). This means that God's demands have been met and therefore His wrath has been turned aside. Hostilities between God and man are ended.

b. Introduction and establishment in grace (v. 2). Through the Redeemer we have liberty of access to God. The fullness of His grace meets us in the justified state.

c. Rejoicing in the hope of the coming glory (v. 2). Hope beyond this life is limited to those in Christ.

d. Enables the believer to glory in tribulation (vv. 3-5). Tribulation is not a pleasant experience but it works beneficent ends. It is a proof of sonship.

e. Absolute assurance of God's love (vv. 6-10). If when we were guilty and under condemnation, Christ died for us we may be doubly sure that now in a justified state, He will not cast us off.

f. Joy in God (v. 11). This justified one not only rejoices in God's glory, but has joy in God Himself.

2. Made Members of a New Race (5:12-21; Heb. 2:16).

The human race is concerned with but two men—Adam and Christ. Our destinies are bound up with them. Sin and death are our inheritance from Adam. Universal sin and death passed upon the race through Adam's sin (vv. 12-15). However, this disaster is more than compensated for through Jesus Christ (vv. 15-21). This argument here stands or falls upon the integrity of Genesis 3. All of the ills of the race spring from one man, so all the blessings of redemption come through one Person Jesus Christ. Observe the following contrasts:

a. Adam and Christ (vv. 12-14).

b. Trespass and gifts (v. 15).

c. Condemnation and justification (v. 16).

d. Death and life (v. 17).

e. Condemnation upon all men and justification of life upon all men (v. 18).

f. Disobedience of one made many sinners and obedience of One made many righteous (v. 19).

g. Abounding sin and more abounding grace (v. 20).

h. Reigning sin unto death and reigning grace unto eternal life (v. 21).

3. Gracious Justification by Faith Makes a Sinful Course in Life Impossible (6:1-23).

Note the vicious inference of verse 1. This inference is on the surface, a plausible one from what is said in 5:20, 21. Paul anticipates it and refutes it.

a. A life of sin is impossible because the believer is organically united to Jesus Christ in death and resurrection (vv. 1-14).

b. Gracious justification is a powerful incentive to a life of holiness (vv. 15-23). In justification the believer is freed from the guilt of sin. This freedom becomes an incentive for one to free himself from the power of sin. Christ indwells the believer by the Holy Spirit. Being set free from the bondage of sin, the believer becomes the bondservant of Jesus Christ.

4. The Believer's Relation to the Law As a Means of Sanctification (7:1-25). Observe:

a. The believer has two natures: the one, his constitutional being as depraved by sin; the other is the nature gained in regeneration. The depraved nature is the common heritage of every descendant of Adam through the law of heredity. This new nature is the result of the sovereign grace of God through faith in Jesus Christ. The new nature gained in regeneration is in mortal conflict with indwelling sin. A freedom from the Law is a condition of life through union with Christ in death and resurrection (vv. 1-6).

b. The character and action of the Law (vv. 7-13). The Law reveals sin, slays the sinner and yet is holy just and good.

c. The struggle for sanctification on the ground of Law observance and its result (vv. 14-25). This struggle is not that of the unregenerate man. The "renewed man is two men." It is the renewed man knowing, approving and struggling but failing. He has not sought the aid of Christ and the Holy Spirit. All Christians more or less understand this struggle when they lay their experiences alongside of this picture.

5. The Standing and State of the Believer (8:1-39).

He has entered into the reality of liberty and victory in Christ through the Holy Spirit.

a. His standing is perfect (8:1). He is absolutely free from condemnation. All that was demanded by the righteous and holy God has been met by Christ. His righteousness in obedience to the Law, and in suffering the penalty of a broken Law has been imputed to the believer.

b. Deliverance from the flesh by the power of the Holy Spirit (vv. 2-13). The depraved nature is a reality with the believer, but the law of the Spirit of life in Christ Jesus gives victory over the old nature. This may be illustrated by the law of gravity holding a balloon to the earth, but as soon as gas is applied to the balloon it soars aloft. A new law which is superior to gravity overcomes the law of gravity. A victorious life for the Christian is possible through the indwelling Holy Spirit.

c. The realization of sonship through the Holy Spirit (vv. 14-17a). It is not a question of getting rid of the flesh in this life, but of having victory over it day by day. The real and only solution is the presence and power of the Holy Spirit.

(1) Sonship realized through a pious walk in the energy of the Spirit (vv. 14, 15).

(2) Sonship confirmed by the testimony of the Holy Spirit to the believers' inner consciousness (v. 16).

(3) The outcome of sonship is heirship with God (v. 17a). How wonderful is the realization of heirship with God! To be an heir of God is the culmination of grace.

d. Preservation in suffering (vv. 17b-30).

(1) The vastness of future glory in contrast with the suffering of the present time (vv. 18-25).

(a) Creation waiting for the manifestation of the sons of God. Why was creation subjected to vanity? (v. 19).

(b) Creation groaning for deliverance (vv. 22, 23). The minor key prevails in all nature. In Heaven all music will be in the major key.

(2) The help of the Holy Spirit meets all our needs (vv. 26, 27).

(3) God controls all things to bring about His people's good (vv. 28-30).

e. The song of triumph (vv. 31-39).

(1) What shall we say to these things? (vv. 31, 32).

(2) Who shall lay anything to the charge of God's elect? (v. 33).

(3) Who is he that condemneth? (v. 34).

(4) Who shall separate? (vv. 35-39).

D. *The Righteousness of God Despised and Rejected, or God's Way with Jews and Gentiles in View of His Gracious Provision of Righteousness and Salvation* (9:1—11:36).

Paul here resumes the consideration of the inquiry raised in chapter 3: "What advantage then hath the Jew?" Note the reconciliation of the doctrine of election (8:28-30) with the apparent failure of the Jews.

1. Paul's Sorrow for His Brethren (9:1-5).

Not many of them were sharing the blessings of Christ's redemption. He could wish himself accursed from Christ for their sakes if that would avail anything. Compare Moses' statement with Paul's utterance (Exod. 32:32). In answer to the question, "What advantage then hath the Jew?", note the wonderful distinctions ascribed to Israel in verses 4 and 5.

a. They were Israelites. *Israel* means "prevailed with God and men" (Gen. 32:28).

b. They were of the adoption "—out of Egypt have I called my son."

c. "The glory"—meaning the Shekinah glory (v. 4).

d. "The covenants," for example, the covenants with Abraham, Moses, and David.

e. Giving of the Law. Nothing today compares with the Law as a code of morals.

f. Service of God, meaning the sacred system of types.

g. Promises such as concerning Palestine, the Messiah.

h. Fathers including the patriarchs, prophets, and kings.

2. No Failure on the Part of God's Promises (9:6-18).

Some were elected and others were passed by. This was God's method from the beginning. It was not a natural seed but one according to promise. This finds illustration in the case of Isaac (vv. 10-13). There is no unrighteousness with God though He so acts (v. 14). God acts according to His own will (vv. 15-18). No explanation of His acts needed. What God does is absolutely right.

3. God's Justice and Mercy Vindicated Against the Attack of the Vicious Objector (9:19-33).

a. The sin and folly of arraigning God (vv. 19-21).

b. The justice of God dare not be questioned (vv. 22-24).

c. A remnant of Israel already saved according to the prophetic prediction (vv. 25-33). Observe:

(1) The Gentiles obtained righteousness through faith (v. 30).

(2) The Jews failed in obtaining righteousness because they sought it by works (v. 32).

4. Why Israel Failed (10:1-21).

The answer is summed up in the word *unbelief*. During this period of rejection both Jews and Gentiles are on the same level—saved through faith in Jesus Christ. The Jews failed. They are not cast off forever. Their rejection is not final. They have passed and are passing through fiery trials. Though the "bush" has been burning through the centuries it is still not consumed. The Jew is indestructible.

5. The Solution of the Problem of the Ages (11:1-35).

a. Though nationally rejected, individuals are being saved from every generation (vv. 1-10). Paul stands out as an illustrious example. As it was in the period of idolatry when Elijah lived 7,000 had not bowed to Baal, so more are being saved from among the

Jews than we suspect. It is the remnant according to the election of grace (v. 5).

b. Their rejection is not final (vv. 11-36). There is a coming day of restoration. God is overruling the sins of His people for good.

(1) Their fall is the occasion of blessing to the Gentiles (vv. 11, 12). Salvation now flows to the Gentiles, but the conversion of the world awaits the conversion of Israel. In view of this what folly and sin to hate and despoil the Jew. The Jew constitutes God's touch stone. Remember Abraham's covenant. There should be no boasting over the Jew, and there should be no disposition on the part of the Gentiles to appropriate the promises made to the Jews.

(2) Israel's rightful place is in the olive tree (v. 24).

(3) The hardening of Israel is only temporary (v. 25). It still goes on but will cease.

(4) The conclusion (v. 26). "All Israel shall be saved." The guarantee of this is:

(a) God's promise of a Redeemer to save Israel (vv. 26, 27).

(b) God's love for them though they are in unbelief (v. 28). They are "beloved for the fathers' sakes."

III. THE RESULT OF RECEIVING GOD'S RIGHTEOUSNESS (12:1—16:27).

Note the behavior of those who have experienced the salvation provided in Jesus Christ. Receiving God's righteousness makes possible a godly walk. The proof of the reality of salvation is in holy living. The *therefore* shows that sacrificial living proves the reality of salvation.

A. *The Willing Offering of Oneself As a Living Sacrifice* (12: 1, 2).

This means the repudiation of the world's spirit and maxims and the deliberate entering into the power of a transformed life.

B. *The Right Use of Spiritual Gifts* (12:3-8).

The church is an organism. God sets in order the members of Christ's Body as He wills (I Cor. 12:18). The members of the Church are interdependent. Each one is to do faithfully and humbly the work given him. There is a wide diversity of gifts (v. 4).

C. *Personal and Individual Duties* (12:9–13:14).

1. Love without hypocrisy (v. 9).
2. Abhor the evil and cleave to the good (v. 9).
3. Unselfish—self-abasing (v. 10).
4. Not slothful in business—fervent in spirit (v. 11).
5. Rejoicing in hope, patient in tribulation (v. 12).
6. Given to hospitality (v. 13).
7. Do good for evil (v. 14).
8. Be sympathetic (v. 15).
9. Each to think better of the other (v. 16).
10. Live honestly and in peace (vv. 17, 18).
11. Be not vindictive (vv. 19-21).
12. Be in subjection to civil authority (13:1-7). Civil government is from God. Being a Christian does not relieve one of his duties as a citizen.
13. Real love in the heart is the fulfillment of the law (13:8-14). The grand incentive prompting all right living is that the night of Christ's absence is drawing to a close.

D. *The Duties of the Enlightened Toward Those Weak in the Faith* (14:1–15:13).

Some among the Roman Christians were vegetarians—some were afraid to eat meat which had been dedicated to idols—some were conscientious about feast days—some had scruples about the sabbath, etc. The remedy for such difficulties is that neither party should judge the others. This is enforced by the following telling arguments:

1. All Must Stand Before the Tribunal of God (14:12).
2. Assertion of One's Liberty Is Dangerous (14:15).
3. Christ Is the Supreme Example (15:3).

E. *Sundry Explanations and Personal Greetings* (15:14–16:27).

FIRST EPISTLE TO THE CORINTHIANS

PART ONE—INTRODUCTORY MATTERS

THE TEACHINGS OF PAUL in I Corinthians are of perennial interest to the Bible student and Christian worker because of their practical bearing upon church life and activity. It is here that we see Christianity in conflict with heathenism—the Church established in the midst of a refined and corrupt people. It was natural that under such circumstances questions should arise touching the relations of Christians to the surrounding heathen.

In this epistle are unfolded principles which relate to the proper discipline of the church; the correct basis of social intercourse; the rights and claims of the marriage relation; the proper decorum in the public assembly; the origin and exercise of spiritual gifts; and the nature of the resurrection body. Here the foreign missionary can learn the proper method to use in the founding of a church, even in the midst of a cultured people. The Christian pastor can find the proper methods to use in the solution of the problems which confront him in church life. The principles involved in Paul's acts and decisions are of universal application and will answer as guides in all ages.

The church can expect to have to deal with party spirit; to administer discipline; to correct the social relations of her members; to maintain church order; to set forth the true significance of the Lord's Supper; to exhibit the nature of the Body of Christ as an organism; to instruct as to the origin and right use of spiritual gifts; and to emphasize the truth of the resurrection of the body.

The teachings of this book have a practical bearing upon the establishing of the church in foreign lands, as well as the direction of its affairs in Christian homelands, becoming a manual for foreign missionaries and Christian pastors at home.

I. History of the City of Corinth

In Paul's time it was the largest city in Greece. The Roman general Mummius destroyed it in 146 B.C. It lay in ruins for a hundred years until rebuilt by Julius Caesar in 46 B.C. Its situation determined its greatness. It was located on the Isthmus of Corinth, which had an important seaport on each side through which the commerce of the world flowed. Because of its situation it could impose toll on all goods passing through, which resulted in the piling up of vast wealth. Its population was mixed. Traders from all parts of the commercial world met there.

Corinth was a veritable hot-bed of all sorts of vice, being notoriously licentious. A word was coined to express this condition. To play "the Corinthian" meant to be guilty of the deepest immorality. "The vice of the East and West met and clasped hands in the work of human degradation." Religion itself was turned into prostitution. A great temple was erected where thousands of fallen women ministered as priestesses. This temple was dedicated to the goddess Aphrodite corresponding to the Roman Venus. "Greek philosophy in its decay showed itself in endless discussion about words, non-essentials, a tendency to set intellectual above moral distinctions, and a denial of the future life for the sake of an unlimited enjoyment of the present." This gives some idea of the conditions which Paul had to meet about the middle of the first century.

II. History of the Founding of the Church at Corinth

This is recorded in Acts 18. Coming from Athens to Corinth on his second missionary journey, Paul was joined by Timothy and Silas (Acts 18:5). A stranger in this city and without the means of support, Paul associated himself with Aquila, a Jew who, with Priscilla his wife, was banished from Rome by the edict of Claudius. He joined with them in the making of tents, for he was of the same craft. A business tie, as well as a natural one, joined these people. Every Jewish boy was taught some trade regardless of the social and financial standing of his father. One of their rabbis said that he who failed to teach his boy a trade taught him to steal—wholesome advice for this age.

On the sabbaths Paul would reason in the synagogue and persuade Jews and Greeks. His preaching of the doctrine of the Messiahship of Jesus aroused bitter opposition, whereupon he shook the dust from his feet and went to the Gentiles. Instead of the synagogue he now made the house of Justus the center of his teaching. Here his work was attended with great success. Crispus, the ruler of the synagogue, with many people of prominence, believed and was baptized. A vision from the Lord, showing him that He had much people there, caused Paul to remain in this city a year and six months. The remarkable success attending his ministry in this city so incited the enmity of these Jews that they arraigned him before the Roman governor. As soon as the governor learned the nature of their charge against him, they were dismissed in a disgraceful manner. This gave encouragement to the bystanders and they beat Sosthenes, the ruler of the synagogue. Notwithstanding this, Paul still remained many days.

From Corinth Paul, in company with Aquila and Priscilla, sailed to Ephesus. After a short stay there, he sailed to Caesarea, then to Jerusalem. Soon after Paul's departure from Ephesus, Apollos came and preached in that city. Eloquent and mighty in the Scriptures he needed more knowledge of the truth, for he knew only the baptism of John. Perceiving this serious defect, Priscilla and Aquila instructed him in the way of the Lord. They gave him letters of introduction to Corinth. Here he "powerfully confuted the Jews, publicly showing by the Scriptures that Jesus was the Christ."

Paul returned to Ephesus and remained three years. While there he heard of the state of the Corinthian church. The commercial interests of the two cities brought them into close contact. Besides, the church addressed some letters of inquiry to him. Then, too, the household of Chloe had given him some information concerning the party spirit which was arising in that church. He seems to have written a letter to them which is no longer in existence, and likely he visited them. Most assuredly he sent Timothy to them (4:17; cf. Acts 19:22).

III. THE OCCASION OF THIS WRITING

A. *The Existence of Rival Factions Contending Against Each Other.*

B. *Their Failure to Carry Out Church Discipline.*

C. *Their Going To Law with Each Other.*

D. *Indifference to the Gross Immoralities of the Corinthians.*

E. *Letters from Them Requesting Information as to:*

1. Marriage and Divorce.
2. Food Connected with Heathen Sacrifices and Festivals.
3. The exercise of Spiritual Gifts.

F. *Disorders in the Public Assembly:*

1. Improper behavior.
2. Unseemly dress of the women .
3. Abuse of the Lord's Supper.

G. *The Presence in the Church of Certain Ones Who Denied the Resurrection of the Dead.*

PART TWO—DETAILED OUTLINE OF BOOK

I. THE TRUE CHURCH OF GOD (1:1-3).

Our discussion of the problems of the modern church will be from the viewpoint of the true Church. So many things have been tacked on to the church that much that is called "the church" is not really the Church. In the light of New Testament revelation, by "the Church" is meant believers in Christ, the Body of called-out people from among all nations united to Jesus Christ as Head and to each other as members of the organism by the Holy Spirit. The Old Testament prophets told of the kingdom to be set up with Messiah at its Head and Israel at its center. In the Gospels we have the kingdom offered to Israel, but they refused it and crucified the King. The kingdom was then withdrawn—placed in abeyance—and only in the Book of the Revelation do we see its establishment. Between its beginning and its consummation there is a great parenthetical interval in which the Church comes into view, which had its beginning after Christ's ascension, and its translation will take place at His coming. The Church is, therefore, something different, separate, and apart from the kingdom.

In I Corinthians 1:1-9, the preface of the book, we have the characteristics of the true Church. The epistle was addressed to the Church of God (v. 2). These messages were directed to those who had been brought into the fellowship of Jesus Christ and therefore were members of His Body, the Church. The statement, "with all that call upon the name of the Lord Jesus Christ in every place," shows that while the application was intended primarily for the church at Corinth, and was therefore local, its underlying principles are applicable to the entire Church for all time. That we may know the extent of its application, we note the following distinguishing features of the Church of God.

A. *Characteristics of the True Church* (1:2).

These give us an unfailing test whereby we may know the people composing the Body of Christ.

1. They Were Consecrated (1:2).

The word *sanctify* here bears the primary scriptural meaning, namely, to set apart for a specific and holy use, to dedicate. Thus we see that the Church of God is composed of men and women set apart for a holy use. They are called out from among other people to maintain before the world lives reflecting Christ and to be witnesses for Him. The supreme aim of every member of the Church should be to attain to this end. It should not be a matter of seeing how much of the world's enjoyments he can gain and how many honors he can attain. This consecration is God's act, no one can consecrate himself, it must be done by the living God. The utmost that one can do is to yield to God's will. It is only as this is done that Christ's purpose for us can be realized.

2. A Holy People (1:2).

One consecrated to God must become holy, for God is holy. The members of the Church of God partake of the divine nature, therefore should exhibit in human life this fundamental trait of God. To belong to the Church of God is not only to be dedicated to God's sacred use, but positively to manifest God's holiness. Many today, as in the church of Corinth, seem to have forgotten this, for even the common moral requirements are ignored. The members of the true Church are not dominated by the passions of the world, but constantly are to show the divine purpose in their calling and sanctification. This is the all-comprehensive purpose of God in man's redemption—the exhibition of His own glorious excellence. The purpose does not terminate upon man, but upon God. The fact that we are called by the name of Christ ought to impel to a holy life. The one, therefore, who really is a member of the Body of Christ will put away all filthiness of habit or conduct and every act that does not positively enhance God's glory. If this really were believed today by people professing godliness, all vile conversation, attendance at places of questionable propriety, the using of questionable methods in business, and tobacco-using, and liquor would be done away with.

3. Universality (1:2).

The Body of true believers is not confined to one nationality or race, nor to one age, but is composed of some out of all kindred and tongues and out of all ages. One of the new songs in glory will be, "Thou art worthy to take the book, and to open the seals thereof: for thou wast slain, and hast redeemed us to God by thy blood out of every kindred, and tongue, and people, and nation" (Rev. 5:9). This truth, if laid hold upon, will do away with much of the Pharisaism and selfishness so prevalent among Christian people. The one only test is calling upon the name of Jesus Christ. All persons, therefore, who really call upon His name belong to the Church. However, calling upon His name means to trust in Him, to look to Him as the supreme Lord. It is belief in Jesus Christ as one Lord, which brings men together as a Christian Church. Happily, no ecclesiastical organization can dictate who shall be members of the Church, for it is not a matter of subscribing to some church polity.

4. Unity (1:2).

Since there is but one Lord, all membership and interests center in and consist in Him. Therefore, there must be unity. Envy and rivalry will disappear when this is realized. Christ is the one Head and the members composing His Body are not divided. By the one Spirit we were all baptized into the one Body (12:13). Since that Body is a united Body, let us inquire as to what that unity consists of. Is it in the minutiae of ecclesiastical polity? No, for if that be true, it is evident that there is but a small body of true Christians in the world, for within denominational circles there are about as many views of the various details as there are members. Our mental proclivities are such as to prevent such union; we must look elsewhere for the basis of true unity. That union must be in Jesus Christ and the great cardinal doctrines of God's Word. If we were to emphasize the principles upon which we are all a unity, we would be surprised how rapidly the small things would adjust themselves to a harmonious working condition.

II. PAUL'S THANKSGIVING (1:4-9).

It was for the grace of God which was bestowed upon them, enriching them in utterance and in knowledge waiting for the coming of Jesus Christ. The apostle considers church character and church equipment. Being enriched in utterance shows that the power of the Church's testimony is from Christ and centers in Him. This shows that the Church not only was equipped intellectually, but gave evidence of experimental knowledge of it. Their utterance, no matter how eloquent, would be of no consequence unless it centered in Christ. Today wherever intellectuality and culture have taken precedence over the preaching of the cross of Christ, such preaching is devoid of power.

III. CHURCH FACTIONS (1:10—4:21).

A. *The Fact Stated* (1:10-12).

The church at Corinth was divided into four parties contending for leadership—some were for Paul, some for Apollos, some for Cephas, and some for Christ. These different men possessed different phases of truth. Such emphasis was not for any selfish purpose, but the result of the Spirit's leading. These people failed to take into consideration that emphasis upon the different phases of truth is essential to its right understanding, the one being complementary of the other.

The Corinthians failed to take this into consideration, as many people do today. Paul, Apollos, and Peter did not pose as rival teachers and leaders. The fault was with the people. Then, there were those who repudiated all human teachers and raised the cry of "Back to Christ." This party, perhaps, became the most sectarian of all. Then, as now, those who repudiate all denominational affiliations were the most unyielding in their demands for party recognition. With dismay Paul hears of this. If he was so affected then, how would he be now? The apostle most deeply deplores this and severely rebukes them for their carnality. We are at no great loss to know why he should do this, for he knew full well that the Devil has no surer way of breaking up a church than by turning men's eyes away from Christ to the men who preach Him.

Men are prone to be occupied more with the messenger than with the message. Sectarianism is an evil to be deplored. The Church was intended to be the unifier of the race. All races, and all kinds of men, were to be gathered within her pale, all united around one common Head, saying, "Our Father." Instead of this the Church has alienated men and races. Men will do business together, dine together, but will not worship together. Because of this factious spirit the strength of the Church is frittered away in strife, her growth is retarded, and her testimony marred. The world looks on and laughs. There can be spiritual growth only as the members fix eyes on Christ alone, and are united in Him.

There were also some people who laid great stress upon the fact that they had been baptized by certain persons. So great did this danger become that Paul delegated that work to others lest people should think of being baptized in the name of the man, rather than the Christ who instituted the ordinance. Many today need to be reminded that the virtue of baptism does not lie in the administrator, but in the faith of the baptized person in the blood of Jesus Christ.

B. *The Problem Considered* (1:13–4:5).

The same causes which broke up the Corinthian church are operative to day. The same remedy proposed by Paul will heal the dissensions. In the consideration of this problem we set forth Paul's teachings in formal propositions as follows:

1. Factions Are Caused by an Improper Comprehension of the Headship of Christ (1:13-16).

Christ is more than a great Teacher. He is the vital Head of an organism—the Church. The Church has but one Head and one source of authority, that is Christ. To place anyone before Christ is the greatest disloyalty. That is just what one does who is controlled by the partisan spirit. This personality of the man eclipses that of Christ. It is not by Christ's teaching and life that men are drawn to

God. It is through His death that He came to have a unique claim upon man. The Church is founded upon the cross. Christ did not die as a martyr, but as Redeemer. He, the representative of God and man, gave His life as a ransom. Failure to grasp this cardinal truth causes divisions. It is when men fail to grasp the Person and work of Jesus Christ that party spirit creeps in. The cure for this evil is the true conception of Christ's authority and headship. Men must see Him as the crucified Saviour, made Head and Lord over all. Only when the thoughts of each one center in the Master can there be unity, which is so essential to growth and development. It was the fear lest men should be drawn away from this conception that caused Paul to refrain from baptizing. It is pitiable to see men and groups of men endeavoring to obtain unity among themselves by church organizations, with systems of teaching, or around teachers.

2. Factions Are Caused by a False Conception of the Gospel (1:17-25).

The Gospel is the proclamation of salvation by faith in the crucified Christ and His resurrection from the dead (see 15:1-4). The express purpose of the Gospel is to save men, not to afford an occasion for the lifting up of their pride (1:21). This Gospel was the heart of Paul's message. His supreme aim was so to carry on his work that the whole matter might stand in the power of God, and not in the wisdom of man. He especially defended himself against having sought to please men. Doubtless with varying circumstances he varied his style, but we are assured that at Corinth, at least, his style was free from rhetorical embellishment.

Though he was pre-eminently qualified to reduce Christian doctrine to a system, so as to appeal to the judgment of the Grecian philosophers, he chose, like his Master, to announce it as good tidings of great joy. He full well knew the nature of man apart from divine aid, and the effectiveness of the salvation which God had provided in His Son. His soul was so wrought upon by the Holy Spirit that he was impelled to announce in the simplest way possible the good news of salvation to a lost world. He refrained from preaching the world's philosophies, for all history and experience had shown that they were unable to bring men to a knowledge of God (v. 21). He showed that the way God determined to save men is by preaching

Christ as crucified. Paul preached a Person, not a mysterious philosophy. What the world needs today is a vision of the cross. When people get a proper vision of Christ on the cross their hearts are melted, they repent and believe.

The cure, then, is to present the Gospel as God's means of salvation, and not as a system of philosophy. However, it is the divinest of philosophies when apprehended by the spiritual mind. Poor, ignorant, and helpless men are unable to understand philosophy, but all can understand the message of the cross, all can understand the helping hand of love. Philosophy has never changed the life of the philosopher, nor the morals of the street upon which he lived; but wherever the Gospel is received there is transformation of life. The preacher himself must experience it before he can proclaim it effectively. Philosophy is confined to the few, while the Gospel of Christ is universal. Not only is it adapted to all nations but to all classes of men in those nations. To see the contrast between philosophy and the Gospel one needs only to place Plato's philosophy over against the Gospel of John, or Peter's preaching with the teaching of Aristotle. The contrast is as great as light and darkness. The contrast is no less great in our own time in the churches where the Gospel is preached and those where human philosophy is taught. To unite the churches, let there be a return to the proclamation of God's evangel and the repudiation of the world's philosophies.

3. Factions Are Caused by an Improper Conception of the Church's Constituent Elements (1:26-31).

Not many wise and noble—not those whose wisdom enables them to find out God and whose nobility of character commends them to God—there is no aristocracy with Him. Before God no flesh can glory. One of the prominent causes of sectarianism today is the failure to declare universal human depravity, and the consequent accentuation of differences in the ability and position of men. The cure is to show that all men are sinners, lost and hopeless, groping in midnight darkness; as unable to help themselves as the blind man is to open his eyes; and man's being in Christ is God's doing—"of him are ye in Christ Jesus." Christ has been made wisdom to those who are ignorant; salvation to those who are in sin; sanctification to those who are unclean; and redemption to those who are entangled in the bondage of sin. Man did not seek God, but God sought him. All that he is and all that he has is of Christ.

4. Factions Are Caused by Failure to Apprehend the Apostle's Ministry (2:1-16).

It was not in words of human wisdom, but in the power and energy of the Holy Spirit. His repudiation of the world's wisdom was misconstrued. In many cases it is so today. The cure is to realize that the Gospel is the true wisdom which man, unaided, could not find. The words of the rhetorician must be set aside for the message and words of the Holy Spirit. Since this wisdom of God cannot be grasped even by the princes of this world, but is revealed by the Spirit, it should be the aim of the minister to create within men the spiritual mind, because the spiritual mind is essential to the understanding of the spiritual message. The supreme need, then, to bring about unity is not teaching, merely, but regeneration. The world today sorely needs preachers like Paul. The worldward drift of the Church is due largely to the absence of such preachers. We may affirm three things of Paul as a preacher.

a. He was a man with a message from God. The preacher of today can and must come with the same message; he must get it from the same source, namely, the infallible Word of God.

b. He was a man who did not doubt the authority of his message. The chief weakness of the modern pulpit message is the lack of positive conviction as to the Word of God. Believing that his message was from God, he was impelled to proclaim the message. Like Jeremiah, the Word of the Lord was in his heart as burning fire shut up in his bones.

c. He was a man who believed in the illumination of the Holy Spirit, which enabled the sinner to apprehend the love of God in Christ Jesus. The Holy Spirit alone can take the things of Christ and show them unto the people.

The preacher who properly honors the Spirit will not spend his greatest energies in the rhetorical embellishment of his sermons. If ever there was a time when the Church needs such preachers it is now.

5. Factions Are Caused by a False Conception of Christian Ministry (3:1–4:5).

To conceive of the ministers as party leaders or teachers of philosophy tends to divisions. Such a view exhibits the low standard of Christianity (3:1-4). Divisions in the church occur when men's eyes are turned from the church of Christ to the men who preach Him—when they are occupied with the messenger rather than with the message—when they respect the authority of the preacher rather than the One who sent him to preach. The cure in such a case is to get a proper conception and estimate of human teachers. They should see them as they really are.

a. Ministers are servants of God (3:5, 6). They are instruments in His hands for the execution of His will, not leaders of men. They are men sent to deliver a message, to perform a definite work. They are not the authors of the system of truth which they teach. When men look away, then, from the ministers to God who sent them, they will not be imbued with the party spirit.

b. Ministers are equal in rank (3:7-9). They are one, called by the same Spirit, to teach the same truth, and stand in the same relationship. The coming of an official hierarchy has no place in the Scriptures. When men once see it as such they will turn away from human teachers to their message.

c. Ministers are accountable to God (3:10-21). Every minister must account to God for his work. If he lay other foundation than Christ, he is not a Christian minister at all. If he build sound doctrine on that foundation he will get a reward. If he build false doctrine, he will suffer loss and be punished. Sorrow and anguish will come to him who builds good material upon a poor foundation, and likewise, to him who builds poor material on a good foundation. Human material and human wisdom have no place in the solemn work of building the Church of God. Worldly-wise teachers destroy God's temple and incur God's wrath (3:16-20).

d. Ministers are owned by the church (3:22, 23). They are her property, and not the church owned by the ministers. We should not, therefore, put confidence in men. We should follow them only as far as they follow Christ.

e. Ministers are God's stewards (4:1-5). Their business is to dispense His truth. They have no right to originate or create the message. God demands fidelity on their part. He will judge them as to their faithfulness.

C. *Conclusion* (4:6-21).

1. He Issues a Sharp Rebuke (4:7-13).

He uses the most cutting irony (4:7, 8) and in which their carnality is shamed by his own apostolic example (4:9-13).

2. His Position As a Father.

He regards the Corinthians as his spiritual children. Looking upon them as such, his parental heart is grieved over the contentions among them.

3. He Appeals to Apostolic Authority (4:18-21).

Having reasoned with them so patiently, pointing out their errors and showing them so clearly their way of shame, then the way to come to a blessed unity in Jesus Christ, the Head, he reminds them of his authority which God vested in him as an apostle.

IV. CHURCH DISCIPLINE (5:1-13).

A. *The Occasion* (5:1, 2).

The church at Corinth was guilty of tolerating within her communion a man who was guilty of incest, an immorality to which even licentious Corinth was a stranger (v. 1). This did not even meet the disapproval of the church, for it seems that they were rather glorying in it. This man may have been rich, educated, and influential. So glad were they to have him as a member of the church that they were willing to condone his sin. The Corinthian church is not the only one which has been remiss in discipline toward the rich, educated, and influential. Seeing the awful end of such remissness of discipline, Paul authoritatively demands that immediate and drastic measures be adopted to rid the church of such scandal. The offender was to be excommunicated, given over to Satan for the destruction of the flesh. This was more than excommunication—it was the infliction of divine judgment.

There is an utter lack of church discipline today in all our churches. This is one of the secrets of the ineffectiveness of her testimony. In many places men and women may conduct their business affairs and live such lives as may please them and yet be regarded as in good standing in the church, especially if they are wealthy and somewhat clever. Members may attend church services only occasionally, may not even take part in prayer meetings or even have prayer in their own homes, scarcely give a mite of their possessions to the Lord's work, yet when they move away from our congregations we give them letters certifying to their good standing. There ought to be an awakening along this line. In chapter 5 of this epistle we have a precedent for church discipline which dare not be ignored.

B. *Authority for Church Discipline* (5:3).

In many quarters there are those who question the right of the church to discipline her members. This is never done by those who have a proper conception of the Word of God, and who are not longing to go after the world. The church has the inherent right to pass judgment upon her members, to determine who shall be members, and as to how they shall live as members. She not only has the inherent right by virtue of her organization as a body, but she has the apostolic precedent and command (5:4). This position is challenged by some who misinterpret Matthew 13:30, saying, "Let the wheat and the tares grow together." They fail to see that the Scripture applies to the *age* in which we live, and not to the members of this called-out Body called the Church. This authority to discipline resides in the congregation—does not inhere in the officials, but in the congregation as a whole. If the congregation has not this authority, Paul was in error when he held that congregation responsible for its administration. To question this is to question Paul's inspiration. He emphatically affirms (14:37) that he was speaking from God, speaking by the Spirit, and he held them responsible for the administration of discipline, and most severely censured them for its neglect.

C. *The Necessity for Church Discipline* (5:4-8).

1. To Save the Individual (5:4, 5).

"In the name of our Lord Jesus Christ, when ye are gathered together, and my spirit, with the power of our Lord Jesus Christ, to deliver such an one to Satan for the destruction of the flesh, that the spirit may be saved in the day of the Lord Jesus." This discipline was for the destruction of the flesh but for the salvation of the spirit. The flesh means the evil passions. He does not say for the destruction of the body, for in chapter 15 he tells us of the glorious resurrection of the body. In all church discipline primary consideration should be given to the good of the individual. This dare not be neglected.

2. To Keep the Church Pure (5:6).

For the church to fail to pass judgment upon her members who sin is to countenance sin. To disregard sin in one means to disregard it in all. Sin is a dreadful contagion. "Know ye not that a little leaven leaveneth the whole lump?" Just as one rotten apple in a barrel of good apples may cause them all to rot, so one sinner in the church, undisciplined, may affect the whole body. As a cancer unremoved may cause death to the whole body, so to preserve her own life, the church must cut off her sinning members. The Lord cannot and will not bless that church which tolerates sin. Achan's sin and its disastrous consequences are a warning to all ages.

The position of the church is analogous to that of the Israelites who were forbidden under penalty of death to eat leaven during the seven days that followed the death of the paschal lamb. Christ is to us what the lamb was to Israel. As no leaven was allowed in the house of Israel, so the Church should remove the sinning member. The death of the paschal lamb put the obligation upon the Israelites to put away the old bread and bring the new; so the death of Christ obliges us to put away sin and live the new life. Sin, like leaven, communicates its nature to all it touches. As every nook and corner were to be searched lest leaven be found, so we should not only search our own hearts, but the church as a body, lest sin be found (5:7, 8). It is this disregard of sin and sinners that has brought the barrenness upon the efforts of the church today. If we are to have a return of the spirit of revival, there must be the judgment for sin, and separation from it.

D. *The Grounds for Church Discipline* (5:9-11).

1. Licentiousness (5:9).

This should be attended to strictly for we are in a very immoral age. Licentiousness is gnawing at the vitals of the home, society, the church, and the nation. Divorce is fearfully prevalent. The records of the Census Bureau show that in the United States, during the twenty years prior to 1908, there were granted on the average, all told, twenty divorces each hour. In Cook County, Illinois, in 1956 up to November 30, there were 14,958 divorce suits filed; during the same time there were 44,180 marriage licenses granted. Statistics of 1950 and 1951 for the state of Illinois show that there was slightly more than one divorce to every four marriages. Recently the statistics show one out of six marriages end in divorce in the country.

2. Covetousness (5:10).

This, too, is a sin of widespread influence. All about us men and women are grasping after money. Even in the church many are more interested in the accumulation of money than in the building up of the cause of Christ.

3. Extortion (5:10).

This has reference to the forceful taking of goods from another. It may be the taking of excessive interest just because one is in the position to demand it. It may be in the manipulation of business affairs so as to bring about forced sales.

4. Idolatry.

This has primary reference to the worship of false gods by the heathen, but has an application to conditions as they exist in many places today. Every man has his god. If it is not the true God, it is a false one. That whch is uppermost in the minds and affections is a god to us. Our activities constitute our worship. Various are the gods which Americans worship today—gold, pleasure, power, lust, beauty, dress, fame.

5. Raillery (5:11).

This applies to slander and abusive speech. Every church member guilty of such conduct should fall immediately into the judgment of the church. If he will not repent, he should be expelled from the church.

6. Drunkenness (5:11).

Everyone who becomes intoxicated is a subject for discipline. However, this requires patient dealing, for many have inherited weaknesses which require great effort to overcome.

E. *The Difficulties of Church Discipline.*

1. Personal guilt.

There is the consciousness of personal guilt on the part of the individual church member. Even those who are leaders in the church frequently feel this, causing them to shrink from bringing others into judgment when they themselves are guilty. Then, too, some may use such circumstances as an occasion to "get even."

2. Human Limitation.

The imperfection of human knowledge renders it extremely difficult to properly discipline members. Sometimes that which seems to be sin on the part of one does not seem so on the part of others, and actually, may not be. While this is difficult, it is not impossible, for the Lord said: "If any of you lack wisdom, let him ask of God." If selfish interests are left out and the mind of God is sought honestly, there will seldom be a mistake.

F. *The Salutary Effects of Church Discipline.*

1. Upon the Person Disciplined.

It seems from II Corinthians that the man disciplined in this case repented and was restored. While great care should be exercised lest one of these little ones who believe in Jesus should be made to stumble, it should be remembered that if one is really a child of God, the discipline will have the effect of working repentance and reconciliation. It was said of a certain pastor, when of necessity he administered discipline to a member of his flock, he earnestly remarked to the offender that his sin was of such a nature as to necessitate his being disfellowshiped, but that the church door stood open for his return whenever he repented and confessed his wrongdoing. However, if he were really a sheep he would come back bleating to get into the fold, and would not, as a pig, endeavor to root out the foundation of the church. The reason why some parties try to destroy the influence of the church itself, when they have fallen into her judgment, is because they never were Christians.

2. Upon the Church Herself.

The best working churches are those where discipline is exercised. It is said of a certain church, where members were disciplined even for gossiping, that scarcely a week passed by without conversions. What a happy effect it would have upon us if for gossiping, prying into other's business, dishonesty, lying, and all acts of immorality and evil conversation, members were brought into judgment! While we would insist upon rigid church discipline, it should be carried out in the spirit of the love of Christ; and great care should be exercised lest the limits of the inspired Word of God be transcended. We should distinguish most carefully between human and divine standards.

V. LITIGATION AMONG CHURCH MEMBERS (6:1-11).

The Corinthians were guilty of carrying their differences into the civil courts for adjudication. Perhaps the case at hand was the carrying into the heathen court the matter mentioned in the previous chapter, namely, the man having his father's wife. The apostle, horrified at such practices, exclaims, "Dare any of you having a matter against another, go to law before the unjust?" The restraining influence of the apostle's teaching needs to be much emphasized today, for it seems there is a greater tendency to disregard this instruction than in former days. The world would be ignorant of many a scandal which the Devil has used to the detriment of the cause of Christ, if Christians had heeded the teaching of the apostle on this important subject. Disputes are to be expected. The occasions for them are manifold. We are constituted so differently that we are liable to see things from different angles. Besides, with the growing complexity of social and business life, interests will be brought into conflict more and more.

A. *The Scandal of It* (6:1).

The very fact that they went to law indicated that there was a bad spirit and a worse practice among them, for "the law is not made for a righteous man, but for the lawless and disobedient, for the ungodly and sinners, for unholy and profane, for murderers of fathers and murderers of mothers, for manslayers, for whoremongers, for them that defile themselves with mankind, for menstealers, for liars, for perjured persons" (I Tim. 1:9, 10). Going to law was bad enough, but when it came to going to law brother with brother, the offense was most aggravated. It is not only a disgraceful thing from without, but it mars brotherly feeling. There are few things which so alienate fraternal affections as contentions at law. Many, even brothers in the flesh, as well as members of the same church, have elbowed each other for years, without speaking, simply because of some litigation before a court. Further, this going to law was before the unbelievers, which would leave a bad impression upon the world. For those who professed to be followers of the Prince of peace, to be quarreling, caused the world to consider their professions to be a sham. The scandal of such a proceeding is seen from the following considerations:

1. It Is Treason Against Christian Brotherhood.

It shows at once that our profession is a farce. If Christ be our Head and we members of His Body, there can be no quarreling and contentions among us. Harmony belongs to the one body. Litigation before the courts on the part of Christians contradicts brotherly love and puts the lie to our profession.

2. It Insults the Dignity of the Church.

The Church contains elements and forces within herself equal to any emergency which may arise. To go before the courts with our troubles is to exhibit the impotency of the Church in her inability to meet the exigencies within her life and activities.

3. It Reproaches Jesus Christ.

He is the Head of the Body. For the members of that Body of which Christ is Head to take their differences before the world, is to show that the Head is not capable of managing the interests of the Body. Jealousy for the honor of the name of Christ will deter us from going to law.

4. It Dishonors God.

Our being joined to Jesus Christ is through the plan and will of God (1:30). Therefore, the failure to bring about harmony reproaches the one who designed it. Any failure of an organism to accomplish the purpose for which it is designed reflects discredit upon the designer.

5. It Outrages the Dignity of the Gospel.

The Gospel purports to be the healer of dissensions. The very song which the angels sang upon the advent of the Lord was, "On earth peace, good will toward men." While there are peace and good will there cannot be contentions at law.

B. *The Absurdity of It* (6:2, 3).

1. It Is Unprofitable.

More is lost in going to law than is ever gained. In the face of such fact, litigation among men is most absurd.

2. It Mars Brotherly Feeling.

The private adjustment of matters would avoid many wounds

which are scarcely ever healed. It is easier to prevent a breach of the affections than to heal it when once made. It is a good thing to have enough grace to live together in peace after there have been contentions, but it is infinitely better to have sufficient grace to prevent them.

3. It Is Incongruous to the Christian Calling and Destiny.

The Christian has been called out of the world to be a light to it. Those, then, who have been called out of the world to be saviours to it should not thus give the lie to their mission. The saints shall judge the world; "if the world shall be judged by you, are ye unworthy to judge the smallest matters?" It is the height of absurdity for those who are destined to be the world's judges to carry their trivial matters to the people of the world for adjustment.

Then, too, it is said that the saints shall judge angels. If we are, then, to be judges of those who have been created our superiors, it is inexpressibly absurd for us to go to the courts of this world for the adjustment of our difficulties. Let those who are disposed to go to law hastily, ponder well these things.

C. *The Remedy for It* (6:5-7).

1. Arbitration (6:5).

Matters upon which Christians cannot agree should be submitted to capable judges. Even the most insignificant of the children of God would come nearer to doing justice than a heathen judge, for the one who is a member of the Body would be sympathetically interested in his fellow members.

2. Suffer Loss.

What cannot be adjusted by arbitration lose rather than disgrace the name of the Lord Jesus Christ. It were better to suffer wrong.

D. *The Penalty of It* (6:8-10).

Verse 8 implies that defrauding by litigation had been going on. Such unrighteousness shuts out from the kingdom of God. The apostle says: "Know ye not that the unrighteous shall not inherit the kingdom of God? Be not deceived: neither fornicators, nor idolaters, nor adulterers, nor effeminate, nor abusers of themselves with mankind, nor thieves, nor covetous, nor drunkards, nor revilers, nor extortioners shall inherit the kingdom of God." He means to say that just as these gross sins—fornication, adultery, etc.—exclude from the kingdom of Heaven, so separation from God is the inevitable doom of those who practice litigation. Furthermore, it reveals the fact that the individuals so engaged have not been born from above and are, therefore, in their sins. May this awful penalty be a solemn warning to all!

VI. The Christians Estimate of His Body (6:12-20).

Licentiousness was a common sin at Corinth. Among its inhabitants it was not reckoned as sin, for it constituted a part of the worship of Aphrodite. Christianity is diametrically opposed to such abominable practices. The Corinthians tried to defend this practice on the ground that since God had made the sexual distinctions, it was right to indulge them. They placed this question on the same basis as food (6:13). They argued that God made the digestive organs and also food. If to eat food is not wrong, then it is not wrong for the sexes to cohabit. This awful error Paul seeks to correct. He leads up to the matter by laying down some general principles. Twice he declares "all things are lawful." By this he meant that all acts in harmony with God's primal purpose were in themselves lawful. Sexual distinctions were made for a high and holy purpose—the procreation of the race. Any indulgence, save in harmony with God's purpose, is criminal.

Under certain circumstances even "lawful things" may not be right for the Christian. First, lawful things may not be expedient; and, second, lawful things must not gain the mastery. In this section of Scripture, the apostle deals mainly with the sin of fornication, only making a passing mention of meats. It should be borne in mind that indulgence in unlawful things has slain its thousands, but wrong indulgence in lawful things has slain its tens of thousands. It is perfectly right to eat, to dress, to have certain occupations, to enjoy certain amusements and recreations, but when they become our masters they become sinful to us. Paul's argument in correcting this evil gathers around the true estimate of the human body. In this day when everything is so completely under the sway of passion, when life itself is only estimated by the amount of pleasure or gain it will bring, it becomes us to take a sober look at what God says about the body.

Human life is very cheap in men's eyes in this age. The body is abused by overwork, by overeating, by overindulgence in pleasures and recreations. In the Scripture the Holy Spirit clearly sets forth some facts touching the human body which, if fully apprehended, will cause all Christians to have a proper regard for their bodies.

A. *The Body Belongs to the Lord* (6:13, 19).

The Christian's body, as well as his soul, is the property of the Lord. Therefore, he is not at liberty to use it for any purpose save to glorify the Lord. Some professing Christians have no higher conception of the body than that it is merely an old garment to be used until worn out and then to be cast aside. Such a view is utterly unscriptural. The Scriptures declare that the body is for the Lord. It is an illegal thing to use the property of another against his consent and for purposes which are dishonoring to him. The Christian's motto is, "Whether, therefore, ye eat or drink, or whatsoever ye do, do all to the glory of God." It was through the body of the Lord that the great facts of our redemption were accomplished. His body was the instrument of the Incarnation and manifestation of God among men, of the death and resurrection by which we are saved. His purpose in our redemption was in part, at least, that our bodies should be the instruments for the accomplishment of His will. This truth realized, as well as the above motto accepted, will sanctify the common relations of life. It will cause us to be just as sincere in our business, pleasures, and mutual relationships in life as when sitting at the Lord's table. "Holiness unto the Lord" ought to be inscribed on our banners, and reverently we ought to approach the so-called common things of life.

B. *The Body Shall Be Resurrected* (6:14).

Physical death is the suspension of the personal union between the soul and the body, but this separation is only temporary. In God's own time He will rebuild the house, which has been taken down in death, on a more glorious plan. That plan will be realized in the resurrection. The body rebuilt, or resurrected, becomes the eternal dwelling place of the spirit. That which God so honors as not to allow it to remain forever in humiliation should receive most careful attention from us. Christ has redeemed both parts of our nature; the body has its share in the great salvation. Heathen philosophers despised the body, esteemed it as an old garment to be cast aside. So do some modern heathen philosophers. Christ's coming in the flesh has swept away such notions forever. This truth touching the resurrection and glorification of the body when fully apprehended has a transforming power over the life.

C. *The Christian's Body Is a Member of Christ* (6:15).

The Church is an organism having many members each performing separate functions and all vitally related to each other, being united to Jesus Christ by the Holy Spirit. Since the believer is a member of Christ, he must touch and use his body with the same reverence as he would that of Christ. Who would not reverently approach the body of the sinless One? In view of this fact who dares practice the sins of uncleanness or in any way abuse his body? What awful sin to take a member of Christ and join it unto a harlot! This solemn truth needs to be set forth clearly for the salvation of many who have never been taught.

D. *The Christian's Body Is the Temple of the Holy Spirit* (6:19).

Marvelous dignity is placed upon the body. God's dwelling place on earth is now the redeemed body instead of the Temple at Jerusalem. The body was bought by Christ's death on Calvary for the purpose of making it a temple of the Holy Spirit. The body of every believer is for that purpose. If the sinless Spirit is to dwell in the body it must be kept clean. He, the Holy Spirit, will not abide in a filthy house. To defile the body is to insult the Holy Spirit. The defiling of the body by fornication is the most awful sacrilege. Such pollution not only deprives us of the sweet companionship of the Spirit but exposes us to God's wrath. "If any man defile the temple of God, him shall God destroy; for the temple of God is holy, which temple ye are" (3:17). This truth apprehended, solves forever the problem of licentiousness, the use of tobacco, gluttony, or abuse in any way whatsoever. In view of this the apostle exclaims: "Flee fornication; every sin that a man doeth is without the body, but he that committeth fornication sinneth against his own body."

E. *The Christian's Body Is Redeemed* (6:20).

The redemption of the body cost much. It was bought at the infinite price of the blood of the Son of God. It is His property; the redeemed body is no longer our own. We are bound to care for it as the property of another. Guarding our health is a part of our religion. We estimate things by what they cost. When we place that estimate on our bodies we will be very jealous of their purity. "Forasmuch as ye know that ye were not redeemed with corruptible things, as silver and gold, from your vain conversation received by tradition from your fathers; but with the precious blood of Christ, as of a lamb without blemish and without spot" (I Peter 1:18, 19).

F. *The Christian's Body Is Intended for the Glory of God* (6:20).

"Therefore, glorify God in your body." The American Standard Version omits "and in your spirit." This places the emphasis where the whole argument rests, namely, upon the body. There is a sense in which we may speak of a loss to God if we prostitute our bodies. The avowed purpose of God in creation and redemption is His glory. To be careless in the use of our bodies, or to prostitute them, will rob Him of His glory. In this section of Scripture we see the mind of the Spirit as to the human body and it should arouse us to the true sense of our duty to it.

VII. MARRIAGE: ADVICE TO THE MARRIED, AND TO THE UNMARRIED (7:1-40).

The oldest and most important institution in the world is the family. It is the foundation stone upon which all other institutions are built. The importance of the family to the church, society, and the nation cannot be overestimated. In the measure that the home is kept pure and strong will the church, society and the nation be pure and strong. Corrupt the home and they are all corrupted together. Corruption at this fountain head is suicidal. Once you tear out the foundation of the building, the whole structure comes tumbling down.

The foundation upon which the home is built is marriage. There is no more important theme in the whole realm of Chrisitan ethics than marriage. Perhaps no subject is more neglected by ministers and teachers than this. As a result few young people entering its sacred relationships understand its significance. In fact, marriage has become a frivolous affair—a mere joke. The magazines, newspapers, radio, and television which come into our homes are filled with articles and suggestions which lower the dignity of the marriage relation. This has become a serious menace to the morals of our land. Then public lecturers have become vitiated with this same virus. It has come to this awful state, where scarcely a lecturer comes before our boys and girls in high school, at the most impressionable age, without in some way making marriage a subject of jesting. It is scarcely better in our colleges. But that which outdistances all is the criminal practice of fathers and mothers who begin to tease their children about being in love with the boys and girls in their tender years, before any such thoughts enter their pure minds. In this way their minds are corrupted from the beginning. Need we wonder that the divorce evil is increasing at such a fearful rate, blighting the morals of our land, when the children are under such pernicious influence from their tenderest years to maturity? It is bad enough that our magazine writers and lecturers have fallen to such an infinite depth, but that fathers and mothers have fallen into this pernicious practice is beyond temperate speech to utter. The least that can be said is, God pity the child who has been so unfortunate as to have such a father and mother. The following are offered as the principal teachings of this chapter on marriage:

A. *Instructions, Chiefly to the Married* (7:1-24).

1. God Intended Men and Women to Marry (7: 4; cf. Gen. 1: 27).

This intention is shown from the fundamental fact of sex. God did not make the sexes out of idle experimentation. He fully knew His intentions before the act of creation. We grant, however, that some specimens of men and women almost seem to have been created without a purpose. One cannot help wondering what some men and women were made for. The one is incomplete without the other. It was of man, in the generic sense, that God said he was created in His own likeness and image. Therefore, that likeness and image can be realized truly only as the male and female are united. Woman is man's complement. When this is realized by her she will not be his competitor, but his helper.

2. God's Purpose Is Monogamy (7:2).

God's thought for the race is one woman for one man and one man for one woman. Any other view is both unscriptural and unnatural, for unless the affections are perverted they cannot be divided. The conjugal love of the man focalizes in the woman and that of the woman focalizes in the man. The law set forth by Christ when He said no man can serve two masters obtains in the marriage relation. No man can really love two women; neither can any women really love two men. Any longing outside of the lawful companion is not love, but lust. Besides, when there is a real union in the case of both husband and wife, never another thought is entertained as to another object upon which to lavish the affections, but all love and devotion center in the object already possessed.

3. The Mutual Relationship of Husband and Wife (7:3, 4). Where there is a real union in the marriage relation, there is a surrender of personality on the part of both husband and wife. There is, likewise, a union of personal traits. Therefore, there is in the ideal marriage a surrender of the baser qualities and a uniting of the virtues of both parties, resulting in a oneness of personality which is better and nobler than either one was alone or, indeed, ever could be. The apostle Peter gives us a very graphic representation of the ideal husband and wife (I Peter 3:1-7). Since the instructions as to obedience to husbands are usually given to wives by ministers today without consideration of what kind of husbands, I shall reverse the order of the teaching of the apostle and set forth:

a. The ideal husband (I Peter 3:7). He will show the following traits:

(1) Reasonableness. "Husbands, dwell with them according to knowledge." Much of the joy of married life is marred by the unreasonableness of husbands. Reason, not passion, should govern the treatment of a wife. A woman cannot respect a man who is unreasonable in his demands. In many cases this is the secret of domestic troubles.

(2) Reverence. "Giving honor to the wife as unto the weaker vessel." An intelligent perception of the mission of woman causes one to pay homage to her. Naturally the presence of virtuous women subdues the coarseness of men. A husband who realizes the complexity of the being of his wife, and the dignity of the sphere God created her to fill, invariably will deal reasonably with her.

(3) Conduct conformable to prayer. "That your prayers be not hindered." This suggests the idea that a man's conduct in

his home may affect his prayers. Many a man's prayers go no higher than his lips because of the tyranny in his home. A man's home life is an indication of his character. What he is there he is everywhere. Many men are kind, polite, and obliging away from home, but are cross, sullen and mean at home.

b. The ideal wife (I Peter 3:1-6). She will show the following characteristics:

(1) Subjection to her husband (7:1). "Wives, be in subjection to your own husbands." God made man to be the head of the family. It is the wife's business to be subject to her husband. This the true woman will always be, when her husband shows the characteristics before mentioned. It is natural for her to be subject to him when he is what God intended him to be. Most people see only the duty and submission of the woman to the man without consideration of what the man should be. When we keep before us what kind of husbands we should be, we can consistently teach submission to our wives.

(2) Purity (7:2). "Chaste conversation." The wife must be pure in heart, thought, and action. No husband can love and reverence an impure woman.[1]

(3) Modesty (7:4). "Meek and quiet spirit." This does not mean submission occasioned by fear. There is nothing servile in meekness. One of the marked characteristics in Jesus was that of meekness, but He was no coward. Someone has defined meekness as being "self-suppression issuing in benevolent service." The quiet spirit is the opposite of loud and boisterous behavior. A man cannot honor a loud woman. If a wife, then, would be reverenced by her husband she dare not display boisterous and masculine qualities.

4. No Separation Allowed (7:5-17).

Divorce is forbidden. Marriage is for life. It is not, mainly, a civil institution. That it is a divine arrangement is seen in the adaptability of sex. It dare not be put off at will. This divine arrangement is seen in the Creator's adaptability of sex, and that God Himself sanctified it by performing the first marriage ceremony. The party guilty of a separation and divorce ought to be dealt with as a crimi-

[1]Smoking and drinking go far to destroy her purity, and ability to be a proper wife and mother.

nal. He or she ought to be ostracized from society. Yea, more, ought to be imprisoned for life at hard work. Public conscience ought to be awakened along this line. The only qualifications put upon this requirement are: a temporary separation for certain ends, and in case of the willful desertion of an unbelieving partner.

5. Be Not Anxious to Change Your Position (7:18-24).

Some ascetics in the church had the idea that since becoming Christians, the marriage relationship should be cast off, thinking it sinful; especially, when the one partner was not a believer. This shows the influence of the materialistic philosophy of the time, which regarded matter as inherently evil. The apostle tells them that, as they were called, they should abide. They should not be anxious to change their estate. He teaches that Christianity does not interfere with the common relations of life, but rather sanctifies them. Urgency of the hope of the coming of the Lord sanctifies everything in life. The one having this hope will sit loose to the things of this life. He will not regard business, or pleasure, or the marriage relationship as the chief things of life, but, seeing these in their true light, will be concerned chiefly with the hope of completed redemption, which occurs when the Lord comes.

B. *Instructions, Chiefly to the Unmarried* (7:25-40).

1. It Is Good for the Present Distress To Remain Single (7:25-27).

"Present distress" has reference to the persecution which was then being waged against the church. Those who were unmarried found escape from these bloody persecutors much easier than if they had families to care for. This instruction does not obtain generally. Under normal conditions it should be the purpose of every man and woman to marry at the proper time, save as the Spirit of God calls certain to work which makes the married life impracticable.

2. Marriage Is Not Sinful (7:28-35).

Some seemed to think that it was sinful to marry. Paul assures them that there is no superior sanctity in the unmarried state. Its advantage consists in that it frees one from many of the distractions in life, giving him greater freedom to engage in the service of the Lord. At the same time, however, he warns them against thinking that marriage is everything in life, the same as he warns them against making business, or pleasure, etc., one's chief object of interest. He insists that the Christian should sit loose to all earthly relationships and callings. In view of this teaching, the Romish claim for celibacy is false to both reason and Scripture.

3. Advice to Fathers As to Their Virgin Daughters (7:36-38).

The father had absolute control over the marriage of his daughter. When circumstances were favorable for the marriage of his daughter, he should feel free to give his consent, as it was not sinful. This is no doubt the plain meaning of these verses. We should guard against the vicious use which is sometimes made of this to justify licentiousness.

4. The Marriage Contract Is Annulled by Death (7:39).

When one or the other of the contracting parties dies, the living party is free from the marriage bond.

5. Marriage Should be Only in the Lord (7:39).

Many times marriage is contracted on the basis of money, title, or social position, instead of that which is right and honorable. None of these things should enter into the marriage contract, for it is not a commercial transaction. The commercializing of marriage has degraded the marriage relation. Successful marriages are made on the basis of a threefold affinity. Anything short of this must eventually result in disaster. There must be:

a. Physical Affinity. There is something in the very physical make-up of men and women that makes them attractive and complementary to each other. This is most important; yet of itself, it is not sufficient.

b. Mental Affinity. Sometimes there may be physical affinity, but mentally there may be no attraction. There should be no union unless there is both physical and mental affinity. Among worldly people, marriages of this sort, may be happy and successful.

c. Spiritual Affinity. The Lord is pleased with marriage only between His children. This is not to say that the non-Christian man and the non-Christian woman should not marry. The Christian has no scriptural right to marry outside of the church. How can a believer be joined to an unbeliever? The physical and mental affinities may be all right, but if the spiritual is lacking the union is not true, for there must be supreme love in every true marriage. If one party hates Jesus Christ, how can the Christian supremely love the one who hates the One who is loved best? Therefore, the union of a believer with an unbeliever should not be. Let it be remembered that the marriage of every Christian with one who is not a Christian is a violation of the commandment of God.

VIII. CHRISTIAN LIBERTY AND FORBEARANCE (8:1–10:33).

This topic might be stated, with reference to its application to present-day life, as the Christian's conscience with reference to amusements, way of spending Sunday, luxury, social affairs, pleasure, kinds of business, ownership of stocks in certain corporations, etc. In our mingling with society, many questions arise such as the above, about which there is no definite agreement among Christians. Our lesson affords principles which are adequate for our guidance in all these problems. The occasion of this teaching was the uncertainty as to the right attitude toward "things sacrificed to idols." These problems were vital while the Christians were in the midst of the heathen; and, with their various modifications, no less vital still.

It was customary to divide the animal offered in sacrifice into three parts. One part was consumed upon the altar, another part was given to the priest, and the third part was kept by the party bringing the offering. The priest's part of it, if he did not need it, was sold in the markets. The part which the offerer kept, sometimes was eaten at home, and sometimes in the court of the temple. The Christian who bought meat in the market was likely to get meat which had been dedicated to the idol god. In fact, it seems that this meat was cheaper than the other meat, making it natural for the poorer people to buy it. Likewise, people who had clear knowledge on the question of idol gods also would buy it. Then, too, one would be invited to eat socially at the table of someone who had kept his portion of the offering, and now set it before the people. Some, with adequate knowledge, had no scruples about it; others, with less knowledge, thought it sinful.

To settle this perplexing question of conscience, the apostle addressed himself in this section. We may not have cases which are identical with these, but the principles set forth are of wide and daily application.

A. *An Idol Is Nothing* (8:1-6).

Paul makes the largest concession to the liberalistic party. They knew that an idol was nothing but a piece of timber or stone. Paul, with all intelligent Christians, knew that there was only the one God, the Creator and sustainer of all things; and that, therefore, an idol was nothing, had no real existence. To such Christians the eating of such meat was a matter of indifference. To eat made them no better, and to refrain from eating made them no worse. This, all because an idol was not real, merely a superstitious figment of the imagination.

It should be remembered that this has reference to things which are indifferent in themselves. We should not make the mistake of widening this principle so as to take in things which are to be condemned in themselves. To apply this principle to things condemnatory in themselves would be a perversion of Paul's teaching. This principle could not be applied to the use of intoxicating liquors, tobacco, and the holding of stocks in certain corporations, and to certain methods and lines of business, because they are injurious and wrong in themselves. This principle may be applied to such things as are harmless in themselves. Even harmless things may become harmful, if they gain the mastery over one.

The necessary instruction is given because something more than knowledge is required to guide us in these matters. Knowledge alone puffeth up, but knowledge controlled by love will be unto edification.

B. *Not All Christians Have Maturity of Discernment* (8:7, 8).

Some Christians still were possessed of the conviction that an idol was really a living and powerful thing. For such persons to sit down to a social meal where such meat was eaten would bring them under bondage to their former sins and practices. The same would be true of those who would purchase any such meat in the market. Further, for such persons to see those who had knowledge of the matter eating such meat would cause them to stumble. Conditions were such that it was highly important that great care should be exercised lest someone for whom Christ died should be made to stumble. Christian liberty is limited by consideration for others. No Christian lives unto himself. He is a member of a Body; a chain of solidarity unites him to others. Even granting that a man might control himself in such matters as gambling and drinking, he is partaking of that which is the cause of untold suffering and crime in the world. He should consider the conscience of the weak brother, avoiding all appearance of evil.

C. *The Christian's Behavior in Such Cases* (8:9-13).

His life should be governed by the principle of love, for love is more important than knowledge (8:1). This love-knowledge will move a man to abridge his liberty for the sake of the weak brother. The one who has a proper understanding of what idols are can eat such meat with impunity, but, lest he should cause his weak brother to stumble, he should deny himself of his rights. Not to do so is to sin against him for whom Christ died, yea, even against Christ Himself. To tempt weak and ignorant Christians is an awful crime. In all our actions, our chief concern and main question should be, not, Will it harm me? but, Will it harm my brother? In connection with such action note three things:

1. The Fate of the Weak Brother (8:11)—*he perishes.*

Human sympathy, let alone Christian love, would move a man to consider such loss.

2. The Relation of the Man to His Slayer—*a brother.*
3. What Christ Did for the Weak Brother—*He died for him.*

Therefore, to sin against a brother is to sin against Christ, because the brother is a member of Christ's Body. Doing that which is innocent in itself, is sinful, if it leads others into sin. If Christ was willing to die for him, should we not be willing to deny ourselves of personal rights for his sake? If we apply this principle to our lives, the question of dancing, theater-going, Sunday liberties, luxurious living, etc., will be solved.

D. *The Teaching Exemplified in Paul's Life* (9:1-27).

At Corinth Paul worked with his own hands, lest his mission to them should be misjudged. He did not ask them for anything in the way of support. By means of his own labors and the donations which he received from the Macedonian churches, he was able to boast that he had not been chargeable to them. They seemed to use this very fact as a proof against his apostleship. He defended himself against this charge by showing that he had a right to have a wife and the enjoyments of a home while they supported him. This right is embodied in a proposition set forth in verse 14. "Even so hath the Lord ordained that they which preach the gospel should live of the gospel." This proposition he sustains by the following unanswerable arguments:

1. Common Rights of the Apostolic Office (9:5).

From his reference to Peter and the other apostles as enjoying such rights, we infer that it was a right which attached to the apostolic office.

2. The Universal Principle of Remuneration (9:7).

The laborer is worthy of his reward. This is set forth under three figures:

a. The soldier, "Who goeth a warfare any time at his own charges?" The soldier who lays down his life on the altar of sacrifice in behalf of his own country is entitled to the support of his government. The right is unchallenged. He is not only supported while in the service, but receives wages in addition, and enjoys a pension when old.

b. The farmer, "Who planteth a vineyard and eateth not of the fruit thereof?" The husbandman who plants a vineyard eats of the fruit without any compunctions of conscience. No one thinks him selfish and greedy for so doing. Even so the minister should receive a reasonable compensation for his work.

c. The shepherd, "Who feedeth a flock and eateth not of the milk of the flock?" The man who feeds his flock has a right to enjoy the benefits thereof. In the same manner, the minister who gives his energy and time to the church should receive his support from her.

3. From the Law (9:8-10).

"Thou shalt not muzzle the mouth of the ox that treadeth out the corn." No one challenges the right of the ox that treadeth out the corn to receive his food. Neither should the right of the minister to compensation be challenged. The apostle asserts that this statement concerning the ox was not only written for the people of that day, but for us as well. For a man to deprive his ox of food and shelter after having plowed all day would seem extremely cruel. It is certainly no less cruel to starve a minister.

4. From the Superiority of Spiritual Things Over Temporal (9:11, 12).

"If others be partakers of this power over you, are not we rather?" Lest someone should object to his placing these things on a parity, he insists that if there be any differences, it is that the minister has even a greater right to receive his support than those who deal with the things of time and sense; for spiritual things have a place which is pre-eminent.

5. From Analogy to the Priest (9:13).

"Do ye not know that they which minister about holy things live of the things of the temple, and they which wait at the altar are partakers with the altar?" The priests filled their office by divine appointment. Therefore, they had a divine right to their support. The Christian minister, if he be a minister at all, is officiating by the appointment of Heaven. Therefore, he has a God-given right to live from the people he serves. Paul makes a very strong case, but tells us that he waived it in the interests of the weak brother. Lest he should be misjudged he denied himself and labored with his own hands. He brought his life under the most rigid control for the sake of others. If, therefore, Paul would deny himself to such an extent, rather than place a difficulty in the way of any man, it is shown that it should be practiced by those who would eat of the meat.

E. *Warnings* (10:1-22).

1. From the Experiences of the Israelites in the Wilderness (10: 1-13).

They failed to enter the Promised Land despite their promising beginning. They disregarded the Lord's directions, and suffered defeat and disaster as a consequence. Their failures and judgments should be a warning to us, lest we through lack of faith and a desire to walk after our own lust should fail likewise. We should not even presume upon God's electing love. The devices of the adversary are many. We should be extremely vigilant. God is faithful and will not allow us to be tempted above that we are able. Through lack of faith and walking after our own lust we may be chastised of God as were the Israelites.

2. From Danger of Lapsing into Idolatry (10:14-22).

It is utterly impossible to have fellowship with Christ in the communion of His body and blood, together with participation in sacrifices and idolatrous feasts. Those who have communed with Christ are under obligation to obey Him and to consider the interests of their fellow Christians, for they are parts of one Body. Whatever the cost the Christian must be entirely separate from anything which is in opposition to Christ and His Church. Sitting at the Lord's Table puts us under solemn obligation to forsake all others. Christ must have first place, or none at all. He is Lord of all, or not Lord at all. Then, too, their partaking with them who sat at the idol's feast brought them under authority of the idol.

The thing which was necessary for the Christian to do was free himself entirely from all entanglements with the doings of the heathen, because of the effect upon his own life and because of the effect upon his brother. Again, we are enabled to apply these principles to the matter of dancing, card-playing, theater-going, etc., because these things are always opposed to Christ and His Church. No man or woman, wholly dedicated to God, ever gave himself to dancing, card-playing, etc.

F. *The Teaching Applied* (10:23—11:1).

The one who has knowledge should bear with the weak one, and at the same time should seek to teach his brother the truth so as to set him free from bondage and superstition. At the same time, he should not allow the whims and superstitious notions of the weaker man to make him a slave. The glory of God should always be kept in view in all things.

1. The Christian's Privilege (10:23).

He can indulge in "lawful things" only as they are expedient and unto edification.

There are many things which may be lawful unto us, but it may not be expedient nor edifying to indulge in them.

2. Unselfishness (10:24).

"Let no man seek his own, but each his neighbor's good." The very principle of love is unselfishness. Therefore, the one wholly controlled by love considers the other's interests rather than his own.

3. Complete Yieldedness (10:31).

"Whether, therefore, ye eat or drink, or whatsoever ye do, do all to the glory of God." The Christian is not at liberty to do that upon which he could not ask God's blessing. It is preposterous to think that you could ask God's blessing upon a winecup, upon dancing, gambling, theater-going, luxurious extravagance, and Sunday desecration.

4. Give No Occasion for Stumbling (10:32).

We should so live that no one can ever say that we have been the occasion of his downfall.

5. Follow the Example of Jesus Christ (11:1).

Christ, through love, gave up all for the sake of others. He did not please Himself. Everyone, therefore, who is Christ's, should imitate Him.

IX. PROPER DECORUM IN THE PUBLIC ASSEMBLY (11:2-34).

Questions of a more public nature now come up for consideration. In this chapter consideration is given to the administration of the affairs of the public assembly. The particular abuses referred to are, the improper dress and behavior of women; and, abuses in the administration of the Lord's Supper. The true Christian will be careful to maintain decency and decorum in public worship. The Church is Christ's witness. His witness cannot afford to be careless in matters which seem trivial. How often her testimony is marred through neglect of the little things! The misconduct of the women was occasioned by a perversion of Paul's doctrine of the spiritual equality of believers. In Galatians 3:26-28 the broad principle of spiritual equality in Christ is enunciated. "For ye are all sons of God through faith in Christ Jesus. For as many of you as were baptized into Christ did put on Christ. There can be neither Jew nor Greek, there can be neither bond nor free, there can be no male and female, for ye all are one man in Christ Jesus" (A.S.V.).

This principle needs decided emphasis today in some quarters. It was quite in contrast with the modes of thought of that day, especially, with reference to woman's position. The women were regarded as men's chattels. When the truth dawned upon the women that they were not mere toys or slaves nor appendages to men's establishments, they overstepped the bounds of propriety. They even appeared in the public assembly unveiled to engage in prayer and prophesying. The spiritual equality of the woman with the man does not destroy the fact of his headship. Man's headship is a divine decree. A disregard for this truth works disaster to human society. Woman's subordination is social, not spiritual. The husband represents his wife in things civil and social, but not in spiritual matters.

In marriage the woman takes the man's name, not the man the woman's name. Woman's freedom in Christ does not dissolve her social relations, but sanctifies them. The boy in the home, becoming a Christian, is still in subordination to his parents. Personal equality is consistent with social subordination.

The application of this principle is Paul's method of dealing with this question. For a woman to appear in the public assembly, disregarding this conventionality—unveiled—was not only indecorous, but expressed a desire on her part to exchange sexes, and a disregard for man's headship. Woman is not inferior to man. She may have equal mental and spiritual endowments, but she exercises them in a different sphere. As Christ, though equal with the Father, is subordinate to Him, so a woman's subordination is not out of keeping with her equality.

A. *Woman's Place and Behavior in the Public Assembly* (11:2-16).

In Paul's effort to correct the abuse which had crept into the Corinthian church, he casts up to light a truth which may be embodied in a formal proposition, as follows: Woman should show her recognition of man's headship, and her consequent subordination to him, by a becoming dress and behavior. The particular dress referred to in this case was the Oriental veil. This proposition is supported by the following arguments:

1. The Divine Order in the Scheme of Redemption (11:3-5). In this order Christ is the supreme and grand center from which the line descends to man, and ascends to God. The Head of the man is Christ; the head of the woman is the man; the Head of Christ is God. Man should not thrust himself into the place of Christ—that would be blasphemy. For the woman to assume man's place would not be blasphemy, but it would be a perversion of the divine order. In the public assembly the woman should recognize her place of subordination by the proper dress and behavior. She should appear

there, as everywhere, as man's companion, not his rival and competitor.

2. From Moral Propriety (11:6-9).

For a woman to appear in the public assembly in that day, unveiled, exposed her to the same shame as if she were shaven. Man is the glory of God, therefore, he should appear unveiled. The woman should be veiled because she is the glory of man. She is man's ornament.

In this we see a reversal of the order of nature. Among the animals the male is the one clothed with glory and splendor, while his female wears the common and ordinary garb. This makes woman to shine forth in her divinely appointed sphere. She is not lower than man, but in her place of social subordination should wear the conventional sign for such position. Let it be forever noted that subordination does not mean inferiority.

Further, the woman was created for the man, not the man for the woman. The true woman now, as always, finds her delight in this; rebellion and insubordination being found only with the imperfect, narrow, and ignoble.

3. From the Example of the Angels (11:10).

As the angels veiled themselves in the presence of Jehovah, to show their subjection, so should the women show their subordination by the proper dress and behavior (see Isa. 6:1-3). She should have the conventional sign which shows her subordination. Observe that, lest woman's position and value be unduly depreciated, the apostle issues the following: "Nevertheless, neither is the woman without the man or the man without the woman in the Lord; for as the woman is of the man, so is the man also by the woman; but all things are of God" (vv. 11, 12). God's arrangement is that the woman is man's complement. In the beginning God declared that it was not good for man to be alone. The unit of society, as God constituted it, is the man and the woman united. Man is not without the woman, neither the woman without the man.

4. From Man's Intuitive Judgment (11:13).

He now appeals to man's judgment, which God gave him. The constitution of man's nature is derived from God. Therefore, the laws which He impressed upon it are His revelations. In our lives we should not go against the fundamental laws which the Creator impressed upon our personalities.

5. From Nature (11:14, 15).

Woman's unalterable physical characteristics indicate her sphere.

a. Her mental characteristics indicate her sphere. Although we find her, here and there through force of circumstance, crowded into the position rightfully belonging to man, and sometimes impelled by her altruistic sympathies; but when left free, she gravitates to her God-appointed sphere—the home.

b. Her physical frame is lighter, the very texture of her body finer, indicating that she was not made for the rougher life.

c. Her long hair. Nature gave her long hair, while it gave to the man short hair. Nature puts a distinction between the sexes. Long hair is a dishonor to a man, while it is a glory to the woman. This distinction should not be ignored even in the church. To do so is to sin against the God of nature. When God became incarnate and the Head of a new race, He appeared not as a woman, but as a man, indicating that in the new race, in the new order of things, man's headship should obtain.

6. From Apostolic Authority (11:16).

Those who were disposed to disregard such powerful arguments were compelled to meet with authority. We should not imagine that now Paul means to give up his arguments, but rather that he appeals to authority to end the controversy, showing that when reason fails, authority must be exercised. May it not be that in the near future, for the restoration and maintenance of the civil and social order, authority must be exercised.

B. *The Proper Observance of the Lord's Supper* (11:17-34).

Fearful abuses had crept into the Corinthian church touching the observance of the Lord's Supper. It was degraded to the level of a common meal. A full meal seems to have preceded the communion, called the love feast, or *agape*. It was a meal of fellowship. It seems to have originated from the paschal supper. However, there is historical intimation that among the Greeks there was some kind of a meal of fellowship. Some were rich and brought much provisions; some were too poor to bring any at all. At first, when the members were controlled by the warmth of first love, the provisions were spread before all, and rich and poor partook on a common level. Soon the spirit of common brotherhood waned, and the rich excessively indulged in their abundant provisions, while the poor were left hungry.

Then, too, divisions were manifesting themselves even in connection with so unifying an ordinance as the communion of the body and blood of the Lord Jesus Christ. This ordinance typified the most intimate relationship and closest communion, but became the manifestation of party spirit. They failed entirely to apprehend the significance of this institution. They not only introduced into the church the practices which were common among the heathen in their feasts, but formed cliques and parties according to their social position, wealth, and doctrinal tenets. The existence of these sects proved that they had no proper recognition of the dignity of the church. Such behavior exposed the poor to open shame. Under such conditions the apostle insists that the Lord's Supper could not be observed. Touching the communion, observe:

1. It Was Instituted by the Lord Himself (11:23).

Given to Paul, it is a unique institution and of divine origin.

2. Its Design (11:24).

a. It was a memorial to the sacrificial death of Jesus (11:24). Everything centers in the death of Jesus. It is His death which makes possible the remission of sins. In fact, it is the very foundation of all vital relationship to God.

b. The present participation in the living Christ (John 6). He is the food of our souls. Our minds, our wills, our hopes center in Him.

c. A prophecy of Christ's coming again (11:26). It is to be observed till He comes again. Thus the cross is linked to the throne of God. We shall drink it anew in the kingdom. Heaven will be a most real and enjoyable feast.

3. It Should Be Preceded by a Self-examination (11:28).

Communicants should enter into a careful examination, not only as to their hearts and lives but as to their apprehension of the purpose of this institution. They should have a proper discernment of the Body of Christ, that is, the Church.

4. Ignorant or Willful Abuse Exposes to the Judgment of God (11:27, 29).

Involved in this judgment is physical affliction. Many are the physical ills which are visited upon our bodies because of our failure to understand the meaning of this ordinance. Then, too, physical death not infrequently is visited upon those who presumptuously approach the Lord's Table. Since in approaching the Lord's Table we approach the Lord Himself, we should approach it with the fullest preparation of heart.

X. SPIRITUAL GIFTS (12:1–14:40).

The remarkable effusion of the Spirit in Messianic times was predicted by the prophet Joel. "And it shall come to pass in the last days, saith God, I will pour out of my Spirit upon all flesh; and your sons and your daughters shall prophesy, and your young men shall see visions, and your old men shall dream dreams: and on my servants and upon my handmaidens I will pour out in those days of my Spirit; and they shall prophesy" (Acts 2:17, 18; cf. Joel 2:28, 29).

The Lord Himself before His crucifixion promised to send the Holy Spirit to be the helper and guide of His people. This was fulfilled historically on the Day of Pentecost.

This new dispensation was marked, first, by a great diffusion of the gifts of the Spirit. They extended to all classes—young and old, male and female, rich and poor, learned and illiterate.

Second, these endowments were marked by great diversity. In a church where such conditions prevailed, it would be quite reasonable to suppose that confusion would arise. Divine life suddenly poured into human nature stirred it to unusual power. The same may be expected today. Some will lay claim to these gifts, under delusion. We see on every hand such pretensions today. Some who are impostors may lay claim to them. Some would become inflated with pride because of their gifts. Some would become dissatisfied with their own gifts and be envious of the gifts of others. Some would not give consideration to the rights of others. To the task of correcting these abuses and irregularities, the apostle addresses himself in these chapters.

A. *The Infallible Criterion* (12:1-3).

When one laid claim to the gift of the Spirit his claim was to be tested. The infallible test which determines whether gifts are spurious or genuine is his conception of, and attitude *toward,* Jesus Christ. Only those who recognize Him as God manifest in the flesh—His vicarious atonement on the cross—and submit to Him as their Lord, the One who actually controls their lives, must be recognized as possessing the gift of the Holy Spirit. If Christ is not Lord of all, He is not Lord at all. Christ said that the supreme business of the Spirit when He came would be to testify of Him—to take of His things and show them unto us. He who does not speak of the divine death on the cross does not speak by the Spirit. The soundness of the faith of a man is the sign of his commission from God. Regardless of eloquence or learning, the man who does not thus view Christ should not be tolerated as a teacher, nor even a member of the Body of Christ. Too frequently in our day a man's learning or his ordination is considered, while his message and personal life are ignored.

B. *The Diversity of Spiritual Gifts* (12:4-11).

In the Church there are those possessing the gift of wisdom, knowledge, faith, healing, power of working miracles, prophecy, discerning of spirits, divers kinds of tongues, and the interpretation of tongues. Whatever the form of the gift, whether of testimony concerning Christ, the working of miracles in demonstration of the power of God, or graces in the life of the individual, they are all manifestations of the same Spirit, dwelling in the Church for the edification of the Body. These gifts are not for the purpose of confusion or to minister to the personal vanity of anyone, but for the edification of all. They are not for the profit of the individual, save as the entire Body may be helped. The utility and efficiency of the Body are greatly increased by the multiplicity of the component membership. So also by the diversity of gifts.

C. *The Unity of the Spirit's Gifts* (12:21-31).

Christian unity is a vital unity, because it is effected by the one indwelling Holy Spirit. This unity amid diversity is represented under the figure of a human body. The Church, the Body of Christ, is an organism as real as the human body. Observe:

1. The Human Body Has Many Members.

Each member performs distinct functions for the good of the body. So also has the Church. A multiplicity of organs cannot make a body, neither can a multitude of people make a Church. The Holy Spirit is the unifying power which pervades the whole organism preventing friction.

2. The Members of the Body Are Mutually Related and Interdependent.

Just so are the members of the Church. The welfare of the one is the welfarc of the other; the shame of the one is the shame of the other; the glory of the one is the glory of the other; they are united by a bond of mutual sympathy.

3. The Members of the Body Have Their Places.

These are not by their own choice, but by the sovereign will and appointment of God. Since the divine will, not theirs, determines their position in the Body, and gifts, there is absolutely no reason for envy and jealousy in the Church. The feet have no right to envy the hands; the ears have no right to envy the tongue; the legs have no right to envy the head; each should be content to do the very best possible in his place, knowing that his place and work have been given him by the all-wise God.

4. The Least Attractive Members in the Body Are the Most Indispensable.

The same is true in the Church—the most attractive gifts are the least useful. In the Church, therefore, there should be no rivalry, for each has its place and work by God's appointment. There should be no indifference toward each other, for they are mutually and sympathetically related. The one possessing superior gifts, should not think himself above the other, because they are but different parts of the one Body.

D. *Love Is Better Than the Most Extraordinary Gifts* (13:1-13).

The apostle does not discourage the earnest desire and struggle for the best gifts; but he shows that there is a gift of the Spirit which is better than any of those mentioned—namely, to have the love of God shed abroad in our hearts. Not all can teach, preach, work miracles, speak with tongues, and interpret tongues, but the gift of love is within the reach of all. The "more excellent way" of 12:31 is the way of love, as set forth in chapter 13. Love is not a mere sentiment or emotion, but a mighty dynamic which transforms the life, expressing itself in practical service to men. Love is the mainspring of all service which counts for anything in the scale of eternal values. Note:

1. The Pre-eminence of Love (13:1-3).

It transcends:

a. Speaking with tongues. For men to possess the loftiest eloquence, to be able to speak in other languages, and to be lacking in love, is to be as sounding brass and a tinkling cymbal. To be able to speak pleasingly and powerfully is desirable, but to love is better.

b. The gift of prophecy. To disclose the events of the future, to be able to unfold all mysteries, to penetrate the mysteries of nature and providence is good, but to love is better.

c. Faith of the most vigorous kind.

d. Philanthropy of the most generous sort, prompting one to surrender all earthly goods for the sake of the poor.

e. Heroic devotion which leads even to martyrdom. All these without love are profitless.

2. The Attributes of Love (13:4-7).

a. It is longsuffering and kind. It means not only to bear long, but to be kind all the while. It is much easier to bear long than to show the spirit of kindness all the while. Patience is a most remarkable virtue.

b. It is free from envy. Those who love are entirely free from that envy which is engendered because of the good, or the success of others.

c. It is free from empty boasting. Love has as its supreme aim the doing of good to all and does not seek their admiration and applause.

d. It is decorous, well behaved. Love is always polite and mannerly. It knows how to behave at all times.

e. It is unselfish. Love is always seeking the good of others and is forgetful of self.

f. Does not give way to passion. It does not allow itself to be aroused to resentment, is not quick tempered.

g. It takes no delight in evil; does not impute evil motives to others; is not suspicious; it is forgiving.

h. It has no sympathy with evil. It sympathizes with that which is true and has a common joy with it. It beareth all things, that is, it encases itself with its own mantle and shuts all evil out.

i. It is trustful, hopeful, and firm.

3. The Permanence of Love (13:8-13).

Prophecy, as prediction, will be fulfilled; prophecy, as teaching, will be brought to an end in the day when teaching is not needed. "And they shall not teach every man his neighbor, and every man his brother, saying, Know the Lord: for all shall know me, from the least to the greatest" (Heb. 8:11; cf. Jer. 31:34). Tongues shall cease, for as the languages of earth were caused by God's judgment for sin, so shall Christ's redemption bring the nations back to one tongue. Knowledge shall be done away with by the coming of a wider and nobler intelligence. The twilight shall be lost in the day. Childhood shall be lost in maturity, for at Christ's coming we shall see Him face to face and be like Him. Love will always abide, for God is love.

E. *The Comparative Value of Prophecy and Tongues* (14:1-25).

Prophecy is set in the highest place, for it is to declare God's will to men. It is not only to declare God's message to men, but to preach it with authority. It mainly means to forthtell. It was the gift which enabled the speaker to bring the mind of the hearer into touch with God. To speak with tongues meant to speak in other languages, to show that God was supernaturally present (v. 22). Prophecy is assigned the highest place because it is to declare God's will to men, to warn sinners and to edify the Church.

F. *Rules for Guidance in the Exercise of Gifts in the Church* (14: 26-40).

1. Everything Was To Be Done Decently and in Order (13:40).

Confusion in the house of God is never right; some praying, some speaking, some singing, some vying with each other to see who could outdo is a reflection upon God. We have some cases similar in our own time, a visit to which would suggest that bedlam had broken loose.

a. With regard to the utterance of tongues, two, and at most three, should speak, and that in succession, while one interpreted. In case no interpreter was present they should refrain from speaking.

b. With regard to prophesying, only two or three were to speak. The rest were to sit in judgment upon what was spoken. Two were not to speak at the same time. Should one receive a new revelation, he did not dare to interrupt the one who was speaking. The power of the Spirit upon them did not destroy their power of self-control. He declares that the spirit of the prophet is under control of the prophet.

2. Everything Must Be Done unto the Edification of All.

Where there was not intelligent speaking, there would not be edification; and where there was the confusion of many speaking at the same time, there would be no possibility of understanding.

3. Women Forbidden To Speak in the Public Assembly (13:34, 35).

This prohibition rests upon the divine establishment of woman's subordination to man. This, no doubt, refers to interruptions in the assembly and assumption of authority. In such cases women were absolutely prohibited from speaking. This should not be so interpreted as to prohibit women from taking an active part in the services of the church. Women have a work to do in the church which alone can be done by them. Those in authority in the church should recognize her place and authorize her to go forward in her work. Man is woman's divinely appointed head, but he should not interfere with her work in the church, that is, should have enough judgment to see that she is unhindered in the performance of her mission. Practically in our modern church life, the only places denied the women are that of pastor and ruling boards.

XI. THE RESURRECTION OF THE BODY (15:1–16:2).

There were some in the Corinthian church who denied the resurrection of the body. The objectors were most likely Grecian philosophers. They seemed to base their objections upon the assumption that a material organization was unsuited to a future state. Then, too, their minds may have been affected by the notion that matter is inherently evil. However, the very presence of these skeptics has given to us this most wonderful apologetic of the resurrection of the body.

Denial of the resurrection of the body is a most deadly heresy. Its denial robs the Christian of his most inspiring hope. Christ's death and resurrection are most closely related. His death was not accidental, neither was His resurrection imaginary. Both were in line of prediction.

A. *The Certainty of the Resurrection* (15:1-22).

The certainty rests upon the fact of Christ's resurrection (vv. 20-22). We have seen in a previous chapter that the Church is an organism, as the human body, with Christ at its Head. If Christ, the Head, arose, it is certain that the body shall arise also, for just as Adam was our head in the old creation, so Christ is our Head in the new creation. Death came through Adam, but life came through Jesus Christ. The proof of the resurrection of the body must, therefore, be the proof for Christ's resurrection. Christ's resurrection is established by the following arguments:

1. Positively (15:1-11).

a. The results which followed Paul's preaching (vv. 1, 2). No more weighty argument could be urged with this people, or with any people. The most powerful testimony for any claim is the result in the lives of men, Paul asserts that he had preached, they had received, and had been saved by a Gospel. That Gospel was that Christ died for our sins, was buried, and arose again. The very essence of his preaching was the death and resurrection of Christ. This they believed, and were saved thereby, leaving no room whatever for them to doubt or deny it, for to do so, was to go back on their own conscious experience.

b. The declaration of the Scriptures (vv. 3, 4). No particular passage of Scripture is cited, since the whole tenor of sacred writing, from Genesis to Malachi, shows that there was coming a Deliverer who was to triumph through suffering. The whole testimony of the Scriptures establishes Christ's resurrection. Christ rebuked His disciples for not believing what Moses and the prophets had spoken on this subject (Luke 24:25-28; see also Ps. 16).

c. The attestation of a large company of living witnesses (vv. 5-8). After His resurrection, He was seen by Peter, then of the twelve, after that by about five hundred brethren at once, most of whom were still living. Following this he was seen by James, then by all of the apostles, and finally by Paul himself. Having been seen by so many different persons, under such varying circumstances, left no possible room for deception. The most remarkable of these appearances was to Paul to whom it would be least expected. He was one who was most unwilling to believe and, furthermore, of a mental make-up least likely to be led away from reason to some fantasy.

d. The transformation of Paul's life (vv. 9-11). He was a strong, resolute man bent on the destruction of the church. While in the very heat of this relentless warfare, Jesus appeared to him. This vision remade his entire life, changing its nature and its course. This fact is most important for our consideration. Mental assent to a doctrine, while denying it in the life, is most destructive. Real belief in the resurrection of Jesus results in the transformation of the life.

2. Negatively (15:12-19).

In these negative considerations the position of these skeptics is placed in such a way as to show its absurdity. He uses that form of argument called *reductio ad absurdum.*

a. Apostolic preaching void (v. 14). The resurrection of Christ was the cardinal truth, the pivotal point of Paul's preaching. If the resurrection of Christ be not a fact, then his preaching was false.

b. Christian faith unreal (v. 14). If Christ did not arise, their faith was empty, unreal and groundless. A risen and living Saviour had been preached. If, therefore, Christ were still in His grave, they were deceived.

c. The apostles would be liars (v. 15). They testified that God had raised Christ from the dead. If He arose from the dead, then resurrection from the dead is possible.

d. All would still be in their sins (v. 17). Christ's resurrection was the proof that His mission was accomplished (Rom. 4:25). If He did not arise, He was defeated; sin was uncanceled; therefore, our guilt still attaches to us; we are still in our sins.

e. Those who had fallen asleep had perished (v. 18). If such be true, these men like Stephen were deceived, and hope for them is utterly baseless. If such monstrous conclusions be true, Christians are most to be pitied of all men. To deny the resurrection of Jesus is to prove Christianity a delusion; but he cannot remain to deny such foolish assertions. The facts were such as to sweep away such assertions and allow faith to triumph.

B. *The Order in Which the Resurrection Will Take Place* (15:23-28).

1. Christ, the First Fruits.

He was the first to arise from the dead. Before Him there had been none to come forth from the grave as He came. In some cases, at His command, the spirit returned to the body, but it was the same old body which had not been set free from the power of corruption and limitations. Christ's body is the new, incorruptible body.

2. Those That Are Christ's at His Coming.

The resurrection of those that are Christ's occurs at His second coming (v. 23; cf. I Thess. 4:16, 17). This is a graphic picture of that time when Christ, as the Captain of our salvation, the Deliverer from death, will be seen leading His own, who follow, in ranks and orders, in the pathway which He opened through His resurrection. This is the first resurrection, and takes place at His coming.

3. Then All the Rest of the Dead at the End (15:24).

Between these events a period of a thousand years intervenes, which will be the millennial kingdom. After He has completed the work for which He came, namely, the bringing of all things under the rule of God; when His mediatorial work is finished, He will hand over the conquered universe to God who will then rule forever. When this is done, Christ will resume His place of co-equality with the Father.

C. *Regenerated and Transformed Lives, the Attestation of the Risen Lord* (15:29-34).

Continuance in sin is evidence that one is ignorant of the true God. God can be known only as men surrender to Him and walk in obedience before Him. We all need to learn that we can make God known to others only as we live in obedience to Him. God is not made known to others by argument. Those who are called His children certainly should know their Father.

D. *The Nature of the Resurrection Body* (15:35-37).

There were those in that church who still raised questions. They inquired: "How are the dead raised, and with what body do they come?" If the dead were raised, they desired to know with what body they came forth from the grave. All are bound to concede that great mysteries surround this matter, but even though we cannot explain, we can and should believe; since God has promised that we shall live beyond this present life, we can rest assured that His Word will not fail.

The trumpet of God will sound and we shall be raised incorruptible. In death there is a suspension of the personal union between the body and soul, and the body is resolved into its chemical elements. In death, then, the body is disorganized, the house thrown down. In the resurrection the body is reorganized, the house built up again. In the rebuilding of the body, such parts and functions as are no longer needed are left out, and the whole is organized upon a different basis adapted to the heavenly life. Whatever changes are made, the identity is not lost. If the doctrine of the bodily resurrection be true, we shall most surely recognize each other in Heaven.

The apostle teaches that the resurrection body will be an incorruptible one, not again subject to decay. It will be glorious—the shame and dishonor which attaches to our bodies here will be removed forever. It will be powerful. Here we are weak, but there our bodies will be strong. In that changed estate our bodies will be spiritual. Spiritual bodies, however, should be distinguished from spirit; spiritual bodies are the habitations of the spirit.

E. *The Practical Effect of Certainty of Conviction Touching the Resurrection of the Body* (15:58–16:2).

1. The Firm Establishment of the Believer in His Internal and Personal Life (15:58).

"Wherefore, my beloved brethren, be ye steadfast, unmovable, always abounding in the work of the Lord, forasmuch as ye know your labor is not in vain in the Lord." Certainty of conviction touching our risen Christ is our sure defense against the assaults on faith. Assurance of life is to all who are united to Him. Christ is the Head of a new and victorious order of humanity.

2. Life of Abounding Service (v. 58).

Belief in Christ's resurrection nerves men for conquests in the name of Christ; knowing that their labor is not in vain in the Lord, they go on to success.

3. Generosity in Financial Support (16:1, 2).

The giving of our means for the support of the Lord's work is to be done in the light of the lofty truth of the resurrection of Christ and His people. Resurrection is the inspiration for this work of unselfishness. This truth has an important bearing upon church life today. In the measure that men deny this truth they become parsimonious with their money. Stinginess, therefore, is a denial of the cardinal truth of Christ's resurrection. Loyalty to Christ means liberality in giving for the support of His work.

The writer begs the reader to think back over the problems considered in this chapter and apply their fundamental teachings to the changing order of things through which the church and society are passing.

As a student of the times he views with deep concern the chaos of the religious and political world; he is filled with hope as to the issue, for God rules. The Church, under God, can do much to strengthen and develop the "things that remain," if she will emphasize the basic principles considered in these pages. His closing exhortation is: "Watch ye; stand fast in the faith; quit you like men; be strong. Let all that ye do be done in love."—"If any man love not the Lord, let him be Anathema Maranatha. The grace of our Lord Jesus Christ be with you. My love be with you all in Christ Jesus."

SECOND EPISTLE TO THE CORINTHIANS

PART ONE—INTRODUCTORY MATTERS

THE INTRODUCTORY MATTER to I Corinthians furnishes the background for II Corinthians. In fact, II Corinthians is a sequel to I Corinthians.

I. Background

Paul's vigorous actions in correcting the errors and irregularities in the Corinthian church provoked violent reactions of that church toward him. These repercussions expressed themselves in wicked charges and severe persecutions. The nature of Paul's personality, methods, and message prevented neutrality on the part of his hearers. The people either loved or hated him. Wherever Paul preached, there was either revival or riot. In this respect he was like his Master. Wherever Jesus Christ is really preached today, the people are either for Him or against Him. Moral indifference is an utter impossibility with human beings. Feigned indifference is for prudential reasons.

How much time elapsed between the writing of I Corinthians and II Corinthians is difficult and perhaps impossible to determine. The implications are that the time was short.

The key word of II Corinthians is *affliction*. Paul's suffering was infinitely more than physical pain. It was the groaning of a wounded and loving soul, which was occasioned by the malicious impugning of his motives. In this vindication of his ministry as the apostle of Jesus Christ, the great servant of the Lord lays bare his heart.

II. Broad Outline

A. *The Introduction* (1:1-11).

B. *Paul's Vindication of His Ministry* (1:12–7:16).
C. *The Collection for the Poor Saints at Jerusalem* (8:1–9:15).
D. *Paul's Defense of His Apostolic Authority* (10:1–13:10).
E. *The Conclusion* (13:11-14).

PART TWO–DETAILED OUTLINE

I. THE INTRODUCTION (1:1-11).

A. *The Greeting* (1:1, 2).

He found it necessary at the beginning of his letter to assert his apostleship by the will of God. He associates Timothy with him in this greeting to show that the church is a brotherhood. He recognized the assembly at Corinth was the church of God even in spite of its carnality. In this greeting Paul expresses the wish that grace and peace from God the Father and from the Lord Jesus Christ might be unto them.

B. *Paul's Praise and Thanksgiving* (1:3-11).

In spite of his great affliction and heavy burden his heart was filled with gratitude to God for His abundant mercies. He assigns two reasons for his thanksgiving:

1. For Divine Comfort (1:3-7).

Some ten times in these verses he mentions comfort. His hymn of praise could only come from one who was conscious that he was suffering for Christ's sake. Every true witness for Christ can expect to suffer. Godly living in Christ Jesus will issue in persecution.

2. For Divine Deliverance (1:8-11).

So grave were the perils which Paul faced that he despaired of his life. In 11:23-33 are enumerated the physical perils which he experienced. In addition to these, his spiritual burdens were extremely heavy. Party spirit, gross immorality, apostasy and hostility were rife in the Corinthian church. In spite of all that he was called upon to suffer, he saw the beneficent hand of God in causing him to look for divine help in God instead of trusting in himself.

II. PAUL'S VINDICATION OF HIS MINISTRY (1:12–7:16).

There are times when it is obligatory for a minister to defend his character. Sometimes suspicion arises because of misunderstanding and a lack of knowledge. A minister should be ready and willing to bring his actions into the light. It is presumptive to assume that God will intervene in behalf of His servants in doing that for them which they can do for themselves.

A. *Paul's Explanation of His Postponed Visit* (1:12–2:4).

His delayed visit was interpreted by some as due to fickleness of mind or duplicity of purpose. He assures them that he had acted in all good conscience before God. His delay was due to change of circumstances. He appealed to God as his witness that his delayed visit was with the same conscientious sincerity as when he and Timothy and Silas had preached the Gospel of Christ among them. The purposed time for his visit was found not to be opportune. It was not his fickleness, but the change of circumstances that delayed his visit. It was to "spare them."

B. *The Penitent Offender* (2:5-13).

As to who was this offender we are not told. Neither are we told the nature of his offense. The Spirit of God speaking through Paul chose to conceal this. However, inferential evidence points to the incestuous person mentioned in I Corinthians 5. In that case Paul commanded the church to discipline him, turning him over to Satan for the destruction of the flesh. It is evident that the discipline had been effective. Therefore they were to forgive the offender and receive him back into fellowship. The abiding principles set forth in this Scripture as shown by Dr. Erdman in his volume on II Corinthians are:

No church should fail to discipline its offending members.

This discipline should be administered by the decision of membership and not by any one man in the church.

The supreme purpose of discipline should be the reformation and reclamation of the offender.

When the offender is penitent, he should be forgiven and treated with affection.

Severity and lack of sympathy may drive the offender to desperation and again place him under the power of Satan.

C. *The Distinguishing Characteristics of Paul's Ministry* (2:14–5:21).

1. Fruitful (2:14-17).

Wherever Paul preached, some were saved. The merit of the Gospel is in what it accomplishes. God made Paul's ministry to triumph in Christ "in every place." Those who preach the Word of God can be assured of success for "the gospel of Christ is the power of God unto salvation to those who believe it." The Gospel is a savor of life unto life or a savor of death unto death.

2. The Credentials of Paul's Ministry (3:1-5).

His credentials were in the lives and character of the people who believed his message. The Corinthian converts were the epistle of Christ written by the Holy Spirit in their hearts. The Christian minister is accredited by the lives of those who believe God's message through him. This ought to be sobering yet challenging to everyone who aspires to be a minister of God's Word.

3. Paul's Ministry Was Glorious (3:6-18).

He was a minister of the new testament. The message of Moses brought condemnation and death. The Gospel of Christ which Paul preached was the power of God unto salvation. That which the Law demanded, the Gospel of Christ provided. Paul's ministry was more glorious than that of Moses. The contrast is not the difference between a literal interpretation of God's Word and a spiritual interpretation, but the difference between the Law and the Gospel. That which the Law could not do is accomplished by the Lord Jesus Christ.

4. Paul's Ministry Was Utterly Frank and Sincere (4:1-6).

He repudiates the charge of deceit and duplicity. He did not preach himself, but Jesus Christ the Lord. He knew that he had no glory to proclaim. He declared the message came directly from God. He had renounced the hidden things of dishonesty and appealed to their own conscience before God.

5. Paul's Ministry Caused Him Great Suffering (4:7-18).

He turns from the glory of the Christian ministry to sufferings which it entails. Suffering comes from anxiety, incessant labor, opposition, persecution. His persistence in preaching the Gospel in spite of the suffering it brought was evidence of his integrity. He looked away from his sufferings to the coming weight of glory.

6. A Ministry of Hope (5:1-10).

The secret of Paul's persistence in preaching the Gospel of Christ in the face of suffering and prospective death was the certainty of the resurrection and the eternal glory. Both will be realized at the coming of the Lord Jesus Christ. The earnest of the Spirit is the guarantee of this fulfillment of redemptive purpose. Paul's supreme purpose was to be well pleasing to the Lord, whether present in the flesh or absent and with the Lord. Death has no terrors for God's devoted servants.

7. Motive of Paul's Ministry (5:11-15).

It was the constraining love of Christ. The Lordship of Christ was such a reality to Paul that, regardless of what men thought of him or did to him, his passion was to persuade men to receive Christ as their Saviour and thus escape the terror of the Lord.

8. A Ministry of Reconciliation (5:16-21).

Paul had experienced regeneration. This was brought about by the act of God in Christ. That which Paul had experienced was the center of his message, and he was God's ambassador beseeching men to be reconciled to God. Paul was acting for Christ in divine grace. This reconciliation to God was effected through Christ the sinless One being made sin for man and man being made the righteousness of God in Christ (v. 21).

D. *Paul's Appeal to the Church at Corinth* (6:1—7:1).

1. Be Reconciled to God (5:20).

In the scheme of redemption provision was made for man's sins in that Christ bore the penalty for sin. That which God's righteousness demanded was provided in Christ, therefore, God was reconciling the world to Himself. Man's responsibility is to accept by faith the offered reconciliation. Man cannot reconcile himself to God. That must be done by God. Man's salvation rests upon his action in receiving Christ as his Saviour. Paul as ambassador for Christ puts his ministry in parallel relation to Christ and God. Every true minister of the Gospel occupies this high position.

2. Receive Not the Grace of God in Vain (6:1-10).

Paul urges them to receive and make good use of God's grace in Christ. To fail to respond to the Gospel invitation and apply God's grace is to receive God's favor in vain. He enforces his entreaty by a quotation from Isaiah 49:8. The Gospel dispensation was God's accepted time—the day of salvation.

Paul enforces his entreaty by giving a summary of his ministry among them (vv. 3-10). All that he did among them was worthy of an ambassador of Christ. The responsibility rested upon the hearers.

3. For Reciprocal Affection (6:11-13).

The success of a Christian minister depends upon the loving confidence of the people. The review of his ministry among them was given with the purpose of stirring up their affection for him. He laid bare his motives in preaching Christ to them and appealed to them to love him in return.

4. For a Separation from Unbelievers (6:14—7:1).

The followers of Christ must not be in close fellowship with those who have rejected Christ—the unbelieving world. Paul enforces this demand by five argumentative questions showing that such fellowship is unnatural, incongruous and perilous. The blessed issue of separation from the world will be fellowship with God's people and a place forever in God's family. This high privilege can only be realized by those who cleanse themselves from all defilement of the flesh and the spirit perfecting holiness in the fear of God. A holy life must not only be desired but sought after.

E. *Paul's Triumph* (7:2-16).

1. Renewal of His Request for Sympathy (7:2-4).

He pleads with them to receive him into their hearts, assuring them of his great love for them and his deep interest in them even though he had used severe language in dealing with them (v. 3).

2. Comforting News Brought by Titus (7:5-12).

He was not only comforted by the presence of Titus but especially by his report of the changed attitude of the church at Corinth toward him. It was most painful to Paul to deal with the saints at Corinth, but the good news of the beneficent effect of his vigorous handling of the matters involved cheered him.

3. His Confidence (7:13-16).

Their treatment of Titus and attitude toward Paul assured him that in spite of the intensity of feeling engendered in the controversy, all was well. The evil had been corrected, and there was mutual good feelings for each other. Paul could say: "I rejoice that in everything I am of good courage concerning you."

III. The Contribution for the Poor at Jerusalem (8:1–9:15).

This section of the epistle is of exceeding great importance, both in its setting forth of every principle and motive entering into the *giving* which has God's sanction and the method of *handling* the church benevolences. Scrupulous care should be exercised in the handling of the money given by the saints, especially that given for the poor. Paul's teaching here is for the church officers in all ages.

A. *Examples of True Christian Benevolences* (8:1-6).

The liberality of these Macedonian churches exhibits practically every grand principle and motive which enter into the giving which has God's sanction. Observe:

1. The Source of True Giving (8:1).

This is said to be the grace of God, by which is meant that the disposition to give freely of our means is created by the Holy Spirit. To give freely of one's money is extremely unnatural. The natural thing for a man to do is to hold on tightly to his money. This puts Christian giving on a much higher plane than that which brings the people under the bondage to the Law to give a tenth. For some to give a tenth would be an unbearable burden, which for others would be the greatest niggardliness.

2. They Gave from the Depths of Their Poverty, Not from the Abundance of Their Riches (8:2).

Their limited means did not cause them to stint in their giving, but their deep poverty abounded unto the "riches of their liberality." On the basis of this philosophy our poverty ought to be a call to greater generosity, for God has promised that if we give liberally, He will give liberally in return. Increase comes not by holding, but by giving. He that soweth sparingly shall reap sparingly, and he that soweth with a free hand shall reap in abundance.

3. Their Willingness Surpassed Their Ability (8:3).

God's gifts are reckoned by the degree of willingness, not by the amount given (II Cor. 8:12; 9:7). If such grace were to be found in the churches today, there would be an abundance of funds to carry on the Lord's work, for there never has been a day when there was such unlimited ability to give. The supreme difficulty is to induce the spirit of willingness. Only the grace of God can make men and women willing to give.

4. They Were Insistent on Being Allowed to Give (8:4).

They did not need to be pressed into giving. How far we have departed from the apostolic method! Today we employ the shrewdest men in financial affairs that can be found to make appeals at our missionary meetings and the dedications of our churches. Christians ought to be taught that to share in the Christian ministry is their high privilege.

5. They First Gave Themselves (8:5).

This is most fundamental to right giving, for when one gives himself to the Lord, there is no reason for withholding his gifts. If one does not give himself to the Lord, there will be the desire to retain as much for self as can be done within the bounds of respectability. The only right method of raising money for the Lord is: first, to induce men and women to give their lives to the Lord, and then to give their possessions. Real devotion involves the pocketbook as well as the soul. The only method that has God's sanction is a consecrated pocketbook. Just as these Christians sought the opportunity of giving, so should Christians be taught that it is their highest privilege to give of their means to the Lord's work.

B. *Emulation of the Benevolence of the Macedonian Churches* (8:7-15).

Moved by the generosity of the Macedonian churches, Paul desired Titus to commend to the Corinthians the same grace. This grace he urges upon them.

1. Not As a Command (8:8).

Giving merely in obedience to a command is not of the highest order. It must be spontaneous, liberal.

2. As a Proof of the Sincerity of Their Love (8:8).

Love is more than mere sentiment; it is benevolent action toward the object loved.

3. As the Completion and Harmony of Christian Character (8:7).

The Corinthian church abounded in spiritual gifts such as faith, utterance, knowledge, diligence, and in love for their ministers. But the grace of liberality was needful for the harmony of their lives. The stingy man is lopsided and unsymmetrical in his character.

4. The Self-sacrificing Example of Christ (8:9).

Self-sacrificing is the test of love. Christ's self-denial and sacrifice is the supreme example of love. All who have enthroned Him as the Lord of their lives (crowned Him Lord of all) will see to it that they imitate Him in all things. Christ was rich, but for our sakes He became poor. He laid aside His heavenly glory because He loved us. We should follow His example.

5. Because the True Principle upon Which Gifts Are Acceptable with God Is a Willing Mind (8:10-12).

God does not estimate the value of the gift on the ground of its intrinsic worth, but on the underlying motive of the giver. The poor before God are therefore on equality with the rich.

6. Because of a Common Equality (8:13-15).

Every Christian should give something. The Law governing the gift is ability to give; "as the Lord has prospered him."

C. *Arrangement for Supervision of the Collection* (8:16–9:5).

The management of the finances of the church requires spiritual vision, enthusiasm, and business capacity. Only God-directed men can succeed in this matter, and they must be free from suspicion as to motive and method. The first officers appointed in the church were to be men of good report, full of the Holy Spirit and wisdom (Acts 6:3). The supervisors appointed for this ministry were Titus, whom the Corinthians knew, and two others whose names are not given. For the integrity of these Paul vouches. The church at Corinth is requested to receive these delegates as partners of Paul in the carrying on of the work of the Lord for Christ's glory (v. 23). The purpose of sending these delegates ahead was that the gifts might be ready when Paul would arrive. Paul had boasted of the liberality of the Macedonians. It would be most humiliating, therefore, to Paul if the collection was not ready.

D. *Encouragement To Give Liberally* (9:6-16).

1. The Volume of Reaping Is Based upon the Sowing (9:6).

Those who sow sparingly cannot expect to reap bountifully.

2. There Should Be a Heart Purpose (9:7).

This calls for intelligence as to the object of giving.

3. Giving Should Not Be of Necessity (9:7).

No particular value accrues to the giver who does it from pressure.

4. God Loves a Cheerful Giver (9:7).

The one who has the right understanding of his responsibility toward God with reference to temporal possessions will regard giving as a glorious privilege.

IV. PAUL'S DEFENSE OF HIS APOSTOLIC AUTHORITY (10:1—12:18).

Paul's enemies accused him of cowardice in not appearing in person to deal with the disorders in the Corinthian church (v. 10), of ignorance of the true Gospel since he had never seen Christ, and of his refusing a salary in order to hide his duplicity. In his defense he shows:

A. *His Authority Was Derived Directly from Jesus Christ* (10:8).

This took place on his way to Damascus with authority to arrest and imprison members of the church (Acts 9:1-16; cf. Gal. 1:12-23). This vision of the Lord Jesus Christ transformed him from a persecutor to a passionate preacher of the Gospel. He knew the Lord Jesus Christ as his personal Saviour and knew the Gospel as the power of God unto salvation. He knew that he was the apostle of Jesus Christ to preach the Gospel to the Gentiles "in the regions beyond" (vv. 14-16). This ministry was entrusted to him by the Lord (v. 18). Consciousness of the divine call is absolutely essential for success in the Christian ministry. The minister must realize that "woe is unto me if I preach not the gospel . . . necessity is laid upon me" (I Cor. 9:16). There is much superficial talk about entering the ministry. It is not a question about entering the ministry, but of the recognition of the divine call.

B. *The Proof of His Apostleship Was His Self-denying Labors* (11:1-33).

1. Paul's Fear.

He was afraid that the minds of the Corinthians might be "corrupted from the simplicity that is in Christ" (v. 3). His godly jealousy moved him to boldly assert his apostolic authority. It is a matter of great grief to a minister of Christ to see the fruits of his labor destroyed. Paul was greatly concerned lest the false teachers should lead the Corinthians away from their single-minded faithfulness to

Christ. It must be borne in mind that Paul is referring to the Church as a whole when he speaks of the "bride of Christ" and not of the individual believer. The subtlety of the Devil was really as manifest in these false teachers as in the case of seducing Eve in the Garden of Eden.

2. Paul's Reason for Refusing a Salary (11:7-12).

Paul forcefully argued that as an apostle he had the right to be maintained by the church he served, but lest his motives be misunderstood he waived his right. He even robbed other churches "taking wages of them to do them service" (v. 8). The Macedonian churches supplied Paul's needs while he served the church at Corinth.

3. Warning Against "False Teachers" (11:13-15).

They are called false apostles, deceitful workers transforming themselves into apostles of Christ. These evil workers even turned Paul's nobility of purpose in refusing a salary into an argument against his apostleship.

4. Paul's Enforced Boasting (11:16—12:10).

a. Its necessity (11:16-21). Paul recoils from this need. Boasting is wrong when it is a rehearsal of personal merits or attainments with the purpose of popularity or praise. However, sometimes it is forced on one to silence critics and convince hearers. In such a case it was right.

b. Grounds of:

(1) His descent (v. 22). His enemies boasted of their ancestry. In this regard they were without advantage over him. The three terms used—*Hebrews, Israelites, Seed of Abraham*—doubtless refer to the pride of race, the peculiar privileges of the covenant people, and the special promise of blessing.

(2) His ministry for Christ (v. 23). They outdistanced the activities of his rivals—he was entitled to greater merit than his enemies.

(3) His sufferings (vv. 23-33). The evidence of his ministry for Christ is shown in the sufferings which he endured for Christ's sake. Their recital amazes one—floggings, imprisonments, perils of death often, stonings, shipwrecks, perils of robbers, perils of the heathen, hunger and cold. Besides these he was burdened with the care of all the churches. There was also hostility on the

part of the civil authorities. The governor of Damascus garrisoned the city in order to apprehend him. He escaped by being let down over the wall in a basket. What had his enemies to offer in comparison? He calls upon God as a witness to his integrity.

C. *His Visions and Revelations Qualified Him as an Apostle* (12:1-12).

Just what these visions and revelations were we have no way of knowing. Paul was caught up to the third Heaven or paradise and heard unspeakable words which were "unlawful for man to utter." It is quite evident that this experience was for the personal benefit of Paul. It took place in his Christian experience some fourteen years before the thrilling escape in Damascus by being let down through the window in a basket. These visions and revelations made him courageous to press on in the face of the fiery trials and sufferings incident to his apostolic ministry. We infer from the Scriptures that the qualifications of an apostle are: (1) called by Christ; (2) a witness of Christ's resurrection; (3) possession of supernatural power. Paul qualified in these particulars (v. 12).

It was in connection with this exalted experience that a "thorn in the flesh" was given to prevent pride.

V. FINAL WARNINGS (12:19—13:10).

Having demonstrated his apostolic authority he issued the following warnings:

1. He Will Not Spare (12:19—13:4).

He intends to visit them again and will deal drastically with those who have not repented of their sins.

2. He Exhorts Them to Self-examination (13:5-10).

He warns against the common sins of the flesh to which all the Corinthians were exposed.

VI. THE FAREWELL (13:11-14).

EPISTLE TO THE GALATIANS

PART ONE—INTRODUCTORY MATTERS

I. Background

THIS EPISTLE WAS WRITTEN to the churches in the district of Asia Minor called Galatia. The country was inhabited by an alien people. In the third century before Christ, people from the northern part of the country now called France poured into Greece and Asia Minor, and when the wave rolled back, some were left. These who were left were confined to the part called Galatia.

These people were quick to receive impressions and quick to lose them. They had the usual Gallic characteristics—intense enthusiasm, affectionateness, and fickleness. This explains such references as 1:6; 3:1; 4:9, and 10.

After the Jerusalem council, Paul went through Galatia on his second missionary journey establishing churches. The occasion of writing this epistle was the defection in these churches caused by certain Judaizing teachers who had found their way into these young Galatian churches.

These teachers insisted that Jewish Law was binding upon Christians. They did not deny Christ's Messiahship but taught that faith in Christ must be supplemented by the works of the Law. In order to carry their point they attacked Paul's apostleship. Paul was equal to the task and wrote this epistle which may appropriately be called the Magna Charta of Christian Liberty.

The study of Galatians and Romans sent Luther forth as the great hero who struck off the chains of slavery from multitudes. A modern Luther is just now needed. The Protestant church is thoroughly Galatianized. Multitudes are ignorant of the relations of Law and grace. The crying need is for preachers who know their Bible and are able to preach it.

PART TWO—DETAILED OUTLINE

I. ANALYSIS

A. *The Apostolic Salutation* (1:1-5).

He sets forth his divine authority as an apostle. It was not of men as to authority; not by men as having been elected or ordained by them, but entirely by Jesus Christ and God the Father (Acts 22:6-15).

He joins with himself all the brethren associated with him in communicating the glorious message of grace and peace from God the Father and Jesus Christ the Son. The sacrifice of the Son was to deliver us from this present evil world or age as well as from the bondage of law-keeping.

B. *The Rebuke* (1:6-9).

Instead of the usual thanksgiving, Paul issues a severe rebuke—instead of a doxology there is a curse invoked. He at the start reveals to them that he has serious matters to present. He rebukes them for three things—the Galatians for their fickleness, the false teachers for their heresy, and his enemies for their false and wicked charge.

Paul as the apostle of Christ had called the Galatians into the grace of Christ. These false teachers were perverting the Gospel by teaching that faith in Christ was not enough; but that it must be supplemented by the works of the Law. Grace means favor extended to the undeserving. The sinner is not only without merit before God, but he deserves separation from God. That which God righteously demands is fully provided by Christ. When the first element of works is added even that of obedience to God's commandments, it is no longer grace. Grace cannot begin until everyone is absolutely speechless before the Law (Rom. 3:19). Grace is God's kindness to those who were *dead* in *trespasses and sins.* Regeneration must take place before there can be obedience at all. These Galatians were being removed from grace in Christ to another gospel or to that which was not a gospel at all. Gospel means good news. There is no good news in being brought under the Law. The attempt to win God's favor by law-keeping is another gospel which has the curse of God upon it. There can be but one Gospel. The Gospel is the good news of life and peace through Jesus Christ. To pervert this good news by any system or rites and ceremonies is to contradict God's Word and expose the one doing it to the fury of God's wrath.

C. *Paul's Divine Commission as an Apostle* (1:10–2:14).

To Paul was committed that body of truth pertaining to the Church (Eph. 3:3-7). He received a special revelation from Christ to make this truth known. In his defense he shows them their mistake in turning from him to false teachers.

1. He was Christ's Loyal, Devoted Servant (1:10).

He—not a "pleaser of men"—sacrificed popularity because of loyalty to Christ and truth.

2. The Divine Origin of His Gospel (1:11, 12).

   a. It was not by tradition (v. 12).

   b. Not man-taught (v. 12).

   c. But received by special revelation of Jesus Christ (v. 12).

3. He Excelled in His Acquaintance with Judaism Itself (1:13, 14).

4. Other Facts Testify to His Apostleship (1:15-20).

The circumstances of his conversion and his intercourse with the apostles show the same truth. The vision of the Christ transformed his life. He was changed from a savage persecutor to a passionate advocate of the Gospel of grace.

5. A Test Was Made of Circumcision and the Law (2:1-5).

Paul went up to Jerusalem where a test was made in the mother church. False brethren entered privately to spy out Paul's liberty and bring the church under bondage. Paul stood against them and was vindicated by receiving the right hand of fellowship and being sent to the Gentiles with the Gospel.

6. His Apostleship Was Recognized by Other Apostles (2:6-10).

Peter, James, and John, two of whom were apostles before him and were foremost among them all, recognized his apostleship.

7. Peter Was Not Infallible (2:11-14).

Since they laid special claim upon the authority of Peter, Paul was obliged to show that Peter was not infallible. Paul was especially called to set forth this truth of grace in Christ. His words were God's words. Let no one misunderstand them.

D. *Justification Is by Faith Without the Works of the Law* (2:15–3:24).

To get the proper meaning of this declaration it is necessary to grasp the scriptural usage of the word *justify*. By reference to the following texts it will be seen that to justify means to *declare* righteous (Deut. 25:1; Isa. 5:23; Rom. 3:21-24). When applied to the believer, justification means that judicial act by which, on account of the merit of Jesus Christ to whom the sinner is united by faith, God declares that the sinner is no longer exposed to the terror of the Law, but is acquitted before Him.

The churches of Galatia were established by Paul. This doctrine he preached was justification by faith. False teachers followed him insisting that faith in Christ should be supplemented by the works of the Law. Observe that they did not deny the need for faith in Christ but that it should be made complete by the works of the Law.

The same condition confronts the church today. Protestant theology is characterized by an admixture of faith and works—grace and Law. The crying need of the hour is a revival of Paul's teaching as to the Gospel in its relation to the Law.

1. Even the Jews Believed in Christ for Justification (2:15, 16).

The Jews, God's covenant people, had to turn to Christ for salvation.

2. The Believer Is Freed from the Law by Death (2:17-20).

Not only is the believer dead and therefore free from the Law, but it was the Law which killed him. However, he is again alive because Christ liveth in him. Christ was made of a woman, made under the Law, that He might redeem us from the curse of the Law. He became man that He might suffer the penalty of death for man.

3. Christ Died in Vain If Righteousness Came by the Law (2:21).

Is anyone ready to say that God made such a blunder? To mingle the works of the Law with grace for justification is to frustrate grace.

4. The Gift of the Spirit Was Received by Faith (3:1-5).

If God had already sealed them by His Spirit, why go back to law-keeping for salvation?

5. Abraham Was Justified by Faith (3:6-9).

Salvation is under the Abrahamic covenant.

6. Those Under the Works of the Law Are Under the Curse of the Law (3:10-14).

The Law curses a man, but Christ bore that curse on the cross. Thereby redemption has been effected. There is a redemption by *price* and a redemption by *power*. Both have been effected by Christ.

7. The Relation of the Law to the Covenant of Grace (3:15-18).

a. It does not add a new condition to the Abrahamic covenant.

b. It does not disannul the covenant of grace through faith.

8. The Purpose of the Law (3:19-24).

a. To reveal sin—it was added because of transgression (vv. 19-23). Sin existed before the Law was given, but it was not imputed to the sinner before the Law was given. The Law brings home to the sinner the knowledge of his guilt (Rom. 7:7; 3:20). We see this manifest in the lives of children. Forbid a child to do a thing which it never thought of doing before, and it will at once desire to do it. Every thoughtful adult knows how this works within himself.

b. To bring us to Christ—it was our schoolmaster (v. 24). The ancient pedagogue had the care of the children—the discipline, as well as the mental and moral training, was in his hands.

E. *Sonship of the Believer Is Realized Through Faith in Christ Jesus* (3:25—4:7).

1. The Believer Is Free from the Rule of the Pedagogue—the Law (3:25).

After faith is come, the believer is free from external discipline.

2. The Believer Is No Longer a Child But an Adult (3:26—4:7).

The child does not differ from a servant while under age, but when maturity is realized through faith in Christ, it comes into the full freedom of the divine family. He is now by adoption given his rightful position in the home. Regeneration gives relationship. Adoption gives position. Adoption literally means the placing as a son.

F. *The Perils of Legalism* (4:8-31).

1. It Puts the Believer into Bondage and Robs Him of His Blessings (4:8-20).

These Galatians may have been saved but they were robbed of their joy and peace. It is so today. Many are saved but have very unsatisfactory experiences. Intelligent faith in the fullness and completeness of Christ's redemptive work brings the *peace of God* to the believer. It is blessed to have peace with God (Rom. 5:1) through justification of faith, but it is infinitely more wonderful to have the *peace of God.* Only those who have this peace can make a success of the Christian life and be effective witnesses for Christ.

2. The Allegory of the Two Covenants Shows That There Is Liberty Alone in Christ (4:21-31).

Law and grace will not mix. The bondwoman must be cast out to make place for the free. The crying need of this hour is pastors and teachers to make known the freedom and liberty which is the birthright of every one who truly receives Christ as his Saviour. The church is almost completely Galatianized.

G. *The Practical Application of the Message of Galatians* (5:1—6:18).

Paul having vindicated his apostleship by showing that he had received his call directly from Jesus Christ, and having shown from other Scriptures and experiences that justification is by faith in Jesus Christ without the works of the Law, appeals to the Galatians to:

1. Stand Fast in the Liberty of Christ (5:1-12).

Stand fast means to persevere in this freedom from the Law as a means of justification. They must be unmoved in this position for to be circumcised would show that Christ profited them nothing and that they became in bondage to keep the whole Law. It meant that they had fallen from grace. To live the Christian life requires definite understanding of the meaning of faith in Christ and positive and courageous effort to persevere.

2. Christian Living Is Not an Occasion to the Flesh But a Powerful Incentive to Obedience (5:13-15).

Liberty in Christ is realized when the believer enthrones Christ as the Lord of his life. The New Testament name of the Saviour is Lord Jesus Christ. Jesus means Saviour. Christ means anointed and Lord means the absolute ruler. God's anointed One becomes the sinner's Saviour in order that He might be his Lord. The Redeemer makes Himself known to the world through the believer's testimony of life and word. This is the wonder of the grace of God.

3. The Believer's Walk in the Holy Spirit (5:16-26).

The sinner's salvation is by the sovereign grace of God, made effective by the Holy Spirit. This salvation begins with regeneration by the Spirit. As soon as the individual is born from above the Spirit takes up His abode in his heart and causes Christ to dwell in his heart by faith, and leads him into a holy and fruitful life. The walk in the Spirit is (*a*) not to fulfill the lusts of flesh (vv.19-21). The indwelling Holy Spirit enables the believer to live a life of victory over the flesh; but (*b*) to bring forth the fruit of the Spirit (vv. 22, 23). Christian living is bearing fruit instead of the so-called "character building." Christian character is not an *edifice* but *fruit*. It is not imitating a model, even Christ, but becoming something.

4. Restore the Erring Brother (6:1).

The word *restore* is a surgical term. It means to reset—restore as the resetting of a broken limb. Believers are members of Christ's Body. We should be just as anxious and willing to restore the one who has fallen into sin as we are to reset and replace a broken bone. This is a life of merit rather than our futile effort to earn God's favor by law-keeping.

5. Bear One Another's Burdens (6:2-5).

Burdens are everywhere. Bearing burdens is peculiarly characteristic of Christianity. Jesus Christ said: "The Son of man came not to be ministered unto, but to minister, and to give his life a ransom for many" (Matt. 20:28). Christ served and died for others.

6. Obligation To Share the Burden of the Christian Ministry (6:6-10).

This obligation is specific and personal. Many Christians fail here. The few always bear the burden in spite of the fact that it is an ordinance of God (I Cor. 9:14). Observe the wonderful significance of verses 7 and 8. They do not give directions to sinners about their sins but to saints about their stinginess. Every act, thought, and deed is seed sown in one or the other soils of the flesh or spirit. The new life in Christ is a life of beneficence (v. 10) to all men, especially to men of the household of faith.

7. Paul's Exultation in the Cross of Christ (6:11-16).

To him it had a double crucifixion—of the world to him and him to the world. We may wonder why he gloried in the cross. We find the answers in this epistle:

a. He had been saved from his sins and delivered from this evil age (1:4). He really had something about which to glory. How can anyone who has a full realization of this keep from saying, Hallelujah!

b. Because there Paul died with Christ (2:19, 20). The Law in slaying Christ slew Paul also. Since it slew him it has no more dominion over him (Rom. 7:1). Should he not glory in this freedom?

c. Because Christ delivered him from the curse of the Law (3:10, 13).

d. Because the cross measured the love of Christ for him (2:20). Who can properly estimate the greatness of this love?

e. Because it made an end of all things between him and the world (6:14). It not only saved him from God's wrath but saved him from the greed, pleasures, and ambitions of the world.

8. The Peace of the New Life (6:16).
9. Warning (6:17).
10. The Benediction (6:18).

EPISTLE TO THE EPHESIANS

PART ONE—INTRODUCTORY MATTERS

I. Author.

The Book of Ephesians was written by Paul from prison at Rome about A.D. 61 or 62 (1:1). It appears to be a circular letter addressed to the saints at Ephesus and the neighboring or daughter churches as indicated by "and the faithful in Christ Jesus."

II. Theme.

It contains the highest church truth—indeed it may rightly be called the spiritual constitution of the church. Its key phrases are "in Christ" and "Christ in you." Its theme is God's masterpiece (2:10). The wonder of God's grace is displayed in the regeneration of those dead in trespasses and sins, and making them to produce good works and live beautiful lives—the believer in Christ and Christ in the believer and the issuing life. It may be called the mystical union of the believer with Christ. It exhibits the members of Christ's Body vitally united to Him by the baptism of the Holy Spirit according to I Corinthians 12:13.

In Ephesians is unfolded the mystery which was hidden in the mind of God before the foundation of the world (3:4-9). Ephesians is one of the mountain-peaks of revelation disclosing the ultimate and crowning purpose of God in Christ in and through the Church.

In the Old Testament the prophets told of the kingdom to be set up with Messiah as its Head and Israel at its center. In the Gospels we have the kingdom offered to Israel and their rejection and crucifixion of Christ the King. The kingdom was then postponed and only the the Book of Revelation do we see its establishment. Between the postponement of the kingdom and its consummation is a great parenthetical interval in which the Church comes into view. We thus see that the Church is something different, separate, and apart from the kingdom. It had its beginning after Christ's ascension, and its translation will take place at Christ's second coming. The apprehension of the Church is absolutely essential to the understanding of the Bible truth. Failure here accounts for the confusion in Christian teaching and objective.

III. ANALYSIS.

Chapter 4 shows the beginning of the hortatory or practical section of the epistle, implying that the first three chapters constitute the doctrinal portion. The doctrinal deals with the *calling* of the Church—the hortatory part has to do with the *walk* of the Church.

This is ever the scheme of Paul's epistles—first doctrinal and then its application to duty—the enunciation of a great truth and then its sanctifying power upon the life.

Some charge the Church with being "other worldly" with no practical concern for the present world. The Church has only a place of glory and power in this world as she keeps her eyes fixed on the world above. Her only hope of affecting the present world for God and righteousness is by perpetually living in the consciousness of the fact that she belongs to the other world. The things that are seen can only be transformed as we live in the power of the unseen.

The fundamental weakness of modern preaching is the attempted practical without the doctrinal basis. The highest doctrine is the motive power for the lowest duty. All moral obligations are based upon our position in the Body of Christ.

PART TWO—DETAILED OUTLINE

I. THE CALLING OF THE CHURCH—DOCTRINAL (1:1—3:21).

A. *God's Eternal Plan and Electing Love in Relation to His Church* (1:1-23).

1. Apostolic Greeting and Salutation (1:1, 2).

Paul, the apostle by the will of God. Consciousness of the divine will was the secret of Paul's devotion and courage. Success in the Christian ministry is dependent upon this consciousness. It is the requirement for strength of human character in all relations of life—domestic, patriotic or missionary. The Puritans' willingness to die for free government is a case in point.

2. Origin of the Church (1:4-6).

a. Where? (v. 5). In the will and mind of God. God had a comprehensive plan for His Church, embracing every member. Every building was first in the architect's mind including every part and stone before a single effort was made.

b. When? (v. 4). Before the foundation of the world the plan for the Church was complete in the mind of God. Man in Christ was divine thought. God's dealing with us was determined and foreseen. The Church is not an afterthought of God.

c. Purpose (v. 6). It was for God's glory. The redemptive purpose primarily terminates upon God, not man. This truth should greatly encourage us.

3. The Respective Work of the Triune God in Building the Church (1:4-14).

a. God the Father (vv. 4-6).

(1) Selected us in Christ before the foundation of the world (v. 4). The purpose of this selection was *holiness* and the proof of this is the *manner of life* we live.

(2) Predestinated us to the place of sons in Christ (v. 5). Adoption means the placing of sons. We become God's children by regeneration (John 1:12, 13), and get our place in His family by adoption.

(3) Made accepted in Christ (v. 6). Our acceptance in God's family is because of our relation to Christ.

b. God, the Son (vv. 7-12).

(1) Redeemed by His blood (v. 7). We were bought back by Christ from the bondage to sin. Redemption is twofold—by price and by power. We now have the first and wait for the second.

(2) Revealed the mystery of the divine will (vv. 8, 9).

(3) Unites the whole universe (v. 10). Christ's redemption is wider than man—it reaches the entire universe.

(4) Inherits us (v. 11). Being in Christ who is rich we have a rich heritage. It is wonderful to have salvation and still more wonderful to be an heir of God.

c. God, the Spirit (vv. 13, 14).

(1) Illumined and quickened in hearing God's Word (2:5).

(2) Sealed us (1:13). Sealing is for a threefold purpose:

(a) To authenticate as genuine and true.

(b) To mark one's property—a token of God's ownership. Not even the Devil dare violate God's property.

(c) To render secure. The Spirit is the earnest of inheritance—the first installment which guarantees the completion of the redemption.

4. Paul's Prayer (1:15-23).

He prays that the divine calling might be realized and that the Ephesians might be spiritually enlightened to apprehend three things:

a. The hope of this calling (v. 18). The understanding of this hope would inspire noble ambitions.

b. Riches of the glory of God's inheritance in the saints (v. 18). The riches of God is that through redeemed sinners He may display His wondrous grace.

c. That the exceeding greatness of His power to usward my be known (v. 19). That power is at the disposal of the believer to work for God in the accomplishment of His purpose in the world. This available power is illustrated in the resurrection and exaltation of Jesus Christ (vv. 20-23). All this power can be realized through the believer's unity with Christ.

B. *Salvation by Grace* (2:1-22).

Sinners are the material out of which God's masterpiece is constructed. The power and skill of a workman is shown by the kind of material used in the construction of something. To create the masterpiece, the Church, out of vile sinners exhibits God's mighty power and consummate skill. Note the connection of power to usward "through Christ's resurrection to raise from sin and death to share His celestial life" (1:19, 20). This mighty work of God in Christ's resurrection is continued in the lives of regenerated creatures.

1. Man's Universal Natural State (2:1-3).

a. Dead on account of trespasses and sins (v. 1). Man is not merely sick and disabled, but dead! Note the characteristics of the dead:

(1) Without sensation (4:19). They were "past feeling." Therefore could neither love God nor hate sin until made alive. God's love and character can no more affect the unregenerate than a sunbeam falling upon the face of a dead man.

(2) Without motion. An unregenerate person is as helpless to move toward God as Lazarus was to get out of the grave.

b. Under the control of fleshly and worldly lusts (v. 2). The principle governing the life of the unregenerate springs out of their corrupt nature.

c. Under the domination of Satan (v. 2). Disobedient to God because they are in bondage to the prince of the power of the air.

d. In a state of condemnation and wrath (v. 3). This is a picture of every human being apart from Christ. The wrath of God hangs over him.

2. Man's State by Grace (2:4-10).

a. "Made alive in Christ" (v. 5).

b. Raised up (v. 6).

c. Associated with Christ in glory (v. 6).

d. The actuating principle of God (v. 4). It was God's pitying love looking down into the world cemetery. Man's salvation is entirely due to God's grace—redeeming love. Even the faith by which salvation is appropriated is God's gift (v. 8). Works are entirely excluded as grounds or means of salvation.

e. Purpose of God in salvation (vv. 7-10).

(1) To display grace in the coming ages (v. 7).

(2) To glorify God through the good works of the redeemed (v. 10 cf. Matt. 5:16).

3. The Relation of Redeemed Sinners to God (2:11-16).

a. No longer Gentiles belonging to the idolatrous world.

b. No longer strangers from the covenant promises.

c. No longer without hope and God, but are nigh through Christ.

4. Means by Which the Change Was Wrought (2:14-18).

This changed condition was not effected by even the teachings of

Christ, nor by the righteous life of Christ, but by the blood of the cross. The death of Christ had a threefold effect:

a. In satisfying divine justice—the reconciliation with God was secured (v. 16).

b. By abolishing the Mosaic institutions as Law, the middle wall of partition between Jew and Gentile was broken down (v. 15). By this means Jew and Gentile are united in one Body.

c. Secured access to God (v. 18).

5. The Glorious Issue of God's Grace (2:19-22).

a. Fellowship with the saints (v. 19). All saved people are on an equality—members of the same Body.

b. Members of God's family (v. 19). All believers enjoy the full privilege of children in the heavenly home. They know God as Father not as a ruler of a kingdom.

c. The constituent parts of a temple in which God dwells by His Spirit (v. 22). That dead, vile, godless and disobedient men could be made fit and builded into a temple where the infinitely holy God dwells is alone of grace. Only God's redeeming grace could make such a thing possible.

C. *The Mystery of God's Masterpiece* (3:1-21).

The wisdom of God is made known through the Church (3:1-21).

1. What It Is (3:6).

Mystery in the Scriptures means truth undiscoverable to human reason, made known by revelation. Mystery here means the Church, the building together of Jews and Gentiles into one Body with Jesus Christ as Head. It was not known in other ages (v. 5).

In the Old Testament Israel's headship among the nations is set forth. The Gentiles were to be blessed through Israel (Gen. 12:1-3; Isa. 60:3-5). In this new Body Gentiles shall be fellow-heirs—joint-partakers of the promises. Promises to Israel shall be fulfilled, but this Body will find its completion and glory before that time. The mystery, the Church, is the Bride of Christ who shall reign with Him in the Messianic kingdom.

2. A Subject of Special Revelation (3:2-5).

This is the content of Paul's Gospel, or the Gospel of the grace of God hidden in other ages or generations (v. 5). The Church was in the counsels of God before time, but not until many ages had elapsed was He pleased to make it known. The Church was not in existence during the Old Testament dispensation. The Incarnation, atonement, exaltation of Christ, and descent of the Holy Spirit were necessary before such a Body could be formed. At Pentecost this purpose became an actuality (I Cor. 12:13). Believers were then and there baptized into the one Body. At that time Christ's prophecy (Matt. 16:18) was fulfilled.

3. Paul the Minister of the Masterpiece (3:7-9).

a. Special gifts of grace were given to him to that end (v. 7). His conversion was effected through His mighty power, and he was especially privileged to see and hear the heavenly mysteries. (See II Cor. 12:1-4.) He was caught up to Paradise to learn this mystery and qualified to reveal it.

b. Paul was especially commissioned to proclaim it (v. 8). Paul stands as the apostle to the Gentiles, a type of the new apostolate. He was converted by the personal appearing of Christ, and then sent to preach to the Gentiles. In like manner shall the whole Jewish nation be converted at the second coming of Jesus Christ and then become a blessing as missionaries heralding the cross to the whole world (Isa. 66:19; Rom. 1:15, 26). In the face of such grace, Paul shows great humility.

4. The Purpose Of (3:9-12).

a. To enlighten men concerning this mystery (v. 9). How necessary is this enlightenment. Ignorance as to this truth results in confusion in Bible interpretation.

b. To make known the manifold wisdom of God to the principalities and powers—the host of angels (v. 10).

Angels seem to be actively interested in the affairs of the earth. They sang for joy in the morning of Creation (Job 38:7). They are ministers of God in the execution of His plans. They seem especially interested in the redeeming work of Christ (I Peter 1:12). Though possessing a high degree of intelligence they could not understand God's intentions toward this world—the Incarnation, the cross of Christ, the outpouring of the Holy Spirit at Pentecost were surprises to them. The Church is the college of wisdom for the universe.

This all centers in Jesus Christ—the very One for whom mankind longed. The whole world of men is bound to the higher spheres through Him. He rules over them. The universe is one. There is a solidarity of rational and moral interests among all intelligences. That which no prophet ever saw—no human being could even imagine—no angel ever could know—is made known by and through the Church. This was all purposed in the Lord Jesus Christ.

5. Paul's Prayer (3:13-21).

a. To whom (vv. 14, 15). It was to God the Father of the Lord Jesus Christ. The divine Fatherhood extends to the angels, for He is the Creator of all intelligent beings (v. 15).

b. For what (vv. 16-19).

(1) The strengthening of the inner man by the Holy Spirit (v. 16). He prays not for outward or material power but for spiritual. Political sovereignty has never been a blessing to the Church. The measure of this strength is as boundless as the ocean—the riches of the glory of Christ.

(2) The indwelling of Christ (v. 17). Christ takes up His abode in the believer, and makes His home—takes possession as the rightful tenant. This is made possible by faith. The Church—the hearts of believers, constitute temples in which Christ dwells.

(3) Believers to be established (v. 17). They are to be rooted and grounded in love.

(4) Apprehension of Christ's love (vv. 18, 19). Love's dimensions are infinite.

(a) Length—from eternity to eternity.

(b) Depth—beyond ability to conceive—never can fully know it.

(c) Height—the Heaven of heavens.

(d) Breadth—infinite, unlimited. He says, "Come unto me, *all.*"

(5) To be filled unto the fullness of God (v. 19). In the measure that Christ dwells in us and we apprehend this love, we shall be filled with this fullness.

c. Triumphant assurance of the realization of Paul's prayer (vv. 20, 21). This realization goes beyond our ability to ask or think. It is all to be accomplished by the indwelling Holy Spirit.

II. THE WALK OF THE CHURCH (4:1–6:24).

The first part presents the high calling of the Church or its position in grace; the second part presents the worthy walk in view of its high calling. Paul now passes from the heavenly calling to the worthy conduct. These two parts are connected by "therefore," showing that the conduct is the logical issue of the calling. The calling is the motive for the conduct. Doctrine and ethics are inseparable. The calling shows what conception the Church should have of herself. The walk shows the conception which God desires the world should have of the Church.

A. *The Believer's Walk in Unity* (4:1-16).

1. Virtues Essential to the Maintenance of Unity (4:1-3).

a. Lowliness (v. 2). It means esteeming oneself as small. Lowliness of mind does not mean low-mindedness. It is the opposite of selfish ambition or vain-glory. With the consciousness of sinfulness one is not unduly concerned with personal interests. He is willing to give place to others where higher interests are involved. Self-importance, the love for position and power, the craving for applause must be put away. These are the seeds of strife and discord.

b. Meekness (v. 2). Meekness is not servile fear, but self-suppression to serve others. It is not timidity or cowardice.

c. Long suffering (v. 2). After all, we live in a world of many individuals. We must endure much. We must bear with the infirmities of others.

d. Loving forbearance (v. 2). This means restraint under just provocation. Love is the sum and substance of that which results in unity.

e. Peaceful endeavor (v. 3). This is more than forbearance. It includes the positive effort to maintain peace.

2. The Fundamental Unities (4:4-6).

This is the basis upon which unity works. This means the unity of which Holy Spirit is the author.

a. One Body—the Church is an organism. The several members have been fused into the one Body of which Christ is the Head by the baptism of the Holy Spirit (I Cor. 12:13).

b. One Spirit. This one Spirit is the Holy Spirit, the third member of the Godhead.

c. One hope of your calling (v. 4; cf. Titus 2:13). Hope is necessary to give energy of endeavor and make progress possible. Nations and societies of the past make no progress. Hope of our completed redemption and the completion of Christ's mediatorial work at His second coming puts energy and purpose in Christian endeavor. All mankind and the whole universe are awaiting the realization of this blessed hope.

d. One Lord—Jesus Christ. He is the only and grand center. He is not Saviour only, He is Lord. If we view Him only as Saviour, we make Him as a means to an end. Such is a utilitarian conception. Many are willing to be saved by Jesus who are not willing to be ruled by Him. We must make Him our Lord Jesus Christ. Disregard of this requirement makes divisions in the Church possible.

e. One faith. This means one instrument by which Christ is appropriated. It does not mean consent to one form of belief. Union of believers is not possible on that line.

f. One baptism—the baptism by the Holy Spirit. By one Spirit all believers are baptized into the one Body of which Christ is the Head (I Cor. 12:13).

g. One God who is the Father of all. He is not a God merely to be pleased, but a Father, pitying and keeping us. God is over all, gathering all things to Himself. We see that Christian unity is not merely assent to logical propositions but ascent into Christ.

3. Unity Amid Diversity (4:7-11).

Unity is not monotonous uniformity. Diversity of gifts is recognized. They are as various as the aspects of personality. The Gospel of Christ can sanctify and use every element and capacity of our nature. The marvelous scope of the gifts is indicated by the measure and scope of Christ's victory accomplished through His Incarnation and exaltation. Note the height and depth (descended and ascended) (vv. 8-10).

a. Every member has a gift (v. 7). The lowliest member has some gift. No one should be idle. Something for everyone to do.

b. Not everyone has the same gift. No room for jealousy (v. 11).

c. No one has all the gifts (v. 7). No one person can run the church.

d. Some gifts enumerated (v. 11).

(1) Apostles for the perfecting of an authoritative system or body of doctrine.

(2) Prophets for the exposition of that doctrine.

(3) Evangelists for the proclamation of the doctrine for the completion of the Body.

(4) Pastors and teachers for the feeding and training of the saints.

4. The Purpose of the Gifts (4:12-16).

a. For the unity of the faith and knowledge of the Son of God (v. 13).

b. For the full-grown man—to attain to measure of the stature of Christ (v. 13).

c. To prevent members from being tossed about by the craftiness and sleight of men in error (v. 14.) These are maladies which prevent or arrest development.

d. Means and conditions of growth (vv. 15, 16).

(1) Speaking the truth in love.

(2) Each member contributing his part maketh increase of the Body. The Church is here compared with the human body which proceeds from the first germ of life through the various stages to full maturity. A faithful and capable ministry in the Church will prevent the inexperienced from being wrought upon by deceivers whose business is to cause them to stumble.

B. *The Believer's Walk as a New Man and Child of God* (4:17–5:14).

The believer is a new man. He is a partaker of Christ. He belongs to a new humanity. He is a member of a new organism, the Church, which is His Body. Therefore, he does not follow after the old man.

1. The Believer Does Not Walk as the Heathen—the Unregenerate (4:17-19).

This has reference to the saved man his renewed nature in conflict with his sinful nature. There is a sense in which the regenerate man is two men—the one in mortal combat with the other. The walk of the unregenerate or Gentiles involved:

a. Their minds (vv. 17, 18), their intellects were confounded; their understanding darkened. They lacked a clear and settled principle or theory of life. They were not rational—were out of their minds—otherwise they would not worship idols and practice sins so odious and ruinous.

b. Their spiritual nature was alienated from the life of God (v. 18). They were ignorant of God. Their condition was most pitiable.

c. Their moral nature (v. 19). They were "past feeling." They gave themselves over to flagrant and shameless profligacy. They gave themselves to gross sensuality as a business. They worked at it with insatiable appetite. They had no love for God or hatred of sin.

2. The Believer Walks as Christ Taught (4:20-24).

Christ is the pattern of holiness and unselfishness.

a. The old man to be put off (v. 22). The old nature is grossly corrupt.

b. The new man to be put on (vv. 23, 24). This new man is known by righteousness and holiness.

3. The New Man Discards the Following Vices (4:25—5:5).

a. Falsehood—lying (v. 25). Truthfulness supplants falsehood and lying. Sound faith makes an honest tongue. Lying is hateful to God. It is not justifiable under any circumstances. Lying even includes the creation of wrong impressions. We are told of a custom in Siam of punishing liars by having their lips sewed together. This would be quite spectacular if done in America.

b. Anger (vv. 26, 27). This does not mean burning indignation against sin, but personal bitterness. If such should enter, get it out before the sun goes down. To have personal bitterness gives place to the Devil. The evil one is watching his chance to enter.

c. Theft (v. 28). The new man will not steal. There are other ways of stealing than that of rifling the cash drawer or taking a pocketbook. Appropriating that which does not belong to one—not giving the right change. Riding on a car and not paying fare is dishonest. Honest toil is demanded. There are three ways of getting property: working for it, receiving it as a gift, or stealing it. The first two are honorable, the last one is criminal.

d. Corrupt speech (vv. 29, 30). This is common today. The

spiritual man will speak only that which he would like his best friends to hear. The inner life is revealed by the speech. Corrupt speech grieves the Holy Spirit. Pure conversation is demanded of the Christian.

e. Malice (vv. 31, 32). This means badness of disposition, expressing itself in bitterness, clamor, and railing. This is to be supplanted with tender-heartedness and kindness. The remedy for malice is to imitate God and walk in love. The supreme example of this is the behavior of Christ (5:1, 2).

f. Impurity and uncleanness (vv. 3, 4). This conduct was common among the heathen of that day and increasingly so today. Jesting and foolish talking are in the same category of sins.

g. Covetousness and licentiousness (vv. 3, 5). Covetousness is inordinate desire for gain. The fornicator is the one under the sway of carnal lust. Neither one has an inheritance in the kingdom of Christ and God.

4. The Walk as Children of Light (5:6-14).

a. Character of children of light (vv. 9, 10).

(1) Goodness.

(2) Righteousness.

(3) Truth.

These virtues are the fruits of union with Christ made effective by the Holy Spirit in the believer.

b. The influence upon the surrounding darkness by the believer's walking in the light (vv. 11-14). The divine method of influencing the world is through the shining of the believer's light—by means of righteous living (Matt. 5:16). This should be a powerful incentive to holy living. The believer must live a separated life.

C. *The Walk of the Believer as Filled with the Spirit* (5:16—6:9).

1. His Outward Life, or Life in Relation to the World (5:15-18a).

a. So as to bear the world's scrutiny (15). It means that every step is to be thoughtfully and prayerfully taken. The believer is to walk with eyes open. Fools walk carelessly. This should be applied to our daily living.

b. Be diligent to seize every opportunity (v. 16). This means watching the time—making it your own. Control it. The wide-awake merchant watches the market favorable for his purchases and sales. So the believer should be on the alert for occasions to further the interest of the Master. This is especially obligatory in the evil days. The Devil is opposed to the Lord and is constantly seeking to hinder the Lord's work.

c. Abstain from the intoxicating cup (v. 18a). This is most imperative today.

2. His Inner Life or Personal State (5:18b-21).

a. Supreme joyousness (v. 19). This joyousness expresses itself in every variety of song—not dancing. The exhiliaration is from within by the Holy Spirit.

b. Thanksgiving to God at all times for all things (v. 20). "All things work together for good" (Rom. 8:28).

c. Lowliness of mind—submissiveness—yieldedness—esteeming others better than himself (v. 21).

3. Married Life (5:22-33).

Conjugal relationship is analogous to that of Christ and the Church. The one illustrates the other. The relative duties of husbands and wives can only be comprehended when their essential oneness is compared with the oneness of Christ and the Church.

a. The wife is to be subject to *her own* husband as the Church is subject to the Lord Jesus Christ (vv. 22-24).

(1) Her motive "as unto the Lord" (v. 22).

(2) Ground of—the husband is the Head (v. 23).

(3) Extent of—all things (v. 24).

This relationship is not temporary but expresses the deep-seated law of human nature. Subjection does not imply inferiority. Woman is man's equal. The man and the woman are parts of a *unit*. The woman is the glory of the man. She, while in subjection, rules by kindness and persuasion. Subjection or submission is not something new but a law of nature reinforced by the law of Christ.

b. The husband is to love his wife (vv. 25-33).

(1) Measure of (vv. 25-27). As Christ loved the Church—He died for it. If husbands were as devoted to their wives as Christ is to the Church, they could better ask submission. Christ is the husband's model. Christ's object is the perfection of the Church.

So the husband's object should be the perfection of his wife's character.

(2) Ground of (vv. 28-33). After all, this is only self-love, for his wife is his own body. True marriage is community of life—not independent of each other. The wife may not be good-looking or even good-natured, but she is to be loved.

4. Domestic Life (6:1-9).

a. Children and parents (vv. 1-4).

(1) Children are to obey and honor their parents.

(a) Ground of—"in the Lord." This means that obedience is ordered and regulated by the Lord. Such obedience is "unto the Lord" because parents stand in the place of God to children.

(b) It is right in itself. Children derive their being from their parents, and parents spend many years in caring for their children—feeding, clothing, and protecting them.

(c) The obligation is imposed by the Lord. The command is accompanied by a promise.

(2) Parents should exercise authority over them (v. 4). This should be done in such a way as not to irritate them. They are charged to "bring them up" in the nurture and admonition of the Lord which means that parents should educate and discipline their children.

b. Servants and masters (vv. 5-9).

(1) Servants (vv. 5-7). Servants were slaves in Paul's time. They were required to obey their masters. This applies in principle to all who are employed as wage earners. This obedience should be characterized by:

(a) Solicitude or anxiety to please the master or employer.

(b) Singleness of mind (v. 5).

(c) As "unto the Lord" (vv. 6, 7). This means that in this way they are serving the Lord. It is indeed a part of their obedience to the Lord.

(2) Masters (v. 9). Slaves—servants—should not be treated with harshness. Masters and servants should recognize that they have a common Master in Heaven to whom account shall be given.

The fulfillment of these requirements would do away with strife between capital and labor.

D. *The Walk of the Believer in Conflict with the Devil* (6:10-20).

The Church has inveterate foes. Salvation is absolutely of grace. Though redemption is free through Christ, yet between its beginning and consummation there is real, severe, and protracted conflict. This conflict is most difficult and dangerous. In it many suffer painful wounds, and many who bear the name Christian give up the struggle. Many because of ignorance of the reality of the conflict and of the methods of carrying it on make grave mistakes and suffer great loss. With reference to this conflict observe that everything is *supernatural.*

1. The Source of Strength (6:10).

We are to be strong in the Lord. Only as a branch is united to the vine—the limb is united to the tree—is there strength of life or conflict. The struggle dare not be attempted in *human strength* and *wisdom.* To rush into battle without regarding oneself as a member of the Body of Christ, deriving its strength and wisdom from Him as Head, is unpardonable folly.

2. The Enemy (6:11, 12).

The Devil is a personal, malicious being with his subordinates—demons.

a. Personality proved by:

(1) Names given him—Devil (slanderer), Satan (adversary), Apollyon (destroyer). Some twenty aliases describing his character show him to be the arch criminal of the universe.

(2) Actions predicated of him: Acts 5:3, filled the heart to lie; I Peter 5:8, walketh about; Matthew 4:11, tempted Christ.

b. His position and power.

(1) Above Michael (Jude 9).
(2) Prince of the power of the air (Eph. 2:2).
(3) Prince of this world (John 12:31).
(4) God of this age (II Cor. 4:4).
(5) Powers exceed that of man (Eph. 6:12).
(6) Power is over all unsaved men (I John 5:19), but limited (Job 1:10-12).

c. His nature.

(1) He is cunning (II Cor. 2:11; Eph. 6:11, 12).
(2) He is the original sinner (I John 3:8).

d. His work.
(1) Brought sin into the world (Gen. 3:1-6).
(2) Author of sickness (Acts 10:38; Luke 13:16).
(3) Power over death (Heb. 2:14).
(4) Personally enters into men (John 13:27).
(5) Lays snares for men (I Tim. 3:7).
(6) Blinds men's eyes (II Cor. 4:4).
(7) Sifts God's servants (Luke 22:31).

e. The means of carrying on his work.
(1) He has a church (Rev. 3:9).
(2) Has ministers (II Cor. 11:14, 15).

f. His destiny.
(1) Now rests under a curse (Gen. 3:14).
(2) Eternal fire awaits him (Matt. 25:41).
(3) Death blow at Christ's death (John 12:31).
(4) Shall be bound when Christ comes (Rev. 20:1-3).
(5) Lake of fire at the end (Rev. 20:10).

3. The Armor (6:13-17).

The means of offense and defense are not of man's devising. Just as strength is from the Lord, so is the armor. The believer *dare* not act, only on the *defensive.* He must attack and subdue his spiritual enemies as well as *resist* their attack. Untold harm has resulted from the use of means of men's devising instead of the armor of the Lord's providing.

a. Some means which human ingenuity has devised:

(1) Asceticism. This means *flight* rather than *fight,* with *failure* and *defeat.*

(2) Celibacy. This likewise always has resulted in failure.

(3) Ritualism. This robs the believer of the means of grace and issues in failure.

(4) Voluntary humility. (See Col. 2:18-23.) These all increase the difficulty instead of lessening it.

b. The panoply of God consists of the following:

(1) Girded with truth (v. 14). The truth of God sincerely and honestly embraced alone will preserve a believer in this con-

flict. Reason, tradition, speculation, and *dead orthodoxy* will fail him in the crucial hour.

(2) Breastplate of Christ's righteousness (v. 14). As the metal plate covered the vital organs, so the righteousness of Christ protects from the assaults of the enemy. The infinite perfection of this righteousness is such that no assault from within or without can succeed. No accusing conscience can weaken because the demands of God have been met in the obedience and suffering of Christ.

(3) Feet shod with the preparation of the Gospel of peace (v. 15). This suggests the firm foothold of the soldier and his readiness to proclaim the Gospel message of peace. He has peace in his own heart, not weakened with doubt.

(4) Shield of faith (v. 16). By this shield he is able to quench all the fiery darts of the wicked one. Christ is the object of that faith—justifying faith. This faith will ward off every burning arrow hurled at the believer.

(5) The helmet of salvation (v. 17). Consciousness of complete and full salvation enables the believer to lift up his head and with confidence vigorously assault the enemy.

The helmet protects the head, the citadel of intelligence; knowing that he is a child of God, a fellow citizen with the saints, he hopes steadfastly to the end.

(6) The Sword of the Spirit (v. 1). This is the Word of God and is the Christian's offensive weapon. With it he can most effectively put the enemy to flight (Matt. 4:4, 7, 10, 11). All the triumphs of the Church have been accomplished by the Word of God. Where used she goes on conquering, but when she falls back upon reason, culture, tradition, science, or the commandments of men, she goes down in defeat before the adversary.

4. The Way to Get Strength (6:18-20).

The only way to get courage to face the foe is to use the armor of God. It is alone through prayer.

a. Every variety and method of prayer should be used—public, private, intercessory, and ejaculatory. It is the constant breathing out that which the Holy Spirit has breathed into him (Rom. 8:26).

b. On every occasion, "always."

c. For our comrades—"all the saints." Christians should stand shoulder to shoulder in praying and fighting.

d. Persistent (vv. 18, 19). Importunity is a requisite for victorious living as well as for witnessing.

E. *Final Greetings and Benediction* (6:21-24).

EPISTLE TO THE PHILIPPIANS

PART ONE—INTRODUCTORY MATTERS

I. The Introduction.

The city of Philippi anciently bore the name of Krenides or "The Little Fountains" because numerous springs surrounded it, but when Philip of Macedon, father of Alexander the Great, seized it, he enlarged it and named it after himself. It was then made the most eastern city of his kingdom. It afterward became famous in Roman history and was raised to the dignity of a Roman colony. It was here that Brutus and Cassius suffered an overwhelming defeat by Anthony and Octavius. It was upon this decisive victory of imperialism over republicanism that the dignity of a Roman colony was given it.

It was here that the Gospel made the first triumphs outside Asia. It was in obedience to the Macedonian cry that Paul and his companions took the Gospel into Europe for the first time about the middle of the first century. (See the account in full in Acts 16.)

The first convert was a woman from Thyatira named Lydia. There was no synagogue there so Paul met with the Jews at the riverside out of town, where they were accustomed to meet for worship—"where prayer was wont to be made." Paul's labors here were crowned with success. A church was established. This church was perhaps the freest from error of any or all of the apostolic churches.

II. Occasion of Writing.

The occasion of the writing of this epistle was the sending of much-needed contribution to Paul at the hand of Epaphroditus for his support while in prison. (See 4:10-18.)

Here Paul could not supply his needs by the labors of his own hands. The church was perhaps small and certainly poor (II Cor. 8:1-3), yet repeatedly sent gifts to him (II Cor. 11:8, 9). This then is a letter from a missionary to a church which had sent means for his support. He gratefully acknowledges his appreciation of it, yet will not let them think that they have done something great. Three things characterize his reaction to their kindness:

A. *Acknowledges Gift.*

Graciously acknowledges their recent gift as well as gifts at former times.

B. *Gives Such Ministry Praise* (4:18).

Calls it "an odor of a sweet smell, a sacrifice acceptable, well-pleasing to God."

C. *Asserts His Independence.*

He will not be brought into slavish obligation in consequence thereof. He tells them that he did not desire a gift—could patiently suffer need (4:11, 12).

The place and time of writing—from Rome about A.D. 60-63.

III. THE THEME.

The outward expression of the Christ-life within the believer, or the real Christian experience in this world of opposition, trials, and persecution, "Yea, and all that will live godly in Christ Jesus shall suffer persecution" (II Tim. 3:12). See the following references: 1:6, 20, 21; 2:5, 13; 3:9; 4:21. The key verse is 1:21.

PART TWO—DETAILED OUTLINE

I. THE SALUTATION (1:1, 2).

A. *From Paul and Timothy* (1:1).

"Servants of Jesus Christ." Note custom of joining himself with Timothy. No suggestion of rank. Believers are members of Christ's Body—all are equal.

B. *"To the Saints in Christ Jesus at Philippi"* (1:1).

Note the expression of a normal church life—"saints with the bishops and deacons." (N.B. "bishops and deacons.") A saint is a believer in Christ. *Saint* means a holy one. The believer is holy because he is in Christ—a member of Christ's Body. Because he is in Christ, he lives a holy life.

C. *The Good Wish for the Saints* (1:2).

"Grace and peace." Grace means the free favor of God—the blessed, the riches of God's love and favor to those in Christ. Peace—the blessed state of those reconciled to God through Christ—the harmony and health of the ones who have entered into the experience of God's grace.

D. *The Fatherhood of God and the Lordship of Jesus Christ* (1:2).

Here Christ is on an equality with God. Lord Jesus Christ is the New Testament name for Christ. God is the Father of those who own Christ as Lord. This can only be done by the Holy Spirit in the believer (I Cor. 12:3).

II. PAUL'S THANKSGIVING (1:3-8).

A. *For Their Fellowship in the Gospel* (1:3-5).

1. Note His Memory of the Believers at Philippi.

The memory of Christian kindness is a precious heritage.

2. His Gratitude (1:3).

He had something to thank God for. He was courteous. Courtesy means much.

3. Supplication for Them (1:4).

He had joy in praying for them.

4. Partnership (1:5).

The Philippians had fellowship with Paul in the Gospel by their gifts.

B. *For the Confidence of Their Completed Redemption* (1:6-8).

This confidence grew out of his experience with God. The time of its realization will be at the second coming of Jesus Christ. Paul saw something in these Philippians which convinced him that they were not quitters (v. 7).

III. PAUL'S PRAYER FOR THEM (1:9-11).

A. *For Abounding in Intelligent Love* (1:9).

This means a flood of love in the bounds of discretion. This is illustrated by a great river within its bounds.

B. *Approval of Right Things* (1:10).

1. For Ourselves.

2. For Others—not duped by others.

C. *Sincere and Without Offense* (1:10).

D. *Filled with the Fruits of Righteousness* (1:11).

IV. HELPED BY OPPOSITION (1:12-20).

Good came out of that which was of evil intent. All that was done to hinder the preaching of the Gospel but furthered its success. "All things work together for good."

A. *Result of Opposition* (1:12).

All that happened to Paul but pushed forward the work. It was opposition that took Paul to Rome. Opposition in Rome "kicked the Gospel upstairs"—Robinson. Even his shipwreck did not stop the progress of the Gospel.

B. *His Chains Proved His Loyalty* (1:13).

His bonds enabled him to express his fidelity to the Christ. There were "sermons in his bands." They showed that he was a prisoner for Christ's sake. They enabled him to tell the soldiers of Christ as he explained his difficulty.

C. *It Stimulated Others to Action* (1:14).

His loyalty to Christ put courage into timid souls. Most of us need such to spur us on to our best endeavor.

D. *Put New Interest in Preaching the Gospel* (1:15-18).

1. Some Through Envy and Strife (1:15, 16).

Two parties: Judaizing teachers had made their way to Rome.

2. Some Through Love (1:17, 18).

Since Christ was being preached, he was filled with joy (v. 18). This is the cure for jealousies and strife among Christian workers.

E. *Paul's Transcendent Aim* (1:21-26).

It was that Christ might be magnified in his body. A standard of life is necessary. To Paul Christ was not only the source of life, but its model, aim, and reward.

1. Living Was To Serve and Honor Christ.

2. Dying Was To Get Gain Because It Would Bring Him to Christ.

3. Quandary About Life (1:20-24).

Living would be gain to the Philippians—dying would be gain for Paul. He really desired to die.

Regardless of our estate there should be a real purpose in life. A realization of this would greatly change our manner of living. Apply by examples.

F. *Duties Enjoined* (1:27–2:16).

1. Conversation (Walk) Worthy of the Gospel of Christ (1:27-30).

This worthy walk consists of:

a. Steadfastness (v. 27). This is always desirable and most needful now.

b. Unity of purpose (v. 27). This is to be expressed everywhere in the home, church, school, shop, civic affairs, and economics. This does not ignore the individuality of the believer. It is a rational unity, a unity of persons "striving together"—not the unity of the sandpit which is but a collection of units held by some external enclosure.

c. Undaunted courage (v. 28). The believer must live his life in the presence of mighty adversaries. The Christian's conflict to the enemy is a sign of perdition, but to the saved it is a "token of God's salvation."

d. Willingness to suffer for Christ's sake (vv. 29, 30). All who will live godly in Christ shall suffer persecution (II Tim. 3:12). It is given to the Christian not only to believe on Christ, but to suffer for His sake. Paul was an example of suffering.

2. Unity and Meekness (2:1, 2).

Paul pleads for unity and declares that their unity would fill his cup of joy.

a. Grounds of his appeal (v. 1).

(1) Reality of their relation to Christ. "In Christ" is basal —unity is the evidence of being in Christ—no hope if the individual is not a member of the Body of Christ.

(2) Love is the incentive to unity.

(3) Participation in the Holy Spirit.

(4) Compassion in the heart. If you have a heart "filled" with the Holy Spirit, there will be unity.

b. Nature of Paul's plea (v. 2).

(1) Likemindedness—think the same things.

(2) Unison of affection in Christ.

(3) Harmony of feeling "one accord."

3. Humility (2:3-11).

The antidote to egotism and party spirit is humility. In lowliness of mind each is to esteem the other better than himself; i.e., consider the other's interests. This does not mean that one should neglect his own interests. Christ is the supreme Example (vv. 5-11).

a. He is our example (v. 5). This means that we should apply the same rule in all of our relations that we see exhibited in Christ.

b. His preincarnate glory (v. 6). By His being in the form of God means that He was the same in essence as God. God has no form. God is Spirit. Christ as to His Person has the same mode of existence as God.

c. His humiliation (vv. 7, 8). Note the details of His humiliation.

d. His exaltation (vv. 9-11). Note the details of His exaltation.

4. Developing Christian Character (2:12-16).

Realizing God's plan in life is not working for salvation, but the outworking of that which God by His sovereign grace began in the individual.

a. There are two kinds of obedience:

(1) That which is rendered while the Master is present.

(2) That which is rendered while the Master is absent. This latter is the true test. The evidence of the servant's conversion was that she now swept under the mats and behind the door.

b. Working out that which has been inworked (v. 13). There is a sense in which God does all in salvation, but the proof that God has done it is that the individual responds to it.

c. Rendering unquestioning obedience (v. 14).

d. Perfect while imperfect (vv. 15, 16). How accomplished (v. 16). "Blameless and harmless" refer to "unmixed," "unadulterated" quality of life, which is to be in the midst of a crooked and perverse nation.

5. The Grand Objective (2:16b-18).

Something to show at the day of Christ. Paul looks forward to his possible execution with joy, as an encouragement to the Philippians to be faithful in their testimony and service even though it issues in death.

G. *Apostolic Example of the Christ-life Within the Believer in its Outworking* (2:17-30).

"In this passage we have a beautiful picture drawn by a master hand of the tender fraternal relations subsisting between true Christian hearts and the sense of obligation instinctively felt by disciples of our Lord to be interested in each other's welfare. So far as it can be done in words, the apostle here sets before us an object lesson, attractive and impressive, of the comfort and power and value in general of the fellowship in which believers in Christ mutually walk and the sympathy they mutually share when overtaken by misfortune and distress"—Dr. Frederick Noble.

Dr. Noble suggests that in preaching upon this passage a suitable subject would be "Fellowship and Sympathy," as illustrated by the various persons whose attitudes and actions are made known to us in this paragraph. The parties concerned are Paul, Timothy, Epaphroditus, and the Philippian church. Paul was a prisoner at Rome. He was permitted to preach but in bonds, handcuffed to a soldier, never permitted alone day or night. Timothy was a spiritual child of Paul. The reciprocal affection of a father and son passed between them. He became an associate of Paul in his ministry to the churches. Paul commended him for his fidelity.

1. Paul's Purpose To Send Timothy to the Philippians (2:19-24).

He had been in prison for some two years and was anxious to know their state. Paul commends Timothy's fidelity.

2. Paul's Purpose To Send Epaphroditus (2:25-30).

He commends Epaphroditus as a fellow soldier, a brother and companion in labor. His return was needful to acquaint the Philippians with his recovery. He had been sick which was caused by endangering his life for Christ's sake in ministering to Paul. May we learn that Christ becomes to believers the strongest bond of fellowship and sympathy known to man and that the time of all times to manifest this fellowship and sympathy is when men are in greatest need.

H. *Some Urgent Exhortations* (3:1—4:7).

"Finally" does not necessarily imply that Paul meant to conclude his letter.

1. Rejoices in the Lord (3:1).

In the Lord means in your Christian privileges. Being in Christ with its issuing privileges outweighs all persecutions, and the sufferings entailed, therefore rejoice!

2. Beware of the Judaizing Teachers (3:2-16).

In the very things they prided themselves, Paul could more than excel them. Though once valuing them he now counts them worthless in comparison with what he has in Christ. He is ambitious to strive after perfection and urges the Spirit upon the Philippians.

3. Beware of Those Who Have False Ideas of the Liberty of the Gospel (3:17-21).

These were those who claimed to be Christians while walking in evil ways, practicing carnal lusts.

4. Stand Fast in the Lord (4:1).

5. To Euodias and Syntyche (4:2).

Exhort them to be of the same mind in the Lord. These two women in the church were not working in harmony. Needed today. Euodias means "prosperous journey" or "sweet fragrance." Syntyche means "good luck." One woman is offended because another woman does not speak to her on the street—the reason for the offense? Maybe she is nearsighted! But thus trouble can start!

6. To Help Certain Women (4:3).

The names of these women are not given. Every minister should make a study of the women who helped with the Gospel in the days of the apostles. "Christianity and Women" would be a good topic.

7. Cheerfulness (4:4).

The message brought by the angels was: "Behold I bring you good tidings of great joy." Christians above all people should be happy and joyous.

8. Moderation or Yieldedness (4:5).

Gentleness is peculiarly a characteristic of the Christian.

9. Prayer (4:6).

"Be careful for nothing but in everything by prayer and supplication with thanksgiving let your requests be made known unto God."

10. The Keeping Power—the Peace of God (4:7).

I. *Virtues Recommended for Their Study and Practice* (4:8, 9).

J. *Paul's Grateful Remembrance of Kindness* (4:10-18).

K. *God the Supplier of Needs* (4:19).

L. *Salutation and Benediction* (4:20-23).

"Glory" is ascribed to God the Father. "Salute every saint in Christ Jesus—all the saints salute you." "The grace of our Lord Jesus Christ be with you."

EPISTLE TO THE COLOSSIANS

PART ONE–INTRODUCTORY MATTERS

I. Introduction.

Location of Colossae. It was situated east of Ephesus in the province of Phrygia in Asia Minor, on the river Lycos (Gorduk), near its junction with the Meander.

Near Colossae lay the towns of Laodicea and Hierapolis (4:13-16), therefore, the influences which pervaded one would more or less pervade the other. Laodicea was famous for its wealth and also for its philosophers, sophists, and rhetoricians. Hierapolis was distinguished as the birthplace of Epictetus the greatest heathen moralist and a contemporary of the great apostle. Phrygia, the "region containing Colossae, had been long famous as the adopted home of oriental mysticism."

Under such influences we would naturally expect that false doctrine would spring up and thrive. The content and character of the epistle show that Paul dealt with just such conditions.

II. Founding of the Church at Colossae

From 2:1 it appears that this church was not founded by Paul. His knowledge was from report (1:4-9), Epaphras their minister was most likely its founder (see 1:7; 4:12). Perhaps Epaphras was a convert of Paul. At least being so near to Ephesus he must have been in close touch with him.

III. Time of Composition

About A.D. 62 or 63 sometime during his first imprisonment (4:3, 7, 18).

IV. THE OCCASION OF THE WRITING

It was the communication to Paul of the state of the church at Colossae. The evil which threatened this church was an admixture of Judaic legalism and oriental mysticism (2:16-18) which may be called Gnosticism. This heresy was characterized by:

A. *A Claim to Superior Knowledge.*

Gnostics, good at knowing, sagacious—they were aristocrats in wisdom, exclusive in spirit.

B. *A Speculative Philosophy.*

It embraces the problems of Creation, evil, and angels. They contended that Creation was not by the supreme God since He could have nothing to do with matter which is inherently evil, but by angelic emanation from Him. They worshiped these emanations or aeons.

C. *Two Principles.*

Either a rigid asceticism because of matter being the abode of evil, or unrestrained licentiousness because of the inherent evil of matter —should not condescend to care for the evil.

The one saturated with these principles, when he became a Christian, would incorporate them with the principles of the Gospel and most grossly pervert them. These errorists were attempting to rob Christ of His deity and assign Him a place as mediator as one of the angelic emanations from God. These same principles widely prevail today and are threatening Christianity. We do well to attend to them in order to be ready to meet the heresies of the age in which we live.

Paul's method in this epistle is to assail these errors and place in opposition to them the true view of Jesus Christ in the dignity of His Person and mediatorial work.

D. *Some Phases of This Heresy As Applied to Man and to Christ.*

Man's spirit is derived from God, combined with a material body and animal soul. By this union the spirit was enslaved and defiled. Redemption means liberation from the body so as to re-enter the sphere of pure spirit. Christ was one of the higher Aeons come into the world. Different views of Christ:

1. Docetists (Docetae).

Christ was a phantom—seemed to be. His whole life was an illusion—no birth—no suffering.

2. Had a Real Body, but Not Material.

3. Two People.

Others, as the Corinthians, held that Jesus and Christ were distinct. Jesus was an ordinary man, son of Joseph and Mary. Christ came upon him at baptism and left him at the cross—the man Jesus —to suffer alone.

PART TWO—DETAILED OUTLINE

I. INTRODUCTION (1:1-14).

A. *The Salutation* (1:1, 2).

1. Paul's Designation of Himself.

"He was an apostle of Jesus Christ by the will of God." This position he occupied by the sovereign will of God or appointment of God.

2. Paul's Designation of Timothy—"the brother."

Beautiful Christian fellowship. No idea of a hierarchy.

3. Paul's Designation of the Christian Believers.

"The saints and faithful in Christ Jesus"—this is given to every believer regardless of the degree of sanctification. It is not because of merit, but because of being under the power of the blood of Christ.

4. Paul's Designation of the Christian's Gifts.

"Grace and peace"—grace issues in peace.

B. *The Thanksgiving* (1:3-8).

Thanksgiving is an important matter in the experience of every true believer. Yet how grossly neglected. Those who experience the peace which grace brings must answer God back. Grace causes the divine life to flow to us, and thanksgiving is merely its flow back to God—its Giver. Would that we were more abundant in its exercise.

1. To Whom He Gave Thanks.

"God and the Father of our Lord Jesus Christ"—this is the Gospel name of God. It shows that the God whom the Gnostics pushed far away from the experiences of men is now in touch with sinful man.

2. For Whom He Gave Thanks (1:2).

For the Colossians—this shows unselfish love of Paul.

3. For What He Gave Thanks.

a. Their faith in Christ—not only believed on Christ, but believed in Him.

b. Their love to the saints. This is a peculiar love—a love for the brotherhood (II Peter 1:7; Gal. 6:10; I Thess. 3:12).

c. Their hope of coming glory and consequent fruitfulness (vv. 5, 6). Their hope of the future made them active in the present.

C. *The Prayer in Their Behalf* (1:9-14).

1. For a Full Knowledge of God's Will (1:9).

This means more than a knowledge of the plan of salvation—the acquaintance with His Word and plans.

2. For a Walk Worthy of the Lord (1:10).

Increasing in the knowledge of God is the only worthy walk. A worthy walk is the practical result of a knowledge of God's Word.

3. For Strength To Joyfully Endure Suffering (1:11).

4. That They Might Be Thankful (1:12-14).

What are the blessings of redemption:

a. The inheritance of the saints in light (v. 12). This is an allotment on the ground of position by birth (I Peter 1:3, 4). "If children then heirs" (Rom. 8:17). This belongs to the saints. Who are saints? We should now live in the power of the truth.

b. Deliverance out of the power of darkness (v. 13). "Power of darkness" includes:

(1) Ignorance of God (I John 3:19).

(2) Gross sins (Rom. 3:12).

(3) Hatred (John 2:11).

(4) Out of fellowship with God (I John 1:6). This includes pride, envy, jealousy, secret sins, etc. Every believer has been delivered from the power of these.

c. Translation into the kingdom of His dear Son (v. 13). This was all accomplished in Christ (v. 14).

II. THE GLORY OF JESUS CHRIST THE SON (1:15-23).

A. *In His Relation to God* (1:15).

He images the invisible God. God is invisible save as manifested through the Son. To profess to know God while denying the Son is folly. He is not this merely in the Incarnation but is such in His eternal relation. Here at the very beginning Paul pulverizes the Gnostic heresy.

B. *In His Relation to Creation* (1:15-17).

1. Lordship over All Creation.

"First-born" suggests pre-eminence. (See Exod. 4:22; Ps. 89:27.)

2. By Him and for Him All Things Were Created (1:16).

He was not among created things—visible nor invisible.

3. He Antedates All Things (1:17).

4. He Is the Upholder of All Things (1:17).

All things consist or hold together by Him. He is the originating cause and upholding power of the whole Creation.

C. *In His Relation to the Church* (1:18).

1. He Is Its Head.

The One who created and upholds the whole universe is the Head of the Church. There is no conflict or contradiction between Creation and redemption. The Church is the Body of Christ, and as such it has organic unity. He is not only its governmental Head, but its vital Head. He thus sustains the same relationship to the Church that He does to Creation. This position was secured through the resurrection, being the "first born from the dead." He occupies this place as a fact. There was no resurrection before Him.

2. He Is Pre-eminent.

The design of this relation was that He might have the pre-eminence. He has the pre-eminence in Creation, in providence, and redemption. In Him all fullness dwells, i.e., in Him dwells the number, plentitude, and perfection of all the attributes of Deity.

D. *In His Work of Reconciliation* (1:20-23).

1. The Ground of His Blood (1:20).

The indwelling of the fullness of the Godhead in the Man Jesus, combined with His wondrous teaching was not sufficient. Blood must be shed because it was God's plan. His death was not by accident—though man had not touched Him—He would have died, for God caused our iniquities to strike upon Him. He was punished at the hand of God. The sinner sees the blood as the basis of God's just dealing with man.

2. The Scope or Extent of the Atonement (1:20, 21).

It is too vast to measure. It is not universal restoration of the alienated and enemies of God, but the demands of the Holy God have been met so that no sinner is beyond redemption.

3. The Means Of (1:22).

Through the body of His flesh—not as a sect of the Gnostics taught that Jesus suffered only in appearance.

4. The Evidence of Reconciliation (1:23).

Steadfastness in the faith.

III. THE MISSION OF PAUL (1:24—2:7).

A. *To Suffer* (1:24).

Suffering to fill up that which was lacking in the afflictions of Christ. What is meant? Christ's sufferings were threefold:

1. From God for sin.
2. From man for righteousness' sake.
3. From weariness, hunger, sorrow, etc. The second is doubtless the true view.

B. *To Reveal God's Mystery* (1:25-27).

What is a mystery? It is here the Church as the medium through which God's glorious purpose will be accomplished. This was peculiarly the truth which Paul was commissioned to make known. (See Rom. 16:25-27; I Cor. 2:7-10; Eph. 3:9, 10.) This Body was unknown until a special revelation was given. The salvation of the Gentile was a thing known, but the formation of a Body composed of Jews and Gentiles on an equality was the thing made known.

C. *To Preach Christ* (1:28—2:7).

(He preached Christ according to that mystery.) This He did by divine power; i.e., by the divine energy in working in Him, enabling Him to bear up under His arduous labors. Here we have set forth the work of the preacher.

1. He Did Not Preach Philosophy, Social Science, or Reform. He preached Christ crucified for sin, not Christ as a great teacher.

2. The Method or Process:

a A warning concerning:

(1) The errors of the times.
(2) The wiles of the Devil.
(3) The deceptions of one's own heart.

b. Teaching—a setting forth of the truth, etc.—much needed today.

3. The Object.

It was to present every man perfect in Christ. To get all the treasures of wisdom.

4. For Their Security Against Delusions (2:4).

5. For Their Stability and Order (2:5-7).

This was much enjoyed by Paul as he beheld it. Every member without self-will, humbly taking his place—no contention as to preeminence. This they did because they had received Christ—were rooted in Him by faith, resulting in being built up in Him. This is a beautiful picture of oneness in Christ.

IV. GRAVE PERILS WHICH THREATENED THE COLOSSIAN CHURCH (2:8-23).

A. *A Vain and Deceitful Philosophy* (2:8-15).

What is philosophy? It has a noble origin for it arose out of Pythagora's humility. He called himself the philosopher, the lover of wisdom. The world's philosophy is vain and empty because it rests upon the reasonings of men handed down on the principles which seem to prevail in a fallen world and is most unsafe. It requires a special revelation and this we have in Jesus Christ.

This warning is of perpetual importance because the proud intellect of man is constantly attempting to measure the facts of Christianity by the standards of human philosophy. The believer being in Christ in whom all the fullness of the Godhead dwells and Christ being in him is absolutely complete. There can be no possible need of human speculation, since all that is needed for poor lost man is provided in Christ, for those who abide in Him.

The believer has been brought into this relationship by a spiritual circumcision which is identification with Christ in death, burial, and resurrection, symbolized in baptism—faith being the bond of connection. This means identification with Christ in death or with His work or reconciliation and identification with His risen life.

This deceitful philosophy was like much that is called philosophy today—an attack upon the Person and dignity of Christ. It should be man's concern to square up his philosophy by God's revelation and not to bend God's revelation to his philosophy.

B. *Legalism* (2:16, 17).

1. As To Eating and Drinking (2:16; see I Tim. 4:1-3).

2. As To Observance of Holy Days (2:16).

This is the imposition of a sacred calendar. We should not allow ourselves to be called to account for these things.

C. *A False Mysticism—Worshiping of Angels* (2:18, 19).

These heretics were putting angels as intermediaries, persuading the people that a becoming humility demanded that Christ be considered as an angel and not as God. Christ should be held as the Head from which all the Body receives nourishment and increment with the increase of God.

D. *Asceticism* (2:20-23).

The root of sin is not in the body but in the soul. No afflictions of the body can ever eradicate sin. Much of the efforts of man today to curb sin by human enactments come under this warning, e.g., such as wearing badges, signing pledges, etc. God says, "Touch not," etc. All these things have a show of wisdom in will worship, humility, and severity to the body. Those dead in Christ need not submit to such things, to do so would be to violate their heavenly citizenship.

V. THE TRUE CHRISTIAN LIFE AS OPPOSED TO THEIR FALSE VIEWS (3:1—4:6).

A. *What It Is* (3:1-4).

1. It Is Union with Christ Through Death and Resurrection (3:1; 2:20).

The *if* of verse 1 is argumentative. Being set free from the bondage to commandments through death they are brought into captivity to Christ's authority through the power of His resurrection life.

2. It Is a Life.

The aspiration and desires of this life are set upon heavenly things; i.e., upon the empire of Christ in union with God, through whose administrations glorious victories shall be achieved. All who possess that life shall share that glory with Him, the vision of which inspires to holy activity. The ideal controls the man.

B. *How To Live It* (3:5-17; 4:6).

1. Mortify—Put to Death Earthly Members (3:5-7).
   a. Fornication
   b. Uncleanness
   c. Lustfulness (inordinate affection)
   d. Evil longings (concupiscence)
   e. Covetousness

Why should this last sin appear in this dark connection? The wrath of God is upon such.

2. Put Off the Sins of the Old Nature (3:8-11).
   a. Anger
   b. Wrath
   c. Malice
   d. Blasphemy (railing)
   e. Filthy communication (shameful speaking)
   f. Lying

These are all put off because the believer is vitally joined to Christ.

3. Put on the Graces of the New Man (3:12-14).

These are the triumphs of the new nature:

   a. Bowels of mercies—a heart of compassion.
   b. Kindness
   c. Humbleness of mind
   d. Meekness (submission to God).
   e. Long suffering
   f. Forbearing one another and forgiving
   g. Love, which is the bond of perfection or perfectness.

4. Let the Peace of God Rule in the Heart (3:15).
5. Be Thankful.
6. Let the Work of Christ Dwell Richly in You (3:16).

Teaching and admonishing and singing with graces.

7. Allow the Proper Spirit to Control all Actions (3:17).

C. *Right Behavior in All Relations in Life* (3:18—4:6).

1. In the Family (3:18-21).

Wives and husbands, children and fathers.

2. Servants and Masters (3:22; 4:1).

Prayer is the spirit in which all these duties should be performed (4:2-4).

3. Social Intercourse (4:5, 6).

D. *Personal Matters and Greetings* (4:7-18).

FIRST EPISTLE TO THE THESSALONIANS

PART ONE–INTRODUCTORY MATTERS

I. City of Thessalonica.

Thessalonica was one of the largest cities in Macedonia. It was a city of great commercial and political importance. Being situated on the Thermaic Gulf, an arm of the Aegean Sea, it commanded a large trade and thus became wealthy and brought to it a mixed population. Also, under the Romans, it was made the capital of one of the four districts of Macedonia, and was too a central station on the Egnatian Road which connected Rome with her eastern dependencies. It was thus fitted to become a radiating center of the Gospel. This explains 1:8. The name was given by Cassander in honor of his wife Thessalonica, a sister of Alexander the Great. This city has largely retained its importance and still retains its name in a modified form—Saloniki.

The church of Thessalonica was founded by Paul, assisted by Silas soon after their release from prison at Philippi on the second missionary journey. For a history of the founding of the church see Acts 17:1-9. The church here seems largely to have been composed of Gentiles (1:9, 10). Paul first spent three sabbaths reasoning with the Jews in the synagogue (Acts 17:2), but no doubt spent some time with the Gentiles (see I Thess. 2:9; II Thess. 3:8; Phil. 4:16). Supplies were sent "once and again" which would require some time as the distance from Philippi was about a hundred miles.

This epistle was written from Corinth after Timothy had returned from visiting the church. (See I Thess. 3:1, 2; Acts 18:5.) It is the earliest of Paul's writings—about A.D. 54.

II. Purpose (1:1, 2, 10).

The purpose of writing was to confirm these Christians in the things already taught them, to exhort them concerning purity of life and the necessity of working (4:1-4, 11); and to comfort them concerning their brethren who had died (4:13-15, 18).

III. THEME.

The apostle's method was to make all his teachings center in the second coming of Christ. Indeed this is the theme of both of his epistles to the Thessalonians as well as the central fact of his preaching at Thessalonica. (See Acts 17:7; cf. with the close of each chapter of I Thess., and this theme is mentioned in each of the chapters of the second epistle.) "The two epistles contain twenty distinct references to the second coming of Christ which is used as a comfort in bereavement, a motive to patience, an inspiration to hope, a security in temptation, a help to purity, a ground of rejoicing, a separating, sanctifying power"—Dr. A. T. Pierson.

PART TWO—DETAILED OUTLINE

I. INTRODUCTION (1:1-4).

A. *Salutation* (1:1).

From Paul, Silas, and Timothy. This does not mean that the three names are coauthors, but the co-workers known to the church of the Thessalonians. This is a fine example of Christian courtesy where the minister of superior rank confers honor upon fellow ministers of a lower rank. Note that the church of the Thessalonians was in God the Father and in the Lord Jesus Christ. The recognition of this truth will have a sobering effect upon the life of every believer. In this salutation Paul fittingly unites grace and peace. Grace is the fountain of peace.

B. *Thanksgiving* (1:2-4).

In his praying to God he mentioned a triad of graces which had been produced in these young Christians, showing for sure their election by God (vv. 3, 4). This trinity of graces was (*a*) "work of faith" (v. 3); (*b*) "labor of love," and (*c*) "patience of hope" (v. 3), made the complement of Christian character. There is such a thing as assurance of salvation. One's testimony must be backed by a consistent life.

II. THE INNER LIFE OF THE THESSALONIANS (1:5-10).

A. *Imitators of Paul and Christ* (1:6, 7).

Having received the Word of God in the power of the Holy Spirit they became imitators of Paul and the Lord that all the saints throughout Greece reaped blessings from their lives. Travelers passing from the Thessalonian church to other parts carried the news of what God had done for them so that Paul's preaching was unnecessary.

B. *They Became Missionaries* (1:8).

It was a missionary church. One who is really saved naturally has a burning desire to get others saved. The primary mission of the church is to evangelize the world. The church is a recruiting center from which evangelizing agents are sent forth and supported. To be a Christian means to be a missionary.

C. *They Were Models in Character* (1:7-9).

They were ensamples to the believers in Macedonia and Achaia. They turned to God from idols to serve the living and true God. This was the proof of their election of God.

D. *They Were Waiting for the Son from Heaven* (1:10).

The supreme, grand incentive for holy living and missionary endeavor is the hope of the second coming of Christ.

III. PAUL'S MINISTRY (2:1-16).

A. *The Nature of Paul's Ministry* (2:1-12).

Here is a portrayal of a model evangelist or minister. Where there is a model church there will usually be found a model preacher, "like people, like priest" (Hosea 4:9).

1. Courageous (2:2).

Still suffering from the treatment which he got at Philippi, he preached the Gospel at Thessalonica. He was bold in God—supernaturally helped. He stands out today as an example.

2. Persevering (2:2).

"With much contention"—striving as with a competitor.

3. Honest and Guileless (2:3).

"Unclean" refers to his motive.

4. Faithful (2:4).

He was a steward of God entrusted with the Gospel. This trust he regarded as sacred—his aim was to please God.

5. Kind and Affectionate (2:7, 8).

His kindness was as a nursing mother with her children. He worked at tent making so as not to be chargeable to them for support.

6. Irreproachable in Character (2:10).

A minister should so live that he can challenge his people to witness to his fidelity.

7. Paul's Fatherly Exhortation (2:11, 12).

This was for them to walk worthy of God.

B. *How His Ministry Was Received* (2:13-16).

1. As the Word of God (2:13).

2. Endured Suffering for the Gospel's Sake (2:14-16).

Paul thanks God for their willingness to suffer for Christ's sake. They proved their fidelity by willingness to endure the same treatment as the churches in Judea.

IV. PAUL'S SOLICITUDE FOR THE SAINTS AT THESSALONICA (2:17–3:13).

This is shown by:

A. *His Earnest Desire To See Them* (2:17-20).

He was taken violently from them. He was as a father bereft of his children. Satan hindered him. The word *hindered* means to cut a trench between oneself and an advancing foe to prevent his progress. The reasons for his earnest desire (vv. 19, 20).

B. *His Sending Timothy To Help and Comfort Them* (3:1-5).

In the midst of their afflictions there was danger of being moved from their faith.

C. *His Rejoicing over Their Good State* (3:6-9).

D. *His Prayer for Them* (3:10-13).

1. For Opportunity To Perfect Their Faith (3:10, 11).
2. For Increase in Love to One Another and to All Men (3:12).
3. To Establish Their Hearts (3:13).

The purpose was that their hearts might be established unblamable at the coming of Christ.

V. SINS REBUKED AND DUTIES ENJOINED (4:1-12).

A. *Fornication* (4:1-8).

This sin includes all sorts of uncleanness in the single as well as in the married state. This sin was common then as now among the heathen. The man's duty is to give the right respect and treatment to his own wife. The one who defrauds his brother in improper conduct with the brother's wife shall be avenged by the Lord at His coming (v. 6).

B. *Duty of Brotherly Love* (4:9, 10).

Love is so important that he urges that it abound—not only love for the brethren, but for all men. Love is the paramount gift of the Holy Spirit (I Cor. 13:1-8). The vulnerable point in our lives is the lack of love.

C. *Disquietude* (4:11).

Paul urges them to study to be quiet—not be stirring up strife causing party division. Many Christians are evangelical in their doctrinal views, upright in their character, but have not a peaceable and quiet behavior. This tends to unhappiness of oneself and those about us. Better confess this to God as sin rather than call it "righteous indignation."

D. *Meddling in Others' Affairs* (4:11).

Those who have the factional spirit are generally busybodies.

E. *Idleness* (4:11).

Idlers are likely to be restless and meddle in others' affairs and tattlers.

Conviction concerning the imminency of the coming of the Lord is the most effective cure for the aforementioned sins. "Watch" (Matt. 24:42); "serve . . . God" (I Thess. 1:9, 10); occupy (Luke 19:30); fidelity (I Tim. 6:14). Work with one's own hands is man's obligation imposed by God. Man should work to pay his debts and also to provide for the future that he be not dependent upon others. "If any man would not work, neither should he eat" (II Thess. 3:10). The crowning sin of this generation is to get on without working.

VI. Doctrinal Error (4:13-18).

This concerns the relation of the dead and the living saints at the second coming of the Lord.

As we saw in stating the theme of this epistle, Paul strongly stressed the second coming of Christ and the glory to the believer which would issue therefrom. Time passed and some died without seeing Christ or partaking of His glory. The friends and relatives of those who died were in great sorrow thinking that the dead would be at a great disadvantage when the Lord came. Paul in meeting this situation states in the most comprehensive and the clearest manner the relation of the dead and living believers at the second coming of Christ. In order to relieve their sorrows he gives them the following instructions:

A. *The Dead in Christ Shall Rise First* (4:16).

The living shall not precede them which are asleep (vv. 15, 16).

B. *Jesus Will Bring the Dead Saints with Him* (4:14).

At death the person of the saint goes immediately to be with Christ which Paul says is far better than to be here in the body (Phil. 1:23).

C. *The Translation of the Living Saints Shall Follow* (4:17, 18).

The living shall be caught up with the resurrected dead to be forever with the Lord. Paul says that this information was given him by the Word of the Lord (v. 15). Wonderful words are these! All controversy on this subject ends with them.

VII. Proper Walk in Light of the Day of the Lord (5:1-11).

A. *Conditions in the World When Christ Returns* (5:1-3).

Paul tells them that it is useless for him to write them anything concerning the times and seasons because they knew perfectly well that the Lord cometh as a thief in the night (v. 2). As Paul delivered to them the things which he had received of Christ (I Cor. 11:23), he was explicit in giving them what Christ had taught; viz., "of that day and hour knoweth no man, no, not the angels of heaven, but my Father only" (Matt. 24:36).

Some are extremely unwise as to say *when* this event shall take place, thereby bringing this glorious doctrine into disrepute and causing men's minds to be prejudiced so as to prevent them from giving serious attention to them. In the face of what Christ has so definitely taught concerning this matter, it is a flagrant presumption or consummate ignorance for anyone to set a time for this event.

While some are making the blunder of setting a time, others are doing even worse by ignoring it entirely. "When they shall say, Peace and safety; then sudden destruction shall come upon them" (v. 3). As far as we know Christ may come for His Church today. Watch, "for in such an hour as ye think not the Son of man cometh" (Matt. 24:44).

B. *The Church Should Not Be Taken Unawares* (5:4-11).

To prevent this the Church should be wide awake concerning the doctrine of the Lord's coming. Christ is the hope of the world.

Wrath awaits the world in that day, while salvation in the fullest sense awaits the Church. Whether alive on the earth when Christ comes or asleep in death and therefore come with Him, we shall live with Him forever.

VIII. CONCLUDING EXHORTATION (5:12-28).

A. *Proper Esteem for Ministers* (5:12, 13).

Due consideration should be given to the minister—that he has been set aside by the Lord for a specific work. He is to be highly esteemed in love for his work's sake.

B. *Duty of Ministers* (5:14-22).

1. Warn the Unruly.
2. Comfort the Feeble-minded.
3. Support the Weak.
4. Patient Toward All Men.
5. Render Not Evil for Evil.
6. Rejoice Evermore.
7. Pray Without Ceasing.
8. Thankful for Everything.
9. Quench Not the Spirit.
10. Despise Not Prophesyings.
11. Cling to That Which Proves To Be Good.
12. Abstain from All Appearance of Evil.

C. *Prayer for Them—Their Entire Sanctification* (5:23).

D. *Request for Prayer* (5:25).

E. *Benediction* (5:28).

SECOND EPISTLE TO THE THESSALONIANS

PART ONE–INTRODUCTORY MATTERS

This epistle was written by Paul shortly after he wrote I Thessalonians and for a similar reason (Acts 17:5-9; cf. I Thess. 1:10). These verses show that Paul preached the second coming of Christ. The people were in error concerning the relation of the living and dead at Christ's coming, which was cleared up in I Thessalonians 4:13–5:12. But another error emerged from the same source, which was fostered by false teachers. These had even forged a letter in Paul's name, saying that the Day of Christ ("Day of the Lord") had already come. This alarmed many, tending to lead them astray (II Thess. 2:1, 2). To meet this need Paul wrote this epistle.

PART TWO–DETAILED OUTLINE

I. Salutation (1:1, 2).

Paul unites names of his missionary companions with his own in his prayer for grace and peace to be given to the Thessalonian believers. They are "in God the Father and in the Lord Jesus Christ." Conditions in the church had not improved. Misunderstanding as to the time of Christ's second coming had become even more serious. Expectation of the immediate return of Christ had led some to live in idleness and disorder. Persecution of the church had increased. The uniting of the names of his companions does not imply that they are coauthors of the epistle. He wishes to show courtesy to his companions and thus strengthen his message by showing that these companions know and endorse what the letter contains and were dear to the hearts of the Thessalonians. Both Silas and Timothy were prominent and respected.

II. THANKSGIVING (1:3, 4).

A. *For Their Growing Faith and Abounding Brotherly Love* (1:3).

B. *For Their Patience and Fidelity in the Midst of Severe Persecutions and Tribulations* (1:4).

III. COMFORT IN PERSECUTION (1:5-12).

A. *It Is a Token of Honor To Suffer for Christ's Sake* (1:5, 6).

B. *The Wicked Persecutors Shall Be Punished* (1:7-10).

"The Lord Jesus shall be revealed from Heaven with His mighty angels in flaming fire taking vengeance on them that know not God and obey not the Gospel of our Lord Jesus Christ, who shall be punished with everlasting destruction from the presence of the Lord, and from the glory of His power; when He shall come to be glorified in His saints and to be admired in all them that believe in that day." Dr. James M. Gray says in *Christian Worker's Commentary:* "But the 'day' Paul now has in mind does not synchronize precisely with the coming of the Lord for His Church as taught in I Thessalonians 4:13-18. In other words, to rehearse what has been taught in other parts of this Commentary, the second coming of Christ is an act of two scenes. There is a 'coming' for His Church when the latter shall be caught up to meet Him in the air, and then, after an interval, how long or short it is impossible to say, there is a 'coming' or a 'revelation' in judgment on the unbelieving and wicked nations of Christendom, that are left behind. It is this latter aspect of the second coming, that associated with judgment, which the Old Testament prophets are ever speaking of as 'The Day of the Lord.' They say nothing about His coming for His Church, as indeed they say nothing about the Church, but focus their attention upon the end of the age, when only Israel and the Gentile nations will be on the earth and the Church shall have been taken away.

"That Paul is speaking of this here is indicated in verses 7-10. The Lord Jesus will be 'revealed from heaven with the angels of His power' (R.V.), 'rendering vengeance.' This shall take the form of 'everlasting destruction from the face of the Lord and from the glory of His power.' This is not annihilation, it is well to observe, but conscious separation from Him. And the time it will take place is 'when he shall have come to be glorified in his saints' (v. 10). The Greek second aorist is used here, indicating that the event spoken of, the glorifying of Christ in His saints shall have taken place. In other words, it is after the translation of the Church, as we understand it, that 'the Day of the Lord' is ushered in with its attendant judgments."

C. *Those Who Suffer for Christ's Sake Shall Be Rewarded* (1:11).

D. *Paul's Prayer for Them* (1:11-12).

To know that Paul was praying for them no doubt encouraged them to be faithful.

IV. THE REVELATION OF THE MAN OF SIN (2:1-12).

Who he is. He is a Devil-filled man—the strong enemy of God and all good.

A. *The Names and Titles Given Him.*

"Man of sin" one of whom sin is the distinguishing feature, in and out, is *sin*. "The son of perdition." He not only leads others to perdition but perdition is his heritage and destiny. He "opposeth and exalteth himself against all that is called God or is worshiped." He is God's foe and antagonist. He is the Antichrist spoken of by John as "denying the Father and the Son" (I John 2:22).

B. *The Amazing Powers Ascribed to Him.*

"His coming is after the working of Satan with all power and signs and lying wonders and with all deceit of unrighteousness."

C. *The Conditions Prevailing at the Time of the Appearing of the Man of Sin.*

1. Apostasy—"a falling away."

This means a defection from the truth of God and from the faith of Christ.

2. A Restraining Influence (2:7).

Just what this means we do not know for sure; most likely it means the restraining influence exerted by the Holy Spirit through the Church. When the Church is called away at the second coming of

Christ, the restraining influence will be removed, and the man of sin will be revealed.

D. *The Doom of the Man of Sin.*

He will be destroyed by the Lord Jesus Christ "whom the Lord shall consume with the spirit of his mouth and shall destroy with the brightness of his coming" (2:8; cf. Isa. 11:4).

It is exceedingly important that distinction be made between Christ's coming for His Church (I Thess. 4:16, 17), and His coming to judge the wicked world (II Thess. 1:8, 9). In chapter 2 we have the reference to false teachers and their teaching. The first two verses should be read in the Revised Version which brings out the meaning clearer, for what the false teachers said was, that "The Day of the Lord *is now present.*" Therefore what the apostle announces to take place before that "Day" comes, does not apply to the coming of Christ for His Church (an advent which, so far as we know, may be very near), but on the ungodly after the Church has been taken away. Such is the significance of verses 3 and 4.

That which is to take place is: (*a*) "a falling away," an apostasy in Christendom, and (*b*), the revelation of "the man of sin" (or lawlessness). This "man of sin," who was foretold by Daniel, by Zechariah, and by Christ Himself as we have seen, is described as opposing and exalting himself against "all that is called God," in the sense that he gives out that he himself is God, and men are ready to believe him. "The temple of God" (v. 4), as we have seen (Dan. 9; Matt. 24), is the Jewish Temple re-erected in Jerusalem, for the Jews are to return there, at first in an unconverted state so far as the acceptance of Jesus as their Messiah is concerned.

The apostle had informed the Thessalonians of these things when he was with them (v. 5), and furthermore that a restraining power was holding back the full development of this man of sin until his time came (v. 6). Just what this power is we are left to conjecture, but doubtless it is the Holy Spirit who dwells in the Church. Imagine the Church translated out of the earth, and the ascent of the Holy Spirit in consequence, and what restraining power would be left to hold back the hordes of wickedness in the earth, and prevent Satan from having his way in the full development of the man of sin? The doom of the latter is given in verse 8, and an added description follows in verses 9 and 10. Satan gives him his power, but he is able to deceive only those who "received not the love of the truth" (v. 10). The truth was revealed to them and rejected, for which reason that moral and spiritual weakness, which made them a prey to the delusion, fell upon them as a divine judgment (vv. 11, 12). There is a solemn warning here for those who are being tempted by Spiritualism, The New Thought, Christian Science, and kindred teachings.

V. CONCLUDING INSTRUCTIONS (3:1-18).

A. *Requests for Prayer* (3:1-4).

1. That the Word of the Lord May Have Free Course and Be Glorified.

The humblest believer can have a part in evangelism by praying for the minister who preaches the Word. This can be done by the housewife or mother as she goes about her household duties.

2. That Paul and His Fellow Missionaries May Be Delivered from Unreasonable and Wicked Men (3:2).

This is a much-needed ministry, for not all men "have the faith."

B. *Paul Prays That the Lord Would Direct Their Hearts into the Love of God and into the Patient Waiting for Christ* (3:5).

C. *Commands Separation* (3:6-15).

In the name of the Lord Jesus Christ Paul commands that there be withdrawal from every brother that walketh disorderly. A case of disorderly walk was idleness—not working to earn one's bread. Paul commanded that "if any man would not work, neither should he eat" (v. 10). This command was endorsed by his own personal example. He wrought with labor and travail night and day, that he might not be chargeable to any of them (vv. 8, 9). Eating without working to earn one's food is immoral not only because it robs others, but gives opportunity to spend time as busybodies. Paul commanded and exhorted by the Lord Jesus Christ that with quietness they work and eat their own bread (v. 12). One of the reasons for the youth problem is that teen-agers are not required to work to help in their support. God said to Adam, "Cursed is the ground for thy sake . . . thorns and thistles shall it bring forth to thee. . . . In the sweat of thy face shalt thou eat bread, till thou return to the ground"

(Gen. 3:17-19). A part of the nurture of the child should be working for a living. Even in our generation we were taught the maxim "an idle brain is the Devil's workshop."

D. *The Benediction* (3:16-18).

"Now the Lord of peace give you peace always by all means. The Lord be with you all."

Note the token of validity was the salutation in his own hand. This would enable the people to know the genuineness of the letter.

FIRST EPISTLE TO TIMOTHY

PART ONE—INTRODUCTORY MATTERS

PASTORAL EPISTLES is the title given to I and II Timothy and Titus because they were addressed to men in charge of the flock. They have become the inspired counsel and directions for the church through the centuries of church history.

I. PERSONAL HISTORY OF TIMOTHY.

He was an inhabitant of Lystra, a native of the province of Iconium (Acts 16:2). He was converted under the preaching of Paul, no doubt during his first missionary journey (Acts 14:6-7; 16:1). The Gospel seed fell upon well-prepared soil (II Tim. 1:5; 3:14, 15). He had been carefully trained in the Scriptures from a child by a godly mother and grandmother. Something can be expected from preaching under such circumstances. He was of mixed parentage—his mother was a Jewess and his father a Greek (Acts 16:1). It was on Paul's second missionary journey that he was chosen as a fellow helper in the Gospel with Paul. From this time on till Paul's death Timothy was his almost constant companion.

II. PURPOSE OF THE BOOK.

The purpose of these writings is seen from the nature of their content—to guide and to encourage Timothy in his pastoral duties. Peculiar dangers were threatening the church. The Jewish teachers were busy with their effort to subvert the faith of the Christians. Many were the duties resting upon Timothy as a pastor. These will emerge as we go on with our study of this epistle. These epistles contain the only inspired instructions for the guidance of the pastor in existence today. Happily they set forth principles which are adequate for the needs of the twentieth century as well as they did for the first century. The same problems are here, perhaps with some added complexity. Every pastor should have a thorough course in pastoral theology and no course is adequate which lacks the mastery of the Pastoral Epistles.

PART TWO—DETAILED OUTLINE

I. Apostolic Salutation (1:1, 2).

Note the two remarkable designations in this greeting. He calls himself an apostle of Jesus Christ by the commandment of God our Saviour and Lord Jesus Christ which is our hope (v. 1). He is our hope, not something which He is going to do for us. Then the designation given to Timothy (v. 2): "My own son in the faith." This reminded Timothy that his salvation was due to hearing the Gospel preached by Paul. He invokes "grace, mercy and peace" upon Timothy. "Grace" denotes the divine favor as the source of his salvation. "Peace" is the experience of the soul in harmony with "God," and "mercy" shows the compassion of God of the unmerited salvation.

II. Timothy's Mission at Ephesus (1:3-11).

Paul besought Timothy to remain at Ephesus and charged him to put a stop to the false teaching, to warn certain men of their ignorance and perversions of the Gospel and to teach them of the true nature and purpose of the Law and its relation to the Gospel. Similar conditions exist today in our churches, especially the confusion of Law and grace. The Law was not made to save sinners nor to rule saints. By the Law is the knowledge of sin, salvation is by the glorious Gospel of the blessed God.

III. Paul an Example of God's Grace (1:12-17).

God's calling of a blasphemer to preach the Gospel gave Timothy hope, for if God's grace could save and transform such a notorious sinner as was Paul, there was hope for the worst among men.

IV. Timothy Charged To Be Faithful (1:18-20).

Paul exhorts him to wage a good warfare and warns him by the example of some who made shipwreck of their faith.

V. PUBLIC WORSHIP—Its Order and Regulations (2:1-15).

A. *Prayer* (2:1-7).

1. Duty of Prayer (2:1).

Prayer should be given a place of pre-eminence in right church life. The church's supreme mission is the preaching of the Gospel. A sound testimony can only be maintained by a praying church. Prayer both public and private is the expression of the life of the church.

2. Scope of Prayer (2:1-7).

For all men—especially those in authority over us—"that we may lead a peaceable and quiet life in all godliness and honesty." The reason for praying for all men is that God "will have all men to be saved and come into the knowledge of the truth." For there is one God—one Mediator who gave Himself a ransom for all. Christ is the medium of all acceptable prayer.

B. *Demeanor of Men and Women in Public Worship* (2:8-15).

1. Men (2:8).

a. To pray everywhere.

b. To lift up holy hands without wrath and doubting. Prayer is hollow mockery if not backed by holiness of life.

2. Women (2:9-11).

a. The women are to appear in the church in modest apparel with shamefacedness and sobriety. "Like manner" means that the women also should show by their lives the integrity of the hearts. The mentioning of men first implies that men should be leaders in public worship.

b. Teaching with authority is denied to the woman (v. 12). This prohibition does not apply to the millions of godly women who are giving their lives by testimony to salvation by faith in the redemption through the blood of Christ. As examples of how women may be teachers see II Timothy 3:14; Titus 2:3, and the several references to the women who had labored with him in the Gospel.

c. Reasons given (vv. 13, 14).

(1) Order of Creation (v. 14).

(2) Eve's place in the fall of man (v. 14).

(3) Promise to the woman (v. 15).

By carefully performing her home duties in contrast to public teaching she shall be preserved "saved" in spite of her trials and sorrows: then, too, in the Incarnation of Christ the Redeemer-Saviour. Woman does not earn salvation through childbearing, but is saved like any other sinner through faith in the finished work of Christ.

VI. CHURCH OFFICERS (3:1-13).

The officers of the apostolic church consisted of ministers and deacons and perhaps deaconesses.

A. *The Minister* (3:1-7).

The minister was known as elder or bishop. Two Greek words appear for the minister: *presbuteros,* meaning "elder," and *episcopos* meaning overseer. The word *elder* or *presbyter* referred to the rank and dignity of the minister; the word *bishop* to the minister's function or duty. "And from Miletus he sent to Ephesus, and called the elders of the church. . . . Take heed therefore unto yourselves, and to all the flock, over the which the Holy Ghost hath made you overseers, to feed the church of God, which he hath purchased with his own blood" (Acts 20:17, 28). "Paul and Timotheus, the servants of Jesus Christ, to all the saints in Christ Jesus which are at Philippi, with the bishops and deacons" (Phil. 1:1). "This is a true saying, If a man desire the office of a bishop, he desireth a good work" (I Tim. 3:1). "For this cause left I thee in Crete, that thou shouldest set in order the things that are wanting, and ordain elders in every city, as I had appointed thee. . . . For a bishop must be blameless, as the steward of God; not self-willed, not soon angry, not given to wine, no striker, not given to filthy lucre" (Titus 1:5, 7). "The elders which are among you I exhort, who am also an elder, and a witness of the sufferings of Christ, and also a partaker of the glory that shall be revealed: feed the flock of God which is among you, taking the oversight thereof, not by constraint, but willingly; not for filthy lucre, but of a ready mind" (I Peter 5:1, 2).

It is evident that when an overseer was desired for the church, the members of the church chose one from among the elders. The number of ministers in a given church was determined by the conditions in the church. A man became an elder by ordination. All men ordained to the Christian ministry are of equal rank. There is absent from the Scriptures records or traces of a hierarchy.

1. Ordination.

The ordination of ministers seems to have consisted in setting apart those divinely called to the work of ministering in the church. "Now there were in the church that was at Antioch certain prophets and teachers, as Barnabas, and Simeon that was called Niger, and Lucius of Cyrene, and Manaen, which had been brought up with Herod the tetrarch, and Saul. As they ministered to the Lord, and fasted, the Holy Ghost said, Separate me Barnabas and Saul for the work whereunto I have called them" (Acts 13:1, 2). "For though I preach the gospel, I have nothing to glory of: for necessity is laid upon me; yea, woe is unto me, if I preach not the gospel" (I Cor. 9:16). "And I thank Christ Jesus our Lord, who hath enabled me, for that he counted me faithful, putting me into the ministry" (I Tim. 1:12). The individual must have a definite conviction that he is called by God. The part that the church had in the ordination was simply to recognize the Lord's hand in calling the individual and to give recognition to the fact of the Lord's call. The church must have definite assurance of the reality of the divine call before proceeding with the ordination.

2. Qualifications of the Minister.

"This is a true saying, If a man desire the office of a bishop, he desireth a good work. A bishop then must be blameless, the husband of one wife, vigilant, sober, of good behavior, given to hospitality, apt to teach; not given to wine, no striker, not greedy of filthy lucre; but patient, not a brawler, not covetous; one that ruleth well his own house, having his children in subjection with all gravity; (for if a man know not how to rule his own house, how shall he take care of the church of God?) not a novice, lest being lifted up with pride he fall into the condemnation of the devil. Moreover he must have a good report of them which are without; lest he fall into reproach and the snare of the devil" (I Tim. 3:1-7). The characteristics set forth in this Scripture constitute the qualifications of the minister.

a. He must be without reproach, that is, blameless.

b. A husband of one wife. No one should be set to rule over a church who is a polygamist.

c. Vigilant. The overseer of the church must be a man of proper alertness. He must give himself with all his capacity to the care of the congregation.

d. Apt to teach. A large part of a minister's duties is teaching the members of his flock the truths of God's Word. The one who lacks teaching ability is manifestly disqualified as an overseer.

e. Temperate, not given to wine. The minister's example must be such as will be helpful to the members of his flock.

f. He is to be no striker. The minister is frequently misunderstood, misjudged, and even persecuted. He must be free from vindictiveness such as would cause him to strike back.

g. Not greedy of filthy lucre. An overseer of the church must not be covetous, grasping after money.

h. He must rule well his own home. The one who is set to be the overseer of a congregation must demonstrate his ability by having his own family under proper discipline.

i. Must have a good reputation from without. The minister should be recognized in the community as a man of integrity in his speech and in his dealing with both the saved and unsaved.

3. The Duties of the Minister.

a. He is to instruct the members of the church in Christian truth. "And how I kept back nothing that was profitable unto you, but have showed you, and have taught you publicly, and from house to house, testifying both to the Jews, and also to the Greeks, repentance toward God, and faith toward our Lord Jesus Christ. . . . Therefore watch, and remember, that by the space of three years I ceased not to warn everyone night and day with tears" (Acts 20:20, 21, 31). "And we beseech you, brethren, to know them which labor among you, and are over you in the Lord, and admonish you" (I Thess. 5:12). "Remember them which have the rule over you, who have spoken unto you the word of God: whose faith follow, considering the end of their conversation. . . . Obey them that have the rule over you, and submit yourselves: for they watch for your souls, as they that must give account, that they may do it with joy, and not with grief: for that is unprofitable for you" (Heb. 13:7, 17). The minister carries the responsibility of instructing his people in the ways of Christian truth. Solemn obligation rests upon him to study to show himself approved of God, rightly dividing the Word of truth. False teaching is widely prevalent. Error is crowding upon believers on every hand. The minister must be capable of setting forth the truths of the Bible so that believers may not only be strong in their own lives, but able to give a proper testimony to others.

b. He is to administer the ordinances of the church. "Go ye therefore, and teach all nations, baptizing them in the name of the Father, and of the Son, and of the Holy Ghost: teaching them to observe all things whatsoever I have commanded you: and, lo, I am with you alway, even unto the end of the world. Amen" (Matt. 28:19, 20). As people are taught the Word of God, it is expected that they will confess the Lord Jesus Christ as Saviour. It is, therefore, the duty of the minister to be able to administer intelligently the rites of Christian baptism and communion to them.

c. He is to administer discipline and execute government. "For if a man know not how to rule his own house, how shall he take care of the church of God?" (I Tim. 3:5). "Let the elders that rule well be counted worthy of double honor, especially they who labor in the word and doctrine" (I Tim. 5:17). "Feed the flock of God which is among you, taking the oversight thereof, not by constraint, but willingly; not for filthy lucre, but of a ready mind; neither as being lords over God's heritage, but being ensamples to the flock" (I Peter 5:2, 3). There is great need for a pastor to present the truths of God's Word to bear upon the daily living of the members and also to execute the matters of government. This is a matter of great importance in the church.

B. *The Deacons* (3:8-13).

The word translated "deacon" in our Bibles means a servant, a messenger. This title was given to New Testament officers who were appointed to serve, having especially the care of the benevolences of the church. "Then the twelve called the multitude of the disciples unto them, and said, It is not reason that we should leave the word of God, and serve tables. Wherefore, brethren, look ye out among you seven men of honest report, full of the Holy Ghost and wisdom, whom we may appoint over this business" (Acts 6:2, 3). Later in the life of the church there may have been women set apart to perform certain services who were called deaconesses.

1. Qualifications of the Deacon.

"Likewise must the deacons be grave, not doubletongued, not given to much wine, not greedy of filthy lucre; holding the mystery of the faith in a pure conscience. And let these also first be proved; then let them use the office of a deacon, being found blameless. Even so must their wives be grave, not slanderers, sober, faithful in all things. Let the deacons be the husbands of one wife, ruling their children and their own houses well. For they that have used the office of a deacon well purchase to themselves a good degree, and great boldness in the faith which is in Christ Jesus" (I Tim. 3:8-13). The qualifications of the deacon correspond to those of the minister. It is therefore unnecessary to repeat them.

2. The Duty of the Deacon.

The temporal interests of the church were administered by the deacons. "And in those days when the number of the disciples were multiplied, there arose a murmuring of the Grecians against the Hebrews, because their widows were neglected in the daily ministration. Then the twelve called the multitude of the disciples unto them, and said, It is not reason that we should leave the word of God, and serve tables. Wherefore, brethren look ye out among you seven men of honest report, full of the Holy Ghost and wisdom, whom we may appoint over this business. But we will give ourselves continually to prayer, and to the ministry of the word" (Acts 6:1-4). The deacons were to look after the poor and the needy particularly. They thus constituted a vital bond between the people and their minister.

VII. THE TRUE DIGNITY OF THE CHURCH (3:14-16).

Paul wrote Timothy of his purpose to shortly pay him a visit, but he recognized that there was the possibility of a long delay, hence he set forth to him the high importance of his charge by showing the true dignity of the church. The fidelity of the true minister is measured by the degree of his apprehension of the worth of that with which he has to do.

A. *The Church is:*

1. The Family of God.

The house of God means the household or family of God. God the Father is the Head. The believers are bound together and to God by the bonds of love. How could there be strife in such a household?

2. "The Church of the Living God."

This implies that the church is not a human institution and therefore must be governed by the divine will.

3. "The Pillar and Ground of the truth."

A pillar is something that supports a roof or foundation. So the society of believers is divinely appointed to sustain in the world the truth which God has revealed to man. This revelation is called a "mystery," which means truth undiscovered by human reason made known by revelation. When a mystery is revealed, it is not mysterious but open and plain.

B. *Mystery Revealed.*

This revealed truth which must be supported by the church centers in the Incarnation of God in Christ (v. 16). This "mystery" Paul calls "great" because of its importance. Furthermore, it is "without controversy," i.e., it is beyond question or doubt. The mystery centers in the Person, the Lord Jesus Christ. This Person was manifest in the flesh, justified in the Spirit, seen of angels, preached unto the nations or Gentiles, believed on in the world, received up into glory. What a responsibility! What a high privilege!

VIII. PROPHECY CONCERNING APOSTASY IN THE LATTER TIMES (4:1-5).

This apostasy is within the church, propagated by false teachers. This false teaching is expressed in:

A. *Forbidding to Marry.*

B. *Commanding to Abstain from Meats.*

There is not much improvement in this age.

IX. TIMOTHY'S OBLIGATION IN VIEW OF SUCH CONDITIONS (4:6-16).

A. *Put the Brethren in Remembrance of These Things* (4:6).

B. *Shun Profane and Old Wives' Fables* (4:7).

C. *Exercise Himself to Godliness* (4:7-11).

D. *Don't Be Intimidated Because of Youth* (4:12).

E. *Be an Example* (4:12).

F. *Personal Directions* (4:13-16).

1. Give attention To Reading of the Scriptures in the Public Assembly (4:13).

2. To Exhortation (4:13).

3. To Doctrine (4:13).

4. Neglect Not the Gift That Is in Thee (4:14).

5. Meditate upon These Things—Digest Them (4:15).

6. Give Thyself Wholly to Them (4:15).

7. Take Heed to Thyself and to the Doctrine (4:16).

8. Continue in Them—To Save Thyself and Them That Hear Thee (4:16).

X. PROPER DEALING WITH VARIOUS CLASSES IN THE CHURCH (5:1—6:21).

A. *Old and Young Men* (5:1).

B. *Old and Young Women* (5:2).

C. *Widows* (5:3-16).

1. Honor Widows That Are Such Indeed (5:3).

2. Those Who Have Children or Nephews Are To Be Cared for by Them (5:4).

3. Occupation of the Widows Who Are Supported by the Church (5:5, 6).

4. Care for One's Family (5:8).

5. Who Are To Receive the Church's Care (5:9, 10).

6. Widows Not To Be Chargeable to the Church (5:11-16).

D. *Ministers* (5:17-22).

1. Elders Who Rule Well Are Worthy of Double Honor (5:17, 18).

2. Accusations Against an Elder.

These should not be entertained unless or except as properly supported by proper witnesses.

3. Openly Rebuke Those Who Sin Openly (5:20).

4. Not To Show Partiality in Dealing with Them (5:21).

5. Be Cautious in Ordaining Elders (5:22).

E. *Personal Duties* (5:23-25).

Timothy was advised to take care of his health. Wine has certain medicinal qualities, Paul advises a little wine for his stomach's sake.

F. *Servants* (6:1, 2).

Servants here mean bondslaves. At this time slavery as an institution was universal throughout the Roman Empire. Slaves were to honor their masters. The master who is a Christian should be regarded as a brother. Christianity is the cure for slavery.

G. *False Teachers Denounced* (6:3-5).

H. *Christian's Attitude Toward Riches* (6:6-10).

I. *Faithfulness Enjoined* (6:11-21).

SECOND EPISTLE TO TIMOTHY

PART ONE—INTRODUCTORY MATTERS

SO FAR AS IS KNOWN this was Paul's last letter. His state has considerably worsened. During his first imprisonment he was accorded considerable liberty—lived in his own hired house—freely mingled with his friends and had some freedom in directing the missionary activities of the church. In his second imprisonment he is an old man chained in a dark dungeon suffering with cold, forsaken by many of his friends and missionary associates. "Only Luke is with me" (v. 11). Perhaps Paul was dictating this farewell message to Luke.

For Timothy as well as Paul, this was a time of testing and discouragement. By Paul's appointment he was pastor of the church at Ephesus. This was a difficult field. False teachers within the church were seeking to corrupt the true Christian doctrine. From without persecutions by bitter enemies were threatening the very existence of the church. Added to this are the atrocious cruelties of the wicked Nero who set fire to Rome and turned suspicion against the Christians as guilty of this crime. This intensified the hatred of the people for the Christians.

This letter to Timothy must have greatly encouraged him. It was the most personal and intensely emotional of all Paul's letters.

Written from Rome about A.D. 67 shortly before Paul's martyrdom.

PART TWO—DETAILED OUTLINE

I. THE INTRODUCTION (1:1-5).

A. *The Salutation* (1:1, 2).

The persons concerned are Paul and Timothy. Paul was now an old man (Phile. 9), languishing in prison, but conscious of his responsibility to the churches which he founded calls himself "an apostle of Jesus Christ" to remind Timothy of his authority, as one sent of Christ. Timothy was a young man in a responsible position, the pastor of the church at Ephesus. Paul calls him "my dearly beloved son" (v. 1), "my own son in the faith" (I Tim. 1:2; 2:22). "As a son with the father he has served with me in the gospel." It was through Paul's ministry, that Timothy was led to Christ. Paul's salutation was a great prayer for Timothy—"grace," "mercy," and "peace"; grace for every service, mercy for every failure; and peace for every circumstance. How greatly Timothy would need them all!

B. *The Thanksgiving* (1:3-5).

For Timothy's genuine faith (1:3-5). Note the dignity placed upon home training. He had motherly and grandmotherly influences brought to bear upon his life. Paul never forgot Timothy's tears of affection shed at Paul's parting from him. Paul expresses the preciousness and the pricelessness of Christian fellowship. Would that Christians would prize more highly the values of the communion of the saints!

II. BOLDNESS IN TESTIMONY ENJOINED (1:6-18).

The gift—which had been given him—is to be stirred up. Perhaps Timothy was somewhat timid—almost shrinking from duty for fear. Spiritual gifts are distributed by the sovereign will of the Holy Spirit (I Cor. 12:11), but the exercise is controlled by the individual possessing them. Timothy is reminded of his ordination hour and assured that God has given, not the spirit of fear, but of "power and of love, and of a sound mind" (v. 7). Many ministers, Sunday school teachers and missionaries today need to "stir up," rekindle, fan into a flame the gifts that are in them.

A. *Because of What Christ Has Done* (1:6-10).

Christ has saved us, called us, abolished death and brought immortality to light through the Gospel. The only hope of the world centers in the Gospel. What an incentive this is to the preaching of the Gospel! "It is the power of God unto salvation" (Rom. 1:16).

B. *Because of Paul's Sufferings* (1:11-14).

Paul knew that the Gospel was God's only way of salvation and that God had appointed him to be a preacher of it and a teacher of the Gentiles. He knew that his awful sufferings were due to his obedience to God's call to preach the Gospel. He said: "I am not ashamed: for I know whom I have believed, and am persuaded that he is able to keep that which I have committed unto him against that day." Paul exhorted Timothy to "hold fast the form of sound words, which thou hast heard from me, in faith and love which is in Christ Jesus."

C. *Paul's Exhortation Enforced by Two Examples* (1:15-18).

The one example is a warning, the other is an encouragement.

III. Timothy Exhorted to Steadfastness and Fidelity (2:1-13).

He is to transmit the truth and be willing to endure hardship for its sake.

A. *Illustrated by:*

1. The Soldier (2:3, 4).
2. The Athlete (2:5).
3. The Farmer (2:6).

B. *Paul's Example* (2:7-10).

Paul endured all things for the elect's sake that they also may obtain salvation which is in Christ Jesus with eternal glory. He suffered trouble as an evildoer even unto bonds. They could bind Paul, but not the Word of God.

C. *Inducement Held Out* (2:11-13).

Efforts for God cannot fail because of the fidelity of God. He remains faithful though we fail; God cannot deny Himself.

IV. Instructions to Timothy as a Preacher of the Word (2:14—4:5).

A. *Study, Be Diligent To Be an Approved Workman* (2:14-19).

The minister must discriminate in his teaching—shun profane and empty babblings which are injurious and even irreligious. Such are dangerous even as a canker—gangrene. Two false teachers are named. The particular error of which they were guilty was a denial of the resurrection "saying that the resurrection is past already." Many in the church today are doing this. Sound teaching is needed. Despite this Paul gives assurance by calling attention to the sure foundation of the church "the pillar and ground of truth."

B. *Proper Attitude* (2:20-24).

The pastor must maintain the proper attitude toward the mixed multitude in the church.

C. *Purity of Life Demanded* (2:22).

Flee youthful lusts which include bodily appetites, pride, and conceit, arrogance, etc.

The antidote for all these is following of righteousness, faith, charity, peace.

D. *How To Behave Before Opposers* (2:23-26).

The true Church has always been opposed. The faithful minister who preaches the Word of God and demands of its members the separated life is bound to meet with opposition. Paul sets down the following rules for Timothy to follow.

1. "Avoid Foolish and Unlearned Questions" (2:23).

"Unlearned" suggests the undisciplined child. The reason for avoiding such questions is that they engender strife. Don't talk and argue in such cases.

2. Gently and Patiently Teach Them the Right Way (2:24).

Follow the example of Christ (Matt. 11:29). Such treatment will likely induce repentance and enable them to recover themselves from the snare of the Devil.

E. *How to Behave in the Coming Perilous Days* (3:1—4:5).

By the "last days" is meant the days immediately preceding the coming of Christ. These times are brought on by false teachers.

1. Description of the Perilous Times (3:1-5).

a. Self-lovers.

b. Covetous—money lovers.

c. Empty boasters.

d. Proud—exalting themselves above their fellows.

e. Blasphemers—speaking evil against God.

f. Disobedient to parents. This is a sign of the last days.

g. Unthankful—true now.

h. Unholy—irreligious.

i. Without natural affection. True of husbands and wives, parents and children.

j. Truce-breakers. Breaking engagements.

k. Slanderers—false accusers.

l. Incontinent—without self-control.

m. Fierce—savage—merciless.

n. Haters of God.

o. Traitors.

p. Heady—precipitate.

q. High-minded. Besotted or beclouded with pride.

r. Pleasure lovers instead of God lovers.

s. Having a form of godliness. Making a profession of godliness but their lives denying their profession.

2. The Method of These False Teachers (3:6-9).

It was to visit certain ones in their homes—especially simple-minded women laden with sins, led away with divers lusts, who never are able to settle down upon the right way and therefore, always a prey to religious cranks and designing men. As Jannes and Jambres withstood Moses by trying to rival Moses, so do these people resort to lying wonders. *Jannes* means "trickster" and *Jambres* means "juggler." Their folly shall be exposed.

3. Paul's Example To Be Followed by Timothy (3:10-13).

This manner of life (suffering, faith, love, and patience) is necessary because "evil men and seducers shall wax worse and worse, deceiving and being deceived" (v. 13). "All that will live godly in Christ shall suffer persecution."

4. The God-inspired Scriptures Are the Minister's Equipment (3:14-17).

They were adequate for Paul and Timothy for such trials and issues and an untold number who have followed in their wake, and they will not fail us.

5. Paul's Charge to Timothy (4:1-5).

This was to preach the Word "in season and out of season" which means to use every opportunity and make opportunity. Preaching the Word is the divinely appointed remedy to meet the need of these difficult days. God works through His Word. Man is helpless, but God's Word is not bound.

The reasons are stated in verses 3 and 4. Time is coming when they will not endure sound doctrine. They will add to teachers having itching ears—will turn away their ears from the truth to fables. What a picture of our time! In view of coming days of peril Timothy is urged to be:

a. On the alert—watchful. Many would need the encouragement of the minister to be faithful and courageous.

b. Willing to suffer hardships for the sake of the Gospel—endure affliction as Paul had done.

c. "Do the work of an evangelist." Evangelist is not a different order of minister but doing the work of preaching the Gospel to the unconverted. Ministers are not to confine themselves to pastoral duties among their own flocks but should be seeking the salvation of the lost.

d. To make full proof of his ministry by fully performing all the functions of the ministry—to accept all its responsibilities and realize all its possibilities.

V. PAUL'S APPROACHING MARTYRDOM (4:6-8).

Paul enforces his charge to Timothy by the solemn announcement of his coming death. He is saying: "I am now laying down my work, I am leaving it to you to carry on. Its success depends upon your fidelity."

In addition to perceiving the effect on Timothy of Paul's approaching death, let us visualize the dying thoughts of Paul the prisoner. To Paul death did not mean cessation of consciousness, or the sleep of the soul, but "to be absent from the body" was to be at home with the Lord (II Cor. 5:8). Paul's thought of his death was:

A. *An Offering to God.*

"I am ready to be offered." His thought was that his blood was about to be poured out as a libation, as a departure; "the time of my departure is at hand." Departure is a going away.

B. *He Thought of the Past.*

1. "I Have Fought a Good Fight."
2. "I have Finished My Course."
3. "I Have Kept the Faith."

C. *He Looked to the Future* (4:8).

"Henceforth there is laid up a crown." He saw before him:

1. Life with God.

Fellowship with God is a prize greatly to be desired.

2. Crown of Righteousness.

This award will be given at the coming of the Lord to all those who love His appearing.

VI. THE CONCLUSION (4:9-22).

A. *Urgently Requests Timothy To Come unto Him* (4:9).

1. Bring Mark.
2. Bring Cloak and Books.

B. *Friends Scattered—Only Luke Was Left.*

C. *Forsaken by Friends at First Trial* (4:16-18).

D. *Closing Messages* (4:19-21).

E. *Benediction* (4:22).

EPISTLE TO TITUS

PART ONE—INTRODUCTORY MATTERS

TITUS WAS A TRUSTED COMPANION of Paul. His parents were Gentiles (Gal. 2:3). He accompanied Paul and Barnabas to the Jerusalem Council where was settled once and for all the relation of the Law to salvation (Gal. 2:1-9). He seems to have been led to the confession of Christ through Paul's ministry (1:4). Titus appears during and after Paul's residence at Ephesus. We learn from II Corinthians 2:13; 7:6, 13; 8:6, 16; 12:18 that Titus had been sent to Corinth to correct certain abuses there which caused anxiety to Paul. His task was a delicate one, and Paul awaited his return with solicitude (II Cor. 2:13). On his return Titus rejoined Paul in Macedonia with good news (II Cor. 7:6, 13, 14), and was sent back to Corinth with II Corinthians (II Cor. 8:6, 18, 23). We do not read again of Titus till after Paul's release from his first Roman imprisonment.

The Epistle of Titus informs us that he had been left in Crete to superintend the organization of the churches in that island. Titus seems to have been Paul's deputy to Crete like Timothy was in Corinth. His mission there was a temporal one as he was to rejoin Paul at Nicopolis. The only other reference to Titus is in II Timothy 4:10 when he is said to have departed into Dalmatia. This departure may have been on a similar mission to that at Crete—not a desertion of Paul. The time of this writing is about A.D. 67.

PART TWO—DETAILED OUTLINE

I. THE APOSTOLIC SALUTATION (1:1-4).

Careful attention should be given to the greetings of these writings. The Holy Spirit speaks just as clearly in the introduction as in the body of the writing. They have no set form, but are varied according to the several occasions.

A. *"A Servant of God."*

This is not found elsewhere. It shows Paul's absolute subservience to God. "An apostle of Jesus Christ according to the faith of God's elect and the acknowledging of the truth." This means a piety which leads to godliness and is based upon the eternal purpose of God.

B. *Result of Paul's Preaching.*

"Manifested in due time through preaching of God's word, according to the obligation imposed by God our Saviour."

C. *Paul's Son in the Faith.*

"To Titus mine own son after the common faith"—common to Jews and Gentiles.

D. *Paul's Greeting.*

"Grace, mercy and peace from God the Father and the Lord Jesus Christ our Saviour."

II. THE MISSION OF TITUS IN CRETE (1:5).

Proper organization of the church is highly important. Efficiency in any enterprise demands organization. Paul's ministry of evangelism was highly successful—many professed conversion throughout the cities of Crete, but he was called away before the task of consolidating his work was completed, therefore, he entrusted to Titus the responsibility of gathering together these converts and setting over them proper officers called elders. With careful detail he describes the qualifications of these officers thus showing the importance of this work.

III. THE QUALIFICATIONS OF ELDERS (1:6-11).

Two Greek words appear in designation of the officers: *presbuteros* meaning elder, and *episcopos* meaning overseer. Two kinds of duties are specified: that of preaching and teaching in the first word; and that of overseeing in the second. Both ministries are required in the church.

A. *Blameless.*

This does not mean faultless. Broken human beings are sinful.

"There is none righteous, no not one." Paul called himself "the chief of sinners."

B. *The Husband of One Wife.*

This means literally, "a man of one woman." The man must be above suspicion as to the marriage relation.

C. *Have Faithful Children.*

The elders should have a commendable family life. If children are unbelieving, disorderly, and accused of rioting, that would be a reflection upon the father.

D. *Not Selfish.*

Not self-willed, self-pleasing, but accommodating his wishes to others.

E. *Not Soon Angry.*

F. *Not Given to Wine.*

G. *No Striker.*

H. *Not Given to Filthy Lucre.*

I. *A Lover of Hospitality.*

J. *A Lover of Good Men,* i.e., *a Lover of All Good.*

K. *Sober-Minded, Self-Restrained.*

L. *Just—Toward Men.*

M. *Holy—Toward God.*

N. *Temperate.*

One should have his passions, hands, tongue and eyes under control.

O. *Hold Fast the Faithful Word* (1:9-11).

There is special need of this. The gainsayers need to be convinced by sound doctrine, the mouths of the vain talkers must be stopped. These evil workers were entering the homes and subverting the people for filthy lucre's sake.

IV. DIFFICULTIES OF TITUS' FIELD (1:12-16).

The Cretians seemingly were a half-civilized people. Epimenides 600 B.C. said that the Cretians:

A. *"Are Always Liars."*

To Cretianize was proverbial for to "lie" as "Corinthianize" was to be dissolute.

B. *"Evil Beasts."*

This means they were brutal.

C. *"Idle Gluttons."*

This means that they were indolent through pampering.

This charge Paul says was true (v. 13). He instructs Titus to "sharply rebuke them" so as to deter from following after Jewish fables and commandments of men, who claim that they know God but by their works deny Him. It is to the glory of the Gospel of Christ that it can transform the lives of heathen and make them witnesses of the saving grace of God.

V. INSTRUCTIONS FOR THE VARIOUS CLASSES (2:1-15).

Titus first deals with proper church organization so that the people may be taught sound doctrine and that doctrine should issue in holy living. This ministry should reach all the people to the end that in all departments of their lives there should be fruit to the glory of God.

A. *The Aged* (2:1-3).

1. The Men Should Be:
   a. Sober.
   b. Grave–Dignified.
   c. Temperate.
   d. Sound in faith.
   e. In charity.
   f. In patience.
2. The Aged Women:

a. Not false accusers–slanderers. This is a besetting sin of many.

b. Not given to much wine.

c. Teachers of good things (2:4, 5). Young women are to be sober, to love their husbands, to love their children, to be discreet, chaste, keepers at home, good, obedient to their husbands. Note the purpose of this (v. 5). Note the wisdom of having the older women teach the young women instead of Titus teaching the young women.

B. *The Young Men* (2:6).

They are to be sober-minded–self-restrained. The tendency of youth is to excessive indulgence–restraint is very necessary.

C. *Ministers* (2: 7, 8).

They should be patterns to all. Titus the young minister was to be a grand model of good works. All teaching is useless unless one's example conforms to the teacher's words.

1. Purity of Motive—Uncorruptness of Doctrine.
2. Gravity, Dignified Sincerity.

The minister should take his commission with earnestness.

3. Sincerity.

He should be free from all admixture—wholly devoted.

4. Sound Speech (2:8).

His speech should conform to his preaching so that the adversary might be ashamed.

D. *Servants* (2:9).

1. "Servants" Here Mean Slaves, and as Slaves They Are:
    a. To be obedient to their masters.
    b. To strive to please them well.
    c. Not to answer again in contradiction.
    d. Not to purloin. This means keeping back something belonging to another. They are to show in every way their integrity. By this means slaves may adorn the doctrine of God our Saviour in all things. The very glory of the Gospel is that it transforms even the heathen into men and women of integrity. Paul bases his exhortations and demands upon the dynamics of the Gospel, a marvelous summary of which he gives in the closing verses of chapter 2.
2. Sermon Outline.

This summary can be presented in a sermon with the subject, "The values of the grace of God."

a. The introduction: Grace means the outgoing of God's favor to the unworthy. The true meaning of this text is seen in the context.

b. The connection between the grace of God and the conduct of the Christian.

(1) God brought salvation to all men (v. 9). "All men" means all classes of men from kings to servants—bondslaves.

(a) Salvation is the starting point of conduct. Right living is only possible as the fruit of the salvation which grace brought.

(b) Salvation must be a reality before there can be right conduct.

(c) Salvation is necessary in order for even the right apprehensions of responsibility and surely for obedience.

(2) Grace teaches right conduct (v. 12).

(a) Negatively considered—it denies ungodliness and worldly lusts. It is the grace of God that enables the believer to say "no" to the temptations and allurements of life. It is the grace of God in the life of the saved man which holds him in check with reference to the evils which surround him. It suppresses improper desires as to wealth, honor, pleasure, and sensual indulgence.

(b) Positively considered—it teaches how to live soberly. "Soberly" refers to the power of the human personality over itself. It means that the saved man has his whole being under control. Sobriety is greatly needed—it is the evidence of real salvation. It teaches how to live righteously. Righteously refers to right relation to all persons around us. Grace of God teaches the child of God to be true in human relations. It teaches how to live godly. "Godly" refers to the believer's relation Godward. It puts the whole life under God's control.

(3) Grace of God furnishes an adequate hope (v. 13). A vitalizing hope is absolutely necessary to enable a man to live a victorious and fruitful life. This is called the blessed hope which is the second coming of Christ. It is the great incentive for all right living and fruitful service. Jesus Christ is to return to this earth. The consciousness of the reality and imminency of Christ's coming causes the Christian to sit loose to the things of this world and to give himself without reserve to the discharge of his moral obligations.

VI. Obedience to Rulers Enjoined (3:1).

"Put them in mind to be in subjection to rulers, to authorities, to be obedient, to be ready unto every good work." The powers that be are ordained of God (Rom. 13:1). The only exception to this obligation is when governments demand that which is morally wrong, then "obey God rather than men."

VII. PEACEABLE AND GENTLE BEHAVIOR TOWARD ALL MEN (3:2-7).

A. *Right Relations.*

It is a Christian's duty to maintain right relations with unbelieving neighbors. One must patiently forbear many things. In this way he may effectively witness for Christ and win them to Christ. The greatest help in getting along with ungodly neighbors is to remember our former sinfulness and present salvation through the free grace of God.

B. *God's Grace* (3:4).

In reminding Titus of God's saving grace, Paul gives another summary of Gospel truth.

1. It Springs from the Kindness and Love of God our Saviour.

This means that the Christian should show the same attitude toward his neighbor that God did toward us in our unsaved state. Salvation appeared through the coming of Christ and His redeeming work which made salvation possible.

2. Sinners Become Recipients of Salvation.

"Not by works of righteousness we have done but according to his mercy he saved us."

3. Method (3:5).

The means by which this salvation is accomplished is the "washing of regeneration and renewing of the Holy Ghost."

VIII. THE MAINTENANCE OF GOOD WORKS, A PRESSING AND PERPETUAL OBLIGATION (3:8).

Note the relation of salvation by grace as the maintenance of good works. Real salvation will show itself in the life—not salvation by works, but a demonstration of it by works.

IX. BEHAVIOR TOWARD ERRORISTS AND HERETICS (3:9-11).

In the church composed of persons of various natural gifts, degrees of culture, inherited tendencies, prejudices, etc., it is to be expected that there will be questions arising, disputings about the meaning of portions of the Bible. The pastor must know how to rightly divide the truth—must patiently help the members into the light. His supreme responsibility is to preach the Word of God. Frequently in the pastoral epistles preaching and teaching are mentioned as the means of giving the right perspective of Christian truth. Most of the questions will be answered in this way. Five times in the pastoral epistles are mentioned "faithful sayings." These where understood in the light of the context will be seen to embrace the range of Christian truth. Two things can be done:

A. *Shun Foolish Questions About the Law.*

Take no time to investigate—avoid.

B. *Reject Heretics* (3:11).

A man who is a heretic after the first and second admonition, reject. A heretic is one who is a leader of factions. His own way of life is his condemnation.

X. PERSONAL MATTERS (3:12-15).

A. *Summons for Titus to Meet Paul at Nicopolis.*

B. *Bring Zenas the Lawyer and Apollos.*

C. *Exhort People To Learn To Maintain Good Works.*

D. *Salutation and Greeting.*

EPISTLE TO PHILEMON

PART ONE—INTRODUCTORY MATTERS

THIS IS A PRIVATE LETTER. Philemon was a member of the church at Colossae. Onesimus, his slave, wronged him, perhaps stole from him and fled to Rome. There he came under Paul's influence and was converted. Paul sent Onesimus back to Philemon with this letter. This is one of the tenderest and most beautiful letters ever written, and the first antislavery petition ever penned.

Every Christian should acquire the ability to witness for Christ by letter to the unsaved, to lead them to Christ as a personal Saviour, and to believers showing them opportunities to do good. This letter of Paul to his friend Philemon is a fine example of Christian witnessing through letter writing.

PART TWO—DETAILED OUTLINE

I. THE SALUTATION (vv. 1-3).

His aim was to touch Philemon's heart, so Paul refers to himself as a prisoner and links Philemon to himself as a fellow laborer in the Gospel of truth. He makes mention of Apphia, Philemon's wife, and Archippus, the son who had already enlisted as a fellow soldier.

II. PHILEMON'S REPUTATION (vv. 4-7).

Paul paid a fine tribute to Philemon, reminding him that he never prayed without bearing him up before God.

A. *His Faith and Love Toward the Lord and All Saints* (v. 5).

It was his hope and desire that this faith might bear fruit in Christ Jesus. With such an approach the way was open to Philemon's heart.

B. *His Ministry to the Saints* (v. 7).

Philemon was generous in his help to the poor saints.

III. PAUL'S REQUEST (vv. 8-16).

He requested Philemon to receive back Onesimus, the runaway slave, as a brother in Christ. Note the incomparable delicacy and courtesy with which Paul approaches Philemon.

A. *He Beseeches Instead of Commands* (vv. 8-10).

Though conscious of his right to enjoin, he pleads as the prisoner of Jesus Christ for love's sake.

B. *He Makes His Plea on the Grounds of Grace* (vv. 11-14).

He admitted that Onesimus had been unprofitable, had forfeited all claim upon Philemon, and that on grounds of justice his plea might well be rejected, and yet because Onesimus was begotten in his bonds (v. 10) and was in a real sense a part of his own suffering nature (v. 12), he ventured to suggest that he should be accepted. Though Onesimus hitherto had been unprofitable to his master, he was now profitable to both Paul and Philemon. Paul would gladly have retained him as a personal attendant, but first sought his friend's permission.

C. *Paul's Desire* (vv. 15, 16).

Paul desired that Onesimus be received back not as a slave, but as a brother in Christ. Here is the real fugitive slave law. Paul never attacked slavery though it was contrary to Christianity, and therefore hateful to him, but emphasized principles which destroyed it. The stablishment of Christianity changes the whole face of human society. The wise thing to do is to get men and women regenerated and thus transform society instead of seeking change by revolution. Social wrongs can only permanently be removed by the creation of a brotherhood, and can only be realized by faith in Jesus Christ. Christ became universal man in order to bring about a brotherhood.

In Paul's request you can hear the pleadings of Christ for us sinners. All men have broken loose, gone astray, and have become unprofitable. We are reconciled to God through the interceding of Christ. He has made us profitable. We have been begotten in "his bonds"; through His passion, agony of heart, we shall be changed. We can see and hear Him now pleading our cause before God's throne for love's sake.

IV. THE BASIS UPON WHICH ONESIMUS IS TO BE RECEIVED (vv. 17-21).

The debt of guilty Onesimus is to be put to the account of Paul, and the merit of Paul is to be put to the account of Onesimus. This is a fine illustration of the atonement of Christ. Whatever wrongs we have committed or debt incurred—all our shortcomings are debited to Him. Jesus Christ on behalf of the whole universe has said to God; "Put that to My account"; "I have written with My pierced hand, I will repay." This is a type of our redemption—all our failures and shortcomings put to Christ's account. Onesimus was taken back, not as a runaway slave, but a beloved brother in Christ.

V. PAUL REQUESTS LODGING (vv. 22-25).

He expected a speedy release from imprisonment and purposed to sojourn with Philemon. In all probability this was realized. What a welcome he must have received! Jesus Christ is saying to everyone of His redeemed ones, "Prepare Me a lodging." How gladly we should prepare that place in our hearts for Him!

EPISTLE TO THE HEBREWS

PART ONE–INTRODUCTORY MATTERS

THE FIRST SENTENCE in this epistle discloses the mission of Jesus Christ. The author declares that "God, who at sundry times and in divers manners spake in time past unto the fathers by the prophets, hath in these last days spoken to us by his Son." The Son, therefore, is God's final word to man. This sentence declares that God is and that God speaks. The self-existent God makes Himself known.

I. AUTHORSHIP.

The human author is unknown to any but God. The book is anonymous. The author seems to be at some pains to conceal himself. It is usually ascribed to Paul. Pauline authorship is supported by tradition and by internal evidence such as style and doctrine. After many centuries of searching investigation, external and internal, we must say with Origen that God alone knows who wrote it.

II. TIME AND PLACE OF WRITING.

A. *Time—about* A.D. 68.

It was evidently before the destruction of Jerusalem or some mention would have been made, for it would have been in line with his argument to show that Judaism had passed. The Temple service was still continued (see 9:8).

B. *Place.*

This is somewhat doubtful. There is only one possible clue. This is in 13:24. "They of Italy," is not absolutely convincing as the phrase may mean "Italians." It does not necessarily mean the people who lived in Italy.

III. TO WHOM ADDRESSED.

Unquestionably this epistle was written to Christian Hebrews, perhaps at Jerusalem. This is determined by the references and illustrations in the writing itself.

IV. THE PURPOSE OF THE WRITING.

This was twofold.

A. *To Comfort.*

Those who were undergoing great affliction through severe persecution needed encouragement. This is seen from the detailed instruction on chastening as set forth in chapter 12.

B. *To Warn of Apostasy.*

To prevent these Hebrew Christians from apostatizing the Christian faith. This gives pertinency to the repeated warnings, especially such as set forth in chapter 6, where the awful consequences of apostasy are mentioned.

V. THE WRITER'S METHOD.

It is to show that the Christian faith and church mark an advance in every respect upon the Jewish dispensation. The key words are *better, perfect, hold fast.* The word *better* is found thirteen times; *perfect,* nine times. The writer urges them to let go of everything else and to hold on to Jesus and the Gospel.

PART TWO—DETAILED OUTLINE

The Book of Hebrews falls into two parts:

Doctrinal 1:1—10:18
Practical 10:19—13:25

In the doctrinal section the author uses one main argument which may be embodied in a proposition somewhat as follows:

I. CHRISTIANITY IS SUPERIOR TO JUDAISM (1:1—10:18).

This proposition the author proves by the following arguments:

A. *Because Christ Its Founder Is Superior to the Prophets* (1:1-3).

The Jews greatly reverenced the prophets. The author does not in any sense disparage them, but he endeavored to show them that Jesus Christ is far in advance, that is, better than the prophets because:

1. He Is the Very Son of God and Not a Stranger.
2. He Is the Heir of All Things.
3. He Created the Worlds—the Universe.
4. He Is the Image of God.
5. He Upholds All Things.
6. He Purged Our Sins.
7. He Sat Down at God's Right Hand.

How different were even the greatest of the prophets! In not one of these particulars did one of them approach unto the dignity of Jesus Christ the Son.

B. *Because Christ Its Founder Is Superior to the Angels* (1:4–2:18).

The angels played a prominent part in God's dealings with His people and were held in great reverence, but Christ is by far their superior because:

1. He Was Given the Better Name, the Son (1:4, 5).

To be the Son is much better than to be the most trusted minister.

2. They Were Commanded to Worship the Son (1:6).

Worship is not even given to equals, much less to those who are inferior.

3. He Is Forever Enthroned (1:8).

4. God Anointed Him with the Oil of Gladness Above His Fellows (1:9).

5. He Is the Eternal God (1:10-12).

This means that He was before all things, even the Almighty Creator, and He shall remain when the heavens and the earth shall have passed away.

6. He Has Been Given a Place at God's Right Hand (1:13, 14).

He now occupies the throne with the Father where He awaits the possession of His mediatorial kingdom.

a. The author's first warning.

It is the author's habit at certain stages in his argument to make a digression in order to solemnly warn the readers against renouncing their faith by showing them the awful consequences of renouncing faith in Jesus Christ and going back to Judaism.

Between the setting forth of the divine glory of Christ and the real humanity of the Redeemer, the writer sounds the warning note.

He impresses upon the hearers that the everlasting God has spoken through His Son, therefore, earnest heed should be taken to the message. They are urged to not let the great salvation slip. He shows them what a great sin the neglect of this great salvation would be.

It is well for us to consider the bearing of these warnings on the assurance of believers. The emphasis is not on the possibility of apostasy but the realization of security through solemn warning. Realizing the greatness of our salvation will induce steadfastness. It is well to note that this salvation has been wrought by the members of the triune God.

7. He Is the Ruler of the Age To Come (2:5-8).

In this coming age all things shall be subjected to Him. The purpose of the mediatorial kingdom of Christ is to subject all things to Him.

8. He Tasted Death (2:9-18).

He, though made for a little time lower than angels, through His Incarnation, sufferings, and death, tasted death for every man that He might lift man above the angels to become members of God's family. He hath destroyed the power of the Devil and is therefore able to succor those who are tempted.

C. *Because Christ Its Founder Is Superior to Moses* (3:1-6).

Moses is a type of Christ (see Deut. 18:15). Three features in this type stand out:

1. He Was Rejected by His Brethren.
2. In His Zeal and Sacrifice for God.
3. In His Willingness To Die for His People.

He is superior to Moses because Moses was but a servant while Christ is the very Son of God. He does not in any way speak disparagingly of Moses, for Moses was a faithful servant over God's house, but Christ the Son is the Lord over His own house. Yea, He is its very builder; He bought the material of which it is built; He dwells in it and is its vital Head.

a. The author's second warning (3:7-19).

Israel's failure and suffering are used to deter these believers from apostasy. The history of Israel in the wilderness is of great importance to us today (see I Cor. 10). We as believers are in the world and therefore exposed to many dangers. The Israelites were a people of high privilege but through unbelief, ingratitude, and hardness of heart went into idolatry and thus tempted the Lord. This warning contains the following:

(1) Exhortation against hardening of the heart (vv. 7-11). It was this that caused Israel's failure.

(2) The need for perseverance (vv. 12-15).

(3) They were to strengthen each other by mutual exhortation. The deceitfulness of sin can be met only by steadfast and aggressive efforts to remain true.

(4) Israel's disobedience and unbelief (vv. 16-19).

D. *Because the "Rest" Which Christ Gives Is Superior to That of Judaism* (4:1-13).

The "rest" in Canaan was only temporary. The days of weary marching were over, but still they faced the necessity of fighting to subdue the enemy. The better rest of Christ was typified by God's creation rest. This better rest we enter by faith (v. 3). Israel failed to find rest under Joshua though he led them into the land where they expected to find it (v. 8). The rest here is in the apprehension of the perfect work of redemption. We rest in this perfect work as God rested after His work of creation (vv. 9-13). When our bodies shall have been liberated and the whole creation delivered from bondage, then shall begin the eternal sabbath which remains for the people of God. The believer is urged to labor to enter into that rest. Observe:

1. This Rest Is Entered into by Faith (4:1-3).

2. Joshua Did Not Bring the People into the Rest of God (4:4-9).

3. The Believer Is Urged To Enter into the Rest (4:10, 11).

4. The Power of God's Word To Judge the Individual Life (4:12, 13).

The believer has need of this judging all along life's way. This judging is so efficient that it pierces to the very center of one's being. As it thus pierces the center it goes both ways, for it is sharper than any two-edged sword.

E. *Because the Priesthood of Christ Is Superior to That of Aaron* (4:14—10:18).

1. Christ Is the True High Priest (4:14—5:10).

Aaron and Melchizedek were but types, and were called and inducted into office to be the types of Christ's priesthood. Two features of that priesthood are thus typified. Aaron represents the work of sacrifice; Melchizedek the work of Christ as the King. Note some qualifications of a true priest which are only fully met in Christ:

a. Capacity for sympathy (4:15–5:2). A real purpose of the Incarnation was to enable the Saviour to enter into sympathy with the saved.

b. His divine appointment (5:3-6). He was not even chosen by the people much less being self-appointed (5:4, 5). His divine selection differentiates Him from all other priests. He received His commission from the heavenly Father (5:6).

c. He possessed the knowledge of experience (5:7-10). He actually suffered.

(1) The author's third warning (5:11–6:20).

In this parenthesis we see the author again interrupting his argument for the purpose of sounding a solemn warning. He in this way shows his great skill.

(a) Reproof for small proficiency in knowledge (5:11-14). This limited knowledge was due to the fact that they were standing still, not making an effort to progress. "Sloth" is usually the cause of retarded growth. Really the human mind cannot stand still. The moment it ceases to go forward it begins the movement backward. His method in rebuking them is to contrast babyhood and maturity. Their experience was long enough to bring them into maturity whereas their state was that of undeveloped infants.

(b) Urgent exhortation to go forward (6:1-3). The only way for widened knowledge, for enlarged mental and spiritual horizon is going forward.

(c) The awful consequence of apostasy (6:4-8). Even after having been brought into touch with Christian influences, it was possible for them to renounce their connections and relations. This should not be recognized as showing the possibility of apostasy, but the effective means of preventing real Christians from apostatizing by inducing them to go forward. Those in whom the grace of

God has wrought will heed the warning and thus be saved from apostasy.

(d) Encouragements (6:9-20).

(i) Persuaded better things (v. 9).

(ii) God is righteous (v. 10).

(iii) Imitate those who persevere to the end (vv. 11, 12).

(iv) God's oath and guarantee (vv. 13-20). God's fidelity is involved in the perseverance of the saint. Salvation is not only begun in God, but perfected by Him. We can be assured that He who hath begun a good work in us will complete it to the day of Jesus Christ. This oath of God is our anchor which will steady us and enable us to enter within the veil.

2. Christ Is the Priest of a Higher Order Than Aaron (7:1-28). He is of a higher order because:

a. He is a kingly type (v. 2).

b. His office is of endless duration (v. 3).

c. He received tithes of Aaron through the loins of Abraham (vv. 4-6).

d. He blessed Abraham (vv. 7-10). The lesser is blessed by the greater.

e. The permanency of this priesthood implies the abrogation of the law of the Levites (vv. 11-17).

f. The priesthood of Christ was made with an oath (vv. 19-22).

g. Jesus Christ is an unchangeable priest (vv. 23-25).

h. He is a sinless priest (vv. 26-28).

3. Christ Is a Priest of a Better Covenant (8:1-13). The new covenant is better because:

a. His place of ministry is in the heavenly sanctuary (vv. 1-3).

b. The new covenant is based on better promises—they are written on the heart rather than upon stones (vv. 6-10).

c. This covenant is universal (v. 11).

d. This covenant brings forgiveness of sins (v. 12).

4. Christ Is a Priest of a Better Tabernacle (9:1-28). This tabernacle is better because:

a. It is not material (v. 11; cf. v. 24).

b. It was consecrated by His own blood rather than that of beasts (v. 12).

c. This blood of consecration secures an eternal inheritance (v. 15).

5. Christ Is a Priest of a Better Sacrifice (10:1-18).

This sacrifice is better than the old, because:

a. Jesus Himself is that sacrifice of which all Old Testament ordinances and ceremonies were but types (vv. 1-9).

b. It has finality. He offered Himself once for all (vv. 10-18). Because of this superior sacrifice those who accept Him are perfected forever. The apprehension of this fact will steady the lives of all. How we should praise His name for the efficiency of His sacrifices!

II. LIFE IN THE POWER OF THE GREAT SALVATION (10:19—13:25).

A. *The New Worship* (10:19-25).

1. The New Way of Access into the Holiest (10:19, 20).

2. A Great High Priest over the House of God (10:21, 22).

3. Life in the Holiest (10:23-25).

a. Hold fast our confession (v. 23).

b. Mutual encouragement—provoke unto love and good works (v. 24).

c. Not forsaking the assembling of ourselves together (v. 25).

d. Exhorting one another (v. 25).

(1) The author's fourth warning—the awful guilt and issue of apostasy (10:26-39).

(a) The danger of sinning willfully (vv. 26-31). It is a fearful thing to fall into the hands of the living God.

(b) Called to boldness and patience (vv. 32-36).

(c) A challenge to faith and an exhortation not to draw back (vv. 37-39).

B. *Faith, the New Dynamic* (11:1-40).

1. The Nature of Faith—the Eye of the Unseen (11:1-3).

2. Faith the Principle of Godly Living in Every Age (11:4-40).

The mighty power of faith finds illustration in the heroes of:

a. The antediluvian age (vv. 4-7).

(1) Abel's faith—how manifested? In worship. He came as a sinner and availed himself of atonement.

(2) Enoch's faith—how manifested? In divine companionship. He walked with God for 300 years.

(3) Noah's faith—how manifested? He believed God when all the world was against him. The flood was against nature's laws. Such a boat as he was instructed to build would not float on the Euphrates or the Tigris. The rationalist of his day doubtless ridiculed him.

b. The Hebrews (11:8-40). Abraham, Sarah, Isaac, Jacob, Moses' parents, Moses, Rahab, etc.

C. *Running the Christian Race* (12:1-13).

In the successful running of this race there must be practiced the patience of hope.

1. Things Laid Aside (12:1).

Distinguish between right and sin.

2. Jesus the Supreme Leader (12:2, 3).

Incentive —a cloud of witnesses; inspiration—Jesus the Leader.

3. Trial—Discipline the Portion of God's Children (12:4-8).

4. Benefits of Chastisement (12:9-13).

Chastisement is an essential part of the Father's discipline. Holiness is its issue.

a. The author's fifth warning (12:14-29).

(1) Falling short of the grace of God (vv. 14, 15). Tender consideration for others and watchfulness enjoined.

(2) Warnings against bartering spiritual privileges for present carnal gratification (vv. 16, 17). Esau an outstanding example.

(3) The splendors of the Mosaic Law in contrast to the glories of the Gospel (vv. 18-29).

(a) "Ye are not come to Mount Sinai" (vv. 18-21).

(b) "Ye are come to Mount Zion" (vv. 22-24).

(c) Fear God—He is a consuming fire (vv. 25-29). In proportion as the spiritual glories of the Gospel outshine the terrific splendors of the Law will the responsibilities of neglecting the Gospel be measured.

D. *Duties and Privileges of Believers* (13:1-8).

1. Living the Love Life (13:1-4).

a. Love to the brethren (v. 1).

b. Love to strangers (v. 2).

c. Love to prisoners (v. 3).

d. Love in the marriage relation (v. 5). Marriage on the basis of true love ennobles life. Marriage without love means the degradation and ruin of both parties.

2. Contentment (13:5, 6).

The Christian should be free from covetousness. He properly estimates the true riches as over against false riches. He trusts God for His daily bread.

3. Imitate the example of Godly Leaders (13:7, 8).

Jesus Christ, whom these leaders represent, is the unchangeable One.

E. *Let the Heart be Established by Grace and Not by Meats* (13:9-16).

The believer goes forth with Jesus without the camp bearing reproach for His sake. All ordinances and ceremonies have only true meaning in Him. The believer therefore should offer the sacrifice of praise.

F. *Final Words and Benediction* (13:17-25).

1. Obey Them That Have the Rule over You (13:17).
2. Pray for Us (13:18, 19).
3. Concluding Prayer and Benediction (13:20-25).

THE EPISTLE OF JAMES

PART ONE—INTRODUCTORY MATTERS

I. The Author.

James, a servant of God and the Lord Jesus Christ" (1:1) shows him to have been a man of prominence in the Church which would differentiate him from all others. He was most likely the James who presided at the Jerusalem Council when the question of the relation of the believer to the Law for justification was settled (Acts 15:13). His name heads the trio—"James, Cephas, and John"—designated as "pillars." This seems to have been the prevailing opinion of the early church.

II. The Time of Writing.

The earliest of the New Testament writings—between A.D. 45 and 50.

III. The Theme.

The relation of faith and works is the theme. Justification is not by faith and works, but by a faith that works. Behavior is the test of faith. Faith appears in works. *Faith* occurs some twenty times in this epistle. Some assume that James wrote to correct Paul's teaching as to justification by faith. This could not be true because it was written too early for that, being the earliest of New Testament writings. Furthermore, James is in entire accord with Paul in Romans. Romans sets forth faith as the actuating principle from which works issue. James sets forth works as a demonstration of faith. Faith is pivotal to both James and Paul. As Guy H. King, of Scotland, said, "Faith is a belief that behaves."

PART TWO—DETAILED OUTLINE

I. THE GREETING (1:1).

A. *From the Bondslave.*

From "James, the servant of God and the Lord Jesus Christ." James uses the word *servant* to denote his position before God and Jesus Christ. He is the bondslave of both the Father and the Son in ministering to the believers in times of great distress.

B. *To the Twelve Tribes of the Dispersion.*

This means to Christian Jews who were "scattered abroad." Not all of the Jews had returned from the Babylonian captivity—they were passing through the fires of persecution—suffering at the hands of the Gentiles and at the hands of their fellow Jews because of their confession of Jesus Christ.

II. CONCERNING TRIALS (1:2-17).

The Christian lives in a world of hatred and opposition. Undying enmity exists between God and the Devil—between the seed of the woman and the seed of the Devil. This fact throws light upon the strife and warfare which persists between good and evil—righteousness and unrighteousness. The history of the human race is but the record of war and strife. This will persist until "the kingdoms of this world are become the kingdoms of our Lord, and of his Christ" (Rev. 11:15).

A. *The Believer's Attitude Toward Trials and Testing* (1:2).

"Count it all joy." This is hard to do because their purpose is not known. We should face courageously testings because of their beneficent results.

1. They Reveal Our Fidelity.
2. They "Worketh" Patience.

This is characteristic of a man who cannot be swerved from his faith by the severest trials and persecutions.

3. They Discipline Us—Make Us Strong.
4. They Develop Patience (1:4).

This results in perfection. It lacks nothing—it is mature and complete.

B. *The Supreme Need in These Trials Is Wisdom* (1:5-8).

Wisdom is the great deficiency in the average Christian. The fear of the Lord is the beginning of wisdom. God-insight will change things with us.

1. God Is the Source of Wisdom.

2. The Means of Supplying This Need Is Asking of God in Faith (1:6-8).

Doubting is to be tossed about like the waves of the sea (v. 6). The doubting double-minded man need not expect to get things from the Lord. He is like the donkey which starved to death between two haystacks, not being able to decide from which to eat.

3. Guarantee of the Supply of That Which Man Is Deficient (1:5).

"God is liberal and upbraideth not; it shall be given him."

C. *The Rich and the Poor Are Sharers Alike in Afflictions* (1:9-11).

Both are to rejoice—the poor in his exaltation, and the rich in his humiliation for "all things work together for good to them who love God" (Rom. 8:28).

D. *The Blessed Reward of Those Who Endure* (1:12).

God is faithful and will not allow the testing to go beyond the capacity to endure.

E. *The Source of Temptations* (1:13-17).

Not from God but from human lust. The word *lust* means natural desire. Note examples of the use of desire. "With desire have I desired to eat" (Luke 22:15); "Having a desire to depart" (Phil. 1:23). Sin is not in the desire, but in the gratification of the desire in an improper way or at the wrong time. In this way a man is "drawn away and enticed." These words indicate the same as snaring animals by the hunter. When lust responds to such enticements sin is conceived and this conception brings forth death. Sin is the gratification of a right propensity in a wrong way. The cry is: "Do not err, my beloved brethren"; "Do not be deceived"; "Watch!"

III. THE NATURE OF THE TRUE CHRISTIAN—THE MAN OF FAITH (1:18-27).

A. *Regenerated by God* (1:18).

There is but one way to be a Christian, that is to be born of God

(John 1:13). This includes God's sovereign choice and His grace in effecting the salvation "of his own will begat he us." "God so loved the world, that he gave his only begotten Son, that whosoever believeth in him should not perish, but have everlasting life" (John 3:16). The instrumental means of this regeneration was the "word of truth." God calls men to preach the Gospel—the Holy Spirit works through the Word in the salvation of the hearer. Faith cometh by hearing the Word. The purpose of this regeneration is "that we should be a kind of first fruits of his creatures."

B. *Behavior of the Man of Faith* (1:19-24).

1. "Swift to Hear" (1:19).

This means the eager learner listening to the Spirit's voice in the pages of the Bible. Let everyone seriously ask himself, "Do I come with eager expectancy to hear the voice of the living Father?" God will bless such reading of His Word.

2. "Slow to Speak."

We have one mouth and two ears. We should be twice as eager to learn as to teach.

3. "Slow to Wrath."

Be not overzealous in argument. Avoid heated disputes.

4. "Lay Apart All Filthiness and Superfluity of Naughtiness" (1:21).

5. "Receive with Meekness the Engrafted Word" (1:21).

Meekness is not weakness. Meekness means the suppression of self in the interest of others.

C. *Obedience to the Word of God the Supreme Test of Faith* (1: 22-25).

To be a hearer of the Word and not a doer is to reveal the unreality of one's life. Such is the hypocrite. The looking glass suggests the laver of cleansing. The mirror of God's Word reveals our sinfulness and points to the way of amendment of life. A *look* into God's holy Word is not enough, there must be a continuation therein to get the blessing. Pretense to godliness without the control of the tongue reveals the emptiness of one's profession: "Pure religion and undefiled before God . . . is this, To visit the fatherless and widows in their affliction, and to keep himself unspotted from the world."

IV. RESPECT OF PERSONS A REVELATION OF THE HEART (2:1-13).

Where there is real faith of the Lord Jesus Christ, there is a fraternal spirit among believers—there is a brotherhood. Respect of persons reveals the absence of the real faith of Jesus Christ.

A. *Examples of* (2:1-4).

1. Treatment of Rich Man.

The appearance in the assembly of a man with a gold ring and goodly apparel is recognized by saying unto him, "Sit thou here in a good place."

2. Treatment of Poor Man.

The appearance in the assembly of a poor man in vile raiment is recognized by saying unto him, "Stand thou there, or sit here under my footstool."

This is common practice today among the worshipers of wealth and position. Such are elected to office and accorded honors. Such respect of persons does much harm. Note that this teaching of James should not be interpreted to mean that there should be no recognition given to *worth* and *position,* e.g., the pastor of the church should have recognition which is not proper to give to his chauffeur. However, should there be a case between them in court there should be no partiality shown.

B. *The Wickedness and Folly of Such Conduct* (2:5-13).

1. It Is Un-Christlike (2:5).

Such conduct shows that connection with Christ is lacking.

2. It Is Unreasonable (2:5-7).

a. God's chosen are mainly from the poor (v. 5).

b. The rich oppress the poor (v. 6).

c. They blaspheme Christ's name. Notwithstanding notable exceptions, riches constitute obstacles to spirituality. With Christ a man's poverty or riches cuts no figure. Relation with God is everything.

3. It Is Unlawful (2:8-13).

Love of Christ in the heart will cause one to treat rich and poor alike. One who shows partiality stands convicted before the Law. The Law of God is one—came forth from the same God—therefore, the breaking of one part is to be guilty of all.

V. THE TRUE NATURE OF SAVING FAITH (2:14-26).

The exposure of a barren orthodoxy. The one who says that he has faith when his works do not comport therewith is a hypocrite. Where there is genuine faith, works are always to be found. Real faith works.

A. *Faith Without Works Is Dead* (2:14-20).

A man's creed may be orthodox, but unless his character and life are such as suggests God's character, it avails nothing.

1. A Comparison (2:14-17).
2. A Challenge (2:18).
3. A Case in Point of Dead Faith (2:19, 20).

B. *Justifying Faith Is a Working Faith* (2:21-26).

This is illustrated by,

1. Abraham (2:21-24).

"Take away faith and Abraham is a murderer or a madman."

2. Rahab (2:25).

"Take away faith and Rahab would be hung in any civilized nation." This would be true in America today.

VI. THE CONTROL OF THE TONGUE A SIGN OF FAITH (3:1-12).

"This is a subject that is in everybody's mouth." Five times in his letter James brings this matter into consideration (1:19, 26; 2:12; 4:11; 5:12). This instruction is particularly addressed to religious teachers. These warnings ought to have a sobering effect upon those who aspire to be teachers. Many teachers are prone to abuse the use of the tongue. It expresses itself in willingness to give advice—no question is so complex or delicate that they cannot at once settle. They even obtrude their advice—they know your business better than you do yourself—they know what you ought to do, etc.

A. *The Control of the Tongue Is a Sign of True Religion* (3:1, 2).

B. *The Power of the Tongue* (3:3, 4).

It is a bit and helm—small things yet control the horse and ship. The tongue is to the body what the bit is to the horse and the helm is to the ship. The Christian's responsibility is to get the tongue under control.

C. *The Peril of the Tongue* (3:5-8).

1. It Is a Fire (3:6).

This finds illustration in the hunter throwing down a lighted match in the woods, or the cow kicking over the lantern in Chicago and the whole city is in flames, or a spark from a passing railway engine and the prairie is on fire.

2. It Is Untamable (3:7, 8).

No man can tame it but the Lord Jesus Christ can. The grace of God is sufficient. Why does it take so long to tame it?

3. It Is Full of Deadly Poison (3: 8).

This deadly poison does not need to be taken in large doses—a drop or two will do the work—an insinuation made, a question raised, and a reputation has been blackened and a friendship has been embittered.

4. The Perversity of the Tongue (5:9-12).

The tongue is nonpersonal and nonmoral. Its use depends upon the quality of the person. The only way to insure the right use is to have the person possessing it brought under the control of God's Spirit. Through the new birth the person becomes a new creation, and therefore uses his tongue to bless God the Father instead of cursing men who bear the image of God. The right use of the tongue proves the reality of regeneration and enables man to use his tongue to glorify God. The same fountain cannot send forth bitter water and sweet at the same time. The wise man shows forth the quality of his being by good conversation. A real Christian is always recognized by the use of his tongue.

VII. EARTHLY AND HEAVENLY WISDOM (3:13-18).

Wisdom is needed to rightly control the tongue.

A. *Test of* (3:13).

Wisdom is the moral aspect of knowledge. The wise show out of a good conversation that they have knowledge from above. Meekness of wisdom means that they have knowledge under control. Meekness means self-suppression issuing in good to others.

B. *Earthly Wisdom* (3:14-16).

This wisdom displays the following characteristics:

1. Bitter Envy and Strife (3:14).

2. It Is Earthly.

It has to do with the things of earth.

3. It Is Sensual.

It has to do with carnal lusts.

4. It Is Devilish.

C. *Heavenly Wisdom* (3:17, 18).

1. It Is Pure.

2. Peaceable.

Stress should be laid upon peace—quarrels are depreciated.

3. Courteous—Gentle, Not Self-willed.

4. Compassionate and Charitable.

5. Impartial.

6. Without Hypocrisy.

The minister should be free from unreality.

7. Fruit of Righteousness.

VIII. STRIFE—WARS AND FIGHTINGS (4:1-12).

A. *Cause of* (4:1-6).

1. Lusts—Worldly aims and Purposes (4:1, 2).

All wars including religious strife originate in lust. It is when one is enticed that the real war begins.

2. Lack of Real Prayer or Prayer with Improper Motives (4:3).

3. Desire for the World's Friendship (4:4).

Consorting with the world is spiritual adultery.

4. Envy (4:5).

5. Pride (4:6).

B. *The Correction* (4:6-12).

1. Be Humble (4:6).

God's grace is sufficient.

2. Submission to God (4:7).

3. Resist the Devil (4:7).

The only way to fight the Devil with success is by surrender to God.

4. Draw Nigh to God in the Spirit of True Penitence (4:8-10).

5. Desist from Censorious Judgments and Unchristian Criticism (4:11, 12).

Strife will remain while evil-speaking is practiced.

IX. LEAVING GOD OUT OF BUSINESS (4:13-17).

James warns against overweaning confidence.

A. *Example of* (4:13).

Proposed to go into a certain city to buy and sell to get gain for a year.

B. *The Folly of Such Action* (4:14).

Man knows not what shall be on the morrow—life itself is uncertain.

C. *Remedy for* (4:15-17).

Make all plans for the future with a recognition of God (4:15).

X. DENUNCIATION OF RICH SINNERS (5:1-6).

Not all riches are of this type. It refers to riches obtained by:

A. *Fraud and Oppression* (5:4).

Dishonest dealing with laboring men and so forth. Such dealing insults the justice of God.

B. *For Own Selfish Life* (5:5).

C. *Condemned and Killed the Just* (5:6).

Riches obtained by injustice and oppression sooner or later curse the possessor—there is no escape.

XI. THE OPPRESSED ARE TO EXERCISE PATIENCE IN VIEW OF THE LORD'S COMING (5:7-16).

A. *The Sure Deliverance Awaits the Oppressed* (5:7, 8).

B. *Grumbling Avails Nothing* (5:9).

Bitter words bring no relief.

C. *Patience and Temperate Speech Enforced by the Example of the Prophets* (5:10, 11).

The issue vindicated the wisdom of the painful process.

XII. SWEARING FORBIDDEN (5:12).

XIII. DIRECTIONS IN CASE OF AFFLICTION—JOY AND SICKNESS (5:13-18).

A. *The Afflicted—Pray* (5:13).

B. *The Merry—Sing Psalms* (5:13).

C. *The Sick* (5:14-18).

1. Call for the Elders of the Church (5:14).
2. Prayer (5:14).
3. Anoint with Oil (5:14).
4. Raised up from Sickness (5:15, 16).

This is not extreme unction but the working of the power of faith.

D. *The Power of Faith Illustrated in Elijah* (5:17, 18).

1. Who Can Pray (5:16).

The righteous ones can—those in right relationship with God and their fellow Christians.

2. How To Pray:
   a. Earnestly.
   b. Definitely—for rain.
   c. Importunately.
   d. Believingly—they pleaded the promises of God.

XIV. DUTY IN REGARD TO THE ERRING BROTHER (5:19, 20).

FIRST EPISTLE OF PETER

PART ONE—INTRODUCTORY MATTERS

I. AUTHOR.

PETER THE SON OF JONAS, one of the twelve chosen by Christ (Matt. 16:17). He introduces himself by the name which the Lord gave him, Peter. He was brought to the Saviour by his brother Andrew (John 1:40, 41). Andrew and his friend John heard the declaration of the Baptist: "Behold the Lamb of God that taketh away the sin of the world" (John 1:29, 36). They followed Jesus and at Jesus' request spent a day with Him. Andrew was pleased with his interview with Jesus and at once acquainted his brother Simon with these remarkable words: "We have found the Messias, which is, being interpreted, the Christ. And he brought him to Jesus." When Jesus beheld him He said: "Thou art Simon the son of Jona: thou shalt be called Cephas."

Peter occupies a distinguished place among the disciples. In the four lists of apostles recorded in the New Testament he stands at the head (see Matt. 10:2-4; Mark 3:16-19; Luke 6:14-16; Acts 1:13). Peter is the chief figure in the first twelve chapters of Acts—he proposes a successor to the fallen Judas—the one who preaches the notable sermon at Pentecost at which three thousand confessed Christ in baptism—he opened the door to the Gentile world in the house of Cornelius—he pronounced sentence upon Ananias and Sapphira, and he rebukes Simon the Sorcerer. It was to him Christ said: "Thou art Peter and on this rock I will build my church."

The minister should make an exhaustive study of Peter's life in order to make clear to himself and the people the teachings of these two epistles bearing the name of Peter. It would be helpful to set forth the steps in Peter's downfall and restoration. I would further recommend the study of articles by Dr. James M. Gray and Dr. William G. Morehead on Simon Peter and the Epistles of Peter in the *International Standard Bible Encyclopedia.*

II. TO WHOM ADDRESSED (1:1).

"To the strangers scattered throughout" the various provinces of Asia Minor—Christian Jews are no doubt meant—the same persons as those to whom James directed his epistle (James 1:1).

III. THE TIME OF WRITING—ABOUT A.D. 64 OR 65.

IV. THE PLACE OF WRITING—BABYLON (5:13).

Babylon on the Euphrates. If this is not literal Babylon, why should the places mentioned in 1:1 be so considered?

V. THE PURPOSE.

It was to establish all such as were passing through great suffering and severe testing. (See 1:7; 3:14; 4:12; 5:10-12.)

In connection with Peter's denial of Christ, Jesus uttered most solemn words: "When once thou hast turned again, establish thy brethren" (Luke 22:32, R.V.) which are now having fulfillment. In both of his epistles he endeavors to do this. His method of accomplishment is twofold (5:12)—"exhorting" and "testifying." "Exhorting" means calling aside or apart. "Testifying" means witnessing. His method therefore was to call aside and witness for Christ. What better method is there for today?

PART TWO—DETAILED OUTLINE

I. THE SALUTATION (1:1, 2).

A. *Personal Introduction* (1:1).

He uses the same name that Jesus gave him and declares his apostleship.

B. *Characteristics of Those Addressed* (1:2).

1. God's Elect.

All believers are the chosen of God—the especial objects of His mercy and love according to His foreknowledge and deliberate purpose.

2. Sanctification (1:2).

Process of realization of this purpose is the sanctification by the Spirit. Sanctification bears its full Bible meaning here which is the separation of the believers from the world and unto God. This is brought about by the Holy Spirit in regeneration and renewal. The Spirit is thus administering the work of Christ "unto obedience and sprinkling of the blood of Jesus Christ." Salvation of the sinner involves the work of the triune God, chosen by God the Father, sanctified by the Holy Spirit, and redeemed by the Son. All that the believer *is* and *enjoys* flows from God's mercy through the redemption of Christ's blood made effectual by the Holy Spirit.

C. *Greeting* (1:2).

"Grace and peace be multiplied." The supply of our needs is unlimited. Our eternal security is underwritten by the infinity of the triune God.

II. THE BLESSINGS AND PRIVILEGES IN CHRIST (1:3–2:10).

A. *The New Life in Christ* (1:3-5).

The reality of this new life has a very important bearing upon the establishment of the believer.

1. Its Source (1:3).

It is a new creation from God. Here Christianity parts company with all so-called religions. It is not a matter of culture but a new birth (John 3:3). Note contrasts between Christianity and all systems of man's origination. *Christianity* versus *Man's Systems of Religions:*

Regeneration–Education.
Transformation–Reform.
Vitalize–Organize.
Bear Fruit–Build Character.

2. The Range of the Possibilities of the New Life (1:3-5).

a. A vitalizing hope—"a living hope" (v. 3). It puts energy and power into the thoughts and will. It is this that tends to establish the believer in the midst of suffering and trials.

b. An enduring inheritance (v. 4). In regeneration we become heirs to a glorious spiritual estate which is imperishable. It is:

(1) Incorruptible—beyond the reach of death. No graves are ever digged on this most excellent estate.

(2) Undefiled—beyond the taint of sin. The robes of the righteous are whiter than snow.

3. A Sure Salvation (1:5).

"Kept by the power of God through faith ready to be revealed in the last times." Guarded by God from the Devil! No one can pluck from the Father's hands.

B. *Perpetual Joy* (1:6-9).

Always rejoicing in the midst of the most fiery trials. Sorrow and rejoicing form a strange wedlock. All the trials and sorrows of life tend toward the betterment of the future hope, for "we know that all things work together for good to them that love God to them who are the called according to his purpose" (Rom. 8:28). "The spiritual joy of the redeemed life is continuous and is not conditioned by the changing moods of the transient day." Funeral bells may be ringing without, but within is the joy of trustful communion with God. The winds of adversity may sweep down upon our lives causing strange bewilderment, but the joy is unbroken. This is all because of being wedded to the Lord in consecrated love—already entering upon the enjoyment of salvation.

C. *Subject of Inquiry* (1:10-12).

This wonderful salvation was a subject of inquiry and research by the prophets. Even the angels desire to look into this. The Holy Spirit in the prophets looked forward to the glorious future when through the sufferings of Christ would come the glorious kingdom of Christ. The purpose of God shall not fail. Preaching the Gospel will entail sore trials—great sufferings—but victory is sure for those who look for Him; Christ shall appear the second time without sin unto salvation (Heb. 9:28).

This was Peter's effort to nerve the believers for the conflict through which they were passing. The establishment of the children of God in the truth brings joy which is mightier than sorrow. This is a challenge to ministers today to preach the fullness of the Gospel, to nerve the believers for coming testings.

D. *Exhortation or Appeal Based upon the Coming Triumph* (1: 13-16).

"Wherefore" gathers up all previous reasonings and bases his appeal upon what had gone before.

1. Gird up the Loins of Your Mind (1:13).

This figure is taken from the flowing garments of the oriental dress. These garments may entangle and hinder, but when taken up and made into a girdle may be serviceable. Our thoughts and affections may be loose and without order, becoming as perilous as flowing robes. How true this is! We should put some strenuousness in our thinking, and our affections should be brought under control.

2. Be Sober (1:13).

This means more than abstinence from intoxicating liquors. Just as drugs and liquors bring the body into a state of stupor, so there are conditions which bring stupor to the soul. Today many are asleep—are unresponsive to the voice from on high. This sleep or stupor is caused by the opiates of pleasure, prosperity, self-serving, pride, greed, etc.

3. Set Your Hope upon the Second Coming (1:13).

Grace shall eventuate at the revelation of Jesus Christ. The hope of the coming of the Lord is a most powerful incentive to holy living.

4. Not Fashioning Oneself According to Former Lusts (1:14).

"Lusts" means carnal longings. These desires may go in various ways. We dare not conform to their demands. The controlling principle in their lives must be that of their new relation to Jesus Christ. As God's children they render obedience to Him.

5. Be Holy in All Manner of Conversation or Life (1:15, 16).

God is the pattern. God demands conformity to that pattern. His command is "be ye holy for I am holy."

E. *Unmerited Redemption a Powerful Incentive to Unfeigned Love of the Brethren* (1:17-25).

Redemption was provided at an enormous cost to God—the most valuable things of the earth as silver and gold are contemptible and pale into insignificance before it. A strong, fervent love would be a mighty factor in their establishment for earth's conflict. Thought for others is a source of strength to us as we pass through trial. "The Lord turned the captivity of Job when he prayed for his friends"

(Job 22:10). The beginning and energy of this affection is the new life implanted by the Word of God whose vitalizing and energizing power never fails because it "liveth and abideth forever." All human life is as grass which withereth away. Not upon "flesh" can we depend—our help is in God.

F. *The Method of Being Established in This Love* (2:1-3).

It is in putting away everything which contradicts love.

1. Malice.

This means badness of feeling, hatred, etc.

2. Guile, Cunning Devices, etc.
3. Hypocrisy, Pretense of Friendship.
4. Envies.
5. Evil Speaking.

Longing for the sustenance of the Word of God, enabling one to grow in grace and brotherly love. The putting away is the negative side, and the positive side is the feeding upon the Word of God. The principle of the new life was conveyed through the Word (1:23). The Word is also the means of the sustenance of that life that love might be strengthened. The love can only be strengthened by the development of the new being. The new being is the sovereign act of the Holy Spirit in effecting the new birth or regeneration. Peter says: "As newborn babes desire the sincere milk of the word that ye may grow thereby." All that a newborn babe needs to reach maturity is proper food and exercise. Happily the inherent attribute of living things is action. The children born in our homes need protection, proper food, and exercise.

G. *The Glorious Church or the Exalted Calling of Believers* (2:4-10).

They are constituted a building in which the glory of God is shed forth. Note the characteristics of this Church:

1. The Living Christ Is Its Chief Cornerstone (2:7).

Peter had not forgotten Christ's words: "Thou art Peter and upon this rock I will build my church" (Matt. 16:18).

2. Believers in Christ Are Living Stones Constituting His Body (2:5).

The living stones derive their preciousness from the chief Cornerstone, the Living Christ. The world saw no beauty or comeliness in

Him, but God, measuring by His right standard, esteemed Him precious because of our union with Christ (see v. 7, A.S.V.). Neither does the world see any preciousness in believers and may reject them as they did Christ.

3. An Elect Race or Generation (2:9).

Being a race it possesses the life principle of propagation.

4. It Is a Royal Priesthood (2:9).

It has the dignity of reigning with Christ in the realm of the Spirit and exercising powerful intercession in the presence of God. This access is by virtue of union with Christ—the Mediator.

5. It Is a Holy Nation Where Just and Righteous Policies Rule (2:9).

6. The Tenant of This House Is the Holy Spirit (2:5).

Surely this is a grand and majestic house which God is building. Would you have a place in it?

III. THE SEEMLY BEHAVIOR OF BELIEVERS IN CHRIST (2:11—4:19).

Believers in Christ are strangers and pilgrims—they do not belong to this world. Therefore their conduct should be seemly—consistent with their high calling.

A. *Abstinence from Fleshly Lusts* (2:11).

This term *lusts* includes the entire army of unclean forces which antagonize the Spirit such as carnal passion, the jealous eye, envy, avarice, selfish ambition, etc.

B. *Behavior Honest Before the Gentiles—the Heathen* (2:12).

Christians should so live before the world that it will be impossible for the world to speak against them as evildoers, but oblige them to glorify God through their good works. Jesus said: "Let your light so shine before men that they may see your good works and glorify your Father which is in heaven" (Matt. 5:16).

C. *Submission to Properly Constituted Authority* (2:13-18).

A Christian man recognizes the necessity of social order and will graciously submit to authority regardless of the form of government, for human government is an ordinance of God (Gen. 9:1-11; Rom. 13:1-7). This he does not through cringing fear, but for the Lord's sake. By freely submitting to rightly constituted authority as a servant of God he puts to silence the ignorance of foolish men. The carrying out of this injunction will keep us in the spirit of reverence and carry us through the entire circle of human relationships.

1. Honor All Men (2:17).

We should see in every man the image of God, and therefore, reverence him. We should show this spirit in all human relations—in the home, among our children and friends. What sanctity of life this would bring!

2. Love the Brotherhood (2:17).

How can one help it? Humanity is an organism; as part of that organism we are interested in each other. In our relationship to that new organism the Church we are doubly bound to love each other.

3. Fear God (2:17).

Bearing the likeness and image of God we have God-consciousness such that we know Him.

4. Honor the King or Ruler (2:17).

5. Servants Be Subject to Your Masters.

This refers to slaves who had been made free in Christ. This he should be and do even though his master was not a good man and unreasonable.

D. *Endure Unmerited Suffering for Christ's Sake* (2:19-25).

Christ is the Christians' supreme example. He was patient under the most terrible afflictions. He vicariously suffered for us—not because of sin in Him. In the midst of it all He committed Himself to God. This is a high ideal—servants when under authority of unreasonable masters should show the spirit in which Christ bore the cross.

E. *The Marriage Relation* (3:1-7).

1. The Ideal Wife (3:1-6).

a. In subjection to her own husband (v. 1). The headship of man is God's order and should not be disregarded. Man's headship obtains in creation and redemption.

b. Chaste in character (v. 2). Purity of life is essential to noble womanhood. Impurity in woman is something which even an impure man will not respect. Not that there are different moral standards for men and women.

c. Modesty (vv. 3-6). Meekness is not servile fear. It is the opposite of the spirit of self-aggression which pushes itself into publicity. It is the opposite of self-advertisement, the opposite of loud ostentatiousness. The loud woman can never make a good wife for no man has respect for such a woman, therefore, there cannot be needed companionship.

d. Restful and rest giving—"the grace of repose." (See v. 6, A.S.V.) "Not put in fear by any terror." This means that she is not "the victim of sudden wild alarms." What an untold blessing is such a woman as a wife! How essential to a man's well-being!

2. The Ideal Husband (3:7).

a. Reasonable—"dwell with them according to knowledge." Reason not passion should control man's behavior to his wife. Unreasonableness of the husband brings great unhappiness to married life. No trouble about a wife being in subjection to such a husband. Her very nature makes her to be in subjection. Sarah is the grand example of the woman's subjection to her husband (v. 6).

b. A spirit of reverence—"giving honor to the wife." The reasonable husband perceives the function of womanhood. When such recognition is given to the wife, the proper honor will be given. Headship implies reasonableness.

c. Conduct in conformity with prayer, "that your prayers be not hindered." When a husband lives with his wife in accordance with his praying there will be fellowship and communion. How few of our prayers are answered because of the miserable inconsistencies of our lives!

F. *Behavior Toward One Another as Members of the Body of Christ* (3:8-22).

1. Elements of (3:8-14).

a. Oneness of mind.

b. Mutual compassion—recognition of each other's frailties will cause forbearance.

c. Loving as brethren.

d. Tenderhearted.

e. Pitiful.

f. Courteous.

g. Not rendering evil for evil—railing for railing, but blessing for blessing.

This is enforced by a quotation from Psalm 34:10-12. The one who thus lives may suffer for righteousness' sake. No harm can come to him, but rather blessing. Be not troubled.

2. How To Bear These Graces (3:15-17).

"Sanctify the Lord God in your hearts." This means to set the heart apart as the territory over which the Lord supremely reigns. By so doing one will be able to give answers "to every man that asketh you a reason for the hope that is in you," and put to shame your revilers.

3. Christ the Supreme Example (3:18-25).

He inspires such conduct in the midst of suffering. His sufferings were more than exemplary—they were substitutionary and saving. Three things are asserted of Him:

a. The sinless suffered for the sinner to bring him to God (v. 18).

b. Following His death, in His life in the Spirit, He preached to the spirits in prison (vv. 19-21).

c. He is enthroned—in supreme authority.

G. *Christian Fidelity Enjoined Regardless of the Treatment of a Hostile World* (4:1-19).

1. Be Patient in Suffering (4:1-6).

For as Christ ultimately triumphed, so shall all who arm themselves with the same mind. This triumph shall be realized when account is rendered to the Judge of the quick and the dead.

Those who were dead were doubtless those who died as a result of the bloody persecutions. This was the "judgment of men" while in the body. The preaching of the Gospel would, therefore, mean such as heard and accepted while living.

In view of the dangers of the judgment, and the glorious triumph of those who crucify the lusts of the flesh, Peter exhorts that they live according to the will of God (4:2-5).

2. Practice Sobriety (4:7).

Why? How?

3. Have Fervent Love (4:8).

Fervent means "tense." Why? Charity covers a multitude of sins.

4. Practice Hospitality (4:9-11).

Hospitality primarily refers to the use of spiritual gifts—ordinary meaning not excluded.

5. Rejoice in Tribulations (4:12-19).

These fiery trials are on account of righteousness. Many suffer because of sin. Even though the believer is free from judgment, yet his works shall be judged. No glory or reward for the sufferings of the saved man who sins.

IV. OFFICIAL DUTIES (5:1-4).

A. *Feed the Flock, Not Fleece Them.*

B. *Watch the Flock* (5:2).

Flocks need the care of a shepherd.

C. *Do Not Lord It over the Flock* (5:3).

D. *Payment Will Be Made at the Coming of the Lord.*

V. HUMILITY AND VIGILANCE ENJOINED (5:5-7).

A. *How?* (5:5).

B. *Why?* (5:6, 7).

VI. THE CHRISTIAN'S CONFLICT (5:8-11).

A. *The Adversary—the Devil* (5:8).

He is a personal being and most active and alert. Goes about "seeking."

B. *His Method* (5:8).

Intimidation. He goes about as a roaring lion—sometimes by craft.

C. *His Purpose.*

Destruction—seeking whom he may devour.

D. *The Christian's Attitude.*

1. Be Sober.

Be free from everything that intoxicates.

2. Watchful.

3. Resist—Steadfast in the Faith.

This all must do until the Devil takes a holiday.

VII. THE SALUTATION (5:12-14).

A. *God of All Grace Make You Perfect, Stablish, Strengthen, and Settle You.*

B. *Ascription of Glory and Dominion to Jesus Christ.*

SECOND EPISTLE OF PETER

PART ONE—INTRODUCTORY MATTERS

THIS LETTER WAS ADDRESSED to the same people or church as was I Peter (see 3:1).

The time of writing was shortly before Peter's death (1:14).

The purpose was to warn and caution (2:1, 2; 3:17, 18).

PART TWO—DETAILED OUTLINE

I. THE SALUTATION (1:1, 2).

A. *From Simon Peter, the Bondservant and Apostle of Jesus Christ.*

B. *To Other Christians.*

To those who had obtained a like precious faith through the righteousness of God and our Saviour Jesus Christ.

C. *Greetings.*

Grace and peace be multiplied unto you through the knowledge of God and Jesus our Lord.

II. PROGRESS IN THE CHRISTIAN LIFE URGED (1:3-21).

The only security against backsliding and apostasy is to grow in grace and the knowledge of God and Jesus Christ our Lord. In order to grow in grace there must be:

A. *Knowledge of God* (1:2-4).

"Grace and peace be multiplied through the knowledge of God and Jesus our Lord"—all things pertaining to life and godliness—all things through which the believer is made partaker of the divine nature.

B. *Lines of Growth* (1:5-9).

Faith is a gift of God. We must add to faith virtue or courage—

to courage, knowledge—to knowledge, temperance—to temperance, patience—to patience, godliness—to godliness, brotherly kindness—to brotherly kindness charity. Growth in all these directions insures fruitfulness of life.

III. GROWTH ISSUES IN ASSURANCE OF OUR CALLING AND ELECTION (1:10, 11).

The proof of life is action and fruitfulness. The unregenerate person is dead. The saved person has been made a partaker of the divine nature—has life from above. "By their lives ye shall know them." The tree is known by its fruit.

IV. PETER'S MOTIVE (1:12-21).

His warning the people of the peril of the failure to grow was to arouse them to diligence—to bring to their remembrance the things he had taught them. Peter knew that the time of his death was near, therefore, he sought to establish them in the truth by:

A. *Giving His Personal Testimony* (1:12-18).

He had been with the Lord on the Mount of the Transfiguration and heard and seen the consummation of the divine purpose.

B. *Giving the Testimony of the Old Testament Prophets* (1:19-21).

These prophets spoke the very message of God.

V. THE REASONS FOR THE WARNING (2:1—3:18).

A. *The Incoming of False Prophets and False Teachers* (2:1-22).

1. They Are Sure To Appear (2:1-3).

They shall secretly bring in damnable heresies—even denying the Lord who bought them.

2. Their Awful Doom (2:4-10).

3. Their Character and Teaching (2:11-22).

B. *Scoffers* (3:1-18).

1. Shall Appear in the Last Days (3:1-3).

2. At What They Scoff (3:4).

Promises of Christ's second coming.

3. The Lord's Delay No Ground for Scoffing (3:5-8).

Time cuts no figure with God.

4. The Certainty of the Lord's Coming a Mighty Incentive to Holy Living (3:9-13).

5. The Lord's Delay Means Salvation (3:14-18).

FIRST EPISTLE OF JOHN

PART ONE–INTRODUCTORY MATTERS

I. The Writer.

Unbroken tradition and internal evidence ascribes the authorship to John the apostle.

Characteristics of John's personality greatly help in the understanding and appreciation of his message.

A. *"I, John Your Brother"* (Rev. 1:9).

He recognized himself as a fellow member of the human family. God is the Father of all members of the race. John took his place in sorrow and suffering with his fellow believers.

B. *He Was Reserved.*

He was decidedly reticent as to himself–giving first thought and place to others.

C. *He Had Keen Mental Penetrative Insight.*

He did not reach conclusions merely by process of reasoning. He was indeed a seer. He had the rare gift of seeing. He could see the truth in its entirety.

D. *He Was the Apostle of Love.*

He said: "Let us love one another: for love is of God" (I John 4:7). His very nature was steeped in the redeeming love of God. This love was not soft, yielding sentiment, but an overmastering passion which seized its object with all its might and repelled whatever tended to disgrace the loved one. This element of his nature accounts for the vehemence of speech in his writings, e.g., "Who is a liar but he that denieth that Jesus is the Christ?" (I John 2:22). His love was not only for God, but for the children of God–his brethren. In fact, love to the brethren was the evidence that he loved God the

Father. He that loveth not his brother whom he has seen is incapable of loving the unseen Father (I John 4:20).

E. *Fiery Vehemence.*

John was not the soft, effeminate, weak man usually thought of, but was capable of displaying fiery zeal. He was thoroughly masculine with strong affection. Note his ambition for pre-eminence in the kingdom (Mark 10:37), and the stern judgment requested against the unhospitable Samaritans (Luke 9:54). He was truly a "Boanerges" so named by the One who truly knew men's inner selves. His love for the Lord would brook no insults or slights by the Samaritans. In the Book of Revelation he pronounces wrath and judgment upon those remaining impenitent (Rev. 21:8).

II. THE POSITION OF JOHN THE APOSTLE.

He might be called pastor—patriarch. His flocks were widely scattered beyond the reach of his voice. His advanced age prevented his journeying among them, therefore, he was obliged to communicate with them by writing—"pen and ink" (see II and III John). John seems to have been the successor to Paul in the churches at Ephesus, etc., in Asia Minor. Paul planted and John nourished the churches. The Lord blessed the work, but the weeds of heresy and contention hindered the growth as Paul had foretold in Acts 20:29, 30. "Grievous wolves" among them—men would arise from among themselves "speaking perverse things." John's letters show this to have been true.

III. JOHN'S MESSAGE TO THIS PRESENT AGE.

No age since John's is more like this, and none greater in need of his message than ours. The same heretical notions as to Christ's Person and work—the same moral insensibility—the same tendency to impurity, and the same lack of brotherly love. False doctrine and wrong living are very closely related. Wrong doctrine will cause wrong living. Doctrine and ethics cannot be divorced. In meeting the heresies of his age, John shows that the real Christian life is fellowship in the Incarnate Word, and that the Christian creed demands faith in the deity, Incarnation, and atonement of the Son of God as manifesting God's love.

IV. JOHN'S PURPOSE IN WRITING.

It was twofold.

A. *To Give Assurance* (5:13).

B. *To Warn* (5:21).

The Gospel of John was written that faith might issue in life (20:31). This epistle was written to exhibit certain tests which might issue in assurance (5:13). By assurance is not meant a certain mystic, self-evidencing acceptance with God, but a conviction based upon grounds simple, definite, and plain. This epistle furnishes definite criteria by which one can satisfy himself of his having been begotten of God.

Because of this John speaks with unqualified assurance. His testimony is positive. He who knows and knows that he knows has the message which the world needs. With reference to Christ there are several classes of people in the world:

1. Those Who Are Too Weak To Deny Him.

The agnostic—not intellectual weakness, but moral; sin in the life makes men cowards.

2. Those Who "Hope," "Guess," "Think."

They are to be pitied. They might and ought to know.

3. Those Who, Like John, "Know" and Know That They Know.

Call the agnostic a philosopher if you like; remain with the "I hope so" class lest you show presumption if you are timid, but as for me I join with John and say "I know."

V. THE TIME.

The exact time of this writing cannot be determined, presumably A.D. 90-95.

VI. THE THEME.

Fellowship in the Life Eternal or The Tests of Eternal Life (1:2, 3; cf. 5:20).

PART TWO— DETAILED OUTLINE

It is imperative that the structure of this epistle be grasped. The thought of the author does not move in straight lines, like Paul's, for example, but revolves around a center. His themes recur again and again—are brought into various relations to each other. His method or style is "spiral"—something like a winding staircase, revolving around a common center, but with each cycle reaching a higher level.

The themes thus operating are righteousness, love, and belief, binding together the thoughts of the epistle. Doing righteousness, loving one another, and believing that Jesus is the Christ come in the flesh are the definite tests which determine as to whether one is a child of God.

I. THE PROLOGUE (1:1-4).

A. *Eternal Life.*

"The spring of being, this animating principle of the universe from the nearest star to the farthest star, from the archangel to the worm in the sod" was now manifested in Jesus Christ. John's method is not *argument,* but to bring the truth with such magnificent splendor as to pulverize and minimize the error. Jesus Christ who is now the source of the spiritual life is also the source of the natural life. He assumes the solidarity of the universe, the unity of the seen and the unseen. Therefore no room is left for the false philosophy which was so rife in Asia Minor at that time, such as Docetism, Manicheism, and the doctrines of the Ebionites.

B. *Manifestation* (1:1, 2).

This eternal life was manifested to competent witnesses—John and his fellow apostles. Their most trustworthy senses corroborated their testimony. They heard, saw and touched—the actuality of what they witnessed could not be doubted.

C. *Participation* (1:3).

Participation in that life brings fellowship with or unto the Father and the Son. Believers are thus introduced through union with Jesus Christ. This union and fellowship are made possible through the Incarnation of God in Christ. The manifestation of this life was to bring men into fellowship with God.

D. *Result* (1:4).

The issue of this fellowship is fullness of joy. Only those who know by experience this joy are truly blessed.

II. FIRST CYCLE OF THOUGHT: FELLOWSHIP IN THE LIFE ETERNAL TESTED BY WALKING IN THE LIGHT (1:5–2:28).

Walking in the light involves.

A. *Doing Righteousness* (1:5–2:6).

This in turn involves:

1. Recognition of His Character (1:5).

Recognition of the character of Him with whom fellowship is enjoyed. "God is light and in him is no darkness at all." He is in wonderful contrast to heathen gods. He is all truth–in Him is no trickery, malice, or wantonness. He can be absolutely trusted. This is serious truth. Yet most grand and sublime. It is highly stimulating to know that through Jesus Christ fellowship with the living God is possible.

2. Being in Accord (1:6-8).

Being in sympathetic accord with the mind and will of God. To have fellowship with a person there must be a likeness. The unreality of one's life is manifested:

a. By hypocritically denying the presence of sin. "If we say we have fellowship with God and walk in darkness, we lie" (v. 6). To profess fellowship with God and be dishonest, unchaste, malicious, spiteful is virtually to declare that God is like himself–to drag God down to his own level. Only clean hands and a pure heart can dwell in God's "holy hill."

b. By boldly denying the principle of sin and the fact of one's actual sins (v. 8). Denying inherent depravity is common today in naturalistic thought and in the doctrine of sinless perfection. Such impertinence *deceives us and makes God a liar.*

3. Recognizing the Nature of Sin (1:9, 10).

Truly recognizing the nature of sin and confession of acutal personal sins to God. Unconfessed sin prevents fellowship with God.

4. Using Advocacy (2:1, 2).

Availing oneself of the advocacy of Christ before the Father. Christ the Mediator acts in behalf of His people. This representation is necessary for the *maintenance* of fellowship and the *only way* it can be restored when once forfeited by *disobedience.*

The relationship of advocate and client involves a personal tie of acquaintanceship and often of kinship between the parties. The Advocate was not a hired pleader, but the head of a clan bound by the claims of honor and family association. Such we have in Jesus Christ. Two conditions in the success of the advocate are:

a. The character and competency; "Jesus Christ the righteous." He appeals on the strict grounds of righteousness.

b. The name of Him to whom the appeal is addressed—the *Father.* Not hard to persuade the Father whose essential nature is *Love.* It is justice pleading with love. The grounds upon which the plea is made is the propitiation of God's own providing satisfaction for sins on the cross of Calvary. The cross is an offense today with many preachers.

5. Obeying God's Commandments (2:3-6).

Keeping commandments is the sure sign of participation in the life of God. Obedience is not a way of *getting* life, but of *expressing* it. Jesus Christ is the supreme Example. Disobedience is the "lie" of life (2:4) just as impenitence is the "lie" of the conscience (1:8). Both are fatal to fellowship. The obedience here is *filial* not *legal.* It is the result of a community of nature.

B. *Loving* (2:7-17).

This is the "old"—"new" commandment. It is as old as creation and is as new as Christ's teaching. Love marks the difference between the Christian and the non-Christian. The one is walking in the light and the other is walking in darkness.

1. The Brethren (2:7-11).

2. Not Loving the World (2:12-17).

By the *world* is not meant the physical universe, business, vocations, society, and home life, but the moral order of things under the dominion of the Devil. In this world there is a trinity of evil:

a. "Lust of the flesh"—all corrupt bodily desires—no one is free from them.

b. "Lust of the eyes." This means the passion to see and enjoy the things of the flesh. This may involve dress, music, and art.

c. "Vainglory of life." This means selfishness expending itself in vain show and pomp. It squanders its wealth in proud display and struts with haughty arrogance. Note the old Puritans' analysis of pride. The pride of race, the pride of place, the pride of face, and the pride of grace. Participation in the life of God excludes the moral life which is dominated by the lust of the flesh, the lust of the eyes, and the pride of life.

C. *Believing* (2:18-28).

Believing in Jesus Christ as the incarnate Son of God. Walking in the light reveals Jesus Christ in His true nature. The Incarnation of the Son of God is the very touch-stone by which all that calls itself Christian is to be tested. Denial of the Incarnation is Antichrist (v. 22). This cannot be overemphasized.

The anointing of the Holy Spirit is essential to the right knowledge of Christ's Person and work. No one who has this anointing will deny the virgin birth.

Believing in Christ is abiding in Him and waiting for His coming. Those who abide in Him and are anointed by the Spirit will not be led astray by the Antichrist and his heresy concerning Christ (vv. 18-28). In this section we see the darkness of sin set over against the true light which combats it at every point—in the individual soul (1:6—2:11); and in the world (2:15-17); and in the anti-Christian movements in the Church which deny the deity of Jesus Christ (2:18-27).

III. SECOND CYCLE OF THOUGHT: FELLOWSHIP IN THE LIFE ETERNAL TESTED BY DIVINE BIRTH (2:29—4:6).

Verse 29 is the transition from the test by walking in the light and the test by divine birth. This is an advance thought upon the first cycle. There the governing thought was based upon what God is to us—the light of the Incarnation. Here the basic thought is what God is in His essential nature. Therefore, John sets forth the characteristics of those who have been "begotten of God." "Born of God" is the key verse.

Three invariable and unfailing tests are again applied:

A. *Doing Righteousness* (2:29—3:10*a*).

Doing righteousness is the ground upon which we know that we have been born of God. A community of nature results in doing righteousness, for God is righteous (2:29). Is every righteous man a child of God? Yes, but distinguish between righteousness and what men call morality. Doing righteous is doing right by God Himself.

Doing righteousness involves:

1. Recognition of Our Sonship (3:1, 2).

We are God's children. It is a matter of amazement that human sinful nature should be brought into such relationship with God. He takes ragged and starving prodigals and gives them not only names as sons but characters as well. "What manner of love hath the Father bestowed upon us that we should be called the sons of God." The origin of such grace is God's love. Note the glory of God's children which is now concealed (v. 1), and then of its future manifestation (v. 2). The future glory in prospect is a mighty impulse to present holy living.

2. Living the Life as Sons of God (3:3-10).

Experiencing the Father's love excludes the practice of sin. Because:

a. Sin will be ruinous to the glorious meeting of the Lord Jesus at His coming in glory. The moral compulsion of this hope leads to a life of absolute righteousness which means conformity to Christ's standards.

b. Sin is illegal (v. 4). Worse still it is rebellion against God.

c. Sin is unchristian (vv. 5-7). The one who practices sin knows not God. There is no sin in Him, therefore, the one who practices sin cannot have fellowship with God.

d. Sin is devilish (vv. 8, 9). The one who practices sin has the nature and is under the power of the Devil—is his child. There are only two classes in the world—the children of God and the children of the Devil. The life of a son of God is one of opposition to sin—sin is of the Devil. Christ came to destroy him and his works. Christ's method of accomplishing this is through the sonship of believers. Righteousness is to be brought into the world by regeneration—not by reformation. The change needed is not so much ethical as biological (see v. 9).

B. *Loving* (3:10*b*—24).

1. Two Fathers in the World—God and the Devil.

The marks which distinguish the children of these respective parents are:

a. Righteousness and Unrighteousness.

b. Brotherly love and hatred.

c. Self-sacrifice and murder (vv. 10*b*-16).

God's children love those born of God—not merely my sect, set, or coterie. Christ is the pattern of love. Love to their brethren is a test of participation in that life. This love is shown in everyday life (3:17, 18), expresses itself in meeting common needs—even in hazarding our lives for the brethren. This truth finds illustration in Cain and Christ—prototypes of hatred and love. Cain is still slaying Abel, and Abel's blood is still crying from the ground in every act of unscrupulous rivalry and extortion from the necessity of others. Thus controversy and hatred go on because the one's deeds are evil and the other's righteous—compromise is impossible, therefore, murder is the climax.

Love is such a strong ground of assurance that when other things fail us—even when our heart condemns us—the consciousness of love —God's knowledge—stays us. Where there is love, God is, for God is love (vv. 19, 20).

2. The Indwelling Holy Spirit (3:24).

He causes the love of God to be shed abroad in our hearts. The Spirit only dwells in the regenerated life. We therefore have the unfailing witness within ourselves that we are God's children.

3. Doing the Things That Please God (3:24).

Keeping His commandments is the expression of love to God.

C. *Believing* (4:1-6).

These verses imply that spiritual discernment is a proof of sonship. The supernatural and divine are not necessarily identical. Truth has its counterfeit. Over against the personal God is the personal Devil. Over against Christ is the Antichrist, and over against the Holy Spirit are the lying spirits.

The right to gauge and test teachers and their doctrine belongs to all believers. Yes, the obligation to do so is enjoined upon them (Matt. 7:15-19). "Believe not" "but try" is John's command (v. 1). Christ foretold the appearance of lying spirits (Matt. 24:24). The world is now filled with them. Some teach part truth, keeping back that which is repugnant to the natural man. Some teach error mainly. Satan transforms himself into an angel of light for he is God's ape. The need of trying the spirits has never been greater than now. Happily the apostle furnishes us with three infallible proofs by which everyone may know the teachers and the teaching (vv. 2-6).

1. Belief in the Incarnation Is an Absolute Test of Sonship.

The Person and work of Christ are the touch-stone. Do they deny Christ's essential deity? His virgin birth? Did Christ come in the flesh? How about blood atonement? Substitution and ransom? His resurrection from the dead? All who do this are of Antichrist—the enemies of the Lord Jesus—therefore, no one sharing their fellowship can have fellowship in the life eternal. This test never fails.

2. The Second Test Is Their Following (4:5).

"The world heareth them." He who is born of God knows the voice of the Son of God through the Gospel testimony.

3. Agreement with Apostolic Teaching (4:6).

"He that is not of God heareth not us." Reception of Christ's servants and message is reception of Him and vice versa. These tests bring into light the historical situation of John's time, e.g., Docetists, Ebionite, Manichaeus, etc. Same heresies appear today under different names.

IV. THIRD CYCLE OF THOUGHT: FELLOWSHIP IN THE LIFE ETERNAL TESTED BY OVERCOMING LIFE (4:7—5:12).

In this cycle the same themes appear but with changed order and different proportions. Righteousness takes a subordinate place giving the chief place to *love* and *belief*. This cycle moves to still a higher plane.

The overcoming life is living:

A. *By Loving* (4:7-21).

Love is the sphere and motive of the new life—it is divine. Twice love has been urged.

1. As the Law of the True Life for Man (2:7-11).
2. As the Sign of a True Birth from God (3:10-18).
3. Apostle Shows Love To Be the Very Essence of God Himself.

All love has been kindled from the fires that burn in the very being of God. "God is love" is the great declaration and "he that dwelleth in love dwelleth in God and God in him" (v. 16).

4. Three Ideas Touching the Love of God Revealed in Christ:
   a. Love's source—the very nature of God (v. 8).
   b. Love's manifestation—the mission of Christ (v. 10).
   c. Love's consummation—Christian brotherhood (v. 12).

5. Born-again Ones Will Live the Love-life.

We love as a consequence of having been made a partaker of the divine nature. This love-life—the commingling of the human and divine through the Holy Spirit—expresses itself in:

a. Testifying that the Father sent His Son to be the world's Saviour (v. 14).

b. Confessing Jesus as the Son of God (v. 15).

c. Assurance of incorporation of God's nature in us (v. 16).

d. Casting out all fear and dread of coming judgment (vv. 17, 18).

e. Uniting God and man in one Person (vv. 19-21). Love to God and man is identical. One born of God will love man made in God's image.

B. *By Believing* (5:1-12).

This world-conquering faith is characterized by having:

1. As Its Object Jesus Christ the Son of God (5:1, 5).

When this faith is lived in the sphere of love there is power to win men from the world. Where it is lacking, the power is absent. This is illustrated by Dr. Chapman's testimony of the New England's defection following the Unitarian heresy. To believe that the one who took my nature and suffered death for me is also one with God is to be gripped with power superior to the world.

2. As Its Grounds, Testimony of the Spirit, the Water, and the Blood (5:8).

The Spirit is the third member of the Godhead; the water signifies the Father's testimony at the Jordan baptism; the blood is that of the cross. The Spirit has this as His supreme business, and is ever active. So is the cross still testifying by gripping men's hearts and saving them. This has been going on all through the centuries of church history. It has pragmatic sanction. Rationalists reject this testimony and make God a liar.

3. As Its Marks:

a. Love as its operating master principle (v. 2). Love for God's children. Love is not animal passion—not corporate selfishness—not mere devotion to friends, class, family, etc., while harsh and unjust to outsiders.

b. Keeps God's commandments (v. 3).

4. As Its Example and Lord—Jesus Christ.

Discipleship spells discipline. Love has its bounds and rules. An army without discipline would be without victory. So-called freedom today is as bad as the antinomianism of John's day. This discipline includes:

a. Guarding the tongue.
b. Honesty in business.
c. Regular attention to home and church duties.
d. Purity of heart and life.
e. Decency of conversation, etc.

The world-conquering faith confesses Jesus Christ as Lord and obeys His requirements.

V. THE EPILOGUE (5:13-21).

The meeting of these tests gloriously issues:

A. *In Assurance of Personal Salvation* (5:13).

Decided differences between faith and assurance of faith. The first may be present while the second is lacking. One may have peace with God and lack the peace *of* God.

Assurance is highly important for the peace and joy of the believer himself and for energy and power to win others to Christ.

B. *In Prevailing Prayer* (5:14, 15).

Assurance of salvation must be put to practical use in interceding for the salvation of others. To see God's children sinning and not pray for them is as great a sin as to have this world's goods and not give to those in need. Christians all about us are in doubt, being tossed to and fro. We should pray for them. Having the nature of Christ we will do the work of a mediator. Christian assurance then is not an end but a condition to an end—great need. We know that we have the petitions.

C. *In Making the Erring Brother Special Object of Prayer* (5:16).

If we see an erring brother sin, pray for him, not tell tales about him and whisper abroad. One limitation—the sin unto death.

D. *In an Experimental Creed* (5:18-21).

1. Begotten of God Does Not Sin—Overcomes the World (5:18).
2. A Holy Life Is the Test of Salvation.

SECOND EPISTLE OF JOHN

PART ONE—INTRODUCTORY MATTERS

THIS IS A PERSONAL, private letter addressed to an unknown Christian woman and her family. Dr. A. T. Pierson, an honored lecturer at the Moody Bible Institute in the days of D. L. Moody, said: "It sets a high value on the piety of a mother and her household; and warns against the abuse of hospitality by those who would undermine holy living and propagate error. It is a tribute to the dignity of womanhood, wifehood, and motherhood. Her home and household are guarded. John warns against those who not only err in doctrine, but who sow the seeds of heresy and iniquity. Hospitality is not forbidden, nor courtesy; but proper guards are placed about a home when evil teachers might work great harm."

PART TWO—DETAILED OUTLINE

I. THE SALUTATION (vv. 1-4).

A. *The Humility of the Writer* (v. 1).

He calls himself the "elder." The most eminent member the church might have said "apostle" but he chose to be known as the "elder," the loving and beloved pastor who mingled with the members of his flock.

B. *Unto the Elect Lady* (v. 1).

This must have been a Christian woman of distinction—of gifts and graces. Her children are included with her in this salutation. John expressed his true Christian affection for the members of this household. It is this undying love which binds together the members of the Body of Christ.

C. *The Greeting* (v. 3).

The three words *grace, mercy* and *peace* include all the blessings to the believer from their source the unmerited favor of God to the "peace which passeth all understanding." This is the experience of those who have accepted Christ as the divine Son of God and are walking in love toward their fellow men.

D. *The Insight into the Elect Lady's Household* (v. 4).

Their spiritual condition was the occasion of great rejoicing to John.

II. THE BURDEN OF JOHN'S HEART-MESSAGE (vv. 5-11).

A. *"That We Love One Another"* (v. 5).

Love is the "old-new" commandment and is a perpetual obligation. The supreme test of the fulfillment of this obligation is rendering obedience to God's commandments.

B. *Witnessing to the True Doctrine of Christ* (vv. 7-10).

Doctrine and life are inseparable. Erroneous thinking issues in wrong living. The supreme test of doctrine is the Incarnation of Christ. To deny that Jesus Christ "is come in the flesh" is to show that one to be a deceiver and an antichrist. The professed minister who rejects the historic doctrine of the virgin birth and the deity of Christ forfeits his right to recognition as a Christian (v. 7).

C. *John Warns Against Extending Courtesy to Such Deceivers* (vv. 9-10).

They are not to be received into the house or bidden God-speed. Those who do so are partakers of the evil deeds of the false teachers.

There has never been a time when John's message has been more needed than now.

III. THE SUPERSCRIPTION (vv. 12, 13).

Having given counsel of Christian love and sounded warning as to compromising in any way with the truth of the Christian faith, he now tells that there were many other things of importance to write but finds that writing with paper and ink was unsatisfactory. Furthermore, he was expecting to visit them at which time he could talk face to face with them. He closes with greetings from the household of their elect sister.

THIRD EPISTLE OF JOHN

PART ONE—INTRODUCTORY MATTERS

THIS STUDY IS INTRODUCED by quoting the first paragraph of Dr. Charles Erdman's treatment of this epistle in his book on the General Epistles. "This precious little fragment of the past may well engage our thoughtful review, for it contains pen portraits from the Apostolic Age which the passing of the centuries has not dimmed, which reflect the life of the early Church, and which bring to Christians of every age and land messages of encouragement and warning and cheer."

PART TWO—DETAILED OUTLINE

I. PERSONAL GREETING (vv. 1-4).

A. *From the Elder or Presbyter.*

Note his humility. Does not call himself apostle, but uses the name by which he was known among the Christians.

B. *To the Well-Beloved Gaius.*

The first pen portrait was of the beloved Gaius. He was the beloved among his fellow believers and especially loved by John—"whom I love in the truth." Truth is the basis of real love and its activating impulse. Note his wish for Gaius (v. 2). It was for "soul-health" and prosperity which includes physical well-being. All these are embraced in the elder's wish. Gaius was loved because of his loyalty to the Lord and also for his generosity to the traveling preachers and evangelists (vv. 5-8). These were strangers to him, but for the sake of the *name* he received them into his home thus furthering the Gospel cause. In II John the Christians are cautioned against receiving into their homes false teachers. Now he praises Gaius for encouragement given to the preachers of the Gospel of Christ. John's highest joy was to hear that his spiritual children were walking in the truth. Gaius was a fellow helper to the truth.

C. *The Second Pen Portrait Was That of Diotrephes* (vv. 9, 10).

His characteristic was pride of place—he loved to have the place of pre-eminence and arbitrarily sought to have his own way. He was an ecclesiastic tyrant. This man was opposed to the teaching of John whom he attacked "with malicious words." This was incipient priesthood which was condemned by John. "He that doeth good is of God, but he that doeth evil hath not seen God" (v. 11).

D. *The Third Pen Portrait Was of Demetrius* (vv. 11, 12).

He was a man held in high esteem of all men. This was corroborated by John himself (v. 12).

"No less striking is the picture of the early Church which the epistle portrays. It appears as a household of brethren, united by bonds of Christian love, separated from the unbelieving world, extending its influence by unselfish service and by gracious hospitality, not free, however, from the perils of ambition and jealousy and faction among its members, but guarded and guided by men of apostolic gifts and graces, strong in love, rejoicing in truth, devoted to Christ."

II. THE CONCLUSION (vv. 13, 14).

A. *The Possible Personal Visit.*

B. *The Salutation.*

THE EPISTLE OF JUDE

PART ONE–INTRODUCTORY MATTERS

I. Author–Brother of James.

He calls himself "the servant of Jesus Christ, and brother of James." Who the James is we are left to conjecture. He recognized a relationship to the Lord Jesus Christ more intimate than that of human kinship.

II. The Time of Writing.

It was perhaps about A.D. 67, certainly before the fall of Jerusalem, or that awful judgment of God upon wickedness would have been mentioned.

III. The Purpose of This Epistle.

It was to warn Christians against false teachers and to urge them to "earnestly contend for the faith." Jude started out with the thought of writing a treatise on the common faith but was directed by the Holy Spirit to impose upon the saints the obligation of contending for the faith.

PART TWO–DETAILED OUTLINE

I. The Introduction (vv. 1, 2).

A. *Persons Addressed* (v. 1).

1. Called (A.S.V.), or Sanctified (A.V.).

This has been because they are beloved in God. Salvation began in the heart of God.

2. Preserved in and Kept for Jesus Christ.

The saints are not only preserved for Christ, but kept in Him.

B. *The Salutation* (v. 2).

"Mercy unto you, and peace, and love, be multiplied."

II. THE OBLIGATION IMPOSED (v. 3).

It was to "earnestly contend for the faith." The word *contend* means to struggle for. It means the passionate effort of the athlete to hold his ground. The way to stay the apostasy is to hold on to the old faith and live such a life of positive testimony as to defeat the opposers.

III. WHAT IS THE FAITH? (v. 4).

It is that body of Christian belief which centers in the Person and work of Jesus Christ. It embraces the Incarnation by means of the historic virgin birth, the salvation through the shedding of His blood, the personal return and the glorification of the saints. Concerning this faith note:

A. *It Was "Delivered" not "Created."*

B. *It Was Delivered to the "Saints"* (v. 3).

Not to theological seminaries, universities, and ecclesiastical organizations and even Bible institutes, but to *all* saints.

C. *This Delivery Was Final*—"once for all."

It is complete in itself. There is no progress in Christian doctrine, but progress in apprchension of that doctrine and in the widening and deepening experience of the life. Conviction as the finality of the faith saves from the many "cults" and "isms."

IV. WHY NECESSARY TO CONTEND FOR THE FAITH (v. 4).

Because evil men had invaded the brotherhood, ungodly men had crept into the church with the stealth of the serpent and the cunning of the beast of prey. The Church's worst enemies are those inside pretending to be its friends while denying the only Lord God and Jesus Christ. Such denial turns the grace of God into lasciviousness. Men who pretend to be Christians and use the pulpit to break down the faith are immoral and ungodly.

V. DOOM OF THE APOSTATES (vv. 5-7).

Having shown that ungodly and unregenerate men had crept into the Church and were turning the grace of God into lasciviousness, even denying the Lord Jesus Christ, Jude now assures his readers that judgment would surely be visited upon the apostates. He enforced his pronouncement of doom by three telling illustrations:

A. *The Unbelieving Israelites Were Judged.*

After their deliverance from Egypt they sinned and were judged.

B. *The Fallen Angels Cast Down to Hell* (II Peter 2:4).

C. *Sodom and Gomorrah Turned into Ashes* (II Peter 2:6).

VI. THE MARKS OF THE FALSE TEACHERS (vv. 8-11).

A. *Defiant of Authority* (vv. 8, 9, 16-19).

B. *Perverters* (v. 10).

C. *Gone in the Way of Cain* (v. 11).

1. Religious But Made His Own Offering.
2. Murderous Envy.

D. *Greedy and Seductive* (v. 11).

As Balaam they were influenced by reward, as honor expected, and applause.

E. *Presumptive as Core* (v. 11).

He repudiated Moses' authority and entered into the priesthood.

F. *Threatens Christians with Shipwreck of Faith and Morals* (vv. 12, 13).

In their false pretense they are like:

1. Shepherds Who Feed Themselves.
2. Clouds Which Bring No Rain.
3. Fruitless Trees.
4. Restless and Noisy as the Surf.
5. Blazing Meteors.

VII. FORETOLD BY ENOCH (vv. 14, 15).

Enoch before the Flood looked forward to the second coming of Christ and the judgment which will be executed upon the ungodly in the church.

VIII. HOW TO CONTEND FOR THE FAITH (vv. 20-23).

A. *Build up Yourselves* (v. 20).

By Bible study and utilizing of every means of grace.

B. *Praying in the Holy Spirit* (v. 20).

C. *Keep Yourselves in the Love of God* (v. 21).
D. *Keep Looking for the Coming of Jesus Christ* (v. 21).
E. *Snatch Lost Men from the Burning Fire* (v. 23). ..

IX. BENEDICTION (vv. 24, 25).

THE REVELATION

PART ONE—INTRODUCTORY MATTERS

I. INTRODUCTORY.

A. *Not Studied.*

PERHAPS NO BOOK of the Bible is studied less than the Book of Revelation—most assuredly, not of the New Testament. Why?

1. Sealed Book.

It is generally regarded as a sealed book, filled with dark and mysterious utterances beyond the capacity of man to comprehend, and therefore, useless.

2. Hidden Truths.

It is said to furnish material for the wildest speculation and fanatical notions. We may soberly ask, are the other books free from the same charge? May we not discard them all on the same ground?

B. *Not Sealed.*

Much of this conclusion is due to the cloudy teaching of expositors. Most of them have proceeded on the assumption that the book contains church truth, when in reality it is kingdom and judgment, mainly. That it is not a sealed book is clear from the following considerations:

1. Its Title.

Consider the title which the Holy Spirit gave it: "The Revelation of Jesus Christ"—not the revelation of the revelation. It is *the* Revelation, not Revelations. *Revelation* means uncovered, unveiled, exposed to view. If, therefore, that which is said to be revealed is sealed, the name which the Holy Spirit gave belies it.

2. Its Blessing.

A special blessing is promised those who read, hear, and keep the sayings of this book (1:3). It is impossible to keep sayings which cannot be understood.

3. Its Sayings.

John was specifically forbidden to seal the sayings of the book (22:10).

We have the following strong and urgent reasons for an earnest, diligent, and reverent study of this book:

a. It contains Christ's last message to man.

b. It is a part of the Word of God. It comes to us in His name and by His authority (1:1). It comes from God and Jesus Christ, and is intended for His servants. It is pre-eminently a servant's book. It can only be understood by those who are actively engaged in His service.

c. Special blessings are promised those who read, hear, and keep the sayings of the book (1:3).

d. A special woe is pronounced against him who would tamper with its contents (22:18, 19).

II. AUTHOR—JOHN.

He calls himself by that name some four times (1:1-4, 9; 22:8). The son of Zebedee, the apostle no doubt, is meant.

III. PLACE OF WRITING.

Patmos, a small island of the Aegean Sea. It was a penal island. Those who were banished there were compelled to work as slaves in the mines. In all probability, John was compelled to work as a slave there.

IV. TIME OF WRITING.

Two dates are assigned, A.D. 68 and A.D. 96. The latter we accept. It has the support of the early fathers and also internal evidence.

V. THEME.

The second coming of Christ—His personal, visible coming in glory (1:1, 7, 10). (Lord's Day). The word *Apocalypse* according to New Testament usage signifies the unveiling of a person. (E.g., II Thess. 1:6-10; I Peter 1:7.) It is the jubilee of victory, "Who for the joy set before him, endured the cross, despising the shame, and is set down at the right hand of the throne of God." It is a divine vindication—a reward for service performed.

VI. ANALYSIS: Key verse (1:19).

A. *The Things Which Thou Hast Seen.*

B. *The Things Which Are.*

C. *The Things Which Shall Be Hereafter.*

PART TWO—DETAILED OUTLINE

I. THE THINGS WHICH THOU HAST SEEN (1:1-20).

A. *Preface* (1:1-3).

Note that verse 3 gives us a landmark to aid us in fixing the date of the composition. No custom like reading in the public assembly before A.D. 70.

B. *Salutation*—"Grace and Peace" (1:4-6).

1. From Him Which Is—Was—and Is To Come.

Same as the "I Am" of Exodus 3 and 6. (Cf. Heb. 9:26, 24, 28.)

2. From the Holy Spirit.

The seven spirits are before the throne—the Holy Spirit in His sevenfold plentitude. Seven is the perfect number. It is the sum of the heavenly 3 and the earthly 4. His sevenfold office is set forth in Isaiah 11:2, also in the Gospel of John, viz: convincing (16:8); regenerating (3:6); comforting (14:16); teaching (14:26); and guiding (16:12).

3. From Jesus Christ.

C. *Theme* (1:7, 8; cf. vv. 1, 10).

D. *The Vision* (1:9-20).

1. Seven Golden Lampstands (1:12).—Not Candlesticks.

The light of a candlestick is self-consumptive, burns down into the socket and goes out. Not so with a lamp—its light remains constant, being perpetually fed by oil. Oil is a symbol of the Holy Spirit. (Note interpretation in v. 20.)

The use of lampstands suggests a time of darkness. We are now living in that time of darkness. The mission of the Church is to let her light shine. Lampstands are not sources of light, but simply bearers of the light. In this vision observe that Christ is the central figure, suggesting that the Church unified by Christ sheds forth her light.

2. The Son of Man Clothed with a Garment Down to the Feet (1:13).

Doubtless this is a robe of royalty, as well as that of the priest (Isa. 22:21), signifying His right to judge and to rule. Observe His girdle is about the breasts which would signify affection and faithfulness. Note His glorious description (vv. 14-16).

a. Head and hair white as wool, etc. (Cf. Dan. 7:9-10.) (Eternity and purity.)

b. Eyes as a flame of fire. This suggests infinite and infallible knowledge—see through and through—detect hidden thoughts—church members cannot hide anything from Him.

c. Feet like burnished brass (v. 15). Brass is a symbol of strength. The judge and king, His power is irresistible.

d. His voice as the sound of many waters (v. 15). Will drown out all sounds—outside of man's control. Illustrate by the Niagara Falls as they sweep resistlessly over the mighty precipice.

e. Seven stars in His right hand (v. 16). According to verse 20 *stars* means the angels or messengers of the churches—pastors, or representatives sent forth from the churches to comfort John in his lonely exile. Note the high honor of the minister to lie in the right hand of Him and listen to His message, and then speak it out again. (Sunday school teachers, preachers, etc.)

f. "Out of his mouth went a sharp two-edged sword" (v. 16). Observe that this is not a hand sword, but a mouth sword. "My words shall judge, etc." (John 12:48). "The word of God is sharper than any two-edged sword, etc." (Heb. 4:12). When studying the messages to the churches, we shall see how sharp the sword is. It has a double edge, double action—condemns the fault and approves the excellence.

g. Countenance was as the sun shineth in his strength. The effect of sunshine is healthful and joyous to some things while it is death and hardening to others.

II. THE THINGS WHICH ARE (2:1—3:22). (Epistolary—Church Age.)

A. *Introductory Remarks.*

Recall the vision of chapter 1. Christ walking in the midst of the seven churches with His penetrating and searching vision. Remember that His office now is that of a judge. The seven epistles set forth His sentence upon the churches as their judge.

These epistles were written to seven historical churches actually existing then in proconsular Asia. If so, why just seven? Were not other churches in existence there? We answer that these seven were intended to be symbolic and representative of the Church universal. These epistles furnish us with pictures of the unfolding of the condition of the Church throughout the successive stages of her history. (Epochs of church history: Apostolic—Ephesus, A.D. 96; persecution period—Smyrna, A.D. 96-316; declension period—Pergamos and Thyatira, 316-1500; reformation period—Sardis, Philadelphia, and Laodicea, 1500 to end of the age.) We may also regard these epistles as giving us pictures of the conditions of church-life as found continuously in the history of the Church of Christ.

B. *Note the Following Characteristics of Each Epistle:*

1. Christ's Title.
2. Christ's Commendation.
3. Christ's Complaint.
4. Christ's Counsel.
5. Christ's Promise to Overcomers.

C. *Addressed to "Angels" of the Churches.*

Note again, that in these epistles Jesus Christ addresses the angels of the churches—not the churches directly. This suggests the relationship of the minister to the church. He stands at the head as the representative of the church. This is the divine appointment. He is not to lord it over Gods' heritage. He is an undershepherd, called to his work by God and not men. Observe, further that serious fault is found with five out of the seven. Two alone pass inspection, and they are in touch with elements which He condemns.

D. *Ephesus* (2:1-7).

1. Christ's Title.

He appears here as "he that holdeth the seven stars in his right hand and walketh in the midst of the seven golden candlesticks [lampstands]."

2. Christ's Commendation (2:2, 3).

a. Works.

b. Toil.

c. Patience.

d. Intolerance of evil men. They rejected impostors.

e. Had not grown weary—endured all for Christ's sake.

f. Hatest the deeds of the Nicolaitanes. What is the meaning of the term? It is composed of two Greek words: *nikan,* meaning to conquer, and *laos,* the people. Official rank in the church oppressed the people—incipient priestcraft.

3. Christ's Complaint (2:4).

Left first love. The church at Ephesus still fulfills church order; outwardly all is right. They had strong impulses toward God, which is shown in their firm discipline and orthodoxy. Notwithstanding this, they were in the "cooling off" process. (Cf. I Thess. 1:3.) The nature of first love is complete absorption. It is the love of espousal, pure and simple. First love is spontaneous. The true wife keeps house and makes home attractive for her husband because she loves him. Her chief delight is in him. She does not do this because the law forbids her to forsake him. Illustrate further by a father and daughter who were much together. At length, for a time the daughter seemed distant. This was a source of grief to her father. When the secret was discovered, it was found that she had been staying away and alone in order to make with her own hands a present for her father. The father declares that he wants her companionship more than her gifts. So the Lord wants us, not our paltry gifts. The home where there is no love is a miserable one. The Lord has no use for the church where there is no love.

4. Christ's Counsel (2:5-7).

"Remember from whence thou art fallen." "Repent." This counsel is endorsed with a solemn warning. "I'll remove thy candlestick." This has been literally fulfilled in the case of Ephesus. (Note her position today.)

5. Christ's Promise to Overcomers.

"Eat of the tree of life."

E. *Smyrna* (2:8-11).

1. Christ's Title.

"First and last, was dead, and is alive." The church at Smyrna was in the very throes of bitter persecution. Christ says, "Fear not, I have passed through the worst and still live."

2. Christ's Commendation.

By silence. It was a little church, reduced to poverty through bitter persecutions, therefore, could not expect much of it.

a. "I know thy tribulation" (v. 9). Tribulation suggests the stones which grind the wheat, or press the blood out of the grapes. Smyrna means bitter (cf. "Myrrh").

b. Poverty. Actual beggary. Suffered the loss of all things—deprived of property rights.

c. Blasphemy of them which say they are Jews. Note the force of the words *I know*. He knew by actual suffering. Note the significance of "synagogue of Satan." Their troubles arose from blaspheming Jews and intolerant pagans—both incited by the Devil. "Thou art rich." (Cf. Rich man with bursting barns.)

3. Christ's Counsel (2:10).

a. "Fear not."

b. "Be thou faithful unto death." As an incentive to faithfulness, a crown of life is offered.

4. Christ's Promise to Overcomers (2:11).

"Shall not be hurt of the second death."

F. *Pergamos* (2:12-17).

1. Christ's Title (2:12).

"The one which hath the sharp sword with two edges." The fitness of this title is seen when we realize that this church is harboring evil. The etymology of the word *Pergamos*, signifies marriage with high things. This was really done when the church and state were united at the professed conversion of Constantine.

2. Christ's Commendation (2:13).

"Holdest fast my name, and hast not denied my faith" even though thou dwellest "where Satan's seat is." Who is Satan? He always has a center of operation. Where is his throne? Not in Hell, for he is not a prisoner there, but in the world. It is always to be found at some strategic point. It is almost invariably at the center of worldly greatness. "In the greatest centers of worldly power, there his eye more particularly watches, his energy more particularly acts, his influence more peculiarly emanates." In Smyrna, he hid behind religion, the synagogue of Satan—opposition. In Pergamos, he enters into alliance. Satan has his seat in places of worldly wealth. "Ye cannot serve God and mammon." The Devil sets up his throne where worldly wealth gathers and from there he rules men. Look at the great evils which blight our land. Back of everyone of them is mammon, e.g., drink traffic, iniquitous crowding of the poor into unsanitary quarters and dwellings. A church is in peril when she enters into alliance with mammon and high things. Many are there now.

3. Christ's Complaint (2:14).

It was that they were yielding to sensual alliances. Many churches are like this one now, married to the world. Dance, theater, and canasta or bingo party on Saturday night and the Communion on Sunday morning. Not whole churches are that way, but some of the members are living such lives, indeed, so many are living such lives that the church is absolutely helpless when it comes to administering discipline. The sin of the church is in fellowshiping with such members.

a. Some were holding to the teachings of the Nicolaitanes.

b. What was the teaching of Balaam? (See Num. 22, 24, 25, and 33.) They held a doctrine which gave license to indulge in sin. The antinomian heresy of a later date is akin to it, which is that you are safe in the name and faith, so it matters little about your conduct.

4. Christ's Counsel (2:16).

Repent. Put away sin. This counsel is enforced by warning, "I will fight against you."

5. Christ's Promises (2:17).

a. Hidden manna.

b. White stone. What is the white stone?

(1) Given as a token of acquittal, after trial.

(2) Reward of victory. Given to one returning from battle.

(3) A token of citizenship.

(4) A token of friendship. The stone was broken—two friends take halves—these were bequeathed to children. Finally when the two stones matched, friendship was founded on basis of long ago.

The Church of Jesus Christ must not tolerate within her borders those who lower the standard of truth's requirements. This is not a question of holding the truth, the church at Pergamos was orthodox, but of making application of the truth. Same error threatens the church today. Many think that if a man's creed is right his conduct does not matter so much. The test of doctrine is purity of conduct.

G. *Thyatira* (2:18-29).

1. Christ's Title (2:18).

"Son of God." Power and authority.

a. Eyes like a flame of fire.

b. Feet like burnished brass, knows the facts and its coming in judgment.

2. Christ's Commendation.

a. "I know thy works."

b. Forces that lie behind that work—love, faith, and patience.

3. Christ's Complaint (2:20).

"Thou sufferest that woman, Jezebel." Who was Jezebel? A woman of the congregation who laid claim to be a prophetess. Doubtless, she was promulgating this new doctrine and seducing the people of God.

a. We must go to the Old Testament for a knowledge of Jezebel. She was a worshiper of Baal. It was nature worship. They did not set aside the worship of Jehovah, but placed Baal worship alongside of it, e.g., Christian Science. Attempts to graft it onto Christianity. What was this licentiousness? Spiritual. Denial of sin.

b. Jezebel's punishment. Will cast her into a bed, indicating that she should perish in her very corruption, which she created. Those who follow her shall go down with her.

c. Jezebel's voice may be heard in most of our churches today. How?

(1) Cry against separation.

(2) Denial that Christ calls us to places of separation and peculiarity.

(3) Holding on to sin and keeping our names with the church. God says, "Come out from among them and be separate." Things at which our fathers shuddered are brought into the church today, e.g., ways of raising money, embracing false doctrine, etc. In the name of God let us keep ourselves separate! Any doctrine

that minimizes sin, or makes an excuse for it, is from Hell, and the church which does not speak out against it is guilty before God.

H. *Sardis* (3:1-6).

1. Christ's Title (3:1).

"He that hath the seven spirits of God and the seven stars."

2. Christ's Complaint (3:1).

"Name that thou livest and art dead." Not devoid of works. "I know thy works." Had an outward form—externals, perfect organization, but no life.

3. Christ's Counsel (3:2).

"Be watchful and strengthen the things that remain." Don't give up the forms of religion, but endow them with life. This counsel is enforced by warnings as to His unexpected coming.

4. Christ's Commendation (3:4).

Always a few who are faithful.

5. Christ's Promise to Overcomers (3:5).

a. White raiment given to him.

b. Not blot out his name.

c. Will confess him.

I. *Philadelphia* (3:7-13).

1. Christ's Title (3:7).

"He that is holy."

2. Christ's Commendation (3:8).

The church here is a little company who have kept the faith. Large company who had departed. They were oppressed by heretical teachers.

3. Christ's Counsel.

"Hold fast that which thou hast, that no man take thy crown." One may lose his crown and yet be saved. He cannot lose his salvation.

4. Christ's Promise to Overcomers (3:12).

Will make him "a pillar in the temple of my God."

J. *Laodicea* (3:14-22).

1. Christ's Title.

"The Amen, the faithful and true witness."

2. Christ's Complaint (3:15).

Lukewarmness. This church, as the name indicates, was ruled by the people. Everything was settled by popular opinion. They were self-righteous. They thought that they were all right, but the testimony of the faithful witness, was that they were naked, poor, and miserable.

3. Christ's Counsel (3:18).

"Buy of me gold tried in the fire that the shame of thy nakedness do not appear." Christ stands at the door and knocks, calling for the faithful ones to come out from the dead mass.

4. Christ's Promise to Overcomers (3:21).

"To sit with me in my throne."

III. THINGS WHICH SHALL BE HEREAFTER (4:1–22:21).

The futurist interpretation of the Revelation seems to be the most satisfactory. This means that all after chapter 4 is still future. History cannot be of help from chapter 4 to the end. We must be content to await fulfillment. It is very important that the Bible student keep this in mind and be alert—watch.

A. *Apocalyptic Premillennial* (4:1–20:3).

1. The Judgment Throne Set (4:1–5:14).

We now come to the third grand division of this Book. In 4:1 the trumpet voice calls the seer to witness the things which shall take place after these things, i.e., after that which we have just been considering, viz: the Church in her whole course. Doubtless this open door in Heaven and the calling of the seer to the skies is to show the manner in which certain are caught out of the Tribulation, according to I Thessalonians 4:16, 17. In chapters 2 and 3 we had before our eyes the Church in her struggles, trials, and sufferings; but here we see her entering upon her heavenly estate and dignity. Note the particulars brought before us in this vision.

a. The throne (v. 2). Wherever there is a throne sovereignty and majesty are suggested. This is the preparation for judgment. It is a parallel to Daniel 7:9.

b. The Occupant of the throne (v. 3).

c. Lightnings and thunderings and voices proceeded from it (v. 5). This indicates that it is a throne of judgment, and that the wrath of God is about to proceed from it. (Cf. Exod. 9:23-28, with Exod. 19:16; also I Sam. 7:10.)

d. Seven torches of fire burning (v. 5), which are the seven spirits of God. This indicates preparation for battle. (See Judges 7:16-20, where Gideon was preparing for battle.) These torches are not for illumination, but for burning (cf. Isa. 4:4). It is the Holy Spirit in all His plentitude. It is the torch which shall set the world on fire (Mal. 4:1).

e. Crystal sea before the throne (v. 6). (See Exod. 24:10, 11; Ezek. 1:22.)

f. A rainbow encircled the throne (v. 3). In Genesis 9:11-17, the bow was a token of God's covenant. So here, while in the midst of terrific judgments, God remembers His covenant. It is a pledge that though the earth goes through mighty throes, its continuity as an organized structure is assured.

g. Around the throne were four and twenty thrones, upon which were four and twenty elders sitting (v. 4). Who are these elders? Negatively, not angels, but human beings, as seen by the songs they sing (5:9). Not patriarchs and apostles only, for they are from every tribe and tongue and people and nation (5:9). Not unfallen human beings, but ransomed sinners, "Thou hast redeemed us by thy blood" (5:9).

Positively, they are elders, i.e., the older ones in the resurrection—the first glorified of the company of the redeemed. They are crowned. Paul says that the crowning occurs when Christ appears (II Tim. 4:8). Why 24? They are representative of a large number. (Cf. the Mosaic economy, I Chron. 23:3, 4, also chapter 24.) There were many priests, but 24 were serving in course at one time. We are informed in Hebrews 9:9, 23, 24 that these things were patterns of things in the heavens. These elders are the associate judges of the world (cf. I Cor. 6:2, 3).

h. In verses 6-8 we find another company of redeemed ones. They sing precisely the same song that the elders do. They are not "beasts," but "living ones." They seem to occupy similar positions in the heavenly order that angels did in the earthly. The faces suggest the figure for the different tribes. (See Num. 2.) These four are again representative. Observe their characteristics:

(1) They are full of eyes before and behind (v. 6). This denotes their intelligence. They look backward and forward, showing their ability to direct their administration with precision.

(2) "Each of them had six wings about him" (v. 8), fitting him for rapid locomotion. These two classes are nearest to God of all the redeemed. The elders seem to occupy positions of counselors, and the living ones to executors. These dignities are open to all who will now repent and believe. Who is willing to lose all this for a little worldly pleasure?

i. In chapter 5 the first thing which attracts our attention is the sealed book "in the right hand of him that sat on the throne." It will help us to a right understanding of this book, if we note that first of all it has to do with redemption. The seal-opener appears as the slain Lamb (v. 6). John wept much because there was no response to the angel's cry. Again observe the use which has been made of books in the Scriptures. In order to fully appreciate this we must inquire into the custom among the Jews concerning estates. They could not be alienated beyond a certain time. The year of Jubilee returned them to their lawful owners. Again it was the right of the one nearest of kin to step in and redeem an estate which had been thus forfeited. When the inheritance was thus disposed of, two books or instruments of writing were made out—one open, and the other sealed—specifying price and condition of redemption. These went into the hands of the one to whom the property was thus made over. The transaction which John witnessed was similar to this. Adam had a noble inheritance, but through his sin it was forfeited. When he thus sinned, the title deeds passed into the hands of Almighty God, and have lain there ever since. This sublime act is but the slain Lamb entering upon His victorious work of redemption. What is redemption? It reaches all creation. Its glorious fullness reaches into the future.

(1) The Lamb has seven horns (v. 6), indicating that something more than sacrifice was now to be His work. Horns are symbols of strength and aggressive power, even imperial power (Deut. 33:17; Zech. 1:18, 19).

(2) He has seven eyes (v. 6). Horns signify kingly and imperial power, and His seven eyes indicate His intelligence. Let us observe in this picture:

(a) Sacrifice for sin.

(b) Strength to overcome all foes.

(c) Universal intelligence.

j. At the sublime act of taking the book, a thrill went through the universe (v. 8). This is what the world has been groaning for, for thousands of years. The elders and living ones fall down before the Lamb. They have vials of odors which are the prayers of the saints. Long have the saints been praying, "Thy kingdom come." Not one prayer offered in truth has been lost. They are carefully treasured in golden bowls. Be encouraged, O ye saints!

A song is sung which never before was sung (v. 9). This sublime anthem was begun by the 24 elders and the 4 living ones around the throne, and soon there is a response from the angels—myriads of myriads. They sing: "Worthy is the Lamb that was slain to receive power, and riches." Wider and still wider the response comes from every holy tongue. Every creature in Heaven, on the earth and in the sea. "We shall reign on the earth."

2. The Opening of the Seals and the Sealing of the 144,000 (6: 1–7:17).

All is in readiness now for the blessed Kinsman-Redeemer to proceed by successive steps to take possession of the purchased possession. The opening of these seals is but so many acts in the judicial proceedings of the Almighty God to rid the earth of its unlawful possessors, the rulers of this darkness, and to restore it to its designed peace and prosperity. It cannot be simply the varying fortunes and experiences of the church, for if our view of the consecutation of this book be true, the Church passed off the stage with the close of chapter 3 and the beginning of chapter 4.

a. Opening of the first seal (vv. 1, 2). We see a rider upon a white horse with a bow in his hand. What significance is attached to the horse in Scripture? (See Job 39:19-25; II Kings 6:15-18.) Swift and irresistible power. Earthly symbols of God's resistless power to judge a proud and unbelieving world. Observe that this horseman alone had a crown, and since he goes forth "conquering and to conquer" his must be conquests of the crown—heavenly conquests. The color of the horse is white which indicates peace and righteousness. Again the rider had in his hand a bow. For the significance of bow see Habakkuk 3:8, 9. What does all this signify? The prophet says: "When thy judgments are in the earth the inhabitants of the world will learn righteousness" (Isa. 26:9). We conclude, therefore, that when the great transaction of the judgment begins, there will be a laying bare of God's Word in such a literal way, that men's hearts will be conquered, and they will turn to the Lord. The effect will be continuous throughout the judgment enactments. Men will then realize that nothing remains for them but to turn to the Lord, the highest dignitics of Heaven already being lost—men's hearts conquered by God's righteous judgments.

b. Opening of the second seal (vv. 3, 4). At the opening of the second seal, the second living one calls into action the red horse. Red is a symbol of vengeance and slaughter. A great sword is given to him and power to take peace out of the earth. This is but the fulfillment of Christ's prediction: "Nation shall rise against nation, and kingdom against kingdom, etc." Imagine a situation when one nation shall be against another, one part of society against the other, one citizen against the other, one man afraid to lie down to sleep because of the hatred of the other, etc., then you have an idea of what shall be in the earth at this stage of the judgment. See samples of this in history (II Chron. 15:3-5), also Josephus on the Syrian troubles. (Seiss' *Lectures,* Vol. 1, page 330.)

c. Opening of the third seal (vv. 5, 6). Now the third living one speaks and the rider upon the black horse goes forth. The picture grows more terrible as the action of judgment proceeds. Black is the symbol of starvation and famine. (See Lam. 5:10; 4:9.) This rider carries a pair of balances in his hand, which indicates a close and careful weighing of provisions. Note also that the price paid for provisions indicates scarcity. The amount of wheat and barley was about the allowance of one man for a day. The price of a measure was a man's wages for a day. Just enough then for himself, his family must starve. Universal war always will be followed by universal famine.

d. Opening of the fourth seal (vv. 7, 8). While these perilous times are being experienced, a fourth seal is broken, and the fourth horseman comes forth to make a still more ghastly appearance. A pale death green is the color of this horse. This is the color of putrefying flesh, a corpse. Following universal war and famine would be bodies rotting all around. The rider here is death, and Hades follows after, swallowing up as a voracious monster. Power is given him over a fourth part of the earth to kill with the sword, with hunger, and with death. Here is a combination of all the evil agencies before mentioned, with the addition of wild and ferocious beasts. The carnage and death before mentioned would have a tendency to incite these beasts to greater terror. These are certainly dark pictures, but as surely as this is the Word of God, they will be displayed in the world in that, perhaps, not distant day. To evade the truth of God's Word is utter folly. There is a way of escape. As there was an Ark for those who listened to the preaching of Noah, so there is a hiding place in the side of the bleeding Lamb for all those who will surrender to Him now. Hide thyself away now. Delay not. The doom is surely coming.

e. Opening of the fifth seal (vv. 9-11). The opening of the fifth seal displays a scene of persecution and martyrdom. These are not the martyrs of the ages gone by, for we have seen them already caught up into glory, crowned and seated with the Judge and taking part in the judgment of the world. These are people, who before the judgment began, were indifferent—caused perhaps by the divisions, errors, etc. of Christendom—but awake now to the true situation of affairs. They begin in earnest to witness for Christ. But men will be then as now, hard of heart, and will be exasperated by the sore judgments which are upon them, and will turn in fury and terror upon those who witness for Jesus, and will slay them.

Note they were slain for the Word of God and the testimony which they held. Doubtless it was the particular testimony which they held that enraged them. What was that particular testimony? It was that because of the long accumulated sin God was visiting wrath upon a godless world. A testimony which said that unless there was immediate and full repentance, everlasting perdition awaited them. Their testimony will not be so different in kind from ours as different in degree. Let a man testify with the fervor of those times even now, and persecution and rejection will be the inevitable outcome (II Tim. 3:12). Observe the state of these persons. They are disembodied souls. The notion that the souls of the dead are in an unconscious state is unscriptural.

They cry for vengeance upon their slayers. Their murderers are still living. This cry is for divine vindication. They are anxious for the hastening of the divine rule and dominion.

f. Opening of the sixth seal (vv. 12-17). At the opening of this seal we observe wonderful physical disturbances. The sun becomes black as sackcloth of hair, the moon becomes as blood, the stars are cast to the ground, the heavens depart as a scroll when it is rolled together and every mountain and island are removed from their places. These are some of the fearful things which shall take place at this time. Let us note the effects produced: The kings of the earth, the great men, the rich men, the chief captains, the mighty men, every bondman, and every freeman hide themselves in the dens and rocks of the mountains, and cry to the mountains and rocks to fall upon them and hide them from the face of Him that sitteth upon the throne and from the wrath of the Lamb. It is well to note the conditions of society at that time. The inequalities of society will still be known; war and carnage will still be common. Let us not be deluded with the idea that the golden age is to be ushered in through the agencies of the present enterprises of men. There will not then be the self-security of godless people as now—they who never before prayed will then call upon the Lord, but then it will be too late.

g. The sealing of the 144,000 (7:1-17). While this takes place under the sixth seal, it is not necessarily a part of it. It is rather an episode.

Let us inquire as to who these 144,000 are? They are literal children of Israel. How are they sealed? Doubtless an extraordinary enduement of spiritual power. (Cf. Eph. 1:13, 14.) The effect of this sealing is great missionary activity. Many conversions. (See v. 9.) Time when nations shall be born in a day. Doubtless Paul belongs to this body (I Cor. 15:8). Christians do not belong to this body. We have a superior calling. Let us ask ourselves as to whether we have the seal of our God? There are those who are faithful. Then there are those who have been baptized, but have no right to this hope. Outwardly they are connected with some church, but are dead branches. Still others, perhaps who have never yet been baptized, are without hope and without God in the world. To all there is this exhortation; flee to Almighty God ere it is too late.

3. The Sounding of the Seven Trumpets (8:1—11:19).

As all that follows in the Book of Revelation is the outcome of the opening of the seventh seal, it seemed wise to end the foregoing with the sixth seal.

At the opening of this seal there is silence in Heaven for the space of about a half an hour. This is the silence of tremendous expectancy. So awful is the judgment scene as it approaches its climax that the heavenly hosts hush their songs to view them. We note here a company of seven angels (v. 2). Who are they? We notice in Matthew 18:10 that there are angels who do always behold the face of the Father. Gabriel is one (see Luke 1:19). They stand, which would indicate readiness for service—ready to go at His bidding. To each angel was given a trumpet. What is the significance of trumpets? Their use was only on important occasions: e.g., connected with war (Num. 10:9); proclamation of great festivals (Rev. 23:24; 25:9); announcement of royalty (I Kings 1:34-39); manifestations of the majesty of God (Exod. 19:16); overthrow of the ungodly (Josh. 6: 13-16). All these were but types which have their fulfillment in these heavenly antitypes.

It is here stated that another angel appears (v. 3). From his standing at the golden altar we conclude that he is the Jehovah Angel who occupies the position of high priest. He offers the prayers of all saints upon the golden altar. Some see in this the prayers of Israel coming into remembrance. Note the double action in this offering. Ascended up before God, he took the censer and filled it with fire and cast it to the ground. This suggests that the punishment is occasioned by the rejection of grace. Out of the altar which they rejected comes their damnation. Their preparation to sound signifies their arrangement as to the part each one was to take in this awful work.

a. Sounding of the first trumpet (v. 7). Hail and fire mingled with blood followed the sounding of the first trumpet. Observe that this is similar to that in Egypt, only here we have it in a larger measure with blood added (see Exod. 9:23-28). As a result of this the third part of all green trees and all green grass was burned up. I accept this as literal.

b. Sounding of the second trumpet (vv. 8, 9). Following

this, a great mountain as it were, burning with fire, caused the third part of all living things in the sea to die and the destruction of the third part of the ships. (Third part of the sea became blood; cf. Exod. 7:20; Zeph. 1:3; Isa. 2:16.)

c. Sounding of the third trumpet (vv. 10, 11). A great star fell from Heaven when the third angel sounded, causing the third part of the rivers and the fountains of waters to become bitter, resulting in great mortality among men.

d. Sounding of the fourth trumpet (vv. 12, 13). Now followed the smiting of the third part of the sun, moon, and stars, producing great darkness. Note that there is a preliminary proclamation to the sounding of the last three trumpets. In the Revised Version we are told that it is an eagle instead of an angel as in the Authorized Version. Are these eagles birds of prey? Or are they such as the Lord tells will be seen at His coming? (Luke 17:34-37; Matt. 24:26-28). It may be that since it occurs under the opening of the seventh seal that they are literal birds of prey and has reference to the gathering to the supper of the great God (19:17). If they are the eagle saints, observe the nature and characteristics of the eagle. They are great watchers, cannot be taken unawares. They fly high—soar aloft, so eagle saints have their citizenship in Heaven. Also, they are strong of wing. Strong of faith.

e. Sounding of the fifth trumpet (9:1). When the fifth angel sounds, a star is seen falling from Heaven to the earth. This is not a meteor, for intelligence is ascribed to him. He takes the key which is given him and acts—opens the bottomless pit. Who or what is this star? (See Job 38:4-7; Jude 6; Eph. 6:6; Matt. 25:41.) Doubtless Satan is here meant. Following this act the pit belched forth smoke to darken the sun and air. And out from the smoke came locusts. These locusts are queer combinations. One of the infernal princes is their king. His name is Apollyon. These locusts have power to sting as a scorpion. The scorpion's sting is terrible. They only are permitted to sting those men who were without the seal of the living God. Though this sting was awful it was not to produce death. So great and terrible will be the suffering that they will even desire to die, but that will be denied them (v. 6).

f. Sounding of the sixth trumpet (v. 13). The loosing of the four angels which are stationed or bound at the Euphrates occurs when the sixth angel sounds. This sets loose an army which the Lord uses in the carrying on of the judgment. Each succeeding stroke of the divine hand seems to be more terrible than the preceding one.

(1) Note the moral condition of the world at this stage of the judgment. This is given in 9:20, 21.

(a) Demon worship. This is the worship of unholy spiritual beings belonging to the kingdom of evil. They in the time of Christ took their position in human beings, causing them to be regarded sometimes as inspired prophets and prophetesses; e.g., the girl at Philippi. There must be something real in this otherwise God would not have spoken against it, as well as kindred evils, such as soothsayers, magicians, etc. In I Timothy 4:1-3 Paul speaks about just such a state of affairs in the last days.

(b) Idolatry. Besides the introduction of actual image worship in this country now, there are many ways in which men worship idols. What is an idol?

(c) Murders. This would show little regard for human life. Murder is now woefully prevalent, and will no doubt increase as the age draws to a close. Note some ways in which this murder will be carried on, such as suicide, infanticide, homicide, etc.

(d) Sorceries. This word carries with it the idea of the use of drugs, such as intoxicants, opiates, etc. The use of drugs also for the carrying on of greater sensual indulgence.

(e) Fornication. This would lead us to the idea of the subversion of the marriage relation and its holy laws. It takes its shape in free love, adultery, divorce, etc. The revival of heathen philosophies will inevitably bring this licentiousness.

(f) Theft. Very common today.

This awful visitation from the altar does not bring repentance to these men. They still are in open rebellion against God. Hell does not have a purgatorial effect. It was not designed as a repentance worker. Final restoration has no suggestion in the Scripture.

(2) In chapter 10 we are introduced to a very remarkable Person. From the description given of Him, we may justly conclude that it is the same Person seen in the vision of chapter 1. Observe

what He does. He sets His right foot upon the sea and His left foot upon the land. This shows His determination to take possession of them. (See Deut. 11:24.) The Book which He holds in His right hand is doubtless the same book seen before, but it is open now. This book contains promises to Israel. Here He holds in His hands the title deeds showing His right and authority to take possession of the purchased possession. Note also His proclamation (vv. 6, 7). He declares that there shall be no longer delay, and that the mystery shall be finished in the time of the seventh trumpet. Doubtless by *mystery* is meant the completion of God's plan for this world.

(3) In chapter 11 we have the measuring of the temple, which no doubt, signifies God's intervention in behalf of His people, Israel. We have here also two remarkable witnesses introduced. By referring to Malachi 4:5 we can identify the one, and by comparing 11:6 with Matthew 17:3, 4, we can pretty certainly identify the other —Moses and Elijah.

g. Sounding of the seventh trumpet (11:15-19).

When the last angel sounded, we hear voices in Heaven. The people in glory cannot keep quiet at this time for they have seen enough of this world's treatment of Christ and His people. While the heavenly beings thus rejoice, the anger of the nations was very great. The kingdom was now about to pass from them to the Lord's Christ, who was the real possessor, and judgment and wrath were about to be poured out upon them.

4. The Woman and the Dragon with Manifestation of the Trinity of Evil (12:1—13:18).

This is a parenthetical section, an episode thrown in.

a. The woman. We have before us now some marvelous pictures. The apostle tells us, specifically, that this is a sign. It is not said that a woman appeared, but that it was the symbol of something beyond itself. When the Scriptures do mean for us to take them literally, it is plainly so indicated. Without a recognition of this fact we cannot arrive at any definite and satisfactory conclusion touching scriptural matters. Let us proceed to inquire into the meaning of this symbol. Doubtless this woman (vv. 1, 2) represents the Jewish race, Israel. It is found in this section where everything is pointing toward the restoration of His people, Israel; she is gorgeously attired. To be clothed with the sun implies universal sovereignty. The moon under her feet would imply the coming into touch with things which reflect light, for the moon has no light of its own—perhaps a suggestion of Israel's ordinances which reflect the light, as coming into recognition. The woman is in a dignified position, gems glitter about her person, and upon her head is a royal crown.

b. Alongside the woman is found an opposing power (vv. 3, 4). This is always found alongside God's people. Satan is always bent on the destruction of God's people. This sign is called the red dragon. He has seven heads and ten horns. For the significance of heads and horns see 17:9, 10, 12. This dragon drew a third part of the stars of Heaven.

Let us now notice his attitude toward the woman. He stands before her ready to destroy her seed. This has striking exemplification all through the history of God's people. It began with Cain in the murder of his brother, and still continues.

c. Who is this Man child? What becomes of him and his mother? (vv. 5, 6). The Man child—Christ—is caught up to God, and the mother fled to the wilderness where God had prepared a place for her.

d. We are now introduced to a scene which is quite remarkable—war in Heaven (vv. 7-12). The forces in conflict are Michael and his angels against the dragon and his angels. Why this struggle? The Devil and his angels must be ejected from Heaven when the Lord's people are being taken to Himself.

e. Note the nature of this battle (v. 13). The Devil is still in the heavenlies, accusing the brethren day and night. They overcome him by the blood of the Lamb. That is the only possible way to overcome him. Our lives are imperfect and give him an opportunity to make accusations, but we can prevail in the blood of the Lamb. The battle issues in utter defeat, and ejection of the dragon and his hosts from Heaven. He is cast down to the earth. When that is done, a voice from Heaven cries, "Woe to the inhabiters of the earth." He is particularly fierce because he knows his time is short. He proceeds at once to the persecution of the woman, and she flees to the wilderness (vv. 14-17).

f. At this juncture we see him organizing his forces for the final conflict. He carries on his work through the beast and the false prophet (13:1-18). They aid in the work of bloody persecution. Who is this beast? This beast comes up out of the sea (v. 1). This is a symbolic representation of the political sovereignty of this world. In this picture we have combination of the four beasts of Daniel. From this we see that this is the sum of this world power as it will be in the last three and one-half years or 42 months. It seems to be an administration under the head of one person. This person is possessed of supernatural power, and is the "man of sin" or Antichrist. Note what he does. He blasphemes God's name, tabernacle, and those who dwell in Heaven (13:6). He wars with the saints (v. 7), and directs the worship of all to himself (v. 8). Let it be remembered that Antichrist is not alone. He has a close companion also called "beast"—another beast. Note his characteristics: two horns like a lamb, speaks like a dragon, has all the power of the first beast, and directs worship not to himself, but to the beast. He has power to do great miracles, so as to deceive the people. He causes all to receive a mark in their foreheads, or right hands.

5. The Lamb on Mount Zion and the Seven Last Plagues (14:1—16:21).

With the contemplation of the scenes of the previous chapter, our hearts almost despaired within us, but as always after the fierce storm has spent itself, there appears the calm, and from behind shines forth the golden luster of the full-orbed day; so in this case, instead of the Hell-trinity, by power, blasphemy, intrigue, and deceit—all the machinations that Hell could furnish—we see the Lamb standing on Mount Zion, and with Him the 144,000 sealed ones, having the Father's name in their foreheads. Who are the 144,000? The same as those in chapter 7.

a. Observe the marks which distinguish them.

(1) By the mark which they have in their foreheads (v. 1). Perhaps this refers to their confession. They witness against the hellish assumptions of the Antichrist and the false prophet.

(2) By their unworldliness, "redeemed from among men." They are still in the world, but severed from it, in heart and life—their citizenship is in Heaven (v. 4).

(3) Their purity. "Not defiled with women." Shall we conclude that the 144,000 are all males who have never married? By no means, celibacy is not the thought here. Marriage is just as pure as abstinence from marriage. Their virginity consists in the fact that they have kept themselves free from the worship of the Anti-christ, and also free from all lewdness.

(4) Their truthfulness. "No guile found in their mouths" (v. 5). This description is far reaching. Lying may be done in many ways. Speaking falsehood is lying, but professing one thing and living another is the worst form of lying.

These 144,000 sing a song which no one else could sing or even learn. They stand with the Lamb on Mount Zion.

b. Following this scene, we listen to angel messages (vv. 6-13).

(1) The first one has the everlasting Gospel to preach, which is this: "Fear God, and give glory to him; for the hour of his judgment is come: and worship him that made heaven and earth, and the sea, and the fountains of waters." When every human voice is still because of the awful oppression of the enemy, the angel sounds forth the message.

(2) The second angel announces the fall of Babylon, and states the reason of her fall.

(3) The third angel announces the woe which comes upon any man who worships the beast or receives the mark in the fore-head or in the hand. Such a man shall drink of the wine of the wrath of God (v. 10), and shall be tormented with fire and brimstone in the presence of the angels and in the presence of the Lamb. This torment is forever and forever—eternal. They have no rest day or night. Men jest at the preacher who believes and preaches an eternal Hell for those who are rebellious against God and reject the grace that is offered in His Son; but here we hear an angel from Heaven, whose message from start to finish is fire and brimstone. After this a voice is heard from Heaven saying: "Blessed are the dead which die in the Lord from henceforth." This is pre-eminently true at this time. Not a text for this present time.

c. We have here now two important visions brought before us, viz; that of the harvest and that of the vintage (vv. 14-20).

(1) The vision of the harvest (vv. 14-16). This is the

harvest of the wicked. The Scriptures set forth a harvest of the wicked as well as of the good. (See Jer. 51:33; and Joel 3:11-16.) In this vision we see one sitting upon a white cloud like unto the Son of man, having a sharp sickle in his hand. As he is thus ready, another angel cries: "Thrust in thy sickle, and reap . . . for the harvest of the earth is ripe."

(2) The vision of the vintage (vv. 17-20). Another angel appears coming out of the temple. He says: "Thrust in thy sharp sickle, and gather the clusters of the vine of the earth; for her grapes are fully ripe." The vine of earth is the opposite of the vine of Heaven. By its being ripe is meant that its wickedness has reached its fullest limit. The angel obeyed, and we see the awful outcome of this treading the winepress as set forth in verse 30.

According to the imagery of the preceding chapter, it would appear that the climax had been reached, but in order to deal with much of the Scripture, especially the prophecies, we must constantly keep in mind a law of recurrence, in which a fact may be stated in a summary way at one time, and then following the same thing may be given in detail, e.g., the creation of man is stated in Genesis 1, and the details are given in Genesis 2. The same peculiarity is to be observed in this book. The struggle in the previous chapter seemed to be over, but in chapters 15 and 16, which go together, we have the successive stages given. This is an important point to consider. All that follows now is still under the last woe. This chapter might well be linked with chapter 11. There the temple was opened, here the same temple is still open.

d. Here now appears another sign, which is seven angels having the seven last plagues (16:1-21). These seven angels come out of the temple. Before the apostle finishes his description of this wonderful sign, he interdicts another vision—the sea of glass, mingled with fire. The image of these beings standing on the shore of this sea suggests at once the children of Israel on the shores of the Red Sea. The song they sing also brings this to mind (Exod. 15:1-11). Here the song has an addition to it. It is now the song of Moses and the Lamb. Let us proceed to notice the plagues as the angels empty their bowls of wrath upon the people.

(1) The first angel pours his vial upon the earth (v. 2).

The effect of which was the producing of a grievous sore upon those who have the mark of the beast, and worship him. This is but the Egyptian ulcers intensified. (See Exod. 9:8-12; Deut. 28:15, 27, 35.) This latter doubtless never has been fulfilled.

(2) The second angel empties his bowl into the sea (v. 3), causing the sea to become as blood, resulting in the death of everything which had life in the sea.

(3) The third angel poured his bowl upon the rivers, etc., and they became blood (vv. 4-7; cf. Exod. 7:19-21). Here we see divine justice vindicated. They who have shed blood are made to drink blood. All Heaven cries out in approval of it.

(4) The fourth angel poured out his bowl upon the sun (vv. 8, 9), causing men to be scorched with fire. This only called forth their blasphemies. It did not produce repentance. One would think that such strokes from the strong hand of the Almighty would break men's hearts.

(5) The fifth angel poured out his bowl upon the seat of the beast (vv. 10, 11), causing great darkness to come upon his kingdom. All these mighty woes and plagues continue in effect. What could be more terrible and unendurable than to be suffering intense agony in the darkness? But all this does not produce repentance. There is no repentance in Hell.

(6) When the sixth angel poured out his bowl upon the Euphrates River, a way was made for the eastern armies (vv. 12-16).

(7) The seventh angel poured out his bowl into the air (vv. 17-21), followed by a voice from the temple, saying, "It is done." The work of judgment is complete. Observe some attendant events. Voices, thunderings and lightnings and a great earthquake, followed by the division of the great city and the falling of the cities of the nations. The islands fled away and the mountains were not found, then followed hail from Heaven upon men the weight of a talent. This only caused men to blaspheme the more.

6. The Fall of Babylon (17:1—18:24).

Twice before we heard of this Babylon. In the chapters upon which we now enter, we deal with the characteristics and particulars of that mystic personage. In the previous accounts the subject was anticipatory, but now we deal with its reality, and find that it reaches backward as well as to the end. It is comprehensive in all its details.

a. The woman. In chapter 12 we had under consideration a woman. Here is another woman. Let us note their parallelism and contrast.

(1) Parallelism. Both are mothers. The first brought forth a son who is to rule all nations; the second is the mother of harlots and of the abominations of the earth. Both are gorgeously arrayed. First is clothed with the sun; the second is clothed with purple and scarlet. Both occupy positions of tremendous influence and power. First has the moon under her feet; the second ruleth over the kings of the earth. Both are sufferers: the first from persecution of the dragon; the second, ultimately, hated by the kings, eat her flesh and burn her with fire.

(2) Contrasts. First is a pure woman; the second is a harlot. First is hated by the powers of the earth; the second is loved and caressed. The first gives birth to a mighty seed which is caught up to heavenly glory; the second produces that which is impure, and calls down the anger and punishment of God. First is helped by celestial wings; the second is carried by the beast. First has the crown of twelve stars; the second bears upon her head the name of the great destroyer. The first finally comes out in the heavenly city, the New Jerusalem; the second comes out in a city of this world which sinks forever under divine wrath, to become the habitation of demons. They seem to be opposites and rivals—the one set over against the other. By recalling the woman of chapter 12 and placing it alongside this one, we see that by the side of the body of God's true people is found a body of the Devil. We read in this book of the synagogue of Satan, ministers of his, etc.

(3) Proofs of Identification. Let us now consider proofs which serve to identify this woman, proofs which are derived from Scripture.

(a) She is characterized by harlotry. She is the mother of harlots. The Scriptures recognize worship of that which is not the true God as spiritual harlotry, called whoredom, adultery, etc. (Jer. 3:6, 8, 9; Ezek. 16:32). Of course where divine laws are ignored, the marriage relation is dishonored, and licentiousness runs riot.

(b) She is the mother of harlots. This goes back to both pagan and papal Rome, to the beginning of all false systems of worship.

(c) The name in her forehead serves also to identify her. For the origin of Babylon we must go back to chapters 10 and 11 of Genesis.

(d) She is made drunk with the blood of the martyrs, saints and prophets. There were martyrs before either papal or pagan Rome.

(e) The inhabitants of the earth were made drunk with the wine of her fornication.

(f) She sits upon many waters. For a definition of waters see verse 15.

(g) She rides the beast full of the names of blasphemy, having seven heads and ten horns. This is the same beast as that in chapter 13.

(4) What do the seven heads and ten horns represent? "The seven heads are seven mountains, on which the woman sitteth. And there are seven kings: five are fallen, and one is, and the other is not yet come; and when he cometh, he must continue a short space. And the beast that was and is not, even he is the eighth, and is of the seven, and goeth into perdition. And the ten horns which thou sawest are ten kings, which have received no kingdom as yet; but receive power as kings one hour with the beast" (17:9-12). By referring to Daniel 2:35; Psalm 30:7; Jeremiah 51:25, what is Babylon? (Cf. 17:18.)

b. Let us now occupy ourselves with the fall of Babylon. We see a glorious angel coming down from Heaven, crying "Babylon the great is fallen" (18:1). Next another voice is heard crying out, "Come out of her my people." After which awful plagues fall upon her (v. 8). In 18:9-24 and 19:1-6 we see the effects of this fall. First we have the wailing and mourning of the kings of the earth (v. 9), and then the weeping of the merchants of the earth (v. 11), and finally, the hosts of Heaven rejoicing over her fall (vv. 20-24).

7. Final Struggle (19:1—20:3).

a. The actual coming of Christ to the earth (19:1-10). The days of the reign of man and the Devil are at an end. Great burden is removed from the hearts of Heaven's throng. The immediate cause of this rejoicing is the time of the marriage of the Lamb.

b. The coming of the saints with Him (19:11-14; cf. I Thess. 4:16, 17).

c. The judgments upon the enemies of Christ (19:15-21). Immediately following this heavenly banquet, the closing scenes of this present age are brought before us. It is the culminating blow which is struck by the powers of Heaven upon the unlawful possessors of Heaven and upon the unlawful possessors of this earth. It is the battle of the Great Day of God Almighty. Let us observe:

(1) The Almighty Conqueror (vv. 12-16).
(2) The heavenly army which follows Him (v. 14).
(3) The opposing armies (v. 19).
(4) The crushing defeat of the enemy (vv. 20, 21).

d. The binding of Satan (20:1-3).

B. *Apocalyptic Millennial—the Thousand Years' Reign* (20:4-6). Note the desirability of the first resurrection (v. 6).

C. *Apocalyptic Postmillennial* (20:7—22:21).

1. The Loosing of Satan (20:7).
2. Man's Final Testing and Judgment (20:8, 9).
3. The Destruction of Satan (20:10).
4. The Judgment of the Wicked Dead (20:11-13).
5. Death and Hades Destroyed (20:14; cf. I Cor. 15:26).
6. The New Heavens and the New Earth (21:1).

The Heaven and the earth not annihilated but rejuvenated, purified. No more sea. Perhaps a pre-Adamite race destroyed by the sea. In the regeneration by the Spirit's brooding over the waters a part was reclaimed for the habitation of man.

7. Descent of the Holy City (21:2-8).

Note the blessedness of those who are permitted within (v. 4), and the doom of those who are excluded (v. 8).

8. Description of the Holy City (21:9—22:5).
9. The Epilogue (22:6-21).

INDEX